T0211654

Lecture Notes of the Institute for Computer Sciences, Social Informatics and Telecommunications Engineering 336

More information about this series at http://www.springer.com/series/8197

Noseong Park · Kun Sun ·
Sara Foresti · Kevin Butler ·
Nitesh Saxena (Eds.)

Security and Privacy in Communication Networks

16th EAI International Conference, SecureComm 2020
Washington, DC, USA, October 21–23, 2020
Proceedings, Part II

 Springer

Editors
Noseong Park
Yonsei University
Seoul, Korea (Republic of)

Sara Foresti
Dipartimento di Informatica
Universita degli Studi
Milan, Milano, Italy

Nitesh Saxena
Division of Nephrology
University of Alabama
Birmingham, AL, USA

Kun Sun
George Mason University
Fairfax, VA, USA

Kevin Butler
University of Florida
Gainesville, FL, USA

ISSN 1867-8211   ISSN 1867-822X   (electronic)
Lecture Notes of the Institute for Computer Sciences, Social Informatics
and Telecommunications Engineering
ISBN 978-3-030-63094-2   ISBN 978-3-030-63095-9   (eBook)
https://doi.org/10.1007/978-3-030-63095-9

This Springer imprint is published by the registered company Springer Nature Switzerland AG
The registered company address is: Gewerbestrasse 11, 6330 Cham, Switzerland

Preface

We are delighted to introduce the proceedings of the 16th EAI International Conference on Security and Privacy in Communication Networks (SecureComm 2020). This conference has brought together researchers, developers, and practitioners from around the world who are leveraging and developing security and privacy technology for a safe and robust system or network.

These proceedings contain 60 papers, which were selected from 120 submissions (an acceptance rate of 50%) from universities, national laboratories, and the private sector from across the USA as well as other countries in Europe and Asia. All the submissions went through an extensive review process by internationally-recognized experts in cybersecurity.

Any successful conference requires the contributions of different stakeholder groups and individuals, who have selflessly volunteered their time and energy in disseminating the call for papers, submitting their research findings, participating in the peer reviews and discussions, etc. First and foremost, we would like to offer our gratitude to the entire Organizing Committee for guiding the entire process of the conference. We are also deeply grateful to all the Technical Program Committee members for their time and effort in reading, commenting, debating, and finally selecting the papers. We also thank all the external reviewers for assisting the Technical Program Committee in their particular areas of expertise as well as all the authors, participants, and session chairs for their valuable contributions. Support from the Steering Committee and EAI staff members was also crucial in ensuring the success of the conference. It was a great privilege to work with such a large group of dedicated and talented individuals.

We hope that you found the discussions and interactions at SecureComm 2020, which was held online, enjoyable and that the proceedings will simulate further research.

October 2020

Kun Sun
Sara Foresti
Kevin Butler
Nitesh Saxena

Organization

Steering Committee

Imrich Chlamtac	University of Trento, Italy
Guofei Gu	Texas A&M University, USA
Peng Liu	Penn State University, USA
Sencun Zhu	Penn State University, USA

Organizing Committee

General Co-chairs

Kun Sun	George Mason University, USA
Sara Foresti	Università degli Studi di Milano, Italy

TPC Chair and Co-chair

Kevin Butler	University of Florida, USA
Nitesh Saxena	University of Alabama at Birmingham, USA

Sponsorship and Exhibit Chair

Liang Zhao	George Mason University, USA

Local Chair

Hemant Purohit	George Mason University, USA

Workshops Chair

Qi Li	Tsinghua University, China

Publicity and Social Media Chairs

Emanuela Marasco	George Mason University, USA
Carol Fung	Virginia Commonwealth University, USA

Publications Chair

Noseong Park	Yonsei University, South Korea

Web Chair

Pengbin Feng	George Mason University, USA

Panels Chair

Massimiliano Albanese	George Mason University, USA

Tutorials Chair

Fabio Scotti   Università degli Studi di Milano, Italy

Technical Program Committee

Adwait Nadkarni	William & Mary, USA
Amro Awad	Sandia National Laboratories, USA
An Wang	Case Western Reserve University, USA
Aziz Mohaisen	University of Central Florida, USA
Birhanu Eshete	University of Michigan - Dearborn, USA
Byron Williams	University of Florida, USA
Cliff Zou	University of Central Florida, USA
Cong Wang	City University of Hong Kong, Hong Kong
Daniel Takabi	Georgia State University, USA
Dave (Jing) Tian	Purdue University, USA
David Barrera	Carleton University, Canada
Debin Gao	Singapore Management University, Singapore
Dinghao Wu	Penn State University, USA
Eric Chan-Tin	Loyola University Chicago, USA
Eugene Vasserman	Kansas State University, USA
Fatima M. Anwar	University of Massachusetts Amherst, USA
Fengyuan Xu	Nanjing University, China
Girish Revadigar	University of New South Wales, Australia
Gokhan Kul	University of Massachusetts Dartmouth, USA
Huacheng Zeng	University of Louisville, USA
Hyoungshick Kim	Sungkyunkwan University, South Korea
Jeffrey Spaulding	Canisius College, USA
Jian Liu	The University of Tennessee at Knoxville, USA
Jiawei Yuan	University of Massachusetts Dartmouth, USA
Jun Dai	California State University, Sacramento, USA
Kai Bu	Zhejiang University, China
Kai Chen	Institute of Information Engineering, Chinese Academy of Sciences, China
Karim Elish	Florida Polytechnic University, USA
Kuan Zhang	University of Nebraska-Lincoln, USA
Le Guan	University of Georgia, USA
Maliheh Shirvanian	Visa Research, USA
Martin Strohmeier	University of Oxford, UK
Mengjun Xie	The University of Tennessee at Chattanooga, USA
Mohamed Shehab	University of North Carolina at Charlotte, USA
Mohammad Mannan	Concordia University, Canada
Murtuza Jadliwala	The University of Texas at San Antonio, USA
Neil Gong	Duke University, USA
Patrick McDaniel	Penn State University, USA
Pierangela Samarati	Università degli Studi di Milano, Italy

Contents – Part II

Contents – Part I

A Practical Machine Learning-Based Framework to Detect DNS Covert Communication in Enterprises

Ruming Tang[1,2], Cheng Huang[3], Yanti Zhou[4], Haoxian Wu[3], Xianglin Lu[1,2], Yongqian Sun[5], Qi Li[1,2(✉)], Jinjin Li[4], Weiyao Huang[4], Siyuan Sun[4], and Dan Pei[1,2]

[1] Tsinghua University, Beijing, China
trm14@mails.tsinghua.edu.cn, {peidan,qli01}@tsinghua.edu.cn
[2] Beijing National Research Center for Information Science and Technology (BNRist), Beijing, China
everl@bupt.edu.cn
[3] BizSeer Technologies Co., Ltd., Beijing, China
huangcheng@bizseer.com, MOVIEGEORGE@pku.edu.cn
[4] Bank of Communications, Shanghai, China
{zhouyt,lijj,huangweiyao,sunsiyuan}@bankcomm.com
[5] Nankai University, Tianjin, China
sunyongqian@nankai.edu.cn

Abstract. DNS is a key protocol of the Internet infrastructure, which ensures network connectivity. However, DNS suffers from various threats. In particular, DNS covert communication is one serious threat in enterprise networks, by which attackers establish stealthy communications between internal hosts and remote servers. In this paper, we propose D^2C^2 (Detection of DNS Covert Communication), a practical and flexible machine learning-based framework to detect DNS covert communications. D^2C^2 is an end-to-end framework contains modular detection models including supervised and unsupervised ones, which detect multiple types of threats efficiently and flexibly. We have deployed D^2C^2 in a large commercial bank with 100 millions of DNS queries per day. During the deployment, D^2C^2 detected over 4k anomalous DNS communications per day, achieving high precision over 0.97 on average. It uncovers a significant number of unnoticed security issues including seven compromised hosts in the enterprise network.

Keywords: DNS · Malicious domain detection · Data exfiltration · DGA

1 Introduction

As a core infrastructure on the Internet, the Domain Name System (DNS) is commonly used in all kinds of Internet applications, to translate easy-to-

© ICST Institute for Computer Sciences, Social Informatics and Telecommunications Engineering 2020
Published by Springer Nature Switzerland AG 2020. All Rights Reserved
N. Park et al. (Eds.): SecureComm 2020, LNICST 336, pp. 1–21, 2020.
https://doi.org/10.1007/978-3-030-63095-9_1

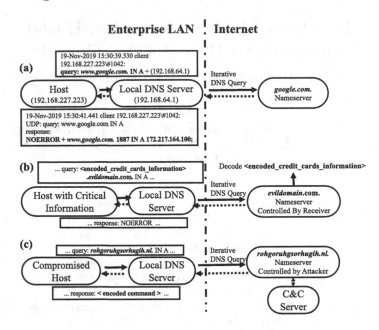

Fig. 1. Examples of (a) normal DNS lookups, (b) DNS-based data exfiltration, and (c) DNS-based C&C.

recognize domain names into IP addresses. Unfortunately, the DNS system suffers from known vulnerabilities, such as DDoS [27], spoofing [24] and other exploits [8,30,36]. To defend against these attacks, approaches such as [10,18,24] have been proposed. Unlike those traditional attacks which target DNS system itself, DNS covert communication is leveraged to transmit messages cross the boundary between an enterprise's LAN (*i.e.*, office network and datacenter) and the Internet, through DNS messages in a stealthy and unauthorized manner. However, the defense against DNS covert communication in enterprises is still not well-studied, and is the focus of this paper.

In enterprises, security tools are commonly deployed to closely monitor the traffic between the enterprise's LAN and the Internet to detect serious security attacks such as *data exfiltration* (which transmits valuable internal data to the Internet), *command-and-control* (C&C) of internal hosts by external attackers, and so on. However, those data exfiltration and C&C using covert communication via the DNS traffic [7,8,22,23,28] are still hard to detect.

Figure 1 shows examples of normal DNS lookup and DNS covert communication. In the normal DNS lookup in Fig. 1(a), a normal host queries its local DNS server about *google.com*, and the local DNS server then iteratively queries DNS root server and *.com* top-level domain server (both are omitted in the figure) and relays the response (which indicates the corresponding IP address is *172.217.164.100*) from the authoritative name server for google.com to the host. Figure 1(b) shows an example of real point of sale (POS) malware, in which POS malware exfiltrated credit card information in the domain names of the DNS queries [20]. Such exfiltration incidents (*e.g.*, MULTIGRAIN [20], UDPoS [28]) caused many loss to the users and providers. The compromised host encodes the stolen credit card information as subdomains in the domain name to be queried, and when the query arrives at the authoritative name server controlled by the attacker, the attacker can then easily decode the credit card information from the queried domain name. Figure 1(c) shows an example of DNS C&C [22] where a malware-infected host talks to and receives command from its C&C server by sending a DNS query message to and receiving corresponding DNS response from the compromised authoritative name server, which is the C&C server. In this example, the seemingly-random domain name (rohgoruhgsorhugih.nl) queried are actually dynamically generated by Domain-Generation-Algorithms (DGAs) and automatically synchronized between the compromised host and the C&C server [9, 13, 29, 30, 35, 36].

Therefore, new detection methods are needed to detect these DNS covert communication because traditional security tools based on blacklists, rules, signatures cannot enumerate or capture the dynamically changing subdomain names in the DNS covert communications exemplified in Fig. 1 (b)(c).

Our intuitive idea in detecting DNS covert communication is to apply machine learning (ML) to capture a suspicious domain based on its features (see the feature list in Table 2, *e.g.*, the length of the domain). Although this idea is promising, previous ML-based approaches along this direction have not been deployed in the real-world enterprises yet, to the best of our knowledge, due to the following the three challenges.

First, the performance of different ML algorithms might be different for different enterprises because the DNS traffic data distribution might be different. Furthermore, the machine learning algorithms used in previous works, supervised models perform better and are preferred for some kinds of known threat types, while unsupervised models are more preferred for some unknown but rare threats. Thus, the algorithms used should be generic and flexible (as opposed to being fixed) in the detection system. Second, different DNS covert communication threats might have different patterns, thus previous machine-leaning based approaches, to the best of our knowledge, so far only focuses on specific types of such attacks, *e.g.*, [7,8] only detect data exfiltration, and [30] only detects DGA domains. However, enterprises in the real-world are interested in detecting various attacks, thus are reluctant to deploy the aforementioned piece-meal approaches that can detect only one type of DNS covert communication. Third, a practical ML-based detection system needs to have feedback mechanisms to either add labeled data for re-training in the supervised approaches and/or tune the parameters in the unsupervised approaches, and also fully utilize (as opposed to replacing) the traditional DNS security tools such as the domain blacklist.

To tackle the above challenges, in this paper we propose a practical, flexible and end-to-end ML-based framework, called D^2C^2 (**D**etecting **DNS C**overt **C**ommunication), to effectively detect various DNS covert communications in enterprises by leveraging supervised and unsupervised classifiers trained by various types of features extracted from DNS logs. It is an end-to-end framework and consists of several modules with an intuitive but efficient workflow, which is easy to be deployed and maintained in enterprise environments. One flexible detection module is used to detect all types of covert communication threats via domain names in DNS traffic. D^2C^2 also uses feedback to take advantage of manual investigations on alerts to improve detection performance. The results of detection are aggregated and visualized, for better display for the operators, to make D^2C^2 more friendly to the users.

In the flexible detection module, modular multiple detection models are used, including supervised and unsupervised approaches so that, for each type of threat, the most suitable model (detector) for it can be applied. Based on all results aggregated from detectors, D^2C^2 is able to reveal covert communication threats in a comprehensive way. The flexible and modular design of multiple detectors also makes it very flexible. Each detector can be adjusted easily and individually for updating or modification, $e.g.$, model tuning or re-training.

Our major contributions can be summarized as follows.

- We propose the first practical, flexible, and end-to-end ML-based framework, D^2C^2, which is easy to be deployed in enterprises to detect DNS covert communication threats, to the best of our knowledge.
- We design a modular threat detection component which consists of supervised and unsupervised methods in series, and can be modified flexibly and individually to handle different data distribution in different enterprises.
- We deployed D^2C^2 in a large commercial bank with more than 25K hosts, detecting more than 100 millions DNS queries per day. D^2C^2 is the first large-scale deployment of DNS covert communication detection system in the wild, to the best of our knowledge.
- Based on our evaluation over 5 billion DNS logs, D^2C^2 detected 4k anomalous logs per day efficiently, and achieved high precision (over 0.97). It uncovered real covert communication threats in the wild, including 7 compromised hosts unknown to the operators previously.

2 Background

2.1 Domain Name System

A DNS log contains several important fields: $NAME$ (the queried domain name), $TYPE$ (A for IPv4 address, $CNAME$ for canonical names, TXT for text records and $etc.$), and $RDATA$ (the resource) [21]. For example, the query in Fig. 1(a) contains the queried name ($www.google.com$), class (IN), type (A). The response log contains the response: RCODE (Response Code), TTL (Time to Live) and the answer, and the corresponding query. The answer is the IPv4 address(es) for the queried name. RCODE indicates the condition of the answer, NOERROR (in this example) means a normal answer, and NXDomain indicates that the queried name does not exist.

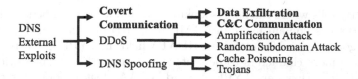

Fig. 2. Typical types of DNS external exploits threats.

Although DNS is a fundamental system that many services rely on, some enterprise operators treat DNS as a "set and forget" infrastructure, and do not update them from time to time with the latest security mechanisms [17]. For example, DNSSEC [12] is one security extension of DNS proposed early, but its adoption is quite slow till recently [10,15]. Some operators may be interested in the availability of DNS only when DNS servers go wrong.

Figure 2 shows some typical exploits against DNS [17]. Attacks against DNS infrastructure itself (*i.e.*, DDoS and spoofing) are much easier to be noticed because it leads to the failures or errors in DNS servers. DDoS (Distributed Denial of Service) attacks compromise the availability of DNS, and spoofing (to redirect users to attackers) leads to wrong or unreachable destinations. Besides these, some attackers take advantage of the lack of monitoring on DNS traffic, and choose DNS as a channel for covert communication (in bold in Fig. 2), which is more difficult to notice.

2.2 Covert Communications in DNS Channel

In this paper, we focus on *DNS Covert Communication*, which is one of the most important DNS-related threats in enterprise environments, where operators pay close attention to malicious communication to the Internet. In a covert communication case, attackers use DNS to establish a communication channel between compromised hosts and remote servers, without being monitored by other security measures.

A common attack is to encode data in certain fields in the DNS packet [8,17,31]. Attackers can simply use the subdomains as payloads, encoding data into the NAME field like *"<encoded...information>.evildomain.com."* as shown in Fig. 1(b), which is known as **data exfiltration**. Such encoded data are usually long strings that are not commonly seen in normal domain names. Some attackers also use DNS channel to transmit **C&C communication** between compromised hosts and remote C&C servers. In this way, the compromised hosts can inform the attackers of their current status. Figure 1(c) shows an example of a host querying a C&C domain, which is generated by an algorithm (IRCBot). Obvious differences can be seen between popular domain names and this domain name, which contains no recognizable words or abbreviation.

In general, malicious communication through DNS channel can be determined by two indicators: whether the DNS packets carry **malicious payloads** or the hosts connect to **malicious destinations**. As mentioned before, the domain name directly tells where the host is looking for, and it also can be used to carry messages. Besides domain name in NAME field, RDATA field in response also provides a good payload for attackers. RDATA fields in TYPE CNAME or TXT packets allow more characters to be sent, which means larger "bandwidth" for attackers [17,23]. However, TYPE A (and AAAA) logs account for the vast majority of all DNS logs (see data trace statistics in Sect. 5), **therefore in this paper we consider anomalies in domain names as our primary threats to be detected in this paper**.

In this paper, we only focus on domains that are related to covert communication threats (mainly data exfiltration and C&C threats). However, not all malicious domains are related to covert communication. Some malicious domains are disguised for phishing, *e.g.*, *Domain Shadowing* (hijack normal domains and create new subdomains to redirect users [19]) and *Typo-Squatting* (register domain names which are similar to popular websites and leverage typos of users [34]), which are not considered as covert communication.

2.3 Related Work

Exfiltration in domain names, by nature, contain more information because of the extra payload, thus are longer than normal ones. Thus, some security engineers detect suspicious domains using a domain name length threshold. However, such signature-based methods do not always work due to the static threshold and can be easily evaded. In recent years, anomaly detection based approaches are proposed to detect exfiltration based on features in DNS traffic. Das *et al.* detect encoded data in DNS traffic related to exfiltration and tunneling [11]. Ahmed *et al.* present an Isolation Forest approach to detecting exfiltration in an enterprise [7,8]. However, these approaches have not been tested on real attacks in the wild, but only on synthetic data generated by toolkits.

Many prior work about **C&C communications** focused on **DGA** [9,13,29, 30,35,36], which are widely used to generate seemingly random domain names (Algorithmically-Generated Domains, AGDs). AGDs appear in many security events, for instance, botnets, to avoid traditional blocking mechanisms like blacklists, sinkholes or signature-based firewalls. Many prior studies used classifiers to detect AGDs because they are different from normal domain names. Antonakakis *et al.* present an approach to detecting DGA based on Bipartite Graph Recursive Clustering and multi-class Alternating Decision Trees from NXDomains (queries for non-existed domains) [9]. Schüppen *et al.* propose FANCI, using Random Forests (RF) and Support Vector Machines (SVM) to detect DGAs with a high accuracy [30]. Sun *et al.* use a Heterogeneous Information Network to model the DGAs and detect them via transductive classification [33]. Tong *et al.* propose D3N, a system using Convolutional Neural Networks (CNN) to detect DGA domains from NXDomains [35]. Most of these classifiers are supervised because researchers can easily get DGA domains as positive samples by synthetic generating, but there are also unsupervised approaches used in detecting them. Gao *et al.* use X-Means to cluster domains, also from NXDomains [13]. Zang *et al.*

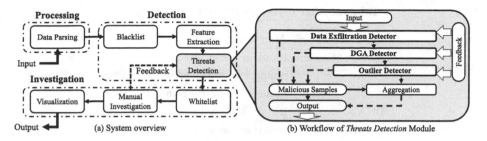

Fig. 3. The framework overview of D^2C^2. Figure (a) shows the overview of three stages in D^2C^2. Figure (b) shows the detailed workflow of the *Threats Detection* module. Dashed lines denote malicious samples detected and dotted denote benign ones.

extract features from domain names and other registration information and use X-Means algorithm to detect AGDs related to Fast-flux [36].

Summary: Each of the aforementioned prior studies focus on just one specific type of anomalous domain names. However, in enterprises, operators have to face threats of all kinds, thus would need lots of efforts to assemble and tune the above "piecemeal" solutions. Therefore, we hope to design a generic framework that is directly deployable, detecting multiple types of covert communication threats with high flexibility.

3   Framework Overview

In this section, we present the core idea for our design and the overview of D^2C^2.

3.1   Design Goal

Our design goal is to **develop a practical framework to detect covert communication in DNS traffic** in enterprise environments. Such a framework should be easy to deploy in real-world enterprise environments, and it should be able to achieve high performance with low overhead.

DNS covert communication consists of data exfiltration, C&C communication and other kinds of threats. To detect these threats, a multi-class classifier seems suitable. However, using one detection model for all the above threats will be inflexible, and such a complex model makes it hard for parameter tuning, which we want to avoid as much as we can, since data distribution changes over time and over different enterprises. Therefore, we use multiple individual detection models (each one is called a detector and focuses on certain types of DNS covert communication threats) instead of one complex model. For each detector, we can choose the most effective algorithm, based on their performance and feedback. Such a modular detection module enables us to update or replace models flexibly. For example, in case the data distribution changes (*e.g.*, over time or

Table 1. Alternative models for each detector.

Detector	Alternative models
Data exfiltration	Random forest (RF)
	Support vector machine (SVM)
	Multi-layer perceptron (MLP)
DGA	RF, SVM & MLP
Outlier	Isolation forest (iForest)
	X-Means

when new APIs deployed), the re-training or model tuning can be done individually, without the need to adjust the overall system workflow. Such updates can be triggered periodically or manually based on the feedback. As a result, the workflow of D^2C^2 stays the same, making it easy to be deployed in practice. Meanwhile, our detection models are very flexible for modification to achieve better performance in real-world detection.

The manual investigation is very necessary for a security system to confirm, analyze and mitigate reported threats. We hope that D^2C^2 is able to learn from these manual investigations. Thus we design D^2C^2 as a human-in-the-loop (HITL) one with feedback from security engineers. All investigation results can be further utilized for threshold adjusting, model tuning or re-training.

3.2 Overview

An system overview of D^2C^2 is shown in Fig. 3(a), which can be divided into three major stages: *Processing Stage* is used to read and parse raw data. *Detection Stage* is used to extract certain features and detect threats in DNS logs via machine learning based algorithms. *Investigation Stage* is to confirm the results from detection results and generate the overall reports to operators.

Processing Stage: This stage has only one **Data Parsing** module. First, D^2C^2 parses the raw data, extracting user demographics, DNS packets and other network information. The raw data consists of both DNS queries and DNS responses. As mentioned in Sect. 2.1, a DNS response already contains its corresponding query, thus for a query which has a response, D^2C^2 only parses the response as the input. A query without response (due to time-out or other errors) will be used directly as input with an added tag "no response".

Detection Stage: The detection stage is composed of three modules: Blacklist, Feature Extraction and Threats Detection. **Blacklist** module first filters the logs, to efficiently detect known malicious domains with low overhead. It is created from the enterprise blacklist maintained by the operators and is updated by manual investigation feedback and threat intelligence. Second, **Feature Extraction** module extracts features from the remaining logs. Last, we detect multiple

Table 2. Features extracted from the domain names.

#	Feature	Type	D-Exfil	D-DGA
1	Length of domain name	Integer	✓	✓
2	Length of subdomain	Integer	✓	
3	No. of labels	Integer	✓	✓
4	Longest label length	Integer	✓	✓
5	Contains one-character label	Boolean		
6	Contains IPv4	Boolean		
7	Has "WWW" prefix	Boolean		
8	Alphabet size	Integer	✓	
9	No. of uppercase characters	Integer	✓	
10	The ratio of digits	Float	✓	✓
11	Ratio of hexadecimal parts	Float		✓
12	Ratio of vowels	Float		✓
13	Ratio of underscore	Float		
14	Ratio of repeat characters	Float		✓
15	Ratio of consecutive consonants	Float		✓
16	Ratio of consecutive digits	Float	✓	✓
17	Shannon entropy [16]	Float	✓	✓
18	Gibberish score [26]	Float		✓
19	Bigram of domain name	Vector		✓

types of threats using **Threats Detection** module. The threats detection module contains multiple chosen classifiers (detectors), each of which focuses on one or more specific types of threats. Detectors can be modified according to the change of data. Results combined from all detectors will be aggregated and then sent for further investigation.

A more detailed architecture of *Threats Detection* is shown in Fig. 3(b), with three detectors in series. Simply, a sample detected as malicious by one detector will be stored, and a benign sample will be moved to the next detector. After all detectors are done, the results will be aggregated and sent to the investigation module. For each detector, different models can be applied based on their performance in practice. Table 1 lists the algorithms we used for these detectors during deployment. The detector workflow will be described in Sect. 4.

Investigation Stage: The investigation stage is divided into three modules: Whitelist, Manual Investigation and Visualization. When receiving the detection results, **Whitelist** module is used to flag some certain samples before them reaching the operators. This is because some queries generated by certain trusted applications (usually security products from different vendors) whose behavior is similar to that of the attackers, *e.g.*, sending data through DNS channel, which may result in unnecessary alerts. Similar to the blacklist module, the whitelist is created and updated based on enterprise operators. The remaining results are further reported to **Manual Investigation** module, where operators and security engineers are involved. Operators and security engineers check the detection results. The false alerts are used as feedback to our detectors, which may trigger alterations of thresholds, feature weights or even re-training of the machine learning algorithms. True threats confirmed are reported and visualized for analysis and display in **Visualization** module.

4   Features and Detectors

In this section, we first present the features we extract from domain names. Then we explain the detailed implementation workflow of threat detectors and alternative algorithms used in these detectors.

4.1   Features Extraction

The performance of machine learning-based detection relies on feature engineering. Thus the feature extraction module must be carefully designed. Queried domain names indicate whether the host is connecting to a dangerous target or not. Therefore, if we can flag a suspicious domain, we are able to flag a suspicious DNS query as well. Data exfiltration domains, which encode messages in the sub-domain names, are likely to contain more characters in their domains. On the other hand, domain names generated by DGAs, as mentioned in Sect. 2.3, often appear more random than normal domains. For example, the ratio of numerical characters and the length of the longest meaningful substring (LMS) show DGA domains' disparities from others [17], which indicate the different construction of suspicious domain names. In summary, we choose features widely used in data exfiltration detection [7,8] and DGA detections [9,25,29,30] for our detectors. Not all features from prior work are used, some of them are removed because of their low feature importances via the evaluation feedback on small scale of labeled data experiments. In addition, we added two features, feature #18 and #19 in Table 2, where we list all the features used in D^2C^2. Note that we do not claim the features in Table 2 as our contributions.

Structural Features: The differences in the construction of domains can be indicated by structural features. *Length* (#1 & #2 in Table 2) is an important feature since more characters mean more information, and many DGA families generate domains in a certain range of length. #3 & #4 are structural features of *Labels* (split by dot, *e.g.*, "www.foo.com" has three labels: "www", "foo" and "com"), since certain patterns in labels can be observed in data exfiltration traffic [7]. #5-7 check whether the domain names contain a certain pattern.

Linguistics Features: As domain names can be treated as strings, we also extract linguistics features (#8-16) to capture the differences in types of characters, including uppercase character, digit, hex, vowel, consonant and underscore.

Most features are self-explanatory, and we discuss the rest. *Alphabet size* is the number of unique characters in the domain name. *Ratio of repeat characters* (#14) is defined as the number of unique characters (each of which is repeated) divided by alphabet size. *Ratio of consecutive consonants* (#15) is defined as the sum of all lengths of consequent consonants (which larger than 1), divided by the domain name length. *Ratio of consecutive digits* (#16) is similar to #15.

Statistics Features: We choose three statistics features commonly used in determining the information in a sequence, *Shannon Entropy* (#17), *Gibberish Score* (#18) and *N-Gram*. The *Gibberish Score* we implemented is based on Hidden Markov Chain [6,26]. It is used to determine the "meaningful" contents from domains, and a string with more meaningful words will get a higher score. Furthermore, we use *bigram* (#19) in feature extraction. We calculated the top-200 bigrams on historical benign domains and Majestic Top Websites [5]. Then we checked the presences of these 200 bigrams in each domain name to form a $N \times 200$ matrix (N denotes the number of all domains for feature extraction). While not all of the bigrams have high feature importance, to lower the overhead, we use Principal Component Analysis (PCA) to reduce the 200 dimensions to 15. Thus for each domain name, we get a 1×15 vector as its feature.

Different features are used for different detectors, based on feature importance. The features used for *Data Exfiltration Detector* (*D-Exfil*) and *DGA Detector* (*D-DGA*) are marked in Table 2. As *Outlier Detector* aims to catch any threats missed by the two previous detectors, it uses all features in the list.

4.2   Anomaly Detection Methods

As mentioned before, in enterprise environments, two popular targets of covert communication are *Data Exfiltration* and *C&C Communication*, and *DGA domains* are most commonly seen in C&C scenarios while other manually forged domain names are very rare. Therefore we design two specific detectors, the **Data Exfiltration Detector** and the **DGA Detector** for these two main threats, respectively. For other suspicious domains left in the DNS logs, we use an extra **Outlier Detector** in order to cover as many threats as possible.

The implementation of multiple standalone detectors grants D^2C^2 with high flexibility. For each individual detector, the algorithm can be updated or replaced easily, according to the performance of different algorithms.

During our study, the chosen algorithms are listed in Table 1. To better evaluate the flexibility and performance of our system, for each detector, we picked several popular algorithms for these detectors based on the prior research [8,19,30,32]. Detectors for *Data Exfiltration* and *DGA Communication* use supervised algorithms, including **random forest (RF)**, **support vector machine (SVM)** and **multi-layer perceptron (MLP)**. *Outlier Detector* uses unsupervised algorithms, including **isolation forest (iForest)** and **X-Means**. Note that X-Means is a clustering algorithm, thus we calculate the distances from each sample to its clustering center as an indicator of anomaly in two ways: 1) if the distance is larger than a given threshold, then the sample is labeled as an outlier; 2) if the average of all samples in the same cluster is larger than the threshold, then the whole cluster is marked as an outlier cluster. The other algorithms are all binary classifiers and we directly use their predicted labels as classified results. All these methods use features described in Sect. 4.1.

4.3 Workflow of All Detectors

The threat detection module is the primary module in D^2C^2 and is also one main contribution in this paper. It contains multiple detectors, including supervised and unsupervised approaches. Thus the workflow of all detectors should be well designed to make them work together efficiently. The general idea of different approaches' cooperation is: supervised approaches focus on detecting known threats, while unsupervised approaches trying to catch rare unknown threats.

All three detectors are to flag covert communication threats based on suspicious domains, which are mainly data exfiltration and C&C communication cases. As mentioned before, supervised methods are more suitable in detecting known threats, thus we implemented two supervised detectors (*Data Exfiltration Detector* and *DGA Detector*) for these two primary types of threats. While there will be other suspicious domains that do not fall into these two categories, we use an unsupervised outlier detection model (*Outlier Detector*) to capture these domains with no specific types.

Figure 3(b) shows the implementation of threats detection module in D^2C^2 framework, consisting of the three detectors running in series. During the detection, all malicious samples detected by a detector will be stored in a database, and all benign samples remaining will be sent to the next detector for testing. The first two supervised detectors will detect known threats which are majorities of all the threats. Thus they will filter most of the threats in the data. The remaining suspicious domains are very rare compared to the other normal domains. Such distribution of data will be suitable for the unsupervised outlier detection algorithm. After all detectors are applied, the results will be aggregated and sent to the next stage for investigation and visualization. Besides, the detected outliers could also be used to improve the supervised approaches, in cases that some missed data exfiltration or DGA threats (which are false negatives of the two detectors) are caught as outliers and then confirmed by the manual investigation, thus are used as feedback.

5   Deployment in a Large Enterprise

In this section, we evaluate our design by a real-world deployment in a large enterprise environment with substantial DNS traffic. Then we present insights into the threats and security issues in the enterprise environments.

5.1   Data Trace

We have deployed D^2C^2 in an enterprise environment with a large scale of Internet traffic. In this enterprise, there are more than 25k hosts, including servers

Table 3. Distribution of different DNS types in a one-month dataset.

Types	# of Queries (Responses)	Total	%
A	2,310,206,811 (2,175,715,764)	4,485,922,575	75.98%
AAAA	443,000,848 (441,857,308)	884,858,156	14.98%
PTR	245,185,527 (244,886,490)	490,072,017	8.30%
SOA	5,751,338 (5,722,695)	11,474,033	0.19%
SRV	5,651,489 (5,611,368)	11,262,857	0.19%
NS	4,790,185 (4,788,276)	9,578,461	0.16%
TXT	3,392,785 (3,389,870)	6,782,655	0.11%
CNAME	630,267 (630,246)	1,260,513	0.02%
MX	327,305 (320,792)	648,097	0.01%
Other	958,983 (963,691)	1,922,674	0.03%
Total	3,019,895,538 (2,883,886,500)	5,903,782,038	–

in IDC and desktops/laptops in office networks. Some sensors were deployed in the DNS servers controlled by this enterprise to collect DNS logs in its network from all hosts. The average number of DNS logs per day is around 100 millions.

The detailed statistics for 1-month dataset with over 5 billion DNS logs are shown in Table 3. The number of queries is ~5% more than that of responses. This is because not all queries have responses due to time-out, packet loss or other kinds of network errors. As mentioned before, all responses will be input into D^2C^2, since each response contains its corresponding query. For queries without responses, the queries will be input into D^2C^2 directly. We also count different types in DNS logs, and list the numbers in Table 3. Type A (IPv4 address) and type $AAAA$ (IPv6 address) dominate in all logs, take up 75.98% and 14.98%, respectively. PTR (pointer) also accounts for 8.30% among all types. PTR query is commonly used for reverse DNS lookups, which are the opposite of A or AAAA queries. It is also used for DNS service discovery, replying with service names. The ratios of other types, $i.e.$, $CNAME$ (canonical name), MX (mail exchange), NS (name server), SOA (state of authority), SRV (service locator) and TXT (descriptive text), are all very small. "Other" contains multiple types which are very rare in our traffic, including $TKEY$ (transaction key), SPF (sender policy framework) and $etc..$.

The operators and security engineers in the enterprise also maintain a blacklist and a whitelist. Both lists are parsed and all the entries are fed into D^2C^2 as the domain names in $Blacklist$ module and $Whitelist$ module. The blacklist consists of known malicious domains found previously or reported in take-downs and security databases including DGArchive [25], 360 Netlab Opendata [4] and other threat intelligence services used by the enterprise. The whitelist contains domains controlled by the studied enterprise, security vendors and several popular websites from Majestic Top Websites [5].

Table 4. Evaluation metrics on labeled dataset.

Detector		Precision	Recall	Accuracy	F1
D-Exfil	**RF**	**1.0000**	**1.0000**	**1.0000**	**1.0000**
	MLP	**0.9999**	**0.9995**	**0.9995**	**0.9993**
	SVM	0.9997	0.9998	0.9998	0.9997
D-DGA	**RF**	**0.9580**	**0.9787**	**0.9945**	**0.9682**
	MLP	**0.9290**	**0.9660**	**0.9910**	**0.9471**
	SVM	0.8049	0.9558	0.9765	0.8793
D-Outlier	**iForest**	**0.8495**	**0.9190**	**0.9988**	**0.8829**
	X-Means	0.6708	0.5371	0.9981	0.5965

Table 5. Processing speed of different models on labeled dataset.

Model		Processing speed (logs/s)
Supervised	RF	49344.9
	MLP	9210.2
	SVM	24150.2
Unsupervised	iForest	9149.0
	X-Means	4090.6

5.2 Evaluation Results

During the deployment, we used the following evaluation metrics:

– $precision = |TP|/(|TP| + |FP|)$, $recall = |TP|/(|TP| + |FN|)$
– $accuracy = (|TP| + |TN|)/(|TP| + |FP| + |TN| + |FN|)$
– $f1\text{-}measure = (2 \times precision \times recall)/(precision + recall)$

TP, FP, TN and FN stand for true positives, false positives, true negatives and false negatives, respectively.

Because in a large volume of real-world traffic, it is difficult to get all data labeled. Thus we evaluate our models in two ways: on a **labeled historical data** (an extra trace of over 764k labeled logs) and on the **un-labeled real-time traffic for a month** (which is shown in Table 3). The labeled historical data trace were collected in the enterprise before D^2C^2 was deployed. It consists of historical logs previously labeled and verified by operators. This data trace is used to evaluate all the algorithms we chose in Sect. 4.2. However, during deployment, it is very difficult to label all logs because of the large volume of traffic. In this case, since all positives (alerts) will be checked by operators according to the workflow of D^2C^2, the precision is accurate. But the recall can only be approximately obtained (since there may be unlabeled threats in the dataset). So we only present precision for these detection results.

For a practical detection framework used in the real world, the *false alert rate* is also a critical metric. This is because all alerts need to be investigated

Table 6. Deployment results of detectors.

Detector		Precision	#TP/day	#FP/day
D-Exfil	**RF**	**0.9755**	**155.6**	**3.9**
	MLP	0.9934	1070.0	7.1
D-DGA	**RF**	**0.9986**	**3958.9**	**5.6**
	MLP	0.9764	3871.0	93.5
D-Outlier	**iForest**	**0.9214**	**29.3**	**2.5**
Total (RF + iForest)		**0.9971**	**4143.8**	**12.0**

by operators, and too many alerts will overwhelm the operators. On average, it takes over 20 min for an operator to investigate one security alert [14]. Thus we present *number of true positives and false positives per day* for our models (#TP/day and #FP/day in Table 6).

Evaluation of Algorithms on Historical Labeled Data: Table 4 shows the precision, recall, accuracy and F1-measure of all chosen models on the labeled historical data set. From this table we can see that all models achieve high accuracy in the evaluation experiments. This is because of the imbalance of positives and negatives in the data, and the numbers of true negatives dominate in the calculation of the accuracy. In this case, F1 Measure values (last column in Table 4) show more disparities among these methods.

In general, all three binary classifier models used in the data exfiltration detector (*D-Exfil*) achieve high precision and recall, with an average F1-measure over 0.99. The results in DGA detector (*D-DGA*) show that random forest (RF) and multi-layer perceptron (MLP) still achieve high performance. But the performance of support vector machine (SVM) is worse, especially in precision, which is only 0.80. This is because some DGA domains also have differences between each other (due to DGA families), which influence SVM's performance.

For the outlier detector (*D-Outlier*), isolation forest model (iForest) achieves much higher performance than X-Means, with a precision of 0.85 and a recall of 0.92. This is mainly because that X-Means is basically a clustering method. The clustering results of X-Means are highly influenced by the distribution of different patterns of samples, and the static thresholds used for anomaly detection may not be suitable for all clusters.

The evaluation results on labeled data trace demonstrated which chosen algorithms are efficient in our environment. That is, based on the above results, RF, MLP and iForest (in bold in Table 4) could be more suitable in the enterprise where we deployed D^2C^2, because of their higher precision and recall values in both detection of exfiltration and DGA domains.

Another concern of a practical framework is the **overhead**. Since systems with high overhead are not suitable to be deployed in practice, especially in enterprise environments. Thus we also tested these models' overheads *on the historical data*, by calculating the processing speeds (using *numbers of logs processed per* *second*). The tests were done on a server with two Intel(R) Xeon(R) Gold 6148 CPU 2.40 GHz and 512 GB RAM, and the results are shown in Table 5. For those three supervised models used in *D-Exfil* and *D-DGA*, RF achieves the fastest speed, with a processing speed of 49344.9 logs/s, following by SVM (24150.2) and MLP (9210.2). Although SVM has a relatively high speed during the evaluation on historical data, please note that the time complexity of SVM is actually much higher than others, which is $O(n^2)$. Thus the processing speed of SVM decreases rapidly as the data size increases. The two models in *D-Outlier*, iForest and X-Means, achieve speeds of 9149.0 logs/s and 4090.6 logs/s, respectively. As a reference, the average number of input DNS logs during the deployment is 1165.1 logs/s.

Considering both detection performance and overhead, RF and MLP models are more practical for *D-Exfil* and *D-DGA*, and iForest is more suitable for *D-Outlier*. Thus we picked these algorithms for the real-world deployment.

Results on Real-Time Traffic During Deployment: Based on the performance and overhead of different methods shown above, during real-world deployment, we picked random forests (RF) and multi-layer perceptron (MLP) for *D-Exfil* and *D-DGA*, and isolation forest (iForest) for *D-Outlier*. SVM and X-Means models are not used due to their lower precisions and higher overheads.

The results in Table 6 show that all chosen models achieve high precisions during the deployment (over 0.97 on average) with low false positives. iForest model has the least FPs, only 2.5 per day. RF models in two detectors both got less FPs than MLP models (3.9 and 5.6 per day, respectively), which demonstrates that RF models are more practical considering the investigation labor cost (12.0 FPs in total per day).

Considering true positives, *D-Outlier* has 29.3 TPs/day on average. *D-Exfil* has more (155.6 if use RF, 1070.0 if use MLP), while *D-DGA* has much more. This is due to the data distribution in our data trace: in which data exfiltration related domains and DGA-domains are more common. For exfiltration, the hosts often send multiple DNS queries for a large file or a series of multiple small files. While DGA often generates a large number of AGDs in a certain time interval.

As a result, considering performance, overhead and false alerts altogether, random forest model and isolation forest model appear more practical in the studied enterprise (which are shown in bold in Table 6).

5.3   Detection Results on Different Types of Threats

On average, over 4k logs were detected as malicious per day. D^2C^2 further aggregates these results based on internal hosts and remote IPs to reduce the investigation overhead for operators, and generate visualized results. Based on the results of different detectors, we list several types of threats below.

Data Exfiltration: The data exfiltration samples detected (TPs in Table 6) during our deployment are all conversations by security vendors (*e.g.*, McAfee [3] and Asiainfo [1]). They use DNS to transmit messages with their servers for a fast connection (usually UDP) bypassing the firewalls. This situation is also observed in other prior work [8]. These domain names were detected as malicious by D^2C^2's detectors, and then labeled as benign in the investigate phase, and then added to D^2C^2's whitelist, so that these samples did not trigger alerts of D^2C^2. Please note different enterprises might have different security vendors thus would end up with different whitelists.

DGA-Domains: DGA-domains are usually used to establish a connection with remote C&C servers. Persistent attempts of AGD querying indicate the host is likely compromised. D^2C^2 further aggregated them based on source and destination IPs for visualization and analysis, as shown in Fig. 4. From these results, we found that AGDs queries are mainly sent from 10 hosts. The top 2 of them are local DNS servers, but the remaining 8 hosts are desktop or data servers, which are very likely to have been compromised. Many of those domains are related to C&C and botnets. However, only 1 of these hosts was reported as malicious by other security measures (*e.g.*, Capsa Enterprise Edition by Colasoft [2]). That is, D^2C^2 detected at least 7 compromised internal hosts previously unknown to the operators of the enterprise.

Outliers: The *Outlier Detector* does not focus on one specific type, but tries to catch all samples deviated from normal ones. The results are further divided into the following categories:

FNs of Exfiltration and AGDs are those threats of data exfiltration or DGA-domains missed by the first two detectors. This may be caused by the labels in training data, which cannot cover *all* kinds of threats in the wild. Thus these results were used as feedback during our periodic updating and re-training, to improve the performance of the former two detectors.

Malware Related domains are related to some malicious activities, *e.g.*, trojans or worms, and are detected because of their abnormal strings hidden in their domains, which indicate malicious resource files or other contents.

Illegal Formats are those queried "domains" which are not actually domain names. Most of these domain-like strings contain illegal characters/substrings which are uncommon in normal domain names. These queries are usually caused by mistakes of employees, or configuration errors and bugs in hosts or other services (*e.g.*, a wrong hyperlink in an e-mail).

Typos are misspelling of popular websites. Some attackers register some domains which are very similar to popular websites for phishing. We further check the *RCODE* of the responses and find that they are actually harmless, mainly caused by the manual misspelling of the enterprise's name.

5.4   Visualization on Hosts

To better understand the causes of all these threats, and the impact on hosts in the enterprise, we built a visualization tool to display the relationships between hosts, remote IPs and threats. A snapshot of our visualized results on malicious domains is shown in Fig. 4, which is a graph displaying the relationship between hosts and remote IPs, with the different conditions in responses. Dots stand for hosts, remote IPs and connection state (RCODE), edges stand for DNS logs.

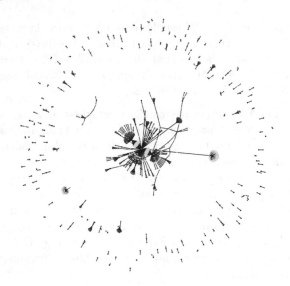

Fig. 4. A snapshot of threat graph generated by D^2C^2. Black dots denote hosts, red dots denote remote IPs and others denote RCODE (pink for NOERROR, blue for NXDOMAIN, green for SERVFAIL and yellow for REFUSED). An edge denotes a query or a response. (Color figure online)

The center cluster (highlighted due to its large number of related dots and edges) in Fig. 4 show a same remote IP which is the query response of multiple malicious domains (detected by D^2C^2), queried by dozens of hosts in the enterprise. We can see obviously that two of these hosts generated a large volume of malicious DNS query logs to this remote IP. Actually, these are DGA-domains (the types of detected anomalies are also labeled in the visualization, but are not shown in Fig. 4 due to the limited size of this figure). Based on such figures, the operators could further determine which of those threats are more urgent and have more security impact. In our deployment, most of these threats are from certain internal hosts, which are likely to be compromised. On the other hand, many hosts only have one or two attempts of malicious domain query. Operators can also tell which of those threats are from the same attackers, indicated by the shared vertexes of the corresponding edges in the visualization graph.

One byproduct of D^2C^2's visualization is that other suspicious activities (*e.g.*, cache poisoning) could also be found. For example, some remote IPs are the query responses not only for many malicious domains detected by D^2C^2 but also for benign domains. These are likely to be **cache poisoning**. For example, in the studied enterprise, one of such IPs we found is seen in the responses for 101k different domain names.

6 Conclusion

In this paper, we present a practical machine learning based framework, D^2C^2, to detect DNS covert communication threats. D^2C^2 is an end-to-end framework, which is easy to be deployed in enterprise environments and has high flexibility. D^2C^2 has been deployed in a large enterprise network with more than 25k hosts and more than 100 million DNS logs per day. We extensively evaluated D^2C^2 based on over 5 billion real-world DNS logs during a month. D^2C^2 achieved a high precision over 0.97. Furthermore, D^2C^2 successfully detected over 4k malicious DNS logs per day on average with low overhead and captured real-world security issues which are previously unknown to the operators, including seven compromised hosts with multiple C&C communication attempts.

Acknowledgment. This work has been supported by the National Key R&D Program of China (2019YFB1802504), the Beijing National Research Center for Information Science and Technology (BNRist) key projects, and has been partially supported by National Natural Science Foundation of China (grants U1736209 & 61572278). We are also very thankful for all those anonymous reviewers who have given valuable comments on this work.

References

1. Asiainfo technologies. https://www.asiainfo.com/en_us/index.html
2. Capsa network analyzer. http://www.colasoft.com/capsa/
3. Mcafee global threat intelligence. https://www.mcafee.com/enterprise/en-gb/threat-center/global-threat-intelligence-technology.html
4. Netlab opendata project. https://data.netlab.360.com/
5. Top 1 million website in the world. https://majestic.com/reports/majestic-million
6. Ahmadian, M.M., Shahriari, H.R., Ghaffarian, S.M.: Connection-monitor & connection-breaker: a novel approach for prevention and detection of high survivable ransomwares. In: 12th International Iranian Society of Cryptology Conference on Information Security and Cryptology (ISCISC), pp. 79–84. IEEE (2015)
7. Ahmed, J., Gharakheili, H.H., Raza, Q., Russell, C., Sivaraman, V.: Real-time detection of DNS exfiltration and tunneling from enterprise networks. In: 2019 IFIP/IEEE Symposium on Integrated Network and Service Management (IM), pp. 649–653. IEEE (2019)
8. Ahmed, J., Gharakheili, H.H., Raza, Q., Russell, C., Sivaraman, V.: Monitoring enterprise DNS queries for detecting data exfiltration from internal hosts. IEEE Trans. Netw. Serv. Manage. **17**, 265–279 (2019)
9. Antonakakis, M., et al.: From throw-away traffic to bots: detecting the rise of DGA-based malware. In: USENIX Security 12, pp. 491–506 (2012)
10. Chung, T., et al.: A longitudinal, end-to-end view of the DNSSEC ecosystem. In: USENIX Security 17, pp. 1307–1322 (2017)
11. Das, A., Shen, M.Y., Shashanka, M., Wang, J.: Detection of exfiltration and tunneling over DNS. In: International Conference on Machine Learning and Applications (ICMLA), pp. 737–742. IEEE (2017)
12. Eastlake, D.: RFC2535. Domain name system security extensions (1999)

13. Gao, H., et al.: An empirical reexamination of global DNS behavior. In: Proceedings of the ACM SIGCOMM 2013, pp. 267–278 (2013)
14. Hassan, W.U., et al.: NoDoze: combatting threat alert fatigue with automated provenance triage. In: NDSS (2019)
15. Lian, W., Rescorla, E., Shacham, H., Savage, S.: Measuring the practical impact of DNSSEC deployment. In: USENIX Security 13, pp. 573–588 (2013)
16. Lin, J.: Divergence measures based on the Shannon entropy. IEEE Trans. Inf. Theor. **37**(1), 145–151 (1991)
17. Liska, A., Stowe, G.: DNS Security: Defending the Domain Name System. Syngress (2016)
18. Liu, B., et al.: Who is answering my queries: understanding and characterizing interception of the DNS resolution path. In: USENIX Security 18, pp. 1113–1128 (2018)
19. Liu, D., Li, Z., Du, K., Wang, H., Liu, B., Duan, H.: Don't let one rotten apple spoil the whole barrel: towards automated detection of shadowed domains. In: ACM CCS (2017)
20. Lynch, C., Andonov, D., Teodorescu, C.: Multigrain - point of sale attackers make an unhealthy addition to the pantry (2016). https://www.fireeye.com/blog/threat-research/2016/04/multigrain_pointo.html
21. Mockapetris, P., et al.: Domain names-implementation and specification. STD 13, RFC 1035 (November 1987)
22. Oprea, A., Li, Z., Yen, T.F., Chin, S.H., Alrwais, S.: Detection of early-stage enterprise infection by mining large-scale log data. In: 45th Annual IEEE/IFIP International Conference on Dependable Systems and Networks, pp. 45–56. IEEE (2015)
23. Paxson, V., et al.: Practical comprehensive bounds on surreptitious communication over DNS. In: USENIX Security 13, pp. 17–32 (2013)
24. Pearce, P., et al.: Global measurement of DNS manipulation. In: USENIX Security 17, pp. 307–323 (2017)
25. Plohmann, D., Yakdan, K., Klatt, M., Bader, J., Gerhards-Padilla, E.: A comprehensive measurement study of domain generating malware. In: USENIX Security 16, pp. 263–278 (2016)
26. Renaud, R.: Gibberish detector. Website (2015). https://github.com/rrenaud/Gibberish-Detector
27. van Rijswijk-Deij, R., Sperotto, A., Pras, A.: DNSSEC and its potential for DDoS attacks: a comprehensive measurement study. In: IMC 2014, pp. 449–460 (2014)
28. Robert, N., Luke, S.: UDPoS - exfiltrating credit card data via DNS (2018). https://www.forcepoint.com/blog/x-labs/udpos-exfiltrating-credit-card-data-dns
29. Schiavoni, S., Maggi, F., Cavallaro, L., Zanero, S.: Phoenix: DGA-based botnet tracking and intelligence. In: Dietrich, S. (ed.) DIMVA 2014. LNCS, vol. 8550, pp. 192–211. Springer, Cham (2014). https://doi.org/10.1007/978-3-319-08509-8_11
30. Schüppen, S., Teubert, D., Herrmann, P., Meyer, U.: FANCI: feature-based automated NXDomain classification and intelligence. In: USENIX Security 18, pp. 1165–1181 (2018)
31. Sheridan, S., Keane, A.: Detection of DNS based covert channels. In: European Conference on Cyber Warfare and Security, p. 267. Academic Conferences International Limited (2015)
32. Sivakorn, S., et al.: Countering malicious processes with process-DNS association. In: NDSS (2019)
33. Sun, X., Tong, M., Yang, J., Xinran, L., Heng, L.: HinDom: a robust malicious domain detection system based on heterogeneous information network with transductive classification. In: RAID 2019, pp. 399–412 (2019)

34. Szurdi, J., Kocso, B., Cseh, G., Spring, J., Felegyhazi, M., Kanich, C.: The long "taile" of typosquatting domain names. In: USENIX Security 14, pp. 191–206 (2014)
35. Tong, M., et al.: D3N: DGA detection with deep-learning through NXDomain. In: Douligeris, C., Karagiannis, D., Apostolou, D. (eds.) KSEM 2019. LNCS (LNAI), vol. 11775, pp. 464–471. Springer, Cham (2019). https://doi.org/10.1007/978-3-030-29551-6_41
36. Zang, X.D., Gong, J., Mo, S.H., Jakalan, A., Ding, D.L.: Identifying fast-flux botnet with AGD names at the upper DNS hierarchy. IEEE Access 6, 69713–69727 (2018)

CacheLoc: Leveraging CDN Edge Servers for User Geolocation

Mingkui Wei[1]([✉])[ID], Khaled Rabieh[2][ID], and Faisal Kaleem[2][ID]

[1] Cyber Forensics Intelligent Center, Computer Science,
Sam Houston State University, Huntsville, TX, USA
mwei@shsu.edu
[2] Computer Science and Cybersecurity, Metropolitan State University,
Saint Paul, MN, USA
{khaled.rabieh,faisal.kaleem}@metrostate.edu

Abstract. In nowadays' Internet, websites rely more and more on obtaining users' geolocation to provide customized services. However, besides Internet giants such as Google, who retains a large amount of detailed user information, most websites still rely on IP addresses for user geolocation, which is proven inaccurate and misleading by existing studies. In this paper, we propose a novel approach, namely *CacheLoc*, for coarse-grained user geolocation leveraging widely-deployed content delivery networks (CDNs). This work is motivated by the fact that CDN providers deploy a number of edge servers that are geographically distributed across the world. Many of these edge servers are assigned with unique identifiers that are tied to their location, which can be easily retrieved by inspecting HTTP responses headers served by these edge servers. As a result, a website can infer coarse-grained user location by asking a user to send an HTTP request to an arbitrary domain that is known being served by a CDN, and inspecting the corresponding responses. To evaluate the usability and accuracy of the cache-based user geolocation, we conducted practical experiments based on a commercial VPN with over 160 endpoints distributed in 94 countries. Our experiments demonstrate that cache-based geolocation can achieve at least accurate country-level granularity in the regions where CDN edge servers are densely deployed. Our work sheds light on a novel light-weight and self-contained user geolocation solution.

Keywords: Content delivery networks · User geolocation

1 Introduction

Websites in today's Internet rely more and more on obtaining users' geolocation to provide customized services, such as regional campaigns or promotional activities. Currently, the primary method to obtain a user's location is based on the user's IP address, to which there are two major approaches. The first approach

N. Park et al. (Eds.): SecureComm 2020, LNICST 336, pp. 22–40, 2020.
https://doi.org/10.1007/978-3-030-63095-9_2

is to directly obtain the user's IP address, and search it against known databases such as IP2Location [1] and Whois [2]. And the second approach is to leverage web APIs provided by Internet giants such as Google, who maintains substantial user information collected via multiple means (WiFi war-driving [3], for example). Both approaches, however, have their shortages. For the former IP-based user geolocation, the major issues lie in the lack of official ground truth to validate the correctness and accuracy of existing databases. It has been found by existing studies that for the same IP address, the distance between the locations obtained from two different databases can be as large as 800 Km [4]. The API-based approach, one the other hand, can obtain very accurate results. However, modern browsers have built-in mechanisms to block such APIs from operating. For instance, Google's geolocation API [5] will trigger a pop-up window asking the user's permission to explicitly allow his/her location to be shared with the website he is visiting. As Internet users' concern regarding their privacy is daily increasing, more likely than not, the user is going to block such location requests unless there are legitimate reasons to allow them.

In this paper, we propose a novel approach for user geolocation by leveraging the popularly used content delivery networks (CDNs). The new cache-based geolocation, namely the *CacheLoc*, is motivated by the fact that CDN providers deploy a large number of edge servers geographically distributed. Many of these edge servers are assigned with unique identifiers that are tied to their geolocation, which can be easily retrieved from HTTP responses served by these edge servers. By asking a client to issue a regular HTTP request to a domain that is served by CDNs and inspect corresponding response headers, a website can infer the location of the user who is currently visiting it. Such cache-based geolocation, although coarse-grained, can be sufficient for purposes such as regional campaign or advertisement. Furthermore, it can be used as a side-channel knowledge to cross-validate the results obtained from conventional IP-based geolocations.

Compared to conventional IP-based user geolocation, the cache-based approach has the following advantages.

1. The mechanism of the cache-based geolocation is very straightforward. While IP-based geolocation requires a website to interact with databases leveraging web APIs, the cache-based approach can be implemented with just a few lines of JavaScript embedded in the web document, which asks the client to issue one regular HTTP request and retrieve one value from response headers.
2. IP-based geolocation relies on third party databases that may incur subscription fees, while the cache-based approach is self-contained and completely free since all that required is to ask the user to issue an HTTP request to a public domain.
3. The correctness and accuracy of IP-based geolocation are hard to be validated because there lacks any official ground truth. Cache-based approach, on the other hand, is based on publicly known and reliable information and therefore bears higher reliability.

In the following, we present the details of the cache-based user geolocation solution. The content of the rest of this paper is organized as follows. In Sect. 2, we introduce necessary background knowledge that assist the reader to understand *CacheLoc*. In Sect. 3, we present the details of the novel cache-based user geolocation. In Sect. 4, we discuss the usability of *CacheLoc* with preliminary experiment results. We conduct practical experiments and present their results in Sect. 5 to evaluate the accuracy and granularity of *CacheLoc*. Finally, we conclude our work in Sect. 6.

2   Background

In this section, we briefly introduce related works in user geolocation and the necessary background knowledge for content delivery networks.

2.1   Existing Works in User Geolocation

Most browsers use IP addresses to determine a user's location due to its simplicity. For IP-based user geolocation, the webserver subscribes to the access to geolocation IP databases, which maps ranges of IP addresses with the corresponding latitudes and longitudes coordinates. The pair of coordinates provides the sever with the location of the IP address, such as time, country, and city [6]. There are abundantly available IP geolocation databases, including ip2c.org, GeoLite2Geo Targetly, IP2Location Lite, and GeoIP Nekudo. While using such databases allows a server to locate a user without the need for GPS receivers or complicated configuration switching, it suffers from plentiful of drawbacks. For instance, IP-based geolocation is far from reliable and accurate since it only provides a rough estimate of users' locations. For example, the literature in [7, 8] shows that the locations obtained from different databases suffer huge accuracy errors up to 800 km in some cases. During our experiments, we also experienced many such cases. For instance, we found one IP address was located in Hong Kong by one database, but Australia by another. Further, IP databases come with many operation overheads such as paid subscriptions for support, frequent updates to guarantee better data accuracy, scalability, and management issues.

Li et al. [4] proposed city-level IP geolocation based on network topology community detection method to improve the accuracy of geolocation. They use the community detection algorithm in complex networks to find the different communities in the network topology and determine the location of the communities. The geographical position of target IP is obtained according to the communities of target IP. The experiment shows that its location accuracy ratio is above 96%. Triukose et al. examine IP address allocation in cellular data networks, with emphasis on understanding the feasibility of IP-based geolocation techniques. The authors used two commercial IP geolocation databases, MaxMind [9] and IPinfoDB [10] to test the ability of the databases to determine the ability of these databases to return host location based on IP addresses seen by the application's server.

API-based geolocation is a new approach that uses the browser's HTML5 Geo-location feature along with the Maps JavaScript API [11] to detect users' locations, all leveraged by Google's comprehensive database about the user's profile. While this approach brings higher location accuracy, the location is only shared if the user allows location sharing in a pop-up window. With more and more Internet users begin to concern about their privacy, a user will likely deny such request unless necessary.

2.2 Content Delivery Networks

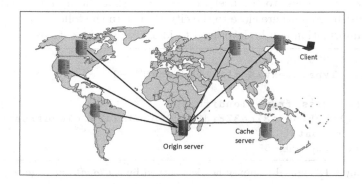

Fig. 1. Content delivery network

Content delivery network, or CDN, is a type of web cache that has undergone substantial growth in the recent decade [12]. It provides a scalable and cost-effective mechanism for accelerating web document dissemination among the Internet [13] by deploying a large number of edge servers around the globe. These edge servers sit between HTTP clients and origin servers, which cache static web documents served by origin servers, and use the cached copies to serve subsequent duplicate requests. Consequently, requests sent by a user in a certain location will always be served by the nearest CDN edge server, regardless of the origin server location. For example, as shown in Fig. 1, users located in the U.S. will be served by the servers in North America instead of the origin server in Africa. As a result, users will not only experience shorter page loading time, but the origin server will also see reduced workload in terms of the volume of HTTP requests. Because of these advantages, CDN has been adopted by a plethora of websites in recent years.

3 Cache Based Client Geolocation

The idea of CacheLoc is motivated by the fact that HTTP responses served by CDN edge servers are usually appended with CDN specific information. For some CDNs, such information reveals the location of the edge servers by whom the request was served. For example, Listing 1.1 presents typical response headers served by a Cloudfront's [14] edge server, where the request was sent via an HTTP proxy that locates in Texas, U.S. As highlighted in line 6, the `X-Amz-Cf-Pop` response header is a customized header appended by all edge servers belong to Amazon Cloudfront, and whose value indicates the request is served by the edge server `DFW55-C1`. This header value implies that the request is served by the edge server near Dallas, TX, because it is a common practice among many CDNs to name their edge servers with the three-letter IATA airport codes that are close by [15], and `DFW` refers to the Dallas/Fort Worth International Airport. Furthermore, because CDNs always serve HTTP requests with the edge servers closest to the user, we can infer that the user who issued the request must be somewhere close to the city Dallas. In the following, we describe how such information can be leveraged to identify users' locations.

```
1  HTTP/1.1 200 OK
2  Content-Type: text/html; charset=UTF-8
3  ...
4  X-Cache: Miss from cloudfront
5  Via: 1.1 5d52966f37c4378fd883294634452d6b.cloudfront.net (
      CloudFront)
6  X-Amz-Cf-Pop: DFW55-C1
```

Listing 1.1. Typical response headers served by a *Cloudfront* edge server.

3.1   Mechanism of CacheLoc

In Fig. 2, we present the flowchart explaining how a website can infer a user's geolocation leveraging CDN response headers. To facilitate the following illustration, we use the term *publisher* to refer the owner of the website that is visited by a user and wants to infer the user's location. We assume the publisher owns the domain `origin.com`. We also assume another domain, i.e., `pilot.com`, is a domain that is served by a CDN whose edge servers append location related headers to the responses.

As shown in Fig. 2, a user visits `origin.com`'s default main page (i.e., `index.html`) by sending a HTTP `GET` request, and the webserver will respond with the requested document once the request is received. In order to infer the user's location, the webserver inserts a JavaScript snippet as a part of *index.html*, which requests the user to issue an HTTP request to the pilot domain `pilot.com`. Because we are only interested in the response header, a `HEAD` request is sufficient.

After the document `origin.com/index.html` is received by the user's browser, the browser will execute the JavaScript and issue the request, which will be served by the closest edge server and append customized header indicating its identity. Once the response from the edge server is received at the user's browser, the JavaScript will inspect the response headers, retrieve the edge server identifier, and send it back to `origin.com`, which can be attached as the content of a `POST` request, or simply appended as a query string using a `GET` request. The

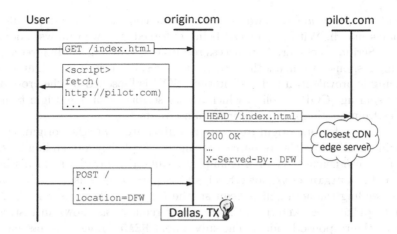

Fig. 2. Flowchart

publisher, knowing that `DFW` implies Dallas, can then infer the user is located in Texas and close to the city Dallas.

We demonstrate the necessary requirements of the pilot domain in order to implement *CacheLoc* in the following.

3.2   Pilot Domain Configuration

As depicted in Fig. 2, `origin.com` takes two steps to infer the user's geolocation: 1) it requests the user to issue an HTTP request to a pilot domain, and 2) it inspects the response to retrieve the value of a specific response header. While issuing the request and inspect response header can be easily done with just a few lines of JavaScript as presented in Listing 1.2, a barrier that may prevent the header information from being accessed lies in the same-origin policy (SOP) set forth by most modern web browsers [16].

```
1  var xhr = new XMLHttpRequest();
2  var url = 'https://pilot.com/';
3  xhr.open('HEAD', url);
4  xhr.send()
5  xhr.onreadystatechange = function() {
6   if(xhr.readyState == 4 ) {
7    var p = xhr.getResponseHeader('X-Served-By');
8   }
```

Listing 1.2. Typical response headers served by a *Cloudfront* edge server.

In specific, the same-origin policy is a critical security mechanism that is implemented on all modern web browsers, which restricts the interaction between a resource request issued from one origin and the actual resources reside on another origin, where the *origin* is composed of the three parts: *scheme*, the *host*, and the *port number*. Two origins are not considered identical unless all three parts match. With strict SOP being enforced, the web browser does not allow JavaScripts in one origin to access resources, including sending requests to or reading responses from, another origin. However, because cross-origin resource referencing is prevalent in today's Internet, SOP is loosened by the cross origin resource sharing (CORS) policy, which allows scripts from one origin to access resources from another origin under certain circumstances.

Particularly, for one origin to access resources from another origin, the latter origin must allow the resource sharing by explicitly appending a set of CORS response headers [17]. For example, assume the JavaScript in Listing 1.2 is included in `origin.com/index.html` and is parsed by a user's web browser. Prior to sending the actual `HEAD` request, the browser will first send a `OPTIONS` request to `pilot.com` (known as the *pre-flight* request) as shown in Listing 1.3, and check the response headers. The subsequent `HEAD` request will be sent only if the header `Access-Control-Allow-Origin` exists in the response and either `origin.com` or the wildcard symbol * presents as the value. Otherwise, the browser will not sent the `HEAD` request at all because `pilot.com` does not allow `origin.com` to access its resources.

```
1  OPTIONS /index.html
2  Access-Control-Request-Method: GET
3  Origin: https://example.com
4  ...
```

Listing 1.3. Typical response headers served by a *Cloudfront* edge server.

Furthermore, even if `Access-Control-Allow-Origin` exists and `origin.com` is explicitly allowed, the browser still restricts `origin.com` that only the 7 CORS-safelisted response headers [18] can be accessed: `Cache-Control`, `Content-Language`, `Content-Length`, `Content-Type`, `Expires`, `Last-Modified`, and `Pragma`. In order to access the CDN specific header, for example, the `X-Served-By` header, another CORS header, i.e., `Access-Control-Expose-Headers`, must also exist and explicitly specify either `X-Served-By` or * as the value.

Therefore, in order to successfully obtain the CDN related response header by issuing HTTP request and reading the response, `origin.com` must find a pilot domain that explicitly appends the headers `Access-Control-Allow-Origin` and `Access-Control-Expose-Headers`, and specify `origin.com` or *, and `X-Served-By` or * as the values, correspondingly.

The most straightforward way to obtain such a pilot domain is for the publisher to set up a dedicated domain and subscribe to CDN services, where the pilot domain can simply be a subdomain of `origin.com`. For instance, the publisher can create the subdomain `cloudfront.origin.com` and subscribed it to Cloudfront's service. Because this domain is entirely controlled by the publisher, the two CORS headers can be directly inserted into response headers by configuring the webserver. Because `origin.com` is only interested in the response headers, the pilot domain does not need to be substantiated with any real content. For example, a completely blank HTML page will suffice the purpose. Because many CDNs offers free tier services based on limited traffic amount or cost (for example, Cloudflare offers free tier service, Fastly provide $50 worth credit for new customers, and Cloudfront set the first 50GB traffic free of charge), a HEAD request only incurs minimal traffic and negligible cost at best.

Another approach to find a suitable pilot domain is to scan the Internet and attempt to find an independent domain that subscribed to a specific CDN service, and also includes the two headers `Access-Control-Allow-Origin` and `Access-Control-Expose-Headers` and the desired value (which should be *, because the specific value `origin.com` and `X-Served-By` is unlikely to be set by an independent third-party domain). This task could be laborious but not impossible. For instance, by scanning the first 50K domains against the *Majestic Million* domain list [19], we found the domain `cwtv.com` is subscribed to Cloudflare's CDN service, and has the above two headers being present and value set to be *. Compared with the first approach, this approach only requires a one time task and is simpler since it eliminates the complexities to set up the subdomain and subscribe to CDN services.

4   CacheLoc Usability

Compared with conventional IP-based user geolocation, the cache-based geolocation has the advantages that 1) It incurs very low overhead. The publisher only needs to insert a few lines of JavaScript code, while the user only needs to issue two HTTP requests, one to the pilot domain to obtain CDN related information and one to the publisher to inform such information. 2) It is self-contained and does not rely on any third party service. And 3) It's information is obtained from CDN edge servers, which is publicly available and thus verifiable. On the other hand, it is evident that the granularity of cache-based geolocation is limited by the edge server's density and distribution, and is unlikely to achieve high accuracy. Nevertheless, we argue that such coarse-grained granularity may be sufficient in many scenarios. For example, a political campaign or commercial advertisement may target a broad region where fine-grained user location is favorable but unnecessary. Further, this cache-based geolocation can also serve as cross-validations to conventional IP-based geolocation to improve the results' reliability. For instance, during our experiment, we encounter many cases where an IP address was located in two different countries, where the cache-based geolocation can then be used to narrow down the results to the correct one. We discuss the usability and limitations of cache-based geolocation in the following.

4.1   Suitable CDN Services for CacheLoc

CDN is a relatively new business model emerged in recent decade [12], and their distribution of services shows strong regional characters. Major CDN providers in North America include both traditional Internet companies, including Google, Amazon, and Akamai, and relatively new ones founded in the last decade, such as Cloudflare and Fastly. According to an online survey [20], currently, there are 23 CDN providers in the United States, however, not all of them are suitable for geolocation purposes. In order to be used for user geolocation, a CDN must present the following two properties: its edge servers' locations are publicly known, and their locations are identifiable from HTTP response headers.

For the first factor, i.e., publishing edge servers' information, different CDN shows different tendencies. Some providers are very transparent and actively publish detailed information regarding their CDN network. For example, Cloudflare publishes its up-to-date data centers' location (also known as the point of presence, or PoP) and the number of servers at each location [21]. On the other hand, providers such as Akamai are relatively conservative and only provide very brief information about their data centers' location.

For the second factor, different CDN providers also take different approaches. Some providers, including Cloudflare, Cloudfront, and Fastly, append a customized response header to identify the edge server that served the request. In particular, Cloudflare appends the `CF-RAY` header, for example, `CF-RAY: 572244ec8cadd266-DFW`, whose last section identifies the edge server; Cloudfront appends `X-Amz-Cf-Pop` header, for example, `X-Amz-Cf-Pop: DFW55-C2`, to indicate not only the location (i.e., `DFW`), but also specific edge server at this location (i.e., `C2`); and Fastly inserts `X-Served-By` header, for example, `X-Served-By: cache-dfw18677-DFW`, whose last section identifies the edge server. On the other hand, CDN providers such as Googles' Cloud CDN only inserts a simple `Via: 1.1 google` header to indicate the request is served by Google, Akamai does not have any header that reveals its edge server's identification either.

4.2 CDN's Data Center Locations

Based on the above discussions, in this study, we chose three CDNs to validate the proposed cache-based user geolocation, which are Cloudflare [22], Cloudfront [14], and Fastly [23]. In order to obtain a preliminary knowledge of the accuracy the cache-based geolocation can achieve, our first step is to collect and analyze information regarding each CDN, as described in the following.

Table 1. Statistics from website description. (* one cite can have multiple PoPs.)

	Cloudflare	Cloudfront	Fastly
Number of PoPs*	N/A	216	75
Number of countries	90	42	N/A
Number of cities	200	84	60

To begin with, we collected information regarding the data centers' location from each CDN's official website, and present the result in Table 1. Comparing the three, Cloudflare has the largest CDN network, which spans over 200 cities in more than 90 countries. A CDN provider may place multiple PoPs in one city, but may not necessarily differentiate them. For instance, according to the website description, Cloudfront has 6 PoPs in Dallas, TX, and during our experiment, we found these data centers are assigned with different names including DFW3, DFW50, DFW52, DFW53, DFW55 (we were only able to see 5 PoP names). On the other hand, Flastly states that it has 2 PoPs present at Dallas, but we were only able to see the unified identifier DFW and thus unable to distinguish the two servers.

Based on our preliminary evaluation, we suspect that the information published on CDN providers' website may not be up-to-date. Therefore, as the second step, we conducted a live scan to verify existing and identify new information. In specific, all three providers publish the range of IP addresses they owned on their website [24–26]. We start the experiment by scanning the whole IP range for TCP port 80. In specific, Cloudflare, Cloudfront and Flastly have 1,786,881, 1,422,793, and 222,208 unique IP addresses, respectively, among which 96,671, 140,347, and 65,969 are alive, i.e., responded to the scan. Note that these results are likely transient because CDN providers usually dynamically assign IP addresses to edge servers due to reasons such as load balancing [27], however, our results provide a snapshot of these CDN networks, based on which we can conduct the following analysis.

Then, we wrote a simple python script leveraging the *requests* library to send a HEAD request to each live IP address. For simplicity purposes, for each request, we set the Host header to be a random string (e.g., Host: aaa) rather than any valid host names. Because the host header is not recognizable by the edge servers, whey will respond with an error page indicating the specified host name is not accessible (500 Domain Not Found from Fastly, 409 Conflict from Cloudflare, and 403 Forbidden from Cloudfront), which nonetheless satisfied our purpose because even the error page still contains response header that includes edge servers' identifier. After we received all responses, we inspect the response headers and strip edge servers' identifier and summarize the result in Table 2. Specifically, we obtained a total of 283 unique edge server IDs from Cloudfront, which is much larger than the number of PoPs stated on its website (i.e., 216), implying the information on its website is obsolete. We also observe Fastly presents a slight difference, i.e., 78 obtained by scanning *v.s.* 75 stated on the website. We were not able to scan Cloudflare's CDN network because Cloudflare's CDN network uses Anycast [28]. As a result, even though we specifically send a request to a specific IP address, the request will always be routed to and served by the closest edge server. Therefore, we can only see the single edge server identifiers that is closest to us.

4.3 Limitation

From the edge server maps of the three CDNs [21, 29, 30], it is evident that their edge servers are densely deployed only in North America and Europe. Therefore, we can only expect higher accuracy and finer granularity in these regions. However, as a proof of concept, we do not aim to practically geolocate

Table 2. Statistics from experiment.

	Cloudflare	Cloudfront	Fastly
Total IP addresses	1,786,881	1,422,793	222,208
Live IP addresses	96,671	140,347	65,969
Unique IDs	N/A	283	78

users worldwide. Further, such a shortage can be easily addressed by leveraging more regional CDNs. For example, Alibaba CDN, a China-based cloud service provider, has 39 data centers deployed in major cities in China [31], which can be used to geolocate China-based users with much higher accuracy.

5   Experiment

In this section, we conduct empirical experiments to evaluate the usability and accuracy of the cache-based user geolocation.

5.1   Experiment Setup

In order to evaluate the usability and accuracy of the cache-based geolocation, the ideal approach would be issuing HTTP requests at multiple locations around the world and verify if the correct location could be obtained. Originally, we planned to leverage the Planet Lab [32], a research project incorporated more than 2000 research institutions across the world, where a user can request access to any of these nodes. However, it seemed to us the Planet Lab project had been discontinued, as we have attempted a few times to email the support staff and never get any reply. Therefore, we finally decided to take an alternative approach by using VPN services. In specific, we purchased access to Express VPN [33], a VPN provider that has 160 VPN endpoints across 94 countries, which has the largest number of endpoints among all VPN providers that we are aware of. Express VPN also has a Linux command-line interface that allows us to write scripts and conduct experiments in batch.

Because we do not own a domain by ourselves, we are unable to completely replicate the scenario described as in Fig. 2. However, since our objectives are to validate the usability and evaluate the accuracy of the cache-based user geolocation, we design the following experiment as an alternative, which achieves our objectives nonetheless.

In specific, we first scan against the *Majestic Million* domain list [19] as mentioned above, and find three arbitrary domains that use Cloudfront, Cloudflare, and Fastly's service, respectively. Then, we wrote a script, which can automatically log in to each VNP endpoint, and issue three HTTP requests to each of these three domains. Then, we collect the response from these three domains, and extract the edge server identifier and save them into a log file.

It is noteworthy that because we do not know the exact location of any of these VPN endpoints, but only the country (or city, for a few cases) each endpoint is placed, in this experiment, we do not seek to pinpoint or verify their accurate locations using cache-based geolocation. Instead, our objective is to evaluate to what extent these 160 locations can be uniquely differentiated using the proposed cache-based geolocation method. However, we argue that this restricted experiment does not diminish the effectiveness of the cache-based geolocation as a general solution for user geolocation. This is because as long as we can uniquely differentiate these endpoints, knowing the identity and accurate location is only a trivial and laborious task. For instance, a capable publisher can gradually build its own database based on users' information. Specifically, the publisher can enable the cache-based location and still ask to access the user's GPS based location. Although such requests may be rejected by most users, it is still likely to be allowed by a few users due to reasons such as carelessness or by accident. Once the publisher obtains one accurate location, it can associate this accurate location with the specific CDN edge server identifier, and be informed that users with the same CDN identifier must from a place that is close to this known accurate location. Gradually, the publisher is able to build a quite accurate geolocation map, which can be further refined each time a user allows his/her accurate location to be accessed.

5.2 Experiment Results and Analysis

Statistical and Geological Results. During our experiment, we were able to successfully connect to 148 endpoints among 160 that is claimed on Express VPN's official website [33], and collected a total of 444 HTTP responses. These 148 endpoints span in 93 countries, which covers most countries in America and Europe, many countries in Southeast Asia, and a few countries in the Middle East and Africa, which is consistent with the official website description. Most endpoints were named by the country name where they locate. Figure 3 presents the countries that were covered by Express VPN's endpoints. Among these 93 countries, 13 countries have more than one VPN endpoints present, in which case, these endpoints were named by the country name append with the city's name and a numerical index. In the following, we analyze the usability and accuracy of cache-based geolocation from both the country level and the city level.

Country Level Geolocation. As explained, the three CDNs that we have chosen, i.e., Cloudfront, Cloudflare, and Fastly, are U.S. based CDN providers and have their market focus in North America and Europe. Therefore, we expect the accuracy of cache-based geolocation bears much higher accuracy in differentiating European countries. In the following description, we separately demonstrate the results for European countries and the rest of the world.

We first present the geolocation result with a single CDN. In total, these 93 countries were served by 41 Cloudfront edge servers, 24 Fastly edge servers,

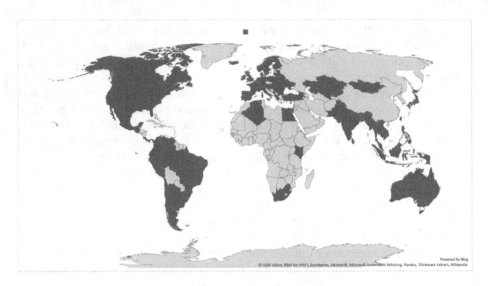

Fig. 3. Countries where Express VPN's endpoints present.

and 31 Cloudflare edge servers, respectively. Among which, 46 European countries were served by 23, 12, and 18 edge servers from Cloudfront, Fastly, and Cloudflare, and 47 non-European countries were served by 20, 14, and 15 edge serves from the same three CDN providers. This implies that, for example, using Cloudfront's edger server, we are able to at least narrow a user's location down to two countries on average, if the user is within Europe (i.e, $46/23/ = 2$). We present the visualized map of Cloudfront's result in Fig. 4, in where we use different colors to identify countries being served by different edge servers. The same result from Fastly and Cloudflare are presented in the Appendix as in Figs. 8 and 7.

Observing these figures, we are able to find edge server deployment does present strong regional characters. Take Fig. 7 as an example, we can observe that the few adjacent countries in middle Europe including Austria, Slovenia, Croatia, Serbia, and Slovakia are all served by one edge server (i.e., all colored with the same Grey color). Furthermore, by comparing the maps between different CDNs, we notice different CDN's have different edge server deployment strategies. For instance, in Fastly's edge server map, we can see while Austria and Slovakia are still served by the same edge server, Solvenia was instead served by the edge server that also serves Italy. And Croatia and Serbia were served by another different edge server. This implies that a finer granularity of user geolocation can be achieved by leveraging multiple CDNs, similar to user location using cellular towers with triangulation [34].

In specific, by holistically considering these 3 CDNs, the 93 countries now see 57 different Cloudfront-Cloudflare-Fastly edge server combinations, a higher resolution than any of the three single CDNs. For the 46 European countries, they can now be separated into 35 categories, a 25% increase in accuracy, i.e.,

a European user can now be narrowed down into an average 1.3 countries. For
the 47 non-European countries, they can be separated into 23 categories. We
present the new geolocation map leveraging all 3 CDNs in Fig. 5. Comparing
with Figs. 4, 7, and 8, it is obvious that higher accuracy has been achieved, as
less adjacent countries shares the same color.

Fig. 4. European countries served by different Cloudfront's edge servers.

State and City Level Geolocation. Next, we present the result to identify
states and cities in the U.S. Totally, Express VPN has 27 endpoints locates
within the United States, which were distributed among 13 cities that belong to
10 states (excluding Washington, D.C.). Metropolitan cities such as Los Angeles
have more than one endpoint. Shown in Fig. 6 is the result when all 3 CDNs
are leveraged to geolocate the states where these endpoints are located. Because
these states are geographically sparse, we found any one of the 3 CDNs alone
is capable of uniquely identify these states. Among these ten states, Florida
State has two endpoints located in Tampa and Miami. California State has two
endpoints located in Los Angeles and San Francisco. All these cities can also be
uniquely identified by either one of these 3 CDNs.

Sub-city Level Geolocation. Finally, we evaluate the accuracy of cache-
based geolocation within the sub-city level. In particular, within the U.S., five
metropolitan cities have more than one endpoints, which are: Los Angeles that
has seven endpoints, Dallas, Miami, New York, and Washington, D.C., each has
two endpoints. According to our experiment result, Cloudflare has the lowest resolution in identifying sub-city level locations, for example, all seven endpoints in

Fig. 5. European countries served by leveraging 3 CDNs' edge servers.

Los Angeles were served by the edge server LAX, while Cloudfront has the highest resolution on the other hand, which alone can identify five endpoints located in LA. When putting together, the seven endpoints can be differentiated into six categories, implying satisfactory resolution in high population cities. Detailed such result is demonstrated in Table 3. For the other four cities, except the two endpoints in New York, all other endpoints can be uniquely identified when three CDNs being utilized.

Table 3. 7 VPN endpoints in Los Angeles served by 3 CDN edge serves.

Endpoints' name	Cloudfront	Fastly	Cloudflare
Los Angeles	LAX3-C1	BUR	LAX
Los Angeles-1	LAX3-C3	LAX	LAX
Los Angeles-2	LAX3-C4	BUR	LAX
Los Angeles-3	LAX3-C1	BUR	LAX
Los Angeles-4	LAX50-C1	BUR	LAX
Los Angeles-5	LAX3-C3	BUR	LAX
Santa Monica	LAX3-C2	LAX	LAX

5.3 Discussion and Future Works

As demonstrated by the experiments, the cache-based user geolocation is able to achieve *at least* country-level granularity in the regions where CDN servers are

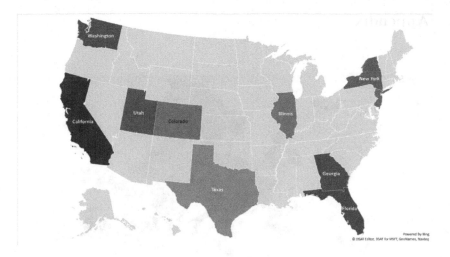

Fig. 6. U.S. states identified by leveraging 3 CDNs.

densely deployed. Due to our limited resource, we were not able to evaluate at smaller granularity, however, based on the results we have obtained, it is evident that finer granularity can be achieved. In specific, the VPN we used only has 46 endpoints present in Europe, which touched only 23, 12, and 18 edge servers belong to Cloudfront, Fastly, and Cloudflare, respectively. However, according to their official websites, these 3 CDNs posses 59, 13, and 47 total edge servers in Europe correspondingly. Therefore, if we were able to obtain more endpoints for evaluation, we can achieve much finer granularity. As such, our future work will focus on seeking more endpoints and conduct more comprehensive evaluations.

6   Conclusions

In this paper, we proposed the *CacheLoc* as a novel user geolocation solution. This cache-based user geolocation solution is easier, cost-free, and more reliable compared to conventional IP-based ones. With limited resources, we conducted multiple experiments to evaluate the usability and accuracy of *CacheLoc*, and our results demonstrate the cache-based approach is feasible and effective for coarse-grained user geolocation. We will be focusing on obtaining more resources for more comprehensive *CacheLoc* evaluation for our future works.

A   Appendix

Fig. 7. European countries served by different Cloudflare's edge servers.

Fig. 8. European countries served by different Fastly's edge servers.

References

1. IP2Location: Ip2location (2020). https://www.ip2location.com/
2. Whois: Whois (2020). https://www.whois.net/

3. Schwartz, M.J.: Google wardriving: how engineering trumped privacy (2020). https://www.darkreading.com/risk-management/google-wardriving-how-engineering-trumped-privacy/d/d-id/1104126
4. Li, M., Luo, X., Shi, W., Chai, L.: City-level IP geolocation based on network topology community detection. In: 2017 International Conference on Information Networking (ICOIN), pp. 578–583. IEEE (2017)
5. Google: Geolocation API developer guide (2020). https://developers.google.com/maps/documentation/geolocation/intro
6. Taylor, J., Devlin, J., Curran, K.: Bringing location to IP addresses withIP geolocation. J. Emerg. Technol. Web Intell. **4**, 273–277 (2012)
7. Poese, I., Uhlig, S., Kaafar, M.A., Donnet, B., Gueye, B.: IP geolocation databases: unreliable? ACM SIGCOMM Comput. Commun. Rev. **41**(2), 53–56 (2011)
8. Shavitt, Y., Zilberman, N.: A geolocation databases study. IEEE J. Sel. Areas Commun. (JSAC) **29**, 2044–2056 (2011)
9. MaxMind: Maxmind (2020). https://www.maxmind.com/en/home
10. Ipinfodb: Ipinfodb (2020). https://ipinfodb.com/
11. Google maps platform. https://developers.google.com/maps/documentation/javascript/geolocation
12. Bizety: CDN market size in 2015 and 2019 (2020). https://www.bizety.com/2015/08/15/cdn-market-size-in-2015-and-2019-2/
13. Loulloudes, N., Pallis, G., Dikaiakos, M.D.: Information dissemination in mobile CDNs. In: Buyya, R., Pathan, M., Vakali, A. (eds.) Content Delivery Networks. LNEE, vol. 9, pp. 343–366. Springer, Heidelberg (2008). https://doi.org/10.1007/978-3-540-77887-5_14
14. Amazon: Amazon cloudfront (2020). https://www.godaddy.com/
15. How fastly builds pops
16. Same origin policy
17. MDN web docs: Cross-origin resource sharing (CORS) (2020). https://developer.mozilla.org/en-US/docs/Web/HTTP/CORS
18. MDN web docs: Access-control-expose-headers (2020). https://developer.mozilla.org/en-US/docs/Web/HTTP/Headers/Access-Control-Expose-Headers
19. The majestic million. https://majestic.com/reports/majestic-million
20. United states CDN. https://www.cdnplanet.com/geo/united-states-cdn/
21. The cloudflare global anycast network. https://www.cloudflare.com/network/
22. Cloudflare: Cloudflare (2020). https://www.cloudflare.com/
23. Fastly: Fastly (2020). https://www.fastly.com/
24. Accessing Fastly's IP ranges. https://docs.fastly.com/en/guides/accessing-fastlys-ip-ranges
25. Locations and IP address ranges of CloudFront edge servers. https://docs.aws.amazon.com/AmazonCloudFront/latest/DeveloperGuide/LocationsOfEdgeServers.html
26. Cloudflare IP ranges. https://www.cloudflare.com/ips/
27. Holowczak, J., Houmansadr, A.: Cachebrowser: bypassing chinese censorship without proxies using cached content. In: Proceedings of the 22nd ACM SIGSAC Conference on Computer and Communications Security, pp. 70–83 (2015)
28. What is anycast? How does anycast work? https://www.cloudflare.com/learning/cdn/glossary/anycast-network/
29. A new architecture for the modern internet. https://www.fastly.com/network-map
30. Amazon CloudFront key features. https://aws.amazon.com/cloudfront/features/
31. Alibaba: Alibaba cloud's global infrastructure (2020). https://www.alibabacloud.com/global-locations

32. Planet Lab: Planet lab (2020). https://www.planet-lab.org/
33. Express VPN: Express VPN (2020). https://www.expressvpn.com/vpn-server
34. 4n6.com: Cell phone triangulation (2020). https://4n6.com/cell-phone-triangu
    lation/

Modeling Mission Impact of Cyber Attacks on Energy Delivery Systems

Md Ariful Haque[1]($\boxtimes$), Sachin Shetty[1], Charles A. Kamhoua[2],
and Kimberly Gold[3]

[1] Department of Computational Modeling and Simulation Engineering,
Old Dominion University, Norfolk, VA, USA
mhaqu001,sshetty@odu.edu
[2] Network Security Research, The U.S. Army Research Laboratory,
Adelphi, MD, USA
charles.a.kamhoua.civ@mail.mil
[3] Naval Surface Warfare Center, Crane Division, Crane, IN, USA
kimberly.gold@navy.mil

Abstract. Today energy delivery systems (EDS) face challenges in dealing with cyberattacks that originate by exploiting the communication network assets. Traditional power systems are highly complex and heterogeneous. These systems focus on reliability, availability, and continuous performance and, thus, not designed to handle security issues. Network administrators often utilize attack graphs to analyze security in EDS. Although attack graphs are useful tools to generate attack paths and estimate possible consequences in a networked system, they lack incorporating the operational or functional dependencies. Localizing the dependencies among operational missions, tasks, and the hosting devices in a large-scale cyber-physical network is also challenging. Current research works handle the system dependency and the attack scenario modeling separately using dependency graphs and attack graphs, respectively. To address the gap of incorporating the mission operational dependencies with possible attack scenarios, in this work, we offer an approach to assess the cyberattack impact on the operational mission of the EDS by combining the logical attack graph and mission functional dependency graph. We provide the graphical modeling details and illustrate the approach using a case study of SCADA (supervisory control and data acquisition) operations within an EDS environment.

Keywords: Energy delivery systems · Attack graph · Mission dependency · Impact propagation graph · Impact assessment · Operability

1 Introduction

The energy delivery systems (EDS) increasingly rely on the communication network for monitoring, operation, and control. The EDS broadly divides itself

© ICST Institute for Computer Sciences, Social Informatics and Telecommunications Engineering 2020
Published by Springer Nature Switzerland AG 2020. All Rights Reserved
N. Park et al. (Eds.): SecureComm 2020, LNICST 336, pp. 41–61, 2020.
https://doi.org/10.1007/978-3-030-63095-9_3

into the physical, control, and cyber layer. The physical layer is responsible for supporting power generation, transmission, and distribution. The control layer is responsible for sensing and reporting field-level data and corrects the setpoints as necessary through automated or manually initiated commands. At the same time, the cyber layer comprises the communication networks to monitor and evaluate performances of the physical layer devices and business-level operations. EDS's key component is the supervisory control and data acquisition (SCADA) system, which provides facilities to monitor, report, and controls different types of physical processes simultaneously. Therefore, the power system's reliable operation is heavily dependent on the attack-resilient functioning of the SCADA and the associated cyber systems.

Because of the heterogeneity and complex interconnectivity among the cyber and physical layers, the energy systems face challenges in assessing the overall mission impact of cyberattacks originating from the cyber layer. There are two research questions as yet not entirely analyzed by the research community:

1. How could we incorporate the critical operational dependencies to the traditional security analysis models to get a comprehensive assessment of mission impact and cyber resilience due to a potential exploit? Here, by dependencies, we mean mapping of the business mission to operation-critical functions/tasks, tasks to software programs/applications/services, and services to the underlying devices.
2. To develop preventive resilience methodologies, how could we assess and quantify the effects of cyberattacks on the operations of the physical layer, which comes from the stepping-stone exploitation of the cyber layer?

To identify the potential exploitable attack paths in the enterprise networks and CIs, researchers often rely on the analysis based on attack graph techniques. Although attack graphs provide insights in analyzing the network security flaws, they do not incorporate the mission-specific operational dependencies while depicting the attack paths. Thus, there remains a gap in evaluating overall mission impact and system operability during adverse attack scenarios. To address the gap of incorporation of mission dependency in attack graph analysis, Sun et al. [1] propose a technique to model the dependency relations by utilizing the service dependency graph and attack graph. Cao et al. [2] present a quantitative metric for business process impact assessment for Enterprize networks using attack graphs and entity dependency graphs. Both the works give a concrete reason to incorporate the dependency into the attack graph. Still, the works lack in providing formal guidance on how to correlate the attack graph and dependency graph; thus, it is not clear how to apply the methods in a specific cyber-physical systems environment.

In this work, we have addressed some of the above research gaps. We introduce new graph types specific to mission, more specifically, mission functional dependency graph, mission impact propagation graph, and mission impact assessment graph. We have developed a NIST defense-in-depth [3] architecture-based SCADA operational case study illustrating the approaches that we formalize under the context of this paper. The main contributions of this work are as follows:

i) A graph-theoretic modeling approach to incorporate the critical mission dependencies (e.g., mapping the mission to tasks, tasks to applications, and applications to hosts) to the logical attack graph model

ii) Quantifying the overall mission impact of cyberattacks and operability of EDS originating by exploiting the communication network assets and

iii) A realistic SCADA operations case study to systematically illustrate the modeling approach and ways to implement.

We organize the rest of the paper as follows. Section 2 presents the definitions and assumptions. Section 3 describes the system model for mission impact assessment. Section 4 explains the modeling approach in detail. Section 5 illustrates the case study and analysis. Section 6 provides some insights on the related works. Finally, Section 7 concludes the article with future directions.

2 Preliminaries: Definitions and Assumptions

Definition 1. *Mission: A mission is an objective to maintain the operational functionality of the constituent parts of the system through securing the performance of the required tasks according to the design or specifications. A mission relies on a set of functions termed as 'tasks' to get accomplished.*

Definition 2. *Task: A task is the component of a mission that has its specific function/functions to be carried out to maintain the proper operational level of the underlying programs/processes/devices.*

Definition 3. *Application: An application is an individual or combined licensed or open-source software (commonly known as 'programs') in use by the network that supports the functions of the task. Here, we use the term 'application' instead of 'program' or 'service' to mean the same.*

Definition 4. *Host: A host is a network device that houses programs or software applications. The types of hosts include but not limited to:*

- *IT Devices: Servers, desktops, databases, other computing devices, etc.*
- *Network Devices: Firewalls, routers, switches, Wi-Fi access points, etc.*
- *SCADA Devices: Historians, human-machine interfaces (HMI), engineering workstations, master terminal units (MTU), etc.*
- *Physical Controllers: PLC (programmable logic controller), RTU (remote terminal unit), IED (intelligent electronic device), PMU (phasor measurement unit), sensors, transducers, actuators, etc.*

Definition 5. *Operability: Operability is the state of a host functioning at some level of performance. The unit of operability is equivalent to a von Neumann-Morgenstern utility measure (expressed in utils as in FDNA [4]). We denote here the utils as a real-valued number within the interval [0,1].*

Definition 6. *Present Operational Capability (POC):* *POC is a time-dependent operational capability of the host indicating the operability level of the host/device at the given time instant. POC 1.0 means fully operable and POC 0.0 means fully inoperable.*

Definition 7. *Strength of Dependency (SOD):* *It depicts to what extent the operability level of the parent node can influence the child node's operability level. For example, an SOD between a task and a host indicates the extent/fraction of the operability level of the host that can be reduced due to the malfunction/compromise/impact on the task.*

Definition 8. *Impact Factor:* *'Impact' means the effect or consequence of an event, incident, or occurrences on the operability of the constituent parts of the system or network. The impact factor is the fraction or amount of loss or reduction in the associated device's performance/operability.*

Assumption 1. Paths between single component nodes of mission graphs are acyclic. For example, if there is an inter-dependency of task t_1 on application a_1, then there is no reverse path of dependency from a_1 to t_1. Similarly, if there is an intra-dependency of task t_1 to t_2, then there exists only one path from $t_1 \rightarrow t_2$, and no paths from $t_2 \rightarrow t_1$.

3   System Mission Impact Assessment Model

We provide a high-level mission impact assessment model in Fig. 1. The input system comprises network vulnerability and mission dependency data. We utilize open-source network scanning tools (such as Nessus[1], OpenVAS[2], etc.) to collect

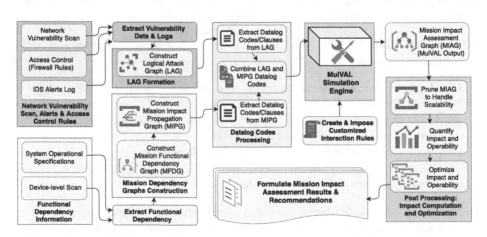

Fig. 1. System mission impact assessment model

---

[1] NESSUS Vulnerability Assessment (https://www.tenable.com/products/nessus).
[2] OpenVAS - Open Vulnerability Assessment Scanner (https://www.openvas.org/).

the network vulnerability information. We use Snort for IDS (intrusion detection system) alerts. There are other vulnerability scanning tools available specific to the ICS environment, such as Nextnine's ICS shield, Radiflow, Darktrace ICS, and Splunk, etc. We extract the required network logs from vulnerability scan, IDS alert, and firewall rules to generate the logical attack graph (LAG). We use quantitative score of the vulnerabilities from CVSS[3] and NVD[4]. We utilize host-level scanning and system operational documents to identify the mission-critical operational tasks and their dependencies on the devices. There are some open-source/commercial tools to identify the network application-level dependencies, such as ManageEnige's application discovery and dependency mapping (ADDM), Device42, AppDynamics, etc. The extracted system dependency data leads to the modeling of the mission functional dependency graph (MFDG). We build the mission impact propagation graph (MIPG) by reversing the edges and using transitivity rules. We combine the logical attack graph (LAG) and mission impact propagation graph (MIPG) using Datalog[5] clauses. We also define and add our custom interaction rules for the open-source MulVAL [5] security analyzer. The MulVAL provides the mission impact assessment graph (MIAG) as an output. Based on the network size, we may need to prune the mission impact assessment graph to handle the scalability issue. We then compute the tasks' impacts and relate that to the operability of hosts and impact on the mission as we provide in Subsect. 4.6 and 4.7.

Let us consider an example of the operation & maintenance of a manufacturing plant (i.e., the mission). The process depends on real-time data collections by the sensor devices, and a historian device stores those data (i.e., the task). The historian is of 'SIEMENS,' and the historian software application is 'SIMATIC 2014 SP3 Basic' (i.e., the app). This application is installed and running in a Windows Server 2008 SP2 (i.e., the host). The Windows Server software has a 'remote code execution' vulnerability with the ID 'CVE-2017-0148'. In this case, the attack graph depicts a vulnerability that would lead to the privilege of code execution in the Windows Server. The **'Network Vulnerability'** block captures these pieces of information in the above diagram. Now, the operational mission depends on data collection and storing tasks, which again depend on the 'SIMATIC' application, which is hosted by Windows-based Server. The MFDG captures these dependency scenarios. Therefore, we find that if there is an executive privilege on the host (i.e., Windows Server), then this privilege would lead to the impact on the associated applications, tasks, and propagate to the overall mission. MIPG captures this scenario, which we construct by reversing the MFDG and using transitivity rule. The block **'Mission Dependency Graph Construction'** reflects this whole dependency scenario. Finally, we consolidate the Datalog codes and use custom made interaction rules in the MulVAL simulation. We present detailed formal definitions of the graphs in Sect. 4.

---

[3] Common Vulnerability Scoring System (https://www.first.org/cvss/).

[4] National Vulnerability Database (https://nvd.nist.gov/).

[5] Declarative Logic Programming.

4   Graphical Modeling Approach Details

In this section, we provide formal definitions of the graph-theoretic modeling approaches and computation processes to derive the mission impact and system operability.

4.1   Logical Attack Graph (LAG)

We utilize the logical attack graph definition by Gonda et al. [6]. The LAG has three types of nodes: (1) **Primitive fact nodes** (N_c) represent **facts** about the system, such as network connectivity, access control or firewall rules, user accounts on host machines, etc.; (2) **Derivation nodes** (N_e) also known as **rule/action/execution/exploit** nodes represent an action the attacker can take or satisfy certain conditions to gain a privilege in the system; (3) **Derived fact nodes** (N_p) (also known as **privilege nodes**) represent a **capability** an attacker gains after performing an action by satisfying the pre-conditions. There are three relationships possible among the nodes. An **'AND'** relation implies that all the pre-conditions need to be satisfied; an **'OR'** relation means that either of the pre-conditions to be fulfilled; a **'FLOW'** relation suggests that the information flows its effects to the successor node. In a LAG, we have:

- Set of vertices, $V = N_c \cup N_e \cup N_p$
- Set of edges, $E \subseteq (N_e \times N_p) \cup ((N_p \cup N_c) \times N_e)$
- If the set of all existing vulnerabilities is V', then vertex intrinsic weight,

$$
f_v = \begin{cases} 1.0 & \text{if } v \in N_c \cup N_p \text{ and } v \notin V' \\ 0.8 & \text{if } v \in N_e, \text{ i.e., } 80\% \text{ probability of exploit as in } MulVAL \\ \frac{CVSS_v}{10} & \text{if } v \in N_c \text{ and } v \in V' \end{cases}
$$

4.2   Mission Functional Dependency Graph (MFDG)

Definition 9.   *A **mission functional dependency graph** G_b is a directed acyclic graph denoted by $G_b = (N_m, N_t, N_a, N_h, E, f_i, w_e, L, \alpha, \gamma)$ where N_m, N_t, N_a, and N_h represent mission, task, application, and host nodes, respectively; E is a set of edges denoted as (u, v) that represents direction of dependency; f_i is a non-negative weights associated with the nodes representing the intrinsic operability of the nodes; w_e is the edge weights; L is a mapping of vertices to the type (AND, OR, FLOW) of logical dependence among the vertices (i.e., mission, task, application, or host); $\alpha : N \times N \to [0,1]$ is the score assignment function representing strength of inter-dependency (inter-SOD). Similarly, $\gamma : N \times N \to [0,1]$ represents strength of intra-dependency (intra-SOD).*

- Set of vertices, $V = N_m \cup N_t \cup N_a \cup N_h$
- If the task t depends on application a (i.e., $t \to a$), and host h is housing application a (means, $a \to h$), then using the *transitivity rule*, we can say, $t \to h$, which means task t has dependency on host h. Thus, we can prune the MFDG to remove the application nodes and establish direct dependency between task to host.

– $N_m \times N_a = \emptyset$, and $N_m \times N_h = \emptyset$; this indicates there is no direct dependence of the mission on the applications or hosts.

4.3   Mission Impact Propagation Graph (MIPG)

We generate the mission impact propagation graph (MIPG) by applying a recursion on the pruned MFDG. Formally, we define the MIPG as follows.

Definition 10. *A mission impact propagation graph.* G_c *is a directed acyclic graph represented by the tuple* $G_c = (N_{hp}, N_{it}, N_{im}, N_d, E, f_v, w_e, \alpha, \gamma, h)$; *node* N_{hp} *represents an execution privilege on host;* N_{it} *is task impact node;* N_{im} *represent mission impact node;* N_d *represents rule node to satisfy to propagate the effect to child node;* E *is a set of edges denoting the direction of dependency;* f_v *is the node intrinsic score as in LAG;* w_e *is the edge weights computed using the logical dependence;* α *is the inter-SOD;* γ *is the intra-SOD, and* h *is a mapping of vertices to the type (i.e., AND, OR, FLOW) of dependence.*

– Set of vertices, $V = N_{hp} \cup N_d \cup N_{it} \cup N_{im}$
– Set of edges, $E \subseteq (N_{hp} \times N_d) \cup (N_d \times N_{it}) \cup (N_{it} \times N_d) \cup (N_d \times N_{im})$

4.4   Integrating LAG and MIPG Using Subgraph Merging Technique to Generate MIAG

We apply here a subgraph merging technique to combine LAG and MIPG. First, we present the types of edges in LAG and MIPG to help the audience understand the merging concepts.

Types of Edges in LAG. There are three types of edges in the LAG as shown in Fig. 2a. An edge (c, e) connecting primitive node (i.e., preconditions) (N_c) to the exploit (i.e., action) node (N_e) implies that by satisfying the condition c an attacker can execute exploit e. An edge (e, p) that connects an exploit node (N_e) to a derived node (i.e., privilege node) (N_p) means that by exploiting e an attacker can gain privilege p. An edge (p, e) from a derived node (N_p) to a exploit (i.e., action or rule) node (N_e) states that p is again a precondition to next exploit e.

Types of Edges in MIPG. In Fig. 2b(1), a gained host execution privilege p leads to exploit the next dependency relation d. In Fig. 2c(2), the dependency relation d implies flow of impact i on the next task or mission node (N_{it}, or N_{im}).

Subgraph Merging. We apply here a subgraph merging techniques utilizing the graph union operation [7]. We consider the LAG as the first subgraph and MIPG as the second subgraph. We then apply the graph union operations on LAG and MIPG to build the combined MIAG. We only consider the nodes and edges for this illustration as the other attributes are same for both LAG and MIPG. Formally, if $LAG\ G_a := G(V_1, E_1)$ where $V_1 = N_c \cup N_e \cup N_p$ and $E_1 \subseteq (N_e \times N_p) \cup ((N_p \cup N_c) \times N_e)$ and MIPG $G_c := G(V_2, E_2)$ where $V_2 = N_{hp} \cup N_d \cup N_{it} \cup N_{im}$ and $E_2 \subseteq (N_{hp} \times N_d) \cup (N_d \times N_{it}) \cup (N_{it} \times N_d) \cup (N_d \times N_{im})$, then we can utilize the sub-graph union operator ($\oplus$) as follows with the help of the mapping function $\lambda : N_p \mapsto N_{hp}$. The mapping function λ indicates that the privilege node N_p (i.e. execution privilege p) in LAG maps to host exploitation node N_{hp} (which is also execution privilege p) in MIPG. Thus, we can formulate the mission impact assessment graph MIAG as $G_d = G(V, E) := G_a \oplus G_c$, where G_a and G_c are the LAG and MIPG respectively. Then, $V := V_1 \oplus V_2 = V_1 \cup (V_2 \setminus u) = N_c \cup N_e \cup N_{hp} \cup N_d \cup N_{it} \cup N_{im}$, $u = N_{hp}$. Also, $E := E_1 \oplus E_2 = E_1 \cup E_2$.

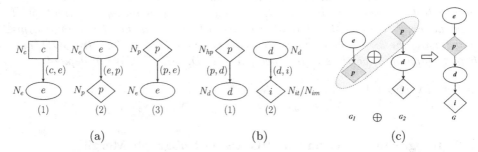

Fig. 2. (a) Edge types in LAG, (b) Edge types in MIPG, (c) Applying subgraph merging technique on LAG and MIPG to get MIAG (Subsect. 4.5)

4.5   Mission Impact Assessment Graph (MIAG)

Definition 11. *A **Mission Impact Assessment Graph (MIAG)** is a directed acyclic graph represented as $G_d = (V, E, f_v, h, \alpha, \gamma, \lambda)$ where V is a set of vertices that represents host information, pre-conditions, vulnerabilities, exploits, impacts on tasks, and impact on missions; E is a set of edges; f_v is a non-negative weights associated with the vertices; h is a mapping of vertices to the type (i.e., AND, OR, FLOW) of logical dependence among the vertices; α represents inter-SOD; γ represents intra-SOD; $\lambda : p \mapsto hp$ is a mapping function that maps an privilege p in LAG to the host privilege hp in MIPG.*

4.6   Impact Score Quantification Process Using MIAG

We associate each node (V) in the MIAG with two scores; the intrinsic score f_v and the derived score $P : V \to [0, 1]$. The intrinsic score stands for the inherent likelihood of an action/exploit e to execute, given that all the pre-conditions required for performing e in the given attack sequence are satisfied. The derived score measures the overall likelihood that an attacker successfully reaches and execute the exploit e and gain privilege p. We assume here that the events that an attacker may execute different exploits are independent of each other for simplicity. For shortening the illustration, we only consider conditions, exploits, and privilege nodes in MIAG to illustrate the computation process, which we also extend for the task and mission nodes. Given an MIAG, we formalize the derived scores for exploit and privilege $P(e)$ and $P(p)$ respectively as below:

- $P(e) = f_v(e) \cdot \prod_{c \in R_e} P(c)$, where $R_e \subseteq (N_c \times N_e) \cup (N_p \times N_e)$
- $P(p) = f_v(p)$, if $R_p(p) = \emptyset$, and $P(p) = f_v(p) \cdot \bigotimes_{e \in R_p(p)} P(e)$ otherwise; where $R_p(p) \subseteq (N_c \times N_p) \cup (N_e \times N_p)$, and the operator $\bigotimes P(e) = P(e_1) \cup P(e_2) = P(e_1) + P(e_2) - P(e_1) \cdot P(e_2)$, where $\{e_1, e_2\} \subseteq R_p(p)$.

Similar computation process we apply for computing the derived scores/ impacts of task nodes.

4.7   Computing Device and System Operability Using Dependency Relations and Task Impacts

We present here six different cases to compute the operability considering the inter and intra-dependency relations among tasks and hosts. Here, we utilize FDNA by Garvey et al. [4] and mission impact assessment by Jakobson et al. [8] to formulate the impact factor and the operability. Here, we use the notations as follows: h_n denotes nth host/device; t_n indicates nth task; I_{t_n} is the impact on task t_n found from MIAG; OC_{h_n} is the computed operability of host h_n; $POC_{h_n}(t)$ depicts present operational capability before any attack incident; $IF_{h_n}(t^+)$ is the impact factor (i.e., the fraction of reduction in operability) on host h_n at time t^+; t^+ are discrete time instances, where $t^+ > t$. There are two different dependency relations: inter-dependency and intra-dependency. $\alpha_{ij} = f(OC_{t_i}, POC_{h_j})$ is the strength of inter-dependency (inter-SOD) (having value in $[0, 1]$) of task t_i on host h_j which is a function of operability of task t_i (i.e, OC_{t_i}), and present operational capability of host h_j (i.e., POC_{h_j}); Similarly, $\gamma_{ij} = g(OC_{t_i}, OC_{t_j})$ is the intra-SOD (having value in $[0, 1]$) of task t_i on another task t_j which is a function of the operability of task t_i (i.e, OC_{t_i}), and task t_j (i.e., OC_{t_j}). We can formulate these values utilizing the feeder-receiver dependency methods described by Guariniello et al. [9]. In case, if we have no way to measure α_{ij}, and γ_{ij}, we can utilize the values of 1.0, 0.5, and 0 for *fully-dependent*, *partially-dependent*, and *non-dependent* cases respectively.

Case I: 'FLOW' Inter-dependency. In Fig. 3(a1) we have a task t_n 'FLOW' depends on the host machine h_n with a strength of dependency between them α_n. Figure 3(a2) shows their dependency in the form of MIDG. Here the impact on task t_n (i.e., I_{t_n}) has a 'FLOW' dependency on the operability of host h_n (i.e., OC_{h_n}). We can compute the operability OC_{h_n} at a discrete time instant t^+ using the present operational capability of h_n (i.e., POC_{h_n}) before the attack incident (i.e., time instant t) and the flow of task impact as follows, where $t^+ > t$.

$$IF_{h_n}(t^+) := \alpha_{nn} I_{t_n}(t^+) \tag{1}$$

$$OC_{h_n}(t^+) := max(POC_{h_n}(t) - IF_{h_n}(t^+), 0) \tag{2}$$

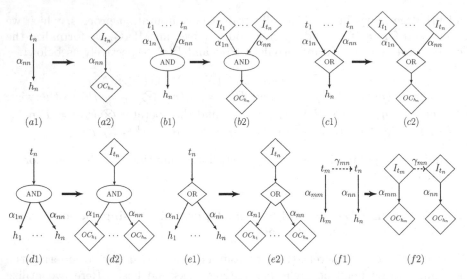

Fig. 3. Dependency relations and operability computation reference figure; (a1) and (a2) task to host 'FLOW' dependency; (b1) and (b2) multiple tasks 'AND' depend on single host; (c1) and (c2) multiple tasks 'OR' depend on single host; (d1) and (d2) single task 'AND' depend on multiple hosts; (e1) and (e2) single task 'OR' depend on multiple hosts; (f1) and (f2) task to task intra-dependency

$$POC_{h_n}(t^+) = OC_{h_n}(t^+) \qquad (3)$$

In Eq. 1, we compute the impact factor at time t^+. We utilize $IF_{h_n}(t^+)$ in Eq. 2 to compute $POC_{h_n}(t^+)$ which is updated operational capability of host h_n after the attack incident reduces the current operability; In Eq. 3, the $POC_{h_n}(t^+)$ is updated with the computed $OC_{h_n}(t^+)$ from Eq. 2, which assist in determining the operability in future time instances. We can get $POC_{h_n}(t)$ from the design documents or initialize to 1.00 if not available otherwise.

Case II: Multiple Tasks to Single Host 'AND' Inter-dependency. As shown in Fig. 3(b1), tasks t_1 to t_n have 'AND' dependencies on host machine h_n with the strength of dependencies α_{1n} to α_{nn}. Figure 3(b2) depicts the relationships in the form of MIDG. We compute the operability of host h_n at the time instant t^+ (i.e., $OC_{h_n}(t^+)$) using $POC_{h_n}(t)$ and the 'AND' dependency of task impacts $\{I_{t_1}(t^+), \ldots, I_{t_1}(t^+)\}$. The combined impact factor due to the 'AND' dependency relations are as follows.

$$IF_{h_n}(t^+) := min(\alpha_{1n}I_{t_1}(t^+), \alpha_{2n}I_{t_2}(t^+), \ldots, \alpha_{nn}I_{t_n}(t^+)) \qquad (4)$$

We utilize $IF_{h_n}(t^+)$ from Eq. 4 in Eq. 2 to compute the operability and in Eq. 3 to update the present operability.

Case III: Multiple Tasks to Single Host 'OR' Inter-dependency. As shown in Fig. 3(c1), tasks t_1 to t_n have an 'OR' dependency on host h_n with the strength of dependencies α_{1n} to α_{nn} respectively. Figure 3(c2) shows the node relationships in the form of MIDG. Similar to previous cases, first we compute the combined impact factor $IF_{h_n}(t^+)$ due to the 'OR' dependency of task impacts $\{I_{t_1}(t^+), \ldots, I_{t_1}(t^+)\}$ as in Eq. 5. We then utilize Eqs. 2 and 3 to compute $OC_{h_n}(t^+)$ using the present operational capability of $POC_{h_n}(t)$.

$$IF_{h_n}(t^+) := max(\alpha_{1n}I_{t_1}(t^+), \alpha_{2n}I_{t_2}(t^+), \ldots, \alpha_{nn}I_{t_n}(t^+)) \tag{5}$$

Case IV: Single Task to Multiple Host 'AND' Inter-dependency. As in Fig. 3(d1) a task t_n has an 'AND' dependency on hosts h_1 to h_n with the strength of dependency α_{1n} to α_{nn}, respectively. Here, we can formulate the impact factor $IF_{h_n}(t^+)$ on host h_n, and operational capability $OC_{h_n}(t^+)$ of h_n as follows.

$$IF_{h_n}(t^+) := min(\alpha_{n1}, \alpha_{n2}, \ldots, \alpha_{nn})I_{t_n}(t^+) \tag{6}$$

We then utilize Eqs. 2 and 3 to compute and update the operability.

Case V: Single Task to Multiple Hosts 'OR' Inter-dependency. Similar to previous case, we can formulate the impact factor $IF_{h_n}(t^+)$ on host h_n as follows.

$$IF_{h_n}(t^+) := max(\alpha_{n1}, \alpha_{n2}, \ldots, \alpha_{nn})I_{t_n}(t^+) \tag{7}$$

Again, we then utilize Eqs. 2 and 3 to compute and update the operability.

Case VI: Single Task to Single Host 'FLOW' Inter-dependency and Task to Task Intra-dependency. As shown in Fig. 3(f1) and (f2), we have two tasks t_m, and t_n having 'FLOW' dependency on host h_m, and h_n. There is also an intra-dependency between tasks t_m and t_n with the strength of intra-dependency γ_{mn}, where t_m precedes t_n, meaning t_m needs to be completed first to perform t_n. Here, we compute the corresponding impact factors as below.

$$\left. \begin{array}{l} IF_{h_m}(t^+) := \alpha_{mm}I_{t_m}(t^+) \\ IF_{h_n}(t^+) := \frac{1}{N}\left[\alpha_{nn}I_{t_n}(t^+) + \gamma_{mn}IF_{h_m}(t^+)\right] \end{array} \right\} \tag{8}$$

In Eq. 8, N is the total number of dependency of task t_n which includes both intra and inter-dependencies, which is equal to 2 in this case. If $\gamma_{mn} = 0$, means there is no intra-dependency, then $N = 1$, and the Eq. 8 becomes same as the 'FLOW' dependency as in Eq. 1. We then compute the operability of h_n and h_m as below.

$$\left. \begin{array}{l} OC_{h_m}(t^+) := max(POC_{h_m}(t) - IF_{t_m}(t^+), 0) \\ OC_{h_n}(t^+) := max(POC_{h_n}(t) - IF_{t_n}(t^+), 0) \end{array} \right\} \tag{9}$$

Mission Impact and Overall Operational Capability. Let us consider, a mission m can be accomplished using a set of task paths $\{TP_1, TP_2, \ldots, TP_n\}$, where each task path TP_n itself includes a sequence of tasks $\{t_{n_1}, t_{n_2}, \ldots, t_{n_m}\}$ to perform to complete the task path TP_n. Also, the corresponding host paths $\{HP_1, HP_2, \ldots, HP_m\}$, where each host path HP_m itself includes a sequence of hosts $\{h_{n_1}, h_{n_2}, \ldots, h_{n_m}\}$. Then, we can compute the overall mission impact $I_m(t^+)$ and overall operational capability measure of the mission $OCM_m(t^+)$ using the below equation.

$$
\left.
\begin{aligned}
I_m(t^+) &= \max_{k \in TP} \left(\frac{\sum_{j \in TP_k} IF_{kj}(t^+)}{|TP_j|} \right) \\
OCM_m(t^+) &= \min_{n \in HP} \left(\frac{\sum_{j \in HP_n} OC_{h_{nj}}(t^+)}{|HP_j|} \right)
\end{aligned}
\right\}
\tag{10}
$$

Here, $|TP_j|$ is the cardinality of the task path TP_j, $IF_{kj}(t^+)$ is the impact factor of task j in task path k. Similarly, $|HP_j|$ is the cardinality of the host path HP_j. $OC_{h_{nj}}(t^+)$ is the operational capability of dependent host j (associated with task j) in host path path n (associated with task path k) at time instance t^+. The interpretation of Eq. 10 is that we take the maximum of the average of all impact factors in the task paths for mission impact computations. We take the minimum of the average of all operability measures for the corresponding host paths to compute system operability due to mission impact.

5   Case Study Formulation and Evaluation

We have set up a case study of SCADA operations in EDS, as shown in Fig. 4. The mission here is to *maintaining proper functioning of the SCADA operations.* Here, we have eight tasks associated with this mission. Task T_1 is to sense the field-device data by the sensors. T_2 is the I/O communications to the sensors. T_3 is to collate information from the sensors and I/O modules and provide them to the control screen in HMI. T_4 presents the real-time graphical schematic/mimic diagrams of the plant operations. T_5 accumulates the time-series historical data. T_6 is the alarm and event log monitoring using real-time and historical data. T_7 is to manually monitor the operational levels of the field-devices by the operators using appropriate CLIs (command-line interface). Finally, T_8 is to initiate supervisory commands to set the operational levels if necessary. Because of redundant operational logic and intra-dependencies of the tasks, the mission can be accomplished by the sequence of tasks $T_3 \rightarrow T_6 \rightarrow T_8$ (i.e., task path1), or $T_3 \rightarrow T_5 \rightarrow T_7 \rightarrow T_8$ (i.e., task path2), where $T_3 := T_1 \wedge T_2$, and $T_6 := T_4 \wedge T_5$. Here, $\wedge$ means logical 'AND'. By task path, we mean the sequence of tasks needed to perform to have the mission successful.

Mission Dependency for the Case Study. The tasks that we have mentioned in Fig. 4 depend on the programs or applications running on the underlying hosts or network devices. Here, we only consider the task-host interdependency bypassing the task-application-host dependency using transitivity rule. For example, the job T_1 of sensing relies on the sensors, T_2 relies on the I/O modules (RTU/IED). T_3 depends on both T_1 and T_2. Similarly, we present other task-host inter-dependencies and task-task intra-dependencies associated with the mission in Fig. 4. The associated network devices are h_1 to h_8, as in Fig. 4.

5.1 Network Architecture and Possible Exploitation Scenarios

We have set up a six subnet EDS network based on NIST recommended defense-in-depth architecture [3] and following the standards IEC 60870-5 (SCADA) in Fig. 5. Here, we have *webServer*, and *workStation1* in the corporate network. The *webServer* allows *http* and *https* traffic from the internet. In the control layer, we have *controlFirewall*, *historian*, and *workStation2*. *historian* allows *ftp* from *workStation1*. *workStation2* allows *ssh* from *workStation1*. The supervisory computers *WS3* collates information from *DataAcquisitionServer(DAS)* which itself collects data from the *sensors* and *PLC/RTU/IED* devices. The *historian* can do *ftp* to *DAS*; *historian* allows pulling data from *workStation2* as they are on the same subnet. Also, *WS3*

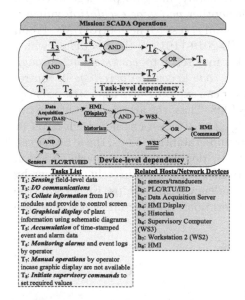

Fig. 4. Mission dependency for the case study. Double underlines indicate direct impact because of the vulnerabilities in associated devices; single underline shows an indirect impact

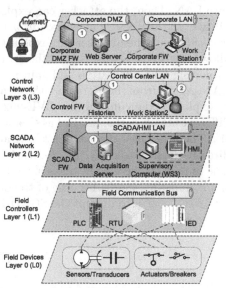

Fig. 5. NIST defense-in-depth architecture based network setup for the case study

Table 1. Network vulnerability information

Vulnerability	CVSS score	Associated host	Exploitation result
CVE-2020-5847[a]	9.8	webServer	Remote code execution
CVE-2019-18822[b]	5.9	workStation1	Privilege escalation
CVE-2020-0796[c]	10.0	workStation2	Remote code execution
CVE-2019-11013[d]	6.5	Historian	Directory traversal
CVE-2020-1008[e]	8.8	DataAcquisitionServer	Remote code execution

[a] https://nvd.nist.gov/vuln/detail/CVE-2020-5847
[b] https://nvd.nist.gov/vuln/detail/CVE-2019-18822
[c] https://nvd.nist.gov/vuln/detail/CVE-2020-0796
[d] https://nvd.nist.gov/vuln/detail/CVE-2019-11013
[e] https://nvd.nist.gov/vuln/detail/CVE-2020-1008

directly connects with the HMI. $workStation2$ houses programs/CLI applications for direct monitoring of PLC/- RTU/IED devices. From the HMI, it is possible to initiate corrective commands to set/adjust the operational levels of some physical devices which pass to the actuators.

Irrespective of the network administrators efforts to make the network free of any exploitation points, there are a couple of vulnerabilities existing on the network, as shown in the Table 1. At first, the attacker can exploit CVE-2020-5847 of the $webServer1$ to by executing codes remotely and gain privilege in corporate LAN. Then, the attacker can exploit another *privilege escalation* vulnerability CVE-2019-18822 in $workStation1$ to gain access to the control LAN. From, $workStation1$ the attacker can exploit CVE-2019-11013 in the *historian*, which allows directory traversal. Also, the attacker may reach to $workstation2$ through exploiting CVE-2020-0796 and gain *remote code execution privilege* in control LAN. Again, from the *historian*, the attacker can exploit $DataAcquisitionServer$ by exploiting the vulnerability CVE-2020-1008. Thus, the attacker can utilize two different attack paths, marked as ① and ②. The attacker can not reach HMI or $WS3$ because these devices don't have any vulnerabilities. Thus, the attacker can directly impact tasks T_3, T_5, T_7, as shown by double underline marks in Fig. 4. The impact on these three tasks impacts tasks T_4, T_6, T_8 indirectly (as shown by single underline mark) because of the dependency relationships. Either way, the attacker's goal is to disrupt the SCADA operations, and our mission is to secure the same.

Table 2. Datalog clauses of Fig. 6

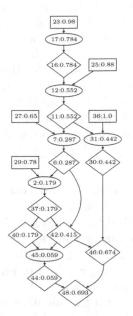

Fig. 6. Pruned mission impact assessment graph for the case study (nodes Datalog clauses are given in Table 2)

Node	Datalog clauses
23	vulExists(webServer,'CVE-2020-5847',httpd,remoteExploit,privEscalation)
17	RULE 2 (remote exploit of a server program)
16	execCode(webServer,root)
25	vulExists(workStation1,'CVE-2019-18822',sshd,remoteExploit,privEscalation)
12	RULE 2 (remote exploit of a server program)
11	execCode(workStation1,root)
36	vulExists(workStation2,'CVE-2020-0796',sshd,remoteExploit,privEscalation)
27	vulExists(historian,'CVE-2019-11013',ftpd,remoteExploit,privEscalation)
7	RULE 2 (remote exploit of a server program)
6	execCode(historian,root)
31	RULE 3 (local exploit of a server program)
30	execCode(workStation2,root)
29	vulExists(dataAcquisitionServer,'CVE-2020-1008',ftpd,remoteExploit,privEscalation)
2	RULE 3 (local exploit of a server program)
37	taskImpact(t3CollateFieldData)
40	taskImpact(t4GraphicDisplay)
42	taskImpact(t5AccumulateEventLogs)
45	RULE 35 (An and-dependent task impacts later task)
44	taskImpact(t6MonitoringAlarms)
46	taskImpact(t7ManualStatusCheck)
48	taskImpact(t8InitiateCorrectiveCommands)

5.2 Result Analysis and Interpretations

We present the complete MIAG in Fig. 8 in Appendix because of space constraints. We utilize a pruning process on the MIAG as in Fig. 6, where we eliminate the condition nodes except the vulnerability nodes; we keep the privilege and task impact nodes, including the dependency rule nodes. On the pruned MIAG, we apply the score quantification process discussed in Subsect. 4.6 and 4.7.

Task Impact Computation: From, Fig. 6, we find the computed derived scores for the task impacts. Thus, $taskImpact(t1Sensing) = 0.0, taskImpact$ $(t2IOCommunication) = 0.0, taskImpact(t3CollateFieldData) = 0.179, task$ $Impact(t4GraphicDisplay) = 0.179, taskImpact(t5AccumulateEventLogs) =$ $0.415, taskImpact(t6MonitoringAlarms) = 0.059, taskImpact(t7ManualSta$ $tusCheck) = 0.674, taskImpact(t8InitiateCorrectiveCommand) = 0.693.$

Task Impact Interpretation: There is no way the attacker can impact T_1 and T_2 because these devices have no vulnerability and exploitation path. Thus, both task impacts are zero. Although task T_3 'AND'-depends on T_1 and T_2, because of the vulnerability exploitation in $DataAcquistionServer$, the task T_3 can be impacted; thus the score is 0.179 as derived from the pruned MIAG graph. T_4 'Flow'-depends on T_3, and has no other associated vulnerability. Thus, the impact on task T_4 is equal to the derived impact of task T_3, which is 0.179. Task T_5 'Flow'-depends on T_3 and also can be impacted by exploitation of *historian*. Thus, the derived score of T_5 is $(6 : execCode(historian, root)) \vee (37 : taskImpact(t3CollateFieldData)) = 0.287 \vee 0.179 = 0.287 + 0.179 - 0.287 * 0.179 = 0.415$. Similarly, we can compute the other derived scores for the task impacts on T_6, T_7, $T8$. From the pruned MIAG, we see that even if T_4, T_6, and T_8 don't have direct vulnerabilities on the associated host devices, but these tasks are getting impacted because of their dependency relations on other preceding tasks. The task impact score represents the fraction of disruption on the task on a scale of 0–1. The higher the score, the greater is the possible disruption on the task.

Overall Mission Impact and Operability Computation and Interpretation: We provide the computed impact factor and operability for the two task paths (i.e., the two ways the mission can be established) in Tables 3, 4, 5, and 6, for different combinations of the strength of dependency factors. Here, scenario ① means all $\alpha_{ii} = 1.0$, and $\gamma_{ij} = 1.0$. Scenario ②, ③, and ④ means all α_{ii} is equal to 0.75, 0.5, and 0.25, respectively keeping $\gamma_{ij} = 1.0$. Finally, we compute the mission impact and overall system operability using Eq. 10 and Tables 3, 4, 5, and 6. We have assumed $POC(h_i) = 1.0$ for this illustration, where $i = 1, 2, \ldots, 8$. For the scenario ① of equal inter-SOD and intra-SOD, the mission impact is $max(0.1382, 0.2305) = 0.2305$, and operational capability is $min(0.8618, 0.7695) = 0.7695$ utils. This means the SCADA operational mission would have 76.95% predictive operability having 23.05% impacts (i.e., disruptions) posed by the existing vulnerabilities during a cyberattack incident.

Table 3. Impact factor for task path1: $T_3 \rightarrow T_6 \rightarrow T_8$ ($T_3 = T_1 \wedge T_2, T_6 = T_4 \wedge T_5$)

Scenario	Impact Factor (IF)							
	IF_{h1}	IF_{h2}	IF_{h3}	IF_{h4}	IF_{h5}	IF_{h6}	IF_{h8}	Average
①	0.00	0.00	0.0895	0.1343	0.2523	0.0966	0.4011	0.1382
②	0.00	0.00	0.0671	0.1007	0.1892	0.0725	0.3008	0.1037
③	0.00	0.00	0.0448	0.0671	0.1261	0.0483	0.2005	0.0691
④	0.00	0.00	0.0224	0.0336	0.0631	0.0242	0.1003	0.0346

Table 4. Impact factor for task path2: $T_3 \rightarrow T_5 \rightarrow T_7 \rightarrow T_8$ ($T_3 = T_1 \wedge T_2$)

Scenario	Impact Factor (IF)						
	IF_{h1}	IF_{h2}	IF_{h3}	IF_{h5}	IF_{h7}	IF_{h8}	Average
①	0.00	0.00	0.0895	0.2523	0.4631	0.5781	0.2305
②	0.00	0.00	0.0671	0.1892	0.3473	0.4335	0.1729
③	0.00	0.00	0.0448	0.1261	0.2316	0.2890	0.1152
④	0.00	0.00	0.0224	0.0631	0.1158	0.1445	0.0576

Table 5. Host operability for task path1: $T_3 \rightarrow T_6 \rightarrow T_8$ ($T_3 = T_1 \wedge T_2, T_6 = T_4 \wedge T_5$), associated hosts $= \{h_1, h_2, h_3, h_4, h_5, h_6, h_8\}$

Scenario	Operational Capability (OC)							
	OC_{h1}	OC_{h2}	OC_{h3}	OC_{h4}	OC_{h5}	OC_{h6}	OC_{h8}	Average
①	1.00	1.00	0.9105	0.8658	0.7478	0.9034	0.6052	0.8618
②	1.00	1.00	0.9329	0.8993	0.8108	0.9275	0.7039	0.8963
③	1.00	1.00	0.9553	0.9329	0.8739	0.9517	0.8026	0.9309
④	1.00	1.00	0.9776	0.9664	0.9369	0.9758	0.9013	0.9654

Table 6. Host operability for task path2: $T_3 \rightarrow T_5 \rightarrow T_7 \rightarrow T_8$ ($T_3 = T_1 \wedge T_2$), associated hosts $= \{h_1, h_2, h_3, h_5, h_7, h_8\}$

Scenario	Operational Capability (OC)						
	OC_{h1}	OC_{h2}	OC_{h3}	OC_{h5}	OC_{h7}	OC_{h8}	Average
①	1.00	1.00	0.9105	0.7478	0.5369	0.4219	0.7695
②	1.00	1.00	0.9329	0.8108	0.6527	0.5665	0.8271
③	1.00	1.00	0.9553	0.8739	0.7684	0.7110	0.8848
④	1.00	1.00	0.9776	0.9369	0.8842	0.8555	0.9424

5.3 Evaluation of Scalability

In our mission impact model, generating the mission impact assessment graph takes time depending on the network size and, thus, related to the scalability. Therefore, we present here a comparison of the simulation time to generate the MIAG. We consider the full SCADA case study as one unit and then replicate and grouped the units together (i.e., no. of simulation units termed as 'NoU').

We utilize an Ubuntu 18.04 OS version Virtual Box (VB) image with 50 GB hard drive and 8 GB memory to install MulVAL and perform the simulation. We use the VB in a Dell Laptop with Windows 10 OS, 16 GB RAM, and 1 TB hard disk. We present the number of nodes and edges and the average graph generation time in Fig. 7. With the increase of simulation units, the graph generation time increases exponentially. Still, as we can see, it can generate the graph with nearly 3000 nodes and 3300 edges in around 182 s (~3 min) on average. Cao et al. [2] also present a detailed evaluation of scalability using the MulVAL simulation platform. We encourage readers to follow the explanations presented by Cao et al. [2] in Subsect. 5.3 to get a good insight on scalability using MulVAL.

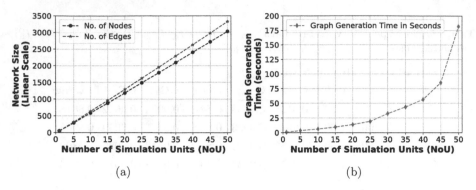

Fig. 7. Evaluation of scalability: (a) Network size in terms of number of nodes and edges, (b) Graph generation time (in sec.) vs. number of simulation units

5.4   Generalization Challenges and Way Forward

We demonstrate the model for energy systems. The model applies to other cyber-physical systems as well. There may be some challenges in identifying the dependencies and determining the strength of dependencies. We can overcome these utilizing artificial intelligence techniques and Hidden-Markov models (HMM) using system process calls. We may also utilize FDNA [4] for dependency modeling. There can be issues with cyclic graphs, and the MulVAL engine is capable of handling the cycling problems [6]. Choosing the right tool to simulate large-scale CPS is also challenging. Open-source tools such as MulVAL, NetworkX can help in this regard. The most critical challenge would be to incorporate real-time services as comprehensive as possible. Rather than considering the complete system as a single mission, dividing the whole mission into several sub-missions and performing mission-critical dependency modeling and impact assessment for each subdivided mission could provide some guidance. The creation of customized rule sets based on the dependency scenario is another challenge to take into considerations.

6   Related Work

Gabriel [8] presents mission security situation assessment using impact dependency graphs. The article presents a conceptual framework for the cyberattack model and uses logical constraint graphs to assess the assets' operational capacity and mission impact. Albanese and Jajodia [10] present a graphical model to evaluate the effects of multi-step attacks. The authors propose an impact assessment graph utilizing the vulnerability dependency graph. Changwei et al. [11] model intrusion evidence dependency using probabilistic evidence graph and attack graph. The use of qualitative evaluation questions the applicability of the model in practical settings. Jajodia et al. [12] present 'Cauldron,' a mission-centric cyber situational awareness tool. Cauldron focuses more on the implementation side and does not disclose the underlying modeling details because of the nature of operations. Haque et al. [13,14] utilize graph theory in analyzing impact and security in cyber-physical systems.

Sun et al. [1,15] propose a technique to model the dependency relations by utilizing the mission or service dependency graph and attack graph. Cao et al. [2] present a quantitative metric for business process impact assessment using the attack graphs and entity dependency graph. The works offer some directions on integrating system dependency in the security models where we get our primary motivations for this work. However, the articles focus on Enterprise networks and lack in providing formal mathematical reasoning to integrate the attack graph and dependency graph. Also, the correlation of the impact with system operability is missing. We have clearly defined different graph types and the integration process to use irrespective of the system type and the simulation platform. Although we have used the MulVAL simulation platform, our detailed mathematical formulations illustrate that the model is implementable regardless of the simulation platform. The significant difference between our model and the previous models is that we relate the impact to system operability. This would guide in developing mitigation strategies and defensive actions. The model is also applicable to the impact assessment of other cyber-physical systems with necessary adjustments.

7 Conclusion and Future Directions

This work addresses two existing modeling problems in the security domain for the energy delivery systems. The first problem deals with the incorporation of the mission functional dependency into the traditional attack graph model. The second problem is to quantify and assess the mission impact and system operability. We provide detailed formal explanations of the graphical models that we use to address the above problems. We offer a case study of SCADA operations for energy delivery systems and present the details of how the mathematical models can help assess the mission impact and system operability in the presence of vulnerabilities on the mission-critical devices. We plan to optimize our model by including control measures that would assist in minimizing the mission impact and maximizing the system operability to provide cyber resilience guidance. We only consider operational dependencies in this work. We have the plan to incorporate strategic and tactical dependencies in our future extension of this work.

Acknowledgment. This material is based upon work supported by the Department of Energy under Award Number DE-OE0000780.

A   Appendix

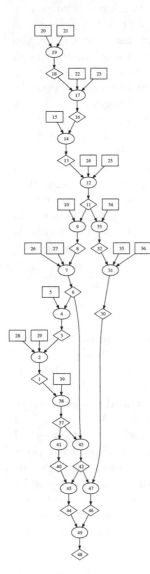

Fig. 8. Complete mission impact assessment graph for the case study (nodes Datalog clauses are given in Table 7)

Table 7. Datalog clauses of Fig. 8

Node	Datalog clauses
20	hacl(internet,webServer,httpProtocol,httpPort)
21	attackerLocated(internet)
19	RULE 11 (direct network access)
18	netAccess(webServer,httpProtocol,httpPort)
22	networkServiceInfo(webServer,httpd,httpProtocol,httpPort,root)
23	vulExists(webServer,'CVE-2020-5847',httpd,remoteExploit,privEscalation)
17	RULE 2 (remote exploit of a server program)
15	hacl(webServer,workStation1,sshProtocol,sshPort)
16	execCode(webServer,root)
14	RULE 10 (multi-hop access)
13	netAccess(workStation1,sshProtocol,sshPort)
24	networkServiceInfo(workStation1,sshd,sshProtocol,sshPort,root)
25	vulExists(workStation1,'CVE-2019-18822',sshd,remoteExploit,privEscalation)
12	RULE 2 (remote exploit of a server program)
10	hacl(workStation1,historian,ftpProtocol,ftpPort)
11	execCode(workStation1,root)
34	hacl(workStation1,workStation2,sshProtocol,sshPort)
9	RULE 10 (multi-hop access)
33	RULE 10 (multi-hop access)
26	networkServiceInfo(historian,ftpd,ftpProtocol,ftpPort,root)
27	vulExists(historian,'CVE-2019-11013',ftpd,remoteExploit,privEscalation)
8	netAccess(historian,ftpProtocol,ftpPort)
32	netAccess(workStation2,sshProtocol,sshPort)
35	networkServiceInfo(workStation2,sshd,sshProtocol,sshPort,root)
36	vulExists(workStation2,'CVE-2020-0796',sshd,remoteExploit,privEscalation)
7	RULE 2 (remote exploit of a server program)
31	RULE 2 (remote exploit of a server program)
5	hacl(historian,dataAcquisitionServer,ftpProtocol,ftpPort)
6	execCode(historian,root)
4	RULE 10 (multi-hop access)
30	execCode(workStation2,root)
28	networkServiceInfo(dataAcquisitionServer,ftpd,ftpProtocol,ftpPort,root)
29	vulExists(dataAcquisitionServer,'CVE-2020-1008',ftpd,remoteExploit,privEscalation)
3	netAccess(dataAcquisitionServer,ftpProtocol,ftpPort)
2	RULE 2 (remote exploit of a server program)
1	execCode(dataAcquisitionServer,root)
39	task(t3CollateFieldData,dependency,dataAcquisitionServer)
38	RULE 32 (An impacted host impacts dependent task)
37	taskImpact(t3CollateFieldData)
41	RULE 33 (An impacted task impacts Flow-dependent succeeding task)
43	RULE 34 (An impacted task or an impacted host impacts dependent task)
40	taskImpact(t4GraphicDisplay)
42	taskImpact(t5AccumulateEventLogs)
45	RULE 35 (An and-dependent task impacts following task)
47	RULE 36 (An impacted task or an impacted host impacts dependent task)
44	taskImpact(t6MonitoringAlarms)
46	taskImpact(t7ManualStatusCheck)
49	RULE 37 (Both impacted tasks impacts dependent task)
48	taskImpact(t8InitiateCorrectiveCommands)

Note: Node numbers are in the order from top to bottom as in Fig. 8

References

1. Sun, X., Liu, P., Singhal, A.: Toward cyberresiliency in the context of cloud computing [resilient security]. IEEE Secur. Priv. **16**(6), 71–75 (2018)
2. Cao, C., Yuan, L.-P., Singhal, A., Liu, P., Sun, X., Zhu, S.: Assessing attack impact on business processes by interconnecting attack graphs and entity dependency graphs. In: Kerschbaum, F., Paraboschi, S. (eds.) DBSec 2018. LNCS, vol. 10980, pp. 330–348. Springer, Cham (2018). https://doi.org/10.1007/978-3-319-95729-6_21
3. Stouffer, K., Falco, J.: Recommended practice: improving industrial control systems cybersecurity with defense-in-depth strategies. Department of Homeland Security, Control systems security program, National cyber security division (2009)
4. Garvey, P.R., Pinto, C.A.: Introduction to functional dependency network analysis. In: The MITRE Corporation and Old Dominion, 2nd International Symposium on Engineering Systems, MIT, Cambridge, Massachusetts, vol. 5 (2009)
5. Ou, X., Govindavajhala, S., Appel, A.W.: MulVAL: a logic-based network security analyzer. In: USENIX Security Symposium, Baltimore, MD, vol. 8, pp. 113–128 (2005)
6. Gonda, T., Pascal, T., Puzis, R., Shani, G., Shapira, B.: Analysis of attack graph representations for ranking vulnerability fixes. In: GCAI, pp. 215–228 (2018)
7. Rao, B., Mitra, A.: An approach to merging of two community subgraphs to form a community graph using graph mining techniques. In: 2014 IEEE International Conference on Computational Intelligence and Computing Research, pp. 1–7. IEEE (2014)
8. Jakobson, G.: Mission-centricity in cyber security: architecting cyber attack resilient missions. In: 2013 5th International Conference on Cyber Conflict, CYCON 2013, pp. 1–18. IEEE (2013)
9. Guariniello, C., DeLaurentis, D.: Supporting design via the system operational dependency analysis methodology. Res. Eng. Des. **28**(1), 53–69 (2017)
10. Albanese, M., Jajodia, S.: A graphical model to assess the impact of multi-step attacks. J. Def. Model. Simul. **15**(1), 79–93 (2018)
11. Liu, C., Singhal, A., Wijesekera, D.: Mapping evidence graphs to attack graphs. In: IEEE International Workshop on Information Forensics and Security, WIFS 2012, pp. 121–126. IEEE (2012)
12. Jajodia, S., Noel, S., Kalapa, P., Albanese, M., Williams, J.: Cauldron mission-centric cyber situational awareness with defense in depth. In: 2011 Military Communications Conference, MILCOM 2011, pp. 1339–1344. IEEE (2011)
13. Haque, M.A., Shetty, S., Krishnappa, B.: Modeling cyber resilience for energy delivery systems using critical system functionality. In: Resilience Week, RWS 2019, vol. 1, pp. 33–41. IEEE (2019)
14. Haque, M.A., Shetty, S., Krishnappa, B.: Cyber-physical system resilience: frameworks, metrics, complexities, challenges, and future directions. In: Complexity Challenges in Cyber Physical Systems: Using Modeling and Simulation (M&S) to Support Intelligence, Adaptation and Autonomy, pp. 301–337 (2019)
15. Sun, X., Singhal, A., Liu, P.: Towards actionable mission impact assessment in the context of cloud computing. In: Livraga, G., Zhu, S. (eds.) DBSec 2017. LNCS, vol. 10359, pp. 259–274. Springer, Cham (2017). https://doi.org/10.1007/978-3-319-61176-1_14

Identifying DApps and User Behaviors on Ethereum via Encrypted Traffic

Yu Wang[1,2], Zhenzhen Li[1,2], Gaopeng Gou[1,2], Gang Xiong[1,2(✉)], Chencheng Wang[1,2], and Zhen Li[1,2]

[1] Institute of Information Engineering, Chinese Academy of Sciences, Beijing, China
{wangyu1996,lizhenzhen,gougaopeng,xionggang,wangchencheng,
lizhen}@iie.ac.cn
[2] School of Cyber Security, University of Chinese Academy of Sciences,
Beijing, China

Abstract. With the surge in popularity of blockchain, more and more Decentralized Applications (DApps) are deployed on blockchain platforms. DApps bring convenience to people, but cause security and efficiency problems. In this paper, we focus on the security and efficiency problems of DApps on Ethereum. Our research is divided into three application scenarios. In DApps classification, we analyze characteristics of DApps and extract efficient features to recognize 11 representative DApps. In DApps user behaviors classification, we propose behavior-sensitive features and improved time features to recognize 88 DApps user behaviors, which would help to identify malicious behaviors in encrypted traffic. In general user behavior classification, different categories of features are proposed to recognize 15 general user behaviors which represent the performance of DApps. DApps developers can obtain valuable data to improve the quality of service through analyzing the classification results. Experimental results in the three application scenarios achieve excellent performance (99.5% accuracy for DApps classification, 95.65% accuracy for DApps user behaviors classification, 98.58% accuracy for general user behaviors classification) and outperform the state-of-the-art methods.

Keywords: DApps and user behaviors · Encrypted traffic classification · Features extraction · Traffic analysis · Machine learning

1 Introduction

Ethereum [4] is the first major blockchain to support the Turing-complete scripting via smart contracts, which allow parties to create virtual trusted third parties that behave according to arbitrary agreed-upon rules. It attracts people to write smart contracts for building Decentralized Applications (DApps), which run on a peer-to-peer network of computers. DApps become one of the development trends of the internet. As of May 2020, there are more than three thousand DApps, and 82% of them are deployed on Ethereum [1].

© ICST Institute for Computer Sciences, Social Informatics and Telecommunications Engineering 2020
Published by Springer Nature Switzerland AG 2020. All Rights Reserved
N. Park et al. (Eds.): SecureComm 2020, LNICST 336, pp. 62–83, 2020.
https://doi.org/10.1007/978-3-030-63095-9_4

DApps deployed on Ethereum use SSL/TLS protocols to encrypt transmission data between entities. There is no difference in encrypted protocol details between different DApps, because these DApps are adopted on the same blockchain platform, so the dissimilarity of encrypted traffic generated by different DApps is reduced. Some traditional classification methods begin to lose effect, such as deep packet inspection [11]. There are lots of research on application identification [3,5,18,21], with few articles mentioned DApps. In [20], the authors use high-dimensional features for DApps classification, which results in low efficiency. So in the case of ensuring high accuracy, how to improve the efficiency of DApps classification is a challenge.

DApps are similar to traditional apps, with privacy and security risks [7,22]. As for the classification on DApps user behaviors, it can identify specific user behaviors (e.g., checking account, communication, purchase, comment) in encrypted traffic, which may help network operators detect suspicious behaviors, thereby enhancing the protection of user privacy. For example, the attacker recruits employees through posts in Ethlance, which are actually phishing posts. This classification may help to identify the dubious behavior which is repeated many times by the same IP in a short period of time. Additionally, some DApps containing Trojan codes disguise as normal DApps, which steal confidential data of unwitting users, and the classification may help to identify suspicious behaviors other than normal ones. The operator could then take appropriate actions to protect user privacy. Researchers have been studying user behaviors classification for many years, but most of them focus on traditional applications [7,8,24]. Due to the invisibility and confusion of DApps user behaviors traffic, some features do not perform well, such as packet sizes [17], packet flags [13,19], statistical features of packet length [21]. Statistical-time features are used to identify Bitcoin wallets and user actions [2], but these statistics have little improvement on DApps user behaviors classification. Therefore, we need to propose a specific set of features according to the characteristics of DApps user behaviors.

Improving Qos is a topic of ongoing interest in many aspects, such as applications [12,15], distributed multimedia services [10], cloud services [16]. As an emerging technology, most DApps cannot provide good quality of user experience. DApps run on a decentralized network and each node can be regarded as a central server, which bring challenges to improve Qos of DApps. As for the classification on general user behaviors, it ignores the differences between DApps. Combined with traffic data, it can provide valuable information (e.g., user preferences, throughput, latency) within an organization. The data is invaluable for network administrators to optimize the networks. For example, the administrators can trigger the automated re-allocation of network resources for priority behaviors after getting user preferences through the usage frequency of general user behaviors. They can obtain the latency of each behavior by extracting time series from the traffic data. Administrators could configure their networks to help DApps perform more efficiently, thereby improving Qos of DApps.

In this paper, we focus on the classification for three application scenarios of DApps encrypted traffic. After analyzing the characteristics of DApps and user behaviors, we propose different sets of features for three scenarios to get better performance. Then, we use three classification models to conduct the classification and compare their performance. In addition, we find that most flows of DApps traffic are short flows through experiment. The contributions of this article are as follows:

- We classify encrypted DApps traffic. After analyzing DApps characteristics and network traffic, we use less features to improve the efficiency of DApps classification. The effectiveness of the proposed features is verified by experimenting on encrypted traffic collected from 11 representative DApps. The experimental results are better than the state-of-the-art methods.
- We explore the fine-grained classification on encrypted DApps traffic and research on DApps user behaviors. After analyzing DApps, 88 available user behaviors are totally extracted. We propose DApps user behaviors-sensitive features and the improved time features, which strengthen the discrimination of DApps user behaviors in encrypted traffic. The experimental results demonstrate that our method can identify DApps user behaviors with up to 95% accuracy. To the best of our knowledge, we are the first one to classify user behaviors of multiple types of DApps.
- We categorize 88 user behaviors into 15 general user behaviors which represent the performance of DApps. Different kinds of features are proposed according to the characteristics of general user behaviors. Compared with the existing methods, the performance of our proposed method is preferable to them, with 98% accuracy. This work is the first to perform classification on general user behaviors.

The rest of this paper is organized as follows. Section 2 briefly reviews related work. Next, we elaborate the process of extracting features for different application scenarios in Sect. 3. Section 4 details the dataset and shows the experimental results. Finally, we conclude this paper in Sect. 5.

2   Related Work

Researches on traffic classification emerge in an endless stream. According to our research, we provide an overview of related work in three aspects: encrypted application traffic classification, application user behavior classification and analysis of network traffic of blockchain.

Encrypted Application Traffic Classification. In [6], Chen et al. found that despite encryption, web applications also suffered from side-channel leakages. They leveraged fundamental features of web applications: stateful communication, low entropy input and significant traffic distinction. But web applications consist of browser-side and server-side components, DApps can be split into browser-side and smart contracts. Cai et al. presented a website fingerprinting attack and proved its effectiveness through traffic analysis countermeasures [5]. They used an SVM with a custom kernel based on an edit-distance. The edit distance allowed for delete and transpose operations, that are supposed to capture drop and re-transmission of packets respectively. Shen et al. incorporated the certificate packet length clustering into the second-order homogeneous Markov chains [18]. The work could lead to a 29% improvement on average compared with existing Markov-based methods, in terms of classification accuracy. In [17], the authors presented a website fingerprinting method at Internet Scale. The accumulated sum of packet sizes was used to represent the progress of webpage loading. Gil et al. extracted time related features such as flow bytes per second, inbound and outbound inter-arrival time to characterize the network traffic by using C4.5 and KNN [9]. They detected six major classes of VPN traffic including browsing, streaming, chat, email, file transfer and VoIP. Alan et al. found that popular Android apps can be identified with 88% accuracy, only using packet sizes of the first 64 packets [3]. Vincent et al. used 54 statistical features of packet length on Random Forest to build an Appscanner [21] which can identify 110 applications with 96% accuracy. They also proved that app fingerprints persist in varying extents across devices and app versions.

Application User Behaviors Classification. Coull et al. utilized the size of exchanged packet between the target user and Apple's server to identify iMessage user actions, such as start writing, stop writing, message sending, attachment sending [8]. In [24], the authors used a suite of inference techniques to reveal a specific user action (i.e., send a tweet) on the Twitter app installed on an Android smartphone. Condi et al. clustered the streams of each application user behavior by clustering methods [7], then they calculated the dynamic warping distance for each stream, in terms of packet length. But they experimented on each app and ignored the similarity of encrypted traffic between different apps. Yan et al. segmented WeChat traffic into several bursts to describe different actions [23], and extracted packet length, number of TCP handshakes, statistics from each burst to identify red packet transactions and fund transfers.

Analysis of Network Traffic of Blockchain. In 2014, Koshy et al. developed heuristics to apply highly conservative constraints to Bitcoin network traffic [14], and they found that nearly 1,000 Bitcoin addresses can be mapped to IPs by leveraging anomalous relaying behaviors. Shen et al. generated high-dimensional features by fusing time series, packet length and packet burst [20]. The accuracy of DApps traffic classification reached 90%. But the training time and testing time of this method is much longer than other methods because of the large input vector, which results in low efficiency. Aiolli et al. identified bitcoin wallet apps and user actions only through statistical-time features, such as length, maximum, minimum, mean, etc. [2]. The classifier was trained by SVM and Random Forest algorithm, and the accuracy achieved 95%.

Due to the same encrypted protocol and blockchain platform, how to effectively and accurately classify DApps and user behaviors in encrypted traffic are challenging. In this paper, we propose suitable features for three application scenarios, and explain them with DApps characteristics.

3   Methodology

In this section, we introduce the features we extracted for three application scenarios: DApps classification, DApps user behaviors classification and general user behaviors classification. The main process of our model is shown in Fig. 1. At first, we collect DApps network traffic and pre-process DApps traffic. After analyzing characteristics of different application scenarios, we propose different features. Finally, we apply different sets of features to the existing machine learning algorithms for different application scenarios classification.

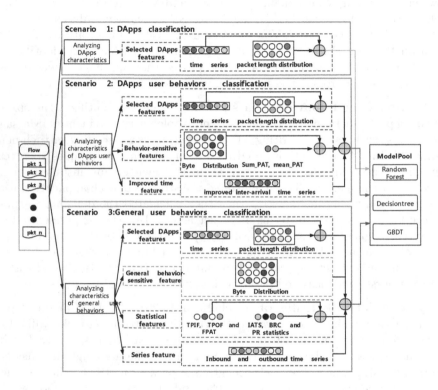

Fig. 1. Main process of Modeling. Sum_PAT, mean_PAT represent sum of packet arrival time, mean of packet arrival time. IATS, BRC and PR statistics represent statistical features of inter-arrival time series, byte rate change and packet rate. TPIF, TPOF and FPAT represent total packets of inbound flow, total packets of outbound flow and the first packet arrival time.

3.1   Feature Extraction for DApps Classification

There are many different characteristics between DApps and traditional applications, such as operation mode (e.g., decentralized), data storage (e.g., Ethereum platform, IPFS), construction (e.g., web applications consist of browser-side and server-side components, DApps consist of browser-side and smart contracts), etc., which result in the differences of packet arrival time and packet length for different DApps.

Selected DApps Features
Selected DApps features consist of packet length distribution and time series. The features are detailed as follows.

Packet Length Distribution. The size of the payloads for the first 100 packets of a session are recorded in dataset. We assume a 1500 byte Maximum Transmission Unit, and create 150 bins of 10 bytes each. Then, the number of packets whose length is in the range [0,10) is taken as the value of the first bin, the number of packets whose length is in the range [10,20) is taken as the value of the second bin, and so on. We get the number of packets that fell into different intervals in a flow. Finally, we construct a length-150 array.

Time Series. The packet arrival time for the first 100 packets of a session are recorded. we construct a length-100 array.

3.2 Feature Extraction for DApps User Behaviors Classification

Compared with DApps classification, DApps user behaviors classification is more fine-grained. We divide proposed features into three categories: selected DApps features, behavior-sensitive features and improved inter-arrival time series.

Selected DApps Features
We use the two features which are mentioned in Sect. 3.1: packet length distribution and time series.

Behavior-Sensitive Features
Behavior-sensitive features consist of sum of packet arrival time, mean of packet arrival time, and byte distribution. The features are detailed as follows.

Sum of Packet Arrival Time and Mean of Packet Arrival Time. For some behaviors, such as creating project, users can submit applications to rent things in Staybit. If other users want to rent, they need to pay through Ethereum accounts. This process causes distinction of transmission data, so sum of packets arrival time may be different. Each behavior has different sequence of actions. For example, behavior 'like the artwork' needs five actions in a precise order, behavior 'comment' needs seven actions, behavior 'open Superrare' needs three actions. An action could be simple (e.g., a click on a button, a selection of edit box) or complex (e.g., a connection of Ethereum wallet, type a text, which is randomly selected from a set of sentences). So the number of packets and response time of each behavior are different. We propose two features: sum of packet arrival time and mean of packet arrival time.

Byte Distribution. DApps utilize encrypted protocol to encrypt transmission data between entities. For different DApps user behaviors, DApps need to call different part of smart contracts, and the action sequence of each behavior is also unique. Although the communication data is encrypted, the encrypted payload is subtle distinction due to the difference of the original payload. So we extract byte distribution which is a length-256 array that keeps a count for each value encountered in the payloads of the packets for each packet in the flow. We use Principal Components Analysis to reduce the 256-dimensional data to 2-dimensional data. Each behavior is represented by two-dimensional data in the figure.

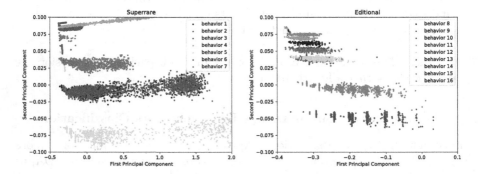

Fig. 2. Byte Distribution of DApps user behaviors. Each color represents a user behavior. Behavior 1–16 refer to the ID in Table 5

We only show the results of 16 DApps user behaviors in Fig. 2 because of space limitation. There are some DApps user behaviors overlap, such as 'open Superrare' and 'view details of the artwork' in Superrare, probably because the action sequences and the required data resources of the two behaviors are similar. However, it can be seen from the figure that the byte distribution is obviously effective in distinguishing DApps user behaviors.

The Improved Inter-arrival Time Series

Users use DApps through web user interface which interacts with wallets (e.g., Metamask, TrustWallet, Imtoken) for some user behaviors (e.g., comment on a post, like or dislike an artwork, etc., but not all user behaviors need this step), then it interacts with blockchain nodes rather than central servers. User behaviors that must connect to wallets are marked with ☆ in Table 5. The back-end code (smart contract) of DApps runs on the nodes of decentralized peer-to-peer network. Some DApps may store data as the metadata of transactions on Ethereum. Some DApps may build separate storage system on IPFS, but the developer needs to consider some complex things while building it, such as access management system. Therefore, the response time from Ethereum nodes to the front-end is different for different user behaviors. we improve inter-arrival time series as follows. We convert the original inter-arrival time series $PTS = (s_1, s_2, \ldots, s_j, \ldots, s_{n-1})$ to the improved inter-arrival time series $G\_PTS = (a_1, a_2, \ldots, a_j, \ldots, a_{n-1})$, where $s_j = t_{j+1} - t_j$. The a_j is computed by:

$$a_j = \Delta t \cdot b + \frac{\Delta t}{2} \tag{1}$$

where b satisfies the condition, $\Delta t \cdot b \leqslant s_j < \Delta t(b+1)$, we select $\Delta t = 0.005\,\mathrm{s}$ after testing.

Figure 3 reports the statistical distribution of the improved inter-arrival time of bidirectional flows for each user behavior. The first quartile, the median and the third quartile are highlighted by using a notched box plot. Some behaviors have a long tail distribution for the improved inter-arrival time such as behavior 33, 34, 46, 50. User behaviors in the same DApps (e.g., Thomas Crown Art, Latium) are very similar, although they are different behaviors. Behavior 7, 35, 60, 65 show a very long inter-arrival time distribution. From the figure we can see that the improved inter-arrival time may be a discriminative feature.

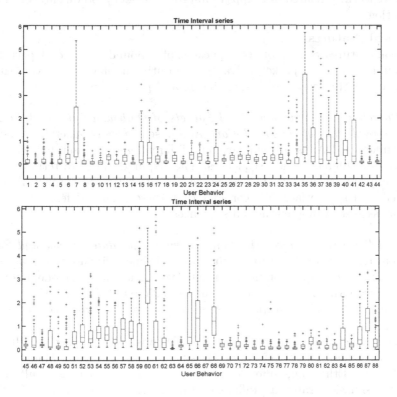

Fig. 3. Statistical distribution of the improved inter-arrival time of bidirectional flows for each user behavior. The median is represented as the red line. First quartile and third quartile are represented as the down and up side of the box. The + represents improved inter-arrival time beyond the first quartile and third quartile. The X-axis label user behavior 1–88 refer to the ID in Table 5 (Color figure online)

3.3   Feature Extraction for General User Behaviors Classification

For this application scenario, we select 15 general user behaviors which represent the performance of these DApps. Each general user behavior consists of the same type of user behavior of different DApps. For example, all DApps exist behavior 'opening DApps' and we group them into a general user behavior. Suitable features are proposed for this scenario, and they are divided into four kinds: selected DApps features, general behavior-sensitive features (behavior-sensitive features without features related to DApps), series features, and statistical features.

Selected DApps Features
We use the two features which are mentioned in Sect. 3.1: packet length distribution and time series.

General Behavior-Sensitive Features
We also use the behavior-sensitive features which are mentioned in Sect. 3.2. But we remove features related to DApps to improve efficiency. So we only select byte distribution.

Statistical Features
Statistical features consist of total packets of inbound flow, total packets of outbound flow, the first packet arrival time of outbound flow, statistical features of inter-arrival time series, byte rate change and packet rate.

Total Packets of Inbound Flow, Total Packets of Outbound Flow, and the First Packet Arrival Time of Outbound Flow. Action sequences of general user behaviors of different DApps are similar, but different general user behaviors are composed of different action sequences. The required data are retrieved from Ethereum peers, then they are transmitted to the front-end through API and displayed on the interface. We consider that these proposed features may be different because of different action sequences.

Statistical Features of Inter-arrival Time Series, Byte Rate Change and Packet Rate. The ten statistical features of inter-arrival time series are the mean, standard deviation, maximum, minimum, length of unique number, mode, frequency of mode, percentile. In particular, we choose 0.25, 0.5, 0.75 percentile of inter-arrival time series. These statistics are also collected for byte rate change and packet rate.

Since there is no central server in DApps, the impact of different DApps on general user behaviors classification is reduced. Many DApps store data on Ethereum, different general user behaviors may result in different transmission rates at different stages. Bytes rate change, $BRC = (\text{brc}_1, \text{brc}_2, \text{brc}_3, \ldots, \text{brc}_{n-1})$, calculated through the bytes rate sequence $BRS = (\text{brs}_1, \text{brs}_2, \text{brs}_3, \ldots, \text{brs}_{n-1})$. brc_i represents the D-value between $brs_{i+1} - brs_i$. brs_i represents rate of bytes in Δt time. We try Δt from 0 to 3 s, and we find the result is the best when $\Delta t = 0.25$ s. However, we do not use this feature directly. Skewness coefficient is a feature that describes the symmetry of data distribution. The skewness brc^s is calculated as follows:

$$brc^s = \frac{\frac{1}{n-1}\sum_{i=1}^{n-1}\left(brc_i - \bar{brc}\right)^3}{\left(\frac{1}{n-2}\sum_{i=1}^{n-1}\left(brc_i - \bar{brc}\right)^2\right)^{\frac{3}{2}}} \qquad (2)$$

Besides, kurtosis is a descriptor of the shape of a probability distribution. The kurtosis brc^k is calculated as follows:

$$brc^k = \frac{\frac{1}{n-1}\sum_{i=1}^{n-1}\left(brc_i - \bar{brc}\right)^4}{\left(\frac{1}{n-1}\sum_{i=1}^{n-1}\left(brc_i - \bar{brc}\right)^2\right)^2} - 3 \qquad (3)$$

Similar to brc^s and brc^k, for packet rate $PR = \left(\mathrm{pr}_1, \mathrm{pr}_2, \mathrm{pr}_3, \ldots, \mathrm{pr}_{n-1}\right)$. The skewness pr^s and the kurtosis pr^k are computed by:

$$pr^s = \frac{\frac{1}{n}\sum_{i=1}^{n}\left(pr_i - \bar{pr}\right)^3}{\left(\frac{1}{n-1}\sum_{i=1}^{n-1}\left(pr_i - \bar{pr}\right)^2\right)^{\frac{3}{2}}}; pr^k = \frac{\frac{1}{n}\sum_{i=1}^{n}\left(pr_i - \bar{pr}\right)^4}{\left(\frac{1}{n}\sum_{i=1}^{n}\left(pr_i - \bar{pr}\right)^2\right)^2} - 3 \qquad (4)$$

Series Features

Inbound and Outbound Arrival Time Series. In order to enhance the impact of the action sequence on classifier, we consider that packet arrival time series play an important role, and the inbound and outbound packet arrival time series have different characteristics. Therefore, we extract not only bidirectional arrival time series, but also inbound and outbound arrival time series.

4   Performance Evaluation

In this section, we first describe how we collect the labeled DApps traffic. Then, in order to evaluate the performance of proposed features for three application scenarios classification, we utilize Precision, Recall, F1-measure and Accuracy. Ten-fold cross validation is used to evaluate our method. We introduce experimental results from the following subsections: results of different models, evaluation of DApps classification, evaluation of DApps user behaviors classification, evaluation of general user behaviors classification and proposed features analysis.

4.1   Dataset

Figure 4 depicts our traffic collection platform. Users use DApps through virtual machines that are connected to the same access point, and all captured files are transferred to the point for traffic pre-processing and experiments. In order to assess our proposed features, we select 11 representative DApps of diverse categories on Ethereum, most of which have a lot of users, and all of them are close to our lives. After analyzing each DApp, we extract 88 available user

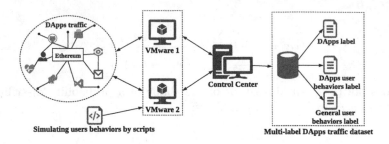

Fig. 4. Process of DApps traffic capture.

behaviors in total. Then, we categorize 88 user behaviors into 15 general user behaviors which represent the performance of these DApps. It is noteworthy that different sets of features proposed for these application scenarios are applicable to all DApps, the 11 representative DApps are used to evaluate our methods.

Table 1. Flow of 11 DApps

DApps	Category	Flow	Percentage (%)
Superrare	Marketplace	17593	9.1
Editional	Social	11066	5.8
John Orion Young	Property	13937	7.2
Thomas Crown Art	Marketplace	12105	6.3
Cryptoboiler	Social	15147	7.9
Ethlance	Social	12349	6.4
Knownorigin	Marketplace	15200	7.9
Staybit	Property	15535	8.1
Crowdholding	Social	24500	12.7
Latium	Exchanges	30245	15.8
Viewly	Media	24696	12.8
Total		**192373**	**100**

In order to achieve a particular target, a user must perform several actions in a precise order, which is the same as the action sequence in the real world. For example, when we comment on a post in Cryptoboiler, we need to perform exactly seven actions before we comment success: 1) open browser 2) enter Cryptoboiler 3) slide window 4) select edit box 5) fill the box with some text, which is randomly selected from a set of sentences 6) click publish button 7) close browser. We write 88 automatic scripts with Microsoft Visual Basic Script Edition, and each script represents a user behavior. Each user behavior is conducted for 200 times. For some user behaviors, we utilize different content to enrich the data set (e.g., for behavior 'select artwork' in Superrare, there is an action in the action sequence to view the detailed information of an artwork, we totally view the detailed information of 40 artworks, five times for each artwork, instead of 200 times for an artwork). The scripts are used to simulate user behaviors within DApps, and the traffic generated by DApps was captured.

For some user behaviors (e.g., comment post in Cryptoboiler, agree article in Crowdholding, like article in Editional), we need two different categories of users. "Passive" user is used to passively use the DApps, by receiving posts or comments. "Active" user simulates the behavior of users that actively use DApps by sending posts, comment, giving "Passive" user a like, etc. The main purpose of this step is to protect the normal use of other users.

Table 2. Flow of 15 general user behaviors (Color figure online)

Behaviors	Flow	Percentage (%)
Open DApps	28426	15
Open market	17176	9
View detail	29502	15
Follow a user	4685	2
Like or dislike	10885	6
Create project	16641	9
Search	22872	12
View homepage	17825	9
Activities	6176	3
Add to cart	2871	1
Watch video	2882	1
Comment	4078	2
DApps introduction	4748	3
Refresh cart	2977	2
Else behaviors	20629	11
Total	**192373**	**100**

We collected 192,373 flows and millions of packets on two virtual machines from August 4, 2019 to September 30, 2019. As seen in Fig. 4, we get the multi-label dataset. For each flow, it has three labels, including DApps label, DApps user behaviors label, and general user behaviors label. By simulating user behaviors through scripts, it is possible to label the flows. Their detailed information is showed in Table 1, Sect. 4.4, and Table 2, respectively. Finally, we extracted data from Wireshark capture files to form the Json file. The data includes time, IP addresses, packet lengths, payload, TCP/IP flags, extension information, etc.

4.2   Results of Different Models

The evaluated classifiers include Random Forest(RF), Gradient Boosting Decision Tree(GBDT), Decision Tree(DT), and the experimental results are shown in Table 3. The Random Forest classifier achieves the best performance for three application scenarios. So we select the Random Forest classifier for the following experiments. The classifier is trained using 100 estimators (the tree number of Random forest).

Table 3. Accuracy of different scenarios with different machine learning algorithms

Accuracy	GBDT	DT	RF
DApps classification	0.9032	0.9884	**0.995**
DApps user behaviors classification	0.8472	0.9483	**0.9565**
General user behaviors classification	0.6878	0.9581	**0.9858**

4.3   Evaluation of DApps Classification

As for the DApps traffic classification, we compare our proposed features with two other methods to classify 11 DApps, which are summarized as follows:

– Appscanner [21], which uses the statistical features of packet length (e.g., mean, percentiles) about incoming, outgoing and bi-directional flows in the RF classifier.

Table 4. Comparison of Appscanner, FFP and our features

DApps	Appscanner			FFP			Our features		
	P	R	F1	P	R	F1	P	R	F1
Superrare	0.9809	0.9039	0.9408	0.9870	0.9903	0.9885	0.9989	0.9989	0.9989
Editional	0.9857	0.9972	0.9915	0.9887	0.9866	0.9876	0.9865	0.9813	0.9838
John Orion Young	0.9914	0.9957	0.9936	0.9906	0.9750	0.9825	0.9958	0.9905	0.9931
Thomas Crown Art	0.9993	0.9921	0.9957	0.9898	0.9915	0.9906	0.9947	0.9969	0.9958
Cryptoboiler	0.9936	0.9984	0.9959	0.9967	0.9956	0.9961	0.9985	0.9980	0.9982
Ethlance	0.9987	0.9928	0.9957	0.9917	0.9892	0.9904	0.9944	0.9935	0.9940
Knownorigin	0.9917	0.9926	0.9922	0.9937	0.9976	0.9956	0.9972	0.9992	0.9982
Staybit	0.9999	0.9993	0.9997	0.9983	0.9979	0.9981	0.9999	0.9988	0.9993
Crowdholding	0.9996	0.9988	0.9992	0.9973	0.9977	0.9975	0.9988	0.9980	0.9984
Latium	0.9912	0.9923	0.9917	0.9886	0.9909	0.9898	0.9918	0.9927	0.9922
Viewly	0.9254	0.9744	0.9492	0.9757	0.9778	0.9766	0.9905	0.9944	0.9925
Average	0.9870	0.9852	0.9859	0.9907	0.9885	0.9902	0.9951	0.9947	0.9949
Accuracy	0.9844			0.9901			0.9950		

*P and R in this table means the metric Precision and Recall.

– FFP [20], which uses three sequence features: time series, packet length and burst. Then these features are fused through a kernel function to become high-dimensional features, which are used in the RF classifier.

As seen in Table 4, all of the methods perform good, the accuracy of the worst classifier reaches 98%. The accuracy of our method is 99.50%, which is higher 1.06% than Appscanner. And our features outperform FFP with about 0.5% improvement. The performance gap between our method and FFP is not large. However, the vector input into the classifier of FFP is much larger than the classifier of our method, so FFP takes longer time to build a model. Our model uses less features to improve efficiency and get better results.

4.4   Evaluation of DApps User Behaviors Classification

To implement our proposed features are better, we compare our approach with AppScanner (AppS) [21] and Aiolli [2] to classify 88 DApps user behaviors. Random forest classifier is used in comparison experiments. Aiolli method is summarized as follows:

– Aiolli, which uses statistical-time features (e.g., mean, median, mode) about incoming, outgoing and bi-directional flows in the RF classifier.

According to Table 5, the precision of our method is more than 98% for most DApps user behaviors. But we can see that the accuracy of behavior 1 (open Superrare) and behavior 3 (select artworks) is really poor according to Table 5. Since the result of DApps classification reaches 99%, the poor results are not caused by the similarity of DApps. Our classifier may confuse the two behaviors, which have similar action sequences. In Fig. 2 and Fig. 3, the distributions of the two behaviors are close to each other, which reflect the distinctiveness of the two features (i.e., byte distribution, the packet inter-arrival time series) in DApps user behaviors classification. The accuracy of the classification is above 95%, so our proposed features can effectively distinguish DApps user behaviors.

The comparison results are shown in Table 5. Our approach achieves the best performance, and outperforms the other methods. The accuracy of the proposed method achieves about 95.66% and the F1 score achieves about 95.53%. Compared to AppScanner and Aiolli, the accuracy of our features increases by 27.58% and 48.06%, and the F1 score of our features increases by 28.89% and 49.28%. The improvement effect is very obvious. Their approaches are prone to misclassification on DApps user behaviors. We think our proposed features (e.g., behavior-sensitive features: byte distribution, the improved inter-arrival time series features) can extract more information and details so that our approach is far more effective than others.

Table 5. Description of user behaviors and classification results with different methods. AppS, AF, OF represent AppScanner, Aiolli features, Our features, respectively.

DApps	ID	User behavior	Description	AppS F1	AF F1	OF F1	Flow
Superrare	1	open superrare	open the Superrare	0.46	0.11	0.54	2819
	2	open market	browse artworks on market page	0.69	0.24	1.00	4268
	3	select artwork	view details of an artwork	0.48	0.19	0.56	3018
	4	☆like artwork	like or dislike an artwork	0.79	0.01	1.00	2841
	5	user homepage	browse one's homepage	0.79	0.68	0.99	1294
	6	view activities	view activities happened in DApp	0.79	0.69	1.00	1498
	7	search	search artworks or artists	0.91	0.63	0.98	1855
		Average		0.70	0.36	0.87	2513
Editional	8	open editional	open the Editional	0.73	0.68	1.00	1419
	9	learn DApp	look Editional introduction	0.82	0.53	0.99	1220
	10	select collectible	view details of a collectible	0.85	0.73	0.98	1238
	11	artist homepage	browse a user homepage	0.75	0.31	0.99	1216
	12	artist create	look collectibles created by artist	0.86	0.46	0.98	1207
	13	artist collect	look collectibles collected by artist	0.80	0.18	0.98	1072
	14	view support page	view the support homepage	0.80	0.65	0.98	1135
	15	search support	search questions on support page	0.71	0.71	0.99	1329
	16	☆like article	like an article and send feedback	0.82	0.70	1.00	1230
		Average		0.79	0.55	0.99	1230
John Orion Young	17	☆add to shopping cart	add things to shopping cart	0.40	0.34	0.99	1428
	18	open market	browse joys on market page	0.89	0.64	0.97	3085
	19	select joy	view details of a joy	0.37	0.36	0.94	1350
	20	open shop	look clothes on the shop page	0.84	0.65	0.94	1342
	21	☆refresh shopping cart	refresh the shopping cart page	0.73	0.29	0.98	1585
	22	open john orion young	open the John Orion Young	0.94	0.48	0.99	2719
	23	view collector	view a collector homepage	0.87	0.68	0.98	2428
		Average		0.72	0.49	0.97	1991
Thomas Crown Art	24	☆add to shopping cart	add artworks to shopping cart	0.76	0.72	0.99	1443
	25	browse all artists	browse all artists on page	0.93	0.47	0.94	1117
	26	browse all artworks	browse all artworks on page	0.87	0.41	0.91	1251
	27	open the DApp	open the Thomas Crown Art	0.85	0.33	0.99	1264
	28	search	search artworks or artists	0.80	0.67	0.99	1491
	29	view blog	view details of a blog	0.74	0.45	0.91	1408
	30	look shopping cart	open the shopping cart page	0.82	0.25	0.97	1392
	31	select artist	view details of an artist	0.82	0.28	0.90	1341
	32	select artwork	view details of an artwork	0.71	0.29	0.99	1398
		Average		0.81	0.43	0.95	1345
Cryptoboiler	33	open Cryptoboiler	open the Cryptoboiler	0.80	0.52	1.00	1329
	34	view questions	view questions page	0.80	0.46	0.99	1398
	35	☆comment post	comment on a post	0.88	0.81	0.99	2735
	36	☆post a problem	post a problem in Cryptoboiler	0.94	0.86	0.99	1631
	37	☆like post	like or dislike a post	0.89	0.82	0.99	1832
	38	user homepage	browse one's homepage	0.70	0.43	0.99	1662
	39	view blog	view details of a blog	0.71	0.73	0.98	1678
	40	view question	view details of a question	0.80	0.40	0.98	1276
	41	search	search by keywords	0.95	0.84	0.99	1606
		Average		0.83	0.65	0.99	1683
Ethlance	42	☆open Ethlance	open the Ethlance	0.47	0.26	0.92	937
	43	☆user homepage	browse one's homepage	0.15	0.27	0.97	659
	44	☆look work	look suitable work	0.06	0.10	0.86	737
	45	☆look worker	look suitable workers	0.32	0.25	0.90	731
	46	☆become employer	fill information to be an employer	0.55	0.29	0.97	2123
	47	☆learn DApp	look Ethlance introduction	0.29	0.14	0.87	976
	48	☆different category	classified by different categories	0.49	0.38	0.70	1926
	49	☆search	search by keywords	0.83	0.36	0.86	2142
	50	☆become employer	fill information to be an employee	0.44	0.33	0.97	2118
		Average		0.40	0.26	0.89	1372

(continued)

Table 5. (*continued*)

DApps	ID	User behavior	Description	AppS F1	AF F1	OF F1	Flow
Knownorigin	51	☆open Knownorigin	open the Knownorigin	0.61	0.49	0.98	1578
	52	☆view gallery	browse all artworks on the page	0.76	0.61	0.91	1388
	53	☆select artwork	view details of an artwork	0.45	0.44	0.85	1714
	54	☆like artwork	like or dislike an artwork	0.05	0.02	0.98	2504
	55	☆view activities	view activities happened in DApp	0.25	0.16	0.99	1592
	56	☆browse all artists	browse all artists on the page	0.71	0.59	0.99	1859
	57	☆select artist	view details of an artist	0.29	0.22	0.99	2761
	58	☆search	search by keywords	0.04	0.02	0.85	1804
	Average			0.40	0.32	0.94	1900
Staybit	59	☆open Staybit	open the Staybit	0.69	0.74	0.98	3909
	60	☆create payment	create a payment request to rent	0.73	0.79	1.00	2706
	61	☆view contract	view my contracts	0.81	0.83	1.00	4632
	62	☆accept payment	retrieve a payment request	0.75	0.76	1.00	4288
	Average			0.75	0.78	1.00	3884
Crowdholding	63	open Crowdholding	open the Crowdholding	0.87	0.70	1.00	2648
	64	select an article	view details of an article	0.62	0.35	0.98	2422
	65	☆comment	comment on an article	0.63	0.46	1.00	1343
	66	☆agree article	agree or disagree an article	0.64	0.39	0.96	2478
	67	user homepage	browse one's homepage	0.58	0.37	0.97	2118
	68	☆follow a person	follow a person in Crowdholding	0.63	0.44	0.97	2391
	69	☆create a project	create a project to find workers	0.35	0.23	0.98	2601
	70	view project	view details of a project	0.54	0.27	1.00	2749
	71	search	search by keywords	0.82	0.73	0.99	3198
	72	learn DApp	look crowdholding introduction	0.59	0.28	1.00	2552
	Average			0.63	0.42	0.99	2450
Latium	73	open Latium	open the Latium	0.55	0.33	0.97	3800
	74	select task	view details of a task	0.60	0.27	0.99	3128
	75	user homepage	browse one's homepage	0.64	0.24	0.93	3749
	76	look transaction web	look transaction page	0.76	0.62	0.96	6761
	77	look my tasks	look my tasks page	0.52	0.26	0.90	3885
	78	homepage	view homepage	0.58	0.40	0.97	4632
	79	☆create a task	create a task to find workers	0.84	0.33	0.98	4290
	Average			0.64	0.35	0.96	4321
Viewly	80	open Viewly	open the Viewly	0.84	0.75	0.98	6004
	81	watch video	watch video	0.68	0.45	0.97	2882
	82	user homepage	browse one's homepage	0.76	0.54	0.98	2420
	83	look video transaction	view video trading information	0.48	0.33	0.98	2475
	84	☆follow person	follow a person in the Viewly	0.69	0.60	0.98	2294
	85	look game rank page	look the rank of distribution game	0.65	0.51	0.97	2887
	86	☆create new channel	create a channel to store video	0.61	0.48	0.99	1329
	87	☆upload video to draft	upload local video to draft	0.73	0.65	0.97	1172
	88	search	search by keyword	0.78	0.67	0.96	3233
	Average			0.69	0.55	0.98	2744
Accuracy				0.6808	0.4760	0.9566	
Precision				0.7027	0.4654	0.9617	
Recall				0.6541	0.4588	0.9565	
F1 score				0.6664	0.4625	0.9553	

*☆ means that users need to connect Ethereum wallet.

4.5 Evaluation of General User Behaviors Classification

Since we are the first one to classify encrypted traffic in this scenario, and in order to confirm the validity of proposed features for general user behaviors classification, we compare our proposed features with Appscanner [21], FFP [20] and the features mentioned in Aiolli [2] to classify 15 general user behaviors. Appscanner represents the conventional traffic analysis approach, FFP and Aiolli are the state-of-the-art classification approaches about blockchain network traffic.

Table 6. Experimental results with different approaches

User behaviors	Appscanner			Aiolli features			FFP			Our features		
	P	R	F1	P	R	F1	P	R	F1	P	R	F1
Open DApps	0.6981	0.5715	0.6081	0.3923	0.394	0.3827	0.642	0.5223	0.5578	0.9861	0.9877	0.9869
Open market	0.6807	0.5843	0.5254	0.3197	0.2942	0.2631	0.6153	0.5394	0.4729	0.9846	0.9809	0.9828
View detail	0.3655	0.3452	0.3357	0.2564	0.2697	0.2538	0.3849	0.327	0.3335	0.9784	0.9847	0.9816
Follow a user	0.6891	0.6073	0.5836	0.5377	0.4822	0.4858	0.6617	0.6065	0.5778	0.9816	0.991	0.9863
Like or dislike	0.5093	0.4668	0.4514	0.2743	0.2593	0.2409	0.4413	0.4865	0.4243	0.992	0.9923	0.9922
Create project	0.6160	0.4895	0.5121	0.3302	0.3186	0.3165	0.5532	0.5091	0.4978	0.9883	0.9899	0.9891
Search	0.6304	0.6076	0.5967	0.5033	0.4811	0.4835	0.656	0.6266	0.6191	0.9903	0.9873	0.9889
View homepage	0.6107	0.5297	0.5434	0.3448	0.3637	0.3447	0.5662	0.5226	0.5271	0.9829	0.9785	0.9807
Activities	0.5923	0.5447	0.5238	0.5172	0.4659	0.4602	0.6089	0.6096	0.5671	0.9864	0.9817	0.984
Add to cart	0.6764	0.4598	0.5050	0.6257	0.4874	0.5380	0.716	0.5929	0.6108	0.9985	0.9833	0.9909
Watch video	0.8488	0.5729	0.6470	0.5823	0.3876	0.4209	0.7895	0.5885	0.6302	0.986	0.9972	0.9916
Comment	0.7108	0.7506	0.6718	0.6353	0.6722	0.6238	0.6693	0.7631	0.6838	0.9972	0.9961	0.9967
DApps introduction	0.6887	0.5233	0.5120	0.3371	0.2612	0.2874	0.5982	0.5396	0.5021	0.9948	0.9753	0.985
Refresh cart	0.8006	0.7910	0.7581	0.4871	0.3445	0.3688	0.8136	0.7844	0.7743	0.9821	0.9902	0.9861
Else behaviors	0.6908	0.7468	0.6980	0.5452	0.5389	0.5178	0.7219	0.6724	0.6750	0.984	0.9847	0.9844
Average	**0.6539**	**0.5727**	**0.5648**	**0.4459**	**0.4014**	**0.3992**	**0.6292**	**0.5794**	**0.5635**	**0.9875**	**0.9867**	**0.9871**
Accuracy	0.5485			0.3826			0.5357			0.9857		

*P and R in this table means the metric Precision and Recall.

The comparison results are shown in Table 6. Our approach outperforms the other methods. The average precision of our method is 98.75%. Compared with Appscanner, FFP and Aiolli method, the precision of our method increases by about 33.36%, 35.83% and 54.16%, respectively. As for F1 score, our method also performs best, which can reach 98.71%. Compared with the other classification methods, the F1 of our method increases by about 42.23%, 42.36% and 58.79%, respectively. The improvement effect is very obvious. According to the classification results, we can intuitively see that our classifier is superior to the current classifiers.

4.6   Proposed Features Analysis

To implement our proposed method is useful and extracted features are better for general user behaviors classification. Seven feature sets are conducted from these features, as you can see in Table 7. PL distribution represents packet length distribution. IO time series represents inbound and outbound time series. IATS, BRC and PR statistics represent statistical features of inter-arrival time series, byte rate change and packet rate. TPIF, TPOF and FPAT represent total packets of inbound flow, total packets of outbound flow and the first packet arrival time.

The experimental results of different feature sets are shown in Fig. 5, and we draw some conclusions.

Table 7. Features information of experiments for 15 user behaviors classification

Feature	F I	F II (base experiment)	F III	F IV	F V	F VI	F VII
Time series	✓	✓	✓	✓	✓	✓	✓
Packet length series	✓	-	-	-	-	-	-
Burst	✓	-	-	-	-	-	-
PL distribution.	-	✓	✓	✓	✓	✓	✓
IO time series	-	-	✓	-	-	-	✓
Byte distribution	-	-	-	✓	-	-	✓
IATS, BRC and PR statistics	-	-	-	-	✓	-	✓
TPIF, TPOF and FPAT	-	-	-	-	-	✓	✓

*F in this table means feature sets.

1. One experiment only used the features mentioned in [20], which is called Feature I. Feature II is called base experiment. In order to know the impact of packet length distribution, we compare Feature I to Feature II. The comparison results show the uselessness of burst and packet length series in this classification. In terms of general user behaviors classification, packet length distribution is more useful than packet length series. As for accuracy, the classifier with Feature II is higher 39.59% points than the classifier with Feature I.

We conduct an additional experiment to find the reason for the poor performance of burst feature. Due to characteristics of DApps user behaviors, which are analyzed in Sect. 3.2, we extract number of packets for each user behavior, and find that more than 60% flows are short flows. The top-5 number of packets for each general user behavior are shown in Fig. 6. Most of flows have less than ten packets. Therefore, the classifier performs bad with this feature.

2. We consider that extracting time series of bidirectional flow may lose detailed information. The model using Feature III is higher 3.42% points than base experiment. So inbound and outbound time series can provide more details for general user behaviors classification.

3. Although transmission data is encrypted, behaviors with different action sequences produce some changes in payload, which cause the changes in traffic. So we use byte distribution to get more details, which can not be obtained from

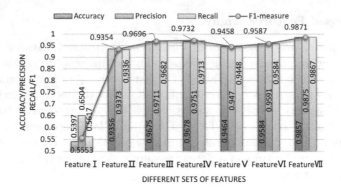

Fig. 5. Comparison results of Random Forest classifier with different sets of features.

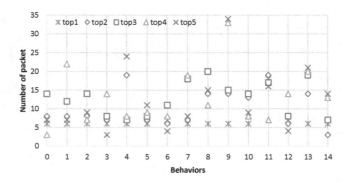

Fig. 6. The top-5 number of packets for each general user behavior. The X-axis label 0–14 represent 15 behaviors: open DApps(0), open market(1), view detail(2), follow a user(3), like or dislike(4), create project(5), search(6), view homepage(7), activities(8), add to cart(9), watch video(10), comment(11), DApps introduction(12), refresh cart(13), and else behaviors(14).

other features. Feature IV have the largest improvement, about 3.78% points in accuracy.

4. Compared with base experiment, Feature V and Feature VI contain different statistical features, and they improved the accuracy of 1.04% and 2.28%, respectively. These features can extract more information to improve the accuracy of the model. For example, byte rate change and packet rate can extract the intensity of user behaviors (i.e., action sequences).

5. According to Fig. 5, we can see that the result of Feature VII is the best. Compared with base experiment, the accuracy of the model is improved by 5.01%, the precision is improved by 5.02%, the recall is improved by 5.31%, the F1 is improved by 5.17%. We think the experiment of Feature VII achieves desirable results case it combines all features then obtains the maximum information.

5   Conclusion

In this paper, we focus on classification of DApps encrypted traffic for three application scenarios: DApps classification, DApps user behaviors classification and general user behaviors classification. For different scenarios, we extract different sets of effective features from DApps encrypted traffic after analyzing DApps characteristics. The experimental results show that our method has achieved satisfactory results in the encrypted traffic collected from 11 representative DApps. The accuracy of DApps classification reaches 99.5%, the accuracy of DApps user behaviors classification reaches 95.65%, and the accuracy of general user behaviors classification reaches 98.58%. The results demonstrate that our proposed features outperform the state-of-the-art methods. In the future, we plan to expand more application scenarios of DApps encrypted traffic classification and improve classification accuracy.

Acknowledgement. This work is supported by The National Natural Science Foundation of China (No. U1636217) and The Development Program for Guangdong Province under grant No. 2019B010137003 and National Key Research and Development Program of China (No. 2016QY05X1000) and The National Natural Science Foundation of China No. 61702501.

References

1. Dapps 2020. https://www.stateofthedapps.com/
2. Aiolli, F., Conti, M., Gangwal, A., Polato, M.: Mind your wallet's privacy: identifying bitcoin wallet apps and user's actions through network traffic analysis. In: Proceedings of the 34th ACM/SIGAPP Symposium on Applied Computing, SAC 2019, Limassol, Cyprus, 8–12 April 2019. pp. 1484–1491 (2019). https://doi.org/10.1145/3297280.3297430
3. Alan H F, K.J.: Can android applications be identified using only TCP/IP headers of their launch time traffic? In: Proceedings of the 9th ACM Conference on Security & Privacy in Wireless and Mobile Networks, WISEC 2016, pp. 61–66 (2016)
4. Buterin, V., et al.: A next-generation smart contract and decentralized application platform. White Paper 3(37) (2014)
5. Cai, X., Zhang, X.C., Joshi, B., Johnson, R.: Touching from a distance: website fingerprinting attacks and defenses. In: the ACM Conference on Computer and Communications Security, CCS 2012, pp. 605–616 (2012). https://doi.org/10.1145/2382196.2382260
6. Chen, S., Wang, R., Wang, X., Zhang, K.: Side-channel leaks in web applications: a reality today, a challenge tomorrow. In: 31st IEEE Symposium on Security and Privacy, S&P 2010, pp. 191–206. IEEE Computer Society (2010), https://doi.org/10.1109/SP.2010.20
7. Conti, M., Mancini, L.V., Spolaor, R., Verde, N.V.: Analyzing android encrypted network traffic to identify user actions. IEEE Trans. Inf. Forensics Secur. 11(1), 114–125 (2016). https://doi.org/10.1109/TIFS.2015.2478741

8. Coull, S.E., Dyer, K.P.: Traffic analysis of encrypted messaging services: Apple iMessage and beyond. Comput. Commun. Rev. **44**(5), 5–11 (2014). https://doi.org/10.1145/2677046.2677048

9. Draper-Gil, G., Lashkari, A.H., Mamun, M.S.I., Ghorbani, A.A.: Characterization of encrypted and VPN traffic using time-related features. In: Proceedings of the 2nd International Conference on Information Systems Security and Privacy, ICISSP 2016, Rome, Italy, 19–21 February 2016, pp. 407–414 (2016)

10. Duflos, S., Gay, V., Kervella, B., Horlait, E.: Integration of security parameters in the service level specification to improve QoS management of secure distributed multimedia services. In: International Conference on Advanced Information Networking & Applications (2017)

11. Finsterbusch, M., Richter, C., Rocha, E., Muller, J.A., Hanssgen, K.: A survey of payload-based traffic classification approaches. IEEE Commun. Surv. Tutor. **16**(2), 1135–1156 (2013)

12. Katsarakis, M., Teixeira, R.C., Papadopouli, M., Christophides, V.: Towards a causal analysis of video QoE from network and application QoS. In: Proceedings of the 2016 Workshop on QoE-Based Analysis and Management of Data Communication Networks, pp. 31–36. ACM (2016)

13. Korczyński, M., Duda, A.: Markov chain fingerprinting to classify encrypted traffic. In: IEEE INFOCOM 2014-IEEE Conference on Computer Communications, pp. 781–789. IEEE (2014)

14. Koshy, P., Koshy, D., McDaniel, P.: An analysis of anonymity in Bitcoin using P2P network traffic. In: Christin, N., Safavi-Naini, R. (eds.) FC 2014. LNCS, vol. 8437, pp. 469–485. Springer, Heidelberg (2014). https://doi.org/10.1007/978-3-662-45472-5_30

15. Liang, Q., Wu, X., Lau, H.C.: Optimizing service systems based on application-level QoS. IEEE Trans. Serv. Comput. **2**(2), 108–121 (2009)

16. Nguyen, B.M., Dang, T., Nguyen, Q.: A strategy for server management to improve cloud service QoS. In: IEEE/ACM International Symposium on Distributed Simulation & Real Time Applications (2015)

17. Panchenko, A., et al.: Website fingerprinting at internet scale. In: NDSS (2016)

18. Shen, M., Wei, M., Zhu, L., Wang, M.: Classification of encrypted traffic with second-order Markov chains and application attribute bigrams. IEEE Trans. Inf. Forensics Secur. **12**(8), 1830–1843 (2017). https://doi.org/10.1109/TIFS.2017.2692682

19. Shen, M., Wei, M., Zhu, L., Wang, M., Li, F.: Certificate-aware encrypted traffic classification using second-order Markov chain. In: 2016 IEEE/ACM 24th International Symposium on Quality of Service (IWQoS), pp. 1–10. IEEE (2016)

20. Shen, M., Zhang, J., Zhu, L., Xu, K., Du, X., Liu, Y.: Encrypted traffic classification of decentralized applications on Ethereum using feature fusion. In: Proceedings of the International Symposium on Quality of Service, IWQoS 2019, pp. 18:1–18:10 (2019). https://doi.org/10.1145/3326285.3329053

21. Taylor, V.F., Spolaor, R., Conti, M., Martinovic, I.: Appscanner: utomatic fingerprinting of smartphone apps from encrypted network traffic. In: IEEE European Symposium on Security and Privacy, EuroS&P 2016. pp. 439–454 (2016). https://doi.org/10.1109/EuroSP.2016.40

22. Wang, Q., Yahyavi, A., Kemme, B., He, W.: I know what you did on your smartphone: inferring app usage over encrypted data traffic. In: 2015 IEEE Conference on Communications and Network Security (CNS) (2015)

23. Yan, F., et al.: Identifying WeChat red packets and fund transfers via analyzing encrypted network traffic. In: 2018 17th IEEE International Conference on Trust, Security and Privacy in Computing and Communications/12th IEEE International Conference on Big Data Science and Engineering (TrustCom/BigDataSE), pp. 1426–1432 (2018)
24. Zhou, X., et al.: Identity, location, disease and more: inferring your secrets from android public resources. In: 2013 ACM SIGSAC Conference on Computer and Communications Security, CCS 2013, pp. 1017–1028. ACM (2013)

TransNet: Unseen Malware Variants Detection Using Deep Transfer Learning

Candong Rong[1,2], Gaopeng Gou[1,2], Mingxin Cui[1,2], Gang Xiong[1,2], Zhen Li[1,2], and Li Guo[1,2(✉)]

[1] Institute of Information Engineering, Chinese Academy of Sciences, Beijing, China
{rongcandong,gougaopeng,cuimingxin,xionggang,
lizhen,guoli}@iie.ac.cn
[2] School of Cyber Security, University of Chinese Academy of Sciences,
Beijing, China

Abstract. The ever-increasing amount and variety of malware on the Internet have presented significant challenges to the interconnected network community. The emergence of unseen malware variants has resulted in a different distribution of features and labels in the training and testing datasets. For widely used machine learning-based detection methods, the issue of dataset shift will render the trained model ineffective in the face of new data. However, it is a laborious and tedious undertaking whether relearning features to describe new data or collecting large amounts of labeled samples to retrain the classifiers. To address these problems, this paper proposes TransNet, a framework based on deep transfer learning for unseen malware variants detection. We first convert the raw traffic represented by sessions containing data from all layers of the OSI model into fixed-size RGB images through data preprocessing. Afterward, based on the ResNet-50 model pre-trained on the ImageNet, we replace Batch Normalization with Transferable Normalization as the normalization layer to construct our deep transfer learning model. In this way, our approach leverages deep learning to avoid the problem of traditional machine learning in relying on expert knowledge and uses transfer learning to address the issue of domain shift. We test the effectiveness of different methods with a thorough set of experiments. TransNet achieves 95.89% accuracy and 96.09% F-measure on two public datasets from the real-world environment, which is higher than comparative methods. Meantime, our method ranks first on all ten subtasks, showing that it can detect unseen malware variants with stable and excellent performance. Moreover, the distribution discrepancy computed by our method is much smaller than other approaches, which illustrates that our method successfully reduces the shift of data distributions.

Keywords: Deep transfer learning · Unseen malware variants detection · Network traffic classification.

© ICST Institute for Computer Sciences, Social Informatics and Telecommunications Engineering 2020
Published by Springer Nature Switzerland AG 2020. All Rights Reserved
N. Park et al. (Eds.): SecureComm 2020, LNICST 336, pp. 84–101, 2020.
https://doi.org/10.1007/978-3-030-63095-9_5

1 Introduction

Malicious software (malware), which is the tool for launching cyber attacks, poses great threats to military, government, and industrial production. Network traffic analysis plays an important role in addressing the issue of detecting malware [1, 2] and is widely used in Intrusion Detection System (IDS) and advanced firewalls [3, 4]. Over the years, including Advanced Persistent Threat (APT) activities and attacks using zero-day vulnerabilities, more and more cyber attacks have evaded detection by making use of the variation and obfuscation of malware [5]. Those variants have taken a toll on the enterprises, e.g., GandCrab that is a variant of ransomware has made 2 billion dollars in one and a half years [6]. Conventional signature-based detection methods are limited to known samples and patterns in the database, so they cannot handle the increasingly sophisticated and diverse malware variants [7]. Therefore, building a novel detection system in a rapidly changing network is essential to weaken the critical challenges that malware variants pose to detection systems.

In recent years, machine learning techniques have been applied to detect malware for improving the detection rate. On the one hand, data-driven supervised learning models rely on large quantities of labeled data, and their results depend on known samples in the training set [8, 9]. Once the malicious samples change behavior, the detection rate of the trained classifiers will drop dramatically, making it impossible to detect malware variants effectively. As a result, it needs recollecting new data to retrain the detection model for accommodating these changes. However, labeled data are often costly to obtain in the real world, especially malicious network traffic, as it represents a tiny small percentage of traffic. On the other hand, unsupervised learning detection methods divide the samples into distinct clusters based on the similarity among them. They can detect new threats, but lots of false alerts limit their practical usefulness [10, 11]. Similar to signature-based methods, traditional machine learning approaches fail to detect unseen threats. Consequently, it is necessary to find out an effective method for understanding and identifying malware variants.

The problem of changing malicious behavior between known malware samples and unseen variants can be solved by *domain adaptation (transfer learning)*. According to the concept of transfer learning, samples in the source domain are considered as already known and labeled, while samples in the target domain are unlabeled and different from those in the source domain. By transferring the knowledge learned from the source domain to the target domain, the task of detecting unseen malware variants is completed. Recently, several papers have focused on utilizing transfer learning to solve the issue of detecting malware variants. For example, Bartos et al. learned domain-invariant statistical feature representation computed from the network traffic to detect unseen malware variants [12]. Li et al. studied a novel method to identify malware variants based on adaptive regularization transfer learning [13]. Zhao et al. proposed a feature-based heterogeneous transfer learning approach HeTL [14] and a hierarchical transfer learning algorithm with clustering enhancement CeHTL [15] to detect unseen variants of attacks. However, the above methods are the combination of traditional machine learning technology and transfer learning. Conventional machine learning techniques are limited in their ability to process natural data in their raw form, as these methods rely on considerable domain expertise to build a system that could detect patterns in the input [16]. Not only are these methods time-consuming and labor-intensive, but they are also not as effective. Meanwhile, with the deployment of TLS 1.3 and ESNI (Encrypted Server Name Indication), some features in the traditional machine learning methods are no longer applicable to the fully encrypted traffic analysis. On the contrary, instead of extracting manually designed features from traffic data, with the help of multiple processing layers, deep learning methods can learn the very complex function to automatically convert the raw input into representations at a higher and more abstract level. Hence, methods of combining deep learning with transfer learning are considered to achieve more satisfactory results.

In the field of network traffic classification, one type of commonly used transfer learning-based approach is to use the models pre-trained on the ImageNet [17] as feature extractors [18,19]. It freezes the convolutional layers of deep neural networks and adapts the last layer to the particular task. In this way, the structure and parameters of pre-trained models are transferred to new tasks, reducing the computational cost of training from scratch while taking advantage of the knowledge that pre-trained models bring. However, such methods do not further consider the variability of data distribution between datasets, so they still cannot effectively address the issue of detecting unseen malware variants.

In this paper, we propose TransNet, a framework based on deep transfer learning to detect unseen malware variants. In the procedure of data preprocessing, we first divide malicious traffic and benign traffic into sessions containing data from all layers of the OSI model, and then do traffic anonymization and remove duplicated files. Afterward, we convert the first 900 bytes of data from each session into fixed-size RGB images. Based on the ResNet-50 [20] model pre-trained on the ImageNet, we use Transferable Normalization [21] to replace Batch Normalization [22] as the normalization layer to form our deep transfer learning model. Finally, these RGB images are used as input of the model to generate the results. The experiments show that our framework TransNet can detect unseen malware variants with superior performance and smaller distribution discrepancy than comparative methods.

In conclusion, the main contributions of our work are briefly summarized as follows:

1. We present a framework based on deep transfer learning for detecting unseen malware variants. It combines deep learning with transfer learning to solve the problem of different data distribution between datasets. It leverages the powerful representation ability of deep neural networks and uses knowledge learned from other domains to make decisions about tasks in new domains. In this way, our method avoids the problem of relying on expert knowledge for feature extraction in traditional machine learning methods and dramatically reduces the cost of manually labeling large amounts of data, enabling it to respond to emerging malware in a relatively short time.

2. Our method is based on the ResNet-50 model pre-trained on the ImageNet, which not only utilizes well-established architecture and parameters but also avoids the computational cost of training from scratch. The decision that uses Transferable Normalization to replace Batch Normalization as the normalization layer has improved the transferability of deep neural networks without increasing additional overhead.

3. Our method achieves 95.89% accuracy and 96.09% F-measure on public datasets from the real-world environment, which is higher than comparison methods. Even though other methods yield good results on the particular subtasks, our method ranks first on all ten subtasks with stable and excellent performance, which shows the superiority of our method in detecting unseen malware variants. Furthermore, MMD (Maximum Mean Discrepancy) of our method is much smaller than other methods on four typical subtasks, which suggests that our method successfully reduces the shift of data distributions.

The rest of this paper is organized as follows. We summarize related work in Sect. 2 and review background knowledge in Sect. 3. In Sect. 4, we describe our deep transfer learning framework. We discuss the experiments in detail and analyze the results in Sect. 5. Finally, we conclude this paper in Sect. 6.

2 Related Work

The issue of detecting unseen malware variants has become a popular topic in recent years. A great effort has been devoted to applying different methods to detect the growing number of variants in the constantly changing network environment. In this section, we retrospect the most relevant work to our method in two parts.

2.1 Conventional Methods for Malware Detection

Traditionally, signature-based methods [7,23] find the threats through the pre-defined signatures extracted from known samples in the database, which means they cannot be effective against novel attacks. Recently, machine learning technology has played a major role in the task of malware detection. They are mainly divided into two parts, namely supervised models [8,9] and unsupervised methods [10,11]. The models based on supervised learning train data-driven classifiers to distinguish malware from the benign samples. New data that are different from the training set will cause the accuracy of the already trained models to decrease. Unsupervised methods divide the samples into different clusters according to the similarity of behavior. They can detect unseen threats, but the high false alarm rate is unbearable in practice. Conventional machine learning-based methods have the same drawback as signature-based methods in that they work poorly in the face of new threats. The increasing number of malware variants has grown up to be a bottleneck in the development of detection systems.

2.2 Transfer Learning for Unseen Malware Detection

Transfer Learning, a novel machine learning technology, aims to build effective learners that can leverage the knowledge of rich labeled data from the source domain and transfer it to the target domain short of labeled data for reducing the shift in data distributions across different domains [24]. Even if transfer learning approaches are widely used in the tasks of computer vision and natural language processing, few studies have utilized them to address the issue of unseen malware detection. In recent papers, Bartos et al. [12] proposed a domain-invariant representation to detect previously unseen malware and behavior changes. The optimization method represented network traffic through the combination of invariant histograms of feature values and feature differences. Li et al. [13] thought it was not enough for knowledge transfer if only considered minimizing the difference between marginal distribution of different domains. Compared to [12], they studied a novel approach to detect unseen variants based on adaptive regularization transfer learning, which could reduce the marginal distribution and conditional distribution between the source and target domains. Zhao et al. proposed HeTL [14] and CeHTL [15] to solve the problem of unknown network attacks detection, respectively. The former method could find optimized representations for both training and testing data by transforming them into a common latent space via the spectral transformation where the difference of distributions could be reduced. The method CeHTL was proposed to make up for the shortcoming that the performance of HeTL depended on manual presettings of hyper-parameters. It was a hierarchical transfer learning algorithm with clustering enhancement, which could cluster the source and target domains and compute the relevance between them.

3 Background

In this section, to better understand the research in this paper, we review the relevant background knowledge. Firstly, we list the definitions related to transfer learning. We then introduce the processing steps of Batch Normalization that has a strong ability to accelerate network training. Finally, we compare Transferable Normalization and Batch Normalization, showing the changes made by the former to improve the transferability of the normalization layer. Table 1 summarizes the notations used in this paper and their corresponding descriptions.

3.1 Definition

In this part, we introduce the definitions related to transfer learning, including the "domain", the "task", and domain adaptation.

Definition 1 (Domain). *A domain $\mathcal{D}$ consists of two components: a feature space $\mathcal{X}$ and a marginal probability distribution $P(\mathbf{x})$, i.e., $\mathcal{D} = \{\mathcal{X}, P(\mathbf{x})\}$, where $\mathbf{x} \in \mathcal{X}$ [25].*

Table 1. Notations used in our paper and their corresponding descriptions

Notation	Description	Notation	Description
$\mathcal{D}_s$	the source domain	$\mathcal{D}_t$	the target domain
$\mathcal{X}$	feature space	P	marginal probability distribution
$\mathcal{T}_s$	the source task	$\mathcal{T}_t$	the target task
$\mathcal{Y}$	label space	f	predictive function
Q	conditional probability distribution	$\mathcal{B}$	mini-batch
k	channel	n	size of mini-batch
μ	mean	σ^2	variance
$\hat{x}$	normalized value	γ	the scaling parameter
β	the shift parameter	d	the domain distance
l	size of channel	α	distance-based probability

In general, if the source domain $\mathcal{D}_s$ and the target domain $\mathcal{D}_t$ are different, then they may have different feature spaces or different marginal probability distributions, i.e., $\mathcal{X}_s \neq \mathcal{X}_t \vee P_s(\mathbf{x}_s) \neq P_t(\mathbf{x}_t)$ [26].

Definition 2 (Task). *Given a specific domain, $\mathcal{D} = \{\mathcal{X}, P(\mathbf{x})\}$, a task $\mathcal{T}$ is composed of two components: a label space $\mathcal{Y}$ and an objective predictive function $f(\mathbf{x})$, i.e., $\mathcal{T} = \{\mathcal{Y}, f(\mathbf{x})\}$. From the probabilistic viewpoint, $f(\mathbf{x}) = Q(y|\mathbf{x})$ can be considered as the conditional probability distribution, where $y \in \mathcal{Y}$, and y is the corresponding label of an instance $\mathbf{x}$ [25].*

In general, if the source task $\mathcal{T}_s$ and the target task $\mathcal{T}_t$ are different, then they may have different label spaces or different conditional probability distributions, i.e., $\mathcal{Y}_s \neq \mathcal{Y}_t \vee Q_s(y_s|\mathbf{x}_s) \neq Q_t(y_t|\mathbf{x}_t)$ [26].

Definition 3 (Domain Adaptation). *Given a labeled source domain $\mathcal{D}_s = \{(\mathbf{x}_1, y_1), \ldots, (\mathbf{x}_n, y_n)\}$ and an unlabeled target domain $\mathcal{D}_t = \{\mathbf{x}_{n+1}, \ldots, \mathbf{x}_{n+m}\}$, where $\mathbf{x}_i$ is an instance and y_i is the corresponding label, the goal of domain adaptation is to utilize the knowledge learned from the source domain $\mathcal{D}_s$ and the source task $\mathcal{T}_s$ for generating a target predictive function $f_t : \mathbf{x}_t \mapsto y_t$ on the target domain $\mathcal{D}_t$ with low error rate, under the assumptions of $\mathcal{X}_s = \mathcal{X}_t$, $\mathcal{Y}_s = \mathcal{Y}_t$, $P_s(\mathbf{x}_s) \neq P_t(\mathbf{x}_t)$, and $Q_s(y_s|\mathbf{x}_s) \neq Q_t(y_t|\mathbf{x}_t)$ [13].*

3.2 Batch Normalization (BN)

Based on the known practice that the network training converges faster if its inputs are whitened [27], Batch Normalization [22] was designed to accelerate the training of deep neural networks. It transforms the inputs of each layer to have zero means and unit variances, and then scales and shifts them with a pair of learnable parameters to restore the representation power of the network. To reduce the expensive computation cost of fully whitening the inputs of each layer, it makes two necessary simplifications: normalize each scalar feature independently in each mini-batch. Specifically, in a mini-batch $\mathcal{B}$ of size n, for a layer with l-dimensional input $\mathbf{x} = \left(x^{(1)} \ldots x^{(l)}\right)$, it focuses on a particular dimension (channel) $x^{(k)}$, which has n values in this channel k. The first is that it calculates two statistics: the expectation $\mu^{(k)}$ and the variance $\sigma^{2(k)}$ for the channel k using the training data in a mini-batch $\mathcal{B}$:

$$\mu^{(k)} = \frac{1}{n} \sum_{i=1}^{n} x_i^{(k)}, \tag{1}$$

$$\sigma^{2(k)} = \frac{1}{n} \sum_{i=1}^{n} \left(x_i^{(k)} - \mu^{(k)}\right)^2. \tag{2}$$

It then utilizes the statistics to normalize the inputs of every layer to have the mean of 0 and the variance of 1. The formula is shown as follows:

$$\widehat{x}^{(k)} = \frac{x^{(k)} - \mu^{(k)}}{\sqrt{\sigma^{2(k)} + \epsilon}}, \tag{3}$$

where ϵ is a constant added to the mini-batch variance for numerical stability. The second step is to learn two trainable parameters for scaling and shifting the normalized value of the channel k to represent the identity transform and preserve the network capacity:

$$y^{(k)} = \gamma\widehat{x}^{(k)} + \beta \equiv \text{BN}_{\gamma,\beta}\left(x^{(k)}\right), \tag{4}$$

where $\text{BN}_{\gamma,\beta}\left(x^{(k)}\right) : x^{(k)} \to y^{(k)}$ is the Batch Normalization Transform.

There is no doubt that Batch Normalization has made outstanding contributions in accelerating network training. However, without considering the difference between the training data and testing data, BN combines them into a single batch to feed as the input of the normalization layer. The representations of data that are following different distributions share the expectation and the variance, which is unsuitable due to the phenomenon known as dataset shift [28]. Additionally, all channels are given the same importance in BN, which is unreasonable in the case of domain adaptation since some channels are more transferable than the others. Therefore, the transferability of BN needs to be improved.

3.3   Transferable Normalization (TransNorm)

In order to overcome the aforesaid shortcomings of Batch Normalization when applied to domain adaptation, Transferable Normalization [21] (TransNorm) was proposed to improve the transferability of deep neural networks. To bridge different domains in domain adaptation, comparing with BN, TransNorm changes the shared mean and variance to domain-specific mean and variance, and assigns different weights to the channels according to the difference of transferability. In this part, we introduce the processing procedure of TransNorm in three steps: domain-specific mean and variance, domain-shared learnable parameters, and domain adaptive weights.

In each BN layer, the inputs coming from the source and target domains are combined into a single batch to calculate the mean and variance. However, due to dataset shift, there exists a significant difference in data distribution across two domains, leading to having different basic statistics between the source and target domains. Instead of straightforwardly sharing the mean and the variance, TransNorm separately calculates domain-specific statistics of each channel: the source statistics μ_s, σ_s^2 and the target statistics μ_t, σ_t^2 as follows (let us focus on the particular channel k and omit k for clarity):

$$\mu_s = \frac{1}{n_s} \sum_{i=1}^{n_s} x_i, \quad \sigma_s^2 = \frac{1}{n_s} \sum_{i=1}^{n_s} (x_i - \mu_s)^2, \tag{5}$$

$$\mu_t = \frac{1}{n_t} \sum_{j=1}^{n_t} x_j, \quad \sigma_t^2 = \frac{1}{n_t} \sum_{j=1}^{n_t} (x_j - \mu_t)^2, \tag{6}$$

where n_s and n_t correspond to the mini-batch size in the source and target domains, respectively. After that, the means and the variances are used to normalize the inputs of each normalization layer independently for each domain:

$$\widehat{x}_s = \frac{x_s - \mu_s}{\sqrt{\sigma_s^2 + \epsilon}}, \quad \widehat{x}_t = \frac{x_t - \mu_t}{\sqrt{\sigma_t^2 + \epsilon}}, \tag{7}$$

where ϵ is a constant added to the mini-batch variance for numerical stability. In this way, the representations from the source and target domains are separately normalized to have the mean of 0 and the variance of 1.

With consideration of simply normalizing each channel of a layer may change what the layer can represent, BN learns a pair of parameters γ and β to scale and shift the normalized values for ensuring the transformation inserted in the network can preserve the representation ability of the network. TransNorm retains the capability of this part of BN, and scales and shifts the normalized values of each normalization layer with domain-shared parameters for different domains:

$$w_s = \gamma \widehat{x}_s + \beta, \quad w_t = \gamma \widehat{x}_t + \beta. \tag{8}$$

Both domain-specific basic statistics and domain-shared learnable parameters treat all channels equally. However, in the context of different channels extract different aspects from the input, the information existing in some aspects is more transferable than the others, resulting in differences in the transferability of different channels. Therefore, in the field of domain adaptation, we need to consider the difference in channel transferability further. To accomplish this, TransNorm reuses the basic statistics from the source and target domains: μ_s, σ_s^2 and μ_t, σ_t^2 to select the channels that are more transferable. For each channel k, TransNorm calculates the distance across domains $d^{(k)}$ as follows:

$$d^{(k)} = \left| \frac{\mu_s^{(k)}}{\sqrt{\sigma_s^2(k) + \epsilon}} - \frac{\mu_t^{(k)}}{\sqrt{\sigma_t^2(k) + \epsilon}} \right|, \quad k = 1, 2, \ldots, l, \tag{9}$$

where l is the size of channels within each TransNorm layer. For enhancing the understandability and applicability of the method, TransNorm utilizes Student t-distribution [29] to convert the channel-wise distances to probabilities. It assigns different weights to the channels according to the transferability calculated by the distance-based probability $\alpha^{(k)}$:

$$\alpha^{(k)} = \frac{l\left(1 + d^{(k)}\right)^{-1}}{\sum_{m=1}^{l}\left(1 + d^{(m)}\right)^{-1}}, \quad k = 1, 2, \ldots, l, \tag{10}$$

where l is the number of channels. In doing so, the channels that are more transferable are assigned with higher weights, improving the transferability of the normalization layer for domain adaptation. Finally, to avoid overly penalizing the channels that are less transferable, TransNorm introduces the residual mechanism to combine the normalized values of Eq. (8) with the transferability-weighted one to generate the output of each normalization layer:

$$y_s = (1 + \alpha)w_s, \quad y_t = (1 + \alpha)w_t. \tag{11}$$

We visually show the differences between Batch Normalization and Transferable Normalization in Fig. 1. Based on BN, the changes made by TransNorm to improve the transferability are reflected in the following two aspects: the first is that TransNorm normalizes the representations from the source and target domains separately, instead of mixing the inputs across domains into a single batch for normalizing like BN. The second is that TransNorm reuses the basic statistics from different domains to calculate the transferability for each channel to select those more transferable channels, making sure the similar patterns are shareable across domains.

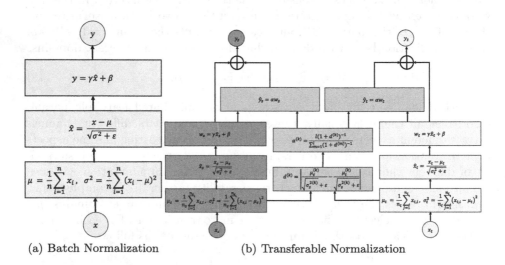

(a) Batch Normalization   (b) Transferable Normalization

Fig. 1. The processing procedure of Batch Normalization is shown in (a). The processing procedure of Transferable Normalization is presented in (b).

4 Design of Framework

In this section, we discuss the design of our framework based on deep transfer learning for unseen malware variants detection. The framework is composed of two crucial components: data preprocessing and deep transfer learning model. As the input of the data preprocessing module, the raw traffic of malware variants and benign applications is converted to images in RGB format. We use Transferable Normalization to replace Batch Normalization in the ResNet-50 model pre-trained on the ImageNet for forming a classification model based on deep transfer learning. The model learns the representations of different types of traffic from the RGB images generated in the previous step, and then produces the final classification results. The architecture of our framework is shown in Fig. 2.

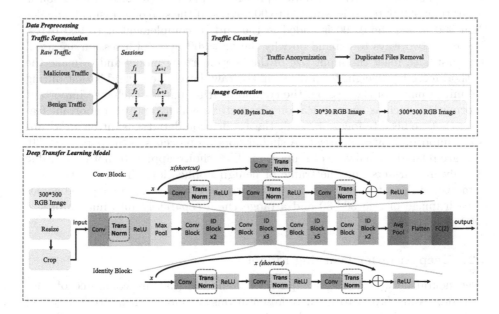

Fig. 2. The architecture of our framework TransNet.

4.1 Data Preprocessing

In the initial stage of data preprocessing, we first need to determine the way of representation for traffic. The flow and the session are commonly used units for traffic splitting in the field of network traffic classification. A flow is a set of packets with the same 5-tuple. The 5-tuple is composed of source IP, source port, destination IP, destination port, and transport layer protocol. Moreover, a session consists of bidirectional flows between two communication hosts. Generally speaking, bidirectional flows contain more interactive information than unidirectional flows. Meanwhile, the representations generated by the data from all layers of the OSI model have more comprehensive traffic features than those from the application layer. Thus, we select the session as the unit for traffic splitting and reserve the data coming from all layers of the OSI model.

As shown in Fig. 2, to convert raw traffic into RGB images with a size of 300 * 300, we need to go through three steps: traffic segmentation, traffic cleaning, and image generation. In the first step, we split raw traffic to large numbers of sessions containing data from all layers of the OSI model. The input and output data formats of this step are packet capture files (pcap). In the stage of traffic cleaning, we first conduct traffic anonymization, that is, randomize MAC addresses in the data link layer and IP addresses in the IP layer. We then remove duplicate files generated by packets with the same content for avoiding biases in the training of deep learning models. In the final step, we first extract the first 900 bytes of data from each session and convert them into RGB images of size 30 * 30. Each byte of original data represents a pixel. If the size of a session is larger than 900 bytes, it is adjusted to 900 bytes. If the size of a session is smaller than 900 bytes, the 0×00 is added in the end to complement it to 900 bytes. There are two ways to expand on why the first 900 bytes of a session are used. The first is to meet the input size of the deep learning model and to make the method more lightweight for processing the raw data. The second is that during the initial phase of the session, the communicating parties exchange important information, such as communication parameters, which contains important features that we need to focus on, while the application data transmitted afterward is less important by comparison. A similar operation occurs in the papers [18,30] that are related to malware classification. This choice applies to both the traffic of malware variants and the traffic of benign applications. To meet the input data size of deep transfer learning model to be used next, we copy 100 copies of each image of size 30 * 30 and arrange them separately into images of size 300 * 300.

4.2 Deep Transfer Learning Model

Deep neural networks allow computational models that are composed of multiple processing layers to learn representations of data with multiple levels of abstraction, and these methods have dramatically improved the state-of-the-art in a wide range of tasks, such as image classification, object detection, and other challenging fields [16]. In recent years, many researchers have proposed numerous deep learning models and made unremitting efforts to improve the performance of the methods. Taking the classic image classification task, ILSVRC (ImageNet Large Scale Visual Recognition Challenge), as an example, different deep neural networks were trained on the ImageNet [17] to reduce the classification error rate, e.g., AlexNet [31], VGG [32], and ResNet [20]. Impressed by the powerful representation capability of deep neural networks, the researchers focusing on network traffic classification utilize them to promote the improvement of performance. In general, the more complex structure the model has, the better performance the model can achieve on a dataset. Meantime, the models pretrained on large datasets have configured structure and parameters, avoiding the cost caused by training from scratch. In our method, after making a trade off between the performance of models and the computational cost of training, we choose the ResNet-50 model pre-trained on the ImageNet as our basic deep learning model.

The purpose of combining deep learning models with transfer learning is to leverage the deep neural networks for cross-domain representation learning. We delve into the architecture design of deep neural networks and use Transferable Normalization (TransNorm) successfully applied in computer vision for reference. TransNorm, which is a more transferable normalization technique, fully considers the difference in data distributions between the source and target domains. Meanwhile, it will not bring additional computational cost and change other network modules. As marked with red boxes in Fig. 2, based on the ResNet-50 model pre-trained on the ImageNet, we propose our deep transfer learning model by leveraging Transferable Normalization as the normalization layer to replace existing Batch Normalization. Our framework can bridge the source and target domains, which will also be confirmed in the experiments. As shown in Fig. 2, the RGB images after being resized and cropped are used as the input of our deep transfer learning model to produce the final results.

5   Evaluation

In this section, we evaluate our method on the real-world datasets. Firstly, we introduce the components of two public datasets used in our experiments and describe the experimental setup. We then construct a series of comparison experiments with different approaches and discuss the corresponding results. The results support the advantage of our deep transfer learning-based method in detecting unseen malware variants with superior performance over comparative methods.

5.1   Dataset and Experimental Setup

In our experiments, we are based on pcap files to carry on the study of malware variants detection from the perspective of network traffic. We use two public datasets for evaluating different methods, where the malicious traffic comes from Malware Capture Facility Project (MCFP) [33], and the benign traffic is composed of data from USTC-TFC2016 [30]. The MCFP is a research project of CTU (Czech Technical University) aiming to collect different kinds of malicious traffic from the real-world network environment. We choose malicious traffic generated by ten types of malware variants from it, including traffic of common categories of malware such as trojan, botnet, and virus. The benign traffic in the USTC-TFC2016 dataset consists of the traffic generated by different classes of normal applications, e.g., data transfer tools, instant messaging applications, email communication systems, databases, and games. As mentioned in Sect. 4.1, we utilize sessions to describe the raw traffic in the aforementioned public datasets. After the data preprocessing, we convert the first 900 bytes of each session into RGB images with a size of 300*300. The RGB images are the input of the deep transfer learning model, and their number is equal to the number of sessions. Table 2 illustrates a general view of datasets used in our experiments.

Table 2. A general view of datasets used in our experiments

Malicious Traffic	Category	Sessions	Benign Traffic	Category	Sessions
MCFP	Cridex	7373	USTC-TFC2016	BitTorrent	7517
	Geodo	9213		Facetime	6000
	Htbot	5730		FTP	15000
	Miuref	6066		Gmail	8629
	Neris	7603		MySQL	15000
	Nsis-ay	5462		Outlook	7524
	Shifu	8671		Skype	6321
	Tinba	7654		SMB	9733
	Virut	7448		Weibo	9988
	Zeus	9873		WorldOfWarcraft	7883

In terms of the experimental setup, the training and testing data contain malicious traffic generated by different malware variants, in other words, for each subtask, we select nine malware variants as a part of training data and another malware variant to be part of testing data. For example, we choose malware variants other than Cridex as part of training data, and Cridex as part of testing data. The purpose of this experimental design is to simulate the scenario of detecting unseen threats created by malware developers for evading current detection methods and systems. Meanwhile, the benign traffic in the training and testing data is also different.

5.2 Basic Result

According to the experimental setup, the evaluation process of each method is divided into ten subtasks. The purpose of every subtask is to utilize nine malware variants to discover another novel variant. As mentioned in the introduction, some features in the methods of combining traditional machine learning technology and transfer learning are no longer suitable for the analysis of fully encrypted traffic. Therefore, in the comparison experiments, to ensure the comparability of methods, we select three pre-trained models commonly used in the studies related to network traffic classification, such as AlexNet, VGG19_bn, and ResNet-50, as the comparative methods. All methods are implemented based on PyTorch. The methods using pre-trained models are model-based transfer learning methods. Table 3 and Table 4 show the accuracy and F-measure of different approaches in the task of detecting unseen malware variants, respectively.

First of all, our method TransNet has achieved the best results among the approaches, with the accuracy of 95.89% and the F-measure of 96.09%. Afterward, the comparison of the average value of indicators of three pre-trained

Table 3. Accuracy (%) on our dataset for unseen malware variants detection

Method	Subtask										
	Cridex	Geodo	Htbot	Miuref	Neris	Nsis-ay	Shifu	Tinba	Virut	Zeus	Avg
AlexNet	71.30	82.10	71.22	80.23	75.54	63.47	74.40	74.26	71.11	66.95	73.06
VGG19_bn	87.75	85.64	88.72	77.02	79.21	71.38	83.66	91.56	87.39	93.36	84.57
ResNet-50	90.49	90.38	90.70	91.62	83.51	65.39	92.32	92.16	79.84	85.94	86.24
TransNet	**96.35**	**90.90**	**95.50**	**95.63**	**97.58**	**89.86**	**99.68**	**96.11**	**99.99**	**97.29**	**95.89**

Table 4. F-measure (%) on our dataset for unseen malware variants detection

Method	Subtask										
	Cridex	Geodo	Htbot	Miuref	Neris	Nsis-ay	Shifu	Tinba	Virut	Zeus	Avg
AlexNet	68.63	78.40	71.97	80.71	74.51	63.50	67.91	69.82	68.95	60.64	70.50
VGG19_bn	87.84	85.73	89.08	72.10	78.06	64.09	83.73	91.68	87.41	92.85	83.26
ResNet-50	90.64	90.27	91.29	92.19	83.35	57.48	92.13	92.26	76.88	85.98	85.25
TransNet	**96.49**	**90.35**	**96.10**	**96.13**	**97.66**	**90.96**	**99.68**	**96.19**	**99.99**	**97.34**	**96.09**

models, AlexNet, VGG19_bn, and ResNet-50, supports the experienced judgment that the increase in model complexity brings the improvement of performance. Although some comparison methods have achieved good results on particular subtasks, e.g., VGG19_bn has the accuracy of 93.36% when used to detect Zeus, but our method ranks first on all subtasks with stable and excellent performance. Our method is achieved by replacing Batch Normalization in the ResNet-50 pre-trained model with Transferable Normalization. The results of these two methods shown in the tables illustrate that TransNorm improves the transferability of deep neural networks. Specifically, TransNorm calculates the basic statistical information of different domains separately and assigns different weights to channels according to the transferability of them. The results show that our method is capable of detecting unseen malware variants at a superior performance. It can relieve the challenge caused by continually increasing malware in the real-world environment through reducing time cost and labor cost of manually labeling data.

5.3 Further Analysis

MMD (Maximum Mean Discrepancy) [34] is proposed as a criterion for comparing different distributions based on the Reproducing Kernel Hilbert Space (RKHS). It is a measure of the cross-domain discrepancy of distributions, which is commonly used in domain adaptation. According to the results in Table 3, among the ten subtasks, our method has the most significant performance gap with the second-ranked method on Neris and Nsis-ay, while our method has the smallest performance gap with the second-ranked method on Geodo and Tinba. Therefore, we compute MMD on the above four subtasks with features of AlexNet, VGG19_bn, ResNet-50, and TransNet. Figure 3 shows the results of MMD calculated by different methods on each subtask.

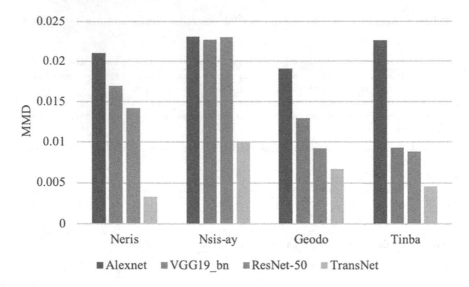

Fig. 3. The results of MMD calculated by different methods on four subtasks.

As shown in Fig. 3, we observe that MMD using TransNet features (our method) is much smaller than MMD using features of other methods, which suggests that TransNet features can close the cross-domain gap more effectively. Meanwhile, the MMD values of TransNet features in Neris and Tinba are smaller than those in Nsis-ay and Geodo, which explains better accuracy of TransNet on the subtasks of detecting Neris and Tinba. Furthermore, compared to the difference of MMD computed by TransNet and other methods on Geodo and Tinba, the MMD values of TransNet on Neris and Nsis-ay differ more significantly from those of other methods, which exactly corresponds to the degree of difference in performance between our method and the second-ranked method in the above four subtasks.

6   Conclusion

In this paper, we present a framework using deep transfer learning, namely TransNet, for unseen malware variants detection. We use data preprocessing to convert the raw traffic into RGB images as the input of our deep transfer learning model. Faced with the problem of identifying unseen malware variants, we delve into the architecture of deep neural networks and find that the operation of the normalization layer needs to take into account the variability of data distribution between different datasets. Consequently, to construct our deep transfer learning model, we replace the Batch Normalization in the ResNet-50 model pre-trained on the ImageNet with Transferable Normalization to improve the transferability of deep neural networks. We test different methods by simulating scenarios where the testing set contains different malware variants from the training set.

Our method achieves 95.89% accuracy and 96.09% F-measure on the public datasets from the real-world environment, which is higher than comparative methods. Meanwhile, our method ranks first on all ten subtasks with stable and excellent performance. The above two points show that our method can detect unseen malware variants. Furthermore, MMD of TransNet is much smaller than MMD of other approaches, which validates that our method successfully reduces the shift of distributions through more transferable representations. When new traffic emerges, instead of re-collecting large amounts of labeled data or learning novel representations, our framework achieves labeling and detecting malicious traffic generated by unseen malware variants with the help of the original trained model and analysis of the distribution of different datasets. In future work, we will conduct a more extensive analysis to discover more malware variants, such as malicious Windows PE (Portable Executable) files and malicious Android APK (Android application package) files. Meanwhile, we will explore the issue of unbalanced data between malicious traffic and benign traffic to improve the possibility of applying our method to the real-world environment.

Acknowledgments. This work is supported by The National Natural Science Foundation of China (No.61702501) and The National Key Research and Development Program of China (No.2016QY05X1000, No.2018YFB1800200).

References

1. Anderson, B., McGrew, D.: Identifying encrypted malware traffic with contextual flow data. Proc. ACM Workshop Artif. Intell. Secur. **2016**, 35–46 (2016)
2. Wang, T.S., Lin, H.T., Cheng, W.T., et al.: DBod: Clustering and detecting DGA-based botnets using DNS traffic analysis. Comput. Secur. **64**, 1–15 (2017)
3. Kovanen, T., David, G., Hämäläinen, T.: Survey: intrusion detection systems in encrypted traffic. In: Galinina, O., Balandin, S., Koucheryavy, Y. (eds.) NEW2AN/ruSMART -2016. LNCS, vol. 9870, pp. 281–293. Springer, Cham (2016). https://doi.org/10.1007/978-3-319-46301-8_23
4. Wang, W., Sheng, Y., Wang, J., et al.: HAST-IDS: Learning hierarchical spatial-temporal features using deep neural networks to improve intrusion detection. IEEE Access **6**, 1792–1806 (2017)
5. Zhao, S., Ma, X., Zou, W., Bai, B.: DeepCG: classifying metamorphic malware through deep learning of call graphs. In: Chen, S., Choo, K.-K.R., Fu, X., Lou, W., Mohaisen, A. (eds.) SecureComm 2019. LNICST, vol. 304, pp. 171–190. Springer, Cham (2019). https://doi.org/10.1007/978-3-030-37228-6_9
6. Tencent Security: https://s.tencent.com/research/report/790.html. August 2019
7. Kumar, V., Sangwan, O.P.: Signature based intrusion detection system using SNORT. Int. J. Comput. Appl. Inf. Technol. **1**(3), 35–41 (2012)
8. Timcenko, V., Gajin, S.: Ensemble classifiers for supervised anomaly based network intrusion detection. In: 2017 13th IEEE International Conference on Intelligent Computer Communication and Processing (ICCP), pp. 13–19. IEEE (2017)
9. AlAhmadi, B.A., Martinovic, I.: Malclassifier: alware family classification using network flow sequence behaviour. In: 2018 APWG Symposium on Electronic Crime Research (eCrime), pp. 1–13. IEEE (2018)

10. Kohout, J, Pevný, T.: Unsupervised detection of malware in persistent web traffic. In: 2015 IEEE International Conference on Acoustics, Speech and Signal Processing (ICASSP), pp. 1757–1761. IEEE (2015)
11. Alom, M.Z., Taha, T.M.: Network intrusion detection for cyber security using unsupervised deep learning approaches. In: 2017 IEEE National Aerospace and Electronics Conference (NAECON), pp. 63–69. IEEE (2017)
12. Bartos, K, Sofka, M, Franc, V.: Optimized invariant representation of network traffic for detecting unseen malware variants. In: 25th USENIX Security Symposium (USENIX Security 16), pp. 807–822 (2016)
13. Li, H., Chen, Z., Spolaor, R., et al.: DART: detecting unseen malware variants using adaptation regularization transfer learning. In: ICC 2019–2019 IEEE International Conference on Communications (ICC), pp. 1–6. IEEE (2019)
14. Zhao, J., Shetty, S., Pan, J.W.: Feature-based transfer learning for network security. In: MILCOM 2017–2017 IEEE Military Communications Conference (MILCOM), pp. 17–22. IEEE (2017)
15. Zhao, J., Shetty, S., Pan, J.W., et al.: Transfer learning for detecting unknown network attacks. EURASIP J. Inf. Secur. **2019**(1), 1 (2019)
16. LeCun, Y., Bengio, Y., Hinton, G.: Deep learning. Nature **521**(7553), 436–444 (2015)
17. Deng, J., Dong, W., Socher, R., et al.: Imagenet: a large-scale hierarchical image database. In: 2009 IEEE Conference on Computer Vision and Pattern Recognition, pp. 248–255. IEEE (2009)
18. Rezende, E., Ruppert, G., Carvalho, T., et al.: Malicious software classification using transfer learning of resnet-50 deep neural network. In: 2017 16th IEEE International Conference on Machine Learning and Applications (ICMLA), pp. 1011–1014. IEEE (2017)
19. Rezende, E., Ruppert, G., Carvalho, T., Theophilo, A., Ramos, F., Geus, P.: Malicious software classification using VGG16 deep neural network's bottleneck features. In: Latifi, S. (ed.) Information Technology - New Generations. AISC, vol. 738, pp. 51–59. Springer, Cham (2018). https://doi.org/10.1007/978-3-319-77028-4_9
20. He, K., Zhang, X., Ren, S., et al.: Deep residual learning for image recognition. In: Proceedings of the IEEE Conference on Computer Vision and Pattern Recognition, pp. 770–778 (2016)
21. Wang, X., Jin, Y., Long, M., et al.: Transferable normalization: towards improving transferability of deep neural networks. In: Advances in Neural Information Processing Systems, pp. 1951–1961 (2019)
22. Ioffe, S., Szegedy, C.: Batch normalization: accelerating deep network training by reducing internal covariate shift. In: International Conference on Machine Learning, pp. 448–456 (2015)
23. Hubballi, N., Suryanarayanan, V.: False alarm minimization techniques in signature-based intrusion detection systems: a survey. Comput. Commun. **49**, 1–17 (2014)
24. Long, M., Zhu, H., Wang, J., et al.: Deep transfer learning with joint adaptation networks. In: Proceedings of the 34th International Conference on Machine Learning, vol. 70, pp. 2208–2217. JMLR. org (2017)
25. Pan, S.J., Yang, Q.: A survey on transfer learning. IEEE Trans. Knowl. Data Eng. **22**(10), 1345–1359 (2009)
26. Long, M., Wang, J., Ding, G., et al.: Adaptation regularization: a general framework for transfer learning. IEEE Trans. Knowl. Data Eng. **26**(5), 1076–1089 (2013)

27. Wiesler, S., Ney, H.: A convergence analysis of log-linear training. In: Advances in Neural Information Processing Systems, pp. 657–665 (2011)
28. Quionero-Candela, J., Sugiyama, M., Schwaighofer, A., et al.: Dataset Shift in Machine Learning. The MIT Press, Cambridge (2009)
29. Student: The probable error of a mean. Biometrika **6**(1), 1–25 (1908)
30. Wang, W., Zhu, M., Zeng, X., et al.: Malware traffic classification using convolutional neural network for representation learning. In: 2017 International Conference on Information Networking (ICOIN), pp. 712–717. IEEE (2017)
31. Krizhevsky, A., Sutskever, I., Hinton, G.E.: Imagenet classification with deep convolutional neural networks. In: Advances in neural information processing systems, pp. 1097–1105 (2012)
32. Simonyan, K., Zisserman, A.: Very deep convolutional networks for large-scale image recognition. arXiv preprint arXiv:1409.1556 (2014)
33. Stratosphere: Stratosphere Laboratory Datasets. (2015). Retrieved March 13, 2020, fromhttps://www.stratosphereips.org/datasets-overview
34. Borgwardt, K.M., Gretton, A., Rasch, M.J., et al.: Integrating structured biological data by kernel maximum mean discrepancy. Bioinformatics **22**(14), e49–e57 (2006)

A Brokerage Approach for Secure Multi-Cloud Storage Resource Management

Muhammad Ihsan Haikal Sukmana[1]([✉]), Kennedy Aondona Torkura[1],
Sezi Dwi Sagarianti Prasetyo[2], Feng Cheng[1], and Christoph Meinel[1]

[1] Hasso Plattner Institute, University of Potsdam, Potsdam, Germany
{muhammad.sukmana,kennedy.torkura,feng.cheng,christoph.meinel}@hpi.de
[2] University of Potsdam, Potsdam, Germany
prasetyo@uni-potsdam.de

Abstract. Nowadays, more cloud customers are utilizing multiple cloud service providers (CSPs) to store their data in the cloud as it provides better data availability and service reliance than storing in the single CSP. However, there are several challenges faced by cloud customers to securely manage their cloud storage resources for cloud end-users (a user or a service) in the multi-cloud scenario, such as diverse APIs and service implementations in multiple CSP as CSP is not required to comply with cloud computing standards and multi-cloud resource management skill gap. In this paper, we present a unified multi-cloud storage resource management framework for managing cloud storage resources and their configurations for Object Storage and Identity and Access Management services following the cloud brokerage approach. We propose a unified cloud storage resource model continuing our previous work to tackle the various data and cloud access control models of cloud storage resources in multiple CSPs. Based on the unified model, we introduce a unified multi-cloud storage resource management platform to manage cloud storage resources and grant/revoke access for the cloud end-user developed for two popular public CSPs: Amazon Web Services and Google Cloud. The unified platform collects and processes information about the cloud storage resources that allows cloud customers to discover, create, delete, modify, evaluate, and monitor cloud storage resources across various CSPs.

Keywords: Multi-cloud storage · Cloud brokerage · Resource management · Access management · Object storage service · Identity and Access Management service · Cloud management platform

1 Introduction

Storage service is one of the most used cloud computing services as it provides cheaper data storage and better data availability and scalability compared to in-house data storage [13]. However, cloud storage services could still be susceptible

N. Park et al. (Eds.): SecureComm 2020, LNICST 336, pp. 102–119, 2020.
https://doi.org/10.1007/978-3-030-63095-9_6

to outage even though they guarantee up to 99.9% uptime. For example, in 2017, Amazon Web Services Simple Storage Service (AWS S3) went down for 4 h causing several web services to be unavailable and massive financial loss [15].

More cloud customers are using storage service from multiple cloud service providers (CSPs) to store their data in the cloud, or commonly known as multi-cloud storage approach [17,19]. The approach provides better data availability and service reliability compared to a single CSP usage as the data could still be accessed in case one or several CSPs are inaccessible due to outage [13,14].

Due to the cloud shared responsibility model [3], cloud customers subscribing to the storage service in a CSP are responsible for securely managing their cloud storage resources, i.e., the buckets and their stored data, the CSP credential, and the resource configurations. Cloud customers must be able to securely create, delete, and modify available cloud storage resources for the cloud end-users, e.g., users, applications, and services, ensure the resources are secure from unauthorized users and monitor resource activities across multiple CSPs.

However, there are several challenges faced by cloud customers to securely adopt and manage their storage resources across multiple CSPs. CSPs are not obligated to follow any cloud computing standards that affect each CSP to have different data models, service implementations, and APIs with other CSPs [22]. Therefore, cloud customers have to deal with the heterogeneity of the CSPs to manage their cloud resources on their own where the complexity is growing with the number of CSPs subscribed by the cloud customers [18]. Meanwhile, multi-cloud orchestration API and tools might not be sufficient to fulfill cloud customer's needs as it does not provide full CSP service functionalities.

In this paper, we present a unified multi-cloud storage resource management framework for securely managing cloud storage resources and its access for Object Storage and Identity and Access Management (IAM) services of various CSPs. Our work provides secure storage resource lifecycle management in a multi-cloud storage environment from the cloud customer's perspective for cloud end-users using the cloud brokerage approach [6].

Our contributions in this paper are as follow:

- We propose a unified cloud storage resource model built on top of the CSP's native API continuing our previous work of unified cloud access control model [21] to manage the information of cloud storage resources and its access for Amazon Web Services (AWS)[1] and Google Cloud (GC)[2].
- We develop a unified multi-cloud storage resource management platform that focuses on four resource management processes: resource discovery, resource orchestration, resource assessment, and resource monitoring.
- We introduce a unified cloud activity log format to normalize cloud activity log messages of different formats from various CSPs.

The structure of this paper is as follows: Sect. 2 presents several related works in the multi-cloud storage resource management area. Section 3 explains

---

[1] https://aws.amazon.com/.
[2] https://cloud.google.com/.

the overview of the multi-cloud storage approach and the challenges faced by cloud customers managing the storage resources in the multi-cloud scenario. In Sect. 4 we present our unified cloud storage resource model based on our previous work [21] to tackle various data and access control models of cloud storage resources from different CSPs. Section 5 introduces our unified multi-cloud cloud resource management platform based on our unified model that allows cloud customers to discover, create, delete, modify, monitor, and evaluate the cloud storage resources across multiple CSPs. Section 6 discusses how our unified platform solves the challenges of multi-cloud storage resource management. Finally, Sect. 7 summarizes our work and the future work of our platform.

2   Related Works

Although there have been several works regarding resource management in a multi-cloud environment, very few works are focusing on the multi-cloud storage resource management and its security area.

Hill and Humprey [7] presented a CSP vendor-agnostic cloud storage abstraction layer (CSAL) that allows an application to access Blob, Table, and Queue storage services in the multiple CSPs. It utilizes a single namespace across all storage services to maintain the metadata of each storage entity. Rafique et al. [17] introduced an adaptive middleware platform for (semi-)autonomous storage architecture management across multiple CSPs for three different scenarios: performance optimization, peak-load condition, and evolving pricing scheme. It continuously monitors the storage system's metrics that allow for identifying the changing condition of the system and optimizing the multi-cloud data placement strategy. Krotsiani and Spanoudakis [10] proposed a certification model for non-repudiation in the cloud storage services to ensure neither data owner nor CSP could deny the activities happening in the CSP. It uses a non-repudiation mechanism based on the fair multi-party non-repudiation scheme and continuous monitoring and assessment to detect the anomaly and suspicious behavior. [4] developed a multi-cloud storage broker API to provide portability and easier migration between different CSPs. It is based on a layered ontological framework to map and abstract common functionalities of object storage service.

Our work is different from the works above as we propose a unified storage resource management framework that would allow cloud customers to securely manage cloud storage resources and its access for cloud end-users in the multi-cloud environment continuing our previous work [21]. We propose a unified cloud storage resource model and a unified cloud activity log format for storing and processing the information of cloud storage resources of various formats in multiple CSPs into a single format. We implement a unified multi-cloud storage resource management platform following the cloud brokerage approach that allows for secure cloud storage resource lifecycle management across multiple CSPs.

3   Background

3.1   Multi-Cloud Storage Resource Management Overview

The usage of storage service from a single CSP is susceptible to vendor lock-in and service unavailability threats as the data could not be retrieved due to the CSP outage [16]. Cloud customers could utilize storage service from more than one CSP to resolve this issue known as the multi-cloud storage approach [17,19]. It provides better data interoperability and availability than utilizing storage service from a single CSP as the data could migrate between CSPs and still be retrieved in case one or several CSPs are unreachable [14,16]. The approach might utilize various data storage strategies by storing multiple objects across various CSPs, e.g., erasure coding, replication, or fragmentation [13,14].

When cloud customers utilize storage services from one or more CSPs, they are responsible to comply with the cloud shared responsibility model implemented by the CSPs [3]. Each CSP is responsible to operate and manage the underlying hardware components to provide the storage services and ensure that cloud customer's storage resources could not be accessed by other unauthorized cloud customers or known as cross-tenant data leakage threats [1,5,22].

Meanwhile, cloud customers are responsible to manage their storage resources across various CSPs from unauthorized users [21,22]. Cloud resource management is a process of managing and allocating available resources in the cloud for the requiring entity to fulfill its requirements and objectives [9,12]. It helps cloud customers to utilize cloud resources efficiently and securely while guaranteeing the Quality of Service for the entities. There are three entities involved in the cloud resource management process [9]:

- **Cloud Service Provider (CSP)**: The CSP manages its infrastructure to provide necessary services and its resources for its customers. It is responsible to fulfill the cloud customer's expected level of service based on the Service Level Agreement (SLA) agreed with cloud customers. We assume that the CSPs are trusted entities as they will execute the commands issued by the cloud customers using the CSP's native APIs and will not unauthorizedly access cloud customer's data.
- **Cloud customers** : Cloud customers subscribe to the CSP to use its services and resources. They are responsible to manage their cloud resources and fulfill the SLA agreed with the cloud end-user.
- **Cloud end-user**: Application, service, or a person that requires certain access to the cloud resources provided by the cloud customers to do its job.

The cloud resource management process for storage service requires cloud customers to orchestrate cloud storage resources, secure the resources from unauthorized users, and monitor its activities [22]. This includes the data uploaded to the cloud, the buckets where the data is stored, the CSP credential(s), and the resource configuration that determines who has what kind of access to the buckets and its stored data. They are also responsible to provide necessary access to the cloud storage resources for the cloud end-user following the agreed SLA between cloud customers and cloud end-users.

3.2   Security Challenges of Multi-Cloud Resource Management

The usage of the multi-cloud storage approach creates several challenges for cloud customers to securely manage their cloud storage resources across various CSPs. Each CSP utilizes various hardware and software resources to build its cloud environments without any obligation to follow any cloud computing standards available in the market [21,22]. This affects each CSP to implement its mechanisms and service implementations of the same cloud service to be different from other CSPs, such as API and data model.

Therefore, cloud customers have to deal with the heterogeneity of the CSPs to manage their cloud resources as several CSPs do not provide cloud interoperability functionality to communicate between services in multiple CSPs [13,22]. The resource management process in a multi-cloud environment requires processing the information coming from CSP's complex environment where it could be difficult to have accurate global information about the cloud resources [12]. They are expected to collect and process the information of the resources across different CSPs by themselves where the management complexity is growing with the number of CSPs subscribed by the cloud customers [18].

Cloud customers are also required to ensure that their cloud storage resources are correctly configured. The configurations of cloud storage resources could follow cloud security best practices and standards available in the market to ensure that it is secure from unauthorized users, such as the Center for Internet Security (CIS) Benchmark[3]. However, cloud customers might lack the knowledge and skill of multi-cloud management and cloud security [12]. They often require to use each CSP's management platform and API to manage the cloud storage resources in various CSPs, which could create limited visibility of cloud storage resources and its activities [3,26]. It could also make it difficult to enforce security and access control towards their cloud resources due to the heterogeneity of the security implementation from various CSPs and the loss of physical access control caused by outsourcing data storage to the cloud [2,22].

There are several multi-cloud APIs and tools available that provide cloud interoperability and multi-cloud orchestration that can be used to manage the resources in the multi-cloud scenario, such as jclouds[4] and Libclouds[5]. However, cloud customers still require to provide an abstraction layer and a unifying environment to achieve multi-cloud resource management while using the APIs and tools [26]. Also, these APIs and tools might not provide full CSP native functionality for all cloud services, e.g., jclouds does not provide user account management in IAM service or bucket storage configuration functionality.

4   Unified Cloud Storage Resource Model

We propose a unified cloud storage resource model continuing our previous work of unified cloud access control model [21] to solve the challenges of various data

---

[3] https://www.cisecurity.org/cis-benchmarks/.

[4] https://jclouds.apache.org/.

[5] https://libcloud.apache.org/.

models of storage resources from different CSPs due to no obligation of CSP to follow any cloud computing standard [22]. It combines the information of cloud storage resources and cloud access control models to solve the challenges of security in multi-cloud storage resource management explained in Sect. 3.

The unified cloud storage resource model helps cloud customers to manage the cloud storage resources across multiple CSPs, such as automated cloud storage resource creation. It also can be used to store the state of cloud storage resources that consists of various data and access control models from different CSPs in a single format. The cloud resource states in the unified format then could be analyzed for different use cases, e.g., discover the relationship between the resources and the entities that have access to it or check the compliance of the resources against cloud security standards and best practices.

We implement our proposed model to manage cloud storage resources available in AWS Simple Storage Service (S3)[6], AWS IAM[7], GC Storage[8], GC IAM[9], and GC Cloud Resource Manager (CRM)[10]. Our unified model could also be extended for Storage and IAM services from other CSPs. The unified cloud storage resource model consists of nine entities as can be seen in Fig. 1.

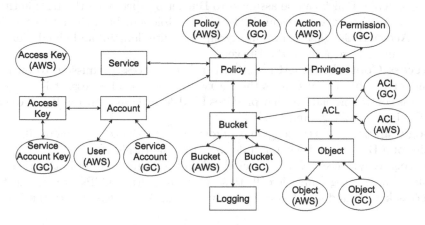

Fig. 1. Unified cloud storage resource model and its implementation on top of Object Storage and Identity and Access Management services in AWS and GC

– **Bucket**: Bucket is a logical abstraction of object storage where the objects are stored in the CSP. It represents Bucket both in AWS[11] and GC[12].

---

[6] https://aws.amazon.com/s3/.
[7] https://aws.amazon.com/iam/.
[8] https://cloud.google.com/storage/.
[9] https://cloud.google.com/iam/.
[10] https://cloud.google.com/resource-manager/.
[11] https://docs.aws.amazon.com/en_pv/AmazonS3/latest/dev/UsingBucket.html.
[12] https://cloud.google.com/storage/docs/json_api/v1/buckets.

- **Object**: Object is the logical abstraction of the file stored in the Bucket. It represents Object in AWS[13] and GC[14].
- **Account**: Account is the identity of an entity created in CSP's IAM service. It consists of User[15] in AWS and Service Account[16] in GC.
- **Service**: Service represents the identity of CSP service.
- **Privilege**: Privilege is the possible action/permission in the CSP's services. It consists of Action[17] in AWS and Permission in GC[18].
- **Policy**: Policy is a set of Privileges and its state (allow/deny) that regulates cloud-level access control between the entity and the cloud resource. Policy is represented as Policy[19] in AWS and Role[20] in GC. In general, there are two types of policy assignment:
    1. *IAM-level Policy*: Policy is attached to an IAM entity that allows or denies access to CSP services and its resources. In AWS, Policy can be assigned directly to User, Group, or Role. In GC, Role can be assigned to Service Account, Google account and group, G Suite domain, and cloud identity domain.
    2. *Resource-level Policy*: Policy is assigned to a resource (e.g., Bucket) and its CSP service that determines who is authorized to access the resource. In AWS, Policy can be assigned to Bucket by specifying the IAM entities or AWS service accessing it. In GC, a Role can be assigned to Service Account, Google account and group, G Suite domain, and cloud identity domain in regards to the Bucket.
- **Access Control List** (ACL): ACL is a list of access permission to buckets and/or its object that defines the entity and its type of access. It is a legacy access control mechanism that predates IAM-level access control. It represents ACL both in AWS[21] and GC[22].
- **Logging**: Logging is the logging configuration of a Bucket[23][24] where all activities of a Bucket are logged and delivered to the target Bucket.
- **Access Key**: Access Key is the credential of Account used for authentication and allowing programmatic calls to services in multiple CSPs. It contains the access key ID and secret key. The privileges of Access Key follow the Policy

---

[13] https://docs.aws.amazon.com/en_pv/AmazonS3/latest/dev/UsingObjects.html.
[14] https://cloud.google.com/storage/docs/json_api/v1/objects.
[15] https://docs.aws.amazon.com/en_pv/IAM/latest/UserGuide/id_users.html.
[16] https://cloud.google.com/iam/docs/service-accounts.
[17] https://docs.aws.amazon.com/en_pv/IAM/latest/UserGuide/reference_policies_actions-resources-contextkeys.html.
[18] https://cloud.google.com/storage/docs/access-control/using-iam-permissions.
[19] https://docs.aws.amazon.com/en_pv/IAM/latest/UserGuide/access_policies.html.
[20] https://cloud.google.com/iam/docs/understanding-roles.
[21] https://docs.aws.amazon.com/AmazonS3/latest/dev/acl-overview.html.
[22] https://cloud.google.com/storage/docs/access-control/lists.
[23] https://docs.aws.amazon.com/AmazonS3/latest/dev/ServerLogs.html.
[24] https://cloud.google.com/storage/docs/access-logs.

set in Account to ensure that it can only access its authorized resources. It represents Access Key[25] in AWS and Service Account Key[26] in GC.

5   Unified Multi-Cloud Storage Resource Management Platform

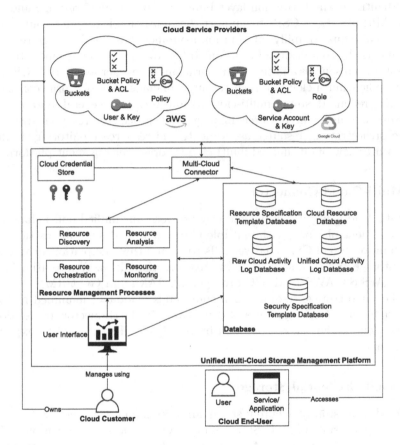

Fig. 2. Overview of unified multi-cloud storage management platform

We propose a unified multi-cloud storage resource management platform to provide cloud customers with holistic visibility and management capabilities for all cloud storage resources across multiple CSPs. It utilizes the unified cloud storage resource model explained in Sect. 4 to manage the information about cloud storage resources across multiple CSPs. Cloud customers only need to use the

---

[25] https://docs.aws.amazon.com/en_pv/IAM/latest/UserGuide/id_credentials_access-keys.html.

[26] https://cloud.google.com/iam/docs/creating-managing-service-account-keys.

unified platform to manage the storage resources in various CSPs instead of utilizing each CSP's management platform and API.

We chose the cloud brokerage approach [6,23] as the basis for our unified platform to manage the relationship between cloud customers, cloud storage resources in multiple CSPs, and cloud end-users. The platform provides centralized multi-cloud management as it collects, pre-processes, and stores the information on cloud storage resources with different data models in a unified format. It utilizes an abstraction layer built on top of Object Storage and IAM services APIs of various CSPs to support the multi-cloud storage resource management. This could simplify information asymmetry of cloud storage resources thus reducing the complexity of decisions taken by the cloud customers to manage the storage resources and their configurations access across multiple CSPs [6].

The unified multi-cloud storage resource management platform consists of the cloud credential store, multi-cloud-connector, and several databases as it focuses on four main resource management processes: resource discovery, resource orchestration, resource assessment, and resource monitoring. Figure 2 shows an overview of our unified multi-cloud storage management platform.

5.1 Multi-Cloud Connector

The multi-cloud connector is the gateway between our unified multi-cloud storage management platform with multiple CSPs. It provides an abstraction layer that is built on top of CSP's native APIs to ensure that the platform can access Object Storage and IAM services full native functionalities. We are utilizing the APIs of AWS S3, AWS IAM, GC Storage, GC IAM, and GC CRM services to access the cloud storage resources. All commands made by the unified platform are translated into CSP's native API commands by the connector. It also downloads the cloud activity logs generated by multiple CSPs that will be explained in Sect. 5.6.

5.2 Cloud Credential Storage

Cloud credential storage securely stores an Access Key for each CSP to allow the unified platform to access Storage and IAM services across various CSPs. The key is generated from the Account with adequate privileges to list, create, modify, and delete cloud storage resources where it can only be accessed via the platform. When the unified management platform issues a request to a CSP, the multi-cloud connector first requests the required Access Key to cloud credential storage before sending the request to the CSP.

5.3 Resource Discovery Process

Resource discovery is the process to detect and register all available created resources for each service in the CSP [11]. The unified multi-cloud storage management platform provides resource discovery by automatically gathering the

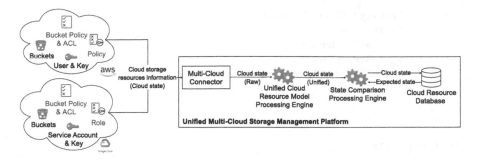

Fig. 3. Overview of resource discovery process

information of all cloud storage resources and their configurations across multiple CSPs in a single format. It runs periodically in the background to monitor any changes in the cloud resources. When it runs for the first time, the platform does not need to have prior knowledge of cloud storage resources owned by cloud customers. Figure 3 shows an overview of the resource discovery process.

Multi-cloud connector first sends a request to each CSP service to retrieve the information of all available cloud storage resources. Depending on the CSP's API capabilities, the information about the cloud resources and their configurations, e.g. name, type, Policy, and ACL, are then retrieved by the multi-cloud connector. Cloud storage resource information that could not be collected during the discovery process due to the limitation of the CSP's API could be added manually later by the cloud customers, e.g., the secret key of Access Key is only available once it is newly generated.

The cloud storage resource's raw information is then processed by the Unified Cloud Resource Model Processing engine to parse the information with different data models from various CSPs to our unified cloud storage resource model as explained in Sect. 4. The processed cloud storage information is then stored in the Cloud Resource database. An example of unified cloud storage information:

```
{
    "name":"exampleBucket",
    "type":"Bucket",
    "csp":"AWS",
    "creationDate":"2019-01-02T21:27:04.000+0000",
    "location":"eu-central-1:Frankfurt",
    "bucketConfiguration":{
        "logging":{
            "enabled":false
        },
        "accessors":[
            {
                "name":"TestUser",
                "effect":"Allow",
                "type":"ACL",
```

```
        "entity":"User Grantee",
        "privileges":[
          "s3:ListBucket",
          "s3:PutObject",
          "s3:DeleteObject"
        ]
      }
    ]
  },
  "deleted":false
}
```

We incorporate the state transition model into our resource discovery process to track the changes made into the cloud storage resource [25]. When the resource discovery process runs for the first time, the cloud storage resource information in a unified format stored in the Cloud Resource database is regarded as the **expected state**. After the initial resource discovery process, the information of storage resource is then regarded as the **cloud state**. These states are then compared using the State Comparison Processing engine. If the states are different, cloud customers could decide whether to store the cloud state in the Cloud Resource database as the expected state or retain the expected state by reversing any changes happening in the storage resources across multiple CSPs.

Using the information of cloud storage resources and their configurations stored in the unified format, cloud customers could then associate the cloud storage resources with the information of the cloud end-users. They could also maintain a consistent and accurate global state of cloud resources across multiple CSPs instead of manually list the created cloud resources and their configurations of each service in each CSP using its management dashboard or API.

5.4 Resource Orchestration Process

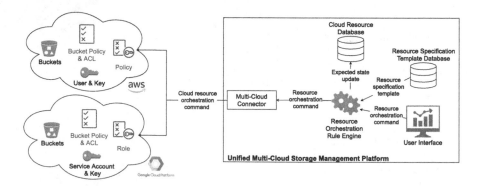

Fig. 4. Overview of resource orchestration process

Resource orchestration is the process of allocating the resources in the CSP to fulfill the requirements of cloud end-users. We follow the unified cloud storage resource model from Sect. 4 to help cloud customers create, delete, and modify cloud storage resources and their configurations for the cloud end-users. Figure 4 shows an overview of the resource orchestration process.

Cloud customers could create, delete, and modify the storage resource in one or multiple CSPs by providing necessary cloud storage resource specification using the user interface to generate resource orchestration command. They could also create a resource specification template for cloud resources and their configurations stored in the Resource Specification Template database. The template is used to automatically create and configure necessary cloud resources for the cloud end-users to reduce the possibility of misconfiguration due to human error.

Cloud customer's resource orchestration command and resource specification template are then processed by Resource Orchestration Rule engine to consolidate the resource orchestration command. It then updates the expected state with the information of created, deleted, or modified cloud storage resources in the Cloud Resource database. The resource orchestration command is then translated by the multi-cloud connector to the specific CSP's API commands.

Cloud customers should follow the least privilege principle, privilege separation concept, or cloud security best practices and standards while orchestrating cloud resources for the cloud end-users [21]. This is to ensure the cloud end-users only have limited access to the authorized cloud resources following their roles or responsibilities, thus avoiding insider threat or over-privileged access.

5.5   Resource Assessment Process

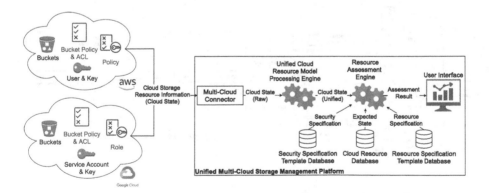

Fig. 5. Overview of resource assessment process

Resource assessment is the process of evaluating the cloud resources against the specifications set by cloud customers. It ensures that the resources are correctly and securely configured that could only be accessed by its authorized cloud end-users [24]. Figure 5 shows an overview of the resource assessment process.

Our method for resource assessment is as follows: the raw information of cloud storage resources and their configurations, or cloud state, is first retrieved periodically and parsed with the Unified Cloud Resource Model Processing engine to follow our unified format. The Resource Assessment engine then compares the unified cloud state with the expected state stored in the Cloud Resource database to detect if there are any unauthorized modifications [25].

The Resource Assessment engine also evaluates the unified cloud state and the expected state against the security specifications and the resource specifications that are fetc.hed from the Security Specification Template and the Resource Specification databases, respectively. The specifications could be derived from cloud computing best security practices or recommendations, such as the Center for Internet Security's AWS benchmark[27]. It could also be derived following the cloud end-users' requirements to ensure the cloud end-users could only access its authorized cloud resources with limited actions.

Finally, the Resource Assessment engine will generate the assessment result for the cloud customers. If there are unauthorized modifications to the cloud state or the cloud storage resource configurations do not comply with the security and resource specifications, the assessment result will include the violations against the security and resource specifications and recommended actions to be taken to address the violations. Cloud customers could take necessary actions to improve the cloud storage resources' configurations to ensure that the resources are secure and can only be accessed by authorized cloud end-users.

5.6 Resource Monitoring Process

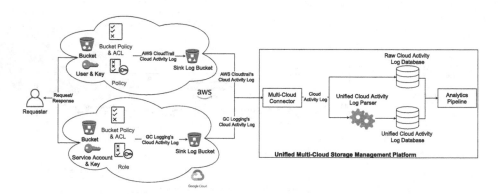

Fig. 6. Overview of resource monitoring process overview

Resource monitoring is a process of monitoring the usage and the activities of the resources in the CSP. As cloud customers outsource their files to the cloud,

---

[27] https://www.cisecurity.org/benchmark/amazon_web_services/.

they lose the full control of files as it could be accessed by anyone. Unauthorized users and authorized cloud end-users could directly interact with the Buckets where the files are stored using the CSP management dashboard, API request using CSP credential or Access Key, signed URL generated from the Access Key, or unauthenticated URL of Buckets and the files. The information provided by the local system owned by the cloud customers might not be enough to give full oversight of cloud activities, therefore they require a new source of information that informs the activities of cloud storage resources [2].

Therefore, we collect cloud activity logs generated by AWS CloudTrail[28] and Google Cloud Logging[29] to monitor the activities happening in cloud storage resources across multiple CSPs. The log contains the detailed information of all activities happening in the CSP's services, e.g., incoming API requests to the cloud resources and its responses in Object Storage service.

However, there are several challenges in processing cloud activity log from different CSPs. Although technically these services are already logging the activities happening in the CSP, the log messages can only be viewed and processed using the CSP's logging and monitoring service. It also requires the cloud customers to actively store or retrieve the log as it may be deleted after a certain period of time[30]. Each CSP has its log format structure and information quality [20], for example, AWS CloudTrail provides more information with better data structure's consistency compared to GC Logging. Cloud customers would be responsible to actively retrieve and process the cloud activity logs while dealing with different cloud logs from various CSPs to gain necessary information about the activities happening in the cloud storage resources.

The resource monitoring process follows the data warehouse method [8], which consists of extraction, transformation, and loading (ETL) steps, to transform semi-structured data of cloud activity log files provided in JSON format to structured data. We propose a unified cloud activity log format to normalize different log formats from various CSPs to a single format. We first select the necessary information needed from the available cloud activity log fields. We then normalize the value that are in different formats or could contain information for multiple log fields. Finally, we combine the information from cloud activity log files from multiple CSPs to give an overview of the events happening to the cloud storage resources in multiple CSPs [20]. Our proposed unified cloud activity log format can be seen in Table 1.

Our method for resource monitoring is as follows: Cloud activity log files are delivered into a specific sink Bucket that provides inexpensive and long-term storage for the log files. Depending on the CSP, the cloud activity log file could be delivered to the Bucket every 5 min[31] up to one hour[32]. Once the cloud log

---

28 https://aws.amazon.com/cloudtrail/.
29 https://cloud.google.com/logging, formerly Google Cloud Stackdriver.
30 https://docs.aws.amazon.com/awscloudtrail/latest/userguide/view-cloudtrail-events.html.
31 https://aws.amazon.com/cloudtrail/faqs.
32 https://cloud.google.com/logging/docs/export/using_exported_logs.

Table 1. Unified cloud activity log format and the parsing from AWS CloudTrail and GC Logging

Unified Cloud Activity Log	AWS CloudTrail	GC Logging	Description
eventId	eventID	–	Event identifier
timestamp	eventTime	timestamp	Event timestamp
csp	"AWS"	"GC"	CSP type
service	eventSource	protoPayload.serviceName	CSP service name
resourceName	requestParameters	protoPayload.request Parameter or protoPayload. resourceName	Resource name
resourceType	requestParameters	protoPayload.request	Resource type
resourceLocation	awsRegion	resource.label.location	Resource location
method	eventName	protoPayload.methodName	Request method
ipAddress	sourceIPAddress	protoPayload.request Metadata.callerIP	Requester IP address
userAgent	userAgent	protoPayload.request Metadata.caller SuppliedAgent	Requester user agent
responseCode	errorCode	protoPayload.status.code	Response status code
responseMessage	errorMessage	protoPayload.status.message	Response message
requesterCredential	userIdentity	protoPayload.authentication Info.principalEmail	Requester identity

file has been delivered to the Bucket, the multi-cloud connector then downloads the log file to our resource management platform.

After the cloud activity log files have been downloaded, it is then stored into Raw Cloud Log Activity database while it is processed by the Unified Cloud Activity Log Parser to parse cloud activity log files into our unified log format and store it in Unified Cloud Log Activity database. Finally, the raw and unified cloud log messages are then pushed into the analytics pipeline for further processing. Figure 6 shows an overview of the resource monitoring process.

6   Discussion

Our unified multi-cloud storage resource management framework could solve the security challenges of managing cloud storage resources across multiple CSPs faced by the cloud customers as explained in Sect. 3.2.

The unified cloud storage resource model helps to normalize various data and cloud access control models of storage resources from different CSPs. We focused on developing our unified model on the storage and IAM services of AWS and GC as both CSPs employ quite a similar cloud access control model following role-based access control, which is useful for associating cloud storage resources with cloud end-users. Our proposed model differs from our previous work of unified cloud access control model [21] as it includes more cloud storage resources types and their configurations that could be utilized for various multi-cloud management strategies, e.g., cloud brokerage [6] or cloud federation [12].

Our unified multi-cloud storage resource management platform provides holistic visibility and secure multi-cloud storage resource management. Our abstraction layer for multiple CSPs implemented in our unified platform is built on top of CSP's native APIs to ensure that the unified platform can access the full functionality of the services provided by the CSP. This is different from the multi-cloud APIs where it provides abstraction by focusing only on the common functionalities and data structure of the CSP's APIs.

The unified platform allows cloud customers to automatically discover created cloud storage resources and orchestrate necessary cloud storage resources for cloud end-users to ensure that the cloud storage resources are not misconfigured due to human error. The cloud resources are also evaluated periodically against cloud computing's security best practices and standards and cloud customer's system requirements to make the resources are secure and accessible only for authorized cloud end-users.

We chose to monitor the cloud storage resources using the cloud activity log instead of the storage event log used in our previous work [20]. This is because the cloud activity log is not limited only to the Bucket and Object operations in the Object Storage service but also other services of the CSPs. Our unified cloud activity log format could be used to normalize cloud activity log files that have semi-structured and complex data in nested JSON format to be simplified and structured data that can be used for monitoring the activities in cloud storage resources. The proposed log format could also be used for different purposes, e.g., cloud forensic and security analytics.

Our unified platform is not as sophisticated as multi-cloud orchestration services available in the market where it provides Infrastructure-as-a-Code abstraction layer where cloud infrastructures could be defined using a human-readable configuration template, such as Terraform[33] or Chef[34]. However, our unified platform focuses on resource discovery, resource assessment, and resource monitoring processes that are not available in multi-cloud orchestration services.

7   Conclusion and Future Works

In the past few years, more cloud customers utilize Object Storage service from multiple CSPs to store their data to provide better data availability. However, cloud customers face several challenges of securely managing their cloud storage resources across different CSPs for the cloud end-users. In this paper, we propose a unified multi-cloud storage resource management framework that allows cloud customers to discover, create, delete, modify, evaluate, and monitor cloud storage resources in various CSPs. We introduce a unified cloud storage resource model that continues our previous model to tackle different data models of various CSPs to determine the state of cloud storage resources. We develop a unified multi-cloud storage resource management platform that collects, pre-processes, stores, and manages the information on cloud storage resources and their configurations

---

[33] https://www.terraform.io/.
[34] https://www.chef.io.

centrally across multiple CSPs. Our unified platform follows the cloud brokerage approach that will help cloud customers to manage cloud storage resources used by the cloud end-users. We also propose a unified cloud activity log format implemented in our platform to normalize cloud activity log messages of different formats from various CSPs.

We are currently researching various security analytics scenarios in a multi-cloud storage environment to ensure the cloud storage resources are secure, such as the correlation process using cloud activity log and storage event log. We are also extending our unified platform to support different resource types in other CSPs, e.g., virtual machine or container in Microsoft Azure and Openstack.

References

1. Amazon Web Services: Shared responsibility model. https://aws.amazon.com/compliance/shared-responsibility-model/ (2020). (Accessed 14 July 2020)
2. Bohli, J.M., Gruschka, N., Jensen, M., Iacono, L.L., Marnau, N.: Security and privacy-enhancing multicloud architectures. IEEE Trans. Dependable Secure Comput. **10**(4), 212–224 (2013)
3. Cloud Security Alliance: Top threats to cloud computing: The egregious 11 (2019). https://cloudsecurityalliance.org/download/artifacts/top-threats-to-cloud-computing-egregious-eleven/
4. Elango, D.M., Fowley, F., Pahl, C.: An ontology-based architecture for an adaptable cloud storage broker. In: Mann, Z.Á., Stolz, V. (eds.) ESOCC 2017. CCIS, vol. 824, pp. 86–101. Springer, Cham (2018). https://doi.org/10.1007/978-3-319-79090-9_6
5. Factor, M., et al.: Secure logical isolation for multi-tenancy in cloud storage. In: 2013 IEEE 29th Symposium on Mass Storage Systems and Technologies (MSST), pp. 1–5. IEEE (2013)
6. Heilig, L., Lalla-Ruiz, E., Voß, S.: A cloud brokerage approach for solving the resource management problem in multi-cloud environments. Comput. Ind. Eng. **95**, 16–26 (2016)
7. Hill, Z., Humphrey, M.: Csal: a cloud storage abstraction layer to enable portable cloud applications. In: 2010 IEEE Second International Conference on Cloud Computing Technology and Science, pp. 504–511. IEEE (2010)
8. Hu, H., Wen, Y., Chua, T.S., Li, X.: Toward scalable systems for big data analytics: a technology tutorial. IEEE Access **2**, 652–687 (2014)
9. Jennings, B., Stadler, R.: Resource management in clouds: survey and research challenges. J. Netw. Syst. Manage. **23**(3), 567–619 (2015)
10. Krotsiani, M., Spanoudakis, G.: Continuous certification of non-repudiation in cloud storage services. In: 2014 IEEE 13th International Conference on Trust, Security and Privacy in Computing and Communications, pp. 921–928. IEEE (2014)
11. Lee, C.A.: Cloud federation management and beyond: requirements, relevant standards, and gaps. IEEE Cloud Comput. **3**(1), 42–49 (2016)
12. Liaqat, M., et al.: Federated cloud resource management: review and discussion. J. Netw. Comput. Appl. **77**, 87–105 (2017)
13. Mansouri, Y., Toosi, A.N., Buyya, R.: Data storage management in cloud environments: taxonomy, survey, and future directions. ACM Comput. Surv. (CSUR) **50**(6), 91 (2018)

14. Nachiappan, R., Javadi, B., Calheiros, R.N., Matawie, K.M.: Cloud storage reliability for big data applications: a state of the art survey. J. Netw. Comput. Appl. **97**, 35–47 (2017)

15. Newton, C.: How a typo took down s3, the backbone of the internet - the verge. https://www.theverge.com/2017/3/2/14792442/amazon-s3-outage-cause-typo-internet-server (2017). (Accessed on 7 August 2020)

16. Petcu, D.: Multi-cloud: expectations and current approaches. In: Proceedings of the 2013 international workshop on Multi-cloud applications and federated clouds, pp. 1–6 (2013)

17. Rafique, A., Van Landuyt, D., Reniers, V., Joosen, W.: Towards an adaptive middleware for efficient multi-cloud data storage. In: Proceedings of the 4th Workshop on CrossCloud Infrastructures & Platforms, pp. 1–6 (2017)

18. Raj, P., Raman, A.: Multi-cloud management: technologies, tools, and techniques. Software-Defined Cloud Centers. CCN, pp. 219–240. Springer, Cham (2018). https://doi.org/10.1007/978-3-319-78637-7_10

19. Schnjakin, M., Korsch, D., Schoenberg, M., Meinel, C.: Implementation of a secure and reliable storage above the untrusted clouds. In: Computer Science & Education (ICCSE), 2013 8th International Conference on, pp. 347–353. IEEE (2013)

20. Sukmana, M.I., Torkura, K.A., Cheng, F., Meinel, C., Graupner, H.: Unified logging system for monitoring multiple cloud storage providers in cloud storage broker. In: 2018 International Conference on Information Networking (ICOIN), pp. 44–49. IEEE (2018)

21. Sukmana, M.I., Torkura, K.A., Graupner, H., Cheng, F., Meinel, C.: Unified cloud access control model for cloud storage broker. In: 2019 International Conference on Information Networking (ICOIN), pp. 60–65. IEEE (2019)

22. Takabi, H., Joshi, J.B., Ahn, G.J.: Security and privacy challenges in cloud computing environments. IEEE Security & Privacy **8**(6), 24–31 (2010)

23. Toosi, A.N., Calheiros, R.N., Buyya, R.: Interconnected cloud computing environments: challenges, taxonomy, and survey. ACM Comput. Surv. (CSUR) **47**(1), 1–47 (2014)

24. Torkura, K.A., Sukmana, M.I., Cheng, F., Meinel, C.: Slingshot-automated threat detection and incident response in multi cloud storage systems. In: 2019 IEEE 18th International Symposium on Network Computing and Applications (NCA), pp. 1–5. IEEE (2019)

25. Torkura, K.A., Sukmana, M.I., Strauss, T., Graupner, H., Cheng, F., Meinel, C.: Csbauditor: proactive security risk analysis for cloud storage broker systems. In: 2018 IEEE 17th International Symposium on Network Computing and Applications (NCA), pp. 1–10. IEEE (2018)

26. Varghese, B., Buyya, R.: Next generation cloud computing: new trends and research directions. Future Gener. Comput. Syst. **79**, 849–861 (2018)

On the Effectiveness of Behavior-Based Ransomware Detection

Jaehyun Han[1]([⊠]), Zhiqiang Lin[2], and Donald E. Porter[1]

[1] The University of North Carolina at Chapel Hill, Chapel Hill, USA
{jaehyun,porter}@cs.unc.edu
[2] The Ohio State University, Columbus, USA
zlin@cse.ohio-state.edu

Abstract. Ransomware has been a growing threat to end-users in the past few years. In response, there is also a burgeoning market for anti-ransomware defense products, as well as research prototypes that explore more advanced, behavioral analyses. Intuitively, ransomware should be amenable to identification through behavioral analysis, since ransomware recursively walks a user's files and encrypts them, overwriting or deleting the plaintext. This paper contributes a study of the effectiveness of these behavior-based ransomware defenses, from both commercial products and academic proposals. We drive the study with a dead simple ransomware, augmented with a number of both straightforward and new evasion techniques. Surprisingly, our results indicate that most commercial products are strikingly ineffective. Ten out of 15 commercial products could not detect our simple ransomware without any evasive techniques; most of the rest were evaded and able to ransom user data with some combination of simple techniques. Only one tool appears to correctly identify our ransomware, but suffers from staggering false positives, including flagging Windows Explorer, Firefox, and Notepad as ransomware during routine operation. Our paper identifies a number of techniques to manipulate entropy to match the original file. The paper further shows that partial encryption, of as little as 3–5% of a file's data is sufficient to ransom most file formats. Finally, we show that a combination of these techniques can render an aggregate malice score that is well below that of a Linux kernel compile. In summary, these results indicate that it is highly likely that ransomware will be able to adapt its behavior to fit within the range of expected benign behaviors, avoiding detection even by future generations of behavioral ransomware detectors.

Keywords: Ransomware · Malware

1 Introduction

Ransomware is a growing threat for computer users, especially smaller businesses and less savvy users. For instance, over 16 million US dollars of bitcoins have been paid in exchange for ransom from roughly 19,750 victims in the years

© ICST Institute for Computer Sciences, Social Informatics and Telecommunications Engineering 2020
Published by Springer Nature Switzerland AG 2020. All Rights Reserved
N. Park et al. (Eds.): SecureComm 2020, LNICST 336, pp. 120–140, 2020.
https://doi.org/10.1007/978-3-030-63095-9_7

2016 and 2017 [13]. In a nutshell, ransomware renders a user's data unavailable, typically by encryption, and then charges the data owner a ransom to recover the data. Encryption is preferred to exfiltrating data, as the attacker need not store or return the ransomed data, but, rather, can simply sell a decryption key to the victim. This strategy is adopted by high-profile ransomware, including CryptoLocker [28], Cerber, and WannaCry [21]. In principle, ransomware should be a non-issue when users and enterprises follow best practices with respect to back-ups and least administrative privilege, as data can be restored from a secured back-up, nullifying the ransomware's leverage over users. Unfortunately, many users and businesses often do not follow these best practices, fall victim to ransomware, and pay the ransom, because the loss of essential data, such as patient or billing records, is more costly than the ransom.

The rising concern about ransomware has led to both commercial products, such as CyberSight RansomStopper, Acronis Ransomware Protection, Check-MAL AppCheck, CryptoDrop [30], and ZoneAlarm Anti-Ransomware as well as research prototypes, including Redemption [16], ShieldFS [5], and RWGuard [20], that purport to detect ransomware, in the same vein as inexpensive commercial virus scanners. Early detection has obvious benefits, primarily that ransomware can be stopped before much data is lost. Because the behavior of ransomware follows a fairly straightforward pattern, namely traversing the file system and encrypting data, there is a basis for optimism that a behavioral malware detector could be effective against ransomware. Indeed, most of the products and prototypes listed above use behavioral detection.

This paper studies the efficacy of these ransomware detectors and their underlying strategies. Although these commercial detectors are generally closed source, we develop a simple ransomware, a python script in less than 100 lines of code, and vary its behavior to infer what these detectors are monitoring. We identify several key features that these detectors use, including file system behavior monitoring and decoy file monitoring. Recent research prototypes have proposed to augment these features with monitoring for changes in file entropy [5,15,16,20,30]. In most designs, systems combine these features. For instance, Redemption [16] calculates a weighted average of these features, or a *malice score*. For each of these principal features, the paper then explores, through more targeted experiments, the degree to which these features can be manipulated or evaded by a more sophisticated ransomware.

In short, our results indicate that, counter-intuitively, the behavioral approach to ransomware detection is fragile in practice, and highly unlikely to work against a sophisticated adversary. First, we find that **several commercial products cannot detect our "textbook" ransomware** (Sect. 4.1). Second, we consider the individual behaviors that are monitored and combined to form a malice score. We demonstrate techniques that can effectively ransom users' data, while staying within a range that is indistinguishable from benign application behavior. Specifically, this paper investigates:

- **Entropy.** (Sects. 3.1 and 3.2) By definition, a good encryption function should yield a high-entropy ciphertext. A number of research prototypes look for a shift in entropy, either in reads versus writes or in original versus overwritten file contents, as an indicator of the presence of ransomware. First, we observe that many common file formats have high entropy (e.g., pdf, jpg), and encrypting these files does not shift their entropy outside of the expected range. Second, for low-entropy files, this paper introduces several techniques to manipulate entropy that still deprive users of their data. For instance, low entropy files are necessarily compressible; if the ransomware first compresses the file, encrypts the compressed contents, and then pads the resulting file to its original length with regular contents, the encrypted output file's entropy will be comparable to the original.

– **File Overwrite or Deletion Rate.** (Sect. 3.3) Another natural monitoring strategy is to identify processes that delete a large swath of files (in the case where the encrypted versions are written elsewhere), or that overwrite a large number of files in place (with the encrypted version). In the case of monitoring for file overwrites, we show that one can evade this detection mechanism by only encrypting portions of a file. For most file formats, there is important metadata that can be encrypted, and that renders the entire file useless, at least for the average user. We show that these techniques are not easily undone by free or inexpensive file recovery tools. Although one might be able to pay an expert to reconstruct this metadata, these costs are often commensurate with the ransom.

– **Decoy Files.** (Sect. 3.4) Another common strategy for ransomware detection is to place decoy files on the users' file system, and monitor whether those specific files are deleted or overwritten. We show that, in practice, the naming and placement of these decoy files is easy to predict and differentiate from the user's "real" data; thus, it is trivial for ransomware to simply avoid these decoy files.

In summary, this paper demonstrates considerable cause for pessimism about the behavioral approach to ransomware protection. Although it is possible that there is room for improvement in behavioral analysis, the margin where it can identify malware without excessive false positives is likely narrow. We do note that backups are not a panacea, as backups without security isolation can themselves be ransomed. On balance, we find that end users would be better served to spend their IT budget on incremental backups within a separate administrative domain and, more generally, securing their infrastructure, than on ransomware-specific products.

2   Background

This paper focuses on ransomware that holds a user's *data* hostage, in order to extort payment from the user. There are other types of ransomware that are either scams, such as misleading the user to believe they have a virus and should pay to remove the virus [17], or that ransom the *system*, such as by locking the bootloader, where the data itself is still available on the file system [29]. In this paper, we focus on ransoming encrypted data, as this is a growing threat and harder for users to recover from [29].

The simple problem is that when users pay to recover their data, generally out of desperation for business-critical data (e.g., billing records) or sentimental data that was not backed up (e.g., baby photos), there is no guarantee they will be able to recover their data. A 2018 report [7] states that more than half of victims who paid a ransom failed to recover their data. There are projects that can decrypt ransomed data for victims of well-known ransomware [23], but these typically rely on flaws in the use of cryptography, such as reuse of a common encryption key; if ransomware makes proper use of cryptography, there is no reason to believe that any reasonable amount of analysis on the ransomware binary or source code will lead to a decryption tool. Thus, research in this space focuses on identifying ransomware attacks as they are in progress, and stopping the ransomware before the data is lost.

As with most malware, we adopt a common assumption that an attacker will be able to install and execute the ransomware. System defenses are not foolproof, and users are prone to exploitable behavior, such as downloading code from the internet that includes malware [2]. Similarly, anti-virus software can scan for known static features of ransomware. Such as signatures of ransomware binaries, encrypted file extensions or static ransom notes. We assume a strong adversary that is evolving the ransomware over time. For instance, the Cerber ransomware generates a new binary with a new signature every 15 s [22].

Based on a mixture of documentation, papers, and our own experiments, Table 1 summarizes the principal features and techniques used by a range of ransomware detectors, namely: file entropy (Sect. 2.1), file system operations (Sect. 2.2), or decoy files (Sect. 2.3). This section explains how each feature is used in greater detail.

Table 1. Detection methods used by state-of-the-art ransomware detection systems

	Data entropy	File system operations	Decoy files
Research prototypes			
Redemption [16]	✓	✓	
ShieldFS [5]	✓	✓	
RWGuard [20]	✓	✓	✓
Commercial products			
CryptoDrop [30]	✓[a]	✓	
CyberSight RansomStopper[b]		✓	✓
Acronis Ransomware Protection[b]		✓	
CheckMAL AppCheck[b]		✓	
ZoneAlarm Anti-Ransomware[b]		✓	✓

[a] CryptoDrop claims to use entropy to detect ransomware. However, we couldn't find evidence that they use entropy in the distributed version.

[b] These are closed-source software and do not document their methods; we base this table on monitoring their behavior.

2.1 Data Entropy

File entropy [31] is a measurement, typically from 0..1, of how uniformly distributed the byte values in a file are. At one extreme, when a content of a file consists of the same byte value, the entropy of the file is 0. At the other, a file with a uniformly random distribution of byte values should have an entropy approaching 1. In principle, any strong encryption algorithm should have high-entropy outputs.

To give a sense of expected entropy values for common file types, we measure the entropy of a corpus of 240 document files, shown in Fig. 1 and grouped by type. We selected the first 30 files of each file type from the Gov-docs1 corpus [11]. As a result, we collected 180 Microsoft Office documents, 30 pdf documents, and 30 jpeg image files. We can see that the entropy is widely distributed.

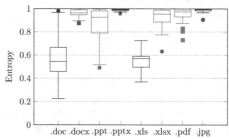

Fig. 1. Entropy distribution of a corpus of 240 document files, grouped by common formats.

Legacy office formats (`.doc` and `.xls`) have the lowest entropy. Most media formats, as well as Microsoft's Office Open XML documents (e.g., docx, pptx, xlsx) use compression, which leads to high entropy.

Since ransomware encrypts files, state-of-the-art ransomware detectors use data entropy as a feature to identify encrypted files by monitoring the entropy. Entropy is typically used in combination with other features, discussed in the following subsections. Some detectors just monitor changes in the entropy of a given file [20]; others, such as Redemption [16] compare the entropy of reads and writes from a given process. In either approach, the detector looks for a significant upward shift in entropy, which would indicate that a file is likely being encrypted. In order to avoid excessive false positives, this approach necessarily involves some sensitivity analysis to "normal" and "abnormal" increases in entropy. This also relies on a flawed assumption that there is room for entropy to increase—i.e., that the file format is not already effectively at entropy 1, as is common for formats such as `.jpg` and `.pptx`. In other words, the efficacy of this feature rests on the assumption that one cannot effectively ransom a file's contents via encryption without significantly raising entropy.

2.2 File Overwrite and Deletion

Another common feature monitored by ransomware detectors is file overwrite and deletion. Intuitively, if one wants to ransom a file by encrypting the contents, the original contents must be overwritten with ciphertext, or, if the ciphertext is in a different location, the original file must be deleted or renamed over.

As with entropy, this monitoring requires some sensitivity to differentiate normal and abnormal behavior. Programs routinely update a portion of a file, or even rewrite an entire file. Speaking generally, we have observed a few common measurement strategies. First, one can measure the percent of bytes overwritten versus the total size of the file, called the *overwrite ratio*. Second, one can monitor the total number of writes or deletions. Third, one can monitor the frequency of write or delete operations. If one of these values rises above a certain threshold, the process is flagged as malicious. Thus, for this feature, the goal for ransomware is to stay below this threshold, but still, deprive the victim of their data.

A related strategy considers the file type or extension written. Benign programs usually write a small number of specific file types only. For example, Microsoft Word will mostly write `*.doc` or `*.docx` files. The detector will flag as potentially malicious a process that writes to multiple different types of files.

Directory Traversal. Some ransomware detectors also monitor for recursive directory scans, typically in concert with other write operations. Because recursive directory scans are also executed by a number of benign applications, including backup utilities and virus scanners, it is easy for this feature to create false positives that irritate users and erode faith in the tool. This paper does not consider directory traversal in great detail, except to show in Sect. 4.5 that spreading this work to a separate process than the encryption work is sufficient to avoid detection by the commercial detectors that use this feature. Moreover, Sect. 5 shows that benign applications, such as git, can easily skew composite metrics based on this behavior.

2.3   Decoy Files

Ransomware detectors may also create a set of decoy files with various file types in the file system and monitor any changes to those files. Ransomware tends to encrypt all documents in the system. Thus when the ransomware tries to encrypt decoy files, the ransomware detector will notice the change in the expected contents of the file, and flag the writing process as ransomware.

2.4   Combining Techniques

As illustrated in Table 1, most ransomware defenses calculate a weighted average of a subset of the above techniques to form a global score, sometimes called a *malice score*. Redemption [16] calculates a malice score using six features. These six features are Entropy Ratio of Data Blocks, File Content Overwrite, Delete Operation, Directory Traversal, Write access to different type of files, and Access Frequency. Redemption scores each of the six features using different formulas, and then uses a weighted average of the six individual scores; if this average is above a threshold, the process is classified as ransomware. In general, combining features can lead to more robust classification, although setting appropriate weights can be a challenge.

3 Avoiding Detection

Section 2 explained the various features that are commonly used by ransomware detectors, typically as a weighted average or score, to flag processes as ransomware. This section explains how each of these mechanisms can be circumvented. We note that each of the avoidance techniques in this section also has a behavior that could be monitored; these behaviors overlap with common, benign patterns, and the heart of the question is whether there are behaviors that clearly delineate ransomware from benign software. Our results indicate that the line between ransomware and benign software is finer than one might expect.

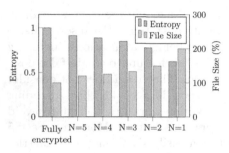
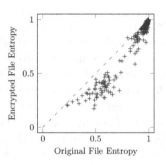

Fig. 2. Entropy and size of an encrypted file with a null, padding byte interleaved after every N bytes of ciphertext. Fully encrypted has no padding bytes interleaved. File size is measured as a percent, relative to the original plaintext. There is a smooth trade-off between size and target entropy, while still withholding the user's data. (Color figure online)

Fig. 3. A comparison of the original and encrypted entropy when using the compress-encrypt-pad strategy, using a corpus of 240 sample files. Points on the $y = x$ line represent an encrypted file with the same entropy and size as the unencrypted file; points below this line represent a reduction in entropy with the same size; points above the line represent an increase in entropy for the same size.

3.1 Entropy Laundering

Monitoring for a shift in entropy has an intuitive appeal, as encrypted outputs are necessarily going to be high entropy. This monitoring can either detect shifts in the contents of specific files, or in the difference between read and written data from a process.

As established in Fig. 1, one fundamental challenge is dealing with high-entropy file formats, such as a compressed Office document. The issue is that these files already have entropy close to 1, and normal file edits can increase small the entropy by small amounts—even as high as 1. In other words, for these file formats, entropy monitoring will have an obnoxiously high false positive rate and is simply not a good feature to monitor in these cases.

Thus, this section focuses on the efficacy of monitoring lower-entropy file formats. In other words, can we encrypt the file contents without changing the overall entropy of the file? Our basic strategy, which we will iteratively refine, is simple: we can encrypt the file (in memory) and then lower the entropy before writing it to disk by appending the same byte value (say zero) to the end of the file (let's call these the *padding bytes*). In practice, a more sophisticated attacker might instead interleave the padding bytes and the ciphertext.

The resulting entropy for interleaving a null padding byte between every N bytes of ciphertext is shown in Fig. 2. *Fully encrypted* shows the entropy and size of an encrypted file with no padding. The file used here is a PowerPoint slide (.ppt) and entropy of the file is 0.55 and the file size is 1.9 MB. We encrypt the file using AES algorithm in CBC mode.

Since entropies of encrypted files are mostly near one, this result is independent of the original file's entropy. When N = 1, this means the resulting file alternates between a byte of ciphertext and a byte of padding, yielding an entropy of about 0.6, or at roughly the first quartile of the lowest entropy formats (e.g., .doc and .xls).

The second, red bar in the figure represents size. There is a fairly smooth curve from N = 5..N = 1 in terms of trading size for lower entropy, and, although not pictured, the trend can be extended beyond N = 1 if needed. If changing the size is no issue, this experiment demonstrates that it is straightforward to ensure an encrypted output with comparable entropy to the input.

Of course, ransomware detectors can also monitor for changes in a file size or file overwrites, which we address in the next two subsections, respectively.

3.2 Maintaining File Size

Because many ransomware detectors also factor in file system operations, growth in a file's size is noticible; we refine the entropy laundering technique to preserve a target file size. We remind the reader that entropy monitoring is only effective for low entropy file formats.

Our second, simple observation is that low entropy files are highly compressible. By using this characteristic, ransomware can first compress then encrypt the smaller data payload, and finally, interleave the contents with padding to lower the entropy and yield an output that matches the original file size.

To evaluate this, we first compress a file using the zlib module in Python. Then we encrypt the compressed contents using the AES algorithm, and then pad the resulting output to match the original file size. Figure 3 compares the original file entropy (on the x-axis) to the encrypted file entropy (on the y-axis). A perfect match in entropy would be a $y = x$ line. The resulting distribution is almost entirely *at or below* $y = x$; i.e., this process often yields a *lower* entropy than the original file, and, in the worst case, the entropy is only raised by 3.4%.

This experiment shows that entropy can be lowered while maintaining the file size, but at the cost of overwriting the entire file. Overwriting the file (or deleting the file after writing these files elsewhere), is still easily detected by several ransomware detectors.

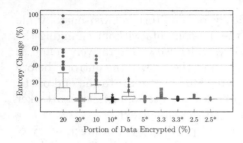

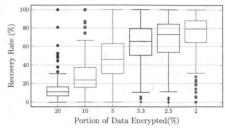

Fig. 4. Entropy changes in percentage value for the partially encrypted file compared to the original file for a corpus of 240 files. We encrypt a portion of the data from 20–2.5%. Star (*) represents that we used the compress-encrypt-pad strategy. The graph shows that the entropy changes are small, even when 20% of the file data is encrypted.

Fig. 5. Recovery rates for partial encryption over a corpus of 200 pdf files, when a portion of the data from 20–2% is encrypted. Block size of 256 bytes is used. Lower is better. The results indicate that, even if only 5–20% of the file is encrypted, roughly half of the data is unrecoverable.

3.3 Partial Encryption

The goal of ransomware is to deny users their file contents. The techniques presented so far accomplish this goal at the cost of overwriting an entire file, which can be detected by common techniques. This Subsection presents a technique that only overwrites a portion of a file, but effectively denies the user access to their data.

We observe that most file formats are brittle, with essential, non-redundant metadata or other data whose interpretation is predicated on the previous bytes. Corrupting (or encrypting) a relatively small portion of the file may be enough to render the file unusable to most end-users. One can thus mimic small updates to a file from a legitimate program with a combination of small updates to critical portions of the file, with the techniques above that can preserve the same average entropy of the encrypted bytes within the same space.

We first note a caveat to this attack: an expert in a given file format may be able to recover part of a file's contents. Specifically, the expert may successfully recover the data structure of the file format; encrypted data cannot be recovered. For instance, an engineer on the Adobe Acrobat team might be able to recover part of a partially encrypted pdf document by hand. We expect that, even if an end-user could find such an engineer, the hourly rate to recover a large data set would quickly approach the cost of the ransom (typically on the order of hundreds for individuals or tens of thousands of dollars for enterprises [9]). Thus, to evaluate the efficacy of this technique, we primarily consider automated file repair tools that are free or inexpensive (hundreds of dollars).

We define the success of this attack as: (1) updating only a small portion of the file (less than 20%), (2) preserving the same size (3) preserving comparable entropy, and (4) rendering most files unopenable and unrepairable by free or inexpensive tools.

As a simple proof-of-concept, we encrypted every N-th block of data in the file to measure its effect on entropy. For instance, when encrypting 20% of the file's data, we encrypted every 5th block. We used the AES algorithm with a block size of 1024 bytes to encrypt data. We also used compress-encrypt-pad for the target portion of data to see the entropy changes.

This is an under-approximation of a more targeted encryption, but allows us to measure the efficacy of the overall approach. Figure 4 shows the entropy changes in percentage value. The entropy of a file is always increased because we still encrypt a part of the file. However, when we use the compress-encrypt-pad strategy described in Sect. 3.2, the maximum entropy change is less than 8% when encrypting 20% of the file data. Most papers do not specify a particular threshold for entropy, except RWGuard, which uses 6 (or 0.75 on our scale from 0..1). In this experiment, entropy shift is at most 0.07, even at an aggressive 20% of encryption. A lower threshold would incur false positives, so we conclude that this change is unlikely to trigger detection.

To measure whether partial encryption is effective at withholding user data, we collected 200 different PDF documents from the web using Common Crawl Document Download [4]. We choose PDF documents with a minimum of 10 pages. We partially encrypted these 200 files and recovered encrypted files using the `pdrepair` utility from pdf-tools [25]. In practice, many documents are partially recoverable or corrupted. In order to conservatively quantify the amount of the document that can be recovered, we measure and compare the ink coverage of the original and recovered documents using `Ghostscript`. Ink coverage is a fraction of paper that is covered in each CMYK ink color.

Figure 5 shows the recovery rate distribution while the amount of encrypted data changes. We used a block size of 256 bytes in this experiment. The recovery rates increase as the amount of encrypted data decreases. We can see the average recovery rate is about 15% when 20% of the file is encrypted. When we encrypted 5% of data, recovery rate increases. However, the average recovery rate is still about 48%. At even lower percentages (3.3% and below), more than 64% of data is recoverable. Thus, we see a "sweet spot" when 5–20% of the file is encrypted, roughly half of the user's data is withheld.

As another point of comparison, and for more visual intuition about the data recovery, we did the same experiments with a JPEG image. The sample encrypted JPEG images are shown in Fig. 6. In this experiment, we change the percent of the file that is encrypted using a 256 bytes block size.

When we encrypt 10% of image data, it is difficult to recognize the image contents. However, when we encrypt 2.5% of image data, an encrypted image is annoying but we can figure out that the original image contains a butterfly and a flower. Overall, encrypting a modest portion of the file (5% or more) is effective at rendering the photograph useless to the average user.

We try to recover the partially encrypted images from the first experiment (Fig. 6a) using Adobe Photoshop. We recover the damaged areas using content-

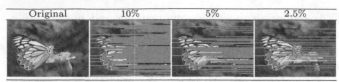

(a) Sample JPEG image after encrypting a portion of the data, from 10–2.5%.

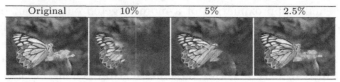

(b) Recovery of partially encrypted images from the first row, using Photoshop.

Fig. 6. Sample images resulting from various partial encryption parameter settings.

aware fill feature [8]. This feature fills a selected area in an image using information from the rest of the image. For all three images, Photoshop generates reasonable images, shown in Fig. 6b. However, Photoshop couldn't recover the details because it doesn't have any information about the damaged area, rather, the encrypted regions appear more blurred together to mask some of the most noticeable artifacts. Nonetheless, for photos with sentimental value, such a baby photos, we expect this level of recovery would be unacceptable and many users would pay a ransom to recover high-quality images.

In summary, the partial encryption technique can avoid detection by only writing to a small portion of a file (effective at 3–5% of total bytes overwritten, which is commensurate with light edits to the file in a legitimate application), preserving the same file size, and rendering the majority of the data unrecoverable for less than the cost of the ransom.

3.4 Decoy Avoidance

Some ransomware detectors generate decoy files in a file system. They monitor these specific files and flag the process when these files are modified. This subsection analyzes decoy files and their generation pattern.

We examine the decoy files generated by three commercial products, CyberSight RansomStopper, Cybereason RansomFree, and ZoneAlarm Anti-Ransomware. All three products create a decoy directory to store decoy files in important user directories, such as "My Documents" or "Desktop". Thus decoy files are not necessarily placed with other user files. In the decoy directory, various types of document and multimedia files are generated as decoy files, because some ransomware encrypts only specific file types. All three ransomware detectors generate one of each file type in the directory. So we start by creating two handwritten rules to detect a decoy directory: if more than three different types of files exist in a directory, and no more than two files of the same type exist in the directory, we conclude that it is a decoy directory. If a directory meets these two conditions, ransomware can just avoid this directory. In short, these decoys in practice are painfully obvious and easy to avoid.

To simulate a more sophisticated ransomware detector, we flatten this directory structure and collect 350 filenames. Filenames of decoy files are generated as a combination of random words. Some detector put a message to not delete the file in every filename, such as "Endpoint_Resume_Do NotRemove.doc". We use collected filenames to train a Naive Bayes classifier. Our classifier can classify files with 88.5% accuracy and 98.3% recall. High recall means a ransomware can detect most of the decoy files with very low false negatives.

Of course, more sophisticated decoy file generation is possible. The challenge is creating files that are truly indistinguishable from a user's data, and it is likely that efforts to improve decoy creation would lead to an "arms race" between decoy detection and decoy generation. The more decoy files look like user files, the harder it will be for ransomware to avoid; on the other hand, this also improves the risk of the user deleting a decoy or editing the decoy by accident, and triggers a false alarm.

3.5 I/O Rate: Slow, Multi-process Attack

In monitoring file system operations, ransomware detectors often factor in the rate of I/O. As a result, recent ransomware is slowing down the encryption process to avoid detection [27].

Similarly, we found that most ransomware detectors are sensitive to spreading the work across multiple processes. Sometimes anti-ransomware monitors a behavior of individual processes. An attacker spreads out the attack on multiple processes. Each process performs small operations and is not suspicious to detector [26].

4   Commercial Products

We evaluated commercial anti-ransomware products, 9 anti-ransomware products: CyberSight RansomStopper (3.1.1), Acronis Ransomware Protection (Build 1700), CheckMAL AppCheck (2.5.35.2), CryptoDrop (1.5.353.1336), ZoneAlarm Anti-Ransomware (1.1.1023.17955), Cybereason RansomFree (2.4.2.0), Bitdefender Anti-ransomware (1.0.12.151), Malwarebytes (3.6.1.2711), and Trend Micro Ransom Buster (12.0.1150) and 6 anti-virus products: Webroot Secure Anywhere (9.0.24.49), Kaspersky Anti-Virus (1.1.534.17681), ESET NOD32 (11.2.49.0), AVG AntiVirus (18.6.3066), Avast Free Antivirus (18.6.2349), and McAfee Total Protection (16.0 R12). We select products that specifically advertise ransomware protection. These software are closed-source, and thus we cannot confirm in all cases whether they monitor behavioral features; that said, some products do specify that they monitor behavioral features (e.g., file activities) in their datasheet or website.

We first test the ability of these products to detect known, real-world ransomware samples. Five ransomware samples are used in this experiment: TeslaCrypt, Jigsaw, Locky, Cerber, and WannaCry. These ransomware families infected a large number of victims and were released on or before 2017 [13,34]. Therefore, we expect they are well-known to the anti-malware industry. All five samples encrypt and ransom user files. We execute these samples on a system running each anti-ransomware product. Except for Bitdefender Anti-Ransomware and Webroot Secure Anywhere, all commercial products can successfully detect all of these real-world ransomware samples. Bitdefender Anti-Ransomware is designed to detect only one of three ransomware families, CTB-Locker, Locky, and TeslaCrypt, but it could not detect any of the five samples. Webroot Secure Anywhere could detect TeslaCrypt and Jigsaw samples but it could not detect Locky, Cerber, and WannaCry samples. Four anti-virus products detect these samples right after the binary file is copied to the system, even before execution, namely: Kaspersky Anti-Virus, ESET NOD32, AVG AntiVirus, and Avast Free Antivirus. This result shows most of the target products are effective for known ransomware.

Second, we evaluate commercial products using a simple, hand-written ransomware in python. Our ransomware recursively encrypts each file in a user's home directory as quickly as possible. The ransomware encrypts a file using the AES algorithm in CBC mode with Python Cryptography Toolkit (pycrypto). When encrypting a file, the ransomware overwrites the file with encrypted contents. Unless otherwise specified, the ransomware uses a block size of 1024 Bytes. We created a Windows 7 VM in Virtual Box and experimented with commercial products in the VM. We place 3,000 files with sizes ranging from 1 KB to 106 MB in the user's home directory. These files are the first 3,000 files from the Govdocs1 corpus [11]. We placed the first 1,000 files in the user's My Documents directory, the next 1,000 files in the user's Downloads directory, the last 1,000 files in the user's desktop. The total size of these files is 1.6 GB. When an anti-ransomware can't detect our ransomware, we ran the test at least two times until seeing the consistent results. We plan to release our ransomware scripts and supporting data upon publication. With this "toy" ransomware, we measure the effectiveness of each of the evasion techniques described in the previous section.

4.1 Basic Ransomware, No Evasion

The most striking result is that our textbook ransomware was not detected by four of the anti-ransomware products: Cybereason RansomFree, Bitdefender Antiransomware, Malwarebytes, and Trend Micro Ransom Buster nor by any of the 6 anti-virus products that advertise ransomware defense. We assume that the reason is that these products solely rely on static features, such as matching known binary signatures in order to detect ransomware. Our hand-written ransomware would not match a known signature. The most likely explanation is that these products are not behavior-based ransomware detectors. Therefore,

Table 2. Commercial anti-ransomware software, and their ability to detect stealthy ransomware. A checkmark in the table means anti-ransomware can detect the ransomware; a percentage indicates the threshold below which the detector could no longer detect the ransomware.

	Basic ransomware	Basic ransomware (New file)	Partial encryption	Decoy avoidance	Slow encryption	Multi-process encryption
Anti-ransomware						
CyberSight RansomStopper	✓	✓	✓		✓	*
Acronis Ransomware Protection	✓	✓	✗ (33%)	✓[a]		
CheckMAL AppCheck	✓	✓	✗ (25%)	✓[a]	✓	
CryptoDrop	✓	✓	✓	✓[a]	✓	✓
ZoneAlarm Anti-Ransomware	✓		✓	✓	✓	

[a] These anti-ransomware products don't use decoy files.

we excluded these products, and did the further analysis on 5 behavior-based ransomware detectors.

AVG AntiVirus has a feature called strict ransomware protection mode. With this mode on, it can detect ransomware but any process that writes to a specified directory is flagged. Consequently, the false positive rate is very high—even a benign word processor is required to get approval to save a document.

Some ransomware creates a new file with encrypted data and deletes the original. Thus, we create a variant of basic ransomware that creates encrypted versions and then deletes the user files. However, most commercial products we tested behave the same toward both variants of the basic ransomware. Only one anti-ransomware product, ZoneAlarm Anti-Ransomware, can't detect ransomware when it creates a new encrypted file and deletes the original.

Table 2 shows these anti-ransomware products and their effectiveness on evasion techniques, explained in more detail below. Anti-ransomware products which couldn't detect the basic ransomware are excluded. A checkmark in the table means that the ransomware detector can detect the ransomware with the feature. In partial encryption, the percentage value indicates the highest portion of encryption that the anti-ransomware cannot detect; a checkmark means the tool can detect any amount of encryption.

4.2   Partial Encryption

We implement partial encryption (Sect. 3.3) in our basic ransomware. Ransom-Stopper, CryptoDrop, and ZoneAlarm Anti-Ransomware can detect the ransomware regardless of the portion of data encrypted. However, Acronis Ransomware Protection cannot detect when $N \geq 3$ which means the ransomware encrypts less than or equal to 33% of file data. AppCheck can't detect when $N \geq 4$ that the ransomware encrypts less than or equal to 25% of file data. As discussed in Sect. 3.3, a user will lose more than 75% of the contents of a file, when only 10% of the data in the file is encrypted.

4.3   Avoiding Decoy Files

Two of the products in Table 2 generate decoy files: CyberSight RansomStopper and ZoneAlarm Anti-Ransomware. Interestingly, these monitors will tolerate small changes to these decoy files without flagging the process as ransomware. Thus deleting or overwriting on one of the decoy files won't trigger the detector. This implies that these detectors monitor a combination of other features to make a decision. This makes some intuitive sense, as decoy files are user-visible and may be accidentally removed by a user.

We avoided encrypting decoy files using the hand-written rules described in Sect. 3.4. This was sufficient to avoid detection by CyberSight RansomStopper. ZoneAlarm can detect the ransomware even when we didn't modify any decoy files.

4.4   Slow Encryption

We measure the impact of encryption rate on the ransomware detectors. We modified the basic ransomware to wait 60 s between encrypting each file. To evaluate slow encryption, we used 300 target files instead of 3000 files. We choose the first 100 files in each of 3 directories. Since we waited 60 s per one file encryption, total encryption time was approximately 330 min, whereas the basic ransomware took less than 10 min to encrypt entire user files (3000 files). This change was sufficient to elide detection in Acronis Ransomware Protection.

4.5   Multi-process Encryption

To measure the sensitivity to dividing the work across processes, one process recursively traverses directories and then forks workers that encrypt a single file and then exit. This was sufficient to evade three of the ransomware detectors: Acronis Ransomware Protection, CheckMAL AppCheck, and ZoneAlarm Anti-Ransomware. A fourth detector, RansomStopper, shows an interesting result: it detects modifications on decoy files, but only kills the worker process, letting processes continue encrypting all of the other files.

4.6   False Positives on CryptoDrop

In the previous experiments, CryptoDrop shows strong performance on detection; it detected all of our evasion strategies. Upon further investigation, however, we find that CryptoDrop is simply monitoring heavy writes to multiple files, and tested whether it would also trigger high false positives. First, we open a new Windows Notepad and write around 1 KB text and save in My Documents directory. When we save copies of this file with 20–30 different names using the "Save As..." menu, CryptoDrop labels Windows Notepad as ransomware. Next, we extract a zip file which consists of 50 files in My Documents directory. We used 7zip and Windows Explorer to extract the file, and CryptoDrop flags both 7zip and Windows Explorer as ransomware. Finally, we browse the web normally using Firefox. We downloaded a file to My Documents directory after every 3–5 pages. When we downloaded the 5th file, CryptoDrop labels Firefox as ransomware.

Although CryptoDrop can detect all of our evasion techniques, it comes at a cost of excessive false positives for users. This result is consistent with the overall hypothesis that there is a very slim range of behaviors that are unique to ransomware.

4.7 Entropy

Although several proposed ransomware detection methods use file entropy as a feature [5,15,16,20], we observed that most commercial ransomware detectors seemed insensitive to the entropy of a file write.

As a simple experiment, we modified our basic ransomware to simply overwrite 25% of file data with null bytes instead of encrypted bytes, which would lower the entropy. In this case, all of the commercial ransomware detectors flagged our ransomware based on the volume of data that was written. Although we cannot confirm that these detectors are not considering data entropy, the fact that they flag code as ransomware that issues large writes but lowers entropy indicates that these tools are likely insensitive to data entropy. It is possible that our ransomware was so simple that entropy detection was not triggered, and a more complex ransomware would trigger entropy monitoring; nonetheless, the observation that the entropy-lowering ransomware is detected is disquieting. We will return to the entropy experiment in Sect. 5, when we consider a state-of-the-art research prototype.

5   Research Prototypes

We contacted the authors of both Redemption [16] and ShieldFS [5]; neither provided us with a source or a binary drop. Thus, we instead did our best to reimplement the malice score as described in the Redemption paper.

To evaluate Redemption's malice score technique, we ran three benign applications and two variants of our basic ransomware: the non-evasive version, and the version that performs partial encryption (at 10% of the files' contents), and at a rate of one file per 2 s. 10% is selected as a relatively generous threshold; our experiments indicate we could easily drop to 3–5% if needed. The three benign applications are a git clone of Linux kernel, Linux kernel build, and bzip2 compression of Linux kernel code. This experiment is done on Linux, and we use strace to trace each process and score features using the trace.

We made two assumptions while scoring because some features are not clearly described in the Redemption paper [16]. First, when measuring the file overwrites, we didn't count newly created files as overwritten. Second, to score a directory traversal, we counted the maximum number of files that are accessed sequentially in the same directory; Redemption scores the "additive inverse of the number of privileged accesses to unique files in a given path." The paper does not provide values for the thresholds.

Redemption calculates a malice score per process. All three benign applications invoke multiple processes. For computing the malice score, we merged I/Os from these processes, treating them as a single application.

The malice score over time is shown in Fig. 7. The highest malice score among the benign applications is a Linux kernel compile, which is consistently around 0.5. This is attributable to the build process frequently writing files in multiple directories. In Fig. 7a, `git clone` does not trigger a high malice score most of the time. Most of the time `git` downloads objects in a file without an extension. At the end of the cloning process, `git` creates a local branch from the `master` branch. At this moment, `git` creates a lot of source code files, with known extensions, in the file system. Consequently, the malice score increases to 0.61. Two features, high scores from directory traversal, and write access to different type of files contribute to git's spike in malice score. Finally, `bzip2` has a low malice score. Unlike other workloads, `bzip2` does not delete any files, writes to a single document class, and only traverses directories with read access. In total, we expect that these applications show the range of expected malice scores. In order to avoid heavy false positives, a ransomware detector would likely need to flag applications that spent significant time over 0.6.

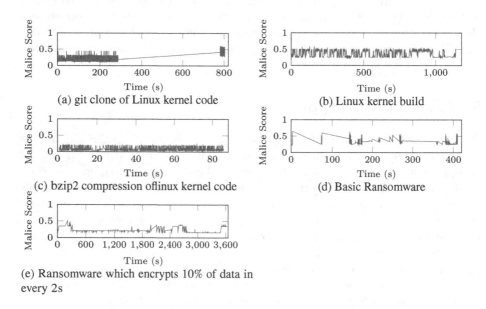

(a) git clone of Linux kernel code

(b) Linux kernel build

(c) bzip2 compression oflinux kernel code

(d) Basic Ransomware

(e) Ransomware which encrypts 10% of data in every 2s

Fig. 7. Redemption [16]'s malice score over time of three benign application executions, a naive ransomware, and a more evasive ransomware. Lower is less likely to be malware. Our evasive ransomware has a consistently lower malice score than a Linux kernel compilation.

Results from our ransomware are in Fig. 7d and e. In the basic ransomware experiment (Fig. 7d), the malice score increases as high as 0.65, and would likely be flagged. This is primarily attributable to the directory traversal component. We observe that the malice score is more sensitive to directory traversal than the entropy ratio.

Partial and slow encryption lowers the malice score—usually at or below 0.4 and, at most, 0.51. Recall that anything below 0.6 is unlikely to be flagged as ransomware with this method.

6 Related Work

Similar to this work, Genç et al. studied ransomware detection and evasion techniques for key-oriented protection and behavioral analysis [12]. Similar to our work, the authors describe two evasion methods: pseudo-random permutation for encryption and partial encryption. Our work advances the state of the art in three ways. First, their proposed permutation method avoids entropy-based detection, but is less robust to reverse engineering by a victim than a standard cipher; our paper shows how to use a standard cipher with the compress-encrypt-pad method and still avoid using entropy-based detection. Second, the authors mentioned 20% encrypted files are unusable, but they didn't discuss the efficacy of the partial encryption. This paper shows that partial encryption is effective to extort user files even when a victim used the recovery tools. Finally, our paper studies additional evasion techniques, such as slow encryption, multi-process encryption, and decoy avoidance to evade more detecting methods.

One significant component of an attack, orthogonal to this paper, is loading malware onto the target system. Malware can get onto a computer by a user's explicit mistake, such as downloading an attachment from a phishing email or malicious website; more stealthily by using a system vulnerability [32]; or via a malware distribution service [2]. Most related to this paper, Gangwar et al. analyze these delivery methods and try to detect ransomware by delivery method [10].

Most ransomware needs to communicate with the ransomers who will collect the payment. Malware often has a command and control (C&C) server to control it remotely. In ransomware, C&C server is used to exchange encryption key or other client details. Several works are available to detect ransomware at the network level by monitoring and identifying these communications between the C&C server and the victim host [1,6]. Our toy ransomware uses a static key and does not perform any network communication. To evade detection by network activity some ransomware locally generates a key instead of getting one from a C&C server [24].

Some anti-ransomware create hooks in common cryptographic libraries. When ransomware tries to encrypt a file, the anti-ransomware can intercept and save the key. Then it decrypts the files using the saved decryption key. Pay-Break [18] successfully retrieves the key from ransomware that uses Microsoft Cryptographic API [33]. The authors showed that it can even detect ransomware that statically links known cryptographic libraries, such as Crypto++.

Cheng et al. studied partial encryption methods on media files [3], in order to reduce encryption/decryption costs. Here, the goal is different—confidentiality of these files—whereas the goal of this paper is to explore the efficacy of partial encryption to ransom a user's data.

A system can implicitly provide a backup. Ransomware needs to overwrite the data in the hard drive. Modern hardware, such as Solid State Drives (SSDs), tend to leave the old files untouched because the device can only erase at the granularity of an erase block. FlashGuard [14] modifies SSD garbage collection to retain the copies of the old files for the file recovery when encrypted by ransomware.

Most general-purpose malware detectors such as signature-based are looking for ransomware. More precisely, for known ransomware. Marpaung et al. survey malware evasion techniques [19]. Since ransomware is a kind of malware, the attacker can use these methods to evade traditional malware detectors.

7   Conclusion

This paper demonstrates that there is considerable cause for pessimism about the effectiveness of host-level ransomware detectors. A "textbook" ransomware cannot be detected by a number of commercial anti-ransomware products; relatively straightforward evasive techniques can thwart the rest, yet still effectively ransom user's data. More sophisticated behavioral analyses are unlikely to fare better; a deeper exploration of each of the features proposed in the literature, as well as aggregate metrics, are unlikely to accurately distinguish ransomware from benign software.

Acknowledgments. We thank the anonymous reviewers, our shepherd Karim Elish, and Bhushan Jain for their insightful comments on previous drafts. This material is based upon work supported by the NSF/VMware Partnership on Software Defined Infrastructure (SDI) as a Foundation for Clean-Slate Computing Security (SDI-CSCS) program under Award "SDI-CSCS: Collaborative Research: S2OS: Enabling Infrastructure-wide Programmable Security with SDI", grant numbers CNS-1700512 and CNS-1834216.

References

1. Cabaj, K., Mazurczyk, W.: Using software-defined networking for ransomware mitigation: the case of CryptoWall. IEEE Netw. **30**(6), 14–20 (2016)
2. Caballero, J., Grier, C., Kreibich, C., Paxson, V.: Measuring pay-per-install: the commoditization of malware distribution. In: USENIX Security Symposium, p. 13 (2011)
3. Cheng, H., Li, X.: Partial encryption of compressed images and videos. IEEE Trans. Signal Process. **48**(8), 2439–2451 (2000)
4. Common Crawl Document Download. https://github.com/centic9/CommonCrawl DocumentDownload

5. Contininella, A., et al.: ShieldFS: a self-healing, ransomware-aware filesystem. In: Proceedings of the 32nd Annual Conference on Computer Security Applications, pp. 336–347. ACM (2016)
6. Cusack, G., Michel, O., Keller, E.: Machine learning-based detection of ransomware using SDN. In: Proceedings of the 2018 ACM International Workshop on Security in Software Defined Networks & Network Function Virtualization, pp. 1–6. ACM (2018)
7. CyberEdge Group: 2018 cyberthreat defense report. Technical report, CyberEdge Group (2018)
8. Ding, M., Tong, R.F.: Content-aware copying and pasting in images. Visual Comput. **26**(6–8), 721–729 (2010)
9. Everett, C.: Ransomware: to pay or not to pay? Comput. Fraud Secur. **2016**(4), 8–12 (2016)
10. Gangwar, K., Mohanty, S., Mohapatra, A.K.: Analysis and detection of ransomware through its delivery methods. In: Panda, B., Sharma, S., Roy, N.R. (eds.) REDSET 2017. CCIS, vol. 799, pp. 353–362. Springer, Singapore (2018). https://doi.org/10.1007/978-981-10-8527-7_29
11. Garfinkel, S., Farrell, P., Roussev, V., Dinolt, G.: Bringing science to digital forensics with standardized forensic corpora. Digit. Investig. **6**, S2–S11 (2009)
12. Genç, Z.A., Lenzini, G., Ryan, P.Y.A.: Next generation cryptographic ransomware. In: Gruschka, N. (ed.) NordSec 2018. LNCS, vol. 11252, pp. 385–401. Springer, Cham (2018). https://doi.org/10.1007/978-3-030-03638-6_24
13. Huang, D.Y., et al.: Tracking ransomware end-to-end. In: Tracking Ransomware End-to-end. IEEE (2018)
14. Huang, J., Xu, J., Xing, X., Liu, P., Qureshi, M.K.: FlashGuard: leveraging intrinsic flash properties to defend against encryption ransomware. In: Proceedings of the 2017 ACM SIGSAC Conference on Computer and Communications Security, pp. 2231–2244. ACM (2017)
15. Kharraz, A., Arshad, S., Mulliner, C., Robertson, W.K., Kirda, E.: UNVEIL: a large-scale, automated approach to detecting ransomware. In: USENIX Security Symposium, pp. 757–772 (2016)
16. Kharraz, A., Kirda, E.: Redemption: real-time protection against ransomware at end-hosts. In: Dacier, M., Bailey, M., Polychronakis, M., Antonakakis, M. (eds.) RAID 2017. LNCS, vol. 10453, pp. 98–119. Springer, Cham (2017). https://doi.org/10.1007/978-3-319-66332-6_5
17. Kharraz, A., Robertson, W., Balzarotti, D., Bilge, L., Kirda, E.: Cutting the gordian knot: a look under the hood of ransomware attacks. In: Almgren, M., Gulisano, V., Maggi, F. (eds.) DIMVA 2015. LNCS, vol. 9148, pp. 3–24. Springer, Cham (2015). https://doi.org/10.1007/978-3-319-20550-2_1
18. Kolodenker, E., Koch, W., Stringhini, G., Egele, M.: PayBreak: defense against cryptographic ransomware. In: Proceedings of the 2017 ACM on Asia Conference on Computer and Communications Security, pp. 599–611. ACM (2017)
19. Marpaung, J.A., Sain, M., Lee, H.J.: Survey on malware evasion techniques: state of the art and challenges. In: 2012 14th International Conference on Advanced Communication Technology (ICACT), pp. 744–749. IEEE (2012)
20. Mehnaz, S., Mudgerikar, A., Bertino, E.: RWGuard: a real-time detection system against cryptographic ransomware. In: Bailey, M., Holz, T., Stamatogiannakis, M., Ioannidis, S. (eds.) RAID 2018. LNCS, vol. 11050, pp. 114–136. Springer, Cham (2018). https://doi.org/10.1007/978-3-030-00470-5_6
21. Mohurle, S., Patil, M.: A brief study of Wannacry threat: ransomware attack 2017. Int. J. Adv. Res. Comput. Sci. **8**(5) (2017)

22. Nieuwenhuizen, D.: A behavioural-based approach to ransomware detection. Whitepaper, MWR Labs Whitepaper (2017)
23. The No More Ransom Project. https://www.nomoreransom.org/en/index.html
24. Offline Ransomware Encrypts Your Data without C&C Communication. https://blog.checkpoint.com/2015/11/04/offline-ransomware-encrypts-your-data-without-cc-communication/
25. PDF Tools. http://www.pdf-tools.com
26. Ramilli, M., Bishop, M., Sun, S.: Multiprocess malware. In: 2011 6th International Conference on Malicious and Unwanted Software (MALWARE), pp. 8–13. IEEE (2011)
27. 11 ransomware trends for 2018. https://www.csoonline.com/article/3267544/ransomware/11-ways-ransomware-is-evolving.html
28. Richardson, R., North, M.: Ransomware: evolution, mitigation and prevention. Int. Manag. Rev. **13**(1), 10–21 (2017)
29. Savage, K., Coogan, P., Lau, H.: The Evolution of Ransomware. Symantec, Mountain View (2015)
30. Scaife, N., Carter, H., Traynor, P., Butler, K.R.: CryptoLock (and drop it): stopping ransomware attacks on user data. In: 2016 IEEE 36th International Conference on Distributed Computing Systems (ICDCS), pp. 303–312. IEEE (2016)
31. Shannon, C.E.: The mathematical theory of communication (1963)
32. Snow, K.Z., Monrose, F., Davi, L., Dmitrienko, A., Liebchen, C., Sadeghi, A.R.: Just-in-time code reuse: on the effectiveness of fine-grained address space layout randomization. In: 2013 IEEE Symposium on Security and Privacy (SP), pp. 574–588. IEEE (2013)
33. Wiewall, E.: Secure your applications with the Microsoft CryptoAPI. Microsoft Dev. Netw. News **5**(96), 3 (1996)
34. Zimba, A., Chishimba, M.: Understanding the evolution of ransomware: paradigm shifts in attack structures. Int. J. Comput. Netw. Inf. Secur. **11**(1), 26–39 (2019)

PoQ: A Consensus Protocol for Private Blockchains Using Intel SGX

Golam Dastoger Bashar, Alejandro Anzola Avila, and Gaby G. Dagher[✉]

CS, Boise State University, Boise, ID 83725, USA
{golambashar,alejandroanzolaa}@u.boisestate.edu,
gabydagher@boisestate.edu

Abstract. In blockchain technology, consensus protocols serve as mechanisms to reach agreements among a distributed network of nodes. Using a centralized party or consortium, private blockchains achieve high transaction throughput and scalability, Hyperledger Sawtooth is a prominent example of private blockchains that uses Proof of Elapsed Time (PoET) (SGX-based) to achieve consensus. In this paper, we propose a novel protocol, called Proof of Queue (PoQ), for private (permissioned) blockchains, that combines the lottery strategy of PoET with a specialized round-robin algorithm where each node has an equal chance to become a leader (who propose valid data blocks to the chain) with equal access. PoQ is relatively scalable without any collision. Similar to PoET, our protocol uses Intel SGX, a Trusted Execution Environment, to generate a secure random waiting time to choose a leader, and fairly distribute the leadership role to everyone on the network. PoQ scales fairness linearly with SGX machines: the more the SGX in the network, the higher the number of chances to be selected as a leader per unit time. Our analysis and experiments show that PoQ provides significant performance improvements over PoET.

Keywords: Blockchain · Consensus · Permissioned · SGX · Fairness

1 Introduction

At the core of any blockchain platform, there is a ledger that is maintained by a trustless P2P network. Due to the untrustworthy nature of the network, there needs to be a way for the nodes in the network to reach an agreement among them on the valid transactions that can be appended to the ledger. Consensus protocols are designed to handle faults in a distributed system and agreeing to a single version of the truth by all nodes on the network. The most common types of consensus protocols are leader election based and traditional Byzantine Fault Tolerance (BFT)-based. In a leader election-based consensus, a leader is chosen randomly (by using a protocol) and proposes final valid blocks. The BFT-based consensus is a more traditional method as per rounds of votes. While existing

© ICST Institute for Computer Sciences, Social Informatics and Telecommunications Engineering 2020
Published by Springer Nature Switzerland AG 2020. All Rights Reserved
N. Park et al. (Eds.): SecureComm 2020, LNICST 336, pp. 141–160, 2020.
https://doi.org/10.1007/978-3-030-63095-9_8

protocols solve the consensus problem fairly well, they also have their own short-comings. A consensus protocol in a blockchain system is typically required to support three properties: *liveness* (transactions are added to the ledger in a reasonable time), *consistency* (all parties have the same view), and *fairness* (all nodes are equally likely to mine the next block) [4].

Public blockchain networks (e.g. Bitcoin [19] and Ethereum [7]) that use proof of work (*PoW*) [19], proof of capacity [15] or proof of activity [6], require a large amount of computational power, which is a misuse of resources and limits transaction throughput (usually expressed as transactions per second). On the other hand, proof of stake [17] and proof of burn[1] [4] are environment-friendly consensus protocols due to the insignificant computation requirements; however, they suffer from the "rich get richer" problem [5].

Private blockchains, on the other hand, require a centralized party (or a consortium of them) to control who joins the system and at what capacity (mine, view, transact, etc). Such reliance on the centralized party leads to a reduced cost for reaching consensus, high transaction throughput, improved scalability to support new nodes and services, and higher efficiency. In private blockchains, the level of access, visibility, and execution can be controlled. Private blockchains are more appropriate to a consortium of organizations, like the banking sector or the insurance industry, where participation is selective with known identity and may operate under a shared governance model [14]. Examples of private blockchains include Ripple (XRP) [20] and Hyperledger [3]. Hyperledger Sawtooth project was introduced by Intel as a modular blockchain that uses Proof of Elapsed Time (*PoET*) consensus protocol to implement a leader election lottery system [8,13]. In *PoET*, each miner node is randomly assigned a `waitTime`, and as soon as this `waitTime` expires, the specific node creates and publishes the next block on the network [8]. The protocol acts as a mix of first-come-first-serve (*FCFS*) and random lottery [21].

Contribution. In this paper, we propose a variant of *PoET*, we call it PoQ, that regulates how nodes compete to finish their `waitTime` (to become a leader) such that the average wait time and number of leadership of each node will remain approximately same after a certain period. Our goal is to optimize the performance of the network concerning *throughput* and *scalability*. PoQ determines which node should execute its `waitTime` when there are multiple run-able nodes in the queue. To achieve this, we introduce the concept of *dynamic Quantum Time* (*QT*) indicating the amount of time a node will get the chance to execute for a single pass, which has a major impact on resource utilization and overall performance of the network. Some of the extended characteristics that differentiate our work over others include fast transaction processing, low energy consumption, fair distribution, and easy verification (deterministic). PoQ avoids high resource utilization and replaces it with a true randomized system. Similar to *PoET*, PoQ uses execution environments in trusted hardware, more specifically Intel *SGX* [10] (secure computing enclave to generate a random wait time and to perform remote attestation), to achieve consensus while preventing tampering. Through the use of Intel SGX enabled CPUs, we enforce correct execution of code and guarantee the "one

---

[1] https://en.bitcoin.it/wiki/Proof_of_burn.

node one machine" policy (to prevent Sybil attacks) for all nodes in the network. We implemented PoQ in a distributed SGX environment, and our analysis and experiment results show that PoQ provides significant performance improvement over PoET.

2   Related Work

In recent years separate approaches are used to extend the performance of *PoET*. Research has been conducted to achieve a good overall performance in a private environment. In addition, there are existing related works that spotlight the perfections behind the intention of Trusted Execution Environment (TEE) design. Hardware-based TEE like ARM TrustZone (available on smartphones) or Trusted Platform Module and Intel SGX (for x86-based computer) are generally obtainable in commodity computing platforms. In the paper [8], authors provide remarks on the design of Sawtooth. In order to reduce potential collision, they discussed waiting times need to be longer. While [12] focusing on reducing the *stale block rate* by restricting the number of nodes which they call *PoET+*. A stale block is an accurate, previously announced block that does not belong as part of the longest chain. A stale block appears at any time when more than one node announces a valid block within a short duration. Proof of Luck (*PoL*) [18] is another consensus protocol based on TEE and similar to *PoET* because it also generates random numbers from SGX into the block referred to as '*luck*' of the block. The protocol selects the chain with the highest accumulative luck as the winner and is determined the luckiest. The luckiest block is then added to the chain. It will generate forks when the network is periodically portioned because the partitions will ensure various largest accumulative luck. In [2], the authors proposed Proof of TEE-Stake (*PoTS*), that leveraging functionality from TEE for public blockchain, where each node in PoTS ensures the same structure to bootstrap a TEE program. In [11], the authors explore the response of throughput of *PoET* and propose a simple adjustment to it (they termed as "*S − PoET*") which leads to a higher throughput as the network becomes larger. According to the authors, if the shortest `waitTime` and another `waitTime` are conflicted by fewer than the propagation delay then that will result in a stale block.

At the beginning, *PoET* was preferred to replace the *PoW* with the exception of the longest-chain rule [22]. Due to its access control nature, it is most appropriate for permissioned blockchains, where certain works will be executed on TEE by certain authenticated nodes. Unlike permissionless, most permissioned blockchains don't require any rewards mechanism. Each consensus protocol is unique based on the way it creates a block, discloses the evidence (block propagation), the procedure of validation inside the network, and the rewards system for an honest effort. Table 1 shows an assessment among some of the protocols designed for TEE based or not [5]. The throughput measurements derive from the complimentary white paper or formal demonstration of the implementation of that protocol and indicate the scales of fastness, i.e. high or low.

Due to dynamic QT in PoQ, all nodes are approximately given the same priority to execute depending on its tier (A relationship engaging level between a set of nodes. PoQ is a multi-tier approach to the early recognition of nodes and provides necessary data to them), thus no nodes are left behind which leads to more speed in the system. PoQ progresses in a round-robin way, wherein each round, a selected node within all the nodes in the network will get a chance to reduce its `waitTime` and if it is successful to reduce all its `waitTime`, then that particular node proposes the potential block (a successive set of transactions). Thus, a node cannot get a total allocation of time above its assigned time. We can say that *PoET* is suitable for a limited network with small `waitTime` while in PoQ arrival time of a node puts great importance on becoming the leader quickly as it maintains a dynamic queue that pushes the nodes based on their arrival time. That means when a node appears in the network it starts to compete with other nodes and the leadership cannot be predetermined. It is suitable for a large number of participants, easy to implement, and also offers similar average `waitTime` and average elapsed time for all its nodes. Due to no hashing is required in PoQ, we can say it also saves energy too. As PoQ is suitable for private blockchain network, it does not provide incentives for participants. To the very best of our knowledge, no work has been done to make the lottery election system fairer for *PoET*.

Table 1. Assessment of blockchain consensus protocols. Symbols for binary values: ✓ means yes, ✗ means no. Symbols for non-binary values: ● means high, ◗ means medium, ○ means low and ⊘ indicates undefined in the protocol white paper.

Concensus Protocols	Type		Block propagation	Block Validation	TEE based	Resource consuming	Rewards	Nodes execution	Throughput (tps)	Fairness
	Public	Private								
Nakamoto (BTC, Litecoin)	✓	✗	PoW	PoW (longest chain)	✗	●	✓	●	○	●
Nakamoto (Etheruem)	✓	✗	PoW (Ethash)	PoW (GHOST)	✗	●	✓	●	○	●
PoET (Hyperledger)	✗	✓	PoET within TEE	TEE certificate	✓	○	⊘	◗	●	●
PoTS	✓	✗	PoTS-based committee election	TEE, eligibility	✓	○	⊘	⊘	⊘	⊘
Chain-based PoS (Nxt)	✓	✗	PoS	PoS (longest chain)	✗	◗	✓	⊘	○	○
PoI (XEM)	✓	✗	PoI Harvesting	Importance score	✗	○	✓	◗	●	●
PoL	✗	✓	PoL	Longest total value of luck	✓	○	⊘	◗	⊘	●
PoQ	✗	✓	PoQ within TEE	Completion of wait time	✓	○	✗	●	●	●

3 Background

3.1 SGX

Intel Software Guard Extension (*SGX*) is fully implemented in the CPU hardware and yields a partial element to execute within an isolated environment, referred to as an enclave [10]. Generally, SGX breaks down an application into

Table 2. Comparison of SGX based system. Symbols: ● means fully-provided, ✗ means unsupported and ⊘ means unspecified.

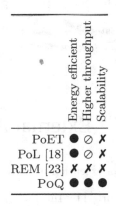

	Energy efficient	Higher throughput	Scalability
PoET	●	⊘	✗
PoL [18]	●	⊘	✗
REM [23]	✗	✗	✗
PoQ	●	●	●

two logical segments: enclave and untrusted part (conventional application). Furthermore, an SGX application can handle 5–20 enclaves. The code in the enclave is used to handle the secret data. On the other hand, the remaining portion of the code, along with all its modules, keeps in the untrusted part. Interaction within these two parts happens via the call gate. A function call that enters the enclave from the untrusted portion is called an Enclave CALL (ECALL). A call within the enclave to an untrusted portion is called an Outside Call (OCALL). Figure 1 provides a high-level view of ECALL and OCALL communication. By definition, an OCALL is made from within an ECALL because an ECALL needs to enter the trusted portion. Figure 2 shows the execution of an SGX application and the way SGX safeguards an enclave from any envious program, including OS, BIOS, drivers, and firmware which pretends to steal application secrets[2] (Table 2).

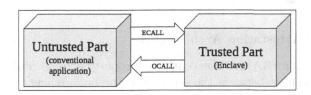

Fig. 1. Interaction between enclave and untrusted part in an SGX application.

SGX depends on remote attestation to prove to remote users that the particular portion of code is executing in a genuine SGX-enabled CPU [10]. It also presents a reliable source of random number via its SGX_READ_RAND API which calls the hardware-based pseudorandom generator (PRNG) over RDRAND on Intel CPUs. Many researchers have already established that this random number generator is secure and cannot be modified from outside the enclave [9].

---

[2] https://software.intel.com/en-us/articles/intel-software-guard-extensions-tutorial-part-1-foundation.

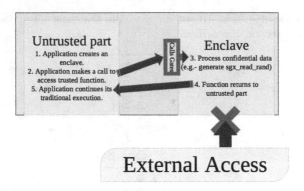

Fig. 2. Flow of execution in SGX application.

Presently, C and C++ are supported by Intel's Software Development Kit (SDK) which is available for both Windows and Linux.

3.2   Abstract Model of PoET

PoET is usually used on the permissioned blockchain networks to determine the leaders of the block on a specific network. After joining the network, each node must ask for a `waitTime` from an enclave and then wait for that randomly chosen `waitTime`. A node who finishes the `waitTime` first – that is, the node with the shortest wait time for an appropriate transaction block, establishes a remote attestation that provides information for verification about its honesty, carries out a new block to the blockchain, and announces the mandatory data to the network. To find the next block, an identical procedure is required. By remote attestation, *PoET* ensures that the nodes select a random `waitTime` (not purposely chosen a curtailed `waitTime`) and the leader has actually waited the allocated `waitTime`.

3.3   Remote Attestation Architecture

Remote attestation (RA) is an exceptional property of Intel SGX, to establish a secure environment between the server and the node (client) [16]. Simply in computing, the term attestation means, a procedure to verify the identity of a software and/or hardware. More specifically, RA is a medium to verify the interaction between the software and the hardware that has been founded on a trustworthy platform. By following remote attestation flow, a client enclave ensures three things: its identity, its pureness (has not been altered), and a certain piece of code executing in a genuine SGX-enabled CPU. A server sends a remote attestation request to a node and it responds to the request by announcing information about the platform configuration. Node executes the client code while the server runs the server's side code. Both parties are interacting over a network, which is not recognized to be part of any side or secured. The whole operation contains fifteen steps with the server (also called challenger) and the

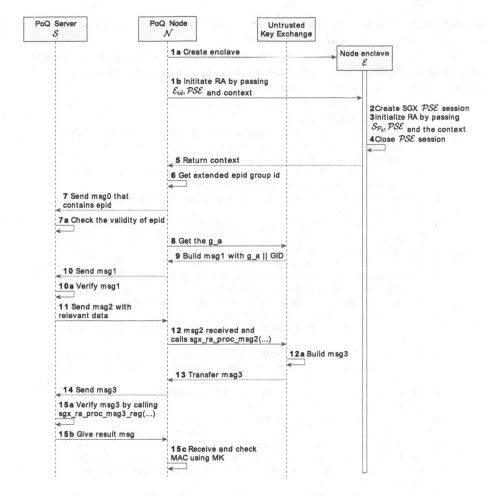

Fig. 3. SGX remote attestation.

node. Figure 3 shows the interactions between the entities engaging in RA. It is worth mentioning that RA adopts a modified version of the sigma protocol to support Diffie-Hellmann key exchange (DHKE) among the node and the server. The sigma protocol is proof that consists of commitment, challenge, and response. SCIFER [1] uses RA to verify the identity of users. Finally, we trust Intel to execute SGX RA service correctly (similar to [1,23]).

4   Consensus Protocol: PoQ

4.1   Overview

This paper introduces a modified version of *PoET* consensus protocol called PoQ based on *SGX*. As part of this protocol, each participating node generates a random `waitTime` using the enclave $\mathcal{E}$, called SGX time $\mathcal{SGX}_t$ and waits for it to be expired. After $\mathcal{SGX}_t$ is finished, the node becomes the leader and is authorized to generate the next block. The `waitTime` and leadership for each node will be approximately the same after a certain period which achieves the equality issue of the consensus protocol.

Remote Attestation Protocol

1. In reply to the challenge request from the server, the node will do the following:

   1a) Initialize the enclave by `sgx_create_enclave (.., enclave_id, ..)` and perform ECALL to go into the encalve.

   1b) Initialize the RA flow by calling `enclave_init_ra(enclave_id,..,b_pse, context)`. Here, *pse* means platform service.

2. If *b_pse* is true then call `sgx_create_pse_session()` before establishing the RA and key session.

3. Call `sgx_ra_init(&sp_pub_key,b_pse,context)` by passing the server's public key. Key is in little-endian byte order and must be hardcoded into enclave.

4. Close PSE session by `sgx_close_pse_session()`.

5. Return *context* to the untrusted part from the enclave.

6. The untrusted part of the node call `sgx_get_extended_epid_group_id()` to get active extended group ID (GID) of enhanced privacy group ID. EPID is an anonymous signature scheme for attestation.

7. This is send to the server as a body of msg0.

   7a) Verify by the server. If it is not valid, server terminate the attestation flow.

8. The untrusted part of the node calls `sgx_ra_get_msg1(...,enclave-id,g_a)` where g_a is a public key of a node enclave and this *enclave_id* is going to be attested.

9. The untrusted Key Exchange (uKE) part of the node builds a message, msg1 that contains g_a || GID.

10. Send msg1 to the server. All elements of msg1 are in little-endian byte order.

    10a) Server translate all elements into little-endian order to check.

11. Server replies with msg2 that contains g_b, *spid*, *quote-type*, *kdf-id*, *sigRL*, etc. The public key of the server, also known as g_b is based on NIST-256. Signature Revocation List (sigRL), is a list of unfaithful signatures, signed by the revocation authority.

12. After receiving msg2, the untrusted part calls the function `sgx_ra_proc_msg2(context,enclave_id,sgx_ra_proc_msg2_trusted_t, sgx_ra_proc_msg3_trusted_t, msg2, msg2_size, ...)`

    12a) By calling `sgx_ra_proc_msg2`, node builds msg3.

13. `sgx_ra_proc_msg2()` builds msg3 that contains mac, g_a, and platform security property.

14. The node sends msg3 to the server and expect to get the attestation result.

15. Upon receiving msg3 from the node, the server will do the following:

    15a) The server verifies the msg3 by calling `sgx_ra_proc_msg3_req(msg2,msg3_size,att_result_msg)`, to compare g_a w.r.t. g_a of msg1 and verify the msg mac using sigma protocol (SMK).

    15b) Send attestation result message to the node.

    15c) The node will receive the result and checks the MAC using MK.

Protocol 1.1: Remote attestation

PoQ Server

Initialization. The server $\mathcal{S}$ establishes a public key directory of permitted nodes, creates an empty Q (contains node id) and $\mathcal{SGX}_\mathrm{T}$, and then starts listening to requests from nodes interested to join the network.

Node Registration $Register(\mathcal{N}_{\mathcal{P}_k}, Sign(\mathcal{N}_{\mathcal{P}_k}))$. Upon receiving a registration request from a node, the server performs the following:

1. Check whether $\mathcal{N}_{\mathcal{P}_k}$ exists in the public key directory. Otherwise terminate the connection.
2. Check the validity of the signature. Otherwise terminate the connection.
3. Create an identification number, $\mathcal{N}_{id}$.
4. Send an acknowledgment back to the node, along with $\mathcal{N}_{id}$ and $\mathcal{SGX}_\mathrm{max}$.

Attestation $Remote\_Att(\mathcal{S}_{\mathcal{P}_k})$. The server and a node jointly execute the RA protocol (Protocol 1.1): Sends a RA request to the client to establish a secure channel.

- The server gets some information from the node which helps to decide whether the program functioning on the node is malicious or fair.

SGX Verification. $Verify(\mathcal{SGX}_t)$. Upon receiving $\mathcal{SGX}_t$, which is a randomly generated time by the node's $\mathcal{E}$ from $\mathcal{N}_{id}$, the server performs the following:

- Check whether $\mathcal{SGX}_t$ is within the range $[\mathcal{SGX}_\mathrm{min}, \mathcal{SGX}_\mathrm{max}]$. Otherwise terminate the connection.
- Add $\mathcal{N}_{id}$ to Q and build $\mathcal{SGX}_\mathrm{T}$ that has $\mathcal{Q}_t$ and $\mathcal{ST}$ for all nodes based on available information.
- Send meta-data $(\mathcal{N}_n, \mathcal{N}_{\mathcal{A}_t}, \mathcal{N}_{\mathcal{Q}_T}, \mathcal{T}_r, \mathcal{N}_{\mathcal{R}\mathcal{T}})$ to $\mathcal{N}_{id}$.

Status. Server will perform the following operation in meta-data:

- Continuously updates the $\mathcal{SGX}_\mathrm{T}$, queue and dequeue the winner nodes to keep a track.
- Broadcast the result to the network.

Protocol 1.2: PoQ Server side protocol.

Random $\mathcal{SGX}_t$. In our protocol, when a node joins the network, it gets a range from the server to generate a random `waitTime`, $\mathcal{SGX}_t$ from its $\mathcal{E}$. After having an $\mathcal{SGX}_t$, the node needs to submit it to the server for further verification. To ensure TEE platforms exists, nodes generally require to register with the hardware manufacturer to set up RA services. For instance, Intel SGX RA service needs registration with Intel Attestation Service (IAS)[3]. During manufacturing, each processor of SGX is equipped with a key that is certified by Intel [1]. After successful verification, the server adds the node id, $\mathcal{N}_{id}$ of that node to the queue, Q as it arrives. Subsequently, the node determines which tier, $\mathcal{T}_i$ it belongs to and then calculates its $\mathcal{Q}_t$ for that particular $\mathcal{T}_i$ for that time being which is

---

[3] Intel, "Software sealing policies– intel® software guard extensions developer guide," 2017. [Online]. Available: https://software.intel.com/en-us/documentation/sgx-developer-guide.

PoQ Node

1. The node signs its public key and then sends a node registration request $Register(\mathcal{N}_{\mathcal{P}_k}, Sign(\mathcal{N}_{\mathcal{P}_k}))$ to $\mathcal{S}$. Upon successful registration, the node receives an acknowledgment with its $\mathcal{N}_{id}$ and $\mathcal{SGX}_{max}$.
2. Initialized by the server, the node jointly executes the $Remote\_Att(\mathcal{S}_{\mathcal{P}_k})$ (Protocol 1.1) with the server to ensures its identity and it is running on an Intel SGX enabled platform without tampering.
3. The node performs the following steps in order to participate into the PoQ protocol:
   (a) Generate a random $\mathcal{SGX}_t$ from $\mathcal{E}$ within a range of $[\mathcal{SGX}_{min}, \mathcal{SGX}_{max}]$.
   (b) Broadcast and request $Verify(\mathcal{SGX}_t)$ to $\mathcal{S}$, hence gets meta-data that states information about the existing nodes in the network.
   (c) Determine tier $\mathcal{T}_i$ it belongs to according to the following:

$$\mathcal{T}_i = \left\lceil \mathcal{T}_r \frac{\mathcal{SGX}_t}{\mathcal{SGX}_{max}} \right\rceil \tag{1}$$

   (d) Calculate the local $\mathcal{Q}_t$ using the following formula:

$$\mathcal{Q}_t = \left\lceil \frac{\sum_{i=1}^{\mathcal{N}_n} \mathcal{RT}}{\mathcal{N}_n^2} \right\rceil \tag{2}$$

   where $\mathcal{N}_n$ is the number of active nodes in the specific $\mathcal{T}_i$.
   (e) Obtain $\mathcal{ST}$ using the information from $\mathcal{SGX}_T$.
4. Once it gets $\mathcal{ST}$, $\mathcal{SGX}_t$ will be reduced for the calculated $\mathcal{Q}_t$. While Remaining Time $\mathcal{RT} \neq 0$, then:
   (a) Generate a new $\mathcal{Q}_t$ and determine the next $\mathcal{ST}$.
   otherwise:
      i. A new block is propagated and the local leadership count is incremented by one.
      ii. Broadcast the winning result to $\mathcal{S}$ and announce new block.
5. To rejoin the network, steps 2 to 4 are repeated.

Protocol 1.3: Individual node side protocol.

equal to the amount of time it can be executed for its first pass. If it remains in the waiting part of the Q and any node joins which belong to its $\mathcal{T}_i$ then it needs to recalculate the $\mathcal{Q}_t$ again based on available data. A new node can also be added at the end of the Q. While a node is executing and a new node joins that belongs to the same $\mathcal{T}_i$ it won't affect the $\mathcal{Q}_t$ of the executing node at that moment. However, if the node is unable to finish the entire $\mathcal{SGX}_t$ during that pass of $\mathcal{Q}_t$, it will be popped up from the Q and added again at the end of it without changing its $\mathcal{T}_i$ but this time it needs to recalculate the $\mathcal{Q}_t$ for its next pass. Then, the node who is in the starting point (starting time, $\mathcal{ST} =$ current time) of the Q will get the chance to reduce its $\mathcal{SGX}_t$. After completion of each node's Q_t, the remaining $\mathcal{SGX}_t$ of the currently executing node is checked. A function "Time Left" keeps track of the *Remaining Time* ($\mathcal{RT}$) over $\mathcal{SGX}_t$ after each pass and once it has zero as its value, it will broadcast the result for claiming the leadership. A participating node is required to finish all its $\mathcal{SGX}_t$ to become the leader and propagates a new block. It is worth mentioning that, the total waiting time of a node is not equal to its $\mathcal{SGX}_t$ (Fig. 5).

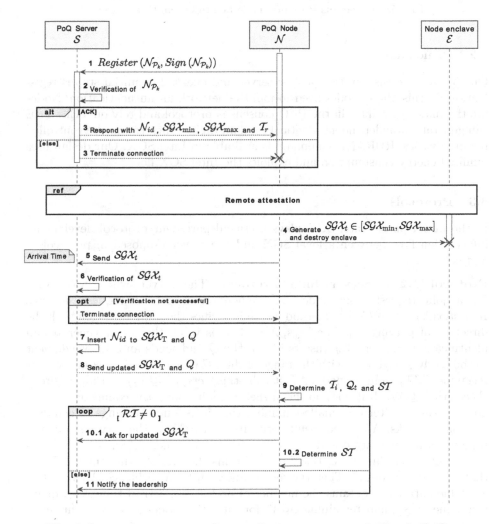

Fig. 4. Interactions corresponding to client-server communication in PoQ.

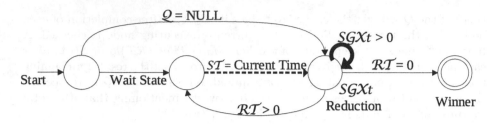

Fig. 5. The various state of a node before becoming a leader.

4.2 Principals

Our protocol consists of two phases: server and client. The initial step is registration. In this phase, nodes need to join the network for authentication. Nodes are the major principals in the PoQ consensus protocol and rely on TEE. TEE can generate an independent identical random digit, which cannot be controlled by an advisory. RDRAND command is available in Intel SGX. Our design uses minimal energy consumption and exploits the Intel SGX floor.

4.3 Protocols

In the initial phase, Intel SGX plays a crucial part. Our protocol develops an information flow between a local SGX and the server proposed in protocols 1 and 2.

Protocol 1.2 - Server Side Protocol. The server will always wait for a join request from nodes, $\mathcal{N}$. Whenever it gets a request, it calls $Register(\mathcal{N}_{\mathcal{P}_k}, Sign(\mathcal{N}_{\mathcal{P}_k}))$ method where it verifies the authentication with the directory of permitted public keys, $\mathcal{N}_{\mathcal{P}_k}$. If it is valid, the server generates an identification number, $\mathcal{N}_{id}$, inserts it into the Q and sends an acknowledgment to the newly joined node with the range of the $\mathcal{SGX}_t$ and $\mathcal{N}_{id}$. Immediately after receiving $\mathcal{SGX}_t$ from an node, $\mathcal{N}'_1$, it calls the $Verify(\mathcal{SGX}_t)$ method where it checks the $\mathcal{SGX}_{t'1}$. If it does not fit in the range, it aborts the connection. Thus, no node can go after the smallest number that is beyond the range to generate too many blocks. After successful verification of $\mathcal{SGX}_{t'1}$, the server stores the time when it's submitted and treats it as its arrival time, $\mathcal{A}_{t'1}$ of $\mathcal{N}'_1$. Then calculates $\mathcal{Q}_{t'1}$ according to its tier $\mathcal{T}_i$ and obtains the first starting time, $\mathcal{ST}'_1$, of that particular node $\mathcal{N}'_1$. Then the server builds an SGX Table, $\mathcal{SGX}_T$ based on available data that contains the number of nodes, $\mathcal{N}_n$, arrival time $\mathcal{N}_{\mathcal{A}_t}$, quantum time, $\mathcal{N}_{\mathcal{Q}_T}$, and remaining $\mathcal{SGX}_t$ for all active nodes $\mathcal{N}_{\mathcal{RT}}$ with numbers of tiers.

The server sends this meta-data to all active nodes. Thus, all $\mathcal{N}_{id}$ have access to a similar database concurrently that server has, and almost every data will replicate to all $\mathcal{N}$ which accelerates the speed of the network. The server always monitors the scheme of finding a new leader. When a new leadership has been claimed, a node $\mathcal{N}'_1$, is supposed to announce that it has completed its $\mathcal{SGX}_{t'1}$, so that it is considered as a leader and get appended to the blockchain and dequeued from the Q. If that particular node wants to rejoin in the network its $\mathcal{N}_{id}$ will remain the same with different credentials. Whenever a new node, $\mathcal{N}_2'$, join or a node $\mathcal{N}_1'$ leaves, the server continuously updates the Q based on all available data. However, the server can compute Average Elapsed Time, $\mathcal{AET}$ and Average Waiting Time, $\mathcal{AWT}$ by the following formulas:

$$\mathcal{AET} = \frac{1}{N} \sum_{i=1}^{N} \mathcal{ET}_i \tag{3}$$

$$\mathcal{AWT} = \frac{1}{N} \sum_{i=1}^{N} \mathcal{WT}_i \tag{4}$$

Definition 4.1. *Waiting Time.* The inactive time of a $\mathcal{N}_i$ after consider its $\mathcal{A}_{ti}$. Simply, the amount of idle time $\mathcal{WT}_i$ spent by a $\mathcal{N}_i$ in the Q before the last pass to finishes its $\mathcal{SGX}_{ti}$ for a single round can be calculated by Eq. (6); where $\mathcal{A}_{ti}$ refers to $\mathcal{A}_t$ of $\mathcal{N}_i$ and $\mathcal{SGX}_{ti}$ refers to the time generated from $\mathcal{E}$ of $\mathcal{N}_i$. $\mathcal{AWT}$ is the average value of wait time of N nodes and can be calculated by Eq. (4).

Definition 4.2. *Elapsed Time.* The entire time requires a $\mathcal{N}_i$ to become a leader. That means the time elapsed between $\mathcal{A}_{ti}$ of a $\mathcal{N}_i$ and its termination. Elapsed time for a $\mathcal{N}_i$ can be calculated by Eq. (5); where $\mathcal{WT}_i$ refers to $\mathcal{WT}$ of $\mathcal{N}_i$ and $\mathcal{SGX}_{ti}$ refers to the time generated from $\mathcal{E}$ of that $\mathcal{N}_i$. The average elapsed time of N nodes $\mathcal{AET}$ can be calculated by using Eq. (3).

Protocol 1.3 - Individual Node Side Protocol. At first, a participant node needs to register for joining the network. After joining, a local SGX acts as a client node that requires to download the PoQ code and execute it. When a local SGX connects to the server, it gets $\mathcal{N}_{id}$ and the range to generate a random $\mathcal{SGX}_t$ (which is subject to change subsequently after each round) from the trusted code inside $\mathcal{E}$ and needs to submit it to the server for verification, which is done on the same platform. If there is more than one node ($\mathcal{N}_2'$, $\mathcal{N}_{21}''$)

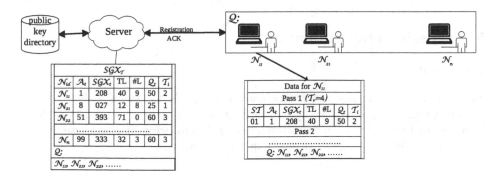

Fig. 6. Top level architectural diagram of the system.

who produces $\mathcal{SGX}_t$ at the same time then they will be added into the Q as ascending order of $\mathcal{N}_{id}$. If Q is null then $\mathcal{N}_{id}$ is added at the front of Q. If Q is not null but the $\mathcal{RT}$ of the current executing node is zero then $\mathcal{N}_{id}$ is added in *FIFO* manner, otherwise, $\mathcal{N}_{id}$ will insert into the Q after the $\mathcal{N}_{id}$ of the executing node. Later, the node gets the $\mathcal{SGX}_T$ from the server that consists of its $\mathcal{Q}_t$, $\mathcal{ST}$ and $\mathcal{A}_t$ along with some meta-data ($\mathcal{N}_n$, $\mathcal{N}_{\mathcal{A}_t}$, $\mathcal{N}_{\mathcal{Q}_T}$, $\mathcal{T}_r$, $\mathcal{N}_{\mathcal{RT}}$). If we consider there are only three nodes ($\mathcal{N}_2'$, $\mathcal{N}_{21}''$, $\mathcal{N}_3'$) in the network where $\mathcal{N}_2'$, $\mathcal{N}_{21}''$ has same $\mathcal{A}_t$ and $\mathcal{N}_3'$ join after two units of time, then the start time of $\mathcal{N}_2'$ which is $\mathcal{ST}'(\mathcal{N}_2')$ immediately when it arrives and $\mathcal{ST}''(\mathcal{N}_{21}'')$ is after the amount of quantum time of $\mathcal{N}_2'$. The $\mathcal{ST}'(\mathcal{N}_3')$ is the addition of all the nodes $\mathcal{Q}_t$ left to execute, who are in front of it in the Q at the moment it arrives. Based on all available information, a particular node, $\mathcal{N}'$, can also calculate which $\mathcal{T}_i$ it belongs to, $\mathcal{Q}_t'$ of that specific $\mathcal{T}_i$ and $\mathcal{ST}'$. For a specific tier whoever comes first will start first. When a new $\mathcal{N}$ is added to a particular $\mathcal{T}_i$, the $\mathcal{Q}_t'$ of that $\mathcal{T}_i$ is recalculated according to the available updated information based on $\mathcal{RT}$ of all nodes in that $\mathcal{T}_i$. When $\mathcal{ST}$ is equivalent to the current time, nodes will execute to reduce its $\mathcal{RT}$. When a node joins, the amount of its $\mathcal{RT}$ is equivalent to its $\mathcal{SGX}_t$.

After a single pass, if a particular node, $\mathcal{N}_1'$, is not able to finish its $\mathcal{SGX}_{t1}'$ as a whole, $\mathcal{RT}_1'$ will be updated by deducting the time spent on that pass and it will put itself at the end of the updated queue, then calculates its next $\mathcal{ST}_1''$ and needs to wait for another pass. If there is no $\mathcal{N}$ in the overall Q than the current node may carry on. It is mentioned that, at any stage, for a particular $\mathcal{N}_1'$, if $\mathcal{SGX}_{t1}'$ or $\mathcal{RT}_n'$ is less than the $\mathcal{Q}_{t\mathcal{T}_i}'$ then the $\mathcal{Q}_{t1}'$ will be updated and assigned to the equal portion of that specific $\mathcal{RT}_n'$. If any node finishes its $\mathcal{SGX}_t$, then it will be withdrawn from the Q and becomes the leader and the number of leadership is assigned to it will be increased by one. Thus, a new block is propagated. Figure 6 elucidates the top-level architecture of PoQ and Fig. 4 shows the inter-process communication between the nodes and server. However, the node can compute its Elapsed Time and Wait Time by the following formulas:

$$\mathcal{ET}_i = \mathcal{SGX}_{ti} + \mathcal{WT}_i \tag{5}$$

$$\mathcal{WT}_i = \text{EndTime}_i - (\mathcal{SGX}_{ti} + \mathcal{A}_{ti}) \tag{6}$$

5   Experimental Evaluation

5.1   Goals

The design of a good consensus protocol must satisfy the following goals: (i) backing up a large-scale network (ii) obtain a higher throughput, and (iii) achieve fairness. To better motivate and illustrate our design, we performs these experiments to achieve those goals throughout the experiments.

5.2 Setup

We built a prototype of PoQ (in C++) to evaluate its performance. All practical experiments performed below were done using a system equipped with SGX PSW 2.X of version 2.5.100.2 and SGX SDK 2.X of version 2.5.100.2 which acts as a in-house client-server network. The system has Windows 10 OS with the latest updates, Intel® Core™ i7-7567U processor (3.5 GHz to 4.0 GHz Turbo, Dual Core 4 MB cache, 28W TDP), 32 GB RAM, 64 Mb Flash EEPROM, and 34.1 GB/s Max Memory Bandwidth[4]. We assume that every full node is a potential validators.

5.3 Throughput

The purpose of this experiment is to measure and compare the throughput of PoQ and PoET. We ran multiple experiments with different parameters. We measure the number of leaderships per second for ten different nodes and three $\mathcal{SGX}_t$ ranges: [1,100], [1,500], and [1,1000]. In the baseline case, we assume that all nodes arrive approximately at the same time: within the first two (Fig. 7.a), ten (Fig. 7.c), and twenty (Fig. 7.e) seconds. Then, we allow those ten nodes to join randomly at different times within a certain range of $\mathcal{A}_t$ with the same $\mathcal{T}_r$ which is 5. We ran each test 50 times where $\mathcal{SGX}_t$ and $\mathcal{A}_t$ were generated randomly. The time duration for each run for Fig. 7.a and b were 90 s ($\mathcal{A}_t \in$ [0,300] s), 450 s ($\mathcal{A}_t \in$ [0,1500] s) for Fig. 7.c and d, and 900 s ($\mathcal{A}_t \in$ [0,3000] s) for Fig. 7.e and f. In Fig. 7, the graph with different arrival times deals with the average result of tests where 20% of nodes leave the network randomly at any time after becoming a leader at least once. Note that the protocol was slightly modified when performed 20% nodes left. For baseline case, experiments were run with the same settings as discussed above and the final result is averaged where node does not leave the network. For comparison, we implement PoET and run the same experiments with the same attributes to evaluate the performance with respect to PoQ.

By comparing PoQ with PoET in Fig. 7, we observe that the throughput of PoQ is higher in both cases: all nodes join approximately at the same time (baseline case), and when they join at different times. The difference between the two protocols' throughput could be as low as 0.3 (Fig. 7.2) and as high as 3.5 (Fig. 7.d).

---

[4] Max Memory Bandwidth is the maximum rate at which data can be read from or stored into a semiconductor memory by the processor (in GB/s).

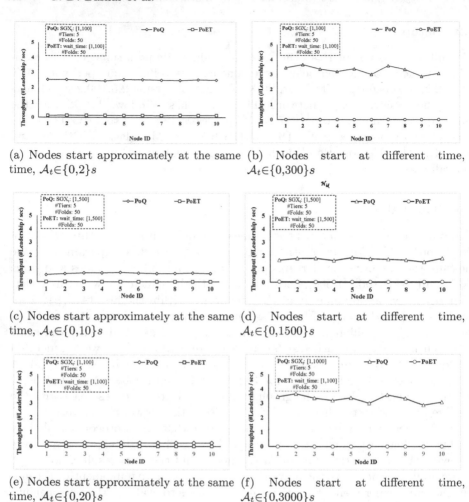

(a) Nodes start approximately at the same time, $\mathcal{A}_t \in \{0,2\}s$

(b) Nodes start at different time, $\mathcal{A}_t \in \{0,300\}s$

(c) Nodes start approximately at the same time, $\mathcal{A}_t \in \{0,10\}s$

(d) Nodes start at different time, $\mathcal{A}_t \in \{0,1500\}s$

(e) Nodes start approximately at the same time, $\mathcal{A}_t \in \{0,20\}s$

(f) Nodes start at different time, $\mathcal{A}_t \in \{0,3000\}s$

Fig. 7. Throughput evaluation results among ten nodes for PoQ and PoET. Each data point in our plots is averaged over 50 independents measurements.

5.4   Scalability

In this section, we evaluate the scalability of our protocol. We start with a network of 2000 nodes then double the network size 5 times, raising to 10,000 nodes in the last setting. In Fig. 8 we keep the same parameters involved in Fig. 7.a but with a larger number of nodes. We ran the experiment only once until all the nodes become exactly one leader. It should be noted that epoch time is longer (e.g., 100 s in 2000 nodes to 504 s in 10,000 nodes) since it requires relatively more times when the total number of nodes increases.

By observing the graph we conclude that $\mathcal{AWT}$, $\mathcal{AET}$ for different sizes of network increase linearly as the network size grows. We also measured RA which takes roughly 2 ms and we did not consider it in result data.

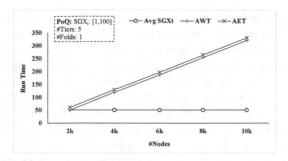

Fig. 8. Overview of bridging between $\mathcal{AWT}$ and $\mathcal{AET}$ in PoQ in response to scalability (up to ten thousands of nodes).

5.5   Fairness

A consensus protocol is fair if a miner/validator with p share of the overall resource ratio can produce a block with a probability p. In this section, we trying to measure the relation between the number of SGX machines a node has and the number of leadership it can reach. We conducted this experiment with the same parameter elaborated in Fig. 7.a. We ran the experiment 50 times and the Fig. 9 reported below are averaged over fifty independent runs. The graph shows the cumulative average leadership of a validator who has a certain number of SGX per node. The X-axis indicates the total number of SGX a node has and the Y-axis shows the average leadership.

After running our experiments, described above, we observe that the probability of being chosen to be a leader scaled linearly, in relation to the number of SGX machines per node.

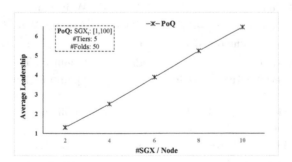

Fig. 9. A linear growth in experimentation over nodes.

6   Conclusions

In this paper, we proposed Proof of Queue (PoQ), a leader based consensus protocol for private (permissioned) blockchains that utilizes Intel SGX to ensure all nodes in the system honestly run trusted code to become a leader. PoQ maintains queues for different tiers, keeps tracks of the quantum times executed by all nodes, and updates the state changes to all nodes. PoQ is specifically designed to avoid the collision in leader election than existing PoET protocol. Also, our protocol is suitable for a large number of nodes with an enormous wait time. The design of PoQ shows that it maintains approximately similar wait times and elapsed times for all the nodes. Finally, based on the simulation and large-scale evaluation of PoQ, we showed that no nodes are left behind. We evaluate PoQ against three metrics; throughput, scalability, and fairness. The results show that PoQ can offer enhanced scalability. Besides, PoQ scales fairness linearly with SGX machines. As future work, we plan to modify the node-side protocol by adjusting the quantum time depending on the time left of executing nodes to optimize the overall fairness of the protocol.

A   Appendix

Abbreviations
The following abbreviations are used in this manuscript (Table 3):

Table 3. Summary of notation used throughout this paper

Symbol	Description	Symbol	Description
Q	Queue	EndTime	End Time
$\mathcal{N}$	SGX Node	$\mathcal{ST}$	Starting Time
$\mathcal{E}$	SGX Node enclave	$\mathcal{RT}$	Remaining Time
$\mathcal{S}$	SGX Server	$\mathcal{AET}$	Average Elapsed Time
$\mathcal{SGX}_t$	SGX time	$\mathcal{WT}$	Wait Time
$\mathcal{SGX}_{min}$	Minimum value of $\mathcal{SGX}_t$	$\mathcal{AWT}$	Average Wait Time
$\mathcal{SGX}_{max}$	Maximum value of $\mathcal{SGX}_t$	σ	Standard deviation
$\mathcal{SGX}_T$	SGX Table	$\mathcal{Q}_t$	Quantum Time
$\mathcal{N}_n$	Number of active nodes in a specific tier	$\mathcal{Q}_T$	Quantum Time of all nodes
$\mathcal{N}_{id}$	Node id generated by the SGX Server	$\mathcal{P}_k$	Public key
$\mathcal{T}_i$	Tier id for i-th node	$\mathcal{S}_k$	Private key
$\mathcal{T}_r$	Total number of tiers available. This value is defined by the SGX Server and is uniformly distributed	$\mathcal{N}_{\mathcal{P}_k}$	Node public key
$\mathcal{A}_t{}^{(i)}$	Arrival Time of i-th node	$\mathcal{N}_{\mathcal{S}_k}$	Node private (secret) key
$\mathcal{A}_t$	Arrival Times from all nodes		
$\mathcal{ET}$	Elapsed Time		

References

1. Ahmed, M., Kostiainen, K.: Identity aging: efficient blockchain consensus (2018)
2. Andreina, S., Bohli, J.M., Karame, G.O., Li, W., Marson, G.A.: PoTS - a secure proof of TEE-stake for permissionless blockchains. IACR Cryptology ePrint Archive **2018**, 1135 (2018)
3. Androulaki, E., et al.: Hyperledger fabric: a distributed operating system for permissioned blockchains. In: Proceedings of the Thirteenth EuroSys Conference, pp. 1–15 (2018)
4. Bano, S., et al.: SoK: consensus in the age of blockchains. In: Proceedings of the 1st ACM Conference on Advances in Financial Technologies, pp. 183–198 (2019)
5. Bashar, G.D., Hill, G., Singha, S., Marella, P.B., Dagher, G.G., Xiao, J.: Contextualizing consensus protocols in blockchain: a short survey. In: 2019 First IEEE International Conference on Trust, Privacy and Security in Intelligent Systems and Applications (TPS-ISA), pp. 190–195 (2019)
6. Bentov, I., Lee, C., Mizrahi, A., Rosenfeld, M.: Proof of activity: extending bitcoin's proof of work via proof of stake [extended abstract] y. ACM SIGMETRICS Perform. Eval. Rev. **42**(3), 34–37 (2014)
7. Buterin, V., et al.: Ethereum: a next-generation smart contract and decentralized application platform, p. 7 (2014)
8. Chen, L., Xu, L., Shah, N., Gao, Z., Lu, Y., Shi, W.: On security analysis of proof-of-elapsed-time (PoET). In: Spirakis, P., Tsigas, P. (eds.) SSS 2017. LNCS, vol. 10616, pp. 282–297. Springer, Cham (2017). https://doi.org/10.1007/978-3-319-69084-1_19
9. Chen, X., Zhao, S.: Scalable, efficient, and consistent consensus for blockchains (2018)
10. Costan, V., Devadas, S.: Intel SGX explained. IACR Cryptology ePrint Archive **2016**(086), 1–118 (2016)
11. Dang, H., Dinh, A., Chang, E.C., Ooi, B.C.: Chain of trust: can trusted hardware help scaling blockchains? arXiv preprint arXiv:1804.00399 (2018)
12. Dang, H., Dinh, T.T.A., Loghin, D., Chang, E.C., Lin, Q., Ooi, B.C.: Towards scaling blockchain systems via sharding. In: Proceedings of the 2019 International Conference on Management of Data, SIGMOD 2019, pp. 123–140. ACM, New York (2019)
13. Dhillon, V., Metcalf, D., Hooper, M.: The hyperledger project. In: Blockchain Enabled Applications, pp. 139–149. Springer, Berkeley (2017). https://doi.org/10.1007/978-1-4842-3081-7_10
14. Dib, O., Brousmiche, K.L., Durand, A., Thea, E., Hamida, E.B.: Consortium blockchains: overview, applications and challenges. Int. J. Adv. Telecommun. **11**(1&2) (2018)
15. Dziembowski, S., Faust, S., Kolmogorov, V., Pietrzak, K.: Proofs of space. In: Gennaro, R., Robshaw, M. (eds.) CRYPTO 2015. LNCS, vol. 9216, pp. 585–605. Springer, Heidelberg (2015). https://doi.org/10.1007/978-3-662-48000-7_29
16. Johnson, S., Scarlata, V., Rozas, C., Brickell, E., Mckeen, F.: Intel® software guard extensions: EPID provisioning and attestation services. White Paper **1**, 1–10 (2016)
17. Kiayias, A., Russell, A., David, B., Oliynykov, R.: Ouroboros: a provably secure proof-of-stake blockchain protocol. In: Katz, J., Shacham, H. (eds.) CRYPTO 2017. LNCS, vol. 10401, pp. 357–388. Springer, Cham (2017). https://doi.org/10.1007/978-3-319-63688-7_12

18. Milutinovic, M., He, W., Wu, H., Kanwal, M.: Proof of luck: an efficient blockchain consensus protocol. In: Proceedings of the 1st Workshop on System Software for Trusted Execution, SysTEX 2016. ACM (2016)
19. Nakamoto, S.: Bitcoin: a peer-to-peer electronic cash system (2008)
20. Schwartz, D., Youngs, N., Britto, A., et al.: The ripple protocol consensus algorithm. White Paper 5(8), Ripple Labs Inc. (2014)
21. Wahab, A., Mehmood, W.: Survey of consensus protocols (2018)
22. Xiao, Y., Zhang, N., Lou, W., Hou, Y.T.: A survey of distributed consensus protocols for blockchain networks (2019)
23. Zhang, F., Eyal, I., Escriva, R., Juels, A., Renesse, R.V.: REM: resource-efficient mining for blockchains. In: 26th USENIX Security Symposium (USENIX Security 2017). USENIX Association, Vancouver (2017)

Share Withholding in Blockchain Mining

Sang-Yoon Chang$^{(\boxtimes)}$

University of Colorado Colorado Springs, Colorado Springs, CO, USA
`schang2@uccs.edu`

Abstract. Cryptocurrency achieves distributed consensus using proof of work or PoW. Prior research in blockchain security identified financially incentivized attacks based on withholding blocks which have the attacker compromise a victim pool and pose as a PoW contributor by submitting the shares (earning credit for mining) but withholding the blocks (no actual contributions to the pool). We advance such threats to generate greater reward advantage to the attackers while undermining the other miners and introduce the share withholding attack (SWH). SWH withholds shares to increase the attacker's reward payout within the pool, in contrast to the prior threats withholding blocks focusing on the inter-pool dynamics. SWH rather builds on the block-withholding threats in order to exploit the information about the impending block submission timing, challenging the popularly established assumption that the block submission time is completely random and unknown to miners. We analyze SWH's incentive compatibility and the vulnerability scope by identifying the critical systems and environmental parameters which determine the attack's impact. Our results show that SWH yields unfair reward advantage at the expense of the protocol-complying victim miners and that a rational miner will selfishly launch SWH to maximize its reward profit. We inform the blockchain and cryptocurrency research of the SWH threat to facilitate further research and development to secure the blockchain consensus protocol.

Keywords: Cryptocurrency · Blockchain · Rational mining · Block withholding

1 Introduction

Blockchain builds a distributed ledger and has emerged as the enabling technology for cryptocurrencies, which generate and process the financial transactions without relying on a centralized authority such as a bank, e.g., Bitcoin [23] and Ethereum [5,26]. Cryptocurrencies operate in a permissionless environment lacking the pre-established trust in identities, and the underlying distributed consensus protocols based on proof of work (PoW) enable the nodes to agree on the ledger transactions by making the consensus fair with respect to the computational power (as opposed to the number of identities/votes); the probability of

N. Park et al. (Eds.): SecureComm 2020, LNICST 336, pp. 161–187, 2020.
https://doi.org/10.1007/978-3-030-63095-9_9

finding a block and winning the corresponding reward is designed to be proportional to the computational power/hash rate by the PoW consensus protocol. Such PoW-based distributed consensus protocol is the most popular consensus protocol in the real-world blockchain implementations. The miners participate in the PoW consensus to generate new currency and process the transactions and are financially incentivized to do so by the block rewards, which are winnings from solving the probabilistic PoW computational puzzles. To lower the variance of such reward income, the miners join and operate as mining pools to share the computational power and the corresponding reward winnings. Within a mining pool, to better estimate the individual miner members' contributions, mining pools use *shares* which correspond to solving the same PoW computations as the blocks but with easier difficulty, providing greater number of samples for the contribution estimation. If a block is found within the mining pool, instead of the miner finding the block getting the entire reward, the reward gets distributed across the shares so that the miners have lower variance in their reward earnings.

Despite the consensus protocol indicating that the miner submits a block (a valid PoW solution) once found [23], recent research in blockchain security identified practical and relevant attacks which have the attacker withhold and control the timing of the block submission (including permanently withholding and discarding the block, as is in the classical block-withholding attack or BWH) for unfair reward advantage over the protocol-complying strategy of immediately submitting the found block. In such block-withholding threats, the attacker compromises a victim mining pool and undermines the pool winnings by posing as a PoW contributor without honestly contributing; while the reward winnings are shared in the victim pool, the attacker additionally has a separate reward channel in its main pool/solo mining, in which it does not need to share the reward with others. These attacks are in the forms of block-withholding attack (BWH), fork-after-withholding (FAW), and uncle-block attack (UBA). FAW builds on selfish mining and BWH to advance and generalize BWH, and UBA further advances FAW by exploiting uncle blocks and making use of all the withheld blocks. These threats are discussed in greater details in Sect. 3.

In this paper, we advance the withholding-based attacks and introduce the *share-withholding* (SWH) attack. SWH withholds and delays the submission of the shares (as opposed to just the blocks) to increase the reward payout within the victim mining pool. In SWH, the misbehaving attacker exploits that it can gain some/probabilistic information about the impending block submission timing, which challenges the previous belief that block arrival timing is completely random to the miners thanks to the block arrival being a Poisson process [23]. Because knowing the block submission timing is critical for incentivizing SWH (as we show in Sect. 7.2), SWH builds on the aforementioned block-withholding threats, in which the attacker withholding and controlling the timing of the block submission opens opportunities for SWH gain. SWH further amplifies the reward gain beyond the state of the art block-withholding threats (where FAW and UBA already outperform protocol compliance and forgo the miner's dilemma) by increasing the attacker reward at the expense of the other miners within the victim pool. The additional reward gain is from the payout/contribution-estimation manipulation within the victim pool (which is different from the source of the reward gain for BWH/FAW/UBA as the block-withholding threats increase the reward of the main pool) as discussed in Sect. 5.

Our analyses show significant gains and incentives for launching SWH even though our reward/payout analyses is conservative in measuring the attacker's performances. For example, we use lower bounds and quantify the performances when the attacker loses the forking race and its fork-after-withheld block (which distinguishes FAW from BWH) does not become the main chain. SWH remains effective even when the probability of the attacker's withheld block becoming main chain is zero (and the FAW attack reduces to the suboptimal BWH). Furthermore, when uncle rewards are implemented (as in Ethereum [5,26]), SWH further exploits the shares for even greater reward advantage than UBA or FAW.

Our work is generally applicable to all mining-based blockchains and to all rational miners. We use formal modeling and analyses to identify the blockchain components which yield the SWH vulnerability, define the attack scope, and determine its impact and the impact dependency on the parameters. Our model is driven by the real-world blockchain system designs and implementations and is applicable to all PoW-consensus-driven blockchains. Throughout the paper, we construct the model and introduce additional complexities/parameters as they are used; the following sections often build on the previous sections and analyses. Furthermore, in addition to sabotaging and undermining the other protocol-complying miners, our threat model supports a rational miner driven by its self profit since we analyze the incentive compatibility. A mining strategy is *incentive compatible* if its expected reward is greater than other known mining strategies, including protocol compliance, and the miners driven by self profit would be incentivized to launch SWH as long as they are uncooperative and willing to diverge from the given protocol. Therefore, our threat model is stronger and more applicable than assuming only malicious and irrational miner which focuses only on disrupting the performances of the other victim miners.

2   Background in Blockchain and Mining

The PoW consensus protocol participation is incentivized by financial rewards for generating a valid PoW which becomes the new block in the ledger. The protocol participation is called *mining* and the participants *miners* because the reward for finding the block include new currencies. Only the miner which solves the PoW puzzle and finds the block the earliest[1] wins the corresponding reward in that round (where each round increases the blockchain's block height by one), since the rest of the miners accept the newly found block and start a new round

---

[1] To determine which block was found the earliest can be a challenge in a distributed environment. To provide greater details about such resolution, we describe forking and how that can be resolved later in this section, and we describe uncle blocks/rewards adopted by Ethereum and newer cryptocurrencies which provide rewards to more than one miner in Sect. 3.

of mining by updating the chain with the found block. The PoW consensus protocol is designed to be computationally fair, distributing the reward winning proportionally to the computational power of the miners in expectation. For example, assuming the protocol compliance of the miners, hundred miners, each of which has an equal hash rate of x H/s, collectively earns the same reward amount as one miner with a hash rate of $100x$ H/s in expectation.

Because a miner is competing with a global-scale group of other miners and the mining difficulty gets adjusted accordingly, solving a block is sporadic and of high variance. To lower the variance and to get a more stable stream of reward income, miners form a pool to combine their computational power and share the corresponding mining rewards. The increased computational power by pooling them together increases the occurrence of winning a block and the corresponding reward gets split across the pool miners according to their computational contributions (which reward split within the pool is called *payout*). To estimate each miner's contributions, the mining pool samples more PoW solutions by using *shares*, which correspond to solving the same computational puzzle with the same block header as the block but with easier difficulty. The PoW solution corresponding to a share fixes fewer number of bit 0's in the most significant bits of the hash output and therefore has a weaker constraint and a greater occurrence/probability than the PoW solution corresponding to a block. In other words, if the block corresponds to finding a preimage/input x which satisfies $H(x) < \tau_{block}$ where τ_{block} is the target threshold of the PoW puzzle, then the share corresponds to finding x satisfying $H(x) < \tau_{share}$, where $\tau_{share} > \tau_{block}$, and thus a block solution is/implies a share but a share is not necessarily a block. To manage the mining pool, the *pool manager* keeps track of the share count, registers/broadcasts the block upon its discovery, and distributes the reward-payout to the pool members according to their share submissions. While optional, joining the mining pool to get a more stable, low-variance reward income is popular; for example, in Bitcoin, more than 89% of the mining computation came from known mining pools [4], which figure is a conservative lower bound because there are unidentified mining pools.

Due to the imperfect/asynchronous networking to submit and broadcast the blocks, *forking* occurs when two block solution propagations result in a collision (i.e., some nodes receive one block earlier than the other while the other nodes receive the other block first), creating a disagreement/partition between the miners on which block was mined first and which to use for its impending round of mining. Forking gets resolved by having the miners choose the longest chain (where the length of the chain can be measured by the number of blocks or the total difficulty), e.g., if one partition finds a second block and propagates that to the other partition, then the miners in the other partition accept that chain which is one block longer than the one that they have been using.

3   Related Work in Blockchain Mining Security

Following the consensus protocol of timely block submissions has been believed to be incentive compatible, as the block submission monotonically increases the reward at the time of the submission. However, given the same computational power, more sophisticated attacks emerged to further increase the mining reward by operating against the protocol and controlling/delaying the timing of block submission, including permanently withholding the submission in certain situations. *Selfish mining* withholds a block so that the miner can get a heads-start on computing the next block and have the rest of the miners discard and switch from the blocks that they were mining [12,16]. However, the confirmation mechanism, introduced by Bitcoin and inherited by most blockchain implementations, resists selfish mining by waiting until multiple blocks are further mined after a block is found, decreasing the probability of successful selfish mining exponentially with the number of blocks needed for confirmation [23].

Against mining pools, there are even more advanced threats. The *block-withholding (BWH) attack* withholds the mined block in the victim pools in order to increase the attacker's overall reward (and specifically that of the main pool) at the expense of the rest of the victim pool members [24]. In BWH, to sabotage the victim mining pool, the attacker simply never submits the found block while submitting the shares. As a consequence, the attacker still reaps the benefits from submitting the shares to the victim pool (pretending to contribute and getting the credit for it) while never actually contributing to the pool (since it never submits the actual block solution which will benefit the victim pool).

Fork-after-withholding (FAW) attack [19] builds on selfish mining and BWH but creates intentional forks in cases when there is a block being broadcasted by a third-party pool (with which the attacker has no association). In other words, while always submitting the shares to gain greater payout on the victim pool, the attacker withholds the found block and either discards it (if the attacker's main pool finds another block or if another miner from the victim pool finds a block) or submits it only when there is another competing block that is being propagated by another third-party pool (creating an intentional fork). Unlike BWH yielding no reward if the third-party pool submits a block, FAW causes a fork to yield a statistically positive reward (i.e., the attacker wins the forking race sometimes) when the third-party finds and submits a block. FAW is significant because it forgoes the miner's dilemma (motivating the pools to cooperate with each other) [11], and there is a real incentive (unfair reward gain) to launch FAW for rational miners.

Uncle-block attack (UBA) [9] exploits the uncle blocks which provide partial rewards for the blocks which got mined but did not become the main chain, e.g., Ethereum to provide greater fairness in the miners' networking conditions. UBA builds on FAW, inheriting the attacker-desirable properties, but advances it to generate greater unfair rewards to the attacker by making use of all the withheld blocks (in contrast to FAW discarding some withheld blocks) and by making it relevant and impactful even when the attacker has suboptimal networking and loses the forking race (in which case, FAW reduces to the suboptimal BWH).

The research and development for defending against such block-withholding threats and aligning the incentives to protocol compliance is ongoing, e.g., [3,6, 8,24]. Rosenfeld [24] (which introduced the aforementioned BWH attack) also introduces payout algorithms to build resistance against pool-hopping attacks, in which the attackers dynamically hop between pools for increased reward. His seminal work and the analyses of the payout schemes are widely adopted in the modern-day mining pool practices. Unfortunately, we later see in Sect. 7.2 that one of Rosenfeld's main inventions for defeating pool hopping (decaying payout, as we call it) yields a critical vulnerability for our novel threat of SWH.

4   Threat Model

We define *honest miners* to be cooperative and follow the consensus protocol and the mining pool protocol, including the timely block and share submissions. The other non-honest miners can launch other mining strategies (e.g., those described in Sect. 3 or SWH) and are rational (choose the strategy achieving greater reward). More specifically, the non-honest miners intelligently control the timing of the PoW solution submissions (blocks or shares). If the non-honest and rational miners violate the consensus protocol, we call them *attackers* as they operate at the expense of the other honest miners.

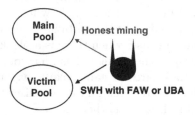

Fig. 1. The SWH setup is the same as BWH, FAW, or UBA and includes compromising the victim pool. The attacker splits its computational power between mining honestly in the main pool and infiltrating the victim pool to launch the mining threats. However, while FAW or UBA increase the reward for the main pool from such infiltration at the expense of the victim pool as a whole, SWH increases the attacker's reward split within the victim pool.

4.1   The Same Setup for SWH as BWH

We investigate the attacks launched by the miners. We assume the threat model of BWH (the same as FAW and UBA), in which the attacker compromises multiple pools and separates the main pool vs. the victim pool, as depicted in Fig. 1. The attacker behaves honestly in the *main pool* while it can launch an attack by diverging from the protocol in the *victim pool*, i.e., the attacker compromises a victim pool by joining the pool with the intention of launching an attack. As a realistic setup and for simplicity, we assume that the main pool is comprised of the attacker only (equivalent to solo mining); the attacker shares the reward winnings in the victim pool while there is no sharing and the attacker takes all the rewards in the main pool. Our model also generalizes to the case of multiple pools/miners (e.g., the main pool or the victim pool can be a collection of mining pools) as long as those comprising the main pool are under the attacker control since the PoW consensus is designed to be power-fair as opposed to identity-fair, as is described in Sect. 2 and captured in our mining-game model in Sect. 6.

The attacker setup is realistic since cryptocurrencies operate in permissionless environments with loose control of identities and is designed for anonymity. For example, in 2014, Eligius became a victim pool of BWH attack and lost 300 BTC [14], which got detected because the attacker only used two accounts for the attack (which resulted in the detection of abnormal behavior where the accounts submitted only shares but no blocks for too long of a time). Combining such attack with Sybil attack (or just simply following Nakamoto's suggestion to use new accounts for new transactions for anonymity [23]) instead of just using two accounts would have made such detection significantly more difficult.

5   Share Withholding Attack

Share withholding attack (SWH) withholds shares in order to manipulate the intra-pool payout (shifting the share-based payout and the reward distribution within the pool), which is in contrast to the prior miner threats withholding blocks in Sect. 3 increasing the probability of winning in the attacker-main pool (at the expense of that of the compromised victim pool). SWH is therefore fundamentally different from the threats withholding blocks and can be launched separately with UBA/FAW/BWH. However, SWH provides reward gain (incentive compatible and relevant to rational miners) if the attacker has some knowledge of the block submission timing as we will see in Sect. 7.2. While there can be other cases to fulfill such condition requirement, we identify the block-withholding-based threats as practical cases where the attacker fulfills the requirement of having knowledge of the block submission time (since the attacker has control over the timing of the withheld blocks). More specifically, when the attacker launches SWH with FAW or UBA, it submits its shares right before its withheld blocks. Therefore, we introduce SWH not only by itself but also in conjunction with the block-withholding-based attacks of UBA/FAW/BWH. When analyzing the impact of SWH in Sects. 8 and 10, we focus more on UBA and FAW because UBA generalizes FAW and FAW generalizes BWH; UBA is more advanced than FAW and FAW more advanced than BWH where, in both cases, the former strategy can be reduced to the latter in certain mining environments (e.g., when uncle reward is zero, UBA gets reduced to FAW).

6   Mining Game

This section builds on and adapts the models in the prior literature analyzing the withholding-based attacks, e.g., [9,19,21]. On the other hand, Sects. 7 and 8 extend the model to introduce a more complex model and a framework to analyze the intra-pool dynamics and SWH. As discussed in Sect. 5, while block withholding increases the main pool reward and focuses on the inter-pool dynamics (this section), SWH manipulates the share-driven reward payouts within the pool (Sects. 7 and 8).

6.1   Mining and Computational Power Model

To investigate the incentive compatibility of the attacks, we model the mining game between the miners and quantify the expected reward. The expected reward depends on the miner's computational power, and we normalize the following variables with respect to the total miner network's computational power, e.g., the entire miner network has a computational power of 1. The attacker's computational power is α (where $0 \leq \alpha \leq 1 - \beta$) while the victim pool's mining power excluding the attacker's power is β (where $0 \leq \beta \leq 1 - \alpha$). The power of the other pools/miners outside of the attacker and the victim pool is therefore $1 - \alpha - \beta$. Building on the attacker setup in Sect. 4.1 and in Fig. 1, the attacker splits its power between its main pool (honest mining) and the victim pool (possibly adopting mining attack strategies to increase the attacker's reward at the expense of the fellow miners in the victim pool), and the fraction of the attacker's power for infiltration of the victim pool is τ (where $0 \leq \tau \leq 1$). Therefore, the attacker's power on the victim pool is $\tau \cdot \alpha$, and the total mining power on the victim pool is $\tau\alpha + \beta$ even though the attacker's power does not fully contribute to the pool earning reward. For example, in the simpler block-withholding attack of BWH, the attacker does not submit block at all in the victim pool so the actual power contributing to block earnings of the pool is only β, while the attacker still earns the reward/credit through share submissions and the reward earning gets split by $\tau\alpha + \beta$.

A miner's expected reward is denoted with R. For example, if an attacker chooses to behave honestly (one of its possible choices), its expected reward (R_{honest}) is proportional to its computational power by the design of the PoW consensus and the mining pools,

$$R_{\text{honest}} = \alpha \tag{1}$$

The following summarizes the variables for analyzing block withholding threats.

α: Attacker's computational power
β: Computational power of the victim pool
τ: Fraction of attacker's power for infiltration of victim
c: Probability that the attacker wins the reward given that there is a fork (collision with another block propagation)

6.2   BWH, FAW, and UBA Analyses

To provide baselines and examples of the use of our model in Sect. 6.1, we analyze the expected reward of BWH and FAW. This section adapts the prior work in the block-withholding-based threats [9,19,21], and we only extract the parts most relevant to our work in this section.

For BWH, the attacker has two possible events for earning a positive reward (in other events, the attacker earns zero reward). The first event is when the attacker finds a block in its honest-mining main pool (A) while the second event corresponds to when another miner from the victim pool, not the attacker, finds a block (B). Because the probability of winning a block is proportional to the computational power spent on mining the block and because $1 - \tau\alpha$ amount of power from all miners actually contributes to finding the block and ending the round (the attacker uses $\tau\alpha$ to only submit shares while withholding the blocks), the probability of A is $\frac{(1-\tau)\alpha}{1-\tau\alpha}$ and the probability of B is $\frac{\beta}{1-\tau\alpha}$. Assuming negligible probability for natural forking, the expected reward for block-withholding attack (R_{BWH}) is:

$$R_{\mathrm{BWH}} = \mathrm{E}[R|A] \cdot \mathrm{Pr}(A) + \mathrm{E}[R|B] \cdot \mathrm{Pr}(B)$$
$$= \frac{(1-\tau)\alpha}{1-\tau\alpha} + \frac{\tau\alpha}{\beta+\tau\alpha} \cdot \frac{\beta}{1-\tau\alpha} \tag{2}$$

The FAW attack builds on the block-withholding attack but provides an extra channel for attacker reward. In addition to the events A and B, the attacker can earn reward by broadcasting the withheld block when a third-party miner outside of the attacker-involved main pool and victim pool finds a block, causing a fork and hence the name fork-after-withholding (FAW). This event of the attacker finding a block *and* a third-party miner finding a block is C. The expected reward for FAW attack (R_{FAW}) is:

$$R_{\mathrm{FAW}} = \frac{(1-\tau)\alpha}{1-\tau\alpha} + \frac{\tau\alpha}{\beta+\tau\alpha} \left(\frac{\beta}{1-\tau\alpha} + c\tau\alpha\frac{1-\alpha-\beta}{1-\tau\alpha} \right) \tag{3}$$

The technical report [7] includes the reward analysis for UBA in Appendix A. We summarize the three events which yield the attacker positive rewards, as we also use them for our analyses of the rewards for the other attacks:

A: Attacker's main pool finds a block
B: Another miner from the victim pool finds a block
C: Third-party miner, not affiliated to attacker, finds a block

7   Mining Pool Game and SWH Scope Analyses

While the mining game model in Sect. 6.1 characterized the miners' activities at the inter-pool level, SWH requires greater details in the modeling of the intra-pool operations at the share/block submission level; the model needs to capture the individual submissions of the blocks/shares and the reward split distribution within the mining pool (which we call *payout*). To support such model, in this section, we introduce the mining pool game and model (Sect. 7.1) and use it to analyze the SWH feasibility and scope (Sect. 7.2). Afterward, we analyze the SWH performance (Sect. 8). Section 8 builds on Sect. 7, focusing on the SWH-vulnerable scope, and provides greater details and increasing complexity in the model and analyses. The variables are introduced as they are used, for example, Sect. 8 focuses on the decaying-payout scheme (which is one of the two types of payout-schemes in Sect. 7.2).

7.1   Mining Pool and Share Model: f and s

In a mining pool, there are n miners, each of which is denoted with $m \in \{1, 2, ..., n\}$. For example, if $n = 1$, then $m \in \{1\}$ and it is solo mining (e.g., the attacker's main pool). We characterize the i-th share submission (s_i) using a pair of random variables: the index of the member who submitted the i-th share m_i and the time of submission t_i (recorded by the mining pool manager). In other words, $s_i = (m_i, t_i)$. The collection of these share submissions over time is denoted with s. In other words, $s = \{s_i\}_i$ is the share history and s grows with the number of share submissions. For example, from the beginning of the round, if the member 4 submitted the first share at time 6 and the member 10 shared the second share at time 9.5, then $s = ((4, 6), (10, 9.5))$ if the second share is the most recent share. The share list s is an implicitly ordered list in the share's time order (i.e., the shares get added at the end as they are found) and continues to grow until the block is found and submitted (the end of the round), after which s resets to $\emptyset$. When a new $i + 1$-th share arrives, s with i submissions/elements gets updated by $s||(m_{i+1}, t_{i+1})$ where $a||b$ denotes the concatenation of a and b. We assume that share rules and validity are enforced so that an invalid share submission (which gets rejected by the mining pool system) is equivalent to no submission.

The *payout* to determine how the pool reward gets split between the pool members (as opposed to the final reward which accounts for the rewards from the other pools as well) depends on the share submissions. To model the payout and generalize it to different payout schemes (how to divide the reward between the share submissions), we introduce the payout function f which divides the reward using the share submissions and produces a vector in which the i-th element corresponds to the payout to the corresponding submitter m_i. In other words, $f : s \to R$, i.e., f uses the share history (s) to generate the reward for each miners (R) where R is either a zero vector if the pool does not win the reward or a vector with non-negative scalar elements with a size of n and $\|R\|_1 = 1$ (the element adds up to one so that each element corresponds to the fraction of the reward winnings). From f, f_j takes the j-th element of R and derives the reward for miner j, i.e., $f_j : s \to R_j$. For example, for Pay-Per-Share (PPS) scheme, f_j counts for the number of shares submitted for each miner member j and, for Proportional payout scheme, f_j counts for the number of shares for each miner j and divides it by the total number of shares.

7.2   SWH Vulnerability Scope

SWH is based on withholding shares and delaying their submissions (in contrast to block-withholding-based attacks which control block submissions). While we study the attack's implementation and impact in Sect. 8, we first investigate if delaying shares can be relevant and incentive-compatible and establish the vulnerability scope in which the share-withholding attack is relevant in this section. We analyze how the payout function f (distributing the pool reward to the members) plays a critical role in determining the system's vulnerability against SWH.

Payout Scheme Definition. The payout function f is designed to increase the reward for a miner when it submits a share. We define f to be *unilaterally increasing* if, given any share history s, the submission of a share monotonically increases (i.e., either increases or remains constant as its input increases) the payout of the submitter of that share. For any miner j, f unilaterally increases with j's share submission if any new share submission by j at time t, corresponding to (j, t) in the share list, monotonically increases j's payout.

Definition 1. f *unilaterally increases the payout with shares if* $f_j(s\|(j,t)) - f_j(s) \geq 0$, $\forall s$, $\forall t$, $\forall j$.

The real-world mining pools implement f so that it unilaterally increases with a share, and any share submission does not harm the subject miner's reward earnings.

f implementation is divided into two classes, which are mutually exclusive and cover all f implementations. The first class of f called fixed payout corresponds to when the payout for each share submission remains the same in time (as long as the share list remains the same) and the other class called decaying payout corresponds to when the share payout gets decayed over time from the time of its submission. We say that the share has a *fixed payout* if the time of the share submission does not affect the share attribution to the payout as long as the share list s remains constant (e.g., a new submission changes the share list s and can further spread the reward between the submissions). Implied in the fixed-payout definition is that the share remains valid and stays within the same round because s remains the same; this is an important clarification for the SWH attack because there is a risk in delaying the share submission and losing its payout value (which occurs if any other miner found a block and the pool moves on to a new block header/round making the attacker's share stale).

Definition 2. f *is a* fixed payout *scheme if* $f_j(s\|(j,t+\Delta t)) - f_j(s\|(j,t)) = 0$, $\forall t$, $\forall \Delta t$, $\forall j, \forall s$.

In real-world f implementations, Proportional, Pay-Per-Share (PPS), Pay-Per-Last-N-Shares (PPLNS) fall within the fixed-payout schemes [24]. In contrast to PPS, the share payout can vary as there are new submissions, e.g., by having the payout depend on the number of shares and the size of s size (which may grow in time), as in the Proportional payout scheme. Even in such cases, the share's payout attribution remains the same as long as the share is submitted within the same round.

On the other hand, other schemes for f has a *decaying payout* [24], i.e., a share's payout value decays in its value in time, and the more recent share submissions have a larger payout than an older share submission.

Definition 3. f *is a* decaying payout *scheme if* $f_j(s\|(j,t+\Delta t)) - f_j(s\|(j,t)) > 0$, $\forall t$, $\forall \Delta t$, $\forall j, \forall s$.

In real-world f implementations, score-based/Slush's payout and Geometric payout fall under decaying-payout schemes.

Fixed Payout Case. We show that the attacker has no incentive to conduct share-withholding attack if f has a fixed payout. In other words, the attacker's choosing $\Delta t > 0$ does not increase its payout.

Theorem 1. *Attacker has no reward gain to delay its share if the payout scheme f unilaterally increases the attacker's payout and has a fixed payout.*

Proof. Suppose the attacker j, for any j, finds a share at time t and it is valid at the time. It is sufficient to show that, given any s and any $\Delta t > 0$, the expected payout is less than that corresponding to $\Delta t = 0$. By definition of f being fixed payout, j's payout for submitting the share at time $t + \Delta t$, $f_j(s||(j, t + \Delta t))$ is either $f_j(s||(j, t + \Delta t)) = f_j(s||(j, t))$ or $f_j(s||(j, t + \Delta t)) = f_j(s)$, the latter of which is smaller than $f_j(s||(j, t))$ because f unilaterally increases with j's share. Since $\mathrm{E}[f_j(s||(j, t))]$ is a linear combination of the payouts corresponding to the two events (which partitions and comprises the entire possibilities - the share either remains valid or becomes invalid, e.g., no longer valid block header because it is a new round) by law of total probability, $\mathrm{E}[f_j(s||(j, t))] \geq \mathrm{E}[f_j(s||(j, t+\Delta t))]$. $\quad\square$

Decaying Payout Case. Suppose the mining pool system uses f such that it unilaterally increases the payout for every miners and has a decaying payout. Given such f, the attacker has an incentive to conduct SWH if the attacker knows the block submission time (the end of the round) ahead of time. The knowledge of the block-submission timing is critical for SWH, as we will see in this section. While there can be other cases where such assumption holds and our analyses still applicable, we identify a concrete case when the attacker does have the block-submission time information in FAW/UBA. In FAW or UBA, an attacker knows the block submission timing and can launch SWH, because an attacker having found and withholding the block has the knowledge of the block submission time. The attacker can further increase its knowledge of the block submission time in advance by combining the withholding with networking-based attacks [2,10,17]. Therefore, we focus on an attacker launching SWH in conjunction with FAW/UBA and analyze the SWH attack impact in such case in Sect. 8.3.

We first analyze the case when the attacker has the *full information* about when the block will get submitted (i.e., the attacker has the correct information about the block submission timing all the time). Then, we build on the full-information case to analyze the case when the attacker has the information sometimes and those cases occur with a non-zero probability (we later introduce c' for such probability when incorporating share-withholding attack with FAW attack in Sect. 8).

Lemma 1. *Given a payout scheme f which unilaterally increases the attacker's payout and has a decaying payout, attacker has a positive reward gain to delay its share if the attacker has full information about when the block will get submitted.*

Proof. Suppose the share is found at time t and the block is found/submitted at t_B, known to the attacker. Let's prove by contradiction. Assume that the attacker choosing $\Delta t = 0$ maximizes the expected payout, which is $\mathrm{E}[f_j(s||(j, t + \Delta t))] = \mathrm{E}[f_j(s||(j,t))]$. Let attacker withhold the share and choose $\Delta t = t_B - t - \epsilon$, $\forall \epsilon > 0$. Then, by definition of f having decaying payout, $f_j(s||(j, t + t_B - t - \epsilon)) = f_j(s||(j, t_B - \epsilon)) > f_j(s||(j,t))$. Therefore, the attacker is incentivized to withhold shares.

Theorem 2. *Given a payout scheme f which unilaterally increases the attacker's payout and has a decaying payout, attacker has a positive reward gain to delay its share if the attacker has the information about when the block will get submitted with a non-zero probability.*

Proof. Lemma 1 states that the attacker is incentivized to launch share-withholding attack if the attacker has the full information of the block submission timing. The attacker can either withhold a share or promptly submit it. If the attacker only withholds shares when it has the knowledge of the block submission timing, then the expected payout of such strategy is a linear combination between the payout when share-withholding attack with perfect knowledge and the payout with no share-withholding, which is greater than the latter (no share-withholding) if there are cases when the attacker has the knowledge with non-zero probability.

7.3   SWH Vulnerable Scope in Real-World Practice

The payout function f is critical in determining whether the mining pool is vulnerable against SWH. More specifically, if f is of decaying payout (as opposed to fixed payout), then the mining pool is vulnerable against SWH. In our investigation, more than 12% of the miner computations in Bitcoin (measured by the computational power) use decaying-payout scheme and are vulnerable against SWH; this is a conservative figure since it only counts the mining pools whose designs are known, and there are many pools which obscure their payout functions. For example, SlushPool (well regarded in cryptocurrency community thanks to its transparency and state of the art security practices) is within the vulnerable against SWH.

8   SWH Payout and Reward

In SWH, the attacker withholds shares for submission until the blocks get submitted in order to increase the payout of the shares. Since the attacker blindly delaying shares risks the shares becoming stale/outdated lowering its payout, we analyze two cases: the case when the attacker has the full information about the block submission timing and the case when the attacker combines share-withholding with block-withholding-based attacks (where the attacker has probabilistic control over the block submission timings). We build on the analyses of the former case for the analyses of the latter case to provide a concrete scenario where the attacker has the information of the block submission timing because it actively controls the submission timing.

SWH is incentivized because the withholding increases the attackers' expected payout. While Sect. 7.2 established the vulnerability scope of SWH (SWH is incentivized when f has a decaying payout and when the attacker knows the block submission timing), we analyze the attack impact in the attacker's payout/reward while assuming that the victim pool adopts decaying payout in this section. We first study SWH payout (within a pool) and then incorporate that to the reward analyses of SWH coupled with FAW and UBA (not only incorporating the payout from the victim pool but also accounting for other reward channels from other pools, e.g., the attacker's main pool).

8.1   Decaying Payout Model

We build on the mining and computational power model in Sect. 6.1 and the mining pool model in Sect. 7.1. This section focuses on the additions to the model to analyze the share-withholding attack. More specifically, it introduces additional parameters to better describe the decaying-payout function f, as opposed to leaving it as an abstract function as in Sect. 7.1.

As described in Sect. 7.2, a payout scheme with a fixed payout is not vulnerable to SWH by a rational, incentive-driven attacker. However, a decaying-payout scheme does incentivize a rational attacker to withhold shares and delay their submissions. A popular implementation of a payout with a decaying payout is in the form of *scores*, which quantify the share values for the payout and have each share experience exponential decay in its payout value. Such scoring-based payout is used in Slush, geometric, and double-geometric payout implementations. In such payout systems, the share's contribution to the payout (the weight for the score) follows the exponential function and decays by de^{-dT} where T is the time elapsed (recorded by the mining pool manager) since the share submission and d is some constant for the decaying factor. In other words, a share which has been submitted at time x will have $e^{-d\Delta x}$ less payout value than the share submitted at time $x + \Delta x$ for any x and any $\Delta x > 0$. Because it decays by exponential, a share's average score is $\frac{1}{d}$. The payout is then distributed proportionally to the shares' contribution to the scores, i.e., the attacker's payout is the sum aggregate of the scores of the shares submitted by the attacker divided by the total sum aggregate of all the shares' scores. The score for any miner j, denoted by S_j, is the sum-aggregate of the scores of the shares submitted by j.

For every block, there are multiple shares by design, and the impact of SWH depends on the number of shares submitted in a round, which number corresponds to $\|s\|$ (where $\|x\|$ is the number of elements of any vector x). We also define γ to be the ratio between the block difficulty and the share difficulty, i.e., $\gamma = \frac{D_{block}}{D_{share}}$ where D_{block} is the measure for difficulty for finding a block and is inversely proportional to the solution threshold τ_{block} (described in Sect. 1) and D_{share} is the share difficulty and inversely proportional to τ_{share}. D_{block} is controlled by the blockchain system, e.g., Bitcoin adjusts D_{block} according to the total computational power so that a block gets mined every ten minutes in expectation, and D_{share} is to increase the contribution-estimation samples to lower the variance, e.g., aggregating more samples converge better to the mean by law of large numbers. $\gamma = \frac{D_{block}}{D_{share}}$ corresponds to the number of shares per blocks, i.e., for every block, a miner finds γ shares on average.

SWH is analyzed within the pool since it unfairly increases the attacker's payout, the attacker's fraction of the victim pool reward. We introduce the *normalized payout* Γ, which is the fraction of f_j with respect to the aggregate-sum of the norm of all the elements of f assuming that the miner j is the attacker. For example, if $\Gamma = 1$, then the attacker earns all the pool reward and no other members within the pool receives the pool reward. To simplify the analyses and focus on the intra-pool perspective, we also introduce an intermediate variable α' which is the attacker's computational power within the victim pool and $\alpha' = \alpha\tau$ (as defined in Sect. 6.1). For example, the victim pool has a computational power of $\alpha' + \beta$ from both the attacker and the other miner members.

To quantify the attacker's reward, we define c' as the attacker's withheld share's payout given that another miner within the victim pool broadcasts a block. In other words, given that the attacker withholds shares and that it detects the block submission from another miner within the victim pool, c' quantifies the fraction of the payout which can be earned from the withheld shares if the attacker submits the shares at the time of the detection. c' is analogous to c from FAW in that it is random and dependent on the attacker's networking topology and environment, e.g., the attacker can increase c' by optimizing routing and forwarding and regularly checking/maintaining the connectivity to the pool manager or, if the attacker is capable of launching a networking-based attack of eclipse attack on the pool manager [17], $c \to 1$ and $c' \to 1$. However, in contrast to c, c' also has a deterministic factor which is the stale share reward given by the mining pools, which can be motivated to do so since the "stale" shares solving the puzzle in the previous round can result in uncle rewards (stale block rewards). c' is lower-bounded by such factor; if the mining pool provides x reward for stale pools where $0 \leq x \leq 1$, then $c' \geq x$. We investigate the impact of c' on SWH and the attacker's reward in Sect. 10.1.

The technical report [7] includes the payout analysis of the honest mining in Appendix B to provide an example case of using our mining-pool model. The following summarizes the additional variables used for the payout/reward analyses.

d: Decaying factor of the share's payout
S_j: Score for the miner j
γ: Ratio of the block difficulty and share difficulty
Γ: Payout to the attacker
α': Attacker's computational power in the victim pool
c': Fraction/probability of payout earned from the withheld shares given that attacker detects another block within the victim pool

8.2   SWH Payout

Suppose the attacker knows when the block will get submitted (t_B). To maximize its reward, the share-withholding attacker submits all the shares right before t_B (at $t_B - \epsilon$ where ϵ is small), so that all shares experience no decay in their payout weight (score) and have the maximum payout weight of one.

While each share's score contribution individually is d times greater than have the attacker behaved honestly and submitted the shares as they were found so that they experienced the decay, the final payout is distributed proportionally to the miner members' scores. Therefore, share-withholding attacker j increases its payout from $\Gamma_{\text{honest}} = \frac{\alpha'}{\beta + \alpha'}$ to $\Gamma_{\text{SWH}} = \mathrm{E}\left[\frac{S_j}{S_j + \sum_{i \neq j} S_i}\right]$ where S_j is from the SWH shares which do not experience decay while S_i are normal shares experiencing decay for the other miners i where $i \neq j$. The share history s and the payout function f determine the attacker's payout, Γ_{SWH}.

Theorem 3. *The expected payout of SWH is:*

$$\Gamma_{SWH} \geq \sum_{y=1}^{\infty} \sum_{x=1}^{y} \binom{y}{x} \frac{x}{x + \frac{y-x}{d}} \cdot \frac{\alpha'^x \beta^{y-x}}{(\alpha' + \beta)^y} \cdot \frac{(\gamma - 1)^{y-1}}{\gamma^y} \tag{4}$$

Proof. The proof is in the technical report [7] in Appendix C.

Corollary 1. *The expected payout of SWH is:*

$$\Gamma_{SWH} \approx \frac{\alpha' d}{\alpha' d + \beta} \tag{5}$$

Proof. The proof is in the technical report [7] in Appendix C.

Corollary 1 provides an approximation of the attacker's payout which is simpler than the iteration-based expression in Eq. 4 and is therefore easier to observe its behaviors with respect to its dependent variables. Using Eq. 5, the SWH attack impact in the payout grows with the attacker's power (α'), decreases with the rest of the mining pool's power (β), and increases with the share score's decaying factor (d). We observe these behaviors in our simulations in the technical report [7] in Appendix F.

8.3   Share and Block Withholding: SWH-FAW and SWH-UBA

FAW attack provides a concrete case when the attacker controls the timing of the block submissions (reactive to a third-party miner submitting a block, causing collision) and is therefore an opportune platform for share-withholding attack (SWH). An FAW attacker submits the withheld block only when it discovers that there is a block getting propagated by a third-party pool. In addition, a share-withholding attacker coupled with FAW attack (SWH-FAW) withholds the shares and submits them right before the withheld blocks.

Building on our analyses of FAW and UBA in Sect. 6.2, the expected reward of SWH-FAW attack is the following, given the SWH attack payout Γ_{SWH} (e.g., Eq. 4):

$$R_{\text{SWH-FAW}} = \frac{(1-\tau)\alpha}{1-\tau\alpha} + \Gamma_{\text{SWH}}\left(c'\frac{\beta}{1-\tau\alpha} + c\tau\alpha\frac{1-\alpha-\beta}{1-\tau\alpha}\right) \tag{6}$$

Similarly, the reward of SWH-UBA attack is the following:

$$R_{\text{SWH-UBA}} \geq \frac{(1-\tau)\alpha}{1-\tau\alpha} + \Gamma_{\text{SWH}}\left(\kappa\frac{(\tau\alpha)^2}{\beta+\tau\alpha}\cdot\frac{(1-\tau)\alpha}{1-\tau\alpha} + c'\frac{\beta}{1-\tau\alpha} + \kappa\tau\alpha\frac{1-\alpha-\beta}{1-\tau\alpha}\right)$$

9   The Equilibrium Analysis

So far we assumed that there exist both rational miners and honest miners (protocol complying and no withholding), i.e., not all miners are rational, because implementing rational miner requires the change in strategy and the update in the mining software from the default code, e.g., for Bitcoin or Ethereum. In this section, we analyze the case where all the miners are rational as a miner's goal is to earn financial profit in general. We summarize our analysis in this section and include more details in the technical report [7] in Appendix D. A rational miner equipped with FAW or UBA (the mining strategies described in Sect. 3 except for BWH) yield the Nash equilibrium where the miners attack each other by launching FAW or UBA without Miner's Dilemma. If the rational miner can also join the mining pool with the greatest aggregate computational power (e.g., because it is an open pool), the rational miners congregate to the pool in Nash equilibrium, resulting in mining centralization [19,20]. SWH only reinforces such equilibrium because it further amplifies the reward gain of the attacks beyond protocol compliance.

10   Simulation Analyses

To analyze SWH, our model introduces environmental parameters (α, β), attacker's control parameters (τ), and the blockchain system control parameters ($\kappa, \lambda, \gamma, d$). We focus our analyses from the attacker's perspective (observing the attacker's reward) and thus vary the attacker's parameters (α, τ) while using $\beta = 0.24$, $\gamma = 2^5$, and $d = 2^5$ (the technical report [7] describes how these system parameters are derived from modern cryptocurrency implementations in Appendix E). The technical report [7] presents our simulation results for analyzing the SWH payout within a pool in Appendix F, while Sect. 10.1 studies the SWH reward performances and compare them with the existing schemes in FAW, UBA, and honest mining.

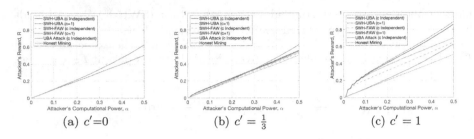

(a) $c'=0$ (b) $c' = \frac{1}{3}$ (c) $c' = 1$

Fig. 2. Reward comparison for SWH combined with block withholding threats (FAW and UBA), UBA only, and honest mining across different c'

10.1   SWH Reward

Because SWH requires the block submission timing information as discussed in Sect. 7.2, we analyze when SWH attack is combined with UBA or FWA. Assuming that the attacker dynamically controls τ, Fig. 2 compares the rewards of the attacks of combining SWH and UBA (SWH-UBA), combining SWH and FAW (SWH-FAW), UBA attack without SWH (UBA), and honest mining with no withholding (honest mining). For the non-SWH strategies, we focus on honest mining and UBA since UBA generalizes and outperforms FAW, which in turn outperforms the original BWH. For SWH-enabled attacks, Fig. 2 shows the worst-case for c (c = 0 which yields the "c independent" reward) and the best-case for c (c = 1) in different curves; any networking environment in between will yield performances between these two extreme reward performances.

We study the attack impact/performances in different environments in c' (which can be influenced by the mining pool implementations and the networking environments, as described in Sect. 8.1). Because it characterizes the general racing condition inside the pool (as opposed to between pools as c does), c' only affects SWH and does not affect the block-withholding based attacks of UBA and FAW. The reward performances behave differently according to the magnitude of c'. When c' is low, the SWH-enabled attacks of SWH-UBA and SWH-FAW force the optimal attacker strategy to become that of either UBA (without SWH) or honest mining (no withholding of blocks and shares), as seen in Fig. 2(a). The SWH-UBA attack becomes better than honest mining when $c' \geq 0.153$ and better than UBA-only attack when $c' \geq 0.201$ when $\alpha = 0.1$; as the attacker's computational capability α increases, the SWH-UBA attack outperforms honest mining and UBA attack with even lower c'. However, an attacker can manipulate networking to increase c' as described in Sect. 8.1. The technical report [7] includes greater details about the reward gain analysis.

For other environments with c' of intermediate magnitudes (e.g., Fig. 2(b)), to maximize its reward, the attacker will choose between SWH-UBA and UBA depending on its power capability α. A lower-power attacker (smaller α) will choose SWH-UBA while a power-capable attacker (large α) will choose UBA attack (without SWH) for maximizing its reward, since the SWH-UBA attack increases more rapidly with α than UBA. The SWH-UBA attacker will opt to UBA-only when $c' \leq 0.201$ at $\alpha = 0.1$, but this changeover point for the optimal attack strategy will occur at greater c' with greater α capabilities (e.g., UBA-only attack is optimal when $c' \leq 0.304$ if $\alpha = 0.24$). In other words, with smaller power capabilities (α), the attacker will more likely choose SWH-UBA over UBA without SWH to optimize its reward capacity with varying pool/networking environments (c'). Lastly, for large c' (e.g., Fig. 2(c)), SWH-UBA attack outperforms UBA attack regardless of α.

11   Conclusion

Blockchain uses PoW to achieve consensus in cryptocurrencies and other permissionless applications. From real-world blockchain and mining system implementations, we identify and analyze the blockchain system components causing vulnerabilities for unfair reward exploitation and introduce the SWH threat. SWH attacks the victim mining pool and increases the payout within the pool, in contrast to the block-withholding based threats which consider the inter-pool dynamics to increase the attacker's main pool reward by sabotaging the victim pool. If launched along with the block-withholding threats, SWH is effective in gaining unfair reward advantage at the expense of the other protocol-complying honest miners and is aligned with the incentives of rational and financially driven miners. Since the attack requirements for launching such threat is comparable to that of BWH, FAW, or UBA (and there are already reported incidents of BWH in real world), we expect the more impactful SWH-UBA or SWH-FAW to occur against vulnerable systems in practice, such as Slush Pool and other mining pools implementing decaying payout.

We intend to inform the blockchain R&D community of the realistic and impactful SWH threat to facilitate further research and development to secure the blockchain's PoW consensus protocol. Potential countermeasures to SWH include the detection based on monitoring the reward, block, or share, the payout and reward control to mitigate or disincentivize SWH, and the cryptographic protocols to make the block and the shares indistinguishable at the time of the submissions. The technical report [7] discusses about these potential countermeasures in greater details in Appendix G.

Acknowledgments. This research is supported in part by Colorado State Bill 18-086. We would also like to thank the anonymous reviewers for their helpful feedback. We publish a technical report to supplement this conference publication [7]. The technical report includes the supplementary additions as appendices to better highlight the differences. The additional materials in the technical report include: more theoretical analyses and proofs, the more detailed Nash equilibrium analyses, the simulations with greater discussions about the setup and the SWH payout results, and the discussions about the potential countermeasures.

Appendix A   UBA Reward Analysis

UBA builds on FAW but adapts its strategy so that the attacker submits the withheld block in Event B and earns additional rewards in Event C. The expected reward for UBA (R_{UBA}) is:

$$R_{UBA} \geq \frac{(1-\tau)\alpha}{1-\tau\alpha} + \frac{\tau\alpha}{\beta+\tau\alpha}\left(\kappa\frac{(\tau\alpha)^2}{\beta+\tau\alpha}\cdot\frac{(1-\tau)\alpha}{1-\tau\alpha}\right.$$

$$\left.+ (1+\kappa\tau\alpha)\frac{\beta}{1-\tau\alpha} + \kappa\tau\alpha\frac{1-\alpha-\beta}{1-\tau\alpha}\right) \tag{7}$$

where $\kappa < 1$ is the partial reward to the uncle blocks. The right-hand side assumes that there is only one uncle block reward, which yields the inequality. If there are more uncle block rewards, e.g., Ethereum's GHOST algorithm, then the reward increases beyond the right-hand side in Eq. 7.

Appendix B   Payout Analysis for Honest Mining

To provide an example case for using the model in Sect. 8.1, we analyze the case of honest mining. We assume decaying payout and each share's score for payout is $\frac{1}{d} = \frac{1}{\gamma}$ in expectation since γ is the expected number of shares per block if the mining pool wins the block (if the mining pool collectively does not find a block, then the payout becomes zero regardless of the share scores). Therefore, $d = \gamma$; while we focus on $d = \gamma$, we analyze the impact of varying d in Appendix F.

An attacker behaving honestly receives a reward of $(\alpha'+\beta)\cdot\frac{1}{\gamma}\cdot\frac{\alpha'}{\alpha'+\beta}\gamma = \alpha'$ in expectation where $\alpha' + \beta$ corresponds to the probability that the pool wins the block (against the other pools), and $\frac{1}{\gamma}$ and $\frac{\alpha'}{\alpha'+\beta}\gamma$ correspond to the reward per share and the number of shares (the total number of shares is γ in expectation), respectively, given that the pool won the block. The resulting expected reward for the attacker behaving honestly is α', which is its computational power invested on the victim pool and agrees with Eq. 1.

With no SWH, the attacker's payout is $\Gamma_{honest} = \frac{\alpha'}{\alpha'+\beta} = \frac{\tau\alpha}{\tau\alpha+\beta}$ in expectation, agreeing with our analyses in Sect. 6.

Appendix C   SWH Payout Analyses: Proofs of Theorem and Corollary

In this appendix section, we prove Theorem 3 and Corollary 1 in Sect. 8.2.

Theorem 4. *The expected payout of SWH is:*

$$\Gamma_{SWH} \geq \sum_{y=1}^{\infty}\sum_{x=1}^{y}\binom{y}{x}\frac{x}{x+\frac{y-x}{d}}\cdot\frac{\alpha'^x\beta^{y-x}}{(\alpha'+\beta)^y}\cdot\frac{(\gamma-1)^{y-1}}{\gamma^y}$$

Proof. The expected payout of the miner j launching SWH with a power of α' is:

$$
\begin{aligned}
\Gamma_{\mathrm{SWH}} &= \mathrm{E}\left[\frac{S_j}{S_j + \sum_{i\neq j} S_i}\right] \\
&= \sum_{y=1}^{\infty}\sum_{x=1}^{y} \mathrm{E}\left[\frac{x}{x + \sum_{i\neq j} S_i}\,\Big|\, S_i = x, \|\boldsymbol{s}\| = y\right] \cdot \Pr[S_j = x \,\big|\, \|\boldsymbol{s}\| = y] \cdot \Pr[\|\boldsymbol{s}\| = y] \\
&= \sum_{y=1}^{\infty}\sum_{x=1}^{y} \mathrm{E}\left[\frac{x}{x + \sum_{i\neq j} S_i}\,\Big|\, S_i = x, \|\boldsymbol{s}\| = y\right] \\
&\qquad \cdot \binom{y}{x}\left(\frac{\alpha'}{\alpha'+\beta}\right)^{x}\left(\frac{\beta}{\alpha'+\beta}\right)^{y-x} \cdot \left(1-\frac{1}{\gamma}\right)^{y-1}\frac{1}{\gamma} \\
&\geq \sum_{y=1}^{\infty}\sum_{x=1}^{y} \frac{x}{x + \mathrm{E}\left[\sum_{i\neq j} S_i\right]} \cdot \binom{y}{x}\left(\frac{\alpha'}{\alpha'+\beta}\right)^{x}\left(\frac{\beta}{\alpha'+\beta}\right)^{y-x} \cdot \left(1-\frac{1}{\gamma}\right)^{y-1}\frac{1}{\gamma} \\
&= \sum_{y=1}^{\infty}\sum_{x=1}^{y} \binom{y}{x} \frac{x}{x + \frac{y-x}{d}} \cdot \frac{\alpha'^{x}\beta^{y-x}}{(\alpha'+\beta)^{y}} \cdot \frac{(\gamma-1)^{y-1}}{\gamma^{y}}
\end{aligned}
$$

$\binom{y}{x}$ is the binomial coefficient, i.e., $\binom{y}{x} = \frac{y!}{x!(y-x)!}$, and $\mathrm{E}[X|Y]$ and $\Pr[X|Y]$, respectively, are the expected value and the probability of event X given event Y for some events X and Y. The second equality is from the Bayes' rule (conditioned on the attacker's final score S_j and the number of shares in the round $\boldsymbol{s}$), and the third equality is derived because S_j has a binomial distribution with y trials and $\frac{\alpha'}{\alpha'+\beta}$ probability (in each share, there is a $\frac{\alpha'}{\alpha'+\beta}$ chance that the share is being submitted by an attacker), given $\|\boldsymbol{s}\| = y$, and $\boldsymbol{s}$ has a geometric distribution with the parameter/probability of $\frac{1}{\gamma} = \frac{D_{\mathrm{share}}}{D_{\mathrm{block}}}$ (the last share in $\boldsymbol{s}$ is the one that is also a block). The inequality is due to Jensen's Inequality and that $\mathrm{E}\left[\frac{S_j}{S_j + \sum_{i\neq j} S_i}\right]$ is convex with $S_j + \sum_{i\neq j} S_i$ given S_j. Finally, linear algebra yields the final equality, which provides a lower bound on the attacker j's payout.

Corollary 2. *The expected payout of SWH is:*

$$
\Gamma_{SWH} \approx \frac{\alpha'd}{\alpha'd + \beta}
$$

Proof. We approximate the gain of SWH with respect to honest mining by taking
$\mathrm{E}\left[\frac{S_j}{S_j+\sum_{i\neq j} S_i}\right] \approx \frac{\mathrm{E}[S_j]}{\mathrm{E}[S_j]+\mathrm{E}[\sum_{i\neq j} S_i]}$.

$$
\begin{aligned}
\Gamma_{\mathrm{SWH}} &\approx \frac{\mathrm{E}[S_j]}{\mathrm{E}[S_j] + \mathrm{E}[\sum_{i\neq j} S_i]} \\
&= \frac{\frac{\alpha'}{\alpha'+\beta}\gamma}{\frac{\alpha'}{\alpha'+\beta}\gamma + \frac{\beta}{\alpha'+\beta}\gamma\frac{1}{d}} \\
&= \frac{\alpha' d}{\alpha' d + \beta}
\end{aligned}
$$

$\mathrm{E}[S_j] = \frac{\alpha'}{\alpha'+\beta}\gamma$ because the expected number of share for the attacker j is $\frac{\alpha'}{\alpha'+\beta}\gamma$ and each share is weighted by one because of no decay, and $\mathrm{E}[\sum_{i\neq j} S_i] = \frac{\beta}{\alpha'+\beta}\gamma\frac{1}{d}$ because the expected number of share fore the rest of the miners excluding j is $\frac{\beta}{\alpha'+\beta}\gamma$ and each share's score contribution is decayed by $\frac{1}{d}$ on average.

Appendix D   The Equilibrium Analysis

In this section, we analyze the case where all the miners are rational as the miner's goal is to earn financial profit. We build on prior research in the mining strategies described in Sect. 3 for our analysis and corroborate with the prior research yielding that rational miners congregate to the mining pool with the greatest computational power resulting in mining centralization [19,20], i.e., SWH only reinforces such equilibrium analyses. (While such analysis is valid, Appendix G discusses a potential measure introducing a distributed mining pool, as opposed to having a centralized pool manager, to mitigate the centralization issue.).

FAW, building on selfish mining and BWH, forgoes the miner's dilemma [11], i.e., the Nash equilibrium of the FAW-capable miners do not result in the suboptimal tragedy-of-the-commons (where collaboration and coordination, as opposed to each miner's adopting their unilateral strategies, would have provided better performances for all the miners involved). As a result, if there is no restriction in joining any pool, the rational miners join and congregate to the mining pool with greater computational power and attack the other pools until no rational miner is left in the other pools. UBA further takes advantage of the rewards for the uncle blocks to further reinforce such Nash equilibrium. (In contrast, for BWH, because of the miner's dilemma, the Nash equilibrium is to leave the mining pools and mine directly in the blockchain's consensus protocol.). SWH, requiring FAW or UBA for incentive compatibility (greater reward than honest mining), only increases the reward beyond FAW and UBA and utilizes an orthogonal channel for the reward gain because, while FAW and UBA increases the chance of the attacker's main pool of winning the reward, SWH increases the attacker's reward payout within the mining pool. Section 7.2 establishes the blockchain- and pool-settings for SWH to be relevant for rational strategy for reward gain, and Sect. 10.1 analyzes the attacker's power and networking conditions which make SWH more profitable than launching UBA or FAW only. Because SWH provides further reward gains for UBA/FAW, it reinforces the Nash equilibrium of UBA/FAW, i.e., the rational miners equipped with the SWH strategies are even more incentivized to congregate to the pool with the greatest mining power. On the other hand, if there is a mechanism to control the joining of the pool (e.g., some closed pools require registration but these pools are rarer because the miner gives up the cryptocurrencies' permissionless and anonymization properties) and the greater-power pool uses such mechanism, then the pools launch SWH and UBA/FAW against each other and the larger pool wins by earning greater reward gains than the smaller pools.

Appendix E   Simulation Setup and Parameters

This section explains the simulations setup and the parameter choices to characterize the blockchain system and the victim pool system under attack.

Our blockchain system simulation setup is influenced by modern blockchain implementations. For the pool system, $\beta = 0.24$, which value corresponds to the strongest mining pool in real-world mining at the time of this manuscript writing [4]. The attacker attacking the stronger pool as its victim pool (as opposed to a weaker pool of $\beta \to 0$) provides greater reward and is aligned with its incentive, which we verify in our simulations and agree with previous literature [3,19]. The pool difficulty of the victim pool corresponds to $\gamma = 2^5$, i.e., the share difficulty is 5 bits (32 times) less than the block difficulty. This falls within the typical range of γ [1], which parameter provides a pool-system-controllable tradeoff between networking/bandwidth and reward variance. The decaying factor for the pool's reward payout is $d = 2^5$; we have $d = \gamma = 2^5$, so that the shares scores decay by e^{-dT} in time T and the scores add up to one in expectation, as described in Sect. 8.1. These parameters are fixed unless otherwise noted (we vary the variables to analyze the dependency and the impacts).

We also consider the 51% attack where the attacker can fully control the blockchain if the attacker's computational power exceeds the 50% of the network's; in our context, the attacker can conduct withholding-based selfish mining to reverse the transactions/blocks on the chain and to waste the other miner's computational resources on blocks that the attacker can reverse and make stale. Therefore, we limit our analyses to $0 \le \alpha \le 0.5$ (the attacker is capable of 51% attack if $\alpha > 0.5$) in addition to the constraint of $\alpha + \beta \le 1$ from the definitions of α and β.

Appendix F   SWH Payout

SWH yields an unfair payout advantage to the attacker. Assuming that the victim pool uses a decaying-payout scheme for distributing the pool reward and that the attacker can submit the shares on time (i.e., $c' = 1$), we study the payout advantage of the SWH attacker. Corollary 1 in Sect. 8.2 provides an

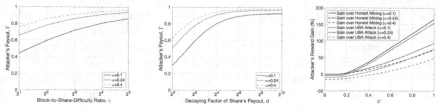

(a) Payout Γ with respect to γ

(b) Payout Γ with respect to the share's decaying factor d

(c) SWH-UBA's reward gain analyses assuming worst-case networking of $c = 0$

Fig. 3. SWH payout analyses (Figs. 3(a) and (b)) and SWH-UBA's reward gain analyses (Fig. 3(c))

approximation for the attacker's payout in Eq. 5, which can characterize the payout's dependency on α, β, and d. For example, the attacker's payout increases with d, the decaying factor of the share's payout, as is also shown in simulations in Fig. 3(b). We observe such behaviors in our simulations. We also summarize our findings here when comparing the approximated payout in Eq. 5 and the more precise payout in Eq. 4. The approximation generally provides a higher payout than the more precise lower bound, and the difference ranges from 0% (when the attacker's power on the victim pool is very low) to 21.1%. Since the difference is significant between the approximation and the lower bound we identified, we use the lower bound in Eq. 4 to quantify the attacker's payout rather than the approximation in Eq. 5. In addition, the resulting payout from launching SWH significantly outperforms honest mining (where the attacker does not withhold shares and submits them as soon as they are found); while there is no payout difference between SWH and honest mining when $\alpha = 0$, the difference quickly becomes the maximum of 0.5813 at $\alpha = 0.06$ and then monotonically decreases and becomes 0.292 at $\alpha = 0.5$.

The block-to-share difficulty ratio γ establishes how often the shares occur for every block/round; in expectation, there are γ shares per block. The greater the number of shares per round the greater the impact of the share-withholding attack, since the share-withholding attack can occur for every shares, as is seen in Fig. 3(a). In practice, mining pools typically control γ and d together so that they are aligned/correlated with each other, i.e., as there are more shares (γ increases), the payout per share decreases more quickly (d increases). However, to isolate the effect of d from γ, Fig. 3(b) plots the payout Γ with respect to d while fixing $\gamma = 2^5$ and shows that the attacker's payout Γ increases with d.

Appendix G   Discussions About Potential Countermeasures

While this paper focuses on the discovery and the analyses of SWH attack, we discuss potential countermeasures for future work in this section.

Behavior-Based Detection of Withholding Threats. The withholding-based threats, including SWH, result in abnormal reward behaviors. For example, SWH decreases the variance and the entropy of the share arrivals. Such phenomenon can be sensed and measured for attack detection, which can be then used for mitigation purposes. While we identify behavior-based detection as promising, we do not recommend relying on identity-based detection and mitigation such as blacklisting public keys or IP addresses because, in permissionless environment, there is no identity control/registration and it is cheap for the attacker to generate multiple identities (Sybil attack).

Payout and Reward Function Control. Controlling the payout and reward functions, for example, the system parameters κ, λ, γ, d in our model, provides a low-overhead countermeasure because it requires the changes in the pool manager only and is backward-compatible to the rest of the miners' software. Prior research [3,25] distinguish between block submissions and share submissions (different weights) against BWH attack. Such approach can not only be used for BWH but also for FAW and UBA, which in turn defends against SWH because SWH relies on FAW or UBA for its incentive compatibility (SWH requires the attacker to have some/probabilistic information of the block arrivals).

Oblivious Share. Similar in purpose to the oblivious transfer protocols and building on commit-and-reveal approach, *oblivious share* deprives the miner of the knowledge of whether it is a block or a share until it submits them [13, 24]. The attacker therefore cannot dynamically adopt the withholding-based threats which require distinguishing the share and the block before submission. While effective against the withholding-based attacks, such approach requires a protocol change (including an additional exchange between the mining pool manager and the miners) and is not backward compatible (does not work with the existing system unless the protocol change/update is made) [19,21], causing protocol/communication overheads and making such schemes undesirable for implementation to the blockchain network (which includes closed pools and solo miners, free of withholding vulnerabilities and thus lacking the incentives for such addition and change).

Unified Distributed Mining Pool. To have all miners join one distributed mining pool eliminates the notion of sabotaging/victimizing another pool. A useful platform for this can be distributed mining pools, e.g., SmartPool [22] and P2Pool, which eliminates the centralized mining pool manager and replaces it with a distributed program/computing, motivated to make the blockchain computing more decentralized without the reliance on trusted third party (the mining pool manager in this case) [15,18]. Since the mining pool is distributed, the mining and the consensus protocol does not have the centralization issue, e.g., there is no centralized pool manager capable of controlling the rewards or blocking/nullifying a share or a block. In fact, the authors of SmartPool [22] envisions that their platform can be used to unify the mining pools citing that the elimination of the mining pool fee (charged by the centralized mining pool manager for their services) and the reduced variance (compared to independent mining) will attract incentive-driven miners. However, despite such desirable properties (and even if the claimed superior performance is true), such approach is a radical solution and it can be difficult to enforce the change in behaviors in the miners and have all miners mine at the designated pool, especially for an existing blockchain implementation with the existing miners having already joined a pool. Enforcing such pool restriction for the miners is not backward-compatible to the existing miners and can also be controversial since it can be viewed as a violation of the freedom of the miners.

References

1. Variable pool difficulty (2012). http://organofcorti.blogspot.com/2012/10/71-variable-pool-difficulty.html
2. Apostolaki, M., Zohar, A., Vanbever, L.: Hijacking bitcoin: routing attacks on cryptocurrencies. In: 2017 IEEE Symposium on Security and Privacy (SP), pp. 375–392 (2017)
3. Bag, S., Sakurai, K.: Yet another note on block withholding attack on Bitcoin mining pools. In: Bishop, M., Nascimento, A.C.A. (eds.) ISC 2016. LNCS, vol. 9866, pp. 167–180. Springer, Cham (2016). https://doi.org/10.1007/978-3-319-45871-7_11
4. blockchain.com. Hash rate distribution. https://www.blockchain.com/en/pools
5. Buterin, V.: Ethereum: a next-generation smart contract and decentralized application platform. https://github.com/ethereum/wiki/wiki/White-Paper (2014). Accessed 22 Aug 2016
6. Buterin, V., Reijsbergen, D., Leonardos, S., Piliouras, G.: Incentives in ethereum's hybrid casper protocol. In: IEEE International Conference on Blockchain and Cryptocurrency (ICBC) (2019). http://arxiv.org/abs/1903.04205
7. Chang, S.-Y.: Share withholding attack in blockchain mining. Technical report (2020)
8. Chang, S.-Y., Park, Y.: Silent timestamping for blockchain mining pool security. In: IEEE International Workshop on Computing, Networking and Communications (CNC) (2019)
9. Chang, S.-Y., Park, Y., Wuthier, S., Chen, C.-W.: Uncle-block attack: blockchain mining threat beyond block withholding for rational and uncooperative miners. In: Proceedings of the 17th International Conference on Applied Cryptography and network Security, Ser. ACNS'19 (2019)
10. Ekparinya, P., Gramoli, V., Jourjon, G.: Impact of man-in-the-middle attacks on ethereum, pp. 11–20 (2018)
11. Eyal, I.: The miner's dilemma. In: Proceedings of the 2015 IEEE Symposium on Security and Privacy, ser. SP '15, pp. 89–103. IEEE Computer Society, Washington, DC, USA (2015). https://doi.org/10.1109/SP.2015.13
12. Eyal, I., Sirer, E.G.: Majority is not enough: bitcoin mining is vulnerable. CoRR, vol. abs/1311.0243 (2013)
13. Eyal, I., Sirer, E.G.: How to disincentivize large bitcoin mining pools (2014)
14. Forum, B.: Eligius: 0% Fee BTC, 105% PPS NMC, No registration, CPPSRB (2014). https://bitcointalk.org/?topic=441465.msg7282674

15. Gervais, A., Karame, G.O., Capkun, V., Capkun, S.: Is bitcoin a decentralized currency? IEEE Secur. Privacy **12**(3), 54–60 (2014)
16. Gervais, A., Karame, G.O., Wüst, K., Glykantzis, V., Ritzdorf, H., Capkun, S.: On the security and performance of proof of work blockchains. In: Proceedings of the 2016 ACM SIGSAC Conference on Computer and Communications Security, ser. CCS '16, pp. 3–16. ACM, New York (2016). http://doi.acm.org/10.1145/2976749.2978341
17. Heilman, E., Kendler, A., Zohar, A., Goldberg, S.: Eclipse attacks on bitcoin's peer-to-peer network. In: 24th USENIX Security Symposium (USENIX Security 15), pp. 129–144. USENIX Association, Washington, D.C. (2015). https://www.usenix.org/conference/usenixsecurity15/technical-sessions/presentation/heilman
18. Bonneau, J., Miller, A., Clark, J., Narayanan, A., Kroll, J.A., Felten, E.W.: Research perspectives and challenges for bitcoin and cryptocurrencies. Cryptology ePrint Archive, Report 2015/261 (2015). https://eprint.iacr.org/2015/261
19. Kwon, Y., Kim, D., Son, Y., Vasserman, E., Kim, Y.: Be selfish and avoid dilemmas: fork after withholding (faw) attacks on bitcoin. In: Proceedings of the 2017 ACM SIGSAC Conference on Computer and Communications Security, ser. CCS '17, pp. 195–209. ACM, New York (2017). https://doi.acm.org/10.1145/3133956.3134019
20. Kwon, Y., Liu, J., Kim, M., Song, D., Kim, Y.: Impossibility of full decentralization in permissionless blockchains. In: AFT 2019 (2019)
21. Luu, L., Saha, R., Parameshwaran, I., Saxena, P., Hobor, A.: On power splitting games in distributed computation: the case of bitcoin pooled mining. In: 2015 IEEE 28th Computer Security Foundations Symposium, July 2015, pp. 397–411 (2015)
22. Luu, L., Velner, Y., Teutsch, J., Saxena, P.: Smartpool: practical decentralized pooled mining. In: 26th USENIX Security Symposium (USENIX Security 17), pp. 1409–1426. USENIX Association, Vancouver, BC (2017). https://www.usenix.org/conference/usenixsecurity17/technical-sessions/presentation/luu
23. Nakamoto, S.: Bitcoin: a peer-to-peer electronic cash system (2008)
24. Rosenfeld, M.: Analysis of bitcoin pooled mining reward systems. CoRR, vol. abs/1112.4980 (2011). http://arxiv.org/abs/1112.4980
25. Sarker, A., Wuthier, S., Chang, S.: Anti-withholding reward system to secure blockchain mining pools. In: 2019 Crypto Valley Conference on Blockchain Technology (CVCBT), June 2019, pp. 43–46 (2019)
26. Wood, G.: Ethereum: a secure decentralised generalised transaction ledger EIP-150 revision (759dccd - 07 Aug 2017) (2017). Accessed 12 May 2018. https://ethereum.github.io/yellowpaper/paper.pdf

PEDR: A Novel Evil Twin Attack Detection Scheme Based on Phase Error Drift Range

Jiahui Zhang[1], Qian Lu[1,2], Ruobing Jiang[1(✉)], and Haipeng Qu[1]

[1] Department of Computer Science and Technology, Ocean University of China,
Qingdao, China
{izjh,luqian}@stu.ouc.edu.cn, {jrb,quhaipeng}@ouc.edu.cn
[2] College of Computer Science and Technology, Qingdao University, Qingdao, China

Abstract. In recent years, wireless local area networks (WLANs) have become one of the important ways to access the Internet. However, the openness of WLANs makes them vulnerable to the threat of the evil twin attack (ETA). Existing effective ETA detection solutions usually rely on physical fingerprints. Especially fingerprints made by information extracted from channel state information (CSI) are more reliable. However, demonstrated by our experiment, the fingerprint of the state-of-the-art ETA detection scheme, which is based on phase error extracted from CSI, is not stable enough, and it results in a large number of false negative results in some cases. In this paper, we present a novel ETA detection scheme, called PEDR, which uses range fingerprint extracted from CSI to identify the evil twin (ET). Inspired by the significant observation that the phase error will drift over time, the concept of drift range fingerprints is proposed and exploited to improve ETA detection accuracy in real-world attack scenarios. Range fingerprints are not affected by drift in phase error and can be uniquely identified. The proposed range fingerprint is implemented and extensive performance evaluation experiments are conducted in the large-scale experiment with 27 devices. The experimental results demonstrate that the detection rate of PEDR is close to 99% and the false negative data is only 1.11%. It is worth mentioning that PEDR is outstanding in the scenario with similar device fingerprints.

Keywords: Evil twin attack · Rogue access point detection · WLAN security · Wi-Fi security · Channel state information

1 Introduction

In recent years, wireless local area networks (WLANs) are rapidly gaining popularity due to the widespread development of wireless network technology and the explosive growth of portable devices. Compared with wired networks, WLAN is more flexible and easier to be installed and expanded, so many wireless access

© ICST Institute for Computer Sciences, Social Informatics and Telecommunications Engineering 2020
Published by Springer Nature Switzerland AG 2020. All Rights Reserved
N. Park et al. (Eds.): SecureComm 2020, LNICST 336, pp. 188–207, 2020.
https://doi.org/10.1007/978-3-030-63095-9_10

points (APs) are deployed in various places such as homes, campuses, hotels, fast food restaurants, airports and shopping centers. As the core device of WLAN, AP provides an effective connection between wired networks and WLANs. Users can access the network freely through APs. Therefore, WLANs provide users with great convenience to access the network and become an integral part of life.

However, the openness and convenience of WLANs bring enormous security risks to wireless users [1]. The ETA is the most prominent one. The ET, also known as the phishing AP, refers to a fraudulent AP established by an attacker. ET tricks wireless users through mimicking the Service Set Identity (SSID) and MAC address (BSSID) of a legitimate AP, as shown in Fig. 1. According to the IEEE 802.11 standard, the client operating system usually selects the AP with the same SSID based on Received Signal Strength Indicator (RSSI). The attacker will exploit this weakness to induce the user to connect to ET by using various means. For example, the attacker can conduct the denial-of-service attack against the legitimate AP or provide a stronger RSSI than the legitimate AP.

Fig. 1. Illustration of ETA attack scene. The attacker establishes ET by imitating the parameters of the legitimate AP. ET attracts users by providing stronger RSSI.

Once a user has inadvertently connected to an ET, she will face serious consequences such as sensitive information leakage, traffic hijacking and other malicious attacks. For example, the attacker can snoop on the sensitive personal information of the victim, such as photos, emails, various login passwords and bank card information, according to the packets sent to ET by the user. The attacker can also manipulate DNS server/communication, launch a DNS spoofing attack [2], hijack the victim to visit the malicious website [3], and cause direct economic loss to the victim. Moreover, the victim connected to ET may suffer SSL Strip Attacks [4], which strip the SSL layer from the original HTTPS connection and force the victim's data to be sent in plain text format. Thus encryption function is deprived.

Because ETA poses a significant threat to wireless users, researchers have done much work on the ETA detection. Based on whether it can be deployed independently on the client and provide real-time detection for wireless users, the existing detection schemes can be divided into two types in this paper: admin-based and client-based. Specifically, although admin-based detection schemes defend ETA to a certain extent, they all require additional hardware equipments or higher permissions to achieve detection. It means that independent real-time detection cannot be provided by admin-based detection schemes. For example, Brik et al. [5] and Nguyen et al. [6] proposed schemes based on radio frequency fingerprint (RFF); In the study [7], researchers determined the target AP's legitimacy according to its network access method which is judged by the wireless traffic flowing through the gateway. On the other hand, some researchers proposed client-based detection schemes. For example, Arackaparambi et al. [8] detected ETA by using inter-packet arrival time (IAT) and clock skew. Lu et al. [9] used the forwarding behavior of ET. ETA can be determined by comparing the 802.11 data frames sent by target APs to users. The state-of-the-art research [10] proposed a detection scheme based on the non-linear phase errors extracted from CSI. Although these schemes can provide users with independent security detection, there are still many limitations in terms of detection rate and attack model.

In this paper, we innovatively use the phase error drift range as the physical device fingerprint for ETA detection on the basis of the study [10]. Specifically, Liu et al. [10] discovered that the non-linear phase error in CSI can be used as the device fingerprint. However, a large number of experimental results confirm that the phase errors have drift phenomenon. Drift phenomenon may cause fingerprints of different devices to overlap each other, and result in failure of Liu's method [10]. In addition, we found that the phase error drift range always remains relatively stable in the time dimension. Based on this observation, PEDR uses the drift range of phase errors as the wireless device fingerprints. In our scheme, the phase error drift range, instead of the phase errors, is used as the device fingerprint, which overcomes the shortcomings of false positives and false negatives due to drift phenomenon. At the same time, PEDR is deployed on the user client, and it can provide users with real-time detection without additional hardware equipments or protocol modification.

In summary, we make the following contributions to the field of WLAN security in our paper:

- Through a large number of experimental observations, we find that the non-linear phase errors extracted from the CSI have drift phenomenon. In other words, if only the phase error is used as the fingerprint, the wireless device cannot be uniquely identified.
- Based on the phase error drift phenomenon, we innovatively use the phase error drift range as the physical fingerprint of the device to identify the ETA. A new detection scheme PEDR deployed on the client is proposed. Compared with admin-based solutions, PEDR can better meet the needs of users, and does not require any additional overhead on wireless devices.

- Extensive simulation experiments are performed with 27 devices. The experimental results prove that the detection rate of ETA by PEDR was close to 99%. Especially for devices with similar phase errors, the detection effect of PEDR is more noticeable than Liu's method [10].

The rest of the paper is organized as follows: Sect. 2 introduces the work related EAT detection. Section 3 briefly introduces the background of CSI and the empirical research of PEDR. Section 4 details the modules of PEDR. In Sect. 5, we demonstrate the feasibility of fingerprints and perform a performance evaluation of PEDR. Finally, we summarize the paper in Sect. 6.

2 Related Work

Due to the great perniciousness of ETA, researchers in the field of wireless network security have conducted extensive research on ETA detection, and they proposed several solutions. A large amount of existing work is usually classified based on the detection model, additional hardware and advanced permissions requirements, etc. [11]. In this paper, whether the detection scheme can provide users with real-time efficient and independent detection is used as the classification standard. We accordingly divide existing detection schemes into two categories: admin-based and client-based.

2.1 Admin-Based ETA Detection Schemes

In the admin-based ETA detection schemes, higher permissions, additional hardware equipments, or protocol modification are required to achieve the ETA detection. In other words, it is difficult for users to conduct real-time ETA detection independently by using admin-based schemes, because most admin-based solutions require information that is hard for ordinary users to collect.

Gonzales et al. proposed a scheme to defend ETA by modifying the existing protocol, called Simple Wireless Authentication Technique (EAP-SWAT) [12,13], which is an extension of the Extensible Authentication Protocol (EAP). EAP-SWAT leverages SSH's Trust On First Use (TOFU) security model. Specifically, if the security of the first connection with the AP can be assured, TOFU can ensure that subsequent connections to this AP will not be spoofed. In addition, researchers in the study [14] also proposed a method that required protocol modification, Secure Open Wireless Access (SOWA). SOWA binds the SSID of the AP with a digital certificate to verify the operator of the AP and determines whether the target AP is legitimate. The solution proposed by Kumar et al. [15] uses a connection count table established between each client and AP to assist users in ETA detection. The connection counts of both parties will increase while the client and the AP are successfully connected. By comparing the values in both tables, the counts of successful connections between each client and AP are confirmed to prevent wireless users from accessing the ET. Unfortunately, this solution has many flaws. For example, both the AP and probe response frame must be adjusted, and the client operating system also needs to be modified to establish a counter. The above solutions could defend ETA to a certain extent, but all need to modify the existing protocol, driver, or firmware. Therefore, all of the above solutions are difficult to be implemented easily.

Some researchers [5, 6, 16] proposed RFF-based methods to identify ETA. By monitoring Radio Frequency (RF) waves, the hardware defects in the network card can be obtained. RFF can be acquired by combining hardware defects and other information such as the SSID and RSSI of the device. In short, the researchers utilize the physical characteristics obtained from the radio signal to identify the ETA. The scheme based on RFF can resist the influence of mobility, noise, and hardware aging, and it achieves a very high detection rate in the experimental scenario. However, the detection in a real scenario requires special wireless sensors to continuously monitor the RF signal sent by the AP. Obviously, this kind of schemes is difficult to be deployed on a large scale.

Wei et al. [7] proposed the method of using the network traffic passing through the gateway to detect ETA, and similar schemes were also proposed in studies [17–22]. Specifically, two parameters, the fraction of TCP flows and the degree of belief that a TCP flow traverses a WLAN inside the network, can be calculated by the iterative Bayesian inference algorithm; they can be used to determine whether client traffic comes from wireless or wired connection according to the difference of network protocol. Unfortunately, capturing the wireless traffic flowing through the gateway requires advanced permissions that ordinary users cannot obtain. In addition, the algorithm used in the study requires a certain amount of time to converge. Therefore, it is difficult to provide users with real-time security detection.

2.2   Client-Based ETA Detection Schemes

The second type of detection scheme is client-based detection schemes which can be independently deployed on the client. Compared with admin-based solutions, it can provide users with real-time ETA detection. However, the existing client-based solutions still have limitations in several aspects, such as detection rates, detection efficiency [23] and detection scenarios, etc.

Jana et al. [24] first used clock skew as the unique fingerprint for ETA detection. Clock skew is calculated by the timing synchronization function timestamp extracted from the beacon frame. Arackaparambil et al. [8] improved the above work and proposed a more accurate detection. It can be achieved by comparing the beacon frame timestamp generated by the AP with the IAT of the client packets. The IAT is extracted from the Radiotap header and represents the difference between the arrival times of two sequential frames. Song et al. [25, 26] believed that additional propagation delays will be introduced due to the wireless connection between ET and legitimate APs. The user can determine whether the client is directly connected to the legitimate AP by using the IAT. Neumann et al. [27] evaluated a variety of network parameters and concluded that using IAT as a signature to identify the ETA is ideal. Although the above methods are effective, the

IAT lacks robustness and will change due to various factors [28], such as the fluctuation of wireless signals and the increase of wireless traffic. Therefore, the detection rates are difficult to satisfy users. In addition, the diversity of attack models will directly cause the failure of the detection.

Alotaibi et al. proposed a method that uses Radiotap length (PLL) as the fingerprint in the study [29]. ETA can be detected by comparing the PLL extracted from the target AP with the legitimate device fingerprint in the fingerprint library. Although this method has a high detection rate and does not require additional equipments, unfortunately, collecting information about all legitimate APs results in a huge amount of work and the scheme is only valid for ETs built by soft APs.

The application of CSI has gradually matured in recent years [30]. As physical layer information, CSI has been widely used in localization and action recognition. Therefore some researchers have begun to use CSI for ETA detection. For example, Liu et al. [31] proposed that the ETA detection can be implemented by using the amplitude information in CSI. Specifically, this solution combines the amplitude and the position information as a device fingerprint to detect ETA. However, multiple monitors are required to collect wireless packets in the scheme. In addition, the scheme requires that the detection terminal equipment must be static, which is impractical in a real scenario. Hua [32] used the carrier frequency offset (CFO) estimated from CSI as the device fingerprint to realize the ETA detection. CFO is based on the instability of the oscillator drift caused by the crystal imperfection. Compared with directly using CSI, CFO is not affected by the environment and remains stable with time. Although the scheme based on CFO achieves successful detection, it is difficult to meet the condition that the equipment needs to be stationary during the detection process, which will lead to unsatisfactory detection results. Zhuo et al. [33] first proposed the existence of non-negligible non-linear phase errors in CSI, and they pointed out that non-linear phase errors are caused by I/Q imbalance. Based on the above achievements, Liu et al. [10] used non-linear phase errors as fingerprints for ETA detection. The phase error is not affected by temperature, physical location, and it can play a good effect on some attack scenarios. However, according to our experiments and observations, the detection scheme will produce false negative results in scenarios where the phase errors of the equipments are similar. The specific content will be detailed in Sect. 3.

3 Empirical Study

In this section, the basic knowledge of CSI is first introduced, and the experiment in the study [10] is reproduced. We describe the phenomenon, phase errors drift, found in the experimental results, and further observe the characteristics of the phase error drift phenomenon.

3.1 Background

CSI is the channel attribute of wireless communication links. It describes the attenuation characteristics of wireless signals on each propagation path. The attenuation characteristics combine multiple effects such as delay, ambient scattering, amplitude attenuation and phase offset. Besides, CSI includes the amplitude and phase information of each subcarrier in the frequency domain space. The amplitude and phase contain the inherent properties of the wireless communication devices. Therefore, CSI is widely used in the fields of localization, identification, and environmental perception.

In the study [10], the non-linear phase errors were proposed as a fingerprint of the hardware device to detect ETA. Non-linear phase errors are caused by the I/Q imbalance and oscillator defects. Liu et al. derived the Eq. (1) for calculating the non-linear phase error E. The equation is as follows:

$$E = \Phi - (2\pi\lambda \cdot K + Z^*), \tag{1}$$

where Φ is the phases of subcarriers measured at the receiver. The parameter K contains subcarrier index. Z^* includes the true phase and a constant. The parameter λ is also a constant and will change across sampled CSIs. It is related to frame detection delay (FDD), sampling frequency offset (SFO) and time of flight (TOF) which affect the phase error. In order to obtain a stable fingerprint, the author used special λ which makes the phase errors of the subcarrier -28 and 28 equal to 0 to remove the effects of FDD, SFO and TOF.

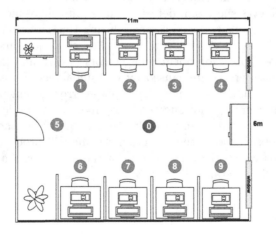

Fig. 2. Experiment scene: 1–9 are the positions of the target devices; 0 is the position of the detection terminal.

3.2 Setup

In order to reproduce the experiment, the same experimental scenario was set up according to the study [10]. The detection terminal of the experiment was a Thinkpad SL410 equipped with Intel 5300 NIC and it ran Ubuntu 12.04 LTS system. The Linux 802.11n CSI Tool was installed to collect CSI. We selected four different wireless devices and placed them in positions 1–4 in Fig. 2. The laptop was placed in position 0 as the detection terminal to connect target devices and collect the CSI information. In order to collect CSI, the detection terminal first sent ICMP messages to the wireless AP and estimated the CSI based on the response frame. The shortest interval of ICMP messages in the experimental scenario of study [10] was 5 ms, and the collection time was 10 s. Therefore, in the verification experiment, we used the same sending interval and collecting time. That is, about 200 frames containing CSI were collected every second. For each wireless AP, a total of 10 groups of data were collected, the interval between each group was 30 s. Each group of data collection took 10 s, and a total of 2000 packets containing CSI information were collected.

3.3   Observation

According to the method mentioned by Liu et al. in the study [10], the expected experimental results are shown in Fig. 3a. The abscissa represents the subcarrier index, and the ordinate represents the value of phase error. Each hardware device has an invariable and unique phase error fingerprint. Unfortunately, from the results of the reproduction experiment, we can observe the following phenomenon which is obviously different from the expected experimental results.

Phase Error Drift Phenomenon (PEDP): PEDP refers to the phenomenon that the phase errors will change to some extent at different times. In other words, the phase error curve will drift instead of staying fixed. This phenomenon will have many effects. For example, devices with similar phase errors will overlap due to PEDP, which will lead to the failure of detection based on phase errors.

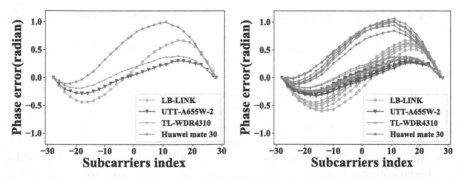

(a) Experimental result obtained by a single collection according to Liu et al.'s method.

(b) Experimental result obtained by multiple collections according to Liu et al.'s method.

Fig. 3. Expected experimental results and actual experimental results.

The common occurrence of PEDP in hardware devices will lead to the failure of detection work based on phase error. Figure 3b depicts the phase errors of four devices. Apparently, all devices produced PEDP with intervals of only 30 s. In addition, it can be clearly observed that the fingerprints of UTT-A655W-2 and TL-WDR4310 partially overlap due to PEDP. In small-scale experiments with only four wireless AP devices, there are two devices that have phase errors overlapping because of the PEDP. Then, the overlapping phenomenon could not be ignored in large-scale experiments. Therefore, in order to verify the universality of overlapping phenomenon caused by the PEDP, we expanded the scale of the experiment to 27 devices. Table 1 shows the specific types and quantities of devices. The experimental results show that the overlapping phenomenon is common in AP equipment. In addition to the overlapping phenomenon of phase errors that occurred in the above equipment, we also found the other two groups of AP equipment also have similar overlapping phenomenon, as shown in Fig. 4a and b. Therefore, attackers can make use of the phenomenon that overlap caused by PEDP to deceive detection. If an attacker deliberately chooses a device with a fingerprint similar to a legitimate AP, Liu's method will generate a lot of false negatives, which will lead to a failure of detection.

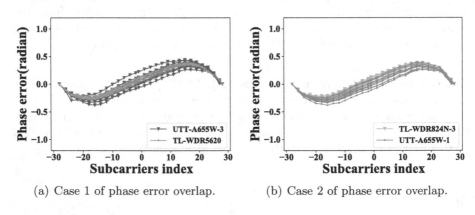

(a) Case 1 of phase error overlap.   (b) Case 2 of phase error overlap.

Fig. 4. Devices with similar phase errors overlap due to PEDP.

In summary, although the scheme based on phase error will achieve a high detection rate when the phase errors between ET and the legitimate device are significantly different, it could produce non-negligible false negatives when the target device and the legitimate device have similar phase errors. In short, due to the instability of the phase error caused by PEDP, the fingerprints will overlap. The overlap phenomenon provides an opportunity for attackers to cause the failure of the Liu's method. At the same time, we found that the drift of the phase error is regular, and the phase error of each device drifts within a unique range. Therefore, we consider that using the drift range of phase errors as the fingerprint will achieve higher accuracy detection.

4   Proposed Approach

A novel ETA detection system PEDR is proposed, which is used to detect the legitimacy of target APs. PEDR uses the drift range of the phase errors as the fingerprint, it overcomes the shortcoming of false negatives caused by PEDP. In this section, we will introduce the components of the PEDR system and the process of detecting the target device.

4.1   Overview of PEDR

The PEDR we proposed is a novel and effective ETA detection scheme. As shown in Fig. 5, PEDR is divided into two parts: the fingerprint library establishment and the legitimacy detection.

Fingerprint Library Establishment: This module is responsible for establishing a legitimate fingerprint library. The legitimate fingerprint library is used for verification and comparison with the fingerprint of target AP during the legitimacy detection process. For each legitimate AP device, fingerprint can be obtained by collecting and processing enough CSI data. The fingerprint is divided into two parts: function expressions and distribution area. The function expressions represent the upper and lower boundaries of the phase error drift range; the distribution area is used to represent the area of the phase error drift. Both are regarded as the fingerprint and added to the legitimate fingerprint database.

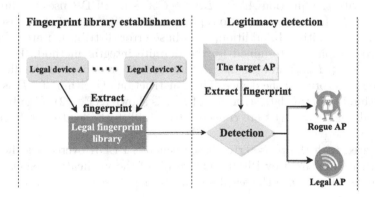

Fig. 5. The overview of PEDR.

Legitimacy Detection: This module is the core part of the PEDR system which is responsible for the legitimacy detection of target APs. The detection terminal collects CSI data by connecting to the target AP and the fingerprint can be made by phase errors extracted from the CSI data. Based on the SSID and MAC of the target AP, the corresponding legitimate fingerprint is extracted from the legitimate fingerprint database, and it will be used to check the legitimacy of the target AP.

Algorithm 1. Generating the device's fingerprint

Require: $Info_{LAP}$: the SSID, MAC and phase error set of legitimate AP;
Ensure: FP_i: Legitimate device fingerprint;
  1: Calculating the max and min phase error values from $Info_{LAP}$ on each subcarrier;
  2: Getting new functions by separately fitting the max and min values with $AX^3 + BX^2 + CX + D$;
  3: $FP_i['F_{max}\,']= \alpha X^3 + \beta X^2 + \gamma X + \theta$;
  4: $FP_i['F_{min}\,']= \alpha' X^3 + \beta' X^2 + \gamma' X + \theta'$;
  5: Calculating the distribution area S by the definite integral;
  6: $FP_i['S']=$ The value of the distribution area S;
  7: Output FP_i;

4.2　Fingerprint Library Establishment

Before the legitimacy detection, each legitimate device needs to be constructed a unique fingerprint to establish the legitimate fingerprint database. PEDR uses the drift range of phase errors as the device fingerprint. The feasibility of the fingerprint is verified in Sect. 5.

For each experimental device, in order to make a fingerprint based on phase error drift range, the maximum range of phase error drift must be obtained. Therefore, the detection terminal needs to collect a sufficient amount of CSI data and estimates the phase error from it. The bound functions (F_{max}, F_{min}) of the drift range are obtained by fitting the extrema of phase errors on each subcarrier with the function $AX^3 + BX^2 + CX + D$. PEDR uses the functions obtained by the fitting technique to represent the drift range of the phase error, which is more intuitive. In addition, the phase error distribution area S on the phase error graph is determined by the definite integral method. The fitting functions (F_{max}, F_{min}) and the distribution area S are stored in the dictionary FP_i as the fingerprint of the device. The construction algorithm of FP_i is shown in Algorithm 1, and the data structure of FP_i is shown as Eq. (2). Finally, fingerprints of all legitimate APs are collected to establish the legitimate fingerprint library.

Compared with the phase error-based scheme, PEDR overcomes the defect of false negatives caused by PEDP. The result of the verification experiment in Sect. 5 further determined the feasibility using the phase error drift range as the fingerprint.

$$
\begin{aligned}
FP_i = \{ &SSID : XXXX, \\
&MAC : XX : XX : XX : XX : XX : XX, \\
&F_{max} : \alpha X^3 + \beta X^2 + \gamma X + \theta, \\
&F_{min} : \alpha' X^3 + \beta' X^2 + \gamma' X + \theta', \\
&S : 0.00 \}
\end{aligned}
\tag{2}
$$

4.3   Legitimacy Detection

The core of legitimacy detection is to compare the target AP fingerprint with the corresponding legitimate fingerprint. The fingerprint of the target AP needs to be made before comparing it with the legitimate fingerprint. When the detection terminal is connected to the target AP, it sends ICMP messages with an interval of 5 ms to the target AP for 10 s. Each time the target AP returns response packets, the detection terminal collects a group of CSI data. The collected data is used to make the fingerprint FP' of the target AP, that is, the upper and lower bound fitting functions (F'_{max}, F'_{min}) and the distribution area S'. The legitimate fingerprint FP_i is extracted from the legitimate fingerprint library according to the SSID and MAC address of the target AP. The first step in comparison verification is determining the difference between two fingerprints based on the number of intersections between the upper and lower bounds of the target AP and the legitimate AP.

On the one hand, if there are three intersections between F_{max} and F'_{max} (or F_{min} and F'_{min}), the two fingerprints are in a cross relationship, as shown in Fig. 6a. PEDR considers that the target AP fingerprint is different from the legitimate AP fingerprint. That is, the target AP is an illegitimate AP. Specifically, since phase errors of subcarriers 28 and -28 are both 0, there are at least two intersections between the boundary functions. Therefore, if there is a third intersection between F_{max} and F'_{max} (or F_{min} and F'_{min}) in the range of subcarriers -28 to 28, it means that the boundaries in the fingerprints crosse each other, and the two fingerprints are clearly different. The target AP is considered an ET.

On the other hand, if there is no third intersection, it means that the target AP fingerprint and the legitimate fingerprint are contained, separated, or partially overlapped, as shown in Fig. 6b, c, d, e and f. The legitimacy of the target AP needs to be further judged. We define the values of $F_{max}(0)$, $F'_{max}(0)$, $F_{min}(0)$, and $F'_{min}(0)$ as the zero value of boundaries, and $F_{max}(0) - F'_{max}(0)$, $F_{min}(0) - F'_{min}(0)$ are respectively defined as the upper and lower bound zero point difference values D_{up}, D_{bot}. Based on this, the specific positional relationship between the two fingerprints can be distinguished. If the result of $D_{up} \times D_{bot}$ is positive, it means that the fingerprints are partially overlapped or separated, and the target device is judged as an ET. Otherwise, the D_{up} is used for further judgment. If $D_{up} < 0$, it means that the upper and lower bounds of the target AP are outside the range of the legitimate fingerprint, as shown in Fig. 6c. The target AP fingerprint contains the legitimate fingerprint, and the device is illegitimate. If $D_{up} > 0$, it means that all phase errors of the target AP are within the range of legitimate fingerprint. In other words, the legitimate fingerprint contains the target fingerprint, but there may be some differences in the fingerprint distribution range, as shown in Fig. 6b and f. Therefore, the phase error distribution area S is used to distinguish the fingerprint distribution of the two devices. At this moment, the threshold TSV is introduced. If the absolute value of the difference between S' and S is less than TSV, PEDR considers that the two fingerprints are coincident and the target AP is legitimate. Otherwise, the

---

Algorithm 2. Detecting the legitimacy of target AP

Require: $Info_{TAP}$: the SSID, MAC and fingerprint of target AP;
      $Dict_{LF}$: the dictionary stored legitimate devices's fingerprints;
Ensure: The legitimacy of the target AP;
 1: Extracting Legitimate fingerprint FP from $Dict_{LF}$ based on the SSID and MAC
    of target AP;
 2: Seeking the intersection number N_{max} of F_{max} and F'_{max} on the subcarriers -28
    to 28;
 3: Seeking the intersection number N_{min} of F_{min} and F'_{min} on the subcarriers -28
    to 28;
 4: **if** $(N_{max} = 3)$ **or** $(N_{min} = 3)$ **then**
 5:     Triggering a rogue AP alarm;
 6:     **Return** rogue AP is detected;
 7: **else**
 8:     calculating $F_{max}(0), F_{min}(0), F'_{max}(0), F'_{min}(0)$;
 9:     calculating $D_{up} = F_{max}(0) - F'_{max}(0)$, $D_{bot} = F_{min}(0) - F'_{min}(0)$;
10:     **if** $(D_{up} \times D_{bot} < 0)$ **and** $(D_{up} > 0)$ **and** $(|S - S'| < S_{TSV})$ **then**
11:         **Return** the target AP is legitimate;
12:     **else**
13:         Triggering a rogue AP alarm;
14:         **Return** rogue AP is detected;
15:     **end if**
16: **end if**

---

fingerprints are considered included, and the target AP is determined to be an ET. The threshold TSV will be discussed in detail in the verification experiment. The process of verifying legitimately is shown in Algorithm 2.

5   Evaluation

In this section, the experimental setup and experimental environment are first described. Then, it is verified that the drift range of phase errors remains relatively stable, so using phase error drift range as the fingerprint is feasible. Finally, the performance evaluation of PEDR was performed in a simulated scenario. We compared the PEDR system with the existing physical fingerprint detection method, and further explained the rationality and superiority of the fingerprint based on phase error drift range.

5.1   Setup

Hardware Implementation: In the experiment, the detection terminal uses the laptop Thinkpad SL410 equipped with Intel 5300 NIC, and the CPU is Intel T6670. It runs Ubuntu 12.04 LTS system. There are 27 devices to be detected, such as wireless routers that can release hotspots, laptops which can turn on soft APs and smartphones. Table 1 shows the specific types and quantities of devices. The validity of fingerprints based on the phase error drift range can be

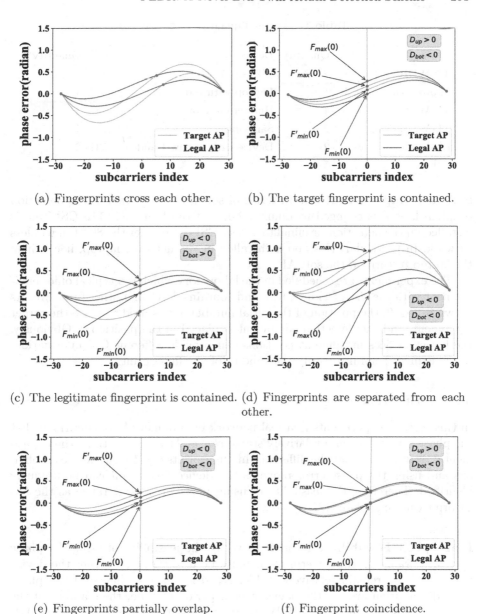

(a) Fingerprints cross each other.   (b) The target fingerprint is contained.

(c) The legitimate fingerprint is contained. (d) Fingerprints are separated from each other.

(e) Fingerprints partially overlap.   (f) Fingerprint coincidence.

Fig. 6. Position relationship of PEDR fingerprint.

more scientifically explained by using different types of devices as target APs. In addition, experiment results verify that device fingerprints of the same model are also different, which means that attackers cannot use the devices with same model to circumvent PEDR.

Table 1. Type and quantity of device.

Device	Quantity	Device	Quantity
TL-WDR5620	2	UTT-A655W	3
Laptop with AR9588	1	Laptop with AR9580	1
TL-WR824N	4	Huawei mate 30	4
TL-WDR4310	2	Samsung	1
LB-LINK	2	Device with openwrt and AR9531	2
Others	5		

Software Implementation: In terms of software, the kernel of the detection terminal laptop is changed to Linux 4.2.0, and the Linux 802.11n CSI Tool is installed on the detection terminal to collect CSI data under the 802.11n wireless network. In particular, Hostapd is installed in the detected laptop, it can help the laptop to turn on the soft AP.

The experiments are scheduled in the laboratory which is a typical office environment with the size of 11 m × 6 m, and contains desks and other furniture. As shown in Fig. 2, the position of the serial number 1–9 is used to place the target equipment, and the detection equipment is placed in the position 0. Obviously, the target devices in different positions can provide different CSI information, which is more helpful to verify the validity of the fingerprint.

5.2 Verification

In this section, experiments in a real network environment have confirmed that the phase errors drift in a relatively stable range. At the same time, the experimental results show that the difference in fingerprints of different devices is obvious and using the phase error range as the device fingerprint can be uniquely identified. Therefore, the feasibility of using phase error drift range as the fingerprint can be explained.

Fingerprint Feasibility: In order to verify the feasibility of using the phase error drift range as the fingerprint, it must be investigated whether the device fingerprint can remain relatively stable. By studying the change of the phase error distribution area of the device over a period of time, the stability of the device fingerprint can be judged. We randomly selected 4 different types of APs and successively placed them in the same place (e.g., position 1 in Fig. 2). For each AP device, data collection was performed daily, and 10 groups of data were collected each time for 15 consecutive days. When collecting each set of data, the detection terminal needed to connect to the target AP. Considering the packet loss rate and network conditions, we set the sending interval to 5 ms. That is, the detection terminal sent the ICMP messages with the interval of 5 ms to the target AP for 10 s. When the target AP returned response packets, the CSI information was collected and processed to obtain the drift range of the phase errors over time. In order to intuitively display the variation of fingerprints, we plotted the change of the phase error distribution area within 15 days, and evaluated the stability of the phase error drift range on the time dimension. Figure 7 shows the curve of the phase error distribution area of the four devices at different time periods. Obviously, the phase error distribution area of the 4 devices can remain stable in the time dimension, and we can design the legitimacy detection threshold TSV accordingly. The experimental results prove that the phase error drift range remains relatively stable in time.

According to our experimental results, the phase error drift range fingerprint is relatively stable, and the fingerprints are significantly different between different devices. Therefore, fingerprints based on the phase error drift range are feasible.

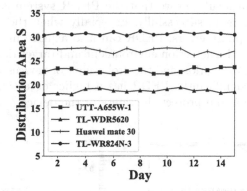

Fig. 7. Variation of phase error distribution area of four devices.

Efficiency: We conducted extensive experiments on the PEDR system, and evaluated both the detection rate and the false negative rate. Besides, we compared PEDR with the latest Liu's method to illustrate the superiority of the fingerprint based on phase error drift range.

The ETA scenario was simulated, and the two parameters, detection rate and false negative rate, were introduced to evaluate the system performance. The detection rate indicates the probability that the detection system can successfully detect the ET in the attack scenario. The false negative rate refers to the probability that ET is not found. In the experiment, 9 devices were randomly selected from 27 experimental devices as illegitimate devices to simulate ETA. In the simulation experiment scenario, the PEDR and Liu's method were used for detection respectively, and the experimental results of the two were compared. During the experiment, the detection terminal extracted CSI information from each target device and made fingerprints to detect its legitimacy. In order to ensure the accuracy and rationality of the experiment, we performed a legitimacy detection experiment 10 times a day for 10 days, and took the average value of the attack detection rate measured multiple times a day for statistics. The results of PEDR and Liu's method are shown in Figs. 8 and 9 respectively. Due to the existence of devices with similar phase errors in the experiment, the phase errors of these devices have overlapped each other due to PEDP. Liu 's method which based on phase error is difficult to distinguish such target devices, and it is easy to generate false negative results. Therefore, the false negative rate of Liu's method is as high as 15.56%, while the attack detection rate is only maintained at about 84.44%. Compared with Liu's method based on phase error, PEDR uses the phase error drift range as the fingerprint. Although it takes a certain amount of time to collect fingerprints, it overcomes the defect of false negative results caused by phase errors drift with time and can achieve more accurate detection. After 10 days of the simulation experiment. The detection rate of PEDR is still stable and as high as 98.89%, and only a few cases have a false negative rate of 1.11%.

The experimental results prove that the PEDR system can implement the legitimacy detection more successfully. Especially when the devices with only slight differences in phase errors, PEDR can also achieve high-precision detection. We believe that the detection environment and target devices will be more complicated in actual scenarios, and the probability of devices with similar phase errors will increase significantly. PEDR has a higher detection rate, which can effectively detect ETA and protect the safety of the device.

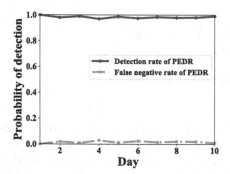

Fig. 8. Detection rate and false negative rate of PEDR.

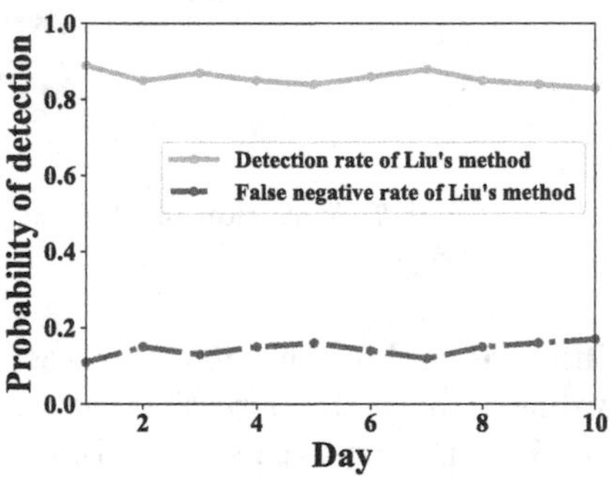

Fig. 9. Detection rate and false negative rate of Liu's method.

6   Conclusion

Validated by our experiments, the phase error drift phenomenon, i.e. PEDP, is widespread in wireless devices, which may cause the failure of detection scheme based on phase errors. In order to achieve higher precision ETA detection, we proposed the legitimacy detection scheme PEDR based on the phase error drift range. Because the phase error drift range remains stable in the time dimension, PEDR can effectively detect ETA. Especially for devices with similar phase errors, the detection effect of PEDR is outstanding. Therefore, attackers cannot use the equipment with the same model to avoid detection, which improves the security between the AP and client devices. In addition, PEDR is based on the user client and does not require additional hardware equipment, which makes it more lightweight and practical. Compared with the active detection scheme, it is not easy for attackers to find and deceive during the entire detection process. We have conducted extensive experiments and proved that the fingerprint based on the phase error drift range is more effective and reliable than the fingerprint only based on phase error for detecting ETA. In the future, we plan to improve the efficiency of legitimacy detection and on the premise of ensuring the detection rate.

Acknowledgment. The work is partly Supported by China Postdoctoral Science Foundation (Grant No. 2019M652475) and the Fundamental Research Funds for the Central Universities (Grant No. 201813021).

References

1. Lu, Q., Jiang, R., Ouyang, Y., et al.: BiRe: a client-side bi-directional SYN reflection mechanism against multi-model evil twin attacks. Comput. Secur. **88**, 101618 (2020)
2. van Rijswijk-Deij, R., Sperotto, A., Pras, A.: DNSSEC and its potential for DDoS attacks: a comprehensive measurement study. In: Proceedings of the 2014 Conference on Internet Measurement Conference, pp. 449–460 (2014)
3. Lu, Q., Qu, H., Ouyang, Y., et al.: SLFAT: client-side evil twin detection approach based on arrival time of special length frames. Secur. Communi. Netw. **2019** (2019)
4. Marlinspike, M.: More tricks for defeating SSL in practice. Black Hat USA (2009)
5. Brik, V., Banerjee, S., Gruteser, M., et al.: Wireless device identification with radiometric signatures. In: Proceedings of the 14th ACM International Conference on Mobile Computing and Networking, pp. 116–127 (2008)
6. Nguyen, N.T., Zheng, G., Han, Z., et al.: Device fingerprinting to enhance wireless security using nonparametric Bayesian method. In: 2011 Proceedings IEEE INFOCOM, pp. 1404–1412. IEEE (2011)
7. Wei, W., Jaiswal, S., Kurose, J.F., et al.: Identifying 802.11 traffic from passive measurements using iterative Bayesian inference. In: INFOCOM (2006)
8. Arackaparambil, C., Bratus, S., Shubina, A., et al.: On the reliability of wireless fingerprinting using clock skews. In: Proceedings of the Third ACM Conference on Wireless Network Security, pp. 169–174 (2010)
9. Lu, Q., Qu, H., Zhuang, Y., et al.: A passive client-based approach to detect evil twin attacks. In: 2017 IEEE Trustcom/BigDataSE/ICESS, pp. 233–239. IEEE (2017)
10. Liu, P., Yang, P., Song, W.Z., et al.: Real-time identification of rogue WiFi connections using environment-independent physical features. In: IEEE INFOCOM 2019-IEEE Conference on Computer Communications, pp. 109–198. IEEE (2019)
11. Agarwal, M., Biswas, S., Nandi, S.: An efficient scheme to detect evil twin rogue access point attack in 802.11 Wi-Fi networks. Int. J. Wirel. Inf. Netw. **25**(2), 130–145 (2018)

12. Bauer, K., Gonzales, H., McCoy, D.: Mitigating evil twin attacks in 802.11. In: 2008 IEEE International Performance, Computing and Communications Conference, pp. 513–516. IEEE (2008)
13. Gonzales, H., Bauer, K., Lindqvist, J., et al.: Practical defenses for evil twin attacks in 802.11. In: 2010 IEEE Global Telecommunications Conference GLOBECOM 2010, pp. 1–6. IEEE (2010)
14. Byrd, C., Cross, T., Takahashi, T.: Secure open wireless networking. Black Hat (2015)
15. Kumar, A., Paul, P.: Security analysis and implementation of a simple method for prevention and detection against Evil Twin attack in IEEE 802.11 wireless LAN. In: 2016 International Conference on Computational Techniques in Information and Communication Technologies (ICCTICT), pp. 176–181. IEEE (2016)
16. Bahl, P., Chandra, R., Padhye, J., et al.: Enhancing the security of corporate Wi-Fi networks using DAIR. In: Proceedings of the 4th International Conference on Mobile Systems, Applications and Services, pp. 1–14 (2006)
17. Wei, W., Wang, B., Zhang, C., et al.: Classification of access network types: ethernet wireless LAN, ADSL, cable modem or dialup? In: Proceedings IEEE 24th Annual Joint Conference of the IEEE Computer and Communications Societies, vol. 2, pp. 1060–1071. IEEE (2005)
18. Wei, W., Suh, K., Wang, B., et al.: Passive online rogue access point detection using sequential hypothesis testing with TCP ACK-pairs. In: Proceedings of the 7th ACM SIGCOMM Conference on Internet Measurement, pp. 365–378 (2007)
19. Yin, H., Chen, G., Wang, J.: Detecting protected layer-3 rogue APs. In: 2007 Fourth International Conference on Broadband Communications, Networks and Systems (BROADNETS'07), pp. 449–458. IEEE (2007)
20. Shetty, S., Song, M., Ma, L.: Rogue access point detection by analyzing network traffic characteristics. In: MILCOM 2007-IEEE Military Communications Conference, pp. 1–7. IEEE (2007)
21. Baiamonte, V., Papagiannaki, K., Iannaccone, G.: Detecting 802.11 wireless hosts from remote passive observations. In: Akyildiz, I.F., Sivakumar, R., Ekici, E., Oliveira, J.C., McNair, J. (eds.) NETWORKING 2007. LNCS, vol. 4479, pp. 356–367. Springer, Heidelberg (2007). https://doi.org/10.1007/978-3-540-72606-7_31
22. Watkins, L., Beyah, R., Corbett, C.: A passive approach to rogue access point detection. In: IEEE GLOBECOM 2007-IEEE Global Telecommunications Conference, pp. 355–360. IEEE (2007)
23. Xia, H., Li, L., Cheng, X., et al.: Modeling and analysis botnet propagation in social Internet of Things. IEEE Internet Things J. **7**, 7470–7481 (2020)
24. Jana, S., Kasera, S.K.: On fast and accurate detection of unauthorized wireless access points using clock skews. IEEE Trans. Mob. Comput. **9**(3), 449–462 (2009)
25. Song, Y., Yang, C., Gu, G.: Who is peeping at your passwords at Starbucks?-To catch an evil twin access point. In: 2010 IEEE/IFIP International Conference on Dependable Systems & Networks (DSN), pp. 323–332. IEEE (2010)
26. Yang, C., Song, Y., Gu, G.: Active user-side evil twin access point detection using statistical techniques. IEEE Trans. Inf. Forensics Secur. **7**(5), 1638–1651 (2012)
27. Neumann, C., Heen, O., Onno, S.: An empirical study of passive 802.11 device fingerprinting. In: 2012 32nd International Conference on Distributed Computing Systems Workshops, pp. 593–602. IEEE (2012)
28. Xia, H., Zhang, R., et al.: Two-stage game design of payoff decision-making scheme for crowdsourcing dilemma. IEEE/ACM Trans. Netw. (2020)
29. Alotaibi, B., Elleithy, K.: A passive fingerprint technique to detect fake access points. In: Wireless Telecommunications Symposium (WTS), pp. 1–8. IEEE (2015)

30. Xia, H., Li, L., Cheng, X., et al.: A dynamic virus propagation model based on social attributes in city IoTs. IEEE Internet Things J. **7**, 8036–8048 (2020)
31. Liu, H., Wang, Y., Liu, J., et al.: Practical user authentication leveraging channel state information (CSI). In: Proceedings of the 9th ACM Symposium on Information, Computer and Communications Security, pp. 389–400 (2014)
32. Hua, J., Sun, H., Shen, Z., et al.: Accurate and efficient wireless device fingerprinting using channel state information. In: IEEE INFOCOM 2018-IEEE Conference on Computer Communications, pp. 1700–1708. IEEE (2018)
33. Zhuo, Y., Zhu, H., Xue, H., et al.: Perceiving accurate CSI phases with commodity WiFi devices. In: IEEE INFOCOM 2017-IEEE Conference on Computer Communications, pp. 1–9. IEEE (2017)

Differentially Private Social Graph Publishing for Community Detection

Xuebin Ma[✉], Jingyu Yang, and Shengyi Guan

School of Computer Science, Inner Mongolia Key Laboratory of Wireless Networking and Mobile Computing, Inner Mongolia University, Hohhot, China
csmaxuebin@imu.edu.cn

Abstract. Social networks typically include a community structure, and the connections between nodes within the same community are very close; however, the connections between communities are sparse. In this study, we analyze the main challenges behind the problem and then resolve it using differential privacy. First, we choose the Louvain algorithm as a benchmark community detection algorithm for the algorithmic perturbation scheme. We introduce an exponential mechanism that uses modularity as a score. Secondly, by transforming each community into a hierarchical random graph model, and its edge connection probability is noisy by differential privacy mechanism to ensure the security of relevant information in the protected community.

Keywords: Differential privacy · Community detection · Social network

1 Introduction

Techniques for identifying the groupings in social networks and then analyzing these groupings for further use have become a key research topic in sociology—this is referred to as "community detection". Through community detection, we can reduce both the network size and the computational complexity of the algorithm used to process it, thereby improving the accuracy of the analysis. However, most of the methods are performed without privacy protection, and the results of community detection are output in the form of the node-set. In order to protect the privacy of users, it is necessary to protect the privacy of community detection.

Existing social network differential privacy protection schemes focus on a centralized model; they assume that third-party data collectors who possess the information are trustworthy, which is a practical assumption of real-world applications. Therefore, we use a local differential privacy (LDP) model to protect the privacy of social networks, by releasing the sanitized graph at local devices after differential privacy processing. The published data mask the interconnections between nodes and preserve the characteristics of the network structure, enabling researchers to achieve a reasonable balance between the utility of the algorithm and its ability to protect privacy when data are used for feature analysis and data mining.

N. Park et al. (Eds.): SecureComm 2020, LNICST 336, pp. 208–214, 2020.
https://doi.org/10.1007/978-3-030-63095-9_11

2 Related Work

2.1 Local Differential Privacy

The differential privacy protection methods applied to social networks can be roughly divided according to two approaches. The first approach focuses on publishing certain types of noisy mining results; these include degree distributions, subgraph counts, frequent graphics patterns, and cut queries [4, 5]. This approach uses the properties of the original graph for general purposes, perturbs the graph, and publishes the aggregated results. It is theoretically proven that noise addition ensures strong privacy preservation. The second approach is to publish the entire social network for general purposes [6, 7]. These methods differ in the intermediate structures used for publishing and the corresponding definitions of differential privacy.

2.2 Community Detection with Differential Privacy

The task of finding node groups using connection relationships in the network is referred to as community detection. The Louvain algorithm [9] is based on multi-level optimization modularity and performs well in terms of efficiency and effectiveness. Moreover, the Louvain algorithm can identify hierarchical community structures; thus, it is considered one of the best community detection algorithms.

Recently, researchers have applied differential privacy for community detection. Nguyen et al. [10] chose the Louvain method as the backend community detection method of the input perturbation scheme and proposed the LouvainDP method. Ye et al. [11] proposed the first LDP-enabled graph metric estimation framework for a variety of graph analysis tasks, which address data correlation among nodes by two efficient perturbation algorithms based on adjacency bit vector and node degree.

3 Preliminaries

3.1 Louvain Algorithm

The Louvain algorithm [9] is based on multi-level optimization modularity, which is efficient to identify hierarchical community structures. According to [9], when assigning node i to a community, the modularity of the community changes as

$$
\begin{aligned}
\Delta Q &= \left[\frac{\sum_{in} + k_{i,in}}{2m} - \left(\frac{\sum_{tot} + k_i}{2m} \right)^2 \right] - \left[\frac{\sum_{in}}{2m} - \left(\frac{\sum_{tot}}{2m} \right)^2 - \left(\frac{k_i}{2m} \right)^2 \right] \\
&= \frac{1}{2m} \left(k_{i,in} - \frac{\sum_{tot} k_i}{m} \right) = \frac{k_{i,in}}{2m} - \frac{\sum_{tot} k_i}{2m^2}.
\end{aligned}
\tag{1}
$$

3.2   Local Differential Privacy

Definition 1 (ϵ-Differential Privacy): Given a random algorithm $\mathcal{A}$, let S represent the set of all output spaces of $\mathcal{A}$ on the two neighbor graphs G_1 and G_2(which differ at most one element). The algorithm $\mathcal{A}$ satisfies ϵ-differential privacy if:

$$\Pr[\mathcal{A}(G_1) \in S] \leq e^{\epsilon} \times \Pr[\mathcal{A}(G_2) \in S] \tag{2}$$

Theorem 1 (Laplace Mechanism): For any function $f : G \rightarrow \mathbb{R}^d$, the mechanism $\mathcal{A}$

$$AG = fG + \left(Lap_1\left(\tfrac{\Delta f}{\epsilon}\right), \ldots, Lap_d\left(\tfrac{\Delta f}{\epsilon}\right) \right) \tag{3}$$

provides ϵ-differential privacy, where $Lap_i\left(\tfrac{\Delta f}{\epsilon}\right)$ represents Laplacian independent and identically distributed variable samples with scale parameter $\tfrac{\Delta f}{\epsilon}$.

Theorem 2 (Exponential Mechanism): Given a function f $: (G \times OS) \rightarrow \mathbb{R}$, where OS is output space. For a graph G, the mechanism $\mathcal{A}$ that samples an output O with a probability proportional to $\exp\left(\tfrac{\epsilon \cdot f(G,O)}{2\Delta f}\right)$ satisfies ϵ-differential privacy.

Theorem 3 (Sequential Composition): Let each $\mathcal{A}_i$ provide ϵ_i-differential privacy. A sequence $\mathcal{A}_i(G)$ over the entire graph G provides $\sum \epsilon_i$-differential privacy.

4   Problem Solution

4.1   Differentially Private Louvain Algorithm

We propose a solution to the privacy problems in community detection. Our scheme is divided into two phases. First, the social network is partitioned into multiple independent communities by adopting the community detection algorithm. Then, the privacy of the edges within each independent community is protected.

Algorithm 1: Differentially Private Louvain Algorithm

Input: Input graph G, privacy parameter ϵ_1
Output: a private partition set $\{P_1,...,P_k\}$
1 Calculate the sensitivity Δf
2 Randomly select initial node sequences and each node as a partition
3 **for** each node i in sequences S **do**
4   **for** neighbor partition P_k from partition set **do**
5   compute the modular gain ΔQ_k
6           $\Delta Q_{max} = \Delta Q_k$ with the probability min $\{1, \dfrac{\exp\left(\frac{\epsilon_1}{2\Delta f}\Delta Q_k\right)}{\exp\left(\frac{\epsilon_1}{2\Delta f}\Delta Q_{max}\right)}\}$
7   Record the partition P_i in which ΔQ_{max} is obtained
8   **end for**
9   move node i into the partition P_i
10   if   the partition of all nodes no longer changes
11   **return** private partition set $\{P_1,...,P_k\}$
12 **end for**

Algorithm 1 first calculates the sensitivity of the social graph according to its number of nodes (Line 1), and we will explain in detail how to calculate Δf later. Based on the first phase of the Louvain algorithm, each node in the original graph is treated as a separate community (Line 2). Then, according to the node sequence, mining the neighboring nodes/communities of each node (lines 3–4). Then moving the node to different communities and calculating the current modularity gain. Finally, we introduce the exponential mechanism, and the maximum modularity gain is selected, otherwise, it is unchanged (lines 5–9). When the movement of all nodes no longer causes changes of the modularity gain, the first round is completed and the results of the first round of community detection are returned (lines 10–12).

4.2 Edge Probability Perturbation

Community detection makes edge connection within the same community more salient and therefore requires additional protection. We use the same model in [15], which converts each community into an HRG model, then combined the generated HRG model with the edge-connection probability by adding Laplace noise in Algorithm 2.

Algorithm 2: Edge Probability Perturbation

Input: Input partition set $\{P_1,...,P_k\}$, privacy parameter ϵ_2
Output: Sanitized graph $\widetilde{G}$
1 **for** each partition P_i in set $\{P_1,...,P_k\}$ **do**
2   Convert to HRG model T_i
3   **for** each internal node r of T_i **do**
4   Calculate noisy probability $\widetilde{p_r} = \min\left\{1, \dfrac{e_r + Lap\left(\frac{1}{\epsilon_2}\right)}{n_{L_r} * n_{R_r}}\right\}$
5   **end for**
6   **for** any two nodes i, j of P_i **do**
7   Find the lowest common ancestor r of i and j
8   Place an edge in P_i between i and j with independent probability $\widetilde{p_r}$
9   **end for**
10 **end for**
11 Connect partition $\widetilde{P_1},...,\widetilde{P_k}$
12 **return** Sanitized graph $\widetilde{G}$

After we convert the community into an HRG model, we calculate the connection probability of each internal node separately. Further, we introduce the Laplacian mechanism. Subsequently, for any two nodes i and j in the community, we find the lowest common ancestor r and establish a connection between the two nodes i and j using the connection probability of the internal node r. Because the inter-community edges are relatively sparse and have low correlations, these direct connections do not provide additional privacy protection.

4.3 Sensitivity Analysis

The sensitivity Δf should be analyzed to complete the selection probability equation, where G' is the neighbor of G. The neighbor of a graph is the graph obtained by changing only one edge. Because the addition or removal operations are similar, only the former is considered in our proof. There are two cases to consider: (1) The connection is an edge inside the community P. (2) The connection is an edge between the community P and S. Finally, we obtain $\Delta f \leq \frac{3}{m}$.

5 Experiment Evaluation

5.1 Experimental Setup

For comparison purposes, two techniques that are similar to our method were implemented as references. They are the basic differential privacy algorithms for the HRG model, which use the same privacy criteria as [13] and the algorithm perturbation presented in [10]; the results of the previously centralized differential privacy scheme and the algorithm perturbation scheme and our proposed scheme are labeled as "DP", "MD" and "LLDP" respectively. We performed experiments on two real datasets to evaluate our algorithm. The details of datasets are shown in Table 1.

Table 1. Statistics of the datasets.

Datasets	Nodes	Edges	Average clustering coefficient
Ego-Facebook [12]	4039	88234	0.6055
Enron [13]	36692	183831	0.4970

5.2 Experiment Evaluation of Community Detection

The real social network dataset we chose did not have standard community detection results. Thus, we chose the output of the Louvain algorithm as a standard control because the evaluation of the data had been performed in [15], and the Louvain method had been proven there to provide high-quality results.

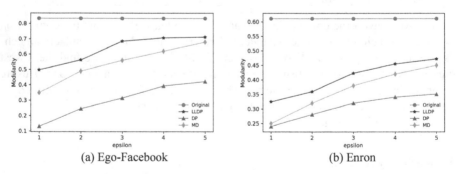

(a) Ego-Facebook   (b) Enron

Fig. 1. The modularity of two social network datasets under different ε

The partitioning results of different privacy budgets are shown in Fig. 1. For both datasets, the results given by our algorithm increased with the increase of the privacy budget and gradually stabilized after reaching a certain value. This provides an effective reference for the selection of a privacy budget. In general, the effectiveness of algorithm perturbations is higher than that of input perturbations. The input disturbance used for comparison also followed a similar trend; however, the overall value was low, which is significantly different from its typical value. Newman [8] suggested that the value of Q in a general network is between 0.3 and 0.7, which can explain a good community structure. Therefore, although the modularity of the results obtained by our algorithm was lower than the real situation, it still retained an effective community structure.

6 Conclusion

We analyzed the privacy problems of community detection can lead to and proposed a differentially private detection procedure based on the Louvain algorithm. Moreover, we proposed to further protect the relational data within the community by converting the individual community into a subgraph of an HRG model and subsequently calculating the edge connection probability by adding Laplacian noise. Experimental results indicated an improved performance on real data.

Acknowledgments. This paper is supported by Inner Mongolia Natural Science Foundation (Grant No. 2018MS06026) and the Science and Technology Program of Inner Mongolia Autonomous Region (Grant No. 2019GG116).

References

1. Newman, M.: Social networks. Oxford Scholarship Online (2018)
2. Kasiviswanathan, S.P., Lee, H.K., Nissim, K., Raskhodnikova, S., Smith, A.: What can we learn privately? SIAM J. Comput. **40**(3), 793–826 (2011)
3. Dwork, C.: Differential privacy: a survey of results. In: Agrawal, M., Du, D., Duan, Z., Li, A. (eds.) Theory and Applications of Models of Computation. Lecture Notes in Computer Science, vol. 4978, pp. 1–19. Springer, Berlin, Heidelberg (2008). https://doi.org/10.1007/978-3-540-79228-4_1
4. Hardt, M., Roth, A.: Beating randomized response on incoherent matrices. In: Proceedings of the 44th symposium on Theory of Computing - STOC'12 (2012)
5. Cai, Z., He, Z., Guan, X., Li, Y.: Collective data-sanitization for preventing sensitive information inference attacks in social networks. IEEE Trans. Dependable Secure Comput. **15**, 1 (2016)
6. Proserpio, D., Goldberg, S., McSherry, F.: A workflow for differentially-private graph synthesis. In: Proceedings of the 2012 ACM Workshop on Workshop on Online Social Networks - WOSN'12 (2012)
7. Wang, Y., Wu, X., Wu, L.: Differential privacy preserving spectral graph analysis. In: Pei, J., Tseng, V.S., Cao, L., Motoda, H., Xu, G. (eds.) Advances in Knowledge Discovery and Data Mining. Lecture Notes in Computer Science, vol. 7819, pp. 329–340. Springer, Berlin, Heidelberg (2013). https://doi.org/10.1007/978-3-642-37456-2_28
8. Newman, M.E.J., Girvan, M.: Finding and evaluating community structure in networks. Phys. Rev. E **69**(2), 026113 (2004)
9. Blondel, V.D., Guillaume, J.-L., Lambiotte, R., Lefebvre, E.: Fast unfolding of communities in large networks. J. Stat. Mech: Theory Exp. **2008**(10), P10008 (2008)

10. Nguyen, H.H., Imine, A., Rusinowitch, M.: Detecting communities under differential privacy. In: Proceedings of the 2016 ACM on Workshop on Privacy in the Electronic Society - WPES'16 (2016)
11. Ye, Q., Hu, H., Au, M.H., Meng, X., Xiao, X.: Towards locally differentially private generic graph metric estimation. In: 2020 IEEE 36th International Conference on Data Engineering (ICDE), Dallas, TX, USA, pp. 1922–1925 (2020)
12. McAuley, J., Leskovec, J.: Learning to discover social circles in ego networks. In: NIPS 2012, pp. 539–547
13. Leskovec, J., Lang, K.J., Dasgupta, A., Mahoney, M.W.: Community structure in large networks: natural cluster sizes and the absence of large well-defined clusters. Internet Math. 6(1), 29–123 (2009)
14. Xiao, Q., Chen, R., Tan, K.-L.: Differentially private network data release via structural inference. In: Proceedings of the 20th ACM SIGKDD International Conference on Knowledge Discovery and Data Mining, pp. 911–920, ACM (2014)
15. Prat-Pérez, A., Dominguez-Sal, D., Larriba-Pey, J.-L.: High quality, scalable and parallel community detection for large real graphs. In: Proceedings of the 23rd international conference on World Wide Web - WWW'14 (2014)

LaaCan: A Lightweight Authentication Architecture for Vehicle Controller Area Network

Syed Akib Anwar Hridoy$^{(\boxtimes)}$ and Mohammad Zulkernine

Queen's Reliable Software Technology (QRST) Lab, School of Computing,
Queen's University, Kingston, ON, Canada
{akib.anwar,mz}@queensu.ca

Abstract. Vehicle manufacturers are installing a large number of Electronic Control Units (ECU) inside vehicles. ECUs communicate among themselves via a Controller Area Network (CAN) to ensure better user experience and safety. CAN is considered as a de facto standard for efficient communication of an embedded control system network. However, it does not have sufficient built-in security features. The major challenges of securing CAN are that the hardware of the ECUs have limited computational power and the size of a CAN message is small. In this paper, a lightweight security solution, LaaCan is designed to secure CAN communication by adopting the Authenticated Encryption with Associated Data (AEAD) approach. The architecture ensures confidentiality, integrity, and authenticity of data transmission. The experimental results show that the delay of LaaCan can be reduced depending on hardware configurations. We consider it lightweight since it adds a low overhead regardless of performing encryption and authentication. We evaluate LaaCan using four metrics: communication overhead, network traffic load, cost of deployment, and compatibility with CAN specification. The evaluation results show that the proposed architecture keeps the network traffic unchanged, has low deployment cost, and is highly compatible with the specification of the protocol.

Keywords: CAN bus · In-vehicle network security · AEAD

1 Introduction

Vehicles were considered as mechanical machines before the introduction of software inside them. Components such as engines, brakes, and gears were assembled into a car in coherence with the principle of mechanics. Yet, the limited accuracy of mechanics led to undetectable failures, and vehicle safety was in threat. The automotive industry moved towards the adaption of digital electronics and software controls in the vehicle to improve the scenario. Manufacturers started installing electronic sensors in vehicles for driving safety and assistance. The

© ICST Institute for Computer Sciences, Social Informatics and Telecommunications Engineering 2020
Published by Springer Nature Switzerland AG 2020. All Rights Reserved
N. Park et al. (Eds.): SecureComm 2020, LNICST 336, pp. 215–234, 2020.
https://doi.org/10.1007/978-3-030-63095-9_12

automotive industry introduced Electronic Control Unit (ECU) in 1970 to collect information from the sensors and control the mechanical components. An ECU can request another ECU for its sensor information to make a collective decision. These ECUs form an in-vehicle network to communicate with each other. For in-vehicle communications, the most widely used medium is the Controller Area Network (CAN).

With the revolution of ECUs, new features are added to vehicles to enable them to make intelligent decisions. These features provide autonomous driving support as well as safety and convenience to users. However, they expose the previously isolated vehicle system to cyberspace, which introduces the opportunity of cyberattacks. These attacks endanger the privacy and safety of a vehicle.

Attacks try to control vehicle functionalities illegally. ECUs are responsible to control these functionalities and they communicate via a CAN bus. Therefore, these attacks highly relate to CAN communications and the security of these communications must be a concern. The two most significant purposes of CAN development were to reduce the wiring complexity and cost. At that time, the security of communication between vehicular components was not a concern as a vehicle was a closed system without communications with other devices or vehicles. Hence, the automotive engineers implemented CAN following the concept of broadcast-based serial communication. As a result, any ECU connected to the network can read or send messages.

In-Vehicle Infotainment (IVI) system is connected to the CAN bus. It increases the security risks as IVI connects external devices through the wireless medium such as Bluetooth and Wi-Fi. There are third-party applications available for IVI to provide entertainment and navigation services [18]. Besides, third party dongles can be plugged into the OBD-II diagnostic port to monitor the status of vehicle systems such as the engine and transmission. These dongles connect to smartphones via Bluetooth. A malicious application installed on a phone that is connected to the OBD-II dongle can help the attacker to read the network traffic [33]. The reverse engineering of recorded communication may lead to an attack. The lack of confidentiality, integrity, and authenticity features in the CAN protocol are the reasons for these attacks.

In this paper, we design LaaCan, a security architecture that implements a lightweight authenticated encryption based on a pre-shared secret key to assure confidentiality, integrity, and authenticity. Authenticated encryption ensures the privacy and authentication of data. It is implemented by adopting Authenticated Encryption with Additional Data (AEAD) cipher. To find the best applicable AEAD cipher in CAN, we explore five AEAD-based ciphers and the analysis shows that ChaCha20-Poly1305 has the best credibility in low powered ECUs. ChaCha20-Poly1305 authenticates data using Message Authentication Code (MAC) that has to be transmitted with the message. The CRC field in CAN frame is used for error detection and error detection is part of data integrity process [23]. Since LaaCan ensures data integrity, we replace the CRC data with MAC that helps to maintain unchanged network traffic and low overhead. The experimental results show that LaaCan provides strong security with low com-

Table 1. Standard CAN frame description.

Field	Length	Description
Start of frame	1 bit	Indicates the beginning of a frame
Arbitration	12 bits	Contains the type and priority of the message
Control	6 bits	Includes the length of the data
Data	64 bits	Holds the transmitted data
CRC	16 bits	Cyclic redundancy check field used for detecting error of the transmitted data
ACK	2 bits	Acknowledges reception of valid CAN messages
EOF	7 bits	Specify the end of the frame

munication overhead and protects the network from the most common form of attacks. The evaluation results show that LaaCan does not have any effect on network traffic load, has low deployment cost, and is highly compatible.

The remainder of the paper is organized as follows. In Sect. 2, we provide an overview of CAN protocol and discuss the related work by providing a classification of existing solutions. Section 3 presents the design of LaaCan. The implementation details and evaluation results are described in Sect. 4. We conclude the paper in Sect. 5 with a discussion on limitations and future work.

2 Related Work

In this section, we discuss the existing CAN security solutions. Here, we compare and contrast LaaCan with the related work qualitatively. Before presenting the related work, we briefly discuss the Controller Area Network (CAN). CAN is a multi-master broadcast-based bus system with a bandwidth up to 1 Mbit/s. It is widely used for embedded system communication as it is efficient and cost-effective. In standard CAN protocol, broadcast messages do not contain any receiver information [7]. Therefore, adding and removing nodes is easier. Table 1 describes each field of a CAN message.

Considering the different implementation techniques of security countermeasures, we present the related work as a classification of existing security solutions. We classify the security measures in terms of security enforcement procedures. Figure 1 depicts the classification. The communication is primarily secured by adopting cryptographic architecture and intrusion detection systems (IDS) or both. The cryptographic architectures mostly involve different ways of encryption and authentication mechanisms to secure network transmission from adversaries. A number of works in this category are discussed in the following subsections. In contrast, the IDS learn the predefined activities and policies to detect

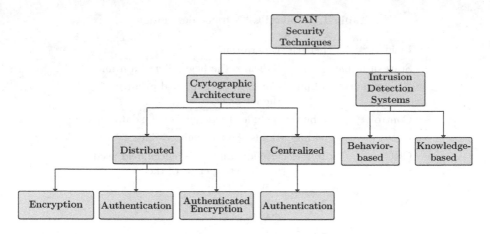

Fig. 1. Classification of CAN security solutions.

and report any malicious activity. The existing IDS of in-vehicle networks can be categorized into behavior-based and knowledge-based techniques [16]. For the sake of space limitation and relevance, we do not discuss the IDS further.

2.1 Distributed Approach

In the distributed cryptographic architecture, security features are implemented inside ECUs and there is no need for a central authority. Although an ECU gets compromised by adversaries, they cannot control the full network. The distributed methods can be further divided into three categories: encryption, authentication, and encrypted-authentication. The encryption-based approaches involve data encryption for security purposes; however, it does not include an authentication mechanism. On the other hand, authentication-based approaches only authenticate data. These approaches lack confidentiality as they do not encrypt data. The authenticated encryption approaches encrypt and authenticate data. Though it may require more processing time, authenticated encryption provides strong security. We present the related work for each category in the following paragraphs.

Distributed Encryption. CANTrack [14] only encrypts the message using the message counter to prevent the replay attacks. It does not include any authentication mechanism. All ECUs maintain a message counter for each message type and use the counters as encryption keys.

Distributed Authentication. VeCure [32] introduces trust-based grouping of ECUs along with Message Authentication Code (MAC) for authentication purposes. It divides ECUs into two groups. ECUs with external interfaces such as OBD-II and infotainment system are assigned to low-trust group. The other

ECUs with no external interfaces are assigned to high-trust group. Authentication is only performed for the communication of high-trust ECUs. They share a common secret key to generate MAC. MAC is transmitted using an *extra message*, which increases network traffic and message processing time. LaaCan does not affect the network traffic as no additional message is used for MAC transmission. Herrewege et al. [31] uses HMAC (Hash-based Message Authentication Code) to generate the message authentication code using shared secret keys. CAN+ [35] is used to share secret keys as it allows additional 120 bits to be attached to a frame. Each message type has a unique secret key, and all secret keys are stored in the participating ECUs. Therefore, compromising of an ECU can reveal all secret keys. Though we use a shared secret key, LaaCan ensures message freshness by involving a counter. The message freshness value makes it harder for attackers when the secret key is compromised as attackers need to keep track of freshness value. LiBrA-CAN [15] authenticates messages using Mixed-Message Authentication Codes (M-MACs). It divides the ECUs into multiple small groups. Each group of ECUs share a secret key. The authentication is performed by employing a helper ECU to compute MAC. Both the sender and the helper computes MAC partially. The receiver ECU performs authentication by merging the partially generated MAC. LiBra-CAN has high communication overhead and uses CAN+ [35], which is not well recognized. Therefore, it is not compatible with the standard CAN.

Distributed Authenticated Encryption. Woo et al. [33] assure data confidentiality, integrity, and authenticity based on MAC. The MAC is transmitted using both the extended ID field and the CRC field. Thus, the payload of the network stays unchanged after the initial key distribution. However, a widely used standard SAE J1939 [17] uses the extended ID field to transmit Parameter Group Number (PGN). Hence, reserving extended id field for MAC excludes existing standards. LASAN [22] ensures three security features as well. A centralized security module authorizes all the general ECUs. AES-128 is used in Cipher Block Chaining (CBC) mode. AES requires hardware support and resource constraint ECUs do not have hardware acceleration support for cryptography [11]. Also, the installation of a central ECU brings hardware change, which increases the deployment cost. LaaCan does not require any hardware support and is adaptable by software updates. TOUCAN [8] assures confidentiality, integrity, and authenticity. It also applies AES-128 for data encryption, and Chaskey [20] for MAC computation. The data payload is reduced to 40 bits to fit 24-bit MAC. However, reducing the size of payload makes it incompatible to existing designed protocols that make use of the full length of the payload. Alam et al. [5] introduce identity-based access control for ECU authorization. The symmetric key cryptography and digital signature are applied to assure confidentiality, integrity, and authenticity. The symmetric keys are shared using elliptic curve-based Public Key Encryption (PKE). Though digital signature ensures non-repudiation, it is slow. LaaCan falls in the category of distributed authenticated encryption. The AES cryptographic algorithm is used by [33] and [8]. AES consumes more resources and requires hardware support to reduce the processing delay. Thus,

AES is not suitable for resource-constrained ECUs. Besides, we avoid using the extended id field to transmit authentication code to assure backward compatibility. We also refrain from reducing payload size, which makes LaaCan adaptable to existing implementations.

2.2 Centralized Approach

In a centralized cryptographic architecture, data is authenticated by central ECU. There is no involvement of encryption in a centralized approach. Although these approaches may involve some processing in participant ECUs related to authentication code generation, the authentication process is served by the central ECU. CaCAN [25] installs a monitor ECU in the bus. The monitor ECU compares both the received and calculated MAC for message authentication. TCAN [9] authenticates based on the physical location of the ECU in the network. Two dedicated node repeater and monitor are used to identify the physical location of ECUs from the message reception time difference. Although TCAN authenticates the messages using the physical location, it involves cryptography for the communication between the general ECUs and the monitor in the initialization phase. CaCAN [25] and TCAN [9] lack confidentiality as messages are not encrypted. Moreover, installing dedicated ECUs for authentication is expensive and not adaptable to already manufactured vehicles. Also, they are vulnerable to man-in-the-middle (MITM) attacks.

3   LaaCan Design

In the preceding section, we discussed existing CAN security solutions and their shortcomings. Among the different approaches of cryptographic implementations, only the distributed authenticated encryption architecture is capable of ensuring confidentiality, integrity, and authenticity. Intrusion detection systems highly depend on the trained model, which is heavy computation for resource constraint devices. Considering the limited resources of ECUs and the consequences of in-vehicle security attacks, we design a lightweight security solution by adopting distributed authenticated encryption architecture.

In this section, the architecture of LaaCan is presented. Since a security architecture should be integrable with the existing standards, the design is analyzed to verify the compliance with standard CAN and AUTOSAR [1]. Later, the design challenges and solution options are explained.

3.1 Authenticated Encryption Design

We propose a lightweight authentication architecture for CAN communication. We implement Authenticated Encryption with Associated Data (AEAD) scheme as it is capable of ensuring confidentiality, integrity, and authenticity. We identify available AEAD schemes used in industry and compare the performance to determine the best fit in CAN protocol. The experimental analysis shows that

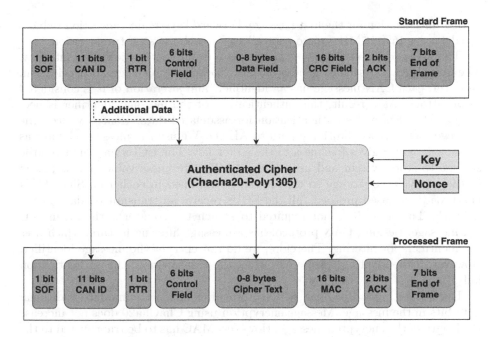

Fig. 2. Design of the authenticated encryption.

among five widely used AEAD algorithms, ChaCha20-Poly1305 has the best performance based on the communication overhead and security measures.

Figure 2 shows the architecture of LaaCan. AEAD requires four inputs: a secret key, nonce, plain text, and additional data. The secret key has to be random. The nonce is used to keep the keystream unique for each operation. Both the sender and the receiver have to know the secret key and nonce. The outputs of AEAD are ciphertext and MAC. The ciphertext is privacy protected plain text, and MAC is a tag to ensure data accuracy.

In the first phase, the message is encrypted using the ChaCha20 stream cipher to assure confidentiality. For encryption, ChaCha20 generates a block using the key block, nonce, and constant characters. Then, it splits the block to form a matrix and runs 20 rounds of alteration between cells. Each round performs four quarter-rounds to process both column and diagonal values. Every quarter-round involves bit operations of add, XOR, and rotate. After the 20 rounds, the matrix is serialized to generate a keystream block. The ChaCha20 performs XOR operation with plain text to generate ciphertext [24]. The keystream block generation process does not involve the plain text. Therefore, it is possible to generate a keystream block earlier to reduce the encryption process delay. After sending a message, a keystream is generated for the next message, which is referred to as a forward key generation. Thus, during the encryption of the next message, the keystream block will be ready to XOR with plain text. Since the forward keystream generation is performed, a keystream block is generated during initialization for the first message. Forward keystream generation reduces the delay by 15% 16 MHz micro-controllers for each message transmission.

The message authentication is necessary to ensure authenticity and integrity. The authentication scheme generates MAC to achieve message authentication. However, each CAN message has an identifier, and alteration of it is considered as an attack. As a result, the authentication of the message identifier is necessary. AEAD provides authentication for associated data. Hence, we feed the message identifier as additional data to AEAD. We use the message counter as the nonce, which gives freshness to the secret key. The ECUs have non-volatile storage to store system and user data [34]. The freshness value can be stored in the non-volatile storage so that it can be retained in each run. Since CAN is a broadcast-based protocol, all the ECUs receive all transmitted data in the network. Therefore, it is not required to attach the counter with a transmitted message. Besides, CAN protocol has a message filtering feature, which uses the identifiers for filtering. Therefore, we do not encrypt the message identifier. However, if the identifier is altered during the transmission, the authentication fails.

Due to the limited payload, CAN protocol cannot accommodate additional data bits in the message. Message encryption using ChaCha20 does not increase the length of the encrypted message. However, MAC has to be transmitted to the receiver to complete the authentication process. Wang et al. [32] used an extra message to carry MAC. Additional message transmission increases the traffic of the network. It also increases the delay in message processing as the receiver has to wait for the MAC. Moreover, no other ECU can communicate between the transmission of the original message and MAC. CAN protocol uses a 15-bit CRC field for error detection of transmitted data. Since LaaCan ensures the integrity of data and error detection is part of data integrity [23], we use the CRC field to attach a 15-bit authentication code. Two existing work [10,33] demonstrated a similar approach of using the CRC field to transmit MAC and showed the feasibility of the solution.

We follow the distributed approach of ensuring security where the network traffic is encrypted and authenticated by all the ECUs. MAC is generated and appended to the message by a sender ECU. There is no need for a central ECU, which allows integrating the solution to existing vehicles with software updates only. Furthermore, LaaCan does not transmit any extra message for security purposes. It does not involve any modified version of the standard protocol also. Therefore, it is feasible to integrate it with the standard CAN protocol as well as standards widely implemented, such as SAE J1939 [17].

3.2   Design Requirement Analysis

To make LaaCan adaptable with the existing systems and standards, we identify two major design requirements: standard CAN and AUTOSAR compliant. The analysis of the design requirements is discussed in the next paragraphs.

Table 2. AUTOSAR profile of LaaCan.

Parameter	Configuration value
Algorithm	ChaCha20-Poly1305
Length of Freshness Value (parameter SecOCFreshnessValueLength)	0 bit
Length of Truncated Freshness Value (parameter SecOCFreshnessValueTxLength)	0 bit
Length of Truncated MAC (parameter SecOCAuthInfoTxLength)	15 bits

Standard CAN Compatibility

The CAN protocol is standardized under ISO (International Organization for Standardization) 11898-1 [2] that describes the data transmission process and message format. The compliance with standard protocol gives solution flexibility of integration with the majority of the existing systems and standards. A security solution should be able to run on existing ECUs and networks to achieve the standard CAN compliance. Some security solutions [15,31] use CAN+ [35] protocol that requires hardware change in transceiver [8]. LaaCan does not require any hardware changes. Unlike some other related work [9,15,22,25,30], we do not install any dedicated ECU. Therefore, we claim LaaCan is standard CAN compliant.

AUTOSAR Compatibility

The AUTOmotive Open System ARchitecture (AUTOSAR) [1] is a development partnership of automotive stakeholders to implement standardized software architectures for ECUs [3]. The specification of AUTOSAR describes standard development practices. To verify the compliance with the AUTOSAR standard, we study the release document of AUTOSAR 4.3.1, Specification of Secure Onboard Communication [6]. According to the specification, sender and receiving nodes require to maintain freshness value. Though, it is not mandatory to add the freshness value to the payload, it has to be considered during the MAC generation. LaaCan maintains a message counter to assure message freshness. In the standard CAN protocol, all the broadcasted messages are received by the participating nodes. Thus, there is no need to add the freshness value to the payload as all the ECUs can maintain the counter. AUTOSAR applies security solution based on the security profile. Table 2 shows the security profile of LaaCan for AUTOSAR. The first parameter "Algorithm" stands for the name of the cryptography algorithm, which is ChaCha20-Poly1305, in this case. SecOCFreshnessValueLength and SecOCFreshnessValueTxLength parameters are related to the freshness value. The configuration values for these parameters are 0 bit as the freshness value is not added to the payload. SecOCAuthInfoTxLength denotes the length of the truncated MAC, and we use 15-bit of the truncated MAC.

3.3 Design Challenges and Solutions

There exist three main challenges in the design of LaaCan: choosing the cryptographic algorithm, deriving the shared secret key, and fixing the MAC size and transmission process. We discuss these challenges and solution choices in the next paragraphs.

Choosing Cryptographic Algorithm

We use authenticated ciphers to ensure data confidentiality, integrity, and authenticity. There are several authenticated ciphers available. However, we need to select one that provides strong security with efficient performance in ECUs.

The in-vehicle communication has to be real-time. However, security measures add a delay in communication. The delay highly depends on the hardware components on which the security solution is running. The vehicle ECUs are resource-constrained. Thus, a solution must have strong security with low communication delay, less memory consumption, and less power consumption. We choose widely used authenticated ciphers and compare the execution time to encrypt and authenticate 8 bytes of data. We take 8 bytes of data because a single CAN frame can have up to 8 bytes of data. We shortlist AES-GCM, Speck-GCM, ChaCha20-Poly1305, Ascon, and Acorn for the comparison as they are widely used. We run the them in three different hardware configurations. We discuss experimental setups in detail in Sect. 4.1.

Figure 3 shows the execution times of the shortlisted ciphers. Chacha20-Poly1305 has the lowest execution time in all three configurations. It is significantly faster than the most widely used AES-GCM. The AES-based ciphers perform better when the hardware has AES support. However, for resource-constrained devices without hardware support, Chacha20-Poly1305 takes less time while consuming low memory and power than some widely used authenticated ciphers [13].

Shared Secret Key

The cryptographic algorithms use a secret key for data encryption. The key selection is essential as the security strength depends on it. The same key can be used for encryption and decryption in case of symmetric-key cryptography. In asymmetric key cryptography, one key is used in the encryption process and a different key is required for the decryption process.

The asymmetric key technique is significantly slower than symmetric key and consumes more resources [27]. Hence, we choose the symmetric key cryptography. In symmetric-key cryptography, the sender and receiver need to share a common secret key. However, key generation and sharing between ECUs is complex as the network is multicast-based, and there is no central authority. If the same key is used throughout the lifetime of the vehicle, an adversary can analyze the network traffic to retrieve the secret key. Therefore, we generate a session key at the starting of a vehicle. To generate a session key, we use a long term symmetric key and a session id of 128 bits each.

A 128-bit session-id allows 2^{20} or 1.04 million distinctive sessions, which are enough for a vehicle lifetime. At the starting of a vehicle, the session-id incre-

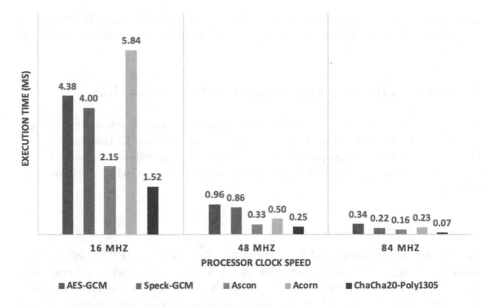

Fig. 3. Execution times of authenticated ciphers.

ments and a session key is generated. ChaCha20 generates the session key using the session id and long term symmetric key. A new session key is also generated when the message counter value reaches its limit. The key establishment and share process are resource consuming and increases the network traffic, which we avoid by deriving the session key. We use the session key for a limited time. Hence, even if an adversary retrieves a key by analyzing network traffic, it can bypass the security measures for only one session as session key changes every time the vehicle starts. The session key generation and key setup process require a maximum of 1.83 ms, which is very low. As it is only done at the starting of the vehicle, it is acceptable.

MAC Size and Transmission
LaaCan authenticates messages based on MAC. The security strength of MAC depends on its length. A MAC with a bigger length has better security strength. However, the size of the CAN frame is limited. CAN frame has a 15-bit CRC field, which provides error detection support only. CRC check can recognize an error that occurs during transmission. LaaCan ensures data accuracy based on MAC. The MAC authentication at the receiver end fails if any bit in the original data changes due to a noisy transmission channel. Therefore, we decide to replace CRC with MAC. The replacement of CRC with MAC allows keeping the traffic of the network the same as standard CAN. Otherwise, data payload has to be reduced [8], or additional message transmission is required [32]. Woo et al. [33] and Bittl [10] also propose overwriting CRC field with MAC.

The probability of guessing MAC is 2^{-mac_length} [20]. We generate 128-bit MAC and truncate it to 15 bits for transmission. Therefore, the probability of guessing MAC is 2^{-15}. In other words, an attacker requires 2^{15} or 32,768 attempts to guess the MAC that is not feasible considering the limited resources available in ECUs.

4   Implementation and Experimental Evaluation

To assess the effectiveness of LaaCan, we validate the security features through experiments and preform security analysis against attacks. In this section, the implementation details are provided and the security analysis is discussed. Later, the evaluation results and comparison with some of the existing work are presented.

4.1   Implementation

LaaCan has to be integrated into Electronic Control Unit (ECU) software by installing in the ECU micro-controller. A micro-controller works as a core processing unit of an ECU. Several exiting work [8,25,30,33] used micro-controllers for experiments. To simulate an in-vehicle network consisting of multiple ECUs connected by a CAN bus, we connect multiple Arduinos by the CAN bus. An Arduino is a programmable micro-controller. However, it does not have the capability of CAN transmission. Hence, we install CAN-Bus Shield V2.0 [28] on top of Arduino that provides CAN transmission ability to Arduino.

Micro-controllers come in different hardware configurations. CAN security researchers mostly use ARM-based micro-controllers with CPU clock speeds between 40–150 MHz for their experiments. However, AVR-based microcontrollers are widely used in vehicle ECUs. Therefore, we consider microcontrollers with three different configurations, which are Arduino Uno (16 MHz 8-bit AVR), Arduino Zero (48 MHz 32-bit ARM), and Arduino Due (84 MHz 32-bit ARM). Among them, Arduino Uno has computationally weak hardware, which helps to verify the performance on resource-constrained devices. Figure 4 demonstrates the diagram of our experimental setup.

4.2   Security Threat Analysis

General Security Requirements

First, we analyze that LaaCan satisfies confidentiality, integrity, and authenticity. For the purpose of analysis, we name the ECUs as ECU_T (transmitter), ECU_R (receiver), and ECU_A (attacker). We assume ECU_T and ECU_R are legitimate nodes and ECU_A is an attacker for the following scenarios.

Confidentiality. ECU_T sends data to ECU_R, and ECU_A tries to sniff the data. We observe that before installing LaaCan, ECU_A receives the original data. After applying LaaCan, ECU_A receives the encrypted data. Encrypted data is completely different from the original data and meaningless to the attacker node.

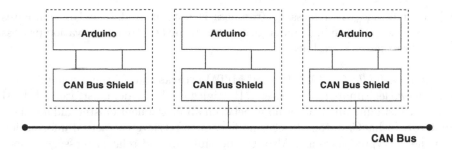

Fig. 4. The experimental setup diagram.

Integrity. ECU_T tries to send data after encryption. However, one or more bit(s) of transmitted data changes due to transmission error or attacker's manipulation and ECU_R receives the fabricated data. We observe that ECU_R does not process the altered data because of the mismatch in the MAC.

Authenticity. Similar to integrity, MAC also ensures data authenticity. ECU_T sends data to ECU_R. However, the message identifier got altered due to transmission error or attacker's manipulation. ECU_R generates the MAC with respect to the altered identifier and discards the message because of mismatch in MAC.

Some Attack Defenses

We analyze the defense potential of LaaCan against five security attacks: eavesdropping, spoofing, replay, Man-in-the-Middle (MITM), and remote attacks. These attacks are considered for protection analysis as they are the most common form of attacks in CAN protocol [4,29]. Denial of Service (DoS) attacks are not considered as preventing them in CAN protocol is impossible [31] and the existing solutions also struggle against it [26].

Eavesdropping Attacks. In a broadcast network, all the participant nodes receive all the transmitted packets. Hence, an adversary ECU can read the data transmission to retrieve information, which may lead to future attacks. Data transmission is encrypted in LaaCan. Therefore, eavesdropping attacks cannot compromise data.

Spoofing Attacks. Spoofing attacks are done by impersonating another ECU. An adversary can mislead a vehicle subsystem by performing this kind of attack. These attacks are possible if the network lacks authenticity and integrity. LaaCan ensures the authenticity and integrity of the transmitted messages to protect against spoofing attacks.

Replay Attacks. In a replay attack, a copy of a previously recorded valid message is transmitted. As messages are exchanged in broadcast form, any attacker node connected to the network can perform a replay attack if no security measures are not taken [19]. The receiving node cannot differentiate between a valid and replayed message when message freshness is not ensured. LaaCan eliminates replay attacks by involving a message counter in the keystream derivation process that assures message freshness.

Man-in-the-Middle (MITM) Attacks. MITM attacks control the communication between two legitimate nodes secretly. Buttigieg et al. [12] demonstrated a MITM attack by installing an attacker node between an instrument cluster and a vehicle simulator. In LaaCan, the attacker node cannot retrieve the actual information from the encrypted message. Also, the possible altered relayed message cannot bypass the authentication process. Hence, LaaCan prevents MITM attacks.

Remote Attacks. Modern vehicles have an OBD-II port that provides self-diagnostic and reporting support. OBD-II is connected to in-vehicle network. Woo et al. [33] presented a remote attack that connects a malicious mobile application to a third party OBD-II diagnostic tool. These attacks are possible due to the lack of data authenticity. LaaCan provides authenticity to prevent these attacks. The secret-key and cryptography mechanism have to be shared with trusted manufacturers of OBD-II dongles to make them compatible with the proposed architecture. If a dongle is vulnerable and a secret key is compromised, then the attacker may bypass the security measures. However, it applies to all the cryptographic approaches to some extent as they operate based on the secret key.

4.3   Evaluation Metrics and Comparison

We evaluate LaaCan based on four metrics: communication overhead, bus load, deployment cost, and compatibility. The metrics are discussed in next paragraphs. Afterwards, it is compared with some existing solutions based on security requirements and performance.

Evaluation Metrics

Communication Overhead. CAN is meant for real-time communication. Therefore, communication overhead is the most important evaluation criteria. LaaCan involves encryption and authentication, which requires processing of every message. It has a total delay of 1.52 ms 16 MHz configuration, 0.25 ms in 48 MHz, and 0.07 ms in 84 MHz. We observe that communication delay significantly depends on the hardware configuration of ECUs. All the delays are for 8 bytes of data, which is the maximum payload of the protocol. We do not include transmission delay here as it solely depends on the setup environment.

Bus Load. If security measures increase the load of the bus, it must have an impact on the message processing latency. Woo et al. [33] use an extra message to transmit MAC for each message, which at least double the traffic of the network. LaaCan avoids transmission of additional messages by replacing the CRC field with the MAC. Hence, LaaCan does not have any effect on the bus load.

Deployment Cost. A huge number of already manufactured vehicles are using CAN protocol. Hence, a new security solution must have a low installation cost. Some of the existing solutions [9, 25] install one or more new dedicated ECUs for security purposes, which is costly. LaaCan has a low deployment cost as it can be integrated by software updates only.

Compatibility.[1] LaaCan integration does not have any impact on the core CAN protocol. No additional bits are added to the message. LaaCan replaces the CRC field with MAC to avoid use of CAN+ [35] or any other customized version of the protocol. However, error checking is part of integrity process and LaaCan assures integrity. Hence, the modification follows the core specification of CAN.

Comparative Analysis

Table 3 illustrates the security features and performance comparison of the proposed design with some related work discussed in Sect. 2. Since LaaCan adapts the cryptographic architecture, IDS-based solutions are excluded from the comparison.

Table 3. Security and performance comparison.

Solution	Confiden tiality	Integrity	Authenti city	Bus load	Deployment cost	Compati bility	Overhead
CANTrack [14]	✓	✗	✗	Unchanged	Low	High	-
VeCure [32]	✗	✓	✓	High	Low	High	0.05 ms (40 MHz)
CANAuth [31]	✗	✓	✓	Unchanged	Low	Low	-
LiBrA-CAN [15]	✗	✓	✓	High	High	Low	2.54 ms
WooCAN [33]	✓	✓	✓	Medium	Low	High	0.38 ms (60 MHz)
LASAN [22]	✓	✓	✓	Medium	Very High	High	4.6 ms (168 MHz)
TOUCAN [8]	✓	✓	✓	Unchanged	Low	Very Low	2.35 ms (168 MHz)
CaCAN [25]	✗	✓	✓	Medium	High	Low	0.03 ms (50 MHz)
TCAN [9]	✗	✗	✓	Medium	Very High	Low	0.03 ms
LaaCan	✓	✓	✓	Unchanged	Low	High	1.52 ms (16 MHz) 0.25 ms (48 MHz) 0.07 ms (84 MHz)

CANTrack [14] only encrypts data to ensure confidentiality. Along with Laa-Can, there are three solutions [8, 22, 33] that ensure confidentiality, integrity, and authenticity. The other solutions implement an authentication mechanism to ensure integrity and authenticity.

The additional message transmission needed for security purposes increases the traffic of the network. CANTrack [14], TOUCAN [8], VeCure [32], and Laa-Can have unchanged network traffic. As CANTrack does not authenticate the message, it does not need to transmit MAC. TOUCAN reduces the payload size to append MAC to it. VeCure and LaaCan replace the CRC field with MAC to avoid additional message transmission.

---

[1] Compatibility indicates the degree of change required in standard CAN protocol and it is a subjective metric.

LASAN [22] and TCAN [9] have very high deployment costs as multiple dedicated ECUs are required to be installed for security. LiBrA-CAN [15] and CaCAN [25] require the installation of one dedicated ECU. Also, the dedicated ECUs used for security purposes increase the coupling among them and general ECUs, which is considered as a weakness [21]. The other considered solutions including LaaCan, have low deployment cost as no hardware changes are required.

The highly compatible solutions do not change the specifications of the standard protocol and do not involve a different variant of the protocol. TOUCAN [8] has very low compatibility as it reduces the payload size. Also, CANAuth [31] and LiBrA-CAN [15] have low compatibility as they use CAN+ [35] that requires hardware changes in transceiver [8]. Though we replace the CRC field with MAC, LaaCan can run on existing hardware and network configurations without any modification. Therefore, LaaCan is highly compatible with standard CAN.

A comparative analysis with other work in terms of communication overhead is challenging as the overhead depends on hardware configurations. Since the clock speed of the processor is considered as one of the significant factors behind the performance, we perform the analysis based on the clock speed. VeCure [32], CaCAN [25], and TCAN [9] outperform LaaCan in terms of overhead. However, they fail to assure at least one feature of confidentiality, integrity, and authenticity. Also, CaCAN and TCAN have high deployment cost, and low compatibility with the standard CAN protocol. Though WooCAN [33], LASAN [22], and TOUCAN [8] ensure the three security features, they have significantly high communication delay than LaaCan.

The remote attacks are usually initiated through the In-Vehicle Infotainment (IVI) system and OBD-II. The secret key and cryptographic mechanism have to be shared with these systems to make them compatible with LaaCan. However, if these systems do not have protected memory and compromise the secret key, then adversaries can bypass the authentication system. VeCure [32] attempts to mitigate this issue by sharing the secret key only with the high-trust ECUs that do not have any external interfaces. It only authenticates the communications between high-trust ECUs and does not assure confidentiality, which makes the ECUs with external interfaces such as IVI and OBD-II vulnerable. Any nontrusted OBD-II tool can read and learn from the data as there is no encryption in place. Also, it can send malicious messages to IVI that will not be discarded as there is no authentication done in IVI.

5   Conclusion and Future Work

5.1   Conclusion

The automotive industry is advancing towards the adoption of information technology and electronic components. The involvement of information technology has opened up the in-vehicle communication networks to the cyber world. Adversaries can gain access to an in-vehicle network by exploiting the vulnerabilities of the Controller Area Network (CAN). In this work, we design a lightweight authentication architecture called LaaCan to secure CAN network communication. We classify the existing security solutions for CAN on the basis of security enforcement procedures in order to compare LaaCan with the existing work. LaaCan is an Authenticated Encryption with Additional Data (AEAD)-based security architecture that implements ChaCha20-Poly1305 for one pass encryption-authentication process. It protects the network from eavesdropping, spoofing, replay, Man-in-the-Middle (MITM), and remote attacks by ensuring the integrity, authenticity, and confidentiality of the transmitted data. The experimental results illustrate that the communication delay can be reduced to 0.07 ms. We evaluate LaaCan based on the communication delay, traffic load, deployment cost, and compatibility with the standard protocol. The comparative analysis shows that the proposed architecture suffers from less overhead compared to the solutions with similar security measures. LaaCan does not increase network traffic. A software update can incorporate the solution without any hardware changes, and it has high compatibility. Lastly, LaaCan is compliant with the CAN and AUTOSAR standards.

5.2   Limitations and Future Work

The cryptographic algorithm requires a secret key, message counter, session id, and session key. These values have to be stored, which consume memory storage. Besides, we generate a session key from the pre-shared secret key. If an adversary compromises a session key, it can bypass the security measures for that particular session. While compromising the session key requires the knowledge of the pre-shared secret key and session id, the attacker may compromise the encryption algorithm that generates the key. We assume that these values are stored in more protected memory. LaaCan uses a message counter to assure message freshness. However, we do not transmit freshness value due to the limited size of a CAN message. Since CAN is a broadcast-based network, all the ECUs receive the transmitted messages in network. Thus, the counter increments upon receiving every message, which keeps all the ECUs synchronized. If an ECU somehow does not receive some messages, then it cannot synchronize with the network.

If the pre-shared key is compromised, an adversary can create a legitimate session key. A sophisticated secret key generation and sharing mechanism can address the issue so that an adversary cannot create a legitimate session key from a compromised pre-shared key. However, the generation of secret keys requires a lot of processing power. As a result, we plan to implement a secret key sharing mechanism for low powered ECUs. Also, we conduct our experiments with microcontrollers that are not real ECUs. Therefore, we plan to install our solutions in ECUs with a real vehicle system running. It will help us reach more concrete conclusions concerning the actual performance and feasibility.

Acknowledgments. This work is partially supported by the Natural Sciences and Engineering Research Council of Canada (NSERC) and the Canada Research Chairs (CRC) program. The authors would also like to thank Farnood Faghihi for reviewing the paper.

References

1. AUTOSAR - enabling innovation. https://www.autosar.org/. Accessed 12 Apr 2020
2. Iso 11898–1:2003 - road vehicles - Controller Area Network (CAN) - part 1: Data link layer and physical signalling. https://www.iso.org/standard/33422.html. Accessed 12 Apr 2020
3. What is AUTOSAR and why is it important. https://www.fpt-software.com/automotive-tech-blog/what-is-autosar-and-why-is-it-important/. Accessed 12 Apr 2020
4. AbdAllah, E.G., Zulkernine, M., Gu, Y.X., Liem, C.: Towards defending connected vehicles against attacks. In: Proceedings of the Fifth European Conference on the Engineering of Computer-Based Systems, pp. 1–9 (2017)
5. Alam, M.S.U., Iqbal, S., Zulkernine, M., Liem, C.: Securing vehicle ECU communications and stored data. In: ICC 2019–2019 IEEE International Conference on Communications (ICC), pp. 1–6. IEEE (2019)
6. AUTOSAR: Specification of secure onboard communication. https://www.autosar.org/fileadmin/user_upload/standards/classic/4-3/AUTOSAR_SWS_SecureOnboardCommunication.pdf
7. Avatefipour, O., Malik, H.: State-of-the-art survey on in-vehicle network communication (CAN-Bus) security and vulnerabilities. Int. J. Comput. Sci. Netw. **6** (2017)
8. Bella, G., Biondi, P., Costantino, G., Matteucci, I.: Toucan: a protocol to secure controller area network (CAN). In: Proceedings of the ACM Workshop on Automotive Cybersecurity. AutoSec 2019, pp. 3–8. ACM, New York (2019)
9. Biham, E., Bitan, S., Gavril, E.: TCAN: authentication without cryptography on a CAN bus based on nodes location on the bus. In: 2018 Embedded Security in Cars, November 2018
10. Bittl, S.: Attack potential and efficient security enhancement of automotive bus networks using short macs with rapid key change. In: Sikora, A., Berbineau, M., Vinel, A., Jonsson, M., Pirovano, A., Aguado, M. (eds.) Communication Technologies for Vehicles. Nets4Cars/Nets4Trains/Nets4Aircraft 2014. LNCS, vol. 8435, pp. 113–125. Springer, Cham (2014). https://doi.org/10.1007/978-3-319-06644-8_11
11. Boldt, B.: Automotive security in a CAN. https://www.electronicdesign.com/markets/automotive/article/21805532/automotive-security-in-a-can. Accessed 07 May 2020
12. Buttigieg, R., Farrugia, M., Meli, C.: Security issues in controller area networks in automobiles. In: 2017 18th International Conference on Sciences and Techniques of Automatic Control and Computer Engineering (STA), pp. 93–98, December 2017
13. De Santis, F., Schauer, A., Sigl, G.: ChaCha20-Poly1305 authenticated encryption for high-speed embedded IoT applications. In: Design, Automation Test in Europe Conference Exhibition (DATE), 2017, pp. 692–697, March 2017
14. Farag, W.A.: Cantrack: enhancing automotive CAN bus security using intuitive encryption algorithms. In: 2017 7th International Conference on Modeling, Simulation, and Applied Optimization (ICMSAO), pp. 1–5. IEEE (2017)

15. Groza, B., Murvay, S., van Herrewege, A., Verbauwhede, I.: LiBrA-CAN: a lightweight broadcast authentication protocol for controller area networks. In: Pieprzyk, J., Sadeghi, A.-R., Manulis, M. (eds.) CANS 2012. LNCS, vol. 7712, pp. 185–200. Springer, Heidelberg (2012). https://doi.org/10.1007/978-3-642-35404-5_15

16. Hu, Q., Luo, F.: Review of secure communication approaches for in-vehicle network. Int. J. Automot. Technol. **19**(5), 879–894 (2018)

17. SAE International: Serial control and communications heavy duty vehicle network (2019)

18. Keller, J.: Best third-party Carplay apps. https://www.imore.com/best-third-party-carplay-apps (2018). Accessed 24 Dec 2019

19. Lin, C., Sangiovanni-Vincentelli, A.: Cyber-security for the controller area network (CAN) communication protocol. In: 2012 International Conference on Cyber Security, pp. 1–7, December 2012

20. Mouha, N., Mennink, B., Van Herrewege, A., Watanabe, D., Preneel, B., Verbauwhede, I.: Chaskey: an efficient MAC algorithm for 32-bit microcontrollers. In: Joux, A., Youssef, A. (eds.) SAC 2014. LNCS, vol. 8781, pp. 306–323. Springer, Cham (2014). https://doi.org/10.1007/978-3-319-13051-4_19

21. Moukahal, L., Zulkernine, M.: Security vulnerability metrics for connected vehicles. In: 2019 IEEE 19th International Conference on Software Quality, Reliability and Security Companion (QRS-C), pp. 17–23. IEEE (2019)

22. Mundhenk, P., et al.: Security in automotive networks: lightweight authentication and authorization. ACM Trans. Des. Autom. Electron. Syst. (TODAES) **22**(2), 25 (2017)

23. NG, C.: What is data integrity and how can you maintain it? https://www.varonis.com/blog/data-integrity/. Accessed 07 May 2020

24. Nir, Y.: ChaCha20 and poly1305 for IETF protocols. https://tools.ietf.org/html/rfc7539

25. R. Kurachi, Y. Matsubara, H.T.N.A.Y.M., Horihata, S.: CaCAN - centralized authentication system in CAN. In: 2014 Embedded Security in Cars, November 2014

26. Radu, A.-I., Garcia, F.D.: LeiA: a lightweight authentication protocol for CAN. In: Askoxylakis, I., Ioannidis, S., Katsikas, S., Meadows, C. (eds.) ESORICS 2016. LNCS, vol. 9879, pp. 283–300. Springer, Cham (2016). https://doi.org/10.1007/978-3-319-45741-3_15

27. Silva, N.B., Pigatto, D.F., Martins, P.S., Branco, K.R.: Case studies of performance evaluation of cryptographic algorithms for an embedded system and a general purpose computer. J. Netw. Comput. Appl. **60**, 130–143 (2016)

28. Studio, S.: CAN-Bus shield v2.0. http://wiki.seeedstudio.com/CAN-BUS_Shield_V2.0/

29. Sun, J., Iqbal, S., Seifollahpour Arabi, N., Zulkernine, M.: A classification of attacks to in-vehicle components (IVCs). Veh. Commun. **25**, 100253 (2020)

30. Ujiie, Y., et al.: A method for disabling malicious can messages by using a centralized monitoring and interceptor ECU. In: 2015 Embedded Security in Cars (2015)

31. Van Herrewege, A., Singelee, D., Verbauwhede, I.: CANAuth-a simple, backward compatible broadcast authentication protocol for CAN bus. In: ECRYPT Workshop on Lightweight Cryptography, vol. 2011 (2011)

32. Wang, Q., Sawhney, S.: VeCure: a practical security framework to protect the CAN bus of vehicles. In: 2014 International Conference on the Internet of Things (IOT), pp. 13–18. IEEE (2014)

33. Woo, S., Jo, H.J., Lee, D.H.: A practical wireless attack on the connected car and security protocol for in-vehicle CAN. IEEE Trans. Intell. Transp. Syst. **16**(2), 993–1006 (2015)
34. Yang, J., et al.: Data management for automotive ECUs based on hybrid RAM-NVM main memory. In: 2016 13th International Conference on Embedded Software and Systems (ICESS), pp. 74–79 (2016)
35. Ziermann, T., Wildermann, S., Teich, J.: CAN+: a new backward-compatible controller area network (CAN) protocol with up to 16x higher data rates. In: Proceedings of the Conference on Design, Automation and Test in Europe, pp. 1088–1093. European Design and Automation Association (2009)

A Machine Learning Based Smartphone App for GPS Spoofing Detection

Javier Campos[1], Kristen Johnson[1], Jonathan Neeley[1], Staci Roesch[1], Farha Jahan[2], Quamar Niyaz[1(✉)], and Khair Al Shamaileh[1]

[1] Purdue University Northwest, Hammond, IN 46323, USA
{jicampos,john1954,neeleyj,sroesch,qniyaz,kalshama}@pnw.edu
[2] The University of Toledo, Toledo, OH 43607, USA
farha.jahan@utoledo.edu

Abstract. With affordable open-source software-defined radio (SDR) devices, the security of civilian Global Position System (GPS) is at risk of spoofing attacks. Spoofed GPS signals from SDR devices have indicated that spoofed signals have higher values of signal-to-noise ratios (SNRs). Utilizing these values along with other parameters, we propose a machine learning (ML) based GPS spoofing detection system for classifying spoofed signals. To build our detection system, we launch spoofing attacks on a GPS receiver using a low-cost SDR device, LimeSDR, and apply ML algorithms on SNR values and the number of tracked and viewed satellites. A performance comparison between different ML algorithms shows that Random Forest (RF) and Support Vector Machine (SVM) achieve 99.5% accuracy, followed by K-Nearest Neighbors (KNN) (99.4%). To demonstrate easy integration of the algorithm with GPS enabled devices, we develop an Android-based smartphone app that successfully notifies the user about the spoofing signals.

Keywords: GPS spoofing · Machine learning · Security · Smartphone app

1 Introduction

From mobile phones to aviation and autonomous vehicles, the use of Global Positioning System (GPS) for navigation and timing has become ubiquitous. As more people and devices rely on GPS, the threat of spoofing attacks increases [2,5]. GPS signals are vulnerable to being spoofed, thus displaying incorrect/inaccurate locations to the user. Civilian GPS signals are not encrypted, and their receiving devices lack effective defense mechanisms, thereby posing a higher risk of a spoofing attack. A GPS defense system must at least detect a spoofed signal and notify the user.

In this work, a machine learning (ML) based GPS spoofing detection mechanism that uses parsed information from the National Marine Electronics Association (NMEA) sentences is proposed. These sentences are standard data format

N. Park et al. (Eds.): SecureComm 2020, LNICST 336, pp. 235–241, 2020.
https://doi.org/10.1007/978-3-030-63095-9_13

supported by most GPS modules. The defense mechanism extracts signal-to-noise ratio (SNR) values and the number of tracked and viewed satellites from NMEA sentences to classify GPS signals. To demonstrate effectiveness of the defense mechanism and its integration flexibility with GPS enabled devices, we implement it as an Android app that notifies the user when a false signal is received and stops updating the spoofed location. Detecting GPS spoofing attacks based on ML techniques have been previously explored in many works [7,9,10]. A work similar to ours demonstrated GPS Spoofing attack on mobile phones, external GPS modules, and car navigation system through RINEX files which provide only raw satellite data [4]. Our work differs in a way that we use ML algorithms for spoofing detection with the help of features extracted from NMEA sentences, which are supported by most GPS modules. Besides, we develop a smartphone app that can use the ML model to detect spoofed GPS signals. A GPS Anti-Spoof app is available on the Google Play that uses celestial navigation instead of analyzing any GPS signals or NMEA sentences [1].

2 Methodology

To design and implement the defense mechanism against a GPS spoofing attack, we setup the necessary hardware and software to generate and collect authentic and spoofed GPS signals. A software-defined radio (SDR) kit, LimeSDR [6], is used. The kit is connected to a PC via a USB cable and integrated with GNU-Radio and GPS-SDR-SIM software. Ephemeris data downloaded from NASA's Archive of Space Geodesy on its Crustal Dynamics Data Information System (CDDIS) is used to launch the spoofing attack. The data provides information on current and predicted location, timing, and health of GPS satellites [8]. The downloaded ephemeris files for the desired date and time are in compressed format. They are first decompressed and converted into binary files of GPS baseband signal data streams using GPS-SDR-SIM. GNURadio converts these binary files into radio frequency signals and transmits such signals to a GPS receiver via LimeSDR. The transmission successfully spoofs the GPS receiver to a false location. Spoofing attacks are also launched using the setup on a smartphone equipped with a built-in GPS module to validate the defense mechanism of our developed app against the attack.

An Arduino microcontroller interfaced with a u-blox NEO-6M GPS module receiver is chosen to collect and parse GPS data. The output of the GPS module is NMEA sentences shown in Fig. 1. These sentences include all the information provided by GPS signals such as latitude, longitude, number of satellites being tracked, and SNR. The two most important NMEA sentences are "GPGGA" and "GPGSV". GPGGA sentences contain location information (latitude, longitude, altitude, and the number of satellites). The GPGSV sentences contain information on the satellites within the view. One of its parameters also describes the SNR of each satellite that played a key role in our ML implementation [3].

```
$GPGSA,A,1,,,,,,,,,,,,,99.99,99.99,99.99*30
$GPGSV,2,1,05,01,,,20,02,,,21,07,,,23,12,,,22*78
$GPGSV,2,2,05,13,,,21*7D
$GPGLL,,,,,,,V,N*64
$GPRMC,,V,,,,,,,,,,N*53
$GPVTG,,,,,,,,,N*30
$GPGGA,,,,,,0,00,99.99,,,,,,*48
$GPGSA,A,1,,,,,,,,,,,,,99.99,99.99,99.99*30
```

Fig. 1. Sample NMEA sentences captured in Arduino interfaced with a GPS receiver.

2.1   Machine Learning Based Defense Mechanism

The stages that are involved to develop the prototype for the defense mechanism against a GPS spoofing attack are as follows:

Capturing GPS Data. The defense mechanism detects a spoof according to the parsed information from NMEA sentences. Thus, NMEA sentences are collected from the GPS module in two scenarios, one of authentic locations and other for spoofed locations. For the former locations, the GPS module is set to operate without interference from the LimeSDR, and NMEA sentences are collected for 20 min each at ten different true geographical locations. After the data for true locations is collected, the LimeSDR is set up about 40 ft from the GPS receiver. False versions of the true locations are generated with the corresponding ephemeris data and transmitted from the LimeSDR. With any distance greater than 40 ft, the GPS receiver was unable to receive signals. NMEA sentences for these false locations were collected for 20 min as well. Later, these NMEA sentences for authentic and false locations are used to prepare the dataset for the development of an ML model.

Detecting Spoofing Attacks Using Machine Learning. The ML algorithm classifies locations as authentic or spoofed based on a given set of input features. These features are extracted from collected NMEA sentences. The information about each satellite is listed in GPGSA and GPGSV sentences including the number of satellites within range and their SNR values. It is observed that a valid GPS signal has lower SNR as compared to spoofed signals by the LimeSDR device. Therefore, for each position in the parsed data, the average SNR value and standard deviation are considered as features to identify a location as spoofed or authentic. Other information from NMEA sentences, such as the number of satellites in view and tracked and horizontal dilution is analyzed. After a close examination, there is not enough evidence to conclude that horizontal dilution could help differentiate between authentic and spoofed locations.

However, the number of satellites in view and being tracked did show promising results. Hence, we created a dataset that consists of one output class for a location to be genuine or spoofed and four input features: i) average SNR, ii) standard deviation in SNR, iii) number of satellites in view, and iv) number of satellites being tracked.

Table 1. Accuracy, precision, recall, and f-measure for each machine learning algorithm

	Accuracy (%)	Precision (%)	Recall (%)	F-measure (%)
KNN	99.46 ± 0.001	99.62	99.57	99.60
RF	99.53 ± 0.002	99.70	99.70	99.67
SVM	99.55 ± 0.002	99.65	99.59	99.62
LR	99.10 ± 0.007	98.46	98.27	98.35
NB	97.83 ± 0.008	98.29	97.97	98.10

From the collected NMEA sentences, 19,925 records are extracted for the dataset. These records are split into training, validation, and testing using a 60-20-20 split, respectively. We considered five traditional ML classification algorithms for the detection mechanism: K-Nearest Neighbors (KNN), Random Forest (RF), Support Vector Machines (SVM), Logistic Regression (LR), and Naïve Bayes (NB). Table 1 displays the performance of each ML algorithm for well-known performance metrics for classification including accuracy, precision, recall, and f-measure. Results are recorded after using cross-validation of five-fold for each classifier using data from the test set. It is found that KNN, RF, and SVM models performed better than LR and NB models in terms of accuracy and f-measure. The first three algorithms achieved an accuracy of around 99.5% and f-measure of 99.6%.

3 Smartphone App Implementation

To implement the ML based detection mechanism in a device, we developed an Android app and installed it on a smartphone. The predefined `LocationListener` interface from Android API detects any location change and updates the smartphone's position (longitude and latitude) regularly through the `onLocationChange()` method. We use Google Maps for a visual display of the location. Once the app is ready to read the GPS data, we broadcast spoofed signals, and the map shows the spoofed location. For the ML algorithm, we used KNN due to its easy implementation and comparable performance with RF and SVM. The KNN algorithm for detection is written in Java as a separate module for integration with the app, and the initial collected data used by the algorithm are stored as a text file. Since the algorithm uses parsed information from NMEA sentences, they are extracted using the `LocationManager` class, which can read the NMEA sentences (code snippet shown in Fig. 2). The app parses each string starting with GPGSA and GPGSV, and extracts information. It then sends the data to the algorithm to predict whether the received signal is faulty or not. An alert pop-up indicates that the GPS signal is spoofed.

```java
if(s.startsWith("$GPGGA")) {
    String[] splitSentence = s.split(",");
    if (!splitSentence[7].isEmpty())
        satellitesTracked = Integer.parseInt(splitSentence[7]);
    else
        satellitesTracked = 0;
}

if(s.startsWith("$GPGSV")) {
    String[] splitSentence = s.split(",");
    if(!splitSentence[3].isEmpty())
        satellitesInView = Integer.parseInt(splitSentence[3]);
    else
        satellitesInView = 0;
    if(NmeaSentenceCount == 0) {
        NmeaSentenceCount = Integer.parseInt(splitSentence[1]);
        NmeaSnr = new ArrayList<Integer>();
    }
    int i = 7;
    while(i < splitSentence.length) {
        if(!splitSentence[i].isEmpty()) {
            Log.d("GPGSV", "String: " + splitSentence[i]);
            NmeaSnr.add(Integer.parseInt(splitSentence[i]));
        }
        i += 4;
    }
    if(Integer.parseInt(splitSentence[2]) == NmeaSentenceCount) {
        checkLocation(NmeaSnr, satellitesInView, satellitesTracked, knn);
        NmeaSentenceCount = 0;
    }
}
```

Fig. 2. Code snippet of the Android app

We evaluated the Android app on a Samsung Galaxy S9 smartphone at one of the author's residence. We downloaded the ephemeris data and followed the steps discussed in Sect. 2 to spoof the location to other place. The spoofed radio frequency signals were received by the smartphone. The Android app successfully identified the spoofed signal and displayed a warning to the user and stopped further location updates. Figure 3 shows the app interfaces before and after the GPS spoofing attack. Airplane mode was turned on to prevent the smartphone from using Wi-Fi and mobile data to refine location estimations.

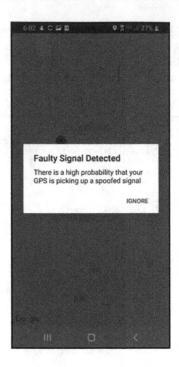

Faulty Signal Detected

There is a high probability that your
GPS is picking up a spoofed signal

IGNORE

Fig. 3. Android app graphical interfaces for genuine and spoofed locations

4   Conclusion and Future Work

In this work, we implemented an ML based defense mechanism against GPS spoofing attack and embedded it in an Android app. We found that ML algorithms such as KNN, RF, and SVM can detect such attacks with an accuracy of around 99.5%, which predominately utilizes SNR values, the number of satellites viewed, and being tracked from NMEA sentences to categorize spoofed signals. We implemented the KNN algorithm in an Android app that would notify the user of a spoofed signal and prevent the map from displaying the spoofed location.

Our experiments and defense mechanism are setup keeping amateur attackers in mind who can launch attacks by using low-cost SDR kits and following the available online resources. The defense mechanism can defend against attacks by those attackers who are not familiar with manipulating hardware and software of SDRs to mimic authentic signals more closely. In future, we will investigate the impact of manipulating SNRs and the number of satellites in view on the ML based defense mechanism to make it robust and widely applicable. Integrating an accelerometer and a gyroscope with the smartphone app can be used to cross-reference measured data from GPS satellites. Furthermore, the app will be profiled to optimize memory and CPU usage for better user experience.

References

1. GPS Anti Spoof. https://play.google.com/store/apps/details?id=com.clockwk. GPSAntiSpoof
2. Woodford, C.: Satellite navigation (2019). https://tinyurl.com/y8wss3wt
3. DePriest, D.: NMEA Data (2019). https://tinyurl.com/b7jvw
4. Goavec-Merou, G., Friedt, J., Meyer, F.: GPS spoofing using software defined radio (2019)
5. Jahan, F., Javaid, A.Y., Sun, W., Alam, M.: GNSSim: an open source GNSS/GPS framework for unmanned aerial vehicular network simulation. ICST Trans. Mob. Commun. Appl. **2**(6), e2 (2015)
6. Lime Microsystems: LimeSDR (2019). https://limemicro.com/products/boards/limesdr/
7. Manesh, M.R., Kenney, J., Hu, W.C., Devabhaktuni, V.K., Kaabouch, N.: Detection of GPS spoofing attacks on unmanned aerial systems. In: 2019 16th IEEE Annual Consumer Communications & Networking Conference (CCNC), pp. 1–6. IEEE (2019)
8. Noll, C.E.: The crustal dynamics data information system: a resource to support scientific analysis using space geodesy. Adv. Space Res. **45**(12), 1421–1440 (2010)
9. Panice, G., et al.: A SVM-based detection approach for GPS spoofing attacks to UAV. In: 2017 23rd International Conference on Automation and Computing (ICAC), pp. 1–11 (2017)
10. Shafiee, E., Mosavi, M., Moazedi, M.: Detection of spoofing attack using machine learning based on multi-layer neural network in single-frequency GPS receivers. J. Navigat. **71**(1), 169–188 (2018)

AOMDroid: Detecting Obfuscation Variants of Android Malware Using Transfer Learning

Yu Jiang[1], Ruixuan Li[1(✉)], Junwei Tang[1], Ali Davanian[2], and Heng Yin[2]

[1] Huazhong University of Science and Technology, Wuhan, China
{m201773045,rxli,junweitang}@hust.edu.cn
[2] University of California, Riverside, Riverside, USA
{adava003,heng}@cs.ucr.edu

Abstract. Android with its large market attracts malware developers. Malware developers employ obfuscation techniques to bypass malware detection mechanisms. Existing systems cannot effectively detect obfuscated Android malware. In this paper, We propose a novel approach to identify obfuscated Android malware. Our proposed approach is based on the intuition that opcode sequences are more resilient to the obfuscation techniques. We first propose an effective approach based on TFIDF algorithm to identify distinctive opcode sequences. Then we represent the opcode sequences as images and reduce the problem of identifying an obfuscated malware to the problem of transforming two images to one another, i.e. unobfuscated malware representation to the obfuscated one. In order to achieve the above, we resort to the transfer learning. We implemented a prototype dubbed AOMDroid based on the proposed approach and extensively evaluated its performance of accuracy and detection time. AOMDroid outperforms four related works that we compared with, and has an accuracy rate of 92.26% in detecting Android obfuscated malware. In addition, AOMDroid supports the detection of 21 Android malware family types. Its malware family detecion accuracy rate is 87.39%. The average time spent by AOMDroid to detect a single Android application is 0.963 s.

Keywords: Android security · Malware detection · Malicious behavior family · Obfuscation · Transfer learning

1 Introduction

Android attracts many attackers. A recent report on Android malware from a security vendor shows that in 2019 alone, a total of 1.809 million malware samples, and 950 million malware attacks on mobile devices [1] were intercepted. In order to detect Android malware, existing systems resort to machine learning and report an acceptable detection rate. However, attackers can use obfuscation techniques to greatly reduce the effectiveness [2].

© ICST Institute for Computer Sciences, Social Informatics and Telecommunications Engineering 2020
Published by Springer Nature Switzerland AG 2020. All Rights Reserved
N. Park et al. (Eds.): SecureComm 2020, LNICST 336, pp. 242–253, 2020.
https://doi.org/10.1007/978-3-030-63095-9_14

We observe that opcodes are more resilient to obfuscation techniques. The ultimate behavior of an application is summarized in the opcode. In addition, we note that learning based on opcodes takes a short time, detection based on opcode features looks promising. Based on above intuitions, we design and implement a method for detecting Android obfuscated malware. We aim to make a correspondence between opcode features before and after obfuscation. A key challenge is an effective feature selection since not all opcodes are distinctive. So we design a feature selection algorithm based on a TFIDF [3] matrix.

Another challenge is making a mapping between opcode features before and after obfuscation. Hence, we resort to transfer learning. The goal of the learning task is effectively transforming obfuscated samples to their unobfuscated ones, or in other words, reducing the difference in opcode features before and after obfuscation. We represent the selected opcode features as images and adopt a domain adaptive method. The underlying assumption is that the source and target domains have the same feature and category space, but there is a certain difference between the feature distribution of two domains. The goal of domain adaptation is to use the labeled source domain data and unlabeled target domain data, to learn a classifier and predict the label of the target domain data. Finally, we take the unobfuscated sample set as the source domain and the obfuscated sample as the target domain. The loss function used in the image transfer model includes the classification loss and the adaptive loss, the adaptive loss represents the difference between the feature distribution of source and target domains.

We implemented our proposed approach in a prototype called AOMDroid, and evaluated it with four different related works. AOMDroid outperforms all related works in terms of detection accuracy of obfuscated malware and the detection time. In summary, our main contributions are:

- We propose a novel anti-obfuscation feature selection algorithm. Our key insight is to apply TFIDF to opcode features before and after obfuscation and group opcode sequences based on constructs such as classes and methods.
- We propose a classification algorithm based on transfer learning that effectively identifies obfuscated malware. Our key idea is to represent the opcode sequences as images, and hence reduce the problem of obfuscated malware detection to the problem of minimizing difference between image pixels before and after obfuscation of an application via an image transformation.
- We implement a prototype based on the proposed approach and evaluate it extensively from accuracy and detection time. In terms of accuracy, our prototype, AOMDroid, achieves 92.26% on obfuscated samples outperforming four related works. For two related works that do not claim anti-obfuscation, AOMDroid is faster in detection time, and offsets their detection accuracy by 16% to 18%. Compared to other two anti-obfuscation related works, AOMDroid is more than 20 times faster while achieving a better accuracy.

2   Background

Obfuscation. Application obfuscation can convert files in the application installation package into forms that functionally equivalent but hard to understand.

It mainly include string encryption, benign code insertion, variable name obfuscation, class name obfuscation, resource obfuscation, API reflection obfuscation, and permission obfuscation. For instance, Permission obfuscation will modify permissions in AndroidManifest.xml. API reflection obfuscation will convert system calls into Java reflection calls. String encryption, variable name obfuscation, and class name obfuscation will obfuscate strings, variable names, and developer-defined class names that is incomprehensible. Due to the low coverage and efficiency in dynamic detection, we consider the static detection method. However, the effect of static detection methods will be significantly reduced due to obfuscation technology. A study shows that attackers can use obfuscation technology for 2000 Android malware samples, to reduce the detection accuracy from 65% to 5.8% of 58 mainstream antivirus engines [2].

Example. We review the malware code for intercepting SMS as shown below. The code uses the Broadcast to steal the SMS, employs the Intent with SMS to start a Service. In addition, It sends SMS content with the device ID to the malicious server. A detection method based on API calls can be constructed by detecting a sequence of getDeviceId, concat and sendData calls. This sequence contains three operations that can describe the behavior of obtaining a device ID, adding it to a message, and sending a message stealing the privacy. When the application adopts obfuscation techniques, it may use benign code obfuscation, insert irrelevant API to interrupt the API subsequence used to judge malicious code. It may also use API reflection obfuscation to convert an API direct call into an indirect API call, which makes it impossible to extract the API features.

```
public class monitorMessage extends BroadcastReceiver {
  public void onReceive(Context context, Intent intent) {
    SmsMessage mSms = SmsMessage.create();
    Intent mIntent = new Intent(Malicious.class);
    mIntent.putExtra("mSms", encrypt(mSms.getMessageBody()));
    startService(mIntent);
  }
}
public class sendMessageToNetwork extends Service {
  public void onStartCommand(Intent intent) {
    TelephonyManager manager = new TelephonyManager();
    String mId = manager.getDeviceId();
    URL maliciousUrl = new URL("http://xxx.com");
    maliciousUrl.sendData(mId.concat(intent.get("mSms")));
  }
}
```

3   Detection Scheme

3.1   Overview

The overview of our system is shown in Fig. 1. It includes: (a) selecting anti-obfuscation features; and, (b) constructing opcode image transfer model. We propose a anti-obfuscation malware classifier. The key idea is to select features for classification that obfuscation would have little effect on them. We start with a set of opcode sequences which represent three constructs: classes, methods and words. Class level, method level and word level opcode sequences refer, respectively, to fragments of opcode sequences for a single class, a single method and a single opcode within the application. We obfuscate a training sample and compare its features before and after obfuscation, and select features that have more weights in identifying malware even with obfuscation in place. We use Term Frequency-Inverse Document Frequency (TFIDF) to assign weights to different features and select those with a higher weight. TF is the frequency of opcode features in applications, and IDF is: if fewer applications contain an opcode feature, the opcode feature are good for distinguishing between categories. Next, we represent selected features as an image before and after obfuscation. Finally, we transfer the problem of classifying malware to image classification.

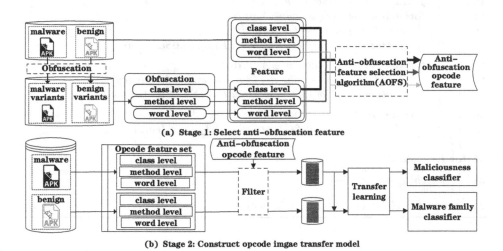

(a) Stage 1: Select anti-obfuscation feature

(b) Stage 2: Construct opcode imgae transfer model

Fig. 1. Structure of the system.

3.2   Anti-obfuscation Feature Selection

Anti-obfuscation Feature Selection (AOFS) follows two design goals. Our selected features can distinguish the unobfuscated sample and be slightly affected by obfuscations. Opcodes, ultimately, characterize the behavior of Android applications and obfuscations impact relatively little on them. For instance, permission obfuscation influence little on opcode features. Yet, our experiments show that feature selection significantly improve the detection effect.

Algorithm 1: AOSF:ANTI-OBFUSCATION FEATURE SELECT

Input: Dictionary array of non-zero frequency features and frequencies of
samples in unobfuscated datasets A_0, dictionary array of all non-zero
frequency features and their frequencies in the set of obfuscated
variants $A_{obfuscation} = [A_1, A_2, \cdot, A_n]$, opcode feature name set
$featureNames$, number of selected features K.

Output: Selected anti-obfuscation opcode feature name set.

1   $n, m, t \leftarrow size(A_{obfuscation}, A_0, featureNames)$

2   initial array $tf_m, idf_m, tfidf_t, diff_t$ as zeros array

3   **for** $i \leftarrow 1$ **to** m **do**

4   **foreach** $name, frequency \in A_0[i]$ **do**

5       $tf[i] \leftarrow tf[i] + frequency$

6       $idf[name] \leftarrow idf[name] + 1$

7   **for** $i \leftarrow 1$ **to** m **do**

8   **foreach** $name, frequency \in A_0[i]$ **do**

9       $tfidf[name] \leftarrow tfidf[name] + \frac{frequency}{tf[i]} * \log_2 \frac{m}{idf[name]+1}$

10   **for** $i \leftarrow 1$ **to** m **do**

11   **for** $j \leftarrow 1$ **to** n **do**

12   initial array $diffTmp_t$ as zeros array

13       $featureFreqNot0Set \leftarrow \Phi$

14   **foreach** $name, frequency \in A_0[i]$ **do**

15         $diffTmp[name] \leftarrow frequency$

16         $featureFreqNot0Set \leftarrow featureFreqNot0Set \cup name$

17   **foreach** $name, frequency \in A_j[i]$ **do**

18         $diffTmp[name] \leftarrow abs(diffTmp[name] - frequency)$

19         $featureFreqNot0Set \leftarrow featureFreqNot0Set \cup name$

20   **foreach** $feature \in featureFreqNot0Set$ **do**

21         $diff[feature] \leftarrow diff[feature] + diffTmp[feature]$

22   **for** $i \leftarrow 1$ **to** t **do**

23     $weight[i] = \frac{\frac{tfidf[i]}{m}+1}{\frac{diff[i]}{m*n}+1}$

24   **return** $topK(weight, K, featureNames)$

We collect opcode features of an application, and categorize them based on
the granularity of obfuscation techniques. obfuscation techniques can be divided
into three levels: class, method and word. In order to collect opcode features, we
apply an obfuscation technique and extract opcode sequences at the same level
of granularity e.g. for a method level obfuscation, we collect opcode sequences of
a method. We use hash values to represent sequences on method or class levels.
For the word-level opcode sequences, the extracted predefined opcode types, such
as invoke-direct and iput-object. We also collect the frequency of each feature.
Because the method level and class level feature frequency matrix is relatively
sparse, we only extract the frequency information of non-zero frequency features.

The details of AOFS algorithm is illustrated in Algorithm 1. First, we compose a TFIDF matrix based on opcode features. The $tfidf_{jk}$ is the TFIDF value of the k_{th} opcode feature of the j_{th} Android application in the unobfuscated dataset. The difference indicators of the opcode features before and after obfuscation is the sum of the absolute values of the frequency differences in the feature frequency matrix before and after obfuscation in the unobfuscated dataset. Assuming that the number of obfuscations in the obfuscation technique set is n, the number of Android applications in the unobfuscated dataset is m, there are t types of opcode features in the obfuscation technique set. Before the obfuscation, the opcode feature frequency matrix is $A^{(0)}$. After the obfuscation, The obfuscated opcode feature frequency matrix is $A^{(1)}, A^{(2)}, \cdots, A^{(n)}$. $A_j^{(i)} = a_{j1}^{(i)}, a_{j2}^{(i)}, \cdots, a_{jt}^{(i)}$ is the opcode feature word frequency vector of the j_{th} Android application in the i_{th} dataset. $a_{jk}^{(i)}$ is frequency of the k_{th} opcode features of the j_{th} Android application in the i_{th} dataset. Assuming that w_k represents weights of the k_{th} opcode features, it is calculated as shown in Formula 1.

$$w_k = \frac{\frac{\sum_{j=1}^{m} tfidf_{jk}}{m} + 1}{\frac{\sum_{j=1}^{m} \sum_{i=1}^{n} |a_{jk}^{(0)} - a_{jk}^{(i)}|}{m*n} + 1} \tag{1}$$

AOSF filters out ineffective features in a hierarchical manner. First, it filters out the class level features that do not meet the preset threshold. Then, it filters out the method level features from remaining classes. Similarly, the word level opcode features are filtered out. Next, we sort opcode features. Features of different class level opcodes are sorted by the class name, and for the same class name, the order of methods in the class is used as the sort basis. Finally, we get opcode sequence to represent the application by connecting opcode features.

3.3   Detection Model

We transfer the problem of malware classification to image domain adaptation. We represent opcode features by the AOSF algorithm as an image. We build a model based on transfer learning [14] with the Resnet [5]. We train it by feeding unobfuscated applications with their obfuscated versions. The model goal is to transfer the obfuscated version to the unobfuscated one with the minimum loss.

Image Representation. We represent the selected opcode sequence features as a grayscale image. We assign a value between 00 and FF to an opcode based on Dalvik bytecode encoding rules [4]. Then, we divide opcode sequences to 256 opcodes per line. If the end line is less than 256 opcodes, we fill it with 0. Finally, The opcode features is converted into a grayscale image, as is shown below.

$$s_{11} \quad s_{12} \quad s_{21} \quad \cdots$$
$$\rightarrow invoke - direct \quad return - void \quad sget - object \quad \cdots$$
$$\rightarrow 112 \quad 14 \quad 98 \quad \cdots$$
$$\rightarrow \text{grayscale image of the opcode sequence}$$

Transfer Learning Model. Android malware detection can be divided into two tasks: the detection of the existence of malware code and malware families. We train a transfer learning model such that these two tasks can be done simultaneously. We feed two inputs into our network: unobfuscated dataset representation as the source domain, and the corresponding obfuscated versions as the target domain. We note that feature and labels of both domains are the same, but the specific distribution of the images and their labels are different. The model realizes the transfer the features from the source (unobfuscated) domain to the target (obfuscated) domain. It can minimize the difference in the distribution between the source and target domains.

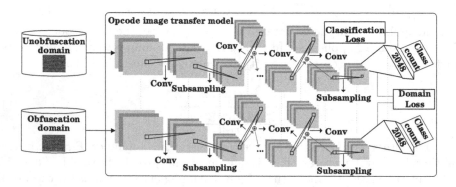

Fig. 2. Training phase of the Android malware obfuscated variants detection model.

Our model is shown in Fig. 2. Both networks share the same network direction and parameters during the training. Our classification network calculates classification loss and domain adaptive loss. Hence, the model can improve the classification accuracy for unobfuscated dataset and reduce the difference of feature distribution before and after obfuscation. The domain adaptive loss is the Maximum Mean Discrepancy (MMD) [13] distance between the data distribution of the unobfuscated application image and the data distribution of the obfuscated application image. As is shown in Eq. 2, the image distributions of the unobfuscated application image and the obfuscated application image are expressed, respectively, by X_U and X_O. $\phi(x)$ represents features of the image after the network's input layer and hidden layer. L is the overall loss function, L_C represents the classification loss, and λ is the weight of the adaptive loss.

$$MMD(X_U, X_O) = ||\frac{\sum_{x_u \in X_U} \phi(x_u)}{|X_U|} - \frac{\sum_{x_o \in X_O} \phi(x_o)}{|X_O|}|| \qquad (2)$$
$$L = L_C + \lambda * MMD^2(X_U, X_O)$$

4   Evaluation

We evaluate AOMDroid, a prototype implementation based on the proposed approach. The evaluation provides insights about the AOMDroid efficiency as well as detection time. Furthermore, we compare AOMDroid with four related works and show that it outperforms all of them in analyzing obfuscated malware.

4.1   Dataset and Configuration

The original dataset contains 5560 malware and 4631 benign samples. We use AVPASS [2] to obfuscate samples. Obfuscation methods include string encryption, inserting benign code obfuscation, variable name obfuscation, class name obfuscation, resource obfuscation, API reflection obfuscation and permission obfuscation. The original malware comes from Drebin [6], and marked with the malware family label. benign samples come from the application market and verified by VirusTotal. AVPASS supports seven obfuscation methods by default that have been cited in the related works [7]. For malware families detection, unobfuscated dataset contains 4615 samples constructed from 21 malware families, the test dataset contains 32513 obfuscated samples.

For the original dataset, we use the successful decompilation samples. The unobfuscated and API reflection obfuscated dataset is used as the source and target domain respectively. All sample labels in the target domain are not added to the training, so seven obfuscated datasets are selected as the test dataset. When the learning rate is 0.01 and the batch size is 16, it reaches the highest accuracy rate. Furthermore, the training epochs are 200. The experiments were done on a computer with an Intel Core(TM) i7-8750H CPU and 16 GB of memory.

Table 1. Effect evaluation of malware detection based on transfer learning. The result is accuracy of detection. U is unobfuscated samples. A is API Reflection obfuscated samples. S is String encryption samples. V is variable obfuscated samples. K is class name obfuscated samples. E is insert benign class code samples. R is resource obfuscated samples. P is permission obfuscated samples. VA is samples of seven obfuscations.

Detection type	U	VA	A	S	V	K	E	R	P
Maliciousness	96.49%	92.26%	91.33%	93.81%	94.20%	83.46%	94.24%	94.30%	94.28%
Malware family	98.22%	87.50%	93.70%	93.81%	55.33%	93.42%	93.83%	93.84%	87.39%

4.2   Detection Effect and Performance of AOMDroid

We measure the accuracy of the proposed model in detecting maliciousness with and without obfuscation. The detection accuracy rate of the existence of malicious code in unobfuscated dataset is 96.49%, and the F value is 96.74%. For obfuscated variants, they are 92.26% and 93.19% respectively, as shown in

Table 1. We apply seven types of obfuscated variants to the unobfuscated dataset. The detection effect on class name obfuscation is low, because the class name obfuscation will change the order of the opcode sequence in the class and change image structure.

Similarly, we measure the malware family detection accuracy both for unobfuscated and obfuscated malware. The detection rate of malicious families against unobfuscated malware is 98.22%, while for seven malware obfuscated variants is 87.50%, as shown in Table 1.

The performance evaluation of AOMDroid considers two parts. The feature selection time is 305.63 s, refers to the time adopted the anti-obfuscation feature selection algorithm. The average time for malware prediction of one application is 0.963 s. Feature selection is in one process. For malware prediction, we divide datasets into 10 subsets, and test in ten processes.

4.3 Comparison with Prior Work

We compare AOMDroid with four related works: Drebin [6], PikaDroid [7], MCSC [8] and RevealDroid [9]. Drebin and PikaDroid are open source but MCSC and RevealDroid are not. We implemented MCSC and tested versus that but for RevealDroid, we rely on their reported numbers. PikaDroid and RevealDroid claim to support anti-obfuscation. Table 2 and 3 summarize the results.

Table 2. Obfuscated malware detection effect and performance evaluation with prior advanced methods that don't claim to support anti-obfuscation. The detection effect is trained on unobfuscated dataset and API reflection obfuscated variants and tested on samples in obfuscated dataset. The predict time is in seconds and tested for average single Android application in unobfuscated dataset by ten progresses.

Method	Average accuracy of malware obfuscated variants detection	Predict time
AOMDroid	**For permission obfuscated and seven obfuscated variants are 94.28% and 92.26% respectively**	**0.96**
Drebin [6]	For permission obfuscated variants is 77.17%	0.99
MCSC [8]	For seven obfuscated variants is 76.64%	3.67

Comparison with Drebin. Drebin and AOMDroid both train by unobfuscated dataset and API reflection dataset. AOMDroid detects permission obfuscated variants with a 94.28% accuracy while Drebin is 77.14%. Drebin is not effective in detecting obfuscated variants because it does not consider the obfuscation techniques. In terms of performance, AOMDroid is more efficient than Drebin in feature extraction. The average prediction time of AOMDroid for a single application is 0.963 s while Drebin is 0.998 s.

Comparison with MCSC. MCSC obfuscated variant detection accuracy is 76.64% while AOMDroid is 92.26%. MCSC is trained by unobfuscated dataset and API reflection dataset, when detecting malware obfuscated variants. In terms of prediction time and detection effectiveness, many hash calculations are required for extracting images in MCSC, so AOMDroid has advantages than MCSC.

Table 3. Obfuscated malware detection effect and performance evaluation with prior advanced methods that claim to support anti-obfuscation. The detection effect of AOMDroid and PikaDroid is based on 200 random unobfuscated samples and 1400 obfuscated samples. The predict time of AOMDroid and PikaDroid is in seconds and tested for average single Android application malware of 1600 samples by sixteen progresses. The detection effect and predict time of RevealDroid are obtained from its paper.

Method	Malware obfuscated variants detection accuracy	Predict time
AOMDroid	**For seven obfuscated variants is 93.56%**	**0.96**
PikaDroid [7]	For seven obfuscated variants is 93.46%	26.39
RevealDroid [9]	For four obfuscated variants drops to 85%	31.37

Comparison with PikaDroid. PikaDroid [7] uses machine learning models to detect Android malware based on API context features. It supports detection of obfuscated malware. We randomly selects 100 benign applications and 100 malicious applications from the original dataset, and uses seven obfuscation methods to generate 1400 obfuscated applications. Unobfuscated applications and permission obfuscated applications are used as source and target domain samples respectively, for training of AOMDroid. PikaDroid uses same training sets. PikaDroid uses program flow graph features based on API context, hence, AOMDroid has obvious advantages in detection time and detection accuracy.

Comparison with RevealDroid. RevealDroid [9] is not open source and reproduction is difficult. Obtaining key insights from the paper, AOMDroid has advantages in anti-obfuscation detection accuracy, the breadth of supporting obfuscation technologies, and the prediction time. RevealDroid detects whether the four obfuscated variants are malicious applications, the accuracy drops by more than 10%. Moreover, AOMDroid takes an average of 0.963 s to predict in parallel, while RevealDroid takes 31.3682 s.

5   Related Work

Android malware detection involves machine learning [6,7,9–12]. DroidAPI Miner [10] offers a machine learning approach based on API call features. Mariconti et al. [11] build markov chains of system APIs to characterize specific logical behaviors. Drebin [6], in addition to detecting maliciousness of Android applications, identifies malicious family. Recently, Hou et al. [12] construct a malware detection system based on heterogeneous information networks with deep learning. The similar work to ours is MCSC [8]. It proposes SimHash to transfer application opcodes to images, and uses convolutional neural networks, but performs poorly. Similar to MCSC, we represent opcode features as images, but our method is anti-obfuscation and feature processing and model are different from MCSC. However, they are all not anti-obfuscation enough.

The accuracy of the aforementioned Android malware detection techniques would deteriorate when the malware is obfuscated. Several related works tried to address this problems [7,9]. PikaDroid [7] uses the API context, but it cannot effectively detect API reflection obfuscated Android malware. Another work, RevealDroid [9] employs multiple features and is resilient to API reflection obfuscation, but still lacks generality.

6 Limitation

AOMDroid would not perform well when analyzing the behavior of packed applications because the packing technologies will hide the actual behavior of the application. AOMDroid analyzes the Android application by static analysis. However, Some application packing technologies encrypt the Android application installation package, and the actual application executable file will be restored only when the application is actually running [15]. Another limitation is analysing Android applications that use dynamic loading technology to load the executable file that does not exist in the original installation package [16].

7 Conclusion

This paper proposes a transfer learning based approach to detect Android malicious obfuscated variants. We design a feature selection algorithm based on TFIDF, and represent selected features as images. Our transfer model learns the transformation between unobfuscated and their obfuscated applications, and hence identifies malware even after obfuscation. We evaluated the effectiveness and efficiency of AOMDroid, a prototype based on our proposed approach, by comparing it with four related works. AOMDroid outperforms all related works in terms of detection accuracy of obfuscated malware and the detection time.

Acknowledgement. This work is supported by the National Key Research and Development Program of China under grants 2016YFB0800402 and 2016QY01W0202, National Natural Science Foundation of China under grants U1836204, U1936108, 61572221, 61433006, U1401258, 61572222 and 61502185, and Major Projects of the National Social Science Foundation under grant 16ZDA092.

References

1. 360, Android malware special report in 2019 (2020). http://blogs.360.cn/post/review_android_malware_of_2019.html. Accessed 3 June 2020

2. Jung, J., Jeon, C., Wolotsky, M., Yun, I., Kim, T.: AVPASS: leaking and bypassing antivirus detection model automatically. In: Black Hat USA Briefings (Black Hat USA) (2017)

3. Salton, G., Yu, C.T.: On the construction of effective vocabularies for information retrieval. In: Proceedings of the 1973 International Conference on Research on Development in Information Retrieval, SIGIR, pp. 48–60. ACM (1973)

4. Google: Dalvik Opcode (2020). https://source.android.com/devices/tech/dalvik/dalvik-bytecode. Accessed 3 June 2020

5. He, K., Zhang, X., Ren, S., Sun, J.: Deep residual learning for image recognition. In: Proceedings of the 2016 IEEE Conference on Computer Vision and Pattern Recognition, CVPR, pp. 770–778. IEEE (2016)

6. Arp, D., Spreitzenbarth, M., Hubner, M., Gascon, H., Rieck, K.: DREBIN: effective and explainable detection of Android malware in your pocket. In: Proceedings of the 21st Annual Network and Distributed System Security Symposium, NDSS. ISOC (2014)

7. Allen, J., Landen, M., Chaba, S., Ji, Y., Chung, S.P.H., Lee, W.: Improving accuracy of Android malware detection with lightweight contextual awareness. In: Proceedings of the 34th Annual Computer Security Applications Conference, ACSAC, pp. 210–221. ACM (2018)

8. Ni, S., Qian, Q., Zhang, R.: Malware identification using visualization images and deep learning. Comput. Secur. **77**, 871–885 (2018)

9. Garcia, J., Hammad, M., Malek, S.: Lightweight, obfuscation-resilient detection and family identification of Android malware. In: Proceedings of the 40th International Conference on Software Engineering, ICSE, p. 497. IEEE/ACM (2018)

10. Aafer, Y., Du, W., Yin, H.: DroidAPIMiner: mining API-level features for robust malware detection in Android. In: Proceedings of the 9th International Conference on Security and Privacy in Communication Networks, SecureComm, pp. 86–103. ACM (2013)

11. Mariconti, E., Onwuzurike, L., Andriotis, P., Cristofaro, E.D., Ross, G.J., Stringhini, G.: MaMaDroid: detecting Android malware by building Markov chains of behavioral models. In: Proceedings of the 24th Annual Network and Distributed System Security Symposium, NDSS. ISOC (2017)

12. Hou, S., Ye, Y., Song, Y., Abdulhayoglu, M.: HinDroid: an intelligent Android malware detection system based on structured heterogeneous information network. In: Proceedings of the 23rd ACM SIGKDD International Conference on Knowledge Discovery and Data Mining, SIGKDD, pp. 1507–1515. ACM (2017)

13. Pan, S.J., Tsang, I.W., Kwok, J.T., Yang, Q.: Domain adaptation via transfer component analysis. IEEE Trans. Neural Networks **22**(2), 199–210 (2011)

14. Tzeng, E., Hoffman, J., Zhang, N., Saenko, K., Darrell, T.: Deep domain confusion: maximizing for domain invariance. arXiv 1412.3474 (2014)

15. Duan, Y., et al.: Things you may not know about Android (Un)packers: a systematic study based on whole-system emulation. In: Proceedings of the 25th Annual Network and Distributed System Security Symposium, NDSS. ISOC (2018)

16. Xue, Y., et al.: Auditing anti-malware tools by evolving Android malware and dynamic loading technique. IEEE Trans. Inf. Forensics Secur. **12**(7), 1529–1544 (2017)

ML-Based Early Detection of IoT Botnets

Ayush Kumar[1](✉) ⓘ, Mrinalini Shridhar[1], Sahithya Swaminathan[1],
and Teng Joon Lim[2]

[1] National University of Singapore, Singapore, Singapore
{ayush.kumar,e0269748,e0269724}@u.nus.edu
[2] University of Sydney, Camperdown, NSW 2008, Australia
tj.lim@sydney.edu.au

Abstract. In this paper, we present EDIMA, an IoT botnet detection
solution to be deployed at the edge gateway installed in home networks
which targets early detection of botnets. EDIMA includes a novel two-
stage machine learning (ML)-based detector which first employs ML
algorithms for aggregate traffic classification and subsequently Autocorrelation Function (ACF)-based tests to detect individual bots. Performance evaluation results show that EDIMA achieves high bot scanning
detection accuracies with a very low false positive rate.

Keywords: Internet of Things · IoT · Malware · Mirai · Botnet
detection · Machine Learning · Anomaly detection · Intrusion detection

1 Introduction

The Internet of things (IoT) refers to the network of low-power, limited processing capability sensing devices which exchange data with each other and/or
systems (e.g., gateways, cloud servers). IoT devices are used in a number of applications such as wearables, home automation and industrial automation. Unfortunately, hackers are increasingly targeting IoT devices using malware (malicious
software) for a number of reasons such as legacy devices connected to the Internet with little or no security updates, low priority given to security within the
development cycle, weak login credentials, etc.

In a widely publicized attack, the IoT malware Mirai was used to launch the
biggest Distributed Denial-of-Service (DDoS) attack on record in 2016 through
infected IoT devices such as IP cameras and DVR recorders. The source code for
Mirai was leaked in 2017 and since then, there has been a proliferation of IoT malware. These malware are usually Mirai variants using a similar brute force technique of scanning random IP addresses for open TELNET ports and attempting
to login using a built-in dictionary of commonly used credentials (e.g., Remaiten,
Hajime), or more sophisticated ones that exploit software vulnerabilities to execute remote command injections on vulnerable devices (e.g., Reaper, Satori,
Masuta, Linux.Darlloz, Amnesia). Bots compromised by Mirai or similar IoT

© ICST Institute for Computer Sciences, Social Informatics and Telecommunications Engineering 2020
Published by Springer Nature Switzerland AG 2020. All Rights Reserved
N. Park et al. (Eds.): SecureComm 2020, LNICST 336, pp. 254–260, 2020.
https://doi.org/10.1007/978-3-030-63095-9_15

malware can be used for DDoS attacks, phishing, spamming and bitcoin mining. These attacks can cause network downtime for long periods which may lead to financial loss to Internet Service Providers (ISP), leakage of users' confidential data, and unauthorized exploitation of computational resources. Furthermore, many of the infected devices are expected to remain infected for a long time.

We propose an IoT botnet detection solution, EDIMA (Early Detection of IoT Malware Scanning and CnC Communication Activity), which is designed to be deployed at the edge gateway installed in home networks and targets the detection of botnets at an early stage of their evolution (scanning and propagation phase) before they can be used for further attacks. EDIMA employs a two-stage detection mechanism which first uses machine learning (ML) algorithms for aggregate traffic classification based on bot scanning traffic patterns, and subsequently Autocorrelation Function (ACF)-based tests which leverage bot-CnC messaging characteristics at the per-device traffic level to detect individual bots. We only target IoT botnets with centralized Command-and-control architecture in this work.

2   EDIMA Architecture

EDIMA is designed to have a modular architecture, as shown in Fig. 1, with the following components:

- **Feature Extractor:** This module extracts features from the aggregate traffic at the gateway. These features are then forwarded to the ML-based Bot Detector (MBD) for classification during the execution phase. The Feature Extractor (FE) also sends features extracted from the aggregate traffic to the *ML Model Constructor* (MC), during the training phase.
- **ML-based Bot Detector:** This is a 2-stage module with the first stage being a *coarse-grained* one that classifies the aggregate traffic samples using the features obtained from FE and the ML model trained and forwarded by the MC. Depending on the result of the classification, the second *fine-grained* stage attempts to identify the infected IoT device(s) from the set of devices connected to the gateway.
- **Traffic Parser:** The traffic parser (TP) sorts the combined gateway traffic into traffic sessions. During the bootstrap (training) phase of EDIMA, it also helps replay malware traffic samples along with normal traffic to generate malicious traffic samples.
- **Malware PCAP Database:** The database stores malware traffic *pcap* files captured from private and professional honeypots targeted at IoT malware.
- **ML Model Constructor:** The ML model used for classifying edge gateway traffic is trained by this module. We assume a publish-subscribe model where multiple gateways subscribe to a MC. A separate ML model is trained for each gateway for optimal performance. Whenever a gateway comes online, it registers with the MC. Malicious traffic samples from the *Malware PCAP Database* (mDB) are sent to the gateway to generate malicious aggregate traffic. The feature vectors extracted from benign (normal traffic with no

malicious scanning packets) and malicious aggregate traffic are subsequently sent by a gateway's FE to the MC. The extracted features are used to train a supervised ML classifier which is then published to the gateway's MBD.

– **Policy Engine:** The policy engine (PE) consists of a list of policies defined by the network administrator, which determine the course of actions to be taken once an IoT device connected to the edge gateway has been detected as a bot.

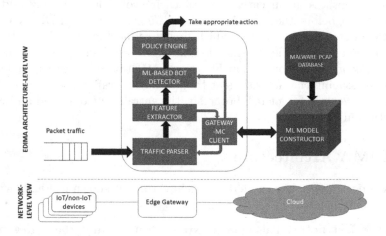

Fig. 1. EDIMA architecture

3   Description of EDIMA's Components

3.1   Detection of Scanning Activity in Aggregate Gateway Traffic

The first coarse-grained stage of the MBD performs classification on aggregate gateway traffic rather than per-device traffic. We define two classes of gateway traffic: *benign* and *malicious*. Benign traffic refers to the gateway traffic which does not include bot scanning packets while malicious traffic refers to gateway traffic that does. The gateway traffic is captured in the form of traffic sessions which are defined statically as the set of ingress/egress packets at a network interface over a fixed time interval. We apply the classification algorithm on these traffic sessions.

In a traffic session, we extract features from TCP packet headers only and not the payloads. The steps used for gateway-level traffic classification are given below:

1. Filter each gateway traffic session to include only TCP packets.
2. Extract the feature vectors for each traffic session.
3. Apply the trained ML classifier on the extracted feature vectors and classify the corresponding sessions.

We have carefully identified the following eight botnet-aware features for ML classification:

- Number of unique TCP SYN destination IP addresses
- Number of packets per unique destination IP address
  - maximum
  - minimum
  - mean
- Number of TCP half-open connections
- TCP packet length
  - maximum
  - minimum
  - mean.

3.2 Detection of Individual Bots Using Bot-CnC Communication Patterns

Once the aggregate traffic at an edge gateway has been classified as *malicious*, the second fine-grained stage of the ML-based bot detector attempts to detect the underlying bots by checking the ingress/egress traffic from each IoT device for the presence of bot-CnC communication patterns. In most existing IoT botnets, including the Mirai-variants, there is a periodic exchange of TCP messages ([PSH, ACK], [ACK]) or UDP messages between the bot and the CnC server. To detect the presence of bot-CnC communication, we propose the following approach: filter the traffic from a potential bot for UDP packets or TCP packets (with PSH and ACK flags *ON*) and exclude IoT application data packets from our analysis using appropriate packet capture filters. Subsequently, sample and encode the filtered packets to produce a uniformly sampled discrete-time signal. To detect periodicity in time series data obtained above, we use the autocorrelation function (ACF) [1].

4 Performance Evaluation

4.1 Testbed Description

To evaluate the performance of EDIMA on real devices, we built a testbed with IoT and non-IoT devices. The devices were used by 3 staff members in our lab over a period of 4 weeks, and thus the traffic data collected from those devices reflects real-world users' behaviour. The edge gateway where the traffic from all the above devices was aggregated was a Linksys WRT32X router running Open-WRT with a 1.8 GHz dual-core processor, 512 MB RAM, and 256 MB NAND flash memory. The testbed schematic is shown in Fig. 2.

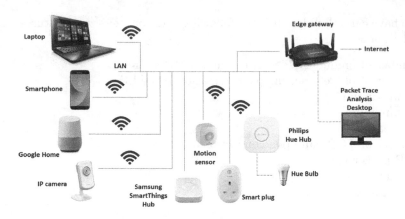

Fig. 2. Schematic of the testbed

4.2 Data Collection and Processing

As mentioned in Sect. 3.1, we classify the aggregate gateway traffic as *benign* or *malicious*. Therefore, we need training data samples to represent both classes. Benign traffic is not difficult to generate as it involves the normal operation of uninfected devices. However, malicious traffic contains both benign traffic as well as scanning/infection packets generated by malware. Towards this, we obtained 23 live IoT malware samples belonging to different malware categories over a period of 3 months (May–July, 2019) from APIs provided by New Sky Security [2] and malware hosting server links posted by Bad Packets Report Twitter account [3]. The FANTASM framework, provided by DeterLab team for safe experimentation with live malware based on their paper [4], was used to run the malware samples and collect the traffic generated by them.

Many of the malware samples were simple variants of each other, as revealed by analysing their traffic using Wireshark. We ended up with two malware samples, called *loligang* and *echobot* by their authors, which exploited TELNET and HTTP POST+GET vulnerabilities respectively. We ran both the malware binaries on the FANTASM testbed for 5 min each and captured the corresponding traffic *pcap* files. Malicious traffic was then generated by replaying the malware traffic collected from FANTASM on the edge gateway using the *tcpreplay* utility. This approach, in effect, emulates an IoT bot connected to the gateway.

We used a traffic session duration of 15 min for this study. 1000 traffic sessions were captured for benign traffic and a further 1000 sessions for malicious traffic through our testbed. The malicious traffic sessions consisted of 400 sessions corresponding to *loligang*, another 400 sessions corresponding to *echobot* and the remaining 200 sessions corresponding to both *loligang* and *echobot* traffic replayed at the OpenWRT router. The features mentioned in Sect. 3.1 were extracted from the captured sessions. Appropriate class labels were assigned to the extracted feature vectors.

The feature vectors were checked for missing values and handled appropriately. Next, all the values in a feature vector were scaled to lie within the range (0,1). Further, the feature vectors were randomly permuted. The combined benign and malicious feature vectors were randomly divided into *training* and *test* datasets using an 80:20 split. We used the χ^2 statistical test to compute the χ^2 test statistic for each feature from the sample data. Subsequently, we selected the best $k=6$ features (having test statistic value more than zero) for training our ML classifiers.

4.3   Results

Scanning Activity Detection Performance. We trained the following ML models using the final feature vectors obtained in the previous section after completing all the data processing steps: Gaussian Naive Bayes' (GNB), Support Vector Machine (SVM) and Random Forest (RForest). Subsequently, the trained ML models are used to predict the class labels of the test dataset and thereby, the detection performance of the models is evaluated and compared. In this work, a 10-fold cross validation approach is used to tune the hyper-parameters of the ML classifiers for achieving the highest possible CV scores. The cross validation is based on training data only without using any information from the test dataset. Using the tuned hyper-parameters' values, the average classification accuracy, precision, recall and F-1 scores obtained for the final classifiers over 50 runs are shown in Table 1. It can be observed that the Random Forest classifier performs the best in terms of classification accuracy followed by SVM classifier and Gaussian Naive Bayes' classifier.

Table 1. Performance of ML classifiers for scanning activity detection

Dataset	Session duration	Method	AC	PR	RC	F1
Testbed	15 min	Rforest	1.0	1.0	1.0	1.0
		SVM	0.99	0.99	1.0	0.99
		GNB	0.97	0.97	1.0	0.97

5   Conclusion

We have proposed EDIMA, a solution for early detection of IoT botnets in home networks. It detects bots connected to an edge gateway in two stages- first by looking for scanning and subsequently bot-CnC server communication traffic patterns. EDIMA consists of a traffic parser, feature extractor, ML-based bot detector, policy engine, ML model constructor and a malware PCAP database. A performance evaluation of EDIMA using our testbed setup revealed that it has a close to 100% accuracy and very low false positive rate in detecting malicious aggregate gateway traffic with ML algorithms such as the Random Forest.

Acknowledgment. This research is supported by the National Research Foundation, Prime Minister's Office, Singapore under its Corporate Laboratory@University Scheme, National University of Singapore, and Singapore Telecommunications Ltd.

References

1. Martin, N., Mailhes, C.: About periodicity and signal to noise ratio - the strength of the autocorrelation function. In: Conference on Condition Monitoring and Machinery Failure Prevention Technologies (CM and MFPT 2010), Stratford-upon-Avon, United Kingdom (2010)
2. New Sky Security: New sky security IoT threat intelligence platform. https://iot.newskysecurity.com/
3. Bad Packets Report (Twitter): Mirai-like botnet hosts. https://tinyurl.com/y5y33omf
4. Alwabel, A., Shi, H., Bartlett, G., Mirkovic, J.: Safe and automated live malware experimentation on public testbeds. In: Proceedings of the 7th Workshop on Cyber Security Experimentation and Test (CSET 2014). USENIX Association, San Diego (2014)

Post-Quantum Cryptography
in WireGuard VPN

Quentin M. Kniep$^{(\boxtimes)}$, Wolf Müller, and Jens-Peter Redlich

Institut für Informatik, Humboldt-Universität zu Berlin, 10099 Berlin, Germany
{kniepque,wolfm,jpr}@informatik.hu-berlin.de
https://sar.informatik.hu-berlin.de

Abstract. WireGuard is a new and promising VPN software. It relies on ECDH for the key agreement and server authentication. This makes the tunnel vulnerable to future attacks with quantum computers.

Three incremental improvements to WireGuard's handshake protocol are proposed, giving differently enhanced levels of post-quantum security. Performance impacts of these are shown to be moderate.

Keywords: Post-quantum cryptography · VPN · Key exchange

1 Introduction

Security features of VPN software can hide your identity, the actual data, and its destination. Well-known implementations are OpenVPN, IPsec, and WireGuard, which was recently integrated into the Linux kernel. We focus on WireGuard (WG) because it is promising for the future. WG's handshake is currently based on ECDH. However, Rötteler et al. [17] have shown that the quantum computer algorithm by Shor can break it. This allows for retroactive attacks. Therefore, we need to use post-quantum (PQ) primitives for the key agreement now. WG allows to use a 256-bit pre-shared key (PSK) [6], which can come from a PQ-secure handshake. While this ensures basic PQ confidentiality, it has neither PFS nor identity hiding. Symmetric encryption and hashes are only somewhat threatened by Grover's algorithm. Also, there are very reasonable doubts raised about its impact [2,18], mainly because of bad parallelizability.

2 Related Work

Mullvad is a VPN provider that allows to use WG with a PQ PSK. Therefore, they also provide neither PFS nor identity hiding. Researchers at Microsoft use OpenVPN with a full PQ key exchange, with all the advantages and disadvantages of OpenVPN compared to WG. Hülsing et al. also propose an adapted WG handshake protocol [10]. The biggest difference to our adaptions is that they aim

N. Park et al. (Eds.): SecureComm 2020, LNICST 336, pp. 261–267, 2020.
https://doi.org/10.1007/978-3-030-63095-9_16

to replace ECDH with PQ primitives. They further prove security under extensions of the models used on WG [7,8]. The proposed solution is very promising for the future. In contrast, we propose a more conservative integration of a full PQ key exchange in WG, which should also guarantee the same security as WG against classical adversaries.

3   Protocol Design

First we define four incremental **levels of security** in a PQ setting:

Level 0 (L0) basic confidentiality (WG specification),
Level 1 (L1) perfect forward secrecy,
Level 2 (L2) identity hiding (same passive security in PQ setting as WG),
Level 3 (L3) active attacks (same security in PQ as WG in classical setting).

Whereas the security levels defined by NIST [12] concern specific costs for breaking primitives, these are about general security properties of handshake protocols. We use *Roman uppercase* numbers **I**, **III**, and **V** for **NIST security levels** and *Arabic* numbers **0**, **1**, **2**, and **3** for **handshake security levels**.

In the following we present three proposed handshake protocols which are extensions of the WG handshake and satisfy L1–L3 respectively. By the Noise construction they are at least as strong as the WG handshake. [15] Note that WG's handshake is an L0 handshake. The protocols are written in Noise notation [15], with the hybrid forward secrecy extension for KEMs [14]. This is further extended with tokens sX, skemX for static public keys and their ciphertexts.

Level 1 Handshake (PFS)

```
<- s
...
-> e, e1, es, s, ss
<- e, ekem1, ee, se, psk
```
PFS is achieved by establishing a shared secret using the PQ KEM with an ephemeral key pair generated by the initiator. For this we need to add the public key to the initiation message and a ciphertext to the response.

Level 2 Handshake (identity hiding)

```
<- s, s1
...
-> e, e1, skem1, es, s, ss
<- e, ekem1, ee, se, psk
```
Identity hiding is achieved by adding a PQ static key pair, in addition to the responder's classical static key pair. The initiator's identity is encrypted with a secret protected under both.

Level 3 Handshake (active attacks)

```
<- s, s1
...
-> e, e1, skem1, es, s, s2, ss
<- e, ekem1, skem2 ee, se, psk
```
For security against active attackers another static PQ key pair is added, this time on the initiator's side. The PQ parts now closely resemble the Noise IK handshake.

4   Performance Analysis

The proof-of-concept implementation is based on BoringTun [5], Cloudflare's Rust implementation of WG, and available on GitHub under the BSD 3-Clause License: https://github.com/qkniep/pqwg-rust. This was originally developed and explained in more detail in my Bachelor's thesis. [11]

Message Sizes. Ciphertexts and public keys of PQ KEMs are hundreds of Bytes large. Since WG is based on UDP and IP packet fragmentation is considered fragile [3], we need to split datagrams on the application layer. In WG there is a 5 s timeout if the handshake fails, e.g. because a datagram was lost. Combined with a study on packet loss [16] this gives about **30 ms per additional datagram**. Choosing cryptographic primitives with small key sizes is thus essential.

Amplification Attacks. To prevent DoS attacks based on amplification, initiation messages should be larger than the response. In the following we always accommodate for the necessary padding in the initiation message.

Memory Exhaustion Attacks. Another problem when splitting messages is the possibility of memory exhaustion attacks. [3] Malicious initiators may send incomplete messages until the responder runs out of memory. WG already has a system against CPU-exhaustion attacks [6], which could be expanded to also prevent memory exhaustion.

4.1   Benchmark Setup

All benchmark results that follow come from a workstation with the following specifications: **CPU** Intel Xeon E3–1230 v3 (4 × 3.3 GHz, 8 MB Cache, AVX2, AES-NI), **RAM** 8 GB DDR3–1600, **OS** Arch Linux x86_64, and **Kernel** 5.3.7–arch1–2–ARCH.

The benchmarks are based on the BoringTun handshake test [5], adapted in the number of packets sent over the WG tunnel, and run through Criterion.rs [9], with *sample size* of 100 and *measurement time* of one minute. Results will be presented only for some of the most interesting cryptographic primitives, based on results from Sect. 4 and the **speed_kem** benchmark in liboqs [13].

4.2   Use Cases

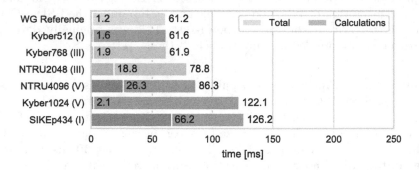

Fig. 1. Time the L1 handshake takes with different PQ cryptographic primitives.

Home VPN Server (L1). Here, identity hiding is not a priority or its impossible anyways. **Kyber-768** seems almost perfect, as it is almost as fast as WG (see Fig. 1), while fitting into one datagram per message. For NIST level V there is a trade-off between computation time and additional datagrams, with **NTRU4096 and Kyber-1024**.

Trusted Network Access (L2). If we want to protect the data and the clients' identities, achieving NIST level V is the most interesting case: It gives the same security guarantees as WG, while also considering the possibility of future quantum-capable attackers. While it could be reasoned to go for level III with Kyber-768, **NTRU4096 or Kyber-1024** both have reasonable cost.

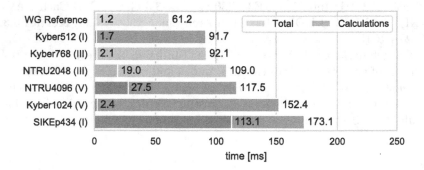

Fig. 2. Time the L2 handshake takes with different PQ cryptographic primitives.

Future Proof System (L3). In cases where a rigid system is built, that can not be adapted once capable quantum computers arrive, it needs to implement an L3 handshake. Such a future-oriented system should reasonably target NIST level V. Then, the handshake needs at least two datagrams more than L2. That is a lot for preventing attacks that are not possible until strong quantum computers are in active use. Only **NTRU4096 and Kyber-1024** seem suitable.

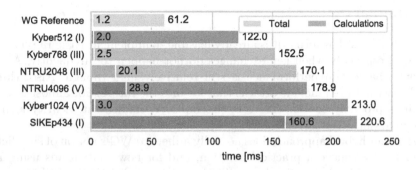

Fig. 3. Time the L3 handshake takes with different PQ cryptographic primitives.

4.3 Throughput, Ping, Reliability

Notably, *nothing* about the symmetric cryptography was changed. Therefore, we expect no noticeable difference in throughput and average packet ping. Especially when measured over the course of a longer networking session.

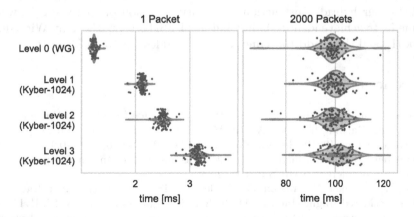

Fig. 4. Runtime of the handshakes with different PQ security levels, each performing the handshake and sending 1 or 2000 packets over the tunnel.

Sending only 2000 packets, it is apparent that the key exchange has little impact in practice. This can be seen in Fig. 4. In these examples packets are sent to *localhost*, latency and its variance link is thus minimal.

WG also has a feature to ensure a failing handshake will, in most cases, not harm transmission throughput over the tunnel: After starting a key exchange there is a sixty second grace period, during which the old key can still be used. [6]

5   Summary

Our analysis has shown that it is already feasible to implement basic PQ security measures, especially when key exchanges do not happen too frequently. At the moment, the cost in performance is still relatively high though. Also, threat models may not even include attacks that far into the future. For almost any use case, it is probably too expensive to preemptively implement security against active quantum adversaries.

While our hybrid approach does not fully adhere to WG's notion of simplicity, we did try to achieve a practical solution, and for now that means using PQ primitives in hybrid. This is also explicitly recommended by the BSI (German Department for IT Security). [4] Once this is no longer necessary, the approach in [10] seems very reasonable.

5.1   Future Work

Results from this work can be used for estimating the cost of including PQ measures into key exchanges. From this point one can decide, whether the gain in security against future attacks is worth the cost in computation and transmission times today. The work by Hülsing et al. [10], which adapts proofs for WG [7,8] to their PQ adaption of WG, could be used as strong foundation to make similar proofs for our hybrid construction. In a future version of this work we would redefine L1 to achieve identity hiding but not PFS, by using the Tiny WireGuard Tweak [1], and then, add the same steps now added for L1 in L2 instead.

References

1. Appelbaum, J., Martindale, C., Wu, P.: Tiny wireguard tweak. In: Buchmann, J., Nitaj, A., Rachidi, T. (eds.) AFRICACRYPT 2019. LNCS, vol. 11627, pp. 3–20. Springer, Cham (2019). https://doi.org/10.1007/978-3-030-23696-0_1
2. Bernstein, D.J.: Cost analysis of hash collisions: will quantum computers make SHARCS obsolete. SHARCS **9**, 105 (2009)
3. Bonica, R., Baker, F., Huston, G., Hinden, R., Troan, O., Gont, F.: IP fragmentation considered fragile. Internet-Draft draft-ietf-intarea-frag-fragile-17, IETF Secretariat, September 2019. http://www.ietf.org/internet-drafts/draft-ietf-intarea-frag-fragile-17.txt
4. Bundesamt für Sicherheit in der Informationstechnik: Migration zu post-quanten-kryptografie. https://www.bsi.bund.de/SharedDocs/Downloads/DE/BSI/Krypto/Post-Quanten-Kryptografie.pdf (2020). Accessed 25 June 2020

5. Cloudflare: Boringtun, March 2019. https://github.com/cloudflare/boringtun. Accessed 25 June 2020
6. Donenfeld, J.A.: WireGuard: next generation kernel network tunnel. In: NDSS (2017)
7. Donenfeld, J.A., Milner, K.: Formal verification of the WireGuard protocol (2017). https://www.wireguard.com/papers/wireguard-formal-verification.pdf. Accessed 25 June 25 2020
8. Dowling, B., Paterson, K.G.: A cryptographic analysis of the wireguard protocol. In: Preneel, B., Vercauteren, F. (eds.) ACNS 2018. LNCS, vol. 10892, pp. 3–21. Springer, Cham (2018). https://doi.org/10.1007/978-3-319-93387-0_1
9. Heisler, B.: Criterion.rs. March 2014. https://github.com/bheisler/criterion.rs. Accessed 25 June 2020
10. Hülsing, A., Ning, K.C., Schwabe, P., Weber, F., Zimmermann, P.R.: Post-quantum WireGuard. Technical report, Cryptology ePrint Archive, Report 2020/379. http://eprint.iacr.org/2020/379 (2020)
11. Kniep, Q.M.: Post-quantum cryptography in WireGuard VPN (2019). https://hu. berlin/PQWireGuard
12. National Institute of Standards and Technology: Submission requirements and evaluation criteria for the post-quantum cryptography standardization process, December 2016. https://csrc.nist.gov/CSRC/media/Projects/Post-Quantum-Cryptography/documents/call-for-proposals-final-dec-2016.pdf. Accessed 25 June 2020
13. Open Quantum Safe: liboqs, August 2016. https://github.com/open-quantum-safe/liboqs/. Accessed 25 June 2020
14. Perrin, T.: KEM-based hybrid forward secrecy for noise (2018). https://github.com/noiseprotocol/noise_hfs_spec/blob/master/output/noise_hfs.pdf. Accessed 25 June 2020
15. Perrin, T.: The Noise protocol framework, July 2018. https://noiseprotocol.org/noise.pdf. Accessed 25 June 2020
16. Raghavendra, R., Belding, E.M.: Characterizing high-bandwidth real-time video traffic in residential broadband networks. In: 8th International Symposium on Modeling and Optimization in Mobile, Ad Hoc, and Wireless Networks, pp. 597–602. IEEE (2010)
17. Roetteler, M., Naehrig, M., Svore, K.M., Lauter, K.: Quantum resource estimates for computing elliptic curve discrete logarithms. arXiv preprint arXiv:1706.06752 (2017)
18. Zalka, C.: Grover's quantum searching algorithm is optimal. Phys. Rev. A $60(4)$, 2746 (1999)

Evaluating the Cost of Personnel Activities in Cybersecurity Management: A Case Study

Rafał Leszczyna[✉][iD]

Gdańsk University of Technology, Faculty of Management and Economics,
Narutowicza 11/12, 80-233 Gdańsk, Poland
rle@zie.pg.gda.pl

Abstract. The methods of cybersecurity costs' evaluation are inclined towards the cost of incidents or technological acquirements. At the same time, there are other, less visible costs related to cybersecurity that require proper recognition. These costs are associated with the actions and the time spent by employees on activities connected to cybersecurity management. The costs form a considerable component of cybersecurity expenditures, but because they become evident only during scrupulous analyses, often they are disregarded. CAsPeA is a method that enables estimating the costs based on a model derived from the Activity-Based Costing (ABC) and the NIST SP 800-53 guidelines. This paper presents the application of CAsPeA in a steel structures manufacturing company.

Keywords: Cybersecurity management · Cost · Estimation · Information security

1 Method Description

CAsPeA – *C*ost *As*sessment of *Pe*rsonnel *A*ctivities in Information Security Management (https://zie.pg.edu.pl/cybsec/caspea) – is a method that complements the portfolio of available methods for estimating the cost of cybersecurity management by enabling the estimation of the costs of human effort and time spent on cybersecurity-related actions during their daily work [1–4]. These costs regard, for instance, employees' participation in cybersecurity training, managing secure configurations of utilised hardware and software or reading cybersecurity policy documents. Such costs constitute a substantial component of cybersecurity spendings, but because they become evident only during scrupulous analyses, often they are neglected. By enabling their estimations, the method should provide a more complete view of the costs of cybersecurity.

To enable the calculations, the Activity-Based Costing (ABC) system was selected and adopted to the costing model [1–4]. The advantage of the ABC is that it recognises activities (human or machine operations) as fundamental

© ICST Institute for Computer Sciences, Social Informatics and Telecommunications Engineering 2020
Published by Springer Nature Switzerland AG 2020. All Rights Reserved
N. Park et al. (Eds.): SecureComm 2020, LNICST 336, pp. 268–274, 2020.
https://doi.org/10.1007/978-3-030-63095-9_17

objects that induce costs in enterprises. In CAsPeA, the total cost in an organisation is calculated as a sum of costs of all activities performed in an enterprise. Then, to derive the costs of activities, proper cost centres must be assigned to them using relevant cost drivers. Duration driver in the form of working time expressed in hours was chosen as the activity cost driver.

For the reference list of the activities to be included in the model, NIST SP's 800-53 list of security controls was chosen after a thorough literature analysis. The list embraces multiple cybersecurity areas that altogether comprehensively address the organisational cybersecurity context. Examples of the areas include the *AT Awareness and Training*, *CM Configuration Management* or *PS Personnel Security* [5]. Another strength of the document is that it is fully compatible with ISO/IEC 27001 (see the mapping between the documents in Appendix H, Table H-1 of NIST SP 800-53) – the most recognised cybersecurity standard worldwide.

The method enables rough estimations based on a small set of input data that characterise an organisation, namely:

- the number of employees with access to the IT system,
- the number of cybersecurity professionals,
- the hire rate (the percentage of personnel hired in the current year),
- the termination rate (the percentage of workers that terminated their employment in the current year),
- the fluctuation rate (associated with employees' promotions, demotions and transfers)
- the mobile devices usage index (the number of employees that use mobile devices divided by the total number of employees),
- and hourly pay rate values for eight categories of employees.

Minimum, maximum, average and usual duration times are assigned to the cost drivers and the posts of personnel performing or responsible for relevant cybersecurity activities (e.g. IT administrators, users or Human Resources Management professionals) associated with resource cost drivers.

Based on the input data, the total cost of staff activities related to information security management, the cost of exclusive IT security professionals' activities, the minimum amount of work time of information security professionals indispensable for assuring sufficient level of information security in an organisation and the related minimum required quantity of information security professionals are calculated. Each of the parameters is represented by its minimum, maximum, average and the usual (typical, based on other organisations) value. The application of the method is presented in the next section.

To facilitate calculations, a spreadsheet was developed and updated periodically. It comprises four worksheets that correspond to subsequent steps of the assessment process. The *Organisation data* worksheet enables entering all required input data, such as the number of employees, human resources metrics or hourly pay rates. The worksheets *List of activities* and *Cost of information security professionals* comprise formulae for calculation of the total cost of activities. In the *Assessment results worksheet* the outcomes of the assessment are presented. More details on CAsPeA can be found in [1–4].

2 Case Study

This section illustrates the application of CAsPeA for a manufacturer of steel structures and filtering devices for water purification in crisis situations. The filters are designed for quick relocation, manoeuvring and deployment. They remove various types of contaminants, including natural, chemical, biological and radioactive. In addition, the company produces devices for storing drinkable water in a field. Figure 1 presents the structure of the IT system of the enterprise. It is worth to note that the main site and the sales office are located in two different cities.

2.1 Input Data

The enterprise employs more than 50 workers. In the first step of the cost evaluation process, the number of posts with access to the IT system needed to be determined. Table 1 presents the extract of the company's employment structure showing the relevant positions. The wanted value is 40. The hire rate, termination rate, fluctuation rate and the mobile devices usage index are subsequently 13%, 8%, 3% and 10%. Finally, the average hourly gross pay rates for eight categories of employees are presented in Table 2.

Table 1. The employment structure of the manufacturer of steel structures and filtering devices (employees that have access to the IT system).

	Position/Department	Number of employees
1	Chief Executive Officer	1
2	Director	3
3	Management Assistant	1
4	Plenipotentiary	2
5	Secretariat	2
6	Quality Control	2
7	Managers	7
8	Specialists	11
9	IT officers	2
10	Other employees	9
	Total	40

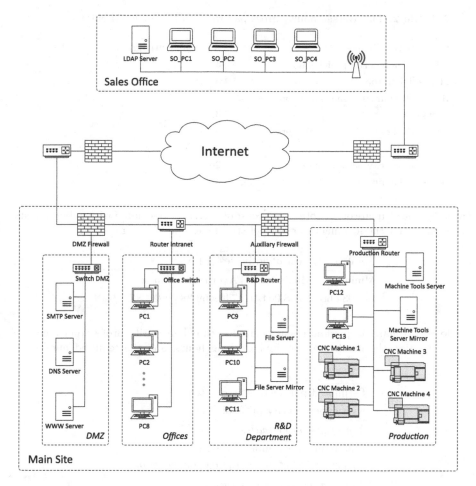

Fig. 1. The IT system of the manufacturer of steel structures and filtering devices for water purification in crisis situations.

2.2   Results

Based on the input data, cost estimates presented in Tables 3 and 4 were obtained. The total cost of personnel activities associated with cybersecurity is 202,287.20 PLN (Polish Złoty) which is equivalent to around 55,000 USD or 46,000 EUR. This cost is calculated based on typical (usual) values from other companies assigned to the activities in the CAsPeA model. Alternatively, the minimum (when baseline cybersecurity level is maintained), maximum (when extensive cybersecurity measures are introduced) and average values are consequently 122,934.66 PLN (around 33,000 USD or 28,000 EUR), 1,358,004.10 PLN (around 370,000 USD or 310,000 EUR) and 740,469.38 PLN (around 200,000 USD or 170,000 EUR). It becomes evident that these values are not negligible. Contrarily, they can become a visible component in a yearly budget. Thus, they

Table 2. The average hourly gross pay rates in the analysed enterprise.

Resource cost drivers	Average hourly gross pay rate [PLN]
Information security professionals	48
IT administrators	51
Human Resources Management professionals	42
Users	32
Senior-level executives or managers	53.5
Physical secuity officers	20
Physical security officers guards	20
Budget Planning and Control professionals	49

Table 3. The estimate of the total yearly cost of activities associated with cybersecurity management for the manufacturer of steel structures and filtering devices.

Total yearly cost of activities [PLN]			
Minimum	Maximum	Average	*Usual*
122,934.66	1,358,004.10	740,469.38	*202,287.20*

Table 4. Estimates of parameters associated with cybersecurity professionals: cost of their activities, the number of required working hours, and the required number of posts.

Estimated parameters associated with cybersecurity professionals			
Yearly cost of activities [PLN]			
Minimum	Maximum	Average	*Usual*
35,553.12	250,516.80	143,034.96	*91,779.60*
Required working hours (yearly)			
Minimum	Maximum	Average	*Usual*
740.69	5,219.10	2,979.90	*1,912.08*
Required positions			
Minimum	Maximum	Average	*Usual*
0.5	3.0	1.5	*1.0*

need to be appropriately considered when planning company activities, cybersecurity strategies etc.

Further analysis of the results reveals that a substantial part of the costs is associated with the activities connected to Physical Access Monitoring and Control (PAMC). These activities include surveillance of both company sites located in two different cities and require continuous presence of security guards and specialists. However, the IT system is one of many assets monitored within

Table 5. The estimate of the total yearly cost of activities associated with cybersecurity management for the manufacturer of steel structures and filtering devices **excluding Physical Access Monitoring and Control (PAMC) activities.**

Total yearly cost of activities excluding PAMC [PLN]			
Minimum	Maximum	Average	*Usual*
44,554.66	296,284.10	170,419.38	*104,607.20*

the activities. Thus, the associated cost can be entirely or partially deduced from the cost of cybersecurity. Table 5 presents the estimate of the total yearly cost of activities associated with cybersecurity management with PAMC excluded.

3   Conclusions

The paper illustrated the application of CAsPeA to an enterprise that specialises in manufacturing steel structures and filtering devices. CAsPeA revealed the hidden costs that normally are not considered, but apparently, constitute a considerable costing component. These costs are associated with employees' daily activities connected to cybersecurity (e.g. getting familiar with cybersecurity policies or 'processing' cybersecurity incidents) and should be taken into account when planning company activities or cybersecurity strategies. Based on a small set of input parameters, a rough estimation of minimum, maximum, average and typical cost values was obtained. Also, indications on the required working hours and posts for cybersecurity officers were provided. Further works on the method include:

- development of ISO/IEC 27001-based version and comparing it to the current, NIST SP 800-53-based edition,
- enhancing CAsPeA with activities linked to the security controls of the secondary and tertiary NIST SP 800-53 baselines,
- and acquiring empirical data on the cost of personnel activities and comparing them to the results from CAsPeA.

References

1. Leszczyna, R.: Cost assessment of computer security activities. Comput. Fraud Secur. **2013**(7), 11–16 (2013). https://doi.org/10.1016/S1361-3723(13)70063-0
2. Leszczyna, R.: Approaching secure industrial control systems. IET Inf. Secur. **9**(1), 81–89 (2015). https://doi.org/10.1049/iet-ifs.2013.0159
3. Leszczyna, R.: Metoda szacowania kosztu zarządzania bezpieczeństwem informacji i przykład jej zastosowania w zakładzie opieki zdrowotnej. Zeszyty Kolegium Analiz Ekonomicznych (2017)

4. Leszczyna, Rafał: Cost of cybersecurity management. Cybersecurity in the Electricity Sector, pp. 127–147. Springer, Cham (2019). https://doi.org/10.1007/978-3-030-19538-0_5
5. National Institute of Standards and Technology (NIST): NIST SP 800–53 Rev. 4 Recommended Security Controls for Federal Information Systems and Organizations. U.S. Government Printing Office (2013)

SGX-Cube: An SGX-Enhanced Single Sign-On System Against Server-Side Credential Leakage

Songsong Liu[1]($\boxtimes$), Qiyang Song[2], Kun Sun[1], and Qi Li[2]

[1] George Mason University, Fairfax, USA
{sliu23,ksun3}@gmu.edu
[2] BNRist, Tsinghua University, Beijing, China
ashes.sqy126@gmail.com, qli01@tsinghua.edu.cn

Abstract. User authentication systems enforce the access control of critical resources over Internet services. The pair of username and password is still the most commonly used user authentication credential for online login systems. Since the credential database has consistently been a main target for attackers, it is critical to protect the security and privacy of credential databases on the servers. In this paper, we propose SGX-Cube, an SGX-enhanced secure Single Sign-On (SSO) login system, to prevent credential leakage directly from the server memory and via brute-force attacks against a stolen credential database. When leveraging Intel SGX to develop a scalable secure SSO system, we solve two main SGX challenges, namely, small secure memory size and the limited number of running threads, by developing a record-based database encrypted scheme and placing only authentication-related functions in the enclave, respectively. We implement an SGX-Cube prototype on a real SGX platform. The experimental results show that SGX-Cube can effectively protect the confidentiality of user credentials on the server side with a small performance overhead.

Keywords: SSO · SGX · Credential leakage

1 Introduction

User authentication is a common security mechanism in Internet applications to restrict unauthorized access to member-only areas on websites. Username/password is still the most commonly used user authentication method for online login systems. After being securely delivered to the authentication system, the user inputted username and password are validated by checking with the credentials stored in a credential file or database.

It continues as a challenge for Internet service providers to protect user credentials including passwords, which may be leaked out from either non-volatile storage (e.g., hard disk) or volatile storage (e.g., RAM). After breaking into

© ICST Institute for Computer Sciences, Social Informatics and Telecommunications Engineering 2020
Published by Springer Nature Switzerland AG 2020. All Rights Reserved
N. Park et al. (Eds.): SecureComm 2020, LNICST 336, pp. 275–290, 2020.
https://doi.org/10.1007/978-3-030-63095-9_18

the target server system, attackers can dump the credential database and then launch offline brute force attacks. Alternatively, attackers can manage to steal user credentials in plaintext from RAM. For instance, attackers can remotely read the memory content from victim servers by exploiting Heartbleed bug in the OpenSSL library [6]. Even worse, when an attacker successfully breaks into the victim server, it can observe the entire credential verification process and easily retrieve credentials from memory. An advanced persistent attacker may collect most user credentials after stealthily residing in the server for a long enough time. In cloud environments, curious-but-honest service providers have the privilege to capture sensitive data in the memory of virtual machines, so it becomes another security concern on protecting user credentials in untrusted clouds.

Considering the difficulty in protecting user credentials, more Internet service providers choose to mitigate the management of various usernames and passwords by using Single Sign-On (SSO) services provided by third-party trusted companies such as Google [1] and Facebook [27]. By verifying a single credential on the SSO site, one user can obtain different authorized tokens to access multiple Internet services. It requires both users and Internet service providers to trust the third-party SSO sites with their credentials. However, similar to traditional online login systems, the SSO service providers are also troubled by the credential leakages from either hard disk or RAM [26]. Protecting the user credential in the SSO system still requires more effort.

Recently, researchers focus more on preventing information leakage during data processing. For instance, homomorphic encryption schemes [7] can ensure the credentials staying in ciphertext when being processed. Though it is promising to enhance the security of sensitive data in memory dramatically, it has to further reduce the overhead before being widely deployed. Another trend is to process sensitive data in an isolated and trusted execution environment. Thus, even if the host OS is malicious, sensitive data can be processed in trusted environments securely. For instance, Intel Software Guard Extensions (SGX) provides a process-level isolation mechanism to protect user-level sensitive code and data from malicious OS [12]. On the client side, SGX has been used to protect password managers [8]. On the server side, SGX has been used to protect a credential encryption module [15]. However, it still requires further studies on using SGX to protect SSO services.

In this paper, we develop SGX-Cube, an SGX-enhanced secure SSO system, to protect user credentials on SSO servers. It can not only successfully prevent credential leakage from memory, but enhance the security of credential databases against offline brute-force attacks. Our system consists of three major components, namely, *authentication server*, *credential database*, and *application server*. As the core of SGX-Cube, the authentication server runs inside the SGX enclave to process authentication requests. It protects the credentials in the memory even if the host OS is compromised. When a user requests to access an application server, the login request will be forwarded to the authentication server. After successful authentication, the authentication server generates and delivers an authorization code to the user. Then the user uses this authorization code to request the corresponding token and access the desired service from the application server.

We implement a prototype of SGX-Cube on a computer supporting SGX v1 instruction set. To protect the transmission of credentials, we implement an HTTPS server inside the enclave. We use a lightweight database management system SQLite as the credential database and a lightweight web server as the application server supporting OAuth 2.0 scheme. SGX-Cube is flexible to support other database systems and application servers. Our test-bed supports up to 4 threads in an enclave concurrently. The experimental results show that SGX-Cube introduces an average 0.6× extra time cost for a single thread in the authentication server. For a single request, it only takes about 1.5 ms for each authentication thread to complete all its tasks. For concurrent 500 requests, the average request processing time is about 1.7 ms. Our security analysis shows that SGX-Cube can effectively increase the security of the SSO system by preventing credential leakage from both memory and hard disk. In summary, we make the following contributions:

- We propose SGX-Cube, an SGX-enhanced secure SSO system, to increase the security and privacy of user credentials on the server by placing operations on credentials inside the SGX enclave. We further propose a record-based encryption scheme to improve authentication efficiency.
- We formulate the security of SGX-Cube in two aspects: confidentiality and integrity. Then, we analyze the security of SGX-Cube against both online attacks and offline attacks.
- We implement a prototype of SGX-Cube using SGX v1. The experimental results show that it is a practical solution with a small performance overhead.

2   Background

2.1   Intel SGX

Intel Software Guard Extensions (SGX) [12] provides user-level isolated execution environments (enclave) to protect the confidentiality and integrity of application code and data in a reserved memory region named the Enclave Page Cache (EPC), which is encrypted and authenticated by a Memory Encryption Engine (MEE) hardware module. SGX protects an application against illegal access from other applications, OS, and hypervisor. An SGX application is divided into two components: *a trusted component* and *an untrusted component*. The trusted component contains the code and data that need to be protected inside the enclave, while the untrusted component contains the rest part. To bridge these two components, SGX uses the enclave entry call (Ecall) and outside call (Ocall) mechanisms, where Ecall is the function call that enters the enclave from outside and Ocall is the function call that calls an untrusted outside function from an enclave. The code inside an enclave can only be executed in the user mode. The maximum EPC size is limited (128 MB for SGX v1, 256 MB for

SGX v2). When the configured enclave size is larger than the EPC size, the performance overhead becomes inevitably high due to paging between EPC and normal memory.

2.2 Single Sign-On (SSO) Systems

A single sign-on (SSO) system provides an authentication process that allows a user to access multiple application servers with one set of login credentials. Therefore, a user only needs to log in once and then gain access to different applications without re-entering the login credentials at each application server. As third-party authentication systems, the SSO systems are trusted by both end users and a number of application servers. One SSO system contains three main parties: *user, identity provider (IDP),* and *relying party (RP)*, where RPs are the applications/websites to be accessed by the users and the IDPs are responsible for providing the authentication services. The workflow is described as follows. First, the client connects to the RP (i.e., application server), which then sends the authorization request to the client. Next, after verifying the IDP (i.e., authentication server) via remote attestation, the client sends its login name and password to the IDP. After successfully verifying the client, the IDP generates an authentication token and sent it to the client. Next, the client forwards the authentication token to the RP. After verifying the client with the provided authentication token, the RP can request the user information (e.g., username) from the IDP and grant the services to the client.

3 Threat Model and Assumption

We focus on protecting the server-side login process and ensuring the confidentiality of user credentials on the server side. In this work, we refer user credentials to the username and password only, though other credentials may also include sensitive information such as PIN or credit card information. The credentials experience three states in the complete login procedure, namely, data-in-motion, data-in-use, and data-in-rest. Therefore, the attacker may commit a series of attacks against each state of credentials to defeat the user authentication process and collect valuable username/password and other user credential information.

In our threat model, we consider a strong attacker, who can commit not only the offline attack but also the online attack. To commit the offline attack, the attacker can extract the credential database from the server, then analyze it with the known information to infer other sensitive information or even brute force the encrypted credentials directly. To commit the online attack, the attacker would compromise the authentication server and users. It targets both the data-in-motion and the data-in-use. The attacker may retrieve plaintext credentials by eavesdropping on the communication channels connected to the authentication server, monitoring the memory of the server, manipulating login requests, or creating new known-plaintext records in our database to launch the chosen-plaintext attack. If it is result-less to reveal the desired credentials, the attacker may try to circumvent the authentication process via manipulating the authentication process in the memory or splicing stored credential records.

We assume the Intel SGX can be trusted. Although the SGX has become vulnerable to high-cost side-channel attacks [18], lots of efforts have been made to mitigate these attacks in both software [22] and hardware [13,19]. We target at protecting the user credentials on the server side, and the credential on the client side can be protected by other SGX-based solution [8].

4   System Design

4.1   System Overview

Figure 1 shows the overall architecture of our SGX-enhanced secure SSO login system. When an application server attempts to use our SSO service, its first step is to authenticate the SSO authentication server. It will request a remote attestation to ensure the integrity of the authentication server running in the SGX enclave. An attestation server may be required to facilitate the attestation [12]. After a successful remote attestation, it can verify the authentication server.

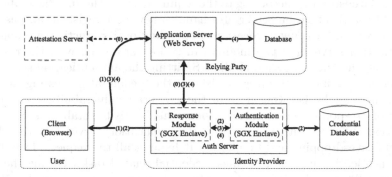

Fig. 1. The Architecture of SGX-Cube. (0) Attestation; (1) Login Request; (2) Credential Handling; (3) Authorization Grant; (4) Service Access.

Based on the standard SSO scheme, our SGX-Cube is divided into three main components: Identity Provider (IDP), Relying Party (RP), and user. These three components interact with each other during the complete login procedure.

Identity Provider (IDP). As the core component of the SSO login system, the IDP consists of two main components, namely, an *enclave-based authentication server* and a *credential database.*

The authentication server runs inside the enclaves. It is responsible for conducting remote attestation, receiving the user's login credentials from clients, verifying user login credentials against the credential database, generating an authentication token, and then sending the token to both the client to facilitate the authentication of the client to the application server. Here, the user

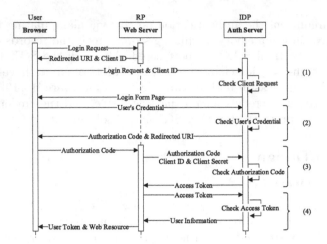

Fig. 2. The flow of user login process

login credential contains the username and the password. The authentication token can be customized according to the requirements of the specific application server. The authentication server also handles new user registration, password update/reset, and account revocation. Depending on its function, we split the authentication server into two modules in two separate enclaves: the response module and the authentication module. Splitting the authentication server into two enclaves, we intend to mitigate risks of the credential processing (authentication module) by isolating it from the potential vulnerabilities of network interaction (response module). The response module is to establish secure communication channels with the outside (the application server and the client) to defend eavesdropping and tampering. It handles all the requests from them. The authentication module processes credential related tasks. During the login procedure, all the credentials are passed from the response module to the authentication module via a secure communication channel of intra-platform.

The credential database stores user credential information for user authentication. The privacy of the database is protected when stored on the hard disk. Instead of encrypting the entire database with one key, we protect each column of the database table with a unique key (subkey). The subkeys are encrypted when stored on disk and in normal memory and are only decrypted inside the enclave. Towards achieving record-based encryption, the fields of one record are bound together [5]; see Sect. 4.3. By using record-based encryption, the query operations can be applied to the encrypted values directly. The credential database can be organized by the default DBMS (database management system) without any modification. After calculating the encrypted value of the inputted username, the authentication server queries the database and reads the encrypted value of the corresponding password into the enclave.

Relying Party (RP). The RP could be any kind of off-the-shelf application server on the internet. It provides Internet services to the user after the user is correctly authenticated by the IDP. All the login requests are redirected to the IDP conducting the credential verification. It only receives the authorization code from the user and verifies the code from IDP via a secure communication channel. If the code is correct, the IDP would allocate the token and corresponding user information to the application server. The user information is used as the user identity on the application server. Based on this identity in its database, the application server creates or updates the record for the authorized user.

User. In our design, the user should get a seamless, out-of-the-box, easy to use client. The client could be a typical browser or self-developed application that supports the SSO scheme. It assists the user to get authorization from IDP and access the desired Internet service of RP.

4.2 Login Procedure

In this section, we discuss each stage of the login procedure. We divide a complete login procedure into four stages, as shown in Fig. 2. While the remote attestation stage is not a part of the login procedure, it is an essential job to be conducted before the login procedure.

Stage 0: Attestation. Before the application server accepts a login request, it is necessary to ensure that the IDP is trustworthy. It conducts the remote attestation to verify that 1) the enclave is running on a genuine SGX enabled platform, and 2) the authentication server code running inside the enclave has not tampered with [14]. Literally, the application server should attest to both two modules of the authentication server. However, since the authentication module is not accessible from the outside, the remote attestation is only conducted on the response module directly. To solve this problem, we let the response module and authentication module to conduct the local attestation [28] for each other during the initialization. Until the dual local attestation is successful, the response module will accept the remote attestation request. The response module will generate a response that contains a signed hash value of the software running inside the enclave and the enclave environment. According to Intel [23], the application server needs to forward the remote attestation response to the response module, which stores the keying material to verify the hash value. To ensure the trustworthiness of IDP, the application server could start the remote attestation periodically (e.g., 24 h). Otherwise, the remote attestation could be conducted by a trusted third-party CA. The application server only needs to verify the certification of the authentication server.

Stage 1: Login Request. When a user requests to access the resource of the application server, the application will check if the request contains a valid token generated by itself. If yes, the user can access the desired Internet service directly. Otherwise, the login request is forwarded to the authentication server. A secure communication channel is established between the user client and the authentication server. The certification of the authentication server will be checked during the connection construction phase. Then the user client sends the login request to the authentication server via the new-built secure communication channel. The authentication server replies to the login request with a login interface (i.e., web page), which will be shown on the user's client.

Stage 2: Credential Handling. After the secure communication channel is established, the user can input the credential on the client side. The secure channel ensures that the user credential is directly delivered into the enclave on the authentication server. Once the authentication server receives the user credential, it encrypts the username and uses it as the key to query the corresponding record from the credential database. The encrypted password is read into the enclave to conduct the password verification. The plaintext of the password won't leak out of the enclave. If the credential is valid, the authentication server will generate an authorization code and return it to this user.

Stage 3: Authorization Grant. For the user, this stage is transparent. No further operations are required. After receiving the authorization code from the authentication server, the user client will resend it to the application server automatically. The application server uses this authorization code to request the access token from the authentication server. Similar to stage 2, a secure communication channel is established between the application server and the authentication server. The authentication server verifies the authorization code. If valid, an access token is generated and allocated to the application server.

Stage 4: Service Access. In this stage, the application server needs to request user information from IDP. The authentication server receives the request of user information with the access token from the application server. If the access token is valid, the application server will receive corresponding user information. The user information is used as the user identity on the application server. The application server stores the user information in its own database allocates a user token and opens the resource access entrance to the user. After that, the user can access the desired Internet service. The whole login procedure is completed.

4.3   Credential Storage

The stored user credentials include three major elements: username, password, and user information. In our scheme, both username and password are encrypted, which increases the entropy of user credentials against brute-force attacks. Moreover, the username may contain sensitive information and provide the attackers with a good hint, directly or indirectly, to speed up the password cracking process [16]. The user information stored in the credential database could be username or other information (e.g., e-mail and address) used in the application server. It is an identity of the user for the application servers.

Since the database is saved on the hard disk, the user credential data inside the database are protected by encryption mechanisms. We use three different subkeys K_u, K_p, and K_i to protect the three columns, i.e., username, password, and user information, respectively. All three subkeys are encrypted by the enclave seal key when stored on the hard disk. First, in the username column, we store the HMAC of the username with subkey K_u. Its saving value is

$$hmac(K_u, username) \tag{1}$$

Since the username serves as the primary key of the database, it should be unique. Next, for the password column, we compute the hash of the combination of subkey K_p and username as the key for the HMAC of password. The password column saves the following value

$$hmac(hash(K_p, username), password) \tag{2}$$

Finally, for the user information column, we encrypt this field with a symmetric encryption scheme. Its key is the hash value of the combination of subkey K_i and username. The saved value is

$$\{userinfo\}_{hash(K_i, username)} \tag{3}$$

We bind the username into both the password and user information to eliminate the possibility of field substitution. It is also equivalent to protect each record with a different key.

5   System Implementation

We develop the SGX-Cube prototype on SGX SDK v2.1.3 [12]. We implement our authentication server running inside the enclave by using around 4K LOC. The total size of binary loading into enclave memory is about 9.8 MB, which includes an OpenSSL library [9]. We use the HTTPS on all communication channels to protect the data transmission and ensure that credentials enter the enclave of the authentication server. We use a lightweight relational database management system, SQLite v3.13.0, as the credential database. We develop a lightweight web server based on python Flask framework v0.12.2 as the application server. Our implementation follows the standard Authorization Code Grant type of OAuth 2.0 [10]. We use 256-bit SHA256 HMAC to protect username and password and 128-bit AES in counter mode to protect user information In our prototype, the authentication server and the credential database are deployed on the same machine, while the application server and clients are deployed on another machine in the same local area network.

6   Performance Evaluation

We evaluate the authentication server performance and overall performance of our SGX-Cube prototype, respectively. We deploy the authentication server on a machine with Intel(R) Core(TM) i7-6500U CPU @ 2.50 GHz and 8 GB RAM. Its size of reserved EPC is set to 128 MB (about 93.5 MB available for applications) on BIOS. The web server and user browser are deployed on another machine with Intel(R) Core(TM) i7-4790 CPU @ 3.6 GHz and 16 GB RAM. All these two machines run 64-bit Ubuntu Linux 16.04 with kernel 4.15.

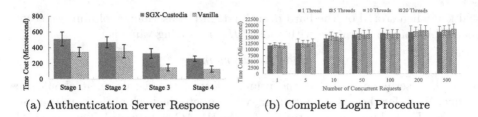

| (a) Authentication Server Response | (b) Complete Login Procedure |

Fig. 3. Time cost of SGX-Cube

6.1   Authentication Server Performance

The authentication server replies to different types of requests in each stage. Therefore, we measured the performance of the authentication server in the login stage. Since there is no built-in timer function in SGX v1, we use the timer function outside the enclave via Ocall. The Ocall introduces the extra overhead around $15\,\mu$s. The extra overhead is compensated in the final results. We run each experiment 100 times and calculate the average values.

Figure 3(a) shows the measurement of the authentication server in each stage. From it, we can observe that Stage 1 has the highest time cost. The authentication server sends a complete HTML login page to the user. Although we only implemented a simplified login page, it is still the largest size of data to be sent in all four stages. As mentioned in Sect. 4.2, the authentication server needs to handle the received credential and access the database in Stage 2. The database access causes the main overhead in this stage. In Stage 3 and 4, the authentication server locates the required information and responses to the corresponding request. Since the authorized user information has been extracted from the credential database and cached inside the enclave, the time cost of Stage is relatively low. We re-implement an authentication server without using SGX as the vanilla SSO system. Compare with it, the overhead of SGX-Cube increases about $0.5\times$ (Stage 1), $0.3\times$ (Stage 2), $1.1\times$ (Stage 3), and $1\times$ (Stage 4). The total overhead increases by about $0.6\times$.

6.2   Overall Performance

To measure the overall time consumption of a complete login procedure, we record the time length from the user starts the login request to the user gains the access of web server. The overall overhead includes the authentication server response, the webserver request handling, and user browser redirection. We measure the time cost of a complete login procedure with a various number of concurrent requests. We also evaluate the performance with multiple threads. The response module and authentication module keep the same number of threads. Note that the number of authentication server threads is limited by the size of the enclave in SGX v1, which includes heap, stack, code/text segments, etc. Although the SDK source code sets 128 GB as the maximum enclave size for the 64-bit program, the enclave size cannot reach this theoretical maximum since the driver did not support the Version Array (VA) page swapping yet. In our experiment, we set 1 MB max heap size and 256 KB max stack size for the enclave. The timer is on the user client. Each thread in the experiment handles 100 requests in total.

As shown in Fig. 3(b), a complete login procedure costs about 11500 μs for a single authentication server thread and a single request. The percentage of authentication server overhead is about 14%. As the number of concurrent requests increases, the average time costs for each request increase. That is because the authentication server cannot handle arriving requests in time. The requests have to wait in the queue. Although we could add more threads to the authentication server, the performance is not improved significantly. Even multiple threads can be created in the authentication server, the number of threads, that can process the login requests concurrently, is limited and decided by the platform. When the number of threads exceeds the number of logical processors, the extra threads will sit idle. In this case, the concurrent requests are processed in sequence to some degree. We will discuss how SGX-Cube could deal with this limitation of concurrent requests in system scalability (Sect. 8).

7   Security Analysis

In this section, we give security definitions and briefly demonstrate the security of SGX-Cube under two types of attacks: offline and online attacks. More details can be found in [25].

7.1   Data Confidentiality Under Offline Attacks

As the records of credential databases are encrypted under secret keys, attackers cannot derive any sensitive information from encrypted records without knowing the keys. To demonstrate the data confidentiality of entire databases under offline attacks, we adopt real world versus ideal world formalization [4] to define the column confidentiality under offline attacks. It is parameterized by a stateful leakage function $\mathcal{L}_1$ describing what information leaks in the protocols. More precisely, we define two games $Real_\mathcal{A}$ and $Ideal_\mathcal{A}$ with a simulator $\mathcal{S}$ [17] and an adversary $\mathcal{A}$. The simulator $\mathcal{S}$ can simulate real protocols and data using a leakage collection, and the adversary $\mathcal{A}$ has the server's view and can interact with real (or simulated) protocols. If $\mathcal{A}$ cannot distinguish the simulated column data from the real column data, then we can say the column achieves $\mathcal{L}_1$-confidentiality under offline attacks. Note that the columns of usernames, passwords, and user information are encrypted by the cryptographic tools HMAC and AES. Therefore, if the adversary $\mathcal{A}$ has finite computational resources and has not held the secret subkeys of each column, it cannot launch chosen plaintext attacks to distinguish the simulated column data from real column data.

7.2 Data Confidentiality Under Online Attacks

Similar to the column confidentiality under offline attacks, the column confidentiality under online attacks is also captured by real world versus ideal world formalization with an attacker $\mathcal{A}_2$ and a simulator $\mathcal{S}$. The attacker $\mathcal{A}_2$ is online, and it has a stronger capability than the online attacker. Specifically, it can compromise both the server and a subset of users and can utilize them to launch chosen-plaintext attacks. Since $\mathcal{A}_2$ can control users to launch chosen-plaintext attacks, it can input arbitrary plaintexts into users' programs and then observe output ciphertexts. Note that the column data of usernames are encrypted by the same subkey, and the subkey is held by all users. Therefore, $\mathcal{A}_2$ can distinguish the simulated column data of usernames from the real column data by running a user's programs. As the column data of passwords and user information are encrypted under the subkeys of different users, if $\mathcal{A}_2$ do not know corresponding subkeys, it cannot distinguish the simulated column data of passwords and user information from the real data.

7.3 Data Integrity Under Online Attacks

Since data can only be manipulated by online attacks, we only demonstrate data integrity under online attacks.

Data Integrity in Memory. The data integrity in memory is guaranteed by the security of the SGX enclave. The whole authentication procedure is completed inside the enclave. The authentication results are delivered to the requester from the enclave directly via secure communication channels. The results are not revealed in the server memory and cannot be tampered. Hence, the attacker can't compromise the data integrity in the memory.

Data Integrity on Disk. The data integrity on disk means that credential databases cannot be manipulated to authenticate a user without a correct pair of username and password. Here, we consider an attacker $\mathcal{A}_3$ who can corrupt both the authentication server and a subset of users. Particularly, $\mathcal{A}_3$ can control a user u_1 to generate a password p_1 from a known string, and then replace an honest user u_2's password with p_1 in the credential database. Next, $\mathcal{A}_3$ may attempt to impersonate u_2 by sending the known string as the password. Recall that the HMAC value of each user's password is generated by a unique secret key. Therefore, attackers have a non-negligible advantage to impersonate an honest user if *HAMC_SHA256* is collision-resistant.

8 Practical Usage

Enclave Migration. In traditional enterprise networks, we can deploy a dedicated physical machine as the authentication server, which is not moved frequently. However, when the entire network is in the cloud environment, authentication server migration should be supported. Usually, the administrators only need to perform an offline server migration by shutting down an enclave on one physical machine and rebooting it on another physical machine, which has different embedded SGX keying materials. Our system design enables a smooth offline enclave migration. First, The credential database can be directly copied or linked to the new enclave without any changes. Second, the subkeys can be securely sent to the new enclave via either a direct secure network connection or an out-of-band communication channel. The new enclave encrypts the subkeys with its own seal key and then saves them on its local storage. We can also support enclave live migration by adopting the migration mechanism proposed by Alder et al. [2].

System Portability. The authentication server can be implemented on any SGX-enabled Intel platform. Moreover, due to the modular design and clear interfaces between modules, our system is flexible to support various Internet services and different database systems. First, in addition to web servers in our prototype system, the application servers could be other types of Internet service, such as mail servers, FTP servers, cloud storage servers, and so on. All they need is a suitable interface supporting the standard SSO scheme. The application server only needs to support a secure communication channel with the authentication server and the client and handle the authentication token, respectively. Second, our system design is flexible to integrate various database systems to store user credentials. Our prototype system uses a lightweight database SQLite, which is good at storing data locally. To achieve a better data management capability, more powerful database systems can be adopted, such as MySQL, SQL Server.

System Scalability. The number of threads in one enclave is limited. Our testbed allows configuring at most 7309 threads, given the 1 MB maximal heap size and 256 KB maximal stack size. In practice, the number of active threads is much smaller than that number. One straightforward solution is to increase the number of active threads by deploying multiple enclaves on the same platform, while those enclaves still share the same EPC. The number of threads running simultaneously is decided by the number of logical CPU cores. Hence, when a large number of requests arrive around the same time, only the first several requests are served, and others have to wait. To serve tens or hundreds of login requests concurrently, we may deploy multiple SGX cards [3] or physical servers.

9   Related Work

To prevent credential leakage, the login credentials must be protected securely on the client, the server, and the transmission channel. On the client side, the credential security mainly depends on how well users could protect their end devices. SGX has been used to protect password managers, which stores all the passwords of end-users on the client [8]. To protect the transmission channel, mature secure protocols (e.g. TLS/SSL) are adopted. On the server side, the key issue is how to process and store the user credentials securely. By porting the credential processing code in trusted execution environments such as

SGX, attackers cannot manipulate the control flow of authentication. To protect credential storage, the common solution is database encryption [24]. Particularly, subkeys have been used to protect different data records or tables in the database [5,11]. CryptDB [21] and Seabed [20] are the database systems supporting encrypted query. Homomorphic encryption [7] allows more other operations on the encrypted data, while the high cost still hinders its wide deployment. Using trusted hardware to protect the credentials is a viable solution with much smaller system overhead. SafeKeeper [15] is the first SGX-based solution for credential protection on the server side. It uses the encryption enclave to replace the PHPass MD5 hash function. To establish a secure channel, SafeKeeper uses DHKE to establish a shared encryption key between browser add-on and enclave. Compared to SafeKeeper, our solution provides a more flexible framework that can integrate with various internet services and database systems. The user can use the original browser without extra add-on installation.

10   Conclusion

This paper demonstrates SGX-Cube, an SGX-enhanced SSO system that targets at preventing user credential leaking from both memory and hard disk on the server side. By utilizing SGX as an isolated execution environment, we can protect the confidentiality of user credentials when they are processed in the memory. Besides, we can protect the control flow of the authentication process. We choose to protect both the username and password to further defeat offline brute-force attacks. We propose a simple but effective record-based encryption scheme to protect user credentials stored on the hard disk. Due to the modular design, it is flexible to port SGX-Cube onto various application servers and database systems. We implement a prototype of SGX-Cube on a real SGX platform. Our experiments show that SGX-Cube can effectively protect the confidentiality of login credentials with a small performance overhead.

Acknowledgments. This work is partially supported by U.S. ONR grants N00014-18-2893, N00014-16-1-3214, and N00014-20-1-2407.

References

1. Google Single Sign-On. https:// cloud. google. com/ identity/ sso/. Accessed Dec 2019
2. Alder, F., Kurnikov, A., Paverd, A., Asokan, N.: Migrating SGX enclaves with persistent state. In: 2018 48th Annual IEEE/IFIP International Conference on Dependable Systems and Networks (DSN), pp. 195–206. IEEE (2018)
3. Chakrabarti, S., Hoekstra, M., Kuvaiskii, D., Vij, M.: Scaling Intel software guard extensions applications with Intel SGX card. In: Proceedings of the 8th International Workshop on Hardware and Architectural Support for Security and Privacy (2019)
4. Curtmola, R., Garay, J., Kamara, S., Ostrovsky, R.: Searchable symmetric encryption: improved definitions and efficient constructions. J. Comput. Secur. **19**(5), 895–934 (2011)

5. Davida, G.I., Wells, D.L., Kam, J.B.: A database encryption system with subkeys. ACM Trans. Database Syst. (TODS) **6**(2), 312–328 (1981)
6. Durumeric, Z., Li, F., Kasten, J., Amann, J., et al.: The matter of heartbleed. In: Proceedings of the 2014 Conference on Internet Measurement Conference, pp. 475–488. ACM (2014)
7. Gentry, C., Boneh, D.: A Fully Homomorphic Encryption Scheme, vol. 20. Stanford University Stanford, CA (2009)
8. Goldberg, J.: Using Intel's SGX to Keep Secrets even Safer (2017). https:// blog. 1password. com/ using- intels- sgx- to- keep- secrets- even- safer/
9. Han, J.: SGX-OpenSSL: Openssl library for SGX application (2017). https:// github. com/ sparkly9399/ SGX- OpenSSL
10. Hardt, D.: RFC 6749: The OAuth 2.0 authorization framework. Internet Eng. Task Force (IETF) **10**, 1721–2070 (2012)
11. Hwang, M.S., Yang, W.P., et al.: Multilevel secure database encryption with subkeys. Data knowl. Eng. **22**(2), 117–131 (1997)
12. Intel: Intel Software Guard Extensions for Linux OS SDK (2018). https:// github. com/ intel/ linux- sgx
13. Intel: Side Channel Mitigation by Product CPU Model (2018). https:// www. intel. com/ content/ www/ us/ en/ architecture- and- technology/ engineering- new- protections- into- hardware. html
14. Johnson, S., Scarlata, V., Rozas, C., Brickell, E., Mckeen, F.: Intel software guard extensions: EPID provisioning and attestation services. White Paper **1**, 1–10 (2016)
15. Krawiecka, K., Kurnikov, A., Paverd, A., Mannan, M., Asokan, N.: Safekeeper: protecting web passwords using trusted execution environments. In: Proceedings of the 2018 World Wide Web Conference on World Wide Web, pp. 349–358 (2018)
16. Li, Y., Wang, H., Sun, K.: A study of personal information in human-chosen passwords and its security implications. In: IEEE INFOCOM 2016 - The 35th Annual IEEE International Conference on Computer Communications, April 2016
17. Lindell, Y.: How to simulate it – a tutorial on the simulation proof technique. Tutorials on the Foundations of Cryptography. ISC, pp. 277–346. Springer, Cham (2017). https:// doi. org/ 10. 1007/ 978- 3- 319- 57048- 8_6
18. Nilsson, A., Bideh, P.N., et al.: A survey of published attacks on Intel SGX (2020)
19. Orenbach, M., Baumann, A., Silberstein, M.: Autarky: closing controlled channels with self-paging enclaves. In: Proceedings of the 15th European Conference on Computer Systems, pp. 1–16 (2020)
20. Papadimitriou, A., Bhagwan, R., Chandran, N., et al.: Big data analytics over encrypted datasets with seabed. In: OSDI, pp. 587–602 (2016)
21. Popa, R.A., Redfield, C., Zeldovich, N., Balakrishnan, H.: Cryptdb: protecting confidentiality with encrypted query processing. In: Proceedings of the 23rd ACM Symposium on Operating Systems Principles, pp. 85–100. ACM (2011)
22. Sasy, S., Gorbunov, S., Fletcher, C.W.: Zerotrace: olivious memory primitives from Intel SGX. IACR Cryptol. ePrint Arch. **2017**, 549 (2017)
23. Scarlata, V., Johnson, S., Beaney, J., et al.: Supporting third party attestation for Intel SGX with Intel data center attestation primitives. White Paper (2018)
24. Shmueli, E., Vaisenberg, R., Elovici, Y., Glezer, C.: Database encryption: an overview of contemporary challenges and design considerations. ACM SIGMOD Rec. **38**(3), 29–34 (2010)
25. Song, Q.: Sgx cube security analysis (2020). https:// github. com/ ashessqy126/ SGX- Cube- Security- Analysis/ blob/ master/ SGX- Cube- Security- Analysis. pdf

26. Winder, D.: Unsecured facebook databases leak data of 419 million users. WIRED, September 2019. https:// www. forbes. com/ sites/ daveywinder/ 2019/ 09/ 05/ facebook- security- snafu- exposes- 419- million- user- phone-numbers/# 3b32d5a1ab7f
27. Workplace by Facebook: Facebook Single Sign-On. https:// www. facebook. com/ workplace/ resources/ tech/ authentication/ sso. Accessed Dec 2019
28. Xing, B.C., Shanahan, M., Leslie-Hurd, R.: Intel software guard extensions (Intel SGX) software support for dynamic memory allocation inside an enclave. In: Proceedings of the Hardware and Architectural Support for Security and Privacy 2016, pp. 1–9 (2016)

EW_{256357}: A New Secure NIST P-256 Compatible Elliptic Curve for VoIP Applications' Security

Nilanjan Sen[1](✉), Ram Dantu[2], and Kirill Morozov[2]

[1] Western Illinois University, Macomb, IL 61455, USA
N-Sen@wiu.edu
[2] University of North Texas, Denton, TX 76207, USA
{ram.dantu,kirill.morozov}@unt.edu

Abstract. Selection of a proper elliptic curve is the most important aspect of Elliptic Curve Cryptography (ECC). Security of ECC is based on the Elliptic Curve Discrete Logarithm Problem which is believed to be unsolvable. Some of the well-known elliptic curve standards are NIST FIPS 186-2, Brainpool, and ANSI X9.62. Among these, NIST-recommended curves are a popular choice for industrial applications, in particular, for Internet security as a part of TLS/SSL, and even in real-time media encryption which uses Voice over IP (VoIP) technology. Specifically, NIST P-256 curve is widely used in these applications. Some NIST curves have disadvantages related to security issues, and therefore it is important to search for secure alternatives. In our work, we propose a new secure short Weierstrass curve EW_{256357} at the 128-bit security level and compare it with the NIST P-256 curve. Our proposed curve is compatible with NIST P-256 curve but features better security. Based on the performance analysis of related curves in our previous and present works in terms of delay and jitter, we say that our proposed curve is suitable for the real-time media encryption.

Keywords: Elliptic curve · Cryptography · ECC · Security

1 Introduction

Elliptic Curve Cryptography (ECC) is a very popular asymmetric encryption scheme proposed separately by Victor Miller [28] and Neal Koblitz [24] in 1985. Since Elliptic curves (EC) have smaller key size and better computational efficiency compare with other asymmetric key encryption techniques such as RSA, the ECC based key exchange protocols, digital signatures, and message encryption have become very popular in the computer and network security field.

Different types of ECs of different security levels are available for commercial or research purposes. Some of the popular ECs are developed by organizations such as National Institute of Standards and Technology (NIST), Teletrust and

© ICST Institute for Computer Sciences, Social Informatics and Telecommunications Engineering 2020
Published by Springer Nature Switzerland AG 2020. All Rights Reserved
N. Park et al. (Eds.): SecureComm 2020, LNICST 336, pp. 291–310, 2020.
https://doi.org/10.1007/978-3-030-63095-9_19

so on. Usually the ECs are used for key exchange and digital signatures. Elliptic Curve Diffie-Hellman Key Exchange (ECDHE) and Elliptic Curve Digital Signature Algorithm (ECDSA) are some well-known applications based on Elliptic curves. Some elliptic curves (other than NIST curves) are Brainpool curves [2], "Curve25519" curve developed by Bernstein [10], "Ed448-Goldilocks" curve developed by Hamburg [21] and so on. NIST's elliptic curves are considered to be the most popular elliptic curves. Some of them are prime curves and some of them are binary curves [1]. However, there are some drawbacks to NIST-recommended curves including debates about the possible presence of backdoor in the NIST-recommended curves [23,25]. These issues drive the researchers to develop more secure elliptic curves. In this work, we have developed a new elliptic curve EW_{256357} at the 128-bit security level, where E stands for Elliptic curve, W stands for Weierstrass curve, and 256357 represents the primary number used in this curve, i.e., $2^{256} - 357$. Our proposed curve is more secure compare with NIST P-256 curve with respect to the security parameters of Elliptic Curve Discrete Logarithm Problem (ECDLP) and some "ECC security" features (relevant to short Weierstrass curves) [12] which are discussed in Sect. 7.1. Based on our present work, we can say that our proposed curve provides better security to VoIP media, which means real-time audio and video.

2   Related Work

The most popular forms of EC are Weierstrass form, Edward form and Montgomery form. Multiple EC standards are available such as SEC2, NIST FIPS 186-2, Brainpool etc. which use one of these EC forms. NIST standards are more popular for industrial applications, but due to some drawbacks in NIST-recommended curves, researchers are developing more secure and efficient curves in terms of EC operations and security. Brainpool curves, developed by Teletrust, are generated over the prime field, use short Weierstrass form and use pseudo-random prime numbers [2]. Bernstein has proposed "Curve25519", a Montgomery curve which uses an efficient Montgomery ladder for ECDHE operation [10]. An Edward curve developed by Hamburg is "Ed448-Goldilocks". It uses Solinas trinomial prime for fast arithmetic operations in both 32 and 64-bit machines [21]. J. W. Bos et al. of Microsoft Research have proposed a set of prime order Weierstrass and (twisted) Edward elliptic curves and analyze them from a performance and security perspective. Their Weierstrass curves are backward compatible with current prime order NIST curves [18]. Their proposed curves provide high security by supporting constant time, exception-free scalar multiplication. The proposed curves' arithmetic operations are faster than the corresponding NIST curves.

3   Motivation

In this work, we propose a short Weierstrass prime curve at the 128-bit security level. A similar type of very popular elliptic curve viz. NIST P-256 curve is widely used but it has some serious drawbacks (discussed in Subsect. 3.1) which motivate us to propose a more secure elliptic curve. In addition, we are interested in real-time media encryption which uses Voice over IP (VoIP) technology. Use of VoIP applications is proliferating in every sector of our daily life such as real-time video streaming, live audio, video-on-demand, webinars and so on. Recent COVID-19 pandemic has increased the use of real-time applications immensely throughout the world. The security of these applications has become a major concern, as well. ECC can be a better choice in this context.

3.1   Some Drawbacks of NIST Curves

- The NIST curve generation process is not fully transparent. The generation of the second curve coefficient b is not justified. NIST uses a random 160-bit seed value and a hash function to generate b. Some researchers fear that if NSA knows any weakness of the curves then the security of the curves may be compromised [13].
  Our curve generation process is fully transparent.
- The so-called "twist security" is an important security feature of ECC [12], the lack of which may lead to twist-security attack. A curve is twist secure if its order and its corresponding twist curve's order are prime [22]. The NIST P-256 curve does not qualify this, so it is weakly twist secure. Bernstein and Lange have also mentioned NIST P-256 curve as a weakly twist secure curve in [13].
  Our proposed curve is twist-secure.
- Bernstein and Lange [13] mentioned that, though OpenSSL is the most popular open-source library (which is used for NIST curves implementation), there are several reports regarding the cryptographic failures in OpenSSL and many of them are still not fixed due to implementation difficulty [13]. OpenSSL team has improved their code quality a few years ago [20] but it is not reported by the coders or researchers yet whether all those issues are resolved or not.
  In our experiment, we have used Java cryptography library "BouncyCastle" to implement our proposed curve.
- Bernstein and Lange [11] also claimed that "NIST's ECC standards create unnecessary complexity in ECC implementations".
  Our proposed curve implementation process is simple and straight forward in nature.
- There have been questions about probable presence of a backdoor in the Dual Elliptic Curve Deterministic Random Bit Generator used in the NIST elliptic curve generation process. This serious matter had been revealed due to the leakage of some NSA documents [23,25]. Steve Lipner, one of the committee members of the Committee of Visitors which was formed to review NIST cryptographic processes, recommended in his report that "NIST should ensure that there are no secret or undocumented components or constants in its cryptographic standards whose origin and effectiveness cannot be explained. (Transparency of product) This recommendation would preclude the issuance

of the EES with its reliance on the then' secret Skipjack algorithm as well as the Dual_EC_DRBG with its reliance on an elliptic curves whose origin was undocumented and whose security could not be verified." [5]. Though the Dual_EC_DRBG is now excluded from the standards, still there are doubts over the other pseudo-random generators used to generate NIST curves, especially after Edward Snowden's revelation [8].
Our curve generation process is transparent and fully described.

In our previous work [26] we showed that the use of ECC based encryption schemes would ensure better real-time media protection. We implemented the ECC encryption scheme in the real-time VoIP systems, and we showed that the ECC implementation worked well in VoIP applications without degrading the quality of the VoIP data. The delay and jitter values were within the range as per the ITU-T G.114 recommendation [4]. Furthermore, we analyzed the performance of the curves in terms of the video data rate as well. The video data rate was the ratio of the received video data rate to that video frame's play time. It was measured in bytes per second. Usually, the high video data rate yields better video quality. In our experiment [26], we noticed that during the video transmission, the video data rates were nearly similar in both AES-encrypted and NIST P-256 curve encrypted streams. Figure 1 [26] depicts the data rate comparison of AES-encrypted video streams and ECC-encrypted video streams using NIST curves. We can see that NIST 256-bit elliptic curve encrypted video streams' data rates are nearly same as AES-encrypted video streams' data rates, but if the EC key size increases, the data rate decreases for the first few frames (e.g. NIST 571-bit curve), that deteriorates the video quality. Hence, 256-bit curve will be more suitable for VoIP media encryption purpose.

This performance has motivated us to develop a new curve which is compatible with the NIST P-256 curve and features better security. *The word "compatible" is used in the sense that our proposed curve will be compatible with the applications which support NIST P-256 curve.* In this work, we have tested and confirmed that our proposed 256-bit curve is suitable for real-time media encryption. We have shown that the proposed curve's performance is faster compare with the NIST P-256 curve in terms of basic elliptic curve arithmetic operations which are essential for elliptic curve key generation and encryption/decryption tasks. We have also compared the performance of the proposed curve with the NIST P-256 curve in terms of real-time audio and video encryption. Furthermore, We have proved that the proposed curve is more secure than NIST P-256 curve.

4   Curve Generation

NIST recommends two types of curves for ECC, the pseudo-random prime curves over $GF(p)$ where p is the prime number, and binary curves over $GF(2^m)$ where m is the degree of the field extension. The coefficients of these types of curves are generated using a cryptographic hash function. NIST recommends the equation

$$y^2 = x^3 - 3x + b \ (mod \ p) \tag{1}$$

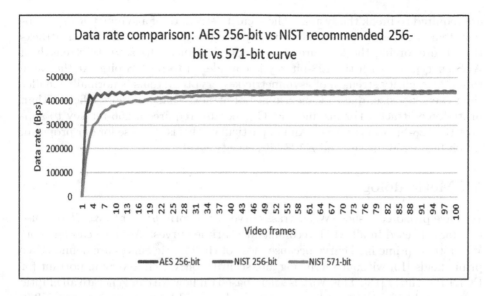

Fig. 1. Data rate comparison between AES and two NIST-recommended curves. Video data rate of ECC NIST 256-bit encrypted video stream is more than that of NIST 571-bit key for first 50–55 frames.

for the pseudo-random prime curve over GF(p). The coefficients of these curves are selected in a way such that the elliptic curve operations' efficiency can be optimized [1].

In this work, we have considered prime curves only. Researchers prefer prime curves over binary curves as the former is more reliable because the discrete logarithm problem can be solved on the binary curves [16]. In general, six parameters are used to generate the prime curves over GF(p) which is represented in a six-tuple notation $< p, r, a, b, G, h >$ where:

1. p is a prime number;
2. r is the prime order of the curve;
3. The first curve coefficient a;
4. The second curve coefficient b;
5. G is the base point where x, y are the coordinates of the base point, denoted as G_x and G_y;
6. h is the cofactor of the curve and h is usually 1.

There are three types of elliptic curves that are commonly used: short Weierstrass curves, twisted Edward curves and Montgomery curves. The short Weierstrass model supports all curves which are defined over large prime fields. At the same time, the twisted Edwards and Montgomery models support only a subset of elliptic curves [18]. In our work, we have used the short Weierstrass model to generate the new curve.

Security strength or security level is the most important aspect of cryptography. By stating that the security strength is "n-bit", we imply that 2^n operations are required to break the system. The security strength of a symmetric key cryptosystem is generally measured as its key size (assuming that no better attacks than brute-forcing the keys are known). For instance, the security strength of AES encryption with the 128-bit key is considered to be 128 bits. At the same time, the security strength of asymmetric key cryptosystems is normally smaller than their key size, due to the existence of attacks that are more efficient than brute-force attacks. For instance, ECC generally requires a 256-bit key to support the 128-bit security level. And in particular, this is the case for our proposal, which has a 256-bit key and a 128-bit security level.

5   Methodology

We have proposed a short Weierstrass curve of the form $y^2 = x^3 - 3x + b$ because this form is used in all NIST-recommended prime curves. We have chosen short Weierstrass prime field curve because most of the elliptic curves are defined over prime fields [19] without sacrificing any security bit which is very important for ECDLP security [18]. This work is solely based on how we can generate an elliptic curve suitable for VoIP media encryption which will be more secure than NIST P-256 curve. Since the NIST P-256 is very popular and widely used curve which uses short Weierstrass form, we have developed a similar type of curve for the compatibility, that means our curve can be implemented in those applications easily which support NIST P-256 curve. No Montgomery or Edward curve is considered in this work for this reason.

Elliptic curve generation procedure includes choosing different curve parameter values. The basic idea of choosing elliptic curve parameter values comes from the work of J. W. Bos et al. [18]. A very important task for elliptic prime curve generation is to choose a prime number. Brainpool curves use pseudorandom prime numbers to generate the prime curves but their performance is not as good as NIST curves. NIST curves use pseudo-Mersenne prime which supports efficient modular arithmetic like fast modular reduction [1]. J. W. Bos et al. [18] used two different forms of primes, pseudo-Mersenne primes, and Montgomery friendly primes. The pseudo-Mersenne primes have the property to make the elliptic curves indistinguishable compared to Montgomery-friendly prime curves, because in Montgomery-friendly prime p, $\dfrac{p+1}{2}$ is not close to 2^n for any value of n [14]. We have used pseudo-Mersenne prime for our proposed curve and have chosen the other parameters of the curve deterministically. The detailed methodology of other curve parameters' selection is described in the next section.

6   New Curve Parameter Selection

6.1   Prime Number Selection

Prime number generation is an important operation in ECC. That prime number is used for the curve's arithmetic modulus operations. Different EC standards use different prime number generation methods. NIST recommends a special type of prime number which is known as generalized Mersenne number. The advantage of these prime numbers over general or random prime numbers is that the fast reduction can be carried out during modular multiplication [1].

There are different forms of primes used for Elliptic curves. One form is $2^\alpha - \gamma$. This type of prime is known as a pseudo-Mersenne prime. Another form of prime is $2^\alpha(2^\beta - \gamma) - 1$, known as a Montgomery friendly prime. The later reduces some computations. The logic behind the Montgomery friendly prime is based on the concept of Montgomery multiplication which states that during modular reduction operations, the division operations can be replaced by logical shift operations which are comparatively less expensive. In both forms α, β, and γ are positive integers [18].

Though Montgomery friendly primes reduce some computations, the pseudo-Mersenne prime curves are better in terms of indistinguishability as discussed in Methodology section [14]. So, in our work, we have used the pseudo-Mersenne prime of the form $2^\alpha - \gamma$. The value of α is 2 times the security level of the curve in terms of bits. For example, for 128-bit security, the value of α is 256. Thus, we can choose a very large prime in this way. Based on their work in [18], J. W. Bos et al. has proposed numsp256d1 curve [17] which uses the largest 256-bit pseudo-Mersenne prime number $2^{256} - 189$, and the property of this curve is already tested with the largest 256-bit pseudo-Mersenne prime. During the curve generation phase we chose the 256-bit second largest pseudo-Mersenne prime number $2^{256} - 357$ and compared its performance with $2^{256} - 189$. *We checked that this prime number was as good as $2^{256} - 189$, and hence we chose $2^{256} - 357$ for our proposed curve. The performance analysis of our proposed curve, NIST P-256 curve and numsp256d1 curves on basic elliptic curve operations are given in* Table 1 *and* Table 2. The chosen prime for our proposed curve is equivalent to 3 mod 4 for efficient modular operations [18]. To check the primality of this number, we have used Miller-Rabin primality test algorithm [6].

6.2 Order of the Curve

Every cryptographically strong prime curve contains a certain number of points, that number must be a prime. This number is known as the order of that curve. Determining the order of the curve for a very large prime is a time-consuming process. One very efficient algorithm, known as Schoof-Elkies-Atkin point counting algorithm based on Schoof's algorithm [27], is used to get the total number of points on that elliptic curve and hence the order of the curve over a finite field. The inputs of this algorithm are values of a, b and the prime p.

The order r is generally calculated as $r = p + 1 - t$, where t is known as trace, where $1 < |t| \leq 2\sqrt{p}$ [18]. In this work, we have used Schoof-Elkies-Atkin (SEA) point counting algorithm to find a prime order curve (i.e., the number of points present in the curve is prime). We have executed the algorithm with $a = -3$ and $b = 1$, and the value of b is incremented by 1 until the prime order is found.

Another feature of the proposed curve is that, it is twist secure, that means for a specific value of b, both $y^2 = x^3 - 3x + b$ and $y^2 = x^3 - 3x - b$ curves have prime order. The second curve is known as the twist of the first curve.

6.3   Coefficients of the Curve

We have chosen the value of the coefficient a as -3 because the elliptic curves of the form $y^2 = x^3 - 3x + b$ provide the fastest elliptic curve arithmetic [3]. NIST and Brainpool prime curves also have the same value for the coefficient a. The parameter b is chosen deterministically, and it belongs to the field F_p. As mentioned in the previous sub-section, we have found b while determining the order of the curve using SEA algorithm. The algorithm started with $b = 1$ and incremented b by 1 until it found the prime order of the curve. Most importantly, the coefficient b should support twist-security feature (discussed later). In our proposed curve, the value of b is 5029.

6.4   Choosing the Base Point

For different applications of the elliptic curve such as key generation or encryption, the base point plays a very important role. The two coordinates of the base point x and y should lie between 0 and p, where p is the prime order of the field F_p. To find the base point of the proposed curve, We started with $x = 1$. We have used Algorithm 1 to find the base point $G(x, y)$.

To check the validity of x, we computed the Legendre symbol $(c|p)$ where $c|p = c^{\frac{p-1}{2}} \pmod{p}$. The Legendre symbol finds whether a number is a quadratic residue modulo an odd prime. As per the rule, if the $(c|p)$ value is either 0 or -1, then c is not a quadratic residue, so we need to repeat the process with the next value of x after incrementing it by 1. To find a valid coordinate x, we used Cipolla's algorithm to find the coordinate y by calculating $y^2 \equiv c \pmod{p}$. Cipolla's algorithm is used to solve the congruence of the form $x^2 \equiv n \pmod{p}$. Since the equation was quadratic, y had two roots. We chose the smallest one. After obtaining y, we checked whether $0 < y < p$, and then selected $G(x, y)$ as the base point.

6.5   Cofactor

The cofactor of the elliptic curve is the ratio of the order of the curve and the order of the base point. We know that the order of the curve is the total number of points that lie on the curve. On the other hand, the order of the base point G of that curve is the smallest value n for which $n.G = \infty$, where ∞ is the point at infinity. For any elliptic curve E over a finite field F_p, if the order of the curve is $\#E(F)$ and the order of the base point is m, then cofactor h is calculated as $\dfrac{\#E(F)}{m}$. The value of the cofactor should be very small and an integer, that means $\#E(F)$ should be divisible by m. As per the NIST specification, the cofactor value should be 1, 2, or 4, and the cofactor of the prime curves must

---

Algorithm 1: Choosing the base point $G(x, y)$

Input: The prime number p, two curve coefficients a and b, and x coordinate of the base point
Output: y coordinate of the base point
$x \leftarrow 1$;
while *true* **do**
$\quad$ $c \leftarrow x^3 + ax + b \ (mod \ p)$;
$\quad$ $l \leftarrow c^{\frac{p-1}{2}} \ (mod \ p)$;
$\quad$ **if** $l = 0 \ or \ l = -1$ **then**
$\quad\quad$ $|\quad x \leftarrow x + 1$;
$\quad$ **else**
$\quad\quad$ $\lfloor$ break the loop;

Solve $y^2 = c \ (mod \ p)$ using Cipolla's algorithm;
y has two roots. Select the smallest one;

---

be 1 [1]. Our proposed curve's cofactor is 1 also. That means the order of the proposed curve and the order of the base point are same.

The curves with cofactor 1 are secure against the well-known small-subgroup attack on Diffie-Hellman. In the small-subgroup attack, the attacker sends a point of small order as his public key to a legitimate user. The user then computes the shared secret key using his private key and the attacker's public key. Since the attacker's public key has small order, the secret key does not have many possibilities, so the attacker can get the information of the user's private key from the secret key. This type of attack can be prevented by the elliptic curves with cofactor 1 [12]. Since the proposed curve's co-factor is 1, it is secure against the small-subgroup attack.

6.6 Proposed New Curve

Based on the requirements and methodology defined above, we have generated a 256-bit twist secure new curve at 128-bit security level whose parameters are given below:

$\quad$ The curve (EW_{256357}): $y^2 = x^3 - 3x + 5029$ over F_p

1. Prime number $p = 115792089237316195423570985008687907853269984665640$
564039457584007913129639579
2. Order of the curve $r = 115792089237316195423570985008687907852793585971$
461506558239498229566154872651
3. $a = -3$
4. $b = 5029$
5. $G_x = 1$
6. $G_y = 101394680058793034172347590806425201075176483002638106094983$
3265392864829636
7. Cofactor $h = 1$

7   Performance Analysis of the New Curve

7.1   Performance Comparison Between EW_{256357} and NIST P-256 Curves Regarding Different Elliptic Curve Operations

We have successfully tested the new curve to check its performance in different elliptic curve operations viz. point addition, point doubling, scalar multiplication, fixed-window based scalar multiplication, Elliptic Curve Diffie-Hellman Key Exchange (ECDHE) and Elliptic Curve Digital Signature Algorithm (ECDSA) for constant execution time, and have compared the performance of the proposed curve with NIST P-256 curve. The corresponding execution times are also shown for numsp256d1 curve proposed by J. W. Bos et al. [17]. The system configuration used for this experiment was Intel 3.40 GHz Core i7-3770 processor, 16 GB main memory, and 64-bit Ubuntu OS. The code was written in Java to implement the curves and the other elliptic curve arithmetic operations. Each operation was executed 1000 times and average execution time was calculated for each of them. The comparison results are given in Table 1 and Table 2, the execution time unit is millisecond.

Table 1. Execution time comparison of different elliptic curve operations (in milliseconds)

Curve	Point addition	Point doubling	Scalar multiplication	Fixed window- based scalar multiplication
EW_{256357}	0.0169	0.0196	6.9298	5.7132
NIST P-256	0.0198	0.0254	6.9564	5.7505
numsp256d1	0.0200	0.0269	7.1362	5.9063

Table 2. Execution time comparison of ECDHE and ECDSA operations (in milliseconds)

Curve	ECDHE	ECDSA
EW_{256357}	12.2958	18.5187
NIST P-256	12.3144	18.5280
numsp256d1	12.3964	18.6591

Scalar multiplication is a very important operation required for elliptic curve key generation and encryption/ decryption operations. Its execution time varies depending on the size of the secret scalar value. An adversary can guess the secret scalar by exploiting that information using side-channel attacks [18]. Fixed window-based scalar multiplication is one of those scalar multiplication algorithms used for constant execution time irrespective of the size of the secret scalar. In this experiment, the window size of the fixed window-based scalar multiplication is 4.

The proposed curve has performed better in basic elliptic curve arithmetic operations, but the execution time differences are not much in two curves. The execution times are so close because the proposed curve and the NIST P-256 curve use short Weierstrass form where the value of the coefficient a is -3. The values of the coefficient b are different for all three curves, but that coefficient is not used in any of the elliptic curve operations. For instance, the two basic elliptic curve arithmetic operations are point addition and point doubling. If we consider two points $P(x_p, y_p)$ and $Q(x_q, y_q)$ on the elliptic curve E where x_p, y_p and x_q, y_q are the x and y coordinates of P and Q respectively, then the addition of P and Q will yield another point $R(x_r, y_r)$ on E. The point R can be calculated as follows [9]:

$$x_r = \left(\frac{y_q - y_p}{x_q - x_p} \right)^2 - x_p - x_q \tag{2}$$

$$y_r = \left(\frac{y_q - y_p}{x_q - x_p} \right).(x_p - x_r) - y_p \tag{3}$$

On the other hand, the point doubling operation, where $P + P = 2P$, $P(x_p, y_p)$ and $2P(x_d, y_d)$ are the points on E and $P \neq -P$, can be calculated as follows [9]:

$$x_d = \left(\frac{x_p^2 + a}{2y_p} \right)^2 - 2x_p \tag{4}$$

$$y_d = \left(\frac{x_p^2 + a}{2y_p} \right).(x_p - x_d) - y_p \tag{5}$$

where a is the coefficient of the short Weierstrass form.

From the last four equations we can see that the coefficient b of short Weierstrass form is not required in the two basic elliptic curve arithmetic operations, the point addition and point doubling, and these two arithmetic operations are used in elliptic curve scalar multiplication, ECDHE and ECDSA. This is the reason why the execution times of different EC arithmetic operations are similar in the two curves. *We have stated earlier that the proposed curve is compatible with the NIST P-256 curve. The primary goal of this work is to propose an elliptic curve which is suitable for VoIP media encryption and more secure than NIST P-256 curve.*

7.2 Comparison Between EW_{256357} and NIST P-256 Curve Regarding ECDLP and ECC Security

D. J. Bernstein and T. Lange have jointly proposed criteria for Elliptic Curves which are safe for cryptographic use [12]. *Since the proposed curve is a prime curve and we have used the short Weierstrass equation, we have considered only those criteria suitable for this curve.* we have considered the Elliptic Curve Discrete Logarithm Problem (ECDLP) security and Elliptic Curve Cryptography (ECC) security criteria to test the proposed curve and compare it with NIST P-256 curve. The comparison result is shown in Table 3.

Though ECDLP is an important property which ensures the security of the ECC, in reality the attackers can break ECC without solving ECDLP [12]. For example, some standard curves may be vulnerable because they may not work properly for some rare curve points, they may reveal secret data for some points which do not lie on those standard curves, or attackers may get secret information through branch or cache timing attacks. These may happen because ECDLP security is more theoretical than practical [12]. Since NIST curves are considered to be the standard curves, they also have the aforementioned problems. Thus, apart from the ECDLP security, we have to ensure ECC security as well. The proposed curve satisfies all required criteria of both ECDLP and ECC security, while the NIST P-256 curve does not satisfy all of the criteria. The security parameters that we have considered are discussed below. The first four parameters are ECDLP security parameters and the last one is the ECC security parameter.

- **Rho Complexity:** The Pollard Rho method is one of the methods used to break ECDLP. Rho complexity is calculated as $\log_2(\sqrt{\pi/4}.\sqrt{r})$ or $0.886\sqrt{r}$ where r is the order of the curve [18]. ECDLP can be broken easily if the value of r is small, because $0.886\sqrt{r}$ number of additions are required to break it. Hence, the value of r should be very large. Since the proposed curve is a 256-bit curve, the Rho complexity of the curve is $2^{127.8}$ as in the NIST P-256 curve, which is large enough for ECDLP security.
- **Transfer:** It is another method where ECDLP can be converted to a linear algebraic group discrete logarithm problem. One of the transfer methods is

Table 3. Comparison of two curves regarding ECDLP and ECC security

Criteria	EW_{256357}	NIST P-256
ECDLP security		
Rho complexity	$2^{127.8}$	$2^{127.8}$
Transfers	Yes	Yes
CM field discriminants	Yes	Yes
Rigidity	Fully rigid	Manipulative
ECC security		
Twist security	Strongly secured	Weakly secured

the Additive Transfer method, where the prime number used to generate the curve over the prime field and the order of that curve are same. Attackers can exploit this to break the ECDLP which is also known as Smart-ASS attack [12]. The proposed curve's prime number and the order of the curve are different, so it is not vulnerable to this attack.

Second type of transfer is the Multiplicative Transfer method where $(p^n - 1)$ is divisible by r, where p is the prime number, r is the order of the curve and n is an integer, $n \geq 1$. The minimum value of n for which $(p^n - 1)$ is divisible by r is known as the embedding degree of the group. If the embedding degree is small, then the curve becomes vulnerable to MOV (Menezes-Okamoto-Vanstone) attack [12]. This attack uses Weil pairing to convert the discrete logarithm problem on the points of an elliptic curve to a discrete logarithm problem on finite fields which can be solved easily [7]. Therefore, the embedding degree value should be very large to prevent MOV attacks. Different standard curves support different embedding degrees. The proposed curve supports embedding degrees large enough to prevent MOV attacks.

- **Complex-Multiplication (CM) field discriminants:** This parameter is applicable to the elliptic curves which have very large endomorphism ring. This is used to find the elliptic curve with proper order. The order of the elliptic curve should be prime for a cryptographically secure elliptic curve. If p is the prime number of the prime group F_p, then the order of the group $r = p + 1 - t$ where t is known as the trace of the curve. According to the Hasse's theorem, $-2\sqrt{p} \leq t \leq 2\sqrt{p}$ [12].

  Algorithm 2 is used to find the CM field discriminant D [12]:

  The value of D is negative. So, the absolute value of D should be large enough to ensure the ECDLP security. As per Bernstein and Lange's approach, the absolute value of D should be more than 2^{100} [12]. The proposed curve's D value is more than 2^{100}.

- **Rigidity:** This feature prevents the generation of multiple curves from a specific curve generation process. If the curve generation process is not rigid, the attackers can generate many curves using that process and can choose a weak curve which is vulnerable to the secret attack. The curve generation process is fully rigid if it explains the generation of all parameters in detail, for instance curve equation, the coefficient of the curve, the base point selection criteria, etc. If the manipulatable curve generation process is not transparent, attackers can potentially generate multiple curves from it.

  Our curve generation process is fully rigid, because we have explained the parameter generation procedures of our proposed curve. At the same time, the NIST P-256 curve generation process is manipulative, because this curve uses a hash function and a 160-bit random seed to generate the coefficient b. The random seed is unexplained, so the hash function may be very strong, but the attackers may try to find a specific seed value from a large set of seed values to find vulnerability for the secret attack [12].

- **Twist security:** Twist security is very important feature with respect to ECC security. It is required to prevent some well-known attacks such as Invalid-curve attacks [12]. Invalid-curve attacks were proposed by Biehl,

Algorithm 2: Calculating CM field discriminant

Input: The prime number p, and trace t
Output: The CM field discriminant D
find the largest integer m where $t^2 - 4p$ is divisible by m^2;

if $\dfrac{t^2 - 4p}{m^2}$ $(mod\ 4) = 1$ then

$\quad\left|\ D \leftarrow \dfrac{t^2 - 4p}{m^2};\right.$

else

$\quad\left|\ D \leftarrow 4.\dfrac{t^2 - 4p}{m^2};\right.$

Meyer and Müller [15]. In this attack, the attacker sends a point Q of small order of another curve to the legitimate user. If the user computes the shared secret key by multiplying his private key n and the point Q, this may reveal the information about the user's private key. For instance, the attacker can send many such invalid points of small order like 2, 3, 4, etc. After getting the corresponding secret keys, he will get the values of $n\ mod\ 2$, $n\ mod\ 3$ and so on. By using Chinese Remainder Theorem, the attacker can compute the private key of the user. A twist secure curve can prevent such attacks.

A curve E is said to be twist secure if both E and its twist E' are cryptographically strong, and the minimum criteria is that their orders must be prime [22]. According to Hasse-Weil theorem, if $y^2 = x^3 + ax + b$ is an elliptic curve E over a prime field F_p, p is a prime number and $p > 3$, then the order of the curve $E = p + 1 + t$, where t is known as trace of Frobenius, and $|t| \leq 2\sqrt{p}$. The corresponding twisted curve of E defined over F_p, represented as E', has its order calculated as $p + 1 - t$.

Our proposed curve is twist secure. The equation of the curve is

$$E : y^2 = x^3 - 3x + 5029 \tag{6}$$

The value of the trace of Frobenius of the proposed curve is
t = 47639869417905748121808577834697476692929.
The corresponding twist of the curve is

$$E' : y^2 = x^3 - 3x - 5029 \tag{7}$$

The orders of both E and E' curves over F_p are prime. But the NIST P-256 curve is not a strongly twist secure curve. The order of the NIST curve $y^2 = x^3 - 3x + b$ is prime (the value of b is given in [1]), but the order of its corresponding twist curve $y^2 = x^3 - 3x - b$ is not prime. So, the NIST P-256 curve has weak twist security. Bernstein and Lange have also mentioned in [13] that NIST P-256 has weaker twist.

7.3 Performance Comparison Between EW_{256357} and NIST P-256 Curves Regarding Real-Time Audio and Video Encryption Using VoIP

We have tested the performance of our proposed curve on the real-time audio and video encryption and compared the performance with the NIST P-256 curve. The experiments are done using client-server architecture. We have used Ubuntu 16.04 (64 bits) operating system on both the server and the client machines. Java and Bouncy Castle (an open-source lightweight cryptography API for Java) are used for curve implementation, key generation and to implement the encryption and decryption processes. We have used Elliptic Curve Integrated Encryption Scheme (ECIES), which was initially proposed by Bellare and Rogaway and later modified by Shoup [9, 29], to encrypt the VoIP packets. Usually, asymmetric key encryption schemes are not directly used for message encryption. But for this experiment, we have encrypted RTP payload using the NIST P-256 curve and our proposed curve to analyze their performance on VoIP applications. In the experimental setup, the server is connected to the network through the Ethernet connection and the client is connected through the institutional Wi-Fi. The audio and video encryption systems follow the same methodology where the server first receives the client's ephemeral elliptic curve public key. The server then encrypts chunks of data using that key and sends the encrypted chunks one by one to the client. The client decrypts the encrypted payload using its ephemeral elliptic curve private key. The encrypted stream is sent to the client as a Real-time Transport Protocol (RTP) payload. UDP is used as the transport layer protocol. MJPEG and WAV files are used for video and audio encryption respectively. The machine configurations are given below:

Server Configuration:

1. Intel 3.40 GHz Core i7-3770 processor
2. 16 GB Main memory

Client Configuration:

1. Intel 2.50 GHz Core i5-2450M processor
2. 6 GB Main memory

We have measured the performance of the curves based on the end-to-end delay and the jitter in milliseconds. We have conducted 5 experiments for each curve (for audio and video encryption) and then calculated the mean of the corresponding results. The end-to-end delay is calculated by adding network latency from the server to the client, the encryption time at the server-end and the decryption time at the client-end. The corresponding results are depicted in Fig. 2, 3, 4 and Fig. 5.

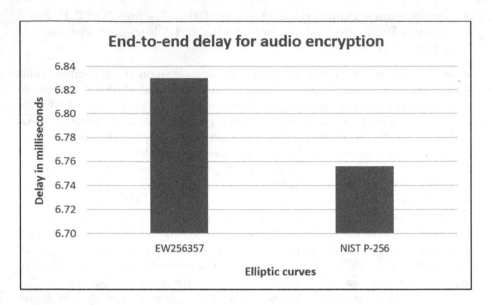

Fig. 2. End-to-end delay graph for audio encryption using EW_{256357} and NIST P-256 curves. The delay of NIST P-256 curve is less than the EW_{256357} curve, but the delay difference between EW_{256357} and NIST P-256 curve is only 0.07 ms.

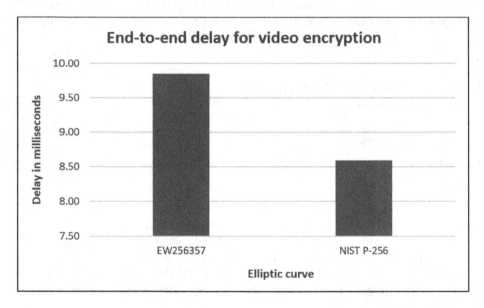

Fig. 3. End-to-end delay graph for video encryption using EW_{256357} and NIST P-256 curves. The delay of NIST P-256 curve is less than the EW_{256357} curve, but the delay difference between EW_{256357} and NIST P-256 curve is only 1.25 ms.

From the two end-to-end delay graphs for audio and video encryption in Fig. 2 and Fig. 3, we can say that the NIST P-256 curve's end-to-end delay is less than the proposed curve. However, the delay differences between the proposed curve and the NIST P-256 curve is only 0.07 ms in audio encryption and 1.25 ms in video encryption, which are negligible. Figure 4 and Fig. 5 depict the jitter plots of two curves. The jitter value of our proposed curve is less than the NIST P-256 curve. The NIST P-256 curve has 0.03 ms and 0.04 ms more jitter than our proposed curve in audio and video encryption, respectively.

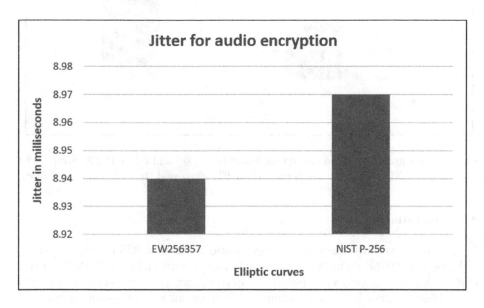

Fig. 4. Jitter graph for audio encryption using EW_{256357} and NIST P-256 curves. The jitter value of NIST P-256 curve is more than EW_{256357} and the difference is 0.03 ms.

The experiments show that our proposed curve's execution time is faster than the NIST P-256 curve in basic EC arithmetic operations. The network jitter is also low in our proposed curve. Our proposed curve's end-to-end delay time is little more than the NIST P-256 curve, but that issue is not as important as far as the curve's security is concerned. Since this work's primary focus is to develop a more secure curve than the NIST P-256 curve, we can see that our proposed curve provides more security than the NIST P-256 curve, and its performance is on a par with the NIST P-256 curve. This experiment proves that the EW_{256357} curve is a better choice for VoIP applications in security and overall performance.

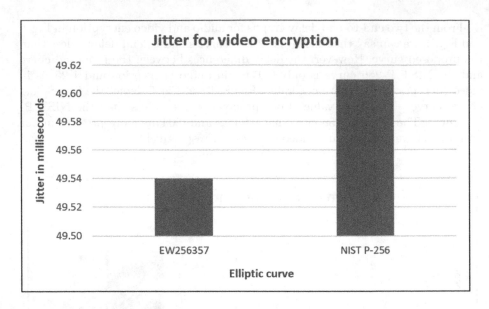

Fig. 5. Jitter graph for video encryption using EW_{256357} and NIST P-256 curves. The jitter value of NIST P-256 curve is more than EW_{256357} and the difference is 0.07 ms.

8 Conclusion

In this work, we have discussed the generation of a new 256-bit elliptic curve EW_{256357} at 128-bit security level, which is more secure than NIST P-256 curve. Our work is based solely on generating a better short Weierstrass curve than the NIST 256-bit curve in terms of security. We have not considered other types of curves like Edward or Montgomery curves. We have tested the performance of our proposed curve and compared it with NIST P-256 curves. We have also shown that the proposed curve's parameters are well explained, and the entire curve generation process is transparent, whereas the NIST P-256 curve generation process is manipulative. The proposed curve is a strongly twist-secure curve but the NIST P-256 curve is not. Based on the performance analysis of related curves, we can conclude that our proposed curve is suitable and a better choice for VoIP media encryption.

The elliptic curves of short Weierstrass form do not support Edward additions. This operation is supported by the Edward curves. Some ECC security features such as completeness or indistinguishability are supported by the Montgomery and Edward curve [12]. Montgomery curves support a scalar multiplication method known as Montgomery ladder which is much faster than the standard multiplication methods used by short Weierstrass curves because unlike short Weierstrass curves, Montgomery ladder method requires only x-coordinate of the elliptic curve point for the scalar multiplication [12]. In the future, we will extend this work to develop Montgomery and Edward curves which will support more ECC security features and will perform better than the existing curves.

Acknowledgement. This research is based upon work supported by the National Science Foundation under awards 1241768 and 1637291.

References

1. Digital Signature Standard (DSS). Federal Information Processing Standards Publication 186–4. https://nvlpubs.nist.gov/nistpubs/fips/nist.fips.186-4.pdf
2. ECC Brainpool. ECC Brainpool Standard Curves and Curve Generation. https://www.teletrust.de/fileadmin/files/oid/oid_ECC-Brainpool-Standard-curves-V1.pdf
3. IEEE 1363–2000: Standard specifications for public key cryptography. https://standards.ieee.org/standard/1363-2000.html
4. ITU-T, Series G: Transmission Systems and Media, Digital Systems and Networks. https://www.itu.int/rec/T-REC-G.114-200305-I
5. Report and Recommendations of the Visiting Committee on Advanced Technology of the National Institute of Standards and Technology. https://www.nist.gov/sites/default/files/documents/2017/05/09/VCAT-Report-on-NIST-Cryptographic-Standards-and-Guidelines-Process.pdf
6. Rabin, M.O.: Probabilistic algorithm for testing primality. J. Number Theory **12**, 128–138 (1980)
7. Lynn, B.: Elliptic Curves - The MOV attack. https://crypto.stanford.edu/pbc/notes/elliptic/movattack.html
8. Hales, C.: The NSA Back Door to NIST. Not. AMS **61**(2), 190–192
9. Hankerson, D., Mcnezes, A., Vanstone, S.: Guide to Elliptic Curve Cryptography. Springer, Heidelberg (2004). https://doi.org/10.1007/b97644
10. Bernstein, D.J.: Curve25519: new Diffie-Hellman speed records. In: Yung, M., Dodis, Y., Kiayias, A., Malkin, T. (eds.) PKC 2006. LNCS, vol. 3958, pp. 207–228. Springer, Heidelberg (2006). https://doi.org/10.1007/11745853_14
11. Bernstein, D.J., Lange, T.: Failures in NIST's ECC standards. https://cr.yp.to/newelliptic/nistecc-20160106.pdf
12. Bernstein, D.J., Lange, T.: SafeCurves: choosing safe curves for elliptic-curve cryptography. https://safecurves.cr.yp.to. Accessed 20 June 2020
13. Bernstein, D.J., Lange, T.: Security dangers of the NIST curves. https://cr.yp.to/talks/2013.05.31/slides-dan+tanja-20130531-4x3.pdf
14. Bernstein, D.J., Hamburg, M., Krasnova, A., Lange, T.: Elligator: elliptic-curve points indistinguishable from uniform random strings. In: ACM Conference on Computer and Communications Security
15. Biehl, I., Meyer, B., Muller, V.: Differential fault attacks on elliptic curve cryptosystems. In: Annual International Cryptology Conference, pp. 131–146 (2000)
16. Faugère, J.-C., Perret, L., Petit, C., Renault, G.: Improving the complexity of index calculus algorithms in elliptic curves over binary fields. In: Pointcheval, D., Johansson, T. (eds.) EUROCRYPT 2012. LNCS, vol. 7237, pp. 27–44. Springer, Heidelberg (2012). https://doi.org/10.1007/978-3-642-29011-4_4
17. Bos, J.W., Costello, C., Longa, P., Naehrig, M.: Specification of curve selection and supported curve parameters in MSR ECCLib. https://www.researchgate.net/publication/281897794_Specification_of_Curve_Selection_and_Supported_Curve_Parameters_in_MSR_ECCLib
18. Bos, J.W., Costello, C., Longa, P., Naehrig, M.: Selecting elliptic curves for cryptography: an efficiency and security analysis. J. Cryptographic Eng. **6**(4), 259–286 (2016)

19. Bos, J.W., Halderman, J.A., Heninger, N., Moore, J., Naehrig, M., Wustrow, E.: Elliptic curve cryptography in practice. https://eprint.iacr.org/2013/734.pdf
20. Caswell, M.: OpenSSL Wins the Levchin Prize. https://www.openssl.org/blog/blog/2018/01/10/levchin/
21. Hamburg, M.: Ed448-Goldilocks, a new elliptic curve. Cryptology ePrint Archive, Report 2015/625 (2015)
22. Lochter, M., Wiemers, A.: Twist Insecurity, International Association for Cryptologic Research. https://pdfs.semanticscholar.org/3428/3663d6d5bfa60c6dfeafadbf50d69e9b9b40.pdf
23. Scott, M.: Backdoors in NIST elliptic curves. https://www.miracl.com/press/backdoors-in-nist-elliptic-curves
24. Koblitz, N.: Elliptic curve cryptosystems. Math. Comput. **48**(177), 203–209 (1987)
25. Perlroth, N.: The New York Times, Government announces steps to restore confidence on encryption standards. http://bits.blogs.nytimes.com/2013/09/10/government-announces-steps-to-restore-confidence-on-encryption-standards
26. Sen, N., Dantu, R., Jagannath, V., Thompson, M.: Performance Analysis of Elliptic Curves for Real-time Video Encryption, pp. 64–71. National Cyber Summit, USA (2018)
27. Schoof, R.: Counting points on elliptic curves over finite fields. J. Theory Numbers Bordeaux **7**, 219–254 (1995)
28. Miller, V.S.: Use of elliptic curves in cryptography. In: Williams, H.C. (ed.) CRYPTO 1985. LNCS, vol. 218, pp. 417–426. Springer, Heidelberg (1986). https://doi.org/10.1007/3-540-39799-X_31
29. Shoup, V.: A Proposal for an ISO Standard for Public Key Encryption. https://www.shoup.net/papers/iso-2_1.pdf. Accessed 15 July 2019

Ucam: A User-Centric, Blockchain-Based and End-to-End Secure Home IP Camera System

Xinxin Fan$^{(\boxtimes)}$ (ID), Zhi Zhong, Qi Chai, and Dong Guo

IoTeX , Menlo Park 94025, USA
{xinxin,zhi,raullen,dong}@iotex.io

Abstract. Home IP cameras are consistently among the most popular smart home devices and recent news stories about home IP cameras getting hacked frequently have posed serious security and privacy concerns for consumers. In this paper, we propose Ucam, a user-centric, blockchain-based and end-to-end secure home IP camera system. Ucam leverages advanced technologies such as blockchain, end-to-end encryption and trusted computing to address a number of vulnerabilities in the existing solutions. In the Ucam design, we replace traditional username/password based login approach with a one-click, blockchain-based passwordless counterpart and apply the resurrecting duckling security model to secure device binding. In particular, we utilize blockchain extensively to manage device ownership and provide integrity protection for the video clips stored locally or remotely. For coping with privacy, the end-to-end encryption, which is coupled with a user-centric, secure element enhanced key management scheme, is implemented in Ucam. Finally, Ucam employs re-encryption with Intel SGX as well as key refreshing to enable the sharing of encrypted video clips and live streaming videos, respectively. The security analysis and performance evaluation demonstrate that Ucam is able to meet the increasing security and privacy requirements for home IP camera systems with negligible performance overhead.

Keywords: Home IP Camera · Blockchain · Passwordless · End-to-end encryption · Integrity protection · Trusted computing

1 Introduction

The growing adoption of smart homes and expanding consciousness regarding security and safety have increased the demand for Internet Protocol (IP) based camera systems at a staggering rate. With packed features from face recognition to various image sensors and multiple connectivity options, home IP cameras offer a number of key benefits such as remote and perimeter video surveillance, intruder detection and alarms, access control and security management, etc.

© ICST Institute for Computer Sciences, Social Informatics and Telecommunications Engineering 2020
Published by Springer Nature Switzerland AG 2020. All Rights Reserved
N. Park et al. (Eds.): SecureComm 2020, LNICST 336, pp. 311–323, 2020.
https://doi.org/10.1007/978-3-030-63095-9_20

While home IP camera systems redefine safety and protection of properties and businesses, security and privacy of those systems continue to be major concerns for consumers [10]. Recent news [8,18,21] about hackers breaking into home IP camera systems has exposed a number of security design issues, including but not limited to poor password policies, problematical login process, vulnerable firmware and leaky database. Those vulnerabilities allow attackers to gain control of devices remotely and put users' personal information at risk.

First of all, the traditional password-based login has become the root cause for many recent hacks against home IP camera systems in which hackers launch so-called credential stuffing attacks [1] to access an account using a list of compromised login credentials. While these attacks could be mitigated by enabling the two-factor authentication mechanism [20], the complexity of the login process has been increased accordingly. Besides cumbersome login hurdles, the device binding mechanism that associates a user's account with his/her IP camera poses another major threat to the device ownership [3]. The third issue involves home IP camera systems that utilize cloud services for storing video clips, in which video files are stored either in plaintext or in encrypted form with the encryption key held by cloud service providers (CSPs) and/or device manufacturers. This practice exposes users' private information to third-party entities and allows them to manipulate the stored video clips in an arbitrary manner. Last but not least, while most home IP camera systems enable owners to share live camera feeds with friends and family, the video clips stored on the local SD card or cloud storage are only accessible by the camera owners. In particular, how to share encrypted video clips and live streaming videos has not been solved. To address the aforementioned issues for the existing home IP camera systems, we propose Ucam, a user-centric and end-to-end secure home IP camera system, in this contribution. Ucam leverages a blockchain wallet generated on the mobile app to enhance security of the user login process by realizing a one-click, password-less user authentication mechanism. Moreover, the resurrecting duckling security model [17] is applied to cameras in the system for securely binding devices with their owners. In particular, the critical device ownership information is directly anchored to the blockchain by cameras in lieu of being maintained by a centralized database server, which reduces the risk that cameras are taken over by attackers significantly. For protecting users' privacy, Ucam realizes end-to-end encryption coupled with a user-centric key management scheme. To thwart potential system errors and misbehavior of CSPs, Ucam allows cameras to periodically commit integrity checkpoints to the blockchain via user configuration, thereby enabling users to check data integrity when downloading video clips from the local or remote storage. Finally, Ucam realizes effective sharing of encrypted video clips and live streaming videos through re-encryption with Intel SGX and key refreshing, respectively.

The rest of the paper is organized as follows. Section 2 gives a brief overview of blockchain, smart contract, and Intel SGX. Section 3 describes the system and attacker models. Section 4 presents the detailed design of the Ucam system. In Sect. 5, we summarize the security and privacy properties of the Ucam design and compare it with other home IP camera solutions. The performance impact of using a secure element in the Ucam system is evaluated in Sect. 6. Finally, we conclude this paper in Sect. 7.

2   Preliminaries

2.1   Blockchain and Smart Contract

Blockchains are tamper evident and tamper resistant digital ledgers implemented in a distributed fashion and usually without a central authority [23]. A blockchain is able to eliminate trusted intermediaries by requiring transactions to be verified by the rest of the blockchain's network. In particular, a distributed consensus protocol, which tolerates faults and adversarial attacks, ensures that all the nodes agree on a unique order in which blocks are appended. The blockchain provides an infrastructure where trust is embodied algorithmically in the transaction itself and effectively liberates data that was previously kept in safeguarded silos. In the context of blockchain, a smart contract [19] represents a piece of code that is stored, verified and executed on a blockchain. While the blockchain holds the storage file of a smart contract, a network of miners execute its business logic and update the blockchain by reaching a consensus. Users can invoke a smart contract by sending transactions to the contract address and each of them triggers the state transition of the contract, with data being written to the contract's internal storage. During the run-time, the smart contract performs predefined logic and may also interact with other accounts by sending messages or transferring funds. As self-executing codes on a blockchain, smart contracts are able to streamline processes that are currently spread across multiple parties and systems.

2.2   Intel SGX

The Intel Software Guard Extensions (SGX) [11] is a set of new x86 instructions provided in newer lines of Intel CPUs that allows application developers to protect sensitive data from unauthorized modification and access from rogue software running at higher privilege levels. SGX aims to provide a trusted execution environment (TEE) for user-space applications by enabling code isolation within virtual containers called enclaves. The program running inside an enclave is cryptographically measured and the generated proofs by the enclave can be reported back to the client. Enclaves feature three salient security properties, namely isolation, sealing and attestation [4]. *Isolation* means that program and data inside an enclave cannot be read/modified by other processes running at the same or higher privilege levels. On the other hand, *sealing* is the process of encrypting enclave secrets for persistent storage to disk, which uses authenticated encryption (i.e., AES-GCM) and thus allows the enclave to detect whether the sealed data has been modified externally. Finally, *attestation* enables an enclave to cryptographically prove that it is a genuine SGX enclave running on an up-to-date platform.

3 System and Attacker Models

3.1 System Model

We consider a blockchain-enabled home IP camera system as shown in Fig. 1, which consists of the following entities:

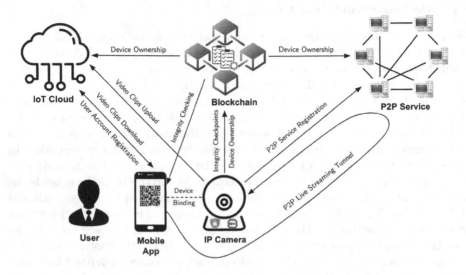

Fig. 1. The system model of a blockchain-enabled home IP camera system

- *IP camera*: An IP camera is a type of digital video camera which can receive control commands and send image data via the Internet.
- *IoT cloud*: An IoT cloud is responsible for user account management, device management, and data storage.
- *Peer-to-peer (P2P) service*: A P2P service simplifies the linkage between IP cameras and mobile devices when a user views camera feeds.
- *Mobile App*: A mobile app facilitates a smartphone user to configure an IP camera, view the captured video clips as well as live streaming videos, and share the video clips with friends and family.
- *User*: A user is the owner of one or multiple IP cameras and utilizes the mobile app to interact with them.
- *Blockchain*: A blockchain is a distributed ledger that is used to record transactions in the order agreed by all the peer computers in the network.

In the above home IP camera system, an IP camera, which is equipped with a secure element for key storage and cryptographic hardware acceleration, starts running once it is initialized and configured by a user via the mobile app. The IP camera records a short video clip (e.g., 10 s) and stores it either in the local storage (e.g., an SD card) or on the remote IoT cloud each time a motion is detected.

The user will receive an alarm and is able to replay the stored video clip using the mobile app. Moreover, the user can also request to view live streaming videos through the P2P streaming service in the system. The IoT cloud provides remote storage and serves users' requests for retrieving video clips. The blockchain, on the other hand, enforces device ownership, facilitates device sharing, and ensures data integrity of the cloud storage.

3.2 Attacker Model

In a typical home IP camera system, an adversary might try to compromise the user account system on the cloud server for taking over the ownership of IP cameras. A nearby adversary may also launch the attacks against the device binding process and take control of the victim's device. In addition, an attacker might eavesdrop on wireless communications between the IP camera and IoT cloud. We also consider the scenario in which a cloud provider could behave maliciously by viewing, inserting, deleting, and modifying the video clips. Furthermore, an attacker may impersonate a legitimate user and try to access the live streaming videos via the P2P service.

4 The Ucam Design

4.1 Passwordless User Authentication

To thwart potential credential stuffing attacks and improve user experience, the Ucam mobile app utilizes the private/public key pair associated with a user's blockchain wallet to implement passwordless login to the IoT cloud. In the Ucam system, the one-click, passwordless user authentication works as follows:

- Once a user opens the Ucam mobile app for the first time, a blockchain wallet is generated automatically, where the private key $priv_U$ is stored in the secure storage of his/her smartphone and the blockchain address $addr_U$, which is derived from the public key pub_U, is passed to the IoT cloud for user account creation. In the Ucam system, each user account consists of a blockchain address $addr_U$ and a random challenge r_U.
- When the user clicks on the login button, an API call to the IoT cloud is made for retrieving the random challenge r_U associated with the blockchain address $addr_U$.
- Upon receiving the random challenge r_U and displaying it on the Ucam mobile app, it requires the user's confirmation for the signed message r_U. If the user accepts it, a signature $\mathsf{Sign}_{priv_U}(r_U)$ is generated and returned to the IoT cloud together with the corresponding blockchain address $addr_U$. Otherwise, the login process is terminated.
- When the IoT cloud receives an authentication response, it first looks up the user account using the blockchain address $addr_U$ and obtains the current random challenge r_U, followed by verifying the authentication response

$\mathsf{Verify}(r_U, addr_U, \mathsf{Sign}_{priv_U}(r_U))$. If the verification succeeds, the user is considered as authenticated and a JSON Web Token (JWT) is issued to the user for accessing the cloud storage. Otherwise, the login attempt is rejected.

- The IoT cloud needs to update the random challenge r_U after each login attempt for thwarting replay attacks.

The above login process uses asymmetric cryptography and blockchain technology to eliminate the need of cumbersome passwords, thereby achieving better usability and security than the traditional username/password based approach.

4.2   Blockchain-Based Ownership Management

In the Ucam system, we bind a home IP camera with a user's account through the out-of-band (OOB) channel and apply the resurrecting duckling security model [17] in the context of IoT device binding. Once the camera is powered on for the first time or the reset button is pressed, the device will look for a valid blockchain address and recognize the device owner as the first entity that provides it. Therefore, when the user opens the Ucam mobile app and adds the camera to his/her account, he/she needs to hold the smartphone in front of the camera and allow his/her blockchain address, which is encoded as a QR code on the Ucam mobile app, to be scanned by the camera. Upon receiving the user's blockchain address $addr_U$, the camera will invoke $\mathsf{SC_{om}}$, an ownership management smart contract deployed by the camera manufacture on the blockchain, with parameters $addr_C$ and $addr_U$, when the internet connection becomes available. Here the camera claims its ownership by creating an association of its blockchain address (i.e., $addr_C$) with its owner's one (i.e., $addr_U$) on the blockchain. The following three cases might occur: i) If $\mathsf{SC_{om}}$ does not have any entry containing $addr_C$, a new entry $(addr_C, addr_U)$ will be created in $\mathsf{SC_{om}}$; ii) If $\mathsf{SC_{om}}$ has already included the same entry $(addr_C, addr_U)$, its means that the camera is reset by its current owner and $\mathsf{SC_{om}}$ does not need to update the state; iii) If $\mathsf{SC_{om}}$ has an entry $(addr_C, addr_U')$ with $addr_U' \neq addr_U$, it implies the transfer of ownership (see Sect. 4.7) and the blockchain address $addr_U$ of the new owner will replace the previous one $addr_U'$ in $\mathsf{SC_{om}}$.

4.3   End-to-End Encryption and User-Centric Key Management

The Ucam system leverages end-to-end encryption to protect confidentiality of both video clips and live stream videos. The raw video data is encrypted using user-specified encryption keys with the aid of a hardware-based cryptographic engine (CE) inside the secure element, before it is stored locally on an SD card, remotely on the cloud storage, or sent to the P2P streaming service. Given a video frame v of l bits and a video encryption key k_V, the cryptographic engine encrypts the video frame as follows:

$$v' = v \oplus \mathsf{KSG}(l, \mathsf{CE}(k_V, IV)),$$

where $\mathsf{KSG}(\cdot)$ is a keystream generator using the underlying CE and the l-bit key stream is XORed with the video frame v to generate the corresponding ciphertext v'. Here CE can be instantiated using a stream cipher or a block cipher operating on the stream cipher mode [5] and IV is an initialization vector.

For enabling a user to update the video encryption key k_V in a secure manner, a Key-Encryption-Key (KEK) k_E is first derived from the user's private key $priv_U$ on the Ucam mobile app, i.e.,

$$k_E = \mathsf{KDF}(priv_U, OtherInput),$$

where KDF can be any standardized key-derivation function [2]. '$OtherInput$' might include a random salt (i.e., a byte string), the length of the derived key, and other context-specific data, depending on the choice of a key-derivation function. Note that k_E is derived immediately after the blockchain wallet is created on the Ucam mobile app and transported to the camera together with the user's blockchain address via the QR code. Upon receiving the KEK k_E, the camera stores it inside the secure element. Whenever a user would like to update the video encryption key k_V, he/she first generates a new key k_V' on the Ucam mobile app and then encrypts it with the KEK k_E, i.e.,

$$c = \mathsf{Enc}(k_E, k_V').$$

The ciphertext c is then sent to the camera through the public channel and replaces the previous encryption key in the file system. As a result, the subsequent video clips or live stream videos will be encrypted with the new key k_V'. Here we utilize two different keys k_C and k_S to encrypt video clips and live streaming videos, respectively, for accommodating the corresponding video sharing mechanisms (see Sects. 4.5 and 4.6) and k_V can be either of those keys.

4.4   Blockchain-Based Data Integrity Protection

For ensuring data integrity of video clips stored locally on an SD card or remotely on the cloud storage, the Ucam system allows the camera to commit integrity checkpoints to the blockchain according to a user-defined time period. To this end, the user needs to first enable the data integrity protection feature on the Ucam mobile app and specify the time period in days for checkpoint commitments, followed by topping up the camera's wallet with a certain amount of cryptocurrency tokens. Note that the shorter the time period is set, the more checkpoints the camera is going to commit on the blockchain.

Once the data integrity protection feature is activated, the camera starts building a Merkle tree [12] dynamically for the encrypted video clips received during the user-specified time period. At the end of each time period, the camera will invoke another manufacture deployed smart contract $\mathsf{SC_{cm}}$, which is responsible for checkpoint management, with parameters (id_{mt}, num, h_r), where id_{mt} is the Merkle tree identifier that is concatenated with a file identifier to indicate which Merkle tree the file belongs to. h_r is the root of the Merkle tree built from num encrypted video files and acts as the integrity checkpoint for the past time period. As soon as integrity checkpoints become available on the blockchain, the user is able to verify data integrity of encrypted video clips retrieved from the SD card or cloud storage. After the user sends a request for downloading an encrypted video clip from the SD card or cloud storage, the camera or cloud server first identifies all the encrypted video clips that are in the same Merkle tree as the one in question using the Merkle tree identifier id_{mt}, followed by the generation of the corresponding Merkle path. The encrypted video clip and Merkle path are then returned to the Ucam mobile app. Before decrypting the video clip, the Ucam mobile app obtains h_r from the smart contract $\mathsf{SC_{cm}}$ and verifies data integrity of the received video clip using h_r and the Merkle path. In this way, the user is confident that the video clip has not been altered.

4.5 Fine-Grained Secure Video Clip Sharing with Intel SGX

Considering the limited video sharing scenarios of home IP cameras, we describe a fine-grained secure video clip sharing scheme through a re-encryption process using the Intel SGX technology. More specifically, we create a data sharing enclave DataShare on the application server of the IoT cloud, which is responsible for re-encrypting the video clip(s) selected by the user for sharing purposes. The video clip sharing process works as follows:

- Whenever a user wants to share the video clip(s) with others, the Ucam mobile app will first perform a remote attestation with the DataShare enclave to verify that the application server has loaded the correct code into the enclave. During this process, a symmetric session key k_{se} is generated on both the Ucam mobile app and DataShare enclave, thereby establishing a secure channel between two entities.
- After the user selects n video clip(s) on the Ucam mobile app and sets a video sharing key k_{sh}, the list of video file identifiers $\{id_{f_1}, \ldots, id_{f_n}\}$, the video sharing key k_{sh}, and the video clip encryption key k_C are encrypted using the session key k_{se} and sent to the application server.
- The application server sends the received information to the DataShare enclave for decryption and retrieves n encrypted video clip(s) from the cloud storage using the identifier list $\{id_{f_1}, \ldots, id_{f_n}\}$. The retrieved n video clip(s) are then decrypted and re-encrypted inside the DataShare enclave using k_C and k_{sh}, respectively.
- The application server stores the re-encrypted video clip(s) in the cloud and returns the Uniform Resource Identifier (URI) to the Ucam mobile app. The user is then able to share the URI and video sharing key k_{sh} with others via various communication channels (e.g., QR code, email, etc.).

To save costs for using cloud storage, the URI for the shared video clip(s) is only valid for a user-defined amount of time and all the shared video clip(s) will be deleted thereafter. The above secure data sharing scheme enables a user to fully control which video clip(s) to share with different entities, thereby minimizing the potential data leakage.

4.6   Secure Live Streaming Video Sharing with Key Refreshing

Due to the real-time requirements for sharing live streaming videos, we employ key refreshing in lieu of re-encryption for sharing cameras with other people. More specifically, the device owner will directly send the current live streaming video encryption key k_S to all the entities with which he/she would like to share the camera. Whenever the device owner decides to revoke access for one or multiple people, a new live streaming video encryption key k'_S will be generated on the fly and distributed to the remaining entities. Moreover, the device owner also needs to update the live streaming video encryption key on the camera as described in Sect. 4.3.

Besides distributing the live streaming video encryption key k_S, the device owner also needs to generate access tokens for authorizing other entities to retrieve live streaming videos via the P2P service. An access token TK_{OR} is a tuple $(pub_O, addr_R, addr_C, T_{exp}, \mathsf{Sign}_{priv_O}(addr_R, addr_C, T_{exp}))$, where pub_O is the device owner's public key. $addr_R$ and $addr_C$ denote the blockchain addresses of the requester and the owner's camera, respectively. T_{exp} is the expiry time of the access token and $\mathsf{Sign}_{priv_O}(addr_R, addr_C, T_{exp})$ is the device owner's signature. A data requester can retrieve live streaming videos with the access token as described below:

- The requester sends a connection request to the P2P service by presenting his/her public key pub_R and access token TK_{OR}.
- The P2P service verifies the validity of the access token TK_{OR} as follows:
  - The P2P service checks T_{exp} to ensure that the access toke TK_{OR} is not expired;
  - The P2P service queries the ownership management smart contract SC_{om} with the device's blockchain address $addr_C$ and then obtains its owner's blockchain address $addr_O$;
  - The P2P service checks that $addr_O$ and $addr_R$ are derived from the public keys pub_O and pub_R, respectively;
  - The P2P service verifies that the signature $\mathsf{Sign}_{priv_O}(addr_R, addr_C, T_{exp})$ is valid.
  If any of the above verification steps fails, the P2P service will reject the connection request.
- The P2P service sends a random challenge r_P to the requester for verifying that he/she is the owner of the blockchain address $addr_R$.
- The requester generates the signature $\mathsf{Sign}_{priv_R}(r_P)$ and sends it to the P2P service as the response.
- The P2P service verifies the validity of the signature $\mathsf{Sign}_{priv_R}(r_P)$ and then grants or rejects the P2P service from the requester accordingly.

4.7   Ownership Transfer

Thanks to the ownership management with the smart contract on the blockchain, the ownership transfer can be easily handled. In the case that the camera is given to another person, the new owner can simply reset the camera, register a user account and restart the ownership claim process (see Sects. 4.1 and 4.2).

5   Security and Privacy Properties

Table 1 presents a comprehensive comparison of Ucam and other popular home IP camera systems in terms of security and privacy properties. Among the existing solutions, Ucam is the only one that utilizes secure hardware for protecting cryptographic keys and blockchain wallet for passwordless user authentication, respectively. While Haicam [7] and Wyze [22] claim the usage of end-to-end encryption, it is not clear how this technology is actually implemented and, in particular, how the encryption key is managed in their systems, due to limited technical information available on their websites. Regarding device ownership management, Ucam takes advantage of the decentralized nature of blockchain to achieve stronger protection of device ownership, when compared to other home IP camera systems in which centralized cloud servers are used for this purpose. Furthermore, Ucam offers additional integrity protection for video clips against storage errors and malicious attacks with the help of integrity checkpoints stored on the blockchain. As for video sharing, Ucam supports fine-grained sharing of encrypted video clips as well as secure sharing of live streaming videos. Although Wyze [22], eufy [6], Ring [15] and Nest [13] also implement (partial) video sharing functionalities, CSPs are still able to access the shared contents. From Table 1, we can see that Ucam provides a number of salient features that improve security and privacy of the state-of-the-art home IP camera systems dramatically.

Table 1. Security and Privacy Properties of Home IP Camera Systems

	Ucam	Haicam [7]	Wyze [22]	eufy [6]	Ring [15]	Nest [13]
Secure Hardware	✓	✗	✗	✗	✗	✗
User Login	Blockchain Wallet	Username/ Password	Username/ Password with 2FA	Username/ Password	Username/ Password with 2FA	Username/ Password with 2FA
End-to-End Encryption	✓	✓	✓	✗	✗	✗
User-Centric Key Management	✓	Unknown	Unknown	N/A	N/A	N/A
Device Ownership Management	Blockchain	Cloud Server				
Data Integrity Protection	✓ (Blockchain)	✗	✗	✗	✗	✗
(Encrypted) Live Streaming Video Sharing	✓ (Key Refreshing)	✗	✓	✓	✓	✓
(Encrypted) Video Clip Sharing	✓ (Re-Encryption)	✗	✗	✓	✓	✓

6   Performance Evaluation

In the Ucam design, a secure element serves as the secure key storage and hardware cryptographic accelerator. More specifically, the secure element is responsible for signing transactions to secure device ownership and commit integrity checkpoints (see Sects. 4.2 and 4.4) as well as generating keystreams in the end-to-end encryption (see Sect. 4.3), respectively. In this section, we use the EdgeLock^{TM} SE050 secure element development board [14] from NXP semiconductors to evaluate the performance impact. In a typical setting, a host controller communicates with an SE050 secure element through an I^{2}C (Inter-Integrated Circuit) interface. At the application level, the host controller exchanges messages with the SE050 secure element using application protocol data units (APDUs) [9]. To simplify the software development, NXP abstracts the interactions between the host controller with the SE050 secure element through the Plug & Trust middleware and associated secure sub-system (SSS) APIs.

For implementing the blockchain-based ownership management and data integrity protection protocols in the Ucam design, the SE050 secure element is used to sign transactions that are sent from the host controller. We configure the SE050 secure element to use the Koblitz curve secp256k1 [16] and test the performance of ECDSA on a message digest of 32 bytes. Our experimental result shows that a digital signature can be generated in around 45.4 ms. In regard to the end-to-end encryption in the Ucam system, we use AES-128 in the counter mode (CTR) [5] to generate keystreams for encrypting video frames. For testing the throughput of the keystream generation on the SE050 secure element, the host controller sends 16-byte messages, each of which consists of a 12-byte nonce and a 4-byte counter, to the AES engine consecutively. The resulting keystream generation throughput is about 11.3 Kbps. Note that all the performance test results take the I^{2}C communication between the host controller and the SE050 secure element into consideration. Based on our experimental results, one can see that secure elements are able to boost security of home IP camera systems dramatically without incurring significant performance overhead.

7   Conclusion

In this paper, we present the design of Ucam, a user-centric, blockchain-based and end-to-end secure home IP camera system. When compared to popular home IP camera solutions, Ucam offers strong security and privacy protection for multiple core functionalities such as user login, device binding, device ownership management, video confidentiality, storage integrity and video sharing. By leveraging blockchain technology, Ucam is able to support passwordless user authentication and protect cameras and videos from various malicious attacks. Moreover, the video data is only accessible by the camera owner and their authorized entities, thanks to the end-to-end encryption and user-centric key management. The secure sharing of encrypted video clips and live streaming videos is addressed using re-encryption based on Intel SGX and key refreshing techniques.

References

1. Avast Security News Team, "What is credential stuffing, and why is my smart security camera vulnerable to it?". https://blog.avast.com/credential-stuffing-and-web-cams, Security News, 4 May 2019
2. Chen, L.: Recommendation for Key Derivation Using Pseudorandom Functions (Revised), NIST Special Publication 800–108, October 2009
3. Chen, J., Sun, M., Zhang, K.: Security analysis of device binding for IP-based IoT devices. In: Proceedings of 2019 IEEE International Conference on Pervasive Computing and Communications Workshops (PerCom Workshops), IEEE Computer Society, pp. 900–905 (2019)
4. Costan, V., Devadas, S.: "Intel SGX Explained", IACR Cryptology ePrint Archive, Report 2016/86 (2016)
5. Dworkin, M.: "Recommendation for Block Cipher Modes of Operation: Methods and Techniques", National Institute of Standards and Technology, NIST Special Publication 800–38A, December 2001
6. eufy Security Indoor Cam 2K Pan & Tilt. https://www.eufylife.com/products/variant/eufycam-2/T8410121
7. Haicam End-to-End Encrypted Home Security Camera. https://haicam.tech/
8. Isidore, C.: Smart camera maker Wyze hit with customer data breach. https://www.cnn.com/2019/12/30/tech/wyze-data-breach/index.html, CNN Business, 30 December 2019
9. ISO/IEC 7816–4:2013, Identification cards - Integrated circuit cards - Part 4: Organization, security and commands for interchange
10. McInnis, K.: Consumer Reports letter to connected camera manufacturers to call for raising security and privacy standards. https://advocacy.consumerreports.org/research/consumer-reports-letter-to-connected-camera-manufacturers-to-call-for-raising-security-and-privacy-standards/, Consumer Reports, 13 January 2020
11. McKeen, F., et al.: Innovative instructions and software model for isolated execution. In: Proceedings of the 2nd International Workshop on Hardware and Architectural Support for Security and Privacy (HASP 2013), p. 10. ACM Press (2013)
12. Merkle, Ralph C.: A digital signature based on a conventional encryption function. In: Pomerance, Carl (ed.) CRYPTO 1987. LNCS, vol. 293, pp. 369–378. Springer, Heidelberg (1988). https://doi.org/10.1007/3-540-48184-2_32
13. Nest Cam Indoor. https://store.google.com/us/product/nest_cam
14. NXP Semiconductors. EdgeLock^{TM} SE050 Development Kit
15. Ring Indoor Cam. https://shop.ring.com/products/mini-indoor-security-camera?variant=30258040832089
16. Standards for Efficient Cryptography. "SEC 2: Recommended Elliptic Curve Domain Parameters, Version 2.0", Certicom Research (2010)
17. Stajano, F., Anderson, R.: The resurrecting duckling: security issues for ubiquitous computing. Computer **35**, 22–26 (2002). IEEE Computer Society
18. Sundby, A.: Hacker spoke to baby, hurled obscenities at couple using Nest camera, dad says. https://www.cbsnews.com/news/nest-camera-hacked-hacker-spoke-to-baby-hurled-obscenities-at-couple-using-nest-camera-dad-says/, CBS News, 31 January 2019
19. Szabo, N.: Smart Contracts: Building Blocks for Digital Markets (1996). http://www.fon.hum.uva.nl/rob/Courses/InformationInSpeech/CDROM/Literature/LOTwinterschool2006/szabo.best.vwh.net/smart_contracts_2.html

20. Thomas, K., Moscicki, A.: New research: how effective is basic account hygiene at preventing hijacking, Google Security Blog, 17 May 2019
21. Vigdor, N.: Somebody's Watching: Hackers Breach Ring Home Security Cameras. https://www.nytimes.com/2019/12/15/us/Hacked-ring-home-security-cameras.html, The New York Times, 15 December 2019
22. Wyze Cam V2. https://wyze.com/wyze-cam.html
23. Yaga, D., Mell, P., Roby, N., Scarfone, K.: Blockchain Technology Overview, National Institute of Standards and Technology, Draft NISTIR 8202, January 2018

Private Global Generator Aggregation from Different Types of Local Models

Chunling Han[1,2(✉)] and Rui Xue[1]

[1] SKLOIS, Institute of Information Engineering, CAS; School of Cyber Security,
University of Chinese Academy of Sciences, Beijing, China
{hanchunling,xuerui}@iie.ac.cn
[2] Indiana University Bloomington, Bloomington, IN 47401, USA

Abstract. Generative Adversary Network (GAN) is a promising field with many practical applications. By using GANs, generated data can replace real sensitive data to be released for outside productive research. However, sometimes sensitive data is distributed among multiple parties, in which global generators are needed. Additionally, generated samples could remember or reflect sensitive features of real data. In this paper, we propose a scheme to aggregate a global generator from distributed local parties without access to local parties' sensitive datasets, and the global generator will not reveal sensitive information of local parties' training data. In our scheme, we separate GAN into two parts: discriminators played by local parties, a global generator played by the global party. Our scheme allows local parties to train different types of discriminators. To prevent generators from stealing sensitive information of real training datasets, we propose noised discriminator loss aggregation, add Gaussian noise to discriminators' loss, then use the average of noised loss to compute global generator's gradients and update its parameters. Our scheme is easy to implement by modifying plain GAN structures. We test our scheme on real-world MNIST and Fashion MNIST datasets, experimental results show that our scheme can achieve high-quality global generators without breaching local parties' training data privacy.

Keywords: GAN · Generator aggregation · Discriminator loss

1 Introduction

Generative Adversary Network (GAN) [9] is a thriving research topic, which can be used to generate fake (synthetic) data to replace sensitive data to be released for outside research [2]. Sometimes, data is distributed among different local parties, developing a global generator can help represent local parties to generate and release fake (synthetic) data.

We illustrate an example to explain why aggregating global generators are useful and will have many applications. We take Covid-19 as an example to explain how global generators can facilitate the understanding of this disease.

N. Park et al. (Eds.): SecureComm 2020, LNICST 336, pp. 324–335, 2020.
https://doi.org/10.1007/978-3-030-63095-9_21

A world organization wishes to use data from some countries to help other countries lack of data and research resources. Some medical research institutes from different countries are willing to contribute. However, due to the concern of patients' privacy, these research institutes are not willing to disclose their data. For this kind of situation, global generators can provide a solution. By developing a global generator, the world organization can generate synthetic data according to real data from those medical research institutes, then use the generated synthetic data to analyze and help other countries.

Here, "Global" can be interpreted from two aspects: firstly, the global generator can be aggregated from only **one** local party, represent this very local party to generate synthetic data; or it can be aggregated from **a group** of local parties, represent them to generate synthetic data reflecting the distribution of data from that group.

You may ask why not let those medical research institutes generate synthetic data themselves, and send the synthetic data to the world organization? The obstacles of this method are: these medical research institutes probably use different models and generate different quality of synthetic data. In addition, the actual amount of generated data needed is unknown at this moment, and every time when new synthetic data is needed, these medical research institutes need to be involved again. Therefore, a centralized global generator will be much easier to organize and manage.

Why Traditional Parameter Aggregation Fails. To aggregate a global generator from different local parties, there are some methods from federated learning can be referred to. Most of those traditional parameter based aggregation methods in federated learning are designed to average local models' parameters to get a global model [1,3,14,16]. They usually assume local parties and the global party develop exactly the same type of model and structure. To prevent private information leaking from local parameters, some works [1,16] release parameters under differential privacy [4–8] by adding noise to gradients. However, in fact, averaging local models' parameters is not always a good choice for model aggregation. Just simply taking the average of local parameters might not directly result in an accurate global model, let alone parameters with noise to achieve differential privacy. **Most importantly**, local parties might use different types of models, in which all different types and structures of parameters can not be averaged. These obstacles in traditional parameter based aggregation methods motivate our work.

Since we can not simply borrow traditional aggregation methods into global generator aggregation, in this paper, we propose a new global generator aggregation method.

To conventionally train a GAN, we usually train the discriminator and the generator together in one party, then use the generator to generate synthetic data. While, in our scheme, we **separate** discriminator and generator among local parties and the global party, allow **multiple** discriminators to one generator. Local parties train discriminators, which can have different types and structures. Meantime, the global party trains the generator. Because the generator might use gradients from discriminators to steal or extract local parties' sensitive information, we let local discriminators add Gaussian noise to their loss. To update global generator's parameters, the discriminators randomly select one discriminator as a representative, this discriminator will collect all discriminators' noised loss, use the average to calculate gradients and help the global generator to update its parameters. After training the global generator, the global party can represent local parties to generate synthetic (fake) data.

We test our scheme on real-world MNIST and Fashion MNIST datasets, experimental results show that our method can achieve high-quality global generators. To test the quality of generated samples output by the global generator, we use generated data to train deep learning models, we can achieve 98.02% and 88.54% accuracies for MNIST and Fashion MNIST test datasets respectively.

The contributions of our work are as follows:

- We solve a problem that aggregating global generators from different types of local discriminators. We achieve two main goals: global generators for local parties, suitable for different types of local discriminators and privacy protection for local parties' sensitive training data.
- We separate GAN into two parts: discriminators in local parties and a global generator in the global party. In this way, we can achieve global generators without access to local parties' private datasets. Since discriminators are probably in different types, parameters can not be used, therefore, we choose discriminator loss as vehicle to aggregate the global generators.
- We add noise to discriminators' loss computed on generated samples, by adding noise to discriminators' loss, we can prevent private information leakage from discriminators.

2 Preliminary

In this section, we briefly describe the basics of generative adversary networks.

Generative Adversarial Network (GAN) [9] consists of two models: generator G and discriminator D. Generator G takes random noise $z \sim p_z(z)$ as input, tries to output fake samples of data with distribution approximates real data's distribution $x \sim p_{data}(x)$. The discriminator D will estimate the probability that a sample is a real data comes from the training dataset rather than a fake data generated from G. These two models are simultaneously trained in a competitive way, the goal of GAN is training G and D playing a two-player minmax game with the value function V(G, D):

$$\min_G \max_D V(G, D) = E_{x \sim p_{data}(x)}[\log(D(x))] + E_{z \sim p_z(z)}[1 - \log(D(G(z)))]$$

3 Our Approach

In this section, we illustrate our approach to global generator aggregation. We design our generator aggregation method for local parties, even they develop different types of discriminators and different structures of parameters.

3.1   Role of Models

There are two roles in our scheme, local parties and the global party. Local parties posses sensitive datasets, the global party is in charge of generator aggregation.

We consider an honest but curious global party, who participates by rules but always wants to steal privacy information from local parties.

We also consider honest but curious local parties, they participate in the system honestly but also want to steal sensitive information from other local parties. They might collude with others but will not destroy their collaboration of aggregation.

3.2   Global Generator Aggregation

In our scheme, we allow local parties to develop different types of discriminators. The global party will develop a global generator generating fake data for discriminators. The global generator and local discriminators form a GAN.

Our scheme is described in Algorithm 1. To train the GAN, **in every training epoch t**, the generator generates a batch of fake data $fake\_data_t$ from random noise $z \sim p_z(z)$, feeds the generated data to discriminators. Every discriminator is trained on a batch of its real data and fake data $fake\_data_t$. Then discriminators are set to be untrainable. Next, the generator generates a new batch of fake data $fake_t$ from noise $z \sim p_z(z)$, feeds the generated data $fake_t$ to the untrainable discriminators. Every discriminator $\{D_i\}_n$ computes the loss function on $fake_t$ as g_loss_i. The output of discriminators are binary class classification (real or fake), we empirically assume all discriminators use binary cross entropy loss function.

To prevent privacy leakage from discriminators, discriminators will add noise to loss g_loss_i:

$$g\_loss_i \leftarrow g\_loss_i + \mathcal{N}(0, \sigma) \tag{1}$$

Where Gaussian noise has distribution with mean 0 and standard deviation σ (we will discuss the noise level σ later).

To compute gradients, those discriminators randomly select one discriminator as a representative to collect other discriminators' noised loss and average all loss values:

$$g\_loss_t = \frac{1}{n} \sum_{1}^{n} g\_loss_i \tag{2}$$

Next, the representative discriminator will use the averaged loss as GAN loss to do backpropagation and compute the gradients. Then the global generator will update its parameters according to the gradients.

Because in every epoch, we randomly choose one discriminator as a representative to collect other discriminators' noised loss and compute gradients for the combination of GAN, it can be seen as this discriminator transfers some knowledge about its sensitive training dataset to the global generator. Because every discriminator is selected by random, after several epochs, every local discriminator can have the same chance to be selected and transfer its knowledge

Algorithm 1. Global Generator Aggregation

Input: n discriminators $\{D_i\}_n$, a generator G, fake dataset fake_data$_t$ for epoch $t \in (0, T)$, real datasets $\{real_1, real_2, ..., real_n\}$ for epoch $t \in (0, T)$

Parameter: Binary cross entropy loss for discriminators.

1: **for** epoch t in range $(0, T)$ **do**
2:     **Generate fake data**
3:     The generator G generates a batch of fake data: fake_data$_t \leftarrow G(z), z \sim p(z)$
4:     **Train n discriminators**
5:     Every discriminator D_i calculates the loss: $d_i\_real \leftarrow D_i(real_i)$ and $d_i\_fake \leftarrow D_i(\text{fake\_data}_t)$
6:     $d_i\_loss_t = \frac{1}{2}(d_i\_real + d_i\_fake)$
7:     Every discriminator D_i computes gradients according to $d_i\_loss_t$ and updates its parameters.
8:     Set discriminators untrainable.
9:     **Generate fake data**
10:     The generator G generates a new batch of fake data from noise z. fake$_t \leftarrow G(z), z \sim p(z)$
11:     **Compute loss**
12:     Every discriminator D_i predicts on that batch of generated fake data and calculates the loss.
13:     $g\_loss_i \leftarrow D_i(\text{fake}_t)$
14:     **Add noise**
15:     $g\_loss_i \leftarrow g\_loss_i + \mathcal{N}(0, \sigma)$
16:     **Average loss**
17:     Randomly select one discriminator D_s to collect other discriminators' noised loss and average the loss.
18:     $g\_loss_t = \frac{1}{n} \sum_1^n g\_loss_i$
19:     **Compute gradients**
20:     The selected discriminator D_s and G calculate the gradients according to g_loss_t for the GAN.
21:     **Generator updates parameters**
22:     The generator G updates its parameters according to the gradients.
23: **end for**
    Output: The global generator G.

to the global generator. Also, the GAN loss is the average of all discriminators' noised loss. Therefore, the global generator can capture the whole distribution features of all local parties' sensitive datasets.

3.3   How We Choose the Noise Level?

Because the scale of loss g_loss_i will change in every epoch of training, here we utilize an adaptive method to set the noise level σ.

As we can see, in every training epoch, the generator actually submits two batches of generated fake samples to discriminators. The first batch is used to train discriminators, while the second batch is the batch used to compute discriminators' loss g_loss_i.

In our scheme, we use the discriminator loss on the **first batch** of generated samples d_i_fake as the scale of noise added to loss g_loss_i, which is computed on the second batch of generated samples. We set $\sigma = 0.5 * d_i$_fake.

As we can see, these two batches of generated fake samples come from the same state of the generator, the loss on the first batch is computed by discriminators before updating, while the loss on the second batch is computed by discriminators after updating. These two loss will be close to each other. Therefore we can use the first batch discriminator loss as a reference to add noise. To avoid adding too much noise, we add a ratio as 0.5 to the noise level. That is because the discriminator loss on the first batch is supposed to be a little bit higher than the loss on the second batch, because the loss for the second batch is computed by the updated discriminator, which is supposed to be better at classifying samples than the discriminator before updating. So we add a ratio (less than 1) to reduce the noise scale. Of course, this ratio can be adjusted in different discriminators.

3.4   Why Adding Noise Can Secure Our Scheme?

Firstly, let's explain why we should provide privacy protection for discriminators. Because discriminators are trained based on local parties' private training datasets, sensitive information of training data could be encoded or reflected into discriminators' parameters. On the other hand, the global generator always tries to steal sensitive information from discriminators and their private training datasets.

What the global generator can obtain are the gradients computed based on discriminators' parameters. Let's see how noised discriminators' noise can prevent the global generator from stealing sensitive information from discriminators' parameters.

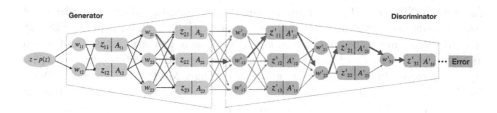

Fig. 1. An example of detailed GAN structure. (Color figure online)

We use a simple example shown in Fig. 1 to demonstrate how noised discriminators' loss will affect gradients. We only draw one discriminator here to represent the selected discriminator and the loss is averaged noised loss from all discriminators.

We take Generator's parameter W_{21} (shown in Fig. 1) as an example to compute gradient for W_{21}. We take one specific line (shown as the green line in Fig. 1) to demonstrate the computation. As we can see, the chain rule is:

$$\frac{\partial E}{\partial A'_{31}} \frac{\partial A'_{31}}{\partial Z'_{31}} \frac{\partial Z'_{31}}{\partial W'_{31}} \frac{\partial W'_{31}}{\partial A'_{21}} \frac{\partial A'_{21}}{\partial Z'_{21}} \frac{\partial Z'_{21}}{\partial W'_{22}} \cdots \frac{\partial Z_{22}}{\partial W_{21}} \tag{3}$$

As we can see, because E (discriminators' loss) in Eq. (3) is noised, $\frac{\partial E}{\partial A'_{31}}$ will be noised, so as $\frac{\partial A'_{31}}{\partial Z'_{31}}$, ... , so as $\frac{\partial Z_{22}}{\partial W_{21}}$, therefore the gradient for W_{21}: $\frac{\partial E}{\partial W_{21}}$ is noised. What the global generator obtained is the noised gradients.

Gradient for W_{11} will be a little bit different, because $Z_{11} = W_{11}X$, in which X are input samples, the gradient for W_{11}: ∂W_{11} will have X as coefficients. Notice that, those input samples X here are generated fake samples, not real samples. Even though the global generator might try to leverage well organized generated fake samples X to extract sensitive information from the gradient ∂W_{11}, because the gradient is noised, this intent will be handicapped due to the noise involved.

Therefore, adding noise to discriminators' loss can protect privacy of local parties' sensitive training datasets.

4 Evaluation

In this section, we evaluate the performance of our scheme on real-world datasets.

4.1 Implementation

We use deep convolutional generative adversarial network as our GAN structure. Deep convolutional generative adversarial network (DCGAN) [15] is an extension of GAN, in which generator and discriminator have deep convolutional network architectures.

We evaluate the performance of our scheme on MNIST and Fashion MNIST datasets. MNIST is a 10-class handwritten digit recognition dataset consisting of 60,000 training examples and 10,000 test examples [12], each example is a 28×28 size greyscale image. Similarly, Fashion MNIST is a 10-class dataset of fashion images, also consisting of 60,000 training examples and 10,000 testing examples [18], each example is a 28×28 size gray-level image. MNIST (produced in 1998) has been as a benchmark for machine learning and data science algorithms for years, and now Fashion MNIST (produced in 2017) serves as a replacement for the MNIST dataset for benchmarking machine learning algorithms.

We program our codes in Python, and execute them on Google Colab with free access to online GPU. We also use Tensorflow and Keras as backend. We develop different types of discriminators, they vary in numbers of layers and numbers of parameters. We equally split the training dataset among local parties, due to the limited number of training samples, we did not assume too many local parties, because more local parties will result in less training samples for every local discriminator and less accurate local discriminators can be achieved.

4.2 Experimental Results

We firstly aggregate a global generator from only one local party, in this case, the local discriminator will use the whole training datasets from MNIST (60,000 samples) and Fashion MNIST (60,000 samples). We train the global generator for 100 epochs with batch size as 256. After obtaining the global generator, we let it generate synthetic samples for MNIST and Fashion MNIST.

We also aggregate global generators from 5 and 10 different local discriminators, every local discriminator has 12,000 (5 local parties) and 6,000 (10 local parties) training samples from MNIST, 12,000 and 6,000 training samples from Fashion MNIST. We train the global generators for 200 epochs with batch size 128. After achieving the global generators, generators generate some fake samples.

In Fig. 2, we show some generated samples from two global generators. The left column are real samples from MNIST and Fashion MNIST. The middle column are generated samples from the global generator aggregated from one local party. The right column are from global generator aggregated from 5 local parties.

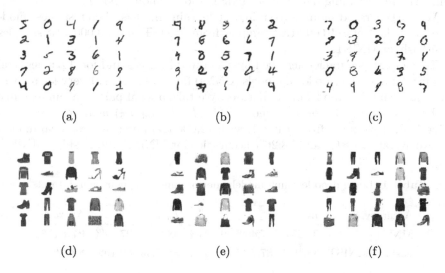

Fig. 2. Comparison between real samples and generated samples from global generators. The left column ((a), (d)) are real samples from MNIST and Fashion MNIST, the middle column ((b), (e)) are generated samples from the global generator aggregated from one local party, the right column ((c), (f)) are generated samples from the global generator aggregated from 5 local parties.

As shown in Fig. 2, generated samples look like real samples from MNIST and Fashion MNIST. Notice that, generated samples are a little bit blurry compared to real samples. The main reasons come from three aspects: firstly, GAN can not perfectly simulate real data, the quality of generated samples depend on the

GAN structure, the number of training epochs, and the training optimizer, etc. Secondly, because we split training datasets among local parties, the quality of generators will be affected by the amount of training data. Finally, the noise added to discriminators' loss will to some extent affect the ability of generators capturing features of real training data.

Compared with generated samples from generator aggregated from 5 local parties (right column of Fig. 2), with more training samples for local discriminators, generator aggregated from one local party produces higher-quality of generated samples (middle column of Fig. 2).

4.3   Performance Evaluation

After aggregating global generators, the global party can use those generators to generate synthetic data. To test the quality of generated synthetic data, we use generated samples to train deep learning models and test accuracies on real samples.

We let global generators generate the same amount of synthetic samples as training samples of MNIST and Fashion MNIST, so that, the global party can mimic the real training datasets of MNIST and Fashion MNIST.

We use generated samples to train deep learning models, then test these models on test datasets (10,000 test samples from MNIST and 10,000 test samples from Fashion MNIST).

To compare accuracies achieved by generated samples and local parties' real training data, we develop local models (CNNs) for local parties. Every local party trains its own CNN model on its dataset. We take 5 local parties as an example to show the accuracies of local models $(L_1, L_2, L_3, L_4, L_5)$ achieved, shown in Table 1. As we can see from Table 1, with 12,000 training samples, local models achieve average 97.81% and 88.26% accuracies for MNIST and Fashion MNIST.

Table 1. Local deep learning models' performance on their own datasets.

Accuracy	L_1	L_2	L_3	L_4	L_5	Average
MNIST	97.65%	97.40%	98.04%	98.21%	97.74%	**97.81%**
Fashion MNIST	88.10%	87.75%	87.59%	88.74%	89.10%	**88.26%**

We list test accuracies achieved by generated samples from global generators, local models' test accuracies and baselines in Table 2. The baselines are accuracies of machine learning models trained on the whole real MNIST and Fashion MNIST datasets and tested on real test datasets.

As seen in Table 2, generated synthetic samples from global generators can achieve accurate models. For MNIST and Fashion MNIST, when there are 5 and 10 local parties, models trained on generated synthetic samples achieve higher accuracies than local models trained solely on local parties' local training datasets. For example, when there are 5 local parties, local models trained on

Table 2. Accuracies achieved by generated samples from global generators.

Dataset	Local party	Local	Global	Baseline	Cmp to local	Cmp to Baseline
MNIST	1	99.20%	98.35%		-0.85%↓	-0.85%↓
	5	97.81%	98.02%	99.20%	+0.21%↑	-1.18%↓
	10	97.48%	97.65%		+0.17%↑	-1.55%↓
Fashion MNIST	1	92.40%	90.16%		-2.24%↓	-2.24%↓
	5	88.26%	88.54%	92.40%	+0.28%↑	-3.86%↓
	10	86.63%	86.87%		+0.24%↑	-5.53%↓

12,000 real samples achieve average 97.81% and 88.26% accuracies for MNIST and Fashion MNIST, while models trained on 60,000 generated samples from aggregated global generators can achieve 98.02% and 88.54% for MNIST and Fashion MNIST, increase 0.21% and 0.28% accuracies respectively. Similar results are shown for 10 local parties as well. These results indicate that aggregated global generators can generate high-quality synthetic samples.

On the other hand, when the global generator is aggregated from only one local party, compared with the local models with accuracies 99.20% and 92.40% trained on the whole training datasets of MNIST and Fashion MNIST, generated samples from global generators achieve less accurate models with 98.35% and 90.16% accuracies for MNIST and Fashion MNIST correspondingly. Generated synthetic samples bring 0.85% and 2.24% declines for MNIST and Fashion MNIST.

Compared with baselines for MNIST and fashion MNIST, which are achieved by whole real training datasets, generated samples from global generators are not as precise as real samples and achieve lower accuracies than baselines.

As a conclusion, from the experimental results, our scheme can achieve global generators with satisfying performance.

5   Related Works and Comparison

In this section, we illustrate some state-of-the-art works related to our study and compare our scheme with some of these related works.

There are some proposed methods for aggregating generators. Work [10] lets discriminators return intermediate feedback results of backpropagation for the generator to update. Work [13,17,19] use differentially private gradient descent (DP-SGD) to achieve differentially private GANs. Work [11] uses differential privacy on majority voting labelling plus a simple classifier to achieve a differentially private GAN.

Notice that, works [10,13] mentioned above only consider aggregating a global generator from same type and structure of discriminators, **while our scheme can generalize their methods and is also suitable for discriminators with different types and structures.** Moreover, in work [10], simply returning discriminators' intermediate feedback is not privacy-preserving for sensitive training datasets.

Works [11,13,17,19] use differential privacy during training, which need to use modified Tensorflow library (Tensorflow Privacy). Using this modified Tensorflow library can be extremely inefficient, according to open codes of work [17], training a differentially private GAN on MNIST can take over two hours on TPU.

We compare the accuracies achieved by generated samples from generators in our work and other three works [13,17,19] mentioned above. The comparison is presented in Table 3. Because these three related works actually achieve differentially private GANs (considered as the global generator aggregated from one local party), we only compare global generators aggregated from one local party. Due to lack of experimental results on Fashion MNIST dataset from these related works, we only list accuracies tested on MNIST dataset.

Table 3. Comparison of accuracies among three related works and ours.

Dataset	Scheme	Accuracy
MNIST	DP-GAN [19]	99.00%
	DP-CGAN [17]	88.16%
	Scalable DP-GAN [13]	80.92%
	Our scheme	**98.35%**

As shown from Table 3, our scheme can achieve higher accuracies compared with works [13,17]. With high privacy loss, work [19] can achieve slightly higher accuracy than our scheme.

6   Conclusion

Motivated by providing methods for global generator aggregation from different types of discriminators. We split GAN into two parts: discriminators in local parties and the global generator in the global party. Since parameters based aggregation fails, we use discriminator loss as vehicle to aggregate the global generator. We achieve two goals, we aggregate a global generator from different types of discriminators, and we achieve high-quality generators, from which generated samples would not reflect private features of local parties' sensitive training data. We test our scheme on two real-world datasets, experiments show that our scheme can achieve high-quality global generators.

References

1. Abadi, M., et al.: Deep learning with differential privacy. In: Proceedings of the 2016 ACM SIGSAC Conference on Computer and Communications Security, pp. 308–318. ACM (2016)

2. Beaulieu-Jones, B.K., Wu, Z.S., Williams, C., Greene, C.S.: Privacy-preserving generative deep neural networks support clinical data sharing. Biorxiv **10**, 159756 (2017)
3. Bonawitz, K., et al.: Practical secure aggregation for privacy-preserving machine learning. In: Proceedings of the 2017 ACM SIGSAC Conference on Computer and Communications Security, pp. 1175–1191. ACM (2017)
4. Dwork, C., Lei, J.: Differential privacy and robust statistics. Stoc **9**, 371–380 (2009)
5. Dwork, C., McSherry, F., Nissim, K., Smith, A.: Calibrating noise to sensitivity in private data analysis. In: Halevi, S., Rabin, T. (eds.) TCC 2006. LNCS, vol. 3876, pp. 265–284. Springer, Heidelberg (2006). https://doi.org/10.1007/11681878_14
6. Dwork, C., Roth, A., et al.: The algorithmic foundations of differential privacy. Found. Trends® Theor. Comput. Sci. **9**(3–4), 211–407 (2014)
7. Dwork, C., Rothblum, G.N.: Concentrated differential privacy (2016). arXiv preprint arXiv:1603.01887
8. Dwork, C., Rothblum, G.N., Vadhan, S.: Boosting and differential privacy. In: 2010 IEEE 51st Annual Symposium on Foundations of Computer Science, pp. 51–60. IEEE (2010)
9. Goodfellow, I., et al.: Generative adversarial nets. In: Advances in neural information processing systems, pp. 2672–2680 (2014)
10. Hardy, C., Le Merrer, E., Sericola, B.: Md-gan: Multi-discriminator generative adversarial networks for distributed datasets. In: 2019 IEEE International Parallel and Distributed Processing Symposium (IPDPS), pp. 866–877. IEEE (2019)
11. Jordon, J., Yoon, J., van der Schaar, M.: Pate-gan: Generating synthetic data with differential privacy guarantees (2018)
12. LeCun, Y., Bottou, L., Bengio, Y., Haffner, P.: Gradient-based learning applied to document recognition. Proc. IEEE **86**(11), 2278–2324 (1998)
13. Long, Y., Lin, S., Yang, Z., Gunter, C.A., Liu, H., Li, B.: Scalable differentially private data generation via private aggregation of teacher ensembles (2020). https://openreview.net/forum?id=Hkl6i0EFPH
14. Pathak, M., Rane, S., Raj, B.: Multiparty differential privacy via aggregation of locally trained classifiers. In: Advances in Neural Information Processing Systems, pp. 1876–1884 (2010)
15. Radford, A., Metz, L., Chintala, S.: Unsupervised representation learning with deep convolutional generative adversarial networks (2015). arXiv preprint arXiv:1511.06434
16. Shokri, R., Shmatikov, V.: Privacy-preserving deep learning. In: Proceedings of the 22nd ACM SIGSAC conference on computer and communications security, pp. 1310–1321. ACM (2015)
17. Torkzadehmahani, R., Kairouz, P., Paten, B.: Dp-cgan: Differentially private synthetic data and label generation. In: Proceedings of the IEEE Conference on Computer Vision and Pattern Recognition Workshops (2019)
18. Xiao, H., Rasul, K., Vollgraf, R.: Fashion-mnist: a novel image dataset for benchmarking machine learning algorithms (2017). arXiv preprint arXiv:1708.07747
19. Xie, L., Lin, K., Wang, S., Wang, F., Zhou, J.: Differentially private generative adversarial network (2018). arXiv preprint arXiv:1802.06739

Perturbing Smart Contract Execution Through the Underlying Runtime

Pinchen Cui$^{(\boxtimes)}$ and David Umphress

Computer Science and Software Engineering, Auburn University,
Auburn, AL 36849, USA
{pinchen,david.umphress}@auburn.edu

Abstract. Because the smart contract is the core element that enables blockchain systems to perform diverse and intelligent operations, the security of smart contracts significantly determines the reliability and availability of the blockchain applications. This work examines security from the perspective that, although a smart contract may be programmatically correct, the environment in which the smart contract is carried out is vulnerable. Adversaries do not need to necessarily concern themselves with how a smart contract is programmed or whether it is vulnerable; the integrity of the smart contract can be undermined by perturbing the output of smart contract execution. Such an approach does not rely on exploiting programming errors or vulnerabilities in smart contract verification and protection frameworks. Instead, it leverages the flaws in the underlying smart contract lifecycle and virtualization mechanisms. The Hyperledger Fabric platform is used to demonstrate the feasibility of the proposed attack.

Keywords: Blockchain · Hyperledger · Docker · Container · Smart contract · Security · Man in the middle

1   Introduction

A "smart contract" is a computation that is performed on a blockchain. The term is an oblique reference to the traditional notion of a legal contract in that it signifies signatories entering into some binding agreement regarding something. "Smart" signifies that software automatically triggered by the agreement carries out a series of actions that define the terms of the agreement; "contract" signifies that the results of the actions are recorded onto an indelible transaction ledger, such as a blockchain. The transactions themselves, once stored onto a blockchain, are considered, for the most part, secure. Executing the smart contract, on the other hand, raises questions. How open to vulnerabilities is the "smart" part of "smart contracts"?

On the one hand, the security of a smart contract relies on how formal and secure the contract has been programmed. Since the smart contract is designed

© ICST Institute for Computer Sciences, Social Informatics and Telecommunications Engineering 2020
Published by Springer Nature Switzerland AG 2020. All Rights Reserved
N. Park et al. (Eds.): SecureComm 2020, LNICST 336, pp. 336–349, 2020.
https://doi.org/10.1007/978-3-030-63095-9_22

to be a public application, any internal programming vulnerabilities can incur enormous influence on all the contract users. Therefore, several evaluation and verification frameworks at the programming level [1–6] have been proposed. These frameworks and tools evaluate the validity and security of smart contracts at the programming level by creating certain rules and boundaries for smart contract programming. With the examination of the smart contract code context, the smart contract can be converted, compiled, and regulated to a secure form. These frameworks focus on the security of the smart contract only in the Ethereum platform[1]. While there exists another platform, Hyperledger[2], which provides competitive smart contract functionalities, no similar smart contract security investigation is evident.

On the other hand, the environment in which the smart contract is carried out also determines security. We take the perspective of an adversary that does not care how the smart contract is programmed, as long as we can interfere or manipulate the output of smart contract execution and thus bypass any verification and protection frameworks that might be in place. We attempt to illustrate the flaws of the underlying smart contract life-cycle or virtualization mechanism (runtime), namely, the Ethereum Virtual Machine in Ethereum and the Docker container environment in Hyperledger Fabric. Since the smart contract installation and execution in Ethereum and Fabric are different, we mainly focus to investigate the potential security risks in the Hyperledger Fabric system.

The contribution of this paper can be summarized as follows:

- We elicit a new attack vector in the smart contract ecosystem. Instead of focusing on smart contract programming, we propose to perturb the smart contract execution at the life-cycle and runtime level.
- A detailed case study on Hyperledger Fabric has been performed, which proves the possibility and feasibility of the proposed attack.
- We briefly discuss and analyze the practicability of launching this attack on Ethereum and other platforms.
- A new threat model of smart contract systems has been created based on the findings in this paper.
- We summarize and demonstrate the limitations and countermeasures of the proposed attack.

2   Background

A smart contract is an automated agreement enforced by tamper-proof execution of computer code [7]. In the context of blockchain, smart contracts are scripts stored on a blockchain system and which enable users to perform general-purpose computations on the blockchain. Smart contracts can be applied to various fields,

---

[1] https://github.com/ethereum/wiki/wiki/White-Paper.
[2] https://www.hyperledger.org.

including B2B international transfers, central clearing, mortgages, and crowd-funding [8]. The use of smart contract enhances the integrity, traceability, and transparency of data, and further benefits the applications in many domains.

To date, only a few platforms provide a full implementation of a smart contract. Two of the most successful and widely deployed implementations are Ethereum and Hyperledger Fabric (or Hyperledger, since many other sub-projects and blockchain applications are developed under the Hyperledger umbrella). Smart contract can be triggered by different nodes in blockchain network, these nodes can be different architecture-based and operating system-based. Ethereum and Hyperledger use different methods to ensure the smart contract can be run on all nodes and generate the same result. However, the core concept is the same: via virtualization. Ethereum adopts a virtual machine mechanism similar to the Java Virtual Machine, named Ethereum Virtual Machine (EVM). EVM is a stack machine that executes bytecode transformed from a high-level smart contract programming language (Solidity or Vyper). EVM is an embedded component of an Ethereum node client, which automatically runs in memory. In contrast, Hyperledger uses a Docker container to execute the smart contract. The smart contract in Hyperledger can be written in Go, Java, or NodeJS. The code is packaged and instantiated as a Docker container in the Hyperledger node's system. Each smart contract runs as a container, more details are described in Sect. 3.

3   Case Study: Attack on Hyperledger Fabric

In this section, we perform a case study on the Hyperledger Fabric platform to investigate the feasibility of perturbing the smart contract execution via runtime

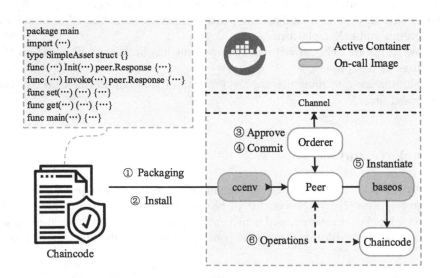

Fig. 1. Chaincode life cycle in hyperledger

vulnerabilities. The entire case study is based on the official Hyperledger network test example, *Byfn* network. We demonstrate the chaincode (the alias for the smart contract in Fabric) life-cycle and Docker environment of Hyperledger Fabric system before introducing the vulnerability itself.

3.1 Chaincode Life Cycle

Figure 1 illustrates the life-cycle of chaincode in the Docker containers that Hyperledger uses as its runtime environment. The following steps transpire when a Hyperledger blockchain peer tries to launch and test a piece of chaincode (starting in the top left corner of Fig. 1):

1. Packaging: The *Peer* first packages the chaincode into a tar format file.
2. Install: The compressed package is delivered to all the peers that need to run/endorse the chaincode. These peers build, compile, and install the chaincode locally.
3. Definition Approve: Corresponding channel members vote on and approve the definition of the chaincode, which includes such information as name, version, and endorsement policy (i.e., who can execute and validate).
4. Commit: Upon a success approval, a commit transaction proposal is submitted to the *Orderer*, which then commits the chaincode definition to the channel.
5. Instantiate: The complied chaincode is added into a base image to create the real instance of chaincode container.
6. Operations: Chaincode invoke and query operations are carried out by the communication between the peer container and chaincode container.

Throughout this procedure, the *Orderer* and *Peer* container are active all the time. The *ccenv* container, which is the chaincode environment container provides the functionalities of installation and instantiation. The *ccenv* is an offline docker image that only becomes an active container when there is a chaincode that needs to be processed. The *baseos* image is always offline.

3.2 Threat Model

In this case study, we identified two threats in the container runtime: insecure communication and loose image management. In the insecure communication threat, we assume the adversary may not have root privilege on the host machine, but he/she has access to the Docker network, images, and containers. This can be achieved using a pre-planted backdoor, malicious docker image, and/or remote control. The communication of the victim can be eavesdropped, intercepted, and modified by the adversary. The adversary can be an unrelated third party or an insider. The prerequisites of these attacks may enable the adversary to damage the system in a more severe and obvious way, but the major motivation of the adversary is to bias, perturb, and stop the service of the chaincode. We further assume the adversary can deliver malicious docker images to victims in the loose image management threat.

The detailed attacks and consequences are presented in Subsects. 3.3, 3.4 and 5.1. For the chaincode invoke operations, the adversary can intercept and manipulate the original input to chaincode using a malicious image, and the faulty data would be added into the blockchain. The adversary can also modify the local chaincode execution result returned to the user using Man-in-the-Middle (MITM) channel (and/or malicious image), thus the transaction proposal of the chaincode invocation will be failed during the endorsement procedure. Namely, the DoS of the smart contract can be achieved.

On the other hand, the adversary can intercept the return results of the chaincode query operations using MITM and/or malicious image, so the query of chaincode data can be manipulated by the adversary.

3.3 Insecure Communication

The operations to an instantiated chaincode in Hyperledger are based on the communication between the *Peer* container and *Chaincode* container. We sniffed the communication traffic between these two containers while a query operation was taking place. As shown in Fig. 2, the communication was TLS v1.2 enabled, the encryption of the communication was based on ECDH Key Exchange, and the authentication was provided by mutual certificate verification. Normally, we should presume the communication is secure and reliable. However, the vulnerability came from a permissioned blockchain and Docker container.

Fig. 2. Communication and handshake between the peer and chaincode containers

The permissioned blockchain requires the network to be a designated group of organizations and entities, and the enforcement of the network regulation relies on authentication. In other words, all the entities need to have corresponding certificates and keys for further verification. All the cryptographic materials are pre-generated and shared in the entire network *by loading them into the container at the point the container is created*. This creates a problem: all the keys and certificates are stored in the user space of both host and container. Figure 3

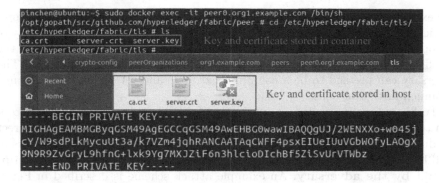

Fig. 3. Unencrypted key and certificates stored in host and containers

shows the accessible keys and certificates stored in host and container, which are also stored in an unencrypted manner.

The Hyperledger project provides a *Cryptogen* binary to help users tailor their cryptographic materials. Users can change the location of the keystore, change the key format and length, and create encrypted keys and certificates, but such information has to be loaded and stored into containers. Hyperledger containers come with root privileges, which provides access to keys. **As long as an adversary has access to any container, he/she has access to this material.** Hyperledger adopts ECDH key exchange, which is secure for

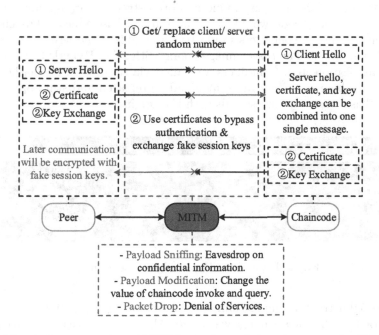

Fig. 4. Demonstration of MITM attack on chaincode communication

key exchange over an unencrypted channel. However, the overall "secure communication" relies on a mutual certificate authentication because the identity of the opposite entity can not be confirmed without it [9]. We discovered that the certificates are accessible on all the containers and can be compromised. The adversary can pretend to be a compromised node and set up a MITM channel to launch further attacks.

Traffic redirection tools (e.g. iptables and ARP spoofing) and TLS interception tools (e.g., SSLProxy[3]) make it relatively easy for an adversary to redirect the duo-direction communication between the *Peer* and *Chaincode* containers to a MITM agent. **All the operations to the chaincode can be then manipulated by the adversary**. An example attack scheme is described in Fig. 4. Note that, besides the *Peer-Chaincode* communication, there is another vulnerable point. **The communication between the *Client* (user command-line tool/ container that used to send the requests to Peer) and *Peer* can be the target of MITM attack as well.**

After this stage, the attack becomes an engineering task of forging all the malicious packets. This is obviously nontrivial, but feasible. We have plans to explore this further in the future; the aim of the current work is to suggest looking to the environment within which the secure contract executes for possible vulnerabilities.

3.4 Loose Image Management

As shown in Fig. 1, the chaincode container is created by loading chaincode binary file into the *baseos* image. One potential strategy for circumventing the integrity of the chaincode would be to poison the base image, thus ensuring subsequent chaincode containers would be vulnerable if the *baseos* image were modified or replaced. The *baseos* image, along with other Hyperledger container images, are ill protected. Containers are called via tags instead of hashes. This means that a benign image can be modified or replaced and still appear to be valid if it has a tag that corresponds with the original.

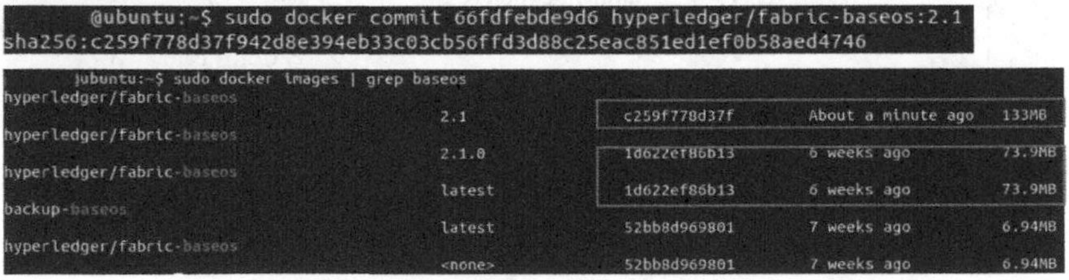

Fig. 5. Replace the Hyperledger baseos image

Figure 5 illustrates a simple example of such an image alteration. The original on Hyperledger v2.1 *baseos* image was Linux Alpine based, with an image size of

---

[3] https://github.com/sonertari/SSLproxy.

6.94 MB. We replaced all the versions of *baseos* image to a Ubuntu-based image of 73.9 MB. In addition, we modified the clean Ubuntu image with Python and some other libraries installed, which also has been committed to *baseos* image version 2.1. **We observed that all the chaincode containers created after this image alteration were installed with Python and additional libraries**.

In this case, if the adversary can either redirect the user to download a malicious image or somehow modify/replace the image, the entire system can be corrupted. The adversary can load customized code, autorun rootkit, revert channel backdoor, and cryptocurrency miner program into the malicious image. These malicious images can lead to denial of services, abuse of resources, unauthorized access, and information leaking. One can also use the malicious image to launch the aforementioned MITM attacks.

Fig. 6. Dev-chaincode containers on-the-fly

This naive attack can work because the Hyperledger container life-cycle environment calls all the images with tags. Image integrity is guaranteed in the Docker container system using hashes. The system can ensure a particular image has not been modified using hash but it cannot stop the tag from being written another image. The adversary can re-assign the corresponding tag to malicious images. Although the hashes are inherently provided by Docker engine, it is apparently more convenient, albeit incautious, to use the human-readable but less secure tags in the life-cycle. Moreover, besides the *baseos* image, all the other Hyperledger images are vulnerable as well. The orderer, CA, and peer images are all free for modification and replacement. Each installed and instantiated chaincode will be mapped with a container image as well (shown in Fig. 6), these images that generated on-the-fly can be also attacked.

3.5 Risks Behind Docker

Hyperledger outsources Docker as the chaincode runtime, and its security is then bounded with Docker container security, which basically doubles the attack surface. The adversary can utilize the vulnerability of Docker to perform much more severe attacks. For example, one can combine a malicious image with reverse shell and Docker escape attack to gain the root access of the host system[4]. This can lead the attacker to have full control of the entire system. An example set up is shown and described in Fig. 7, where upon the invocation of the malicious image, a reverse shell establishes and returns with the root access of the victim's host. If the adversary replaces the *baseos* image with this malicious one,

---

[4] https://cve.mitre.org/cgi-bin/cvename.cgi?name=CVE-2019-5736.

the entire chaincode system is disrupted. Note that the malicious docker images problem has been of concern for some time. By uploading malicious images into Docker Hub, an unscrupulous actor can generate $90,000 dollars from the million downloads and deployments of these malicious images in 10 months[5].

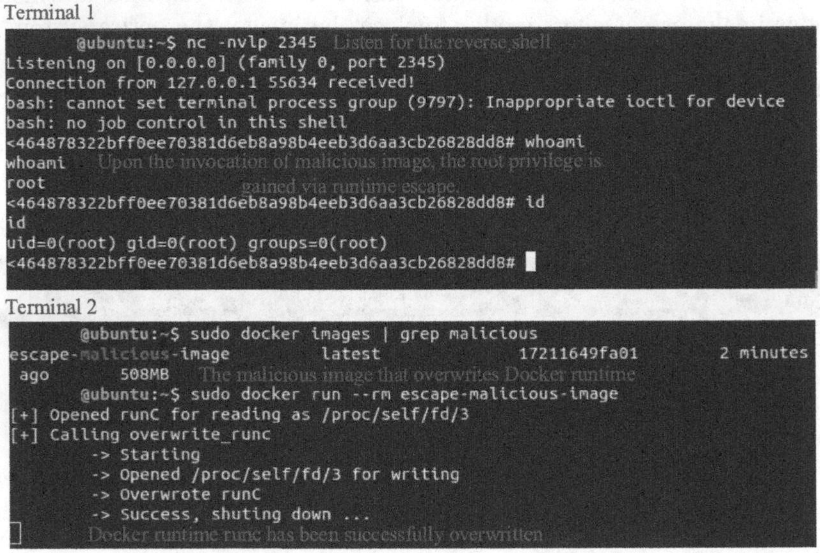

Terminal 1

Terminal 2

Fig. 7. Gain root access on host via malicious image: this attack allows the adversary to inject any code in docker runtime (runc), and the code will be executed on host with root privilege. This example simply injects "$bash - i > \&/dev/tcp/0.0.0.0/23450 > \&1\&$" into runc, and a reverse shell with root access on victim's host will be created.

Complicating things further, Docker and Docker Compose are normally configured to be user-space applications. Since it is not practical, efficient, and secure in a production environment to ask all the persistent container operations for root privileges, the Docker environment can be significantly manipulated even without root access on the host system. Issuing Docker commands on the host can be another threat to the chaincode system. One can stop and re-run a chaincode container to break the established TLS connection with *Peer* container, thus, the sniffing and MITM can be launched at any time. One can run the containers with privileged mode, so the *iptables* and all the other kernel-related system calls are enabled in the container for further malicious objectives (e.g., setup network forwarding rules and divert channels, and load malicious kernel modules).

---

[5] https://arstechnica.com/information-technology/2018/06/backdoored-images-downloaded-5-million-times-finally-removed-from-docker-hub/.

4   What About Ethereum and Others?

Generally, it may seem that Ethereum is more secure than Hyperledger since its runtime, EVM, is a customized in-memory stack machine. We focus on Hyperledger is not only because it is less discussed or arguably less secure, but also due to the fact that EVM has already been attacked in a similar form. Both EVM stack overflow attacks[10,11] and CVE-2018-18920 (an internal flaw of python implementation of EVM)[6] attacks perturb the normal execution of smart contract based on the vulnerabilities in EVM implementation. These two attacks can infinitely trigger the smart contract functions without corresponding gas and payments, which also do not rely on any programming faults in the smart contract. Although these two vulnerabilities have been already fixed, the concept of our proposed attack is verified.

A research question is whether it is possible to attack the EVM without a zero-day vulnerability. Because EVM is a program running in the local system, it can be perturbed if the system owner (or the adversary with the same privilege) decides to do so. Indeed, any program and applications can be attacked in this manner as well, this type of attack is beyond the scope of "attack on the runtime". A smart contract is different from the other application scenarios. **Since the contracts are immutable and reliable hardcoded programs in the blockchain, altering the execution or the result of smart contracts even in a more general manner would still be interesting.** One potential direction is to locate the EVM stack and memory locations in physical memory space and use the *process_vm_writev()* system call to transfer and inject data into that memory location, thus altering execution.

We note that there exist some other smart contract platforms, such as EOSIO and NEO EOSIO adopts a customized web assembly virtual machine (EOS-VM) to transform a C++ smart contract, making the code executable across platforms. NEO uses an enriched EVM-style stack machine to execute the smart contract. Generally, the threats and concerns of all other VM-like runtimes would be similar to the EVM.

5   Lessons Learned

5.1   Limitation and Impact of the Proposed Attack

Altering smart contract execution requires access to the runtime environment and/or certain vulnerabilities present at runtime. Access to the runtime environment may lead to other security concerns and make the perturbation unnecessary. For example, the adversary can simply remove the Docker engine from the victim's system, thus achieving DoS. Similarly, one can block the EVM implementation and Ethereum client from normal functioning by setting up certain network rules or checkpoints (via debugger). We notice that the assumption of having partial access to the system is a strong assumption, but note that all the

---

[6] https://cve.mitre.org/cgi-bin/cvename.cgi?name=CVE-2018-18920.

aforementioned attacks in Hyperledger can still be performed without access to the system, as long as a malicious image is delivered.

The detailed attack consequences depend on the type of container/commu nication compromised by the adversary:

- Orderer Container: Gaining control of the orderer container allows an adversary to i) partially DoS the blockchain network by dropping transactions sent to the orderer node; or ii) perturb the overall transaction propagation in the orderer cluster.
- Peer Container and/or Chaincode Container: The adversary can use a compromised container to send malicious chaincode invocations (the input to chaincode is manipulated), so the final data uploaded into blockchain can be manipulated. Although the users can find out the wrong values added in the blockchain and examine the local system afterward, the faulty data has been already uploaded.
- Communication between Peer and Chaincode Containers: When the user invokes/queries a chaincode, an adversary can DoS or perturb this chaincode execution procedure using the MITM channel. The modification on invocation execution results leads to the failed transaction endorsements, thus DoS of chaincode can be achieved. The modification on query execution results enables the adversary to manipulate the chaincode query functionality and fool the victim.

5.2 Countermeasure to the Proposed Attack

Aforementioned problems can be solved in the following way:

- Malicious Image: The Hyperledger system should regulate all the invocation of containers to be bound with hashes instead of tags. Each time a container image is called, the hash needs to be compared, including the on-the-fly generated chaincode images.
- Access Control: If it is not necessary, all the Hyperledger containers should be run in root-less mode. This may need additional libraries installed on the host and further supports from Docker community [7]. This can limit the adversary from accessing the keys and certificates.
- Communication Security: The adversary can obtain access to the private keys for further communication manipulation due to the confidential cryptographic material loaded into containers. This is a side-effect of malicious image and loose access control, and the problem can be fixed only if the previous two are properly handled. However, the use of containers also adds an additional communication layer between the peer and installed chaincode. Note that, the chaincode is installed locally per Peer, which means the *Chaincode* container and *Peer* container are running in the same machine. For the local system data exchanging between *Chaincode* container and *Peer* container, network-based

---

[7] https://docs.docker.com/engine/security/rootless/.

communication is not the only option. Docker supports shared memory (inter-process communication (IPC) namespace) for inter-container data exchange. Using IPC between *Chaincode* container and *Peer* container can eliminate the risk in network-based communication.

5.3   Threat Model of Smart Contract Systems

Based on the findings in this paper, a new threat model of the smart contract system is established and shown in Fig. 8. The threats can be divided into two levels, smart contract programming level [11], and runtime level. The threats in smart contract programming level are either caused by programming flaws or backdoors. The programming flaws including external dependence (e.g., re-entrancy, delegatecall injection), improper validations (e.g., integer overflow and underflow), and inadequate authentication or authorization (e.g., erroneous visibility, unprotected suicide). The backdoors are intentionally planted malicious functions, they may not violate any programming rules or fall in any programming flaw definitions. However, they can be used to trigger blockchain operations that can potentially prejudice the interests of others.

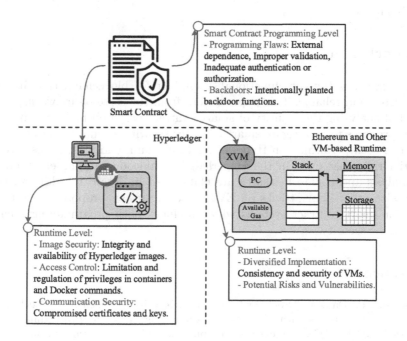

Fig. 8. Threat model of smart contract system

The runtime level threats in Hyperledger-based blockchain are bound to Docker container security. The integrity and availability of Hyperledger images significantly determine the security of the chaincode system. If the access control in the Docker environment is not appropriately configured, keys and certificates can be accessed without authorization. The Docker commands that can be issued as a non-root user can also harm the chaincode system. For example, an evil insider can easily stop the containers to perturb and even DoS the blockchain system. The insecure communication and loose image management threats presented in this paper also need concerns.

On the other hand, the Ethereum-based smart contract system suffers from the diversified EVM implementations. Hyperledger adopts a single standardized runtime Docker as the universal chaincode runtime, whereas Ethereum provides different implementations of EVMs. As stated in [12], the gas and opcode consistency problem have been already found in different EVM implementations. Moreover, maintaining and ensuring the security of all the EVM implementations are non-trivial and challenging tasks. The attack in CVE-2018-18920 just utilizes the flaws in the Python version of EVM implementation. Some of the other potential risks are also indicated in the work [13]. As the development and maintenance of EVM continue, the security of Ethereum runtime needs more concern. Other VM-based runtime blockchains such as EOSIO and NEO may confront the same problems, however, the security analysis on these two platforms is limited.

6   Conclusion

Smart contract is the core functionality enabler for blockchain, thus it needs to be secure and reliable. This paper differs from the state-of-art works, which instead of analyzing the security of smart contract based on programming validation, proposes to investigate smart contract security at runtime level. A case study has been performed on Hyperledger blockchain, and we demonstrate the potential risks that exist in the Hyperledger chaincode runtime environment. The analysis and countermeasures are elaborated in detail. In addition, combining with other prior attacks on EVM mechanism, we propose a new threat model for smart contract systems which includes both programming security and runtime security.

References

1. Tsankov, P., Dan, A., Drachsler-Cohen, D., Gervais, A., Buenzli, F., Vechev, M.: Securify: practical security analysis of smart contracts. In: Proceedings of the 2018 ACM SIGSAC Conference on Computer and Communications Security, ACM (2018)
2. Park, D., Zhang, Y., Saxena, M., Daian, P., Roşu, G.: A formal verification tool for Ethereum VM bytecode. In: Proceedings of the 2018 26th ACM Joint Meeting on European Software Engineering Conference and Symposium on the Foundations of Software Engineering, pp. 912–915. ACM (2018)

3. Hildenbrandt, E. et al.: Kevm: a complete formal semantics of the ethereum virtual machine. In: 2018 IEEE 31st Computer Security Foundations Symposium (CSF), pp. 204–217. IEEE (2018)
4. Wohrer, M., Zdun, U.: Smart contracts: security patterns in the ethereum ecosystem and solidity. In: 2018 International Workshop on Blockchain Oriented Software Engineering (IWBOSE), pp. 2–8. IEEE (2018)
5. Perez, D., Livshits, B.: Smart contract vulnerabilities: Does anyone care? (2019). arXiv preprint arXiv:1902.06710
6. Brent, L. et al.: Vandal: a scalable security analysis framework for smart contracts (2018)
7. Clack, C.D., Bakshi, V.A., Braine, L.: Smart contract templates: foundations, design landscape and research directions (2016)
8. Cui, P., Guin, U., Skjellum, A., Umphress, D.: Blockchain in IoT: current trends, challenges, and future roadmap. J. Hardware Syst. Secur. 3(4), 338–364 (2019). https://doi.org/10.1007/s41635-019-00079-5
9. Adrian, D. et al.: Imperfect forward secrecy: how diffie-hellman fails in practice. In: Proceedings of the 22nd ACM SIGSAC Conference on Computer and Communications Security, pp. 5–17 (2015)
10. Atzei, N., Bartoletti, M., Cimoli, T.: A survey of attacks on Ethereum smart contracts (SoK). In: Maffei, M., Ryan, M. (eds.) POST 2017. LNCS, vol. 10204, pp. 164–186. Springer, Heidelberg (2017). https://doi.org/10.1007/978-3-662-54455-6_8
11. Chen, H., Pendleton, M., Njilla, L., Xu, S.: A survey on Ethereum systems security: vulnerabilities, attacks and defenses. ACM Comput. Surv. 53(3), 1–43 (2020). https://doi.org/10.1145/3391195
12. Fu, Y., Ren, M., Ma, F., Jiang, Y., Shi, H., Sun, J.: Evmfuzz: differential fuzz testing of Ethereum virtual machine (2019)
13. Fu, Y. et al.: Evmfuzzer: detect EVM vulnerabilities via fuzz testing. In: Proceedings of the 2019 27th ACM Joint Meeting on European Software Engineering Conference and Symposium on the Foundations of Software Engineering, pp. 1110–1114 (2019)

Blockchain Based Multi-keyword Similarity Search Scheme over Encrypted Data

Mingyue Li[1,2], Chunfu Jia[1,2(✉)], and Wei Shao[1,2]

[1] College of Cyber Science, Nankai University, Tianjin, China
{limingyue,wei.shao}@mail.nankai.edu.cn, cfjia@nankai.edu.cn
[2] Tianjin Key Laboratory of Network and Data Security Technology,
Nankai University, Tianjin, China

Abstract. Traditional searchable encryption schemes focus on preventing an honest-but-curious server. In practice, cloud servers may delete user data, perform partial queries and even falsify search results to save computing and storage resources. Although there is some previous work to verify the correctness of search results, these verification mechanisms are highly dependent on the specially appointed index structures.

In this paper, we propose a blockchain based multi-keyword similarity search scheme over encrypted data (BMSSED), which is a general scheme that keeps users from worrying about potential misbehaviors of a malicious server. To solve the problem that the size of transactions is limited, we use an index partition method to divide the traditional binary tree index into a plurality of sub-indexes. The new structure of sub-indexes not only circumvents the *gasLimit* problem, but also reduces the dimension of file vectors and improves the search efficiency using smart contracts. In addition, we propose an access control mechanism for transaction data, which is implemented by a new smart contract. It can reduce the computation burden of data owners and prevent the leakage of confidential information. We then define the security model and conduct repeated experiments on real data sets to test the efficiency. Experimental results and theoretical analysis show the practicability and security of our scheme.

Keywords: Searchable encryption · Blockchain · Ethereum · Smart contract · Access control.

1 Introduction

With the rapid development of computer technology and Internet applications, the demand for data access and information storage is increasing [1]. Although cloud computing enables users to enjoy high-quality services and ubiquitous network access, outsourcing data to cloud servers makes data owners lose the control over their sensitive data, resulting in data privacy disclosure [2,3]. To

N. Park et al. (Eds.): SecureComm 2020, LNICST 336, pp. 350–371, 2020.
https://doi.org/10.1007/978-3-030-63095-9_23

protect data privacy, the data owners usually opt to encrypt their data before outsourcing to clouds. This in turn limits the availability of encrypted data, e.g., the widely used keyword retrieval technology of plaintext information cannot be directly applied to encrypted data. To address this problem, Song et al. [4] firstly proposed a searchable encryption scheme based on ciphertext scanning that enables users to store encrypted data in clouds and perform keyword searches on the ciphertext domain. Their scheme is simple to implement and has virtually no additional storage overhead. Subsequently, much effort has been devoted to designing effective mechanisms to enable search over encrypted data.

Traditional searchable encryption (SE) schemes focus on problems brought by an honest-but-curious server. More severely, any insider attacker may use discovered vulnerabilities and unlawfully alter the computations performed over the outsourced data. Recently, there is some work proposing verifiable designs that enable the data owner to verify the correctness and integrity of search results and outsourced data (e.g., using MHST [5] or verifiable matrix [6]). Unfortunately, these verification mechanisms are highly dependent on specially appointed index structures and do not support expressive queries or complex data structures (e.g., fuzzy search [7], similarity search [8,10] or multimedia data [9]).

With the emergence of blockchain, symmetric searchable encryption (SSE) scheme based on Bitcoin was proposed to guarantee the privacy and confidentiality of data. However, the transaction cycle of Bitcoin system is long. Besides, its script language is not Turing complete and cannot be applied to more scenarios. Therefore, Hu et al.[11] proposed a symmetric searchable encryption scheme based on Ethereum blockchain and smart contract. This scheme not only ensures the privacy of data, but also solves the problem of fairness of retrieval. Subsequently, there is some work based on Ethereum [12]. Nevertheless, they focus on single-keyword queries and cannot meet actual demands of users. More importantly, all of the above schemes control who has access to the data through data owners. That is to say, if Bob wants to access transactions of Alice, he has to send the query keywords to Alice. Alice asserts Bob have permissions according to the access control list stored locally and generates trapdoor for executing query (or Alice sends the trapdoor to Bob). Meanwhile, Alice has to pay for $Search(\cdot)$ function in advance. There is no doubt that Alice has a huge computational burden, which violates the original intention of outsourcing.

1.1   Our Contributions

To address the above concerns, we propose a blockchain based multi-keyword similarity search scheme over encrypted data (BMSSED), utilizing smart contracts in Ethereum [11] to allow users of different roles to request access permission and interact with confidential documents. To give an exemplary instantiation, we build BMSSED on the classic binary tree index [10] and design the corresponding smart contract to circumvent various barriers in Ethereum. For example, the size of the binary tree index increases as the amount of data increases. If the size of an index is larger than the maximum of $gasLimit$, then blockchain network will reject the transaction. Therefore, we divide the binary tree in [10] to break the limit (see discussion in Subsect. 3.1 for details). In addition, to reduce the computation burden of client and simplify the query process, we novelly use smart contract to create an access control mechanism, where data owners write access control policy, roles, permissions and other information of data users to a smart contract and install it on each node. Before executing the $Search(\cdot)$ function, the access control policy is executed in advance. Note that our framework is a general one, which can be better applied to many practical scenarios (e.g., management of personal electronic medical profiles). Generally, the main contributions are as follows.

– We design a new index partition method to avoid exceeding $gasLimit$ and improve the query efficiency. If the size of an index tree is greater than the maximum value of $gasLimit$, we divide the traditional binary tree index into multiple sub-indexes and embed each sub-index into transactions. After that the transactions are sorted in ascending order of their keys, added to blocks in turn and written to disk in block order.
– Considering the complicated query process and the huge computational burden of data owners, we novelly use smart contracts to create an access control mechanism. Meanwhile, to simplify the access control mechanism and avoid the complexity of individual authorization policies, we use an effective role-based access control (RBAC) strategy to check whether users have access to transaction data.
– We accomplish a prototype of our scheme and also deploy it to a locally simulated network and an Ethereum test network as [11]. We conduct repeated experiments on real data sets. Experimental results and theoretical analysis show the practicability and security of our scheme over encrypted data.

1.2   Related Work

To fulfill the retrieval of encrypted data, Song et al. [4] firstly proposed a searchable encryption scheme based on ciphertext scanning, where each plaintext is divided into equal length keywords. This scheme uses the double-layered XOR encryption to encrypt each keyword in plaintext by the stream cipher. Authorized users only provide the encrypted keywords to the server. The server makes a linear query for the encrypted files and returns the search results. The cryptographic model of the scheme is simple. There is no additional storage space overhead. However, the statistical distribution of plaintext is vulnerable to attack. In addition, retrieval performance is limited by the size of files. Considering the problems of retrieval efficiency and security, much effort has been devoted to enabling search over encrypted data [13–16].

However, the above schemes are based on the ideal assumption, that is, cloud servers are honest-but-curious. In practice, cloud servers may delete user data and perform partial queries or falsify search results to save computing and storage resources. To verify the correctness and integrity of the search results, Chen and Zhu [5] designed the structure of minimum hash subtree (MHST). The cloud server returns the MHST and the root signature to the data owner (or data user). The client uses the MHST to recalculate the hash value of the node for verification. To resist the malicious behavior of cloud servers, Wan and Deng [8] designed a trusted privacy protection keyword search scheme (VPSearch). The VPSearch scheme generates a binary vector for each keyword and uses homomorphic MAC (Message Authentication Code) technology to check the authenticity of the returned ciphertext. Liu et al. [6] proposed a dynamically verifiable SSE scheme that allows a user to perform a top-k search on a set of dynamic files while effectively verifying the correctness of search results. In this scheme, file nodes are ordered according to their ranks for such a keyword. The information about a node's prior/following neighbor is encoded with the RSA accumulator. Zhang et al. [17] proposed a verifiable keyword ranking retrieval scheme based on deterrence. Throughout the verification process, the cloud server cannot know which data owners, or how many data owners exchange anchor data that will be used for verifying the misbehavior of a cloud server. To recapitulate, these authentication mechanisms are highly dependent on the encrypted query index structure. It lacks a verification mechanism suitable for all search schemes.

The decentralized and tamper-proof characteristics of blockchain can prevent user data from malicious tampering and ensure the correctness of search results. There are many works about blockchain recently. Ron and Shamir [18] made a quantitative analysis of the full Bitcoin transaction graph. Vitalik et al. [19] firstly introduced smart contract to Bitcoin systems and proposed Ethereum. Andrychowicz et al. [20] and Bentov and Kumaresan [21] introduced Bitcoin to multi-party computing to solve the fairness problem. Swan put forward several blockchain schemes that can be applied to [22], one of which is Blockchain health. It provides a framework for storing health medical data on the blockchain. Patients who place their own electronic medical records (EMR) on the blockchain can obtain a certain amount of healthy coin.

Unfortunately, the above schemes fail to give an effective search method. Therefore, Li et al. [23] proposed a searchable symmetric encryption scheme based on blockchain. The scheme stores encrypted data and indexes on the blockchain and realizes the effective query of encrypted data in blocks. However, the script language of Bitcoin is not Turing complete and cannot be applied to more scenarios. Therefore, Tahir and Rajarajan [24] proposed a new privacy protection framework to fulfill keyword search for ciphertext stored on blockchain networks. The framework firstly implements a searchable encryption scheme based on probabilistic trapdoor on Hyperledger Fabric. The probabilistic trapdoor can resist distinguishable attacks and ensure a higher level of security and privacy for the scheme. Hu et al. [11] built a decentralized, reliable and fair search scheme by replacing cloud servers with smart contract to ensure that data owners can obtain correct search results without worrying about malicious servers. Shortly afterwards, Chen [25] proposed blockchain based searchable encryption for electronic health records (EHR) sharing on the basis of Hu et al.'s scheme. The index of EHRs is constructed by complex logical expressions and is stored in smart contract, so that data users can use expressions to search for indexes.

2   Preparatory Knowledge

2.1   Ethereum

Ethereum is a new and open source blockchain platform where users can write code that controls digital assets runs exactly as programmed, and is accessible anywhere in the world. The top layer of its architecture is decentralized applications (DApp) that exchanges through the web3.js with the smart contract layer. All smart contracts run on the EVM and call the Remote Procedure Call (RPC) protocol. The EVM and RPC support four core elements of the Ethereum, including the Blockchain, the Consensus algorithm, the Miner and the Network layer. As a whole, Ethereum provides us with two appealing properties:

- Ethereum does not give users a set of preset operations (such as Bitcoin). It allows users to create complex operations as they wish.
- The design of the Ethereum is very flexible and adaptable. It is easy to create new applications on the Ethereum.

Smart contracts in Ethereum are applications with a state stored in the blockchain that can run automatically on each decentralized network node [26]. Similar to the way of the software library works, developers can create smart contracts to provide functionality for other smart contracts. Alternatively, smart contracts can be simply used as an application to store information on the Ethereum.

Gas system is designed to mitigate Denial-of-Service attack on the Ethereum network. When Alice sends a token, executes a contract or transfers etheric money, each opcode will cost a certain pre-defined amount of *gas*, so that Alice has to pay $gasprice*gasUsed$ for the *gas* used. In addition, to avoid unpredictable fuel consumption caused by errors in contracts, the user sets a maximum allowable gas consumption when sending the transactions, that is, $gasLimit$.

2.2   Notations

Following are the notations used in our manuscript (Table 1).

Table 1. Notations and descriptions

F:	The plaintext collection of m documents $F = \{f_1, ..., f_m\}$. Each file f_i in the collectioncan be considered as a sequence of keywords
m:	The number of files in F.
W:	The dictionary, namely, the set of keywords, denoted as $W = \{w_1, ..., w_n\}$.
n:	The size of W.
C:	The encrypted files collection stored in the blockchain, denoted as $C = \{C_1, ..., C_m\}$.
I:	The index tree encompassing multiple sub-indexes for the whole file collection F, denoted as $I = \{I_1, I_2, ..., I_c\}$
c:	The number of keyword groups.
$\widehat{I}$:	The encrypted form of index tree I.
T_q:	The set of query vector.
$\widehat{T_q}$:	The encrypted form of T_q, named as trapdoor for the search request.
$TXID$:	The identifier of a transaction.
TX_{inx}:	The transaction embedded in index.
TX_{trap}:	The transaction embedded in trapdoor.
K:	The number of files returned.
h:	The number of roles in the access control list.
u:	The dimensions added for the security of the files.
l:	The upper bound of file size

2.3 System Overview

In Fig. 1, we outline the architecture of our system. There are three entities in the system model: data owner (Uo), data user (Us) and Ethereum. The Uo has m files $f_1, ..., f_m$. To protect the privacy of confidential documents, the Uo uses the symmetric encryption algorithm (e.g., AES) to transform them into ciphertext $C_1, ..., C_m$, which will be uploaded to the Ethereum blockchain in the form of transaction $TX_i (i = 1, ..., m)$. After the transactions are successful, each of them will have a corresponding transaction identifier $TXID$. The Uo uses these $TXIDs$ to generate an index I and encrypts the index to $\widehat{I}$. Then, the Uo uploads $\widehat{I}$ to the Ethereum in the form of transaction TX_{ind}. The Us is a data user authorized by the Uo. When the Us queries the encrypted data stored in Ethereum, he/she sends the transaction TX_{trap} embedded in the trapdoor to the Ethereum. After receiving legitimate query requests from Us, the smart contract executes search algorithms with a search token $\widehat{T_q}$ and the previously stored index $\widehat{I}$ and saves the search results (i.e., file identifiers) to its state, which is publicly known including the Uo. After receiving the search results, the Us uses the secret keys to decrypt the documents.

2.4 Threat Models

Depending on what information an adversary (e.g., a malicious server node) knows, we adopt the following two threat models.

Known Ciphertext Model. In this model, the adversary only knows the encrypted file collection C, the encrypted index tree $\widehat{I}$, and the search trapdoor $\widehat{T_q}$ submitted by the Us. It means that the adversary can conduct ciphertext-only attack (COA) [10].

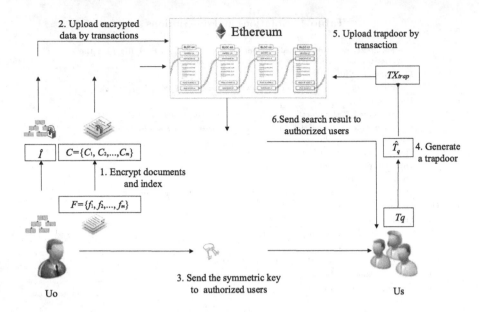

Fig. 1. System overview

Known Background Model. In this stronger model, the adversary not only equips with the knowledge of known ciphertext model, but also some other knowledge, such as the term frequency statistics of the document collection. That is to say, the adversary equipped with such statistical information can record how many documents there are for each term frequency of a specific keyword in F. Specifically, the adversary can conduct term frequency (TF) statistical attack to infer or even identify certain keywords through analyzing histogram and value range of the corresponding frequency distributions [27].

2.5 Design Goals

Soundness. It indicates that if there is a malicious server that does not correctly perform a protocol, it will get caught and obtain nothing. Generally, the previous works achieve this goal through a range of verifications of search results. In this paper, our scheme can obtain correct query results without verification operations and effectively prevent malicious nodes from unauthorized access.

Privacy-Preserving. In our scheme, we aim to protect the index and query confidentiality, query unlinkablitity as well as keywords privacy from adversaries.

- Index and query confidentiality. The adversaries cannot detect or infer the plaintext information about the content of trapdoor and index.
- Query unlinkablitity. The adversaries cannot identify whether or not two trapdoors are from the same search request.
- Keywords privacy. The adversaries cannot deduce whether the specific keyword is contained in a trapdoor through analyzing the TF distribution histogram.

2.6   Vector Space Mode

Vector space model and the $TF \times IDF$ rule are widely used in information retrieval [10]. In vector space model, for each document f_i, the Uo generates an n-dimensional document vector $D_i (1 \le i \le m)$. If the keyword w_j is not included in f_i, $D_i[j] = 0$; otherwise $D_i[j] = p_j == \frac{TF(w_j) \times IDF(w_j)}{\sqrt{\sum_{n=1}^{N} TF(w_i) \times IDF(w_i)}}$, where p_j is the weight of the keyword w_j. The $TF(w_j)$ is the frequency of the characteristic item, that is, the times that the keyword w_j appears in the document. The $IDF(w_j)$ is the inverse document frequency, inversely proportional to the number of documents in which the keyword w_j appears, $IDF = lg \frac{N}{idf}$. N denotes the number of words in the dictionary, and idf denotes the number of documents containing w_j.

3   Design Challenges and Countermeasures

3.1   Binary Indexed Tree

In Ethereum, each operation, including sending/storing data and executing computations, has an upper bound of consumed gas called $gasLimit$ as described in Subsect. 2.1. This restricts the size of transactions and the complexity of designed functions. Therefore, we divide the encrypted data to make privacy-preserving search over a large database feasible. Specifically, the main challenge is to divide the traditional binary index tree into multiple sub-indexes. The index partition method is described in detail as follows.

- The Uo produces an inverted index $INV = (inv(w_1), inv(w_2), ..., inv(w_n))$ for dictionary W, where $inv(w_i)$ is an inverted list of w_i. Each inverted list only stores top-P documents corresponding to keyword wi, where P is a positive integer, $P > K$.
- The Uo divides the set of keywords W into c groups $Wg = \{Wg_1, Wg_2, ..., Wg_c\}$, where each group Wg_i in Wg contains d keywords. Then, according to the inverted index INV, we generate inverted index set $Vg = \{Vg_1, Vg_2, ..., Vg_c\}$ for each group Wg_i.
- For each keyword group Wg_i, the Uo constructs the keyword balance binary (KBB) tree I_i as the sub-index by the top-P documents and obtains the index tree $I = \{I_1, I_2, ..., I_c\}$ for the whole file collection, where $1 \le c$. The number of sub-indexes is determined by the value of d. Suppose N_i represents a node of index I_i and it is in the form of $< TXID, l_N, r_N, value >$, where l_N and r_N are the left and right nodes of N_i, and $value$ is a d-dimensional file vector. If N_i is a leaf node, then $TXID$ is transaction identifier, and $value$ stores the document vector D_i of keyword group Wg_i; else, the N_i is an intermediate node, then the $TXID$ is empty and the $value$ is calculated as follows:

$$value[j] = max\{l_N.value[j], r_N.value[j]\} + |rand()|\%max\{l_N.value[j], r_N.value[j]\}$$

As shown in Fig. 2, we give an example to illustrate the detailed process of partition. In summary, the structure of sub-indexes not only circumvents the

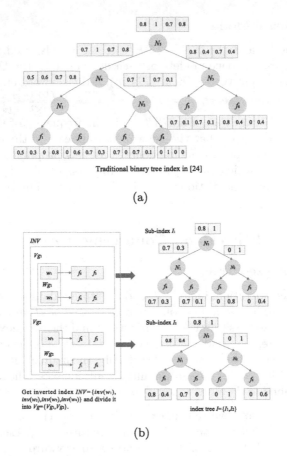

Traditional binary tree index in [24]

(a)

Get inverted index $INV=\{inv(w_1),$
$inv(w_2),inv(w_3),inv(w_4)\}$ and divide it
into $Vg=\{Vg_1,Vg_2\}$.

index tree $I=\{I_1,I_2\}$

(b)

Fig. 2. An example of dividing the traditional binary tree index in [10] with the file set $F = f_1, ..., f_6$ and the dictionary $W = \{w_1, ..., w_4\}$. In the process of constructing the index, we divide (a) the traditional binary tree index into (b) two sub-indexes I_1 and I_2 by dividing the set of keywords W into two groups Wg_1 and Wg_2 (where $P = 2$ and $d = 2$). The sub-index of each group Wgi is generated according to the traditional index generation algorithm in [10]. Note that the file vectors in the figure is unencrypted to simply describe the partition process.

above $gasLimit$, but also reduces the n-dimensional file vector to d-dimensional and lowers the height of index tree to improve the retrieval efficiency in the smart contract.

3.2   Access Control

Due to the restriction of $gasLimit$ in Ethereum, the operation of access control may become significantly expensive when there are abundant and complex expressions in a smart contract. Therefore, to simplify the whole access control mechanism and avoid the complexity of individual authorization, we introduce an effective role-based access control (RBAC) strategy for transaction data. It can assert who have permission to access the requested transactions by checking whether the user roles are the root of the target polynomial. The detailed process is as follows.

Suppose there are h roles in the role set $\widehat{h}$. A data user whose role is in η_i will have the right to query transaction TX_i, where $\eta_i \subseteq \widehat{h}$. Let SC be a smart contract running on the Ethereum network, Uo be the dispatcher of SC and Us be a user authorized to invoke SC. The access control process is as follows.

(1) The Uo writes the access control policies, roles information and permissions of the users to SC and install it on each node.
(2) The Us searches the encrypted data by submitting the transaction TX_{trap} that contains the trapdoor $\widehat{T}_q$, the transaction identifier TX_{ind_i} of the index and its role information z_1.
(3) After receiving the search request of the Us, the SC executes the access control strategy in advance.
   – Construct a variable polynomial of degree z for the transaction TX_{ind_i},

$$\text{denoted as } y_i(z) = \prod_{r_j \in \eta_i} (z - r_j) = \sum_{j=0}^{j=h} \widehat{r}_j z^j \text{ (when } j > |\eta_i|, \widehat{r}_j = 0).$$

   – Substitute the role z_1 of Us into the polynomial $y_i(z)$. If the role z_1 is the root of $y_i(z)$, the Us can access the transaction TX_{ind_i}. Otherwise, the Us is an unauthorized user and does not have permission to access the transaction data.

Therefore, the problem of whether the Us has access permission for TX_{ind_i} can be reduced to the problem to check whether its role is the root of $y_i(z)$.

Correctness. If Us is assigned to a role $z_1 \in \widehat{h}$ and transaction possesses subset η_i, it holds that

$$y_i(z) = \begin{cases} 0 & z_1 \in \eta_i \\ y_i(z_1) \neq 0 & other \end{cases} \tag{1}$$

4   The Detailed Scheme

In this section, we construct a decentralized privacy-preserving search scheme BMSSED that consists of six polynomial-time algorithm = (Setup, EncFiles, EcryptIndex, GenTrapdoor, Query, Dec).

(1) *Setup*(1^λ):
   – The Uo enters the security parameter λ to generate the key $\Pi = \{sk_1, sk_2\}$. Let $\varepsilon = (\varepsilon.Enc, \varepsilon.Dec)$ be a secure symmetric encryption scheme, and sk_1 be the symmetric key of ε for encrypting files. Then, the Uo shares the key to the authorized users. The key $sk_2 = \{S, M_1, M_2\}$ is used to encrypt the index, where S contains the c groups $(d + u + 1)$ dimension vector, denoted $S = \{S_1, S_2, ..., S_c\}$. M_1 and M_2 are two groups of matrices, both of which contain c invertible matrices that are $(d + u + 1) \times (d + u + 1)$. Besides, the Uo sets a price of \$*offer* for each search.

– The Us makes a deposit $\$deposit$ from $\$B_{user}$, where $\$B_{user}$ is the balance of the Us and $\$deposit$ is the deposit currency by the Us.

(2) $EncFiles(sk_1, F) \rightarrow C$: The Uo uses sk_1 to encrypt the document set $F = \{f_1, f_2, ..., f_m\}$ and obtains the ciphertext collection $C = \{C_1, C_2, ..., C_m\}$ as follow. Immediately, the Uo embeds the encrypted documents in C into transactions.

$$C_i = \varepsilon.Enc(sk_1, f_i)(1 \leq i \leq m) \tag{2}$$

– If $C_i > l$, the Uo divides C_i into s blocks $C_{i1}, C_{i2}, ..., C_{is}$, $|C_{ij}| + p \leq l$, $\forall j \in \{1, ..., s\}$, $s = \lfloor |C_i|/p \rfloor$. To store $C_i, C_{i1}, C_{i2}, ..., C_{is}$ are respectively embedded in the transaction $TX_{f_{i,k}} (k = 1, ..., s)$, the process is as follows:

  • When $k = 1$:
    * Embed $C_{i1} \| 0^p$ into the transaction $TX_{f_{i,1}}$.
    * Upload it to the blockchain and record its transaction identifier $TXID_{f_{i,1}}$.
    * For $2 \leq k \leq s$:
    * Embed $C_{ik} \| TXID_{f_{i,k-1}}$ into the transaction $TX_{f_{i,k}}$.
    * Upload it to the blockchain and record its identifier $TXID_{f_{i,k}}$.

– If $|C_i| \leq l(1 \leq i \leq n)$, it is embedded directly into the transaction TX_{f_i} after signing it, upload it to the blockchain and record its corresponding transaction identifier $TXID_i$.

(3) $EncryptIndex(sk_2, S, F) \rightarrow \widehat{I}$:

– The Uo uses the $TXIDs$ of encrypted data to generate index $I = \{I_1, I_2, ..., I_c\}$. The generation process is described in Subsect. 3.1.

– The dimension of each data vector in the sub-index I_i is extended from d to $d + u + 1$. The value of the corresponding positions are randomly set to 0 or 1. The value of the $(d + u + 1)$-th dimension is set to 1.

– We use the secure kNN algorithm in [10] to encrypt the index. Suppose N_i denotes a node in index I_i, ND_i represents the stored data vector and S_i is the i-th vector in S.

  • Split ND_i into two random vectors ND_i' and ND_i'' with the splitting indicator S_i as follow. For $1 < j < d + u + 1$,

$$\begin{cases} ND_i'[j] = ND_i''[j] = ND_i[j], & S_i[j] = 0 \\ ND_i'[j] + ND_i''[j] = ND_i[j], & S_i[j] = 1 \end{cases}$$

  • Encrypt these two vectors as $\{M_{1,i}^T ND_i', M_{2,i}^T ND_i''\}$ and store them on node N_i, where $M_{1,i}^T$ and $M_{2,i}^T$ represent the i-th matrices in the matrix groups M_1 and M_2, respectively. The encryption form of index I is denoted as

$$\begin{aligned} \widehat{I} &= \{\{M_{1,1}^T ND_i', M_{2,1}^T ND_i''\}, ..., \{M_{1,c}^T ND_i', M_{2,c}^T ND_i''\}\} \\ &= \{\widehat{I}_1, ..., \widehat{I}_c\}, \end{aligned} \tag{3}$$

where $\widehat{I}_i \leq l$ and $1 \leq i \leq c$

– For each sub-index $\widehat{I}_i$ in $\widehat{I}$, the Uo embeds it into the transaction TX_{ind_i} and submits to the blockchain.
  • Embed $\widehat{I}_i\|0^p$ into the transaction TX_{ind_1}, upload it to the blockchain and record its transaction identifier $TXID_{ind_1}$ that can be seen as a pointer to the TX_{ind_1}.
  • For each $\widehat{I}_i(2 \leq i \leq c)$, the Uo inserts $\widehat{I}_i\|TXID_{ind_{i-1}}$ into transaction TX_{ind_i}, uploads it to blockchain and records its transaction identifier $TXID_{ind_i}$.

(4) $GenTrapdoor(w_Q, sk_1) \rightarrow TX_{trap}$
– When the Us wants to search with keyword set w_Q, he/she generates the trapdoor $T_q = \{T_{q1}, T_{q2}, ..., T_{qc}\}$, where T_{qi} is a query vector of length d. If $Wg_{i,j}$ exists in the keyword set w_Q, the value of $T_{qi}[j]$ is 1; else, it is 0. We emphasize that when all the dimensions of the query T_{qi} are 0, remove T_{qi} from T_q (see an example in Fig. 3).
– The dimension of each query vector T_{qi} in T_q is extended from d to $d+u+1$. The values of the corresponding positions are randomly set to $\gamma_{i,j}$, where $i \in \{1, ..., c\}$ and $j \in \{1, ..., u\}$. The $(d+u+1)$-th dimension of query T_{qi} is set to another random number ψ_i. Besides, the first $d + u$ dimensions of each vector are multiplied by a random positive number r. The process that the Us encrypts T_{qi} with sk_1 is as follows.
  • Split T_{qi} into two random vectors T'_{qi} and T''_{qi} with the splitting indicator S_i as follow. For $1 < j < d+u+1$,

$$\begin{cases} T'_{qi}[j] + T''_{qi}[j] = T_{qi}[j], & S_i[j] = 0 \\ T'_{qi}[j] = T''_{qi}[j] = T_{qi}[j], & S_i[j] = 1 \end{cases}$$

  • The encryption form of trapdoor T_q is denoted as

$$\begin{aligned} \widehat{T}_q &= \{\{M_{1,1}^{-1}T'_{q1}, M_{2,1}^{-1}T''_{q1}\}, ..., \{M_{1,c}^{-1}T'_{qc}, M_{2,c}^{-1}T''_{qc}\}\} \\ &= \{\widehat{T}_{q1}, ..., \widehat{T}_{q1}\}, \end{aligned} \tag{4}$$

– For each $\widehat{T}_{qi}$ in $\widehat{T}_q$, the Us embeds it into the transaction TX_{trap} and submits it to the smart contract.
  • Specify a time limitation T_1.
  • Embed $(\widehat{T}_q, TXID_{ind}, T_1, z_1)$ into the transaction TX_{trap} and upload it to the smart contract.

(5) $Query(TX_{trap}, TX_{ind}) \rightarrow C_l$:
– Assert current time $T < T_1$.
– Assert that the Us is the authorized user according to the access control policy described in Subsect. 3.2.
– Assert $\$deposit > GL_{srch} \times \$gasPrice + \$offer$, where GL_{srch} is the gasLimit for calling $Search(\cdot)$ function.

– Execute algorithm Search $(\hat{T}_q, \hat{I}, K)$, get search result $Rlist = \{TXID_{\rho 1}, ..., TXID_{\rho K}\}$ and obtain corresponding $C_l = \{C_{l1}, ..., C_{lK}\}$ according to $Rlist$ (see an example in Fig. 3). The relevance score is

$$
\begin{aligned}
Score(\hat{T}_{qi}, \hat{ND}_i) &= (M_{1,i}^{-1}T'_{qi}, M_{2,i}^{-1}T''_{qi}) \cdot (M_{1,i}^T ND'_i, M_{2,i}^T ND''_i) \\
&= r(Score(T_{qi}, ND_i) + \sum_{j=1}^{u} \gamma_{i,j}) + \psi_i,
\end{aligned}
\tag{5}
$$

where $Score(T_{qi}, ND_i)$ is real score.
– Let $\$cost \leftarrow \$offer + G_{srch} \times \$gasPrice$ and send $\$cost$ to $\$B_{owner}$. G_{srch} is the *gascost* for calling $Search(\cdot)$ function.
– Let $\$deposit \leftarrow \$deposit \times \$cost$ and send $\$deposit$ to $\$B_{user}$. .

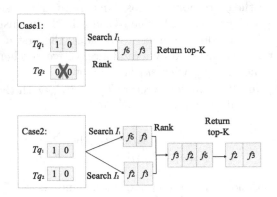

Fig. 3. An example of generating the trapdoor T_q for Case1: $w_Q = \{w_1, w_2\}$ or Case 2: $w_Q = \{w_1, w_3\}$ and returning the search results ($K = 2$) by querying the sub-indexes in Fig. 2.

(6) $Dec(C_l, sk_1) \rightarrow D$:
   After receiving the ciphertext set C_l, the Us uses the screct key to calculate $D_{\rho i} = \varepsilon.Dec(sk_1, C_{\rho i})(1 \le i \le r)$.

Algorithm 1. Search $(\hat{T}_q, \hat{I}, K) \to Rlist$

Require: The query $\hat{T}_q$, the searchable index $\hat{I}$;
Ensure: K transaction identifiers with highest scores.
1: **for** query $\hat{T}_{qi}$ in query group $\hat{T}_q$ **do**
2:     TOPK($\hat{T}_{qi}$, root of $\hat{I}_i$, 0,K)
3:     Merge top-K transaction identifiers $list_i$ of $\hat{T}_q$ into $RList$
4: **end for**
5: **return** top-K transaction identifiers of $RList$
6: TOPK($\hat{T}_{qi}, node, sco, K$)
7: **if** $sco < K$-th score in $list_i$ **then**
8:     return $null$
9: **end if**
10: **if** $node$ is leaf node **then**
11:     Insert the $TXID$ of $node$ into $list_i$
12: **else**
13:     $leftScore = Score(\hat{T}_{qi}, node.l_N)$
14:     $rightScore = Score(\hat{T}_{qi}, node.r_N)$
15:     **if** $leftScore > rightScore$ **then**
16:         TOPK($\hat{T}_{qi}, node.l_N, leftScore, K$)
17:         TOPK($\hat{T}_{qi}, node.r_N, rightScore, K$)
18:     **else**
19:         TOPK($\hat{T}_{qi}, node.r_N, rightScore, K$)
20:         TOPK($\hat{T}_{qi}, node.l_N, leftScore, K$)
21:     **end if**
22: **end if**

---

5   Security Proof

In this section, we analyze the security of the BMSSED protocol.

5.1   Soundness

It is obvious that the security of our scheme depends on Ethereum. Therefore, BMSSED can achieve soundness so long as the security of Ethereum is ensured. When the smart contracts are correctly executed on Ethereum, the decision and search results will be stored as contract states permanently and publicly. Moreover, miners in Ethereum network can verify the data. The consensus property of Ethereum can guarantee that access control policies and search operations are executed correctly.

5.2   Privacy-Preserving

Index Confidentiality and Query Confidentiality. Adversaries can calculate the real values of indexes and queries by establishing liner equations from the exposed ciphertext [10]. In our scheme, we use the $(d+u+1)$-dimensional segmentation indicator vector S_i and the $(d+u+1) \times (d+u+1)$ reversible matrices $(M_{1,i}, M_{2,i})$ to encrypt each subindex I_i in the index I, where each data vector is randomly split into two different $(d+u+1)$-dimensional vectors, ND_i' and ND_i''. That is to say, adversaries can establish $2\varpi(d+u+1)$ equations from the ciphertext of this index, where ϖ represents the number of nodes that sub-index $\widehat{I}_i$ contains. However, subindex $\widehat{I}_i$ contains $2(d+u+1)^2$ unknown numbers in each node. Besides, matrices $M_{1,i}, M_{2,i}$ also have $2(d+u+1)^2$ unknown numbers. It is obvious that the size of unknown numbers is more than the known equations. Similarly, the query vector T_{qi}' and T_{qi}'' can be regarded as two $(d+u+1)$-dimensional random vectors. There are $2(d+u+1)$ unknown numbers in two query vectors and $2(d+u+1)(d+u+1)$ unknowns in matrices $M_{1,i}, M_{2,i}$. However, adversaries have only $2(d+u+1)$ equations, which are less than the unknown numbers. Therefore, there is not enough information to calculate the query vector or matrices $M_{1,i}, M_{2,i}$. Moreover, adversaries always use the known plaintext-ciphertext pair of queries to construct linear equations to calculate the value of index [28]. In our scheme, the relevance scores learned by adversaries are shown in formula (5), where $Score(T_{qi}, ND_i)$ is disturbed by the random value $r, \gamma_{i,j}$ and ψ_i. It means that the corresponding values of $Score(\widehat{T}_{qi}, \widehat{N}_i)$ are different for the same queries. Furthermore, each linear equation may introduce u unknowns $\gamma_{i,j}$, two unknowns r and $\gamma_{i,j}$, that is, the unknowns in equations are always more than the number of linear equations. Therefore, adversaries cannot calculate the real value of index and secret key.

In summary, the BMSSED is strong enough to protect the security of index and query in known ciphertext model.

Query Unlinkability. By introducing the random value $r, \gamma_{i,j}$ and ψ_i, the same search requests will generate different query vectors and receive different relevance score distributions. Thus, adversaries are unable to establish the correspondence between query vectors and documents. However, adversaries can analyze the similarity of search results to judge whether the retrieved results come from the same requests. In the proposed BMSSED scheme, the data user can control the level of unlinkability by adjusting the value of $\sum_{j=1}^{u} \gamma_{i,j}$. This is a trade-off between accuracy and privacy, which is determined by the user.

Keyword Privacy. In the known background model, the adversary is equipped with the TF statistics of the document collection. The proposed BMSSED scheme is designed to obscure the TF distributions of keywords with the randomness of $\sum_{j=1}^{u} \gamma_{i,j}$. In order to maximize the randomness of relevance score distributions, we need to get as many different $\sum_{j=1}^{u} \gamma_{i,j}$ as possible. However, the query accuracy will be reduced. Therefore, data users can balance the trade off between query accuracy and keyword privacy by adjusting the value of u.

6   Performance Evaluation

6.1   Experimental Environment

Implementation. Experiments are performed on a computing system with an Intel(R)Core(TM) i5-6500 CPU(3.2 GHz) processor, and the Windows 10 (64 bit) operation system. We deploy the smart contract to the locally simulated network TestRPC and the official Ethereum test network Rinkeby, where TestRPC is initiated with the default configuration, similar to the configuration of the real Ethereum environment. Its mining block time is set to 0 so that we can focus on the performance of the search part of the smart contract. The smart contract is written in Python and combines with Solidity and Javascript as an intermediate interaction language.

Data. We make an assessment for BMSSED on four different, synthetically generated test data sets provided by the Natural language processing group, international database center, Department of computer information and technology [1]. These data sets have also been used in prior work, such as [8]. A quick summary of the statistics of the data sets, the size of the resulting encrypted databases, and the size of keyword set W are shown in Table 2.

Table 2. Database evaluation

DB name	#DB	EDB	Distinct keywords
DB1	348	5.62 MB	709
DB2	742	11.8 MB	1244
DB3	1184	14.8 MB	2176
DB4	1472	23.0 MB	1802

Table 3. Key differences between our scheme and other blockchain based SE schemes

Scheme	Query support	Application context	Access control
Tahir et al. [24]	Single keyword	General	By data owner
Hu et al. [11]	Single keyword	General	By data owner
Chen et al. [25]	Boolean, range	EHRs	By data owner
Ours	Similarity search	General	By smart contract

6.2   Performance in Ethereum

In this section, we design a number of experiments to test the performance of the proposed BMSSED scheme. It is mainly composed of the overhead on

---

[1] https://download.csdn.net/download/zgj_gutou/12009292.

TestRPC and Rinkeby. The indicators in the experiment are the running time of the algorithm, where we take the average value of 30 independent runs of the algorithm as the running time of the algorithm. Prior to presenting our evaluation, we first provide a comparative summary of our proposed scheme and other blockchain based SE schemes. As shown in Table 3, our scheme supports similarity search for the general data and novelly uses smart contracts to create an access control mechanism, having a certain advantage in terms of function.

On the Locally Simulated Ethereum Network TestRPC. To avoid exceeding *gasLimit*, we experimentally set the limited size of a transaction as $l = 16$ kB and the number of keywords in each sub-index as $d = 34$. Table 4 presents the time overhead for building an index, uploading encrypted data, and generating a trapdoor on different data sets. We can observe from the experimental results that the overhead of uploading the encryption data to the Ethereum blockchain is much higher than other overheads. This is because data owners store their confidential data in blockchain by embedding it into thousands of transactions (e.g., storing DB4 requires 1501 transactions), and each transaction costs about 4 s on average. Besides, we compare the query time overhead corresponding to the change of matching document numbers on different data sets. As shown in Fig. 4, the size of DB4 is the largest, with the longest time of searching. Accordingly, the query time overhead on the DB1 is the least. We explain that by a larger number of mined blocks leads to a longer time for loading.

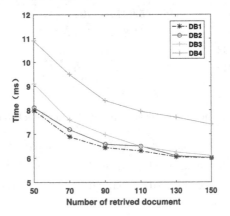

Fig. 4. Search time per matching document in TestRPC

We also observe that the running time of the query algorithm is lower as the size of search result become larger. This is caused by the constant cost of loading past mined blocks from disk into memory before each search runs. After the TestRPC startes, it creates 10 accounts by default and the following *Available Accounts* is the account list. Therefore, we use these default accounts to test the efficiency of access control policies based on smart contracts. As shown in

Table 4. Evaluations in TestRPC

DB name	#Tx	Construct index	#Tx	Upload encrypted files and index	Generate trapdoor	#Tx	Search Time
DB1	359	0.0045 s	10	24 min	≈ 0.001 s	1	7.23 s
DB2	944	0.0078 s	37	65 min	≈ 0.001 s	1	8.13 s
DB3	1258	0.0150 s	64	88 min	≈ 0.001 s	1	8.97 s
DB4	1501	0.0201 s	53	99 min	≈ 0.001 s	1	10.21 s

Fig. 5, in the case where the number of accounts is determined, the access control decision time is evenly distributed around 0.4 s and does not change with the size of the data sets. The exception point in the figure is mainly due to the instability of the network when the contract is running.

Available Accounts

===================

(0) 0x74650142c29e358b8f94a8c5d43345649009a4cd
(1) 0x450f2896c47c6e8763b6d389c40166584d0ced40
......

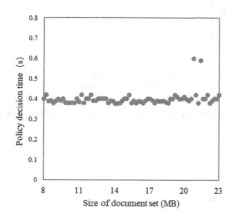

Fig. 5. The efficiency of access control policies based on smart contracts

On the Official Ethereum Test Network Rinkeby. Due to the limited balance, we only use the smallest database DB1 to perform experiments. There are 359 transactions to store database DB1. The average block time for mining is 15 s and it costs 89 min to upload the whole encrypted data set. Besides, each command executed in a smart contract has a specific consumption, counted in units of gas. The average gas usage for a transaction is 4,201,232. However, when the SSE smart contract is deployed to the Ethereum blockchain for the first time, the cost is high. After completing the deployment of the smart contract, the consumption cost that the users invoke the function interface provided by the smart contract is obviously reduced. For instance, the search time is about 10 s, 11 s, and 12.5 s for 50, 110, and 150 matched documents respectively in one transaction. The average gas usage for searching is 1,676,958.

Comparison of Query Efficiency with EDMRS in [10]. As shown in Fig. 6, we compare the search efficiency of our scheme with EDMRS in [10] under different numbers of retrieved documents to demonstrate the validity of our partition algorithm. The experimental results reveal that the sub-index structure is more efficient than the binary tree index of EDMRS. This is because our method divides the query T_q into c queries $\{T_{q1}, ..., T_{qc}\}$ and only sends those that are not empty to the cloud server. Therefore, the server does not have to search all sub-indexes.

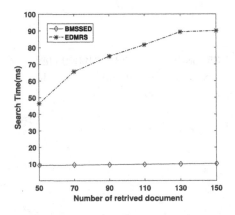

Fig. 6. Time cost of search with different numbers of documents that the Us wants to retrieve

6.3 Search Precision

Data users not only pay attention to search efficiency, but also care about search precision. The higher the similarity among the documents in search result, the higher the search precision. In our scheme, without loss of generality, the search precision SP_k is defined as

$$SP_k = \sum_{i=1}^{K} Score(\hat{T}_{qi}, \hat{ND_i}) / \sum_{i=1}^{K'} Score(T_{qi}, N_i) \tag{6}$$

where K is the top-K file returned by the ciphertext retrieval, and K' is the top-K file returned in the plaintext query. $Score(\hat{T}_{qi}, \hat{ND_i})$ is the similarity between the encrypted query vectors and the returned documents in result set and $Score(T_{qi}, N_i)$ is real score.

As described in Subsect. 3.1, to avoid exceeding *gasLimit* and improving the query efficiency, each sub-index only stores the top-*P* documents. Obviously, this method may lead to lower accuracy of queries whereas the Us in BMSSED can control the accuracy by adjusting the value of P. Figure 7(a) indicates that the Us wants to get a higher retrieval accuracy, he/she just sets a larger value of *P*. Besides, when the value of *P* is beyond a certain point (such as, *P* =90 in Fig. 7(a)), it has little effects on search results. We explain that by the union of search results for one single keyword query embrace most of the top-*K* documents in a multi-keyword query. Note that the search precision of scheme is also affected by the size of the data set with the same *P*. The results are shown in Fig. 7(b). The smaller data set has a higher search precision.

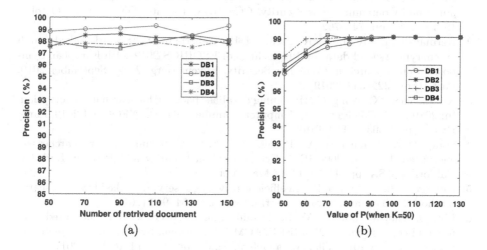

Fig. 7. The impact of the different values *P* (a) and K(b) on precision

7 Conclusion

In this work, we propose a blockchain based multi-keyword similarity search scheme over encrypted data (BMSSED). Different from the existing SSE scheme based on blockchain, our novelty is to use smart contracts to create an access control mechanism and fulfill multi-keyword similarity query. To avoid exceeding *gasLimit*, we divide the traditional binary tree index into a plurality of sub-indexes. The structure of sub-index not only helps us circumvent the *gasLimit*, but also reduces the dimensional of file vector and lower the height of index tree to improve the retrieval efficiency in the smart contracts. In addition, to simplify the whole authorization mechanism, we use the polynomial-based RBAC strategy to assert who have the permission to access the transactions. We conduct repeated experiments on real data sets. Experimental results and theoretical analysis show the practicability and security of our scheme over encrypted data.

The possible further research direction is to establish a protocol that enables access control crossing the domain on the basis of the present work.

Acknowledgments. We would like to thank anonymous reviewers for their helpful comments. This work is supported by National Key R&D Program of China(2018YFA0704703); National Natural Science Foundation of China(61972215, 61702399, 61972073); Natural Science Foundation of TianJin(17JCZDJC30500)

References

1. Shangqi Lai, Sikhar Patranabis, Amin Sakzad. Result pattern hiding searchable encryption for conjunctive queries, in: the 2018 ACM SIGSAC Conference on Computer and Communications Security, CCS 2018, Toronto, ON, Canada, October 15–19, 2018, pp. 745–762
2. Kermanshahi, S.K., Liu, J.K., Steinfeld, R.: Generic multi keyword ranked search on encrypted cloud data, In: Proceedings of ESORICS 2019–24th European Symposium on Research in Computer Security, Luxembourg, 23–27 September 2019, Part II, pp. 322–343 (2019)
3. Xu, L., Yuan, X., Wang, C.: Hardening database padding for searchable encryption. In: 2019 IEEE Conference on Computer Communications, INFOCOM 2019, Paris, France, pp. 2503–2511 (2019)
4. Song, D.X., Wagner, D.A., Perrig, A.: Practical techniques for searches on encrypted data. In: 2000 IEEE Symposium on Security and Privacy, Berkeley, California, USA, pp. 44–55. 14–17 May 2000
5. Chen, C., Zhu, X., Shen, P.: An efficient privacy-preserving ranked keyword search method. IEEE Trans. Parallel Distrib. Syst. **27**, 951–963 (2015)
6. Liu, Q., Nie, X., Liu, X.: Verifiable ranked search over dynamic encrypted data in cloud computing. In: 25th IEEE/ACM International Symposium on Quality of Service, IWQoS 2017, Vilanovaila Geltrú, Spain, pp. 1–6. 14–16 June 2017
7. Homann, D., Wiese, L.: Inference attacks on fuzzy searchable encryption schemes. Trans. Data Priv. **12**(2), 91–115 (2019)
8. Wan, Z., Deng, R.H.: Vpsearch: achieving verifiability for privacy-preserving multi-keyword search over encrypted cloud data. IEEE Trans. Dependable Secure Comput. **15**, 1083–1095 (2016)
9. Wang, Q., He, M., Minxin, D.: Searchable encryption over feature rich data. IEEE Trans. Dependable Sec. Comput. **15**, 496–510 (2018)
10. Xia, Z., Wang, X., Sun, X.: A secure and dynamic multi-keyword ranked search scheme over encrypted cloud data. IEEE Trans. Parallel Distrib. Syst. **27**(2), 340–352 (2016)
11. Hu, S., Cai, C., Wang, Q.: Searching an encrypted cloud meets blockchain: a decentralized, reliable and fair realization. In: 2018 IEEE Conference on Computer Communications, INFOCOM 2018, Honolulu, HI, USA, pp. 792–800 (2018)
12. Jiang, S., Liu, J., Wang, L.: Verifiable search meets blockchain: a privacy-preserving framework for outsourced encrypted data. In: 2019 IEEE International Conference on Communications, ICC 2019, Shanghai, China, pp. 1–6. 20–24 May 2019
13. Lai, S., Patranabis, S., Sakzad, A.: Result pattern hiding searchable encryption for conjunctive queries. In: Proceedings of the ACM Conference on Computer and Communications Security, pp. 745–762 (2018)

14. Kerschbaum, F., Tueno, A.: An efficiently searchable encrypted data structure for range queries. In: Sako, K., Schneider, S., Ryan, P.Y.A. (eds.) ESORICS 2019. LNCS, vol. 11736, pp. 344–364. Springer, Cham (2019). https://doi.org/10.1007/978-3-030-29962-0_17

15. Golle, P., Staddon, J., Waters, B.: Secure conjunctive keyword search over encrypted data. In: Jakobsson, M., Yung, M., Zhou, J. (eds.) ACNS 2004. LNCS, vol. 3089, pp. 31–45. Springer, Heidelberg (2004). https://doi.org/10.1007/978-3-540-24852-1_3

16. Asharov, G., Segev, G., Shahaf, I.: Tight tradeoffs in searchable symmetric encryption. In: Shacham, H., Boldyreva, A. (eds.) CRYPTO 2018. LNCS, vol. 10991, pp. 407–436. Springer, Cham (2018). https://doi.org/10.1007/978-3-319-96884-1_14

17. Zhang, W., Lin, Y., Qi, G.: Catch you if you misbehave: Ranked keyword search results verification in cloud computing. IEEE Trans. Cloud Comput. **6**, 74–86 (2018)

18. Ron, D., Shamir, A.: Quantitative analysis of the full bitcoin transaction graph. In: Sadeghi, A.-R. (ed.) FC 2013. LNCS, vol. 7859, pp. 6–24. Springer, Heidelberg (2013). https://doi.org/10.1007/978-3-642-39884-1_2

19. Lavery, K.: Smart Contracting for Local Government Services: Processes and Experience. Praeger Publishers Inc, Westport (1999)

20. Andrychowicz, M., Dziembowski, S., Malinowski, D., Mazurek, L.: Secure multiparty computations on Bitcoin. Commun. ACM **59**(4), 76–84 (2016)

21. Bentov, I., Kumaresan, R.: How to use Bitcoin to design fair protocols. In: Garay, J.A., Gennaro, R. (eds.) CRYPTO 2014. LNCS, vol. 8617, pp. 421–439. Springer, Heidelberg (2014). https://doi.org/10.1007/978-3-662-44381-1_24

22. Portmann, E.: Rezension blockchain: blueprint for a new economy. HMD Prax. der Wirtschaftsinformatik **55**(6), 1362–1364 (2018). https://doi.org/10.1365/s40702-018-00468-4

23. Li, H., Zhang, F., He, J.: A searchable symmetric encryption scheme using blockchain. CoRR abs/1711.01030 (2017)

24. Tahir, S., Rajarajan, M.: Privacy-preserving searchable encryption framework for permissioned blockchain networks. In: IEEE International Conference on Internet of Things (iThings) and IEEE Green Computing and Communications (Green-Com) and IEEE Cyber, Physical and Social Computing (CPSCom) and IEEE Smart Data (SmartData), iThings/GreenCom/CPSCom/SmartData, Halifax, NS, Canada, pp. 1628–1633 (2018)

25. Chen, L., Lee, W.-K., Chang, C.-C.: Blockchain based searchable encryption for electronic health record sharing. Future Gener. Comput. Syst. **95**, 420–429 (2019)

26. Torres, C.F.: Mathis steichen, radu state: the art of the scam: demystifying honeypots in ethereum smart contracts. In: USENIX Security Symposium, pp. 1591–1607 (2019)

27. Zhang, Q., Fu, S., Jia, N., Xu, M.: A verifiable and dynamic multi-keyword ranked search scheme over encrypted cloud data with accuracy improvement. In: Beyah, R., Chang, B., Li, Y., Zhu, S. (eds.) SecureComm 2018. LNICST, vol. 254, pp. 588–604. Springer, Cham (2018). https://doi.org/10.1007/978-3-030-01701-9_32

28. Yao, B., Li, F., Xiao, X.: Secure nearest neighbor revisited. In: 29th IEEE International Conference on Data Engineering, ICDE 2013, Brisbane, Australia, pp. 733–744 (2013)

Using the Physical Layer to Detect Attacks on Building Automation Networks

Andreas Zdziarstek(✉) , Willi Brekenfelder , and Felix Eibisch

University of Rostock, Rostock, Germany
{andreas.zdziarstek,willi.brekenfelder,felix.eibisch}@uni-rostock.de

Abstract. This work investigates possible methods of adding security features to building automation networks in the form of intrusion or tamper detection by using the physical layer. This is a concept that is widely known in the field of wireless communications but is—as of now—less prevalent in wired environments. We propose three distinct and complementary methods which rely on electrical fingerprinting of devices and the communication medium, as well as active radio-frequency probing of the network. To assess their effectiveness, we conduct a series of experiments in a building automation system test environment.

Keywords: Physical layer security · Network security · Building automation · Network intrusion detection and prevention

1 Introduction

In modern and large public buildings such as hospitals, universities or schools, a high amount of complex electrical signaling may be required to control its internal appliances such as lights, heating, air-treatment, or access controls. To alleviate some of this complexity, there are standards for building automation systems (BASes) which enable the use of multiplexed control lines in a network topology.

Unfortunately, there are major security flaws present within widely adopted BAS protocols [9]. Messages on the network medium are either sent using obsolete forms of encryption or none at all. This enables an attacker with physical access to the cabling to read traffic and potentially send harmful commands to connected devices. In a public building, it is not easy to prevent this kind of access as reaching a BAS endpoint can be as easy as popping off a light switch and connecting to the exposed wires. Even if there are no critical devices connected to that particular bus line, previous research has shown that logging seemingly harmless lighting data over an extended period of time provides information that may raise privacy and security concerns [16]. This is especially true if the building employs motion detectors for lighting control.

N. Park et al. (Eds.): SecureComm 2020, LNICST 336, pp. 372–390, 2020.
https://doi.org/10.1007/978-3-030-63095-9_24

These concerns are now beginning to be addressed by newer standards, examples being KNX Secure [15] and BACnet/SC [7]. But, given the large number of insecure devices already installed and still being sold, widespread practical adoption of secure protocols cannot be expected in the near future.

In this situation, it becomes necessary to think about adding new security features to existing network installations. Generally, it can be assumed that any device-specific modifications—for example adding an encryption layer—would require prohibitive effort and may interfere with other communications on the bus. This limits the possible interventions to adding special devices which monitor the network and either intervene in and/or report any suspicious activity. Such devices can be seen as being a part of an intrusion detection system (IDS) which would safeguard the building network against malicious activity. Generally, these systems operate by analyzing network traffic, matching patterns and detecting unusual activity, i.e. they tend to operate on OSI layer 2 and up.

It is common to just assume the inherent security of BAS networks when they are not directly connected to other wider area networks such as local area networks or the internet. But as mentioned above, especially in publicly accessible buildings this assumption may be treacherous. Nevertheless, a physically isolated and reasonably static network structure does offer unique possibilities of detecting an intrusion. In this paper, we explore ideas on how to make use of the physical layer characteristics of the network and the connected devices for attack detection. Our general assumption is that every network and device has uniquely detectable features when analyzing the bus on an electrical level. At least in the field of wireless networking, previous research has shown the feasibility of such physical layer approaches, for example using radio-frequency (RF) fingerprinting in WLAN networks [12].

2 Related Work

2.1 Device Fingerprinting

As a starting point, it makes sense to look at Physical Layer Security research in wireless networks in the hopes of transporting some of the concepts over to wired systems. For example, experiments by Brik et al. [4] show promising results for their method of distinguishing WLAN transceivers which are of the same model. They are using vector signal analyzer (VSA) hardware devices to capture WiFi signals. Subsequently, they perform signal analysis and machine learning on the data using specific WLAN signal characteristics as classifying features. The authors ascribe the electrical differences between devices to hardware imperfections in the transmitting parts of the chips. While WiFi-specific signal features are not applicable in our case, the general approach of using passive signal measurements and extracting device-specific quirks from the data is relevant to wired use-cases as well.

A method proposed by Wang et al. [21] by contrast does not rely on protocol- or technology-specific characteristics but uses more abstract mathematical features of the captured waveforms. Their method could theoretically be applied to any time-series input. For our use-case, this poses the question of how significant the differences of those features are for technologies other than WLAN.

Also of particular interest is a technique described in a publication by Gerdes et al. [8] as the authors aim to identify wired Ethernet devices according to a waveform comparison of their synchronization signals by implementing a matched filter. On the hardware level they use oscilloscopes with high sample rates to be able to accurately capture the Ethernet waveforms.

The measured device fingerprints in these methods can be seen as a form of physically unclonable function (PUF). In these cases, the PUF would be an intrinsic characteristic of the transmitters in the network stemming from manufacturing variations. This bears some similarity to ring-oscillator PUFs which can be used to uniquely identify FPGAs or ASICs by measuring the variations of internal delay lines [14]. In contrast, though, in the above fingerprinting methods it is not necessarily clear how the variations may present themselves in the measurements.

2.2 Environment Fingerprinting

As described by Campos and Lovisolo in [5], it is also possible to use these kinds of physical layer methods to verify a location. This means the fingerprint is tied to an environment instead of a device. An example of this would be to compare the received RF spectrum of different locations thereby telling them apart.

A US Patent by Bevan et al. [3] specifies a WLAN localization approach by mapping the complex channel frequency response between a network node and multiple static base stations. In a way, this can be applicable to wired environments as cable length, cable type and physical connection topology can have an effect on the frequency response of a wire thereby altering signals traveling on them.

2.3 Tamper Detection

If both environment and device fingerprinting are brought together, then this can be used to detect if the physical network configuration—that is, both physical topology and device hardware—has been tampered with. An example of this for WiFi-networks is proposed by Bagci et al. in [2].

3   Suggested Methods

Given the publications mentioned above, it is safe to say that there is a healthy research interest in physical layer security in wireless communications with a lot of well-developed methods in existence. Research is less easy to find, though, in the area of wired networks and especially communication buses like those used in building automation. Due to the security problems mentioned in Sect. 1, it is worthwhile to explore this avenue.

3.1 Threat Model Definition

In order to come up with specific ideas on how to guard against security threats, we need to define what the scope of possible attacks may be. As a general rule we assume that the network systems our methods are applied in do not have sufficient higher-level security to guarantee secure authentication and/or confidentiality. Also, we assume that in the age of small battery-powered single-board computers with universal internet access, a permanent air gap between any large building network installation and the outside world is near unenforceable, at least in public and semi-public buildings where a potential attacker is likely to find some accessible network tap to install an illicit device.

The most obvious kind of attack on such a system is what we will call an active one, meaning the attacker interacts with other devices in the network by sending messages. In the initial situation, there is no way to disprove the authenticity of those messages, meaning the attacker may instruct connected devices to perform potentially harmful acts. Potential high risk examples would be environmental controls in laboratories, medical facilities, or similar installations. During a medical procedure, even only turning off the lights may cause a catastrophic situation. While this kind of threat clearly has a high potential for serious harm, we also believe it to be the most detectable as the attacker's device needs to openly communicate, thereby revealing its physical layer characteristics.

On the other hand, the possible harmful impact of having an attacker passively listening to the messages on a BAS network may not be as obvious but is a serious issue. An example could be a sensitive facility where an attacker might map guard routes and occupation times of specific offices using the building's motion detectors in preparation for a break-in. In contrast to an active attack, the potential for harm is less direct and momentary but detection may be more complicated as the attacker does not need to openly send data through the network. Nevertheless, it is possible that a connected device does change the electrical characteristics of the medium enough to be detectable.

With the above in mind, we developed three different Physical Layer Security approaches which can be implemented on BAS networks.

3.2 Passive Waveform Fingerprinting

The most basic, general, and non-invasive approach to look at is passive fingerprinting, i.e. using a method like the ones classifying WiFi transmitters and applying it to BAS devices. For this, it is necessary to capture the communication on the bus as analog waveforms. This is possible with a modern digital oscilloscope. As the fingerprint is generally unique with respect to the currently active transmitter, such methods are suited to verifying the identities of known devices in the network. Nevertheless, the cable as the transmission medium does alter the signal due to its impedance characteristic and possible external interference. Moreover, even connected but inactive devices represent an alteration of the network circuit's electrical characteristics that may be large enough to have a measurable impact on the fingerprint of all transmitters. This means, given suitable equipment and data analysis, passive fingerprinting is potentially able to detect all possible physical network changes.

As for feature extraction from the measured data, it is a good starting point to look at very general approaches, such as the *RF-DNA* method [21] mentioned above. It just requires a time-series representation of the signal which is converted to instantaneous phase and instantaneous frequency data using the Hilbert transform. Then the authors calculate the mean, variance, skewness and kurtosis for each of the signal's amplitude, frequency and phase. This results in a 12-dimensional feature vector for each device and physical makeup of the network that is measured.

3.3   Device Noise Characteristics

While the above approach relies on very general signal analysis, it may be beneficial to make use of BAS physical layer specifics. Generally, their local directly-connected parts rely on some form of bit-based serial bus protocol for simplicity and robustness, typical examples being KNX-TP [19] and BACnet MS/TP [13]. This means there is a well-defined bit timing which we can use to determine exactly when a specific device is sourcing or sinking current to alter the bus wire's potential for data transmission. Our assumption is that during these active phases the transmitting device will—in addition to the data signal—emit a certain amount of noise that can be measured. There are multiple forms of noise emissions, some of them caused by semiconductor impurities and doping errors [10] which become apparent when current flows through them. This means each device has a unique noise level and signature that can be detected given sensitive enough measuring equipment. To enhance resolution, a form of over-sampling can be employed by using repeated measurements. For example, it is possible to repeatedly request a serial number or diagnostic information from a device and capture the responses which can then be overlaid.

Formally, we assume each measurement is represented by a time-series

$$\{x_0, \ldots, x_M\}$$

of numerical samples captured with a constant sample rate. This is true for digital oscilloscopes and other analog-digital-conversion-based data capture devices. If N measurements of messages containing the same bit patterns coming from the very same device are then aligned by cross-correlation, each sample becomes a statistical set X_i of measurements where $i, i \leq M$ denotes the sample position in the time-series and $|X_i| = N$. It is possible to compute the sample averages

$$\overline{X}_i = \frac{1}{N} \sum_{j=1}^{N} x_j \text{ with } x_j \in X_i \tag{1}$$

in order to obtain a finer quantization of the data. Now that we have a set of measurements and its mean for each sample point, it is possible to also calculate the sample standard deviations

$$s_{X_i} = \sqrt{\frac{1}{N-1} \sum_{j=1}^{N} \left(x_j - \overline{X}_i\right)^2} \text{ with } x_j \in X_i \tag{2}$$

which gives an indication of the overall noise level during the sampling timepoint i. This measured noise is a sum of every type of noise generated in the measuring circuit, including the oscilloscope's internal components and artifacts of digital quantization. In order to counteract the latter, it is possible to now superimpose all equal symbols within a message and calculate the average standard deviation for every sample point of the active transmission phase, i.e. where the device is sinking or sourcing current.

Formally, find the smallest i_0 where an active transmission phase begins. Depending on the protocol, this could for example be a falling or rising edge which can be detected by calculating the slope between $\overline{X}_{i_0}$ and $\overline{X}_{i_0-1}$. Then find the width of an active transmission phase

$$I = i_e - i_0 \tag{3}$$

where i_e is the endpoint of the active phase following i_0. Now, find the indices of all remaining active phase beginnings $i_m, m \in \mathbb{N}$. Then build a series of sets

$$S_j = \left\{s_{X_{i_0+j}}, \dots, s_{X_{i_m+j}}\right\} \text{ with } j \leq I, j \in \mathbb{N} \cup \{0\} \tag{4}$$

and calculate the means $\overline{S}_j$. The resulting time-series $\left\{\overline{S}_0, \dots, \overline{S}_I\right\}$ can offer a more accurate picture of a device's noise characteristics than simply analyzing a single capture of a bit transmission. If the assumption of detectable differences in noise characteristics due to manufacturing imperfections holds true, this average standard deviation time-series is unique to any given device and can be used for identity verification.

3.4   Active Measurements

The methods described so far all rely·on passive measurements as this is straightforward and does not interfere with normal bus communications. It may be of interest, though, to look into active probing of a network. Specifically, it may be worthwhile to measure the wideband frequency response of the connected bus line as it should be more sensitive to changes in physical network topology, i.e. how the cables are interconnected and where. This is generally done by emitting a test frequency in the RF range at one point in the network and measuring the received magnitude of the signal at another. By sweeping through a range of frequencies, a response curve can be mapped out. As this reveals the characteristic of the whole network medium, this method may be better suited than the others to guard against passive listening attacks.

As the measurements are meant to be done on an active bus, this poses the question of how the RF path can safely coexist with the BAS communication bus on the same medium without impairing either. The technical solution to this problem will likely be unique to a specific bus system.

4   Experiments

Now, to demonstrate the viability of the above methods we present three experiments as proofs-of-concept. As we intend to show applicability to currently
relevant BASes, we decided on KNX-TP as the physical-layer medium.

4.1   KNX

KNX is a well-known BAS standard which is partly derived from the earlier
European Installation Bus (EIB). The standard has been widely adopted, with
a 2019 press release by the KNX Association [11] claiming over 300 million KNX-
ceritified products to be in use around the world. The protocol is designed to work
across different physical media including standards for IP-tunneled, wireless,
and powerline communication. For a regular wired installation on a BAS-specific
medium though, KNX retains the EIB physical layer which is essentially a shared
serial bus using twisted-pair cabling called KNX-TP [19].

4.2   Technical Background

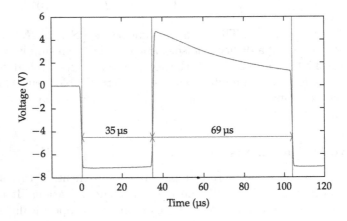

Fig. 1. A KNX-TP zero-bit waveform measured with a digital oscilloscope, averaged
over $N = 171$ measurements, with added timing markers. Note that 0 V in this case
denotes the resting potential of about 30 V DC as the oscilloscope was set to AC
coupling.

The KNX-TP physical layer can be described as a multiplexed serial line including direct-current (DC) power delivery [19]. In order to provide the latter, the
bus has a resting voltage of 30 V DC supplied by a KNX-specific active trans-
former. The current capability of this power supply is usually around a few
hundred milliamperes while KNX devices draw a few tens. This is enough for

most switching, control and communication tasks. Devices meant for more power hungry applications will need an additional external source.

As per the data signaling protocol, the resting potential is interpreted as a digital 1, while a 0 is actively generated by the transmitting device. At the start of every zero bit, the transmitter pulls the bus voltage lower by more than 6 V for exactly 35 μs then stops pulling and waits for 69 μs until the start of the next bit [20].

In this waiting phase, a choke coil in the power supply will generate an equalization pulse which overshoots the resting potential by several volts and then drops off slowly. The reason for this implementation is to ensure that the average bus potential does not drop significantly if the bus carries a lot of data traffic as this might interfere with power delivery. Figure 1 shows a plot of a KNX-TP zero symbol with timing markers superimposed.

4.3   Passive Waveform Fingerprinting

In our first experiment we adapted the method used in [21] for KNX-TP. Our test setup is a single KNX line consisting of a KNX push button sensor controlling a DATEC 1630.03160/61100 switch actuator connected to a MEAN WELL KNX-20E-640 power supply. For the push button sensor we used two identical models (MDT BE-TA5508.01), designated as A and B, only one of which is connected to the line during a test run. To control the amount of variables, the switches are only connected at a single specific spot in the line. This yields 2 possible experiment configurations.

We captured $N = 320$ KNX message waveforms for each configuration with a PicoScope 2206A USB-oscilloscope connected to a single endpoint of the network. Using the Hilbert transform we calculated mean, variance, kurtosis, and skewness for the signal amplitude, instantaneous phase, and instantaneous frequency. For visual inspection of the resulting 12-dimensional data we decided to use principal component analysis (PCA) to find a suitable projection to 2D without having to discard whole dimensions arbitrarily. Practically, we relied on a freely available Python implementation included in the *scikit-learn*[1] toolkit. The aim of PCA is to generate new dimensions (principal components) from the data as linear combinations of the original ones [1]. Ideally, PCA will maximize the explained variance in the first principal components in such a way that the rest may be discarded without much information loss. In our case, two principal components were enough to retain 99.9994% of the explained variance.

Figure 2 shows a scatter plot of the results where each point represents a recorded waveform. It is necessary to note that we discarded one of the data points from the set belonging to Switch B as the measurement seems to be a result of a spurious trigger of the oscilloscope rather than an actual message from the switch.

---

[1] *scikit-learn* is freely available at scikit-learn.org.

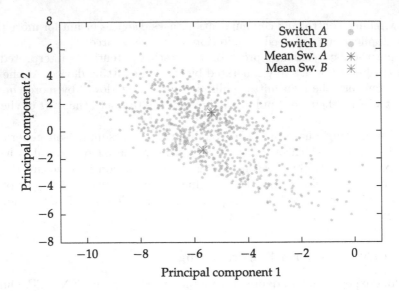

Fig. 2. Dimensionality-reduced scatter plot of the passive device identification test

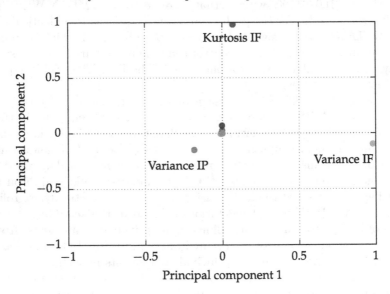

Fig. 3. PCA loadings plot of the passive device identification test

In the diagram, it is easy to see that the point clouds are scattered around two distinct averages and that both clouds are largely separate from each other with only a few outliers. This means, given a high enough N, the two switches are distinguishable using this method.

To explain the meaning of the two principal components (PCs), Fig. 3 shows the corresponding loadings plot of the transform. It indicates that the first PC is mostly influenced by the variance of the instantaneous frequency (IF) and to a much lesser extent by the Kurtosis of the if and the Variance of the instantaneous phase (IP). In contrast, the kurtosis of the IF has the most weight within the second PC together with small influences from IP variance and IF kurtosis. All other original dimensions do not have a sizable effect on either.

4.4 Device Noise Characteristics

Table 1. Configurations of the 2nd experiment

Switch	Experiment	Linecoupler	N
A	E_1	✓	170
	E_2	✗	171
	E_3	✓	349
	E_4	✗	351
B	E_1	✓	178
	E_2	✗	165
	E_3	✓	379
	E_4	✗	325

For the next experiment, we used the technique of comparing active transmission noise characteristics described in Sect. 3.3. The devices and test network were the same as before with the addition of a third device (a KNX linecoupler) that could be connected and disconnected using a switch. This addition allows to check if the method is sensitive to network changes. To also rule out temperature influences on our data, we used a temperature-controlled lab environment and performed two sets of measurements for each possible configuration with different lengths to account for internal device heating. Table 1 lists all 8 test run configurations.

In the KNX-TP physical layer protocol, active transmission phases occur during the first 35 μs of each bit with a value of 0. Throughout that phase the transmitting device needs to sink enough current to drop the bus voltage by about 6V or more (see Sect. 4.2). It is possible to find the indices i_0, i_e by looking for the corresponding rising and falling edges visible in Fig. 1. Formally, find the smallest i_0 such that

$$\overline{X}_{i_0} - \overline{X}_{i_0-1} \leq s \tag{5}$$

where s is a suitable slope threshold value. Now, find the smallest i_e such that

$$\overline{X}_{i_e} - \overline{X}_{i_e-1} \geq s \tag{6}$$

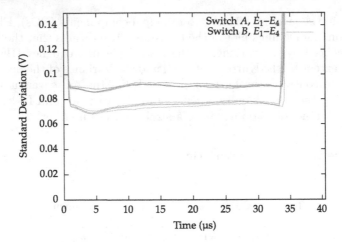

Fig. 4. Results of the transmission noise experiments (Color figure online)

Then use Eq. 3 to determine I and Eq. 4 to build the time series $\{\overline{S}_0, \dots, \overline{S}_I\}$. Figure 4 shows the resulting plots of all experiments. The differences in N and the addition of the linecoupler evidently had only a very small effect on the data when compared to the differences between the two switches. To improve readability, the plots corresponding to the same switch have the same color and are drawn semi-transparently, making superimposed lines visible. From the plotted results, it is easily possible to tell both switches apart graphically.

4.5 Active Measurements Using a NanoVNA

For the third experiment we used a NanoVNA vector network analyzer to measure the frequency response curve of three different test setups, one with a variable device, one with a variable cable length and a third one also with a variable device but connected to a larger network. The NanoVNA is a device which is able to successively transmit a series of radio frequencies and at the same time measure the amplitude of the returned signal in order to map the spectrum. To deal with the problem of interfacing to an active communication bus without functional interference, we developed an RF transmitter amplifier as well as an attenuator with AC coupling on the receiving end. Figure 5 shows the schematics of both circuits.

The TX amplifier is capable of subtracting a small analog waveform from the KNX voltage by modulating a bus load current small enough to not be registered by any KNX devices. To control the load current, we used two bipolar-junction transistors (NTE2633) originally designed for high-frequency video amplification. The transistors are operating in parallel Class A mode with resistor dividers providing biasing. An AC coupling capacitor and a resistor at the input roughly provide a $50\,\Omega$ impedance.

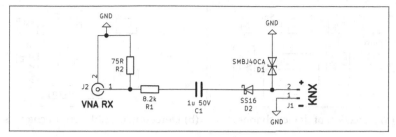

(a) Receiver protection, attenuation and AC coupling circuit

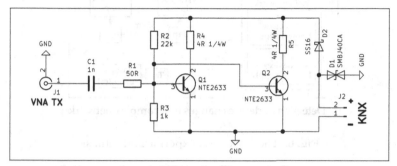

(b) Transmitter amplifier circuit

Fig. 5. Circuit diagrams of the NanoVNA/KNX-Adapters

The receiver-side circuit is a simple passive AC coupling capacitor together with a resistor divider providing at least 40 dB of attenuation or more, depending on the input impedance of the connected receiver. Together this is enough to limit the maximum voltage seen by the receiver to safe levels even during KNX communication causing large AC swings.

To explore if both device and topology changes are significantly reflected in the system's frequency response curve, we performed three sets of experiments. Figure 6 shows their respective setups. As can be seen, the first two have the same general outline, with the TX and RX circuits connected across a 10 m length of KNX-TP wire with a center tap. In the first one (Fig. 6a), two different devices were connected at that position using a 1 m lead. Specifically, the devices were a custom KNX interface board based on NCN5121 transceiver chip by ON Semiconductor [17], and one of the MDT push-button switches from before. In the second one (Fig. 6b) the MDT switch is connected using either a 1 m or a 6 m lead.

The third setup (Fig. 6c) is in essence an extension of the first experiment where we connected the devices to a KNX test line containing 4 permanently installed devices (2 KNX-USB dongles, a quad relay, and a line coupler interconnected with about 1.5 m of cabling in total) and attached both VNA input and output to taps at the far end. Our intention is to determine if a more complex network and a larger amount of connected devices will make small changes like

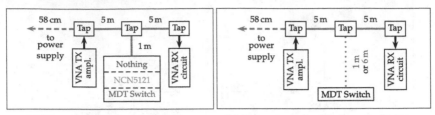

(a) Detection of device changes   (b) Detection of cable length changes

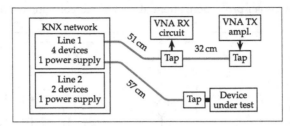

(c) Detection of device changes in a complex network

Fig. 6. The NanoVNA experimental setups

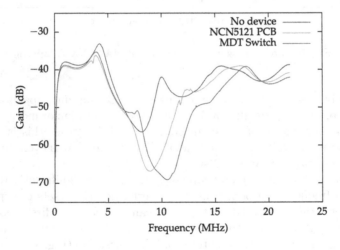

Fig. 7. Results of the NanoVNA frequency sweep with device changes (Color figure online)

swapping out a device less detectable. We also decided to connect both the input and output of the VNA close together as this most closely mirrors a situation where a single intrusion detection device is added at a single point in a network.

In all three parts of the experiment, the NanoVNA was configured to produce a frequency sweep between 50 KHz and 22 MHz in 1010 discrete steps, yielding a resolution of 21.73 KHz/step.

To achieve this resolution, the NanoVNA does in fact perform 10 successive partial sweeps of the spectrum with 101 samples each. The measured quantity is gain in decibels, i.e. the logarithmic power ratio of the signal transmitted by the NanoVNA on its TX side versus what it receives back at its RX side. The signal path includes the damping and amplification circuits as well as the connected KNX network.

Figure 7 shows the results of the device change experiments. Each of the three measurements was taken $N = 100$ times and then averaged per frequency step to improve accuracy. Average sample standard deviations were 0.02 dB for "no device", 0.15 dB for the MDT switch and 0.04 dB for the NCN5121 interface board. Evidently, there is a significant difference in frequency response between devices, i.e. their response curves are unique and—as evidenced by the low standard deviation between measurements—virtually static.

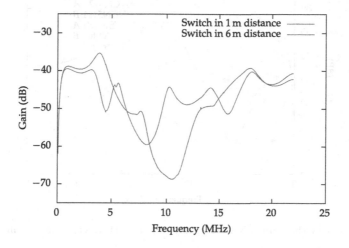

Fig. 8. Results of the NanoVNA frequency sweep with cable length changes

The results of the second experiment plotted in Fig. 8 show that also cable length has an easily detectable impact on the system's frequency response with both plotted curves being largely dissimilar. As before, sample standard deviations are low with an average of 0.12 dB for the 1 m-lead and 0.04 dB for 6 m. The blue line in this plot is nearly congruent with the blue line of Fig. 7 which is expected because the experimental setup is the same (see Fig. 6). Interestingly, some features of the red curve (6 m distance) coincide with the "no devices" plot from Fig. 7. Namely, the local gain minima at about 8 MHz and 12 MHz exist in both cases. Yet, the red curve also has local minima at about 4.5 MHz and 15.8 MHz which are nonexistent in the other. A possible reason for this partial similarity may be that the device's influence on the frequency response was damped by the added resistance of the 5 m lead between it and the measurement path.

The third experiment's results can be seen in Fig. 9, this time with $N = 99$ per curve. Note that in this experiment we have connected two specimens of each device, labeled A and B. As can be seen, differences between two specimens of the same device model are visually undetectable. Differences between the switches, the NCN5121 PCBs, and leaving the tap unconnected, though, are less obvious than before but still easily discernible when looking at the range from 10 MHz to 15 MHz and the location of the minima around 6 MHz. The average sample standard deviations are similarly low to the former experiments with 0.07 dB being the highest. This means, while the visible differences look small, they are orders of magnitude larger than the sample standard deviations and thereby statistically significant.

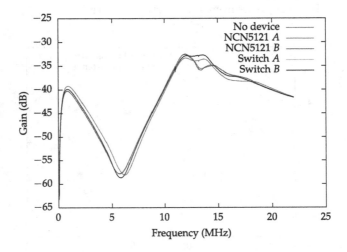

Fig. 9. Results of the NanoVNA frequency sweep with device changes in a complex setup

5   Discussion

Given these results, it is clear that our proposed approaches incorporating passive waveform fingerprinting and device noise characteristics are sensitive to device changes in the network. Furthermore, we have demonstrated that it is possible to detect a swapped-out device even if it is from the same make and model as the original one. This would be a highly valuable feature for tamper and intrusion detection as no attacker would be able to assume a fake device identity without fully taking over a known, present device in the network—a significantly higher hurdle than adding a fake device of their own. With regards to the threat model specified in Sect. 3.1, this method seems to be suited to counteract an active attack.

Similarly, the results also show the active probing approach to be sensitive to both changes in connected devices as well as cabling changes. This means the method can be used to counteract the passive kind of attack defined in Sect. 3.1 as this would at the very least entail tampering with a cable endpoint. It is, though, worth noting that given our limited dataset it is not easily possible to match a change in frequency response to any specific event. This contrasts with the other approaches where the offending device can be pinpointed.

Given their respective limitations, it is advisable to not singularly use any of the methods for attack detection but to combine them with each other. A combined system would be able to alert the user to a wide range of possible suspicious events while also delivering a form of device authentication by hardware identification. Of course, any or all of the concepts can also be added to existing higher level intrusion detection systems to provide additional data points indicating the current network state.

Also, as our practical experiments were limited to KNX networks and devices, the question remains how easily transferable the methods are to other bus systems. Nevertheless the concepts introduced in Sect. 3 are sufficiently generalized to guide the implementation work for any wired electrical bus system. Of course, depending on the systems' technical features this can be more difficult in some cases.

For passive signal analysis, it is necessary to have measuring equipment that is able to sample the waveforms fast enough. With a constant speed of 9600 bit/s, KNX-TP is quite slow when compared to other building, industrial and vehicular serial buses such as RS485/Profibus (up to 12 Mbit/s) and CAN-bus (up to 1 Mbit/s) [6, 18]. Speeds like that would require a considerably higher investment in measurement hardware.

While bus speed is of lesser importance for the active probing method, its practical implementation is very dependent on the electrical specifications of the physical medium. Our self-designed RF amplifier could use the KNX DC level to power itself and modulate an AC waveform on top of it. For other bus systems this might be possible to do in a similar fashion if there is a positive resting potential to exploit such as in the CAN bus [6]. If a bus system uses active-high signaling though the amplifier will need to be powered from an external source which would lead to a more complicated design.

6 Conclusion

In this work, we introduced three different methods for anomaly or attack detection intended for the physical layer of BASes fieldbus networks. Two of those are based on passive observation of the electrical signals on the bus while the third method relies on actively mapping the high-frequency response spectrum of a network. To demonstrate their viability, we performed a series of experiments on a widely adopted BAS fieldbus system. The results comprehensively support our assumption that physical layer security can be a valuable addition to existing BASes to help ensure their integrity.

7 Future Work

The above being said, it is clear that more testing is needed to conclusively verify that the approaches are universally usable among different BAS network types and topologies. Also, it would be useful to have a larger database of network setups and devices with their respective measured characteristics. This could allow us to find feature patterns correlating with certain specific kinds of network changes leading to better insight into what data anomaly indicates which actual event or class of events. We plan to conduct further experiments on more complex setups as well as different physical layer technologies used in fieldbus-type networks.

As these are problems related to classification and pattern matching, we also intend to investigate the benefits of applying different machine-learning algorithms to our data. Especially the *RF-DNA*-derived passive fingerprinting approach may be well complemented by high-dimensional classification methods.

Another area of interest is the methods' practical implementation as a self-contained physical layer intrusion detection device. At least the first two experiments as described in Sect. 4 use comparatively expensive hardware, specifically the oscilloscope. Also all three methods so far rely on offline data analysis using a personal computer. For practical usage, it would be beneficial to limit these costs. Examples for improvements in this area could be to substitute the oscilloscope with cheaper and less versatile analog-digital converters and to use less expensive computation hardware, e.g. embedded controllers or single-board computers. Given such improvements, it may be possible to devise low-cost physical layer security devices that can be easily added to existing networks.

Supplementary Material

The measurements and results of the above experiments can be found at https:// opsci.informatik.uni-rostock.de/repos/datasets/bas-pls/bas-pls-res.zip.

Acknowledgment. This research was funded by a grant from the German Federal Ministry for Economic Affairs and Energy in accordance with a resolution passed by the German federal parliament.

References

1. Abdi, H., Williams, L.J.: Principal component analysis. WIREs Comput. Stat. **2**(4), 433–459 (2010)
2. Bagci, I.E., Roedig, U., Martinovic, I., Schulz, M., Hollick, M.: Using channel state information for tamper detection in the internet of things. In: Proceedings of the 31st Annual Computer Security Applications Conference, pp. 131–140. Association for Computing Machinery, Los Angeles (2015)
3. Bevan, D.D., Averin, I., Lysyakov, D.: RF fingerprinting for location estimation. US Patent 8,170,815 B2 (USA). R.B. LP. May 1, 2012. http://patft1.uspto.gov/netacgi/nph-Parser?patentnumber=8170815. Accessed 14 Feb 2020

4. Brik, V., Banerjee, S., Gruteser, M., Oh, S.: Wireless device identification with radiometric signatures. In: Proceedings of the 14th ACM International Conference on Mobile Computing and Networking, pp. 116–127. Association for Computing Machinery, San Francisco (2008)
5. Campos, R.S., Lovisolo, L.: RF fingerprinting location techniques (chap. 15). In: Handbook of Position Location, pp. 487–520. Wiley (2011). https://doi.org/10.1002/9781118104750. ISBN 9781118104750
6. Corrigan, S.: Introduction to the Controller Area Network (CAN). SLOA101B. Application Report. Texas Instruments Incorporated, May 2016. https://www.ti.com/lit/an/sloa101b/sloa101b.pdf. Accessed 07 Feb 2020
7. Fisher, D., Isler, B., Osborne, M.: BACnet Secure Connect. A Secure Infrastructure for Building Automation. White Paper, version 15. ASHRAE SSPC 135 IT Working Group (2019). https://www.ashrae.org/File%20Library/Technical%20Resources/Bookstore/BACnet-SC-Whitepaper-v15_Final_20190521.pdf. Accessed 03 Apr 2020
8. Gerdes, R.M., Mina, M., Russell, S.F., Daniels, T.E.: Physical-layer identification of wired ethernet devices. IEEE Trans. Inf. Forensics Secur. **7**(4), 1339–1353 (2012)
9. Granzer, W., Praus, F., Kastner, W.: Security in building automation systems. IEEE Tran. Ind. Electron. **57**(11), 3622–3630 (2010)
10. Gray, P.R., Hurst, P.J., Lewis, S.H., Meyer, R.G.: Noise in integrated circuits (chap. 11). In: Analysis and Design of Analog Integrated Circuits, 5th edn., pp. 736–795. Wiley, January 2009. ISBN 978-0-470-24599-6
11. KNX on track for success again in 2019: Sector Coupling and IoT in focus. Press Release, KNX Association Cvba (2019). https://media.knx.org/feed/file/1050. Accessed 13 Feb 2020
12. Lackner, G., Payer, U., Teufl, P.: Combating wireless LAN MAC-layer address spoofing with fingerprinting methods. Int. J. Netw. Secur. **9**(2), 164–172 (2009)
13. Leach, T.: Implementing a BACnet network. ASHRAE J. **59**(3), 40–48 (2017)
14. Maes, R., Verbauwhede, I.: Physically unclonable functions: a study on the state of the art and future research directions. In: Sadeghi, A.R., Naccache, D. (eds.) Towards Hardware-Intrinsic Security. ISC, pp. 3–37. Springer, Heidelberg (2010). https://doi.org/10.1007/978-3-642-14452-3_1. ISBN 978-3-642-14452-3
15. Maximum data protection for smart buildings. Press Release, KNX Association Cvba (2017). https://media.knx.org/feed/file/918. Accessed 03 Apr 2020
16. Mundt, T., Krüger, F., Wollenberg, T.: Who refuses to wash hands? Privacy issues in modern house installation networks. In: 2012 Seventh International Conference on Broadband, Wireless Computing, Communication and Applications, pp. 271–277 (2012)
17. NCN5121. Transceiver for KNX Twisted Pair Networks. Rev. 2. Datasheet. Semiconductor Components Industries, LLC, August 2019. https://www.onsemi.com/pub/Collateral/NCN5121-D.PDF. Accessed 17 Feb 2020
18. PROFIBUS System Description. Technology and Application. 4.332. PROFIBUS Nutzerorganisation e. V. (PNO), April 2016. https://www.profibus.com/index.php?eID=dumpFile&t=f&f=52380&token=4868812e 468cd5e71d2a07c7b3da955b47a8e10d Accessed 07 Feb 2020
19. Sokollik, F., Helm, P., Seela, R.: KNX für die Gebäudesystemtechnik in Wohnund Zweckbau. VDE Verlag GmbH (2017)

20. Szmulewicz, D.: Using MSP on KNX Systems. SWRA497. Application Report. Texas Instruments Incorporated. December 2015. http://www.ti.com/lit/an/swra497/swra497.pdf. Accessed 17 Feb 2020
21. Wang, X., Zhang, Y., Zhang, H., Wei, X., Wang, G.: Identification and authentication for wireless transmission security based on RF-DNA fingerprint. EURASIP J. Wirel. Commun. Netw. **2019**, 230 (2019). https://doi.org/10.1186/s13638-019-1544-8

Formalizing Dynamic Behaviors of Smart Contract Workflow in Smart Healthcare Supply Chain

Mohammad Saidur Rahman[1](✉), Ibrahim Khalil[1], and Abdelaziz Bouras[2]

[1] RMIT University, Melbourne, Australia
{mohammadsaidur.rahman,ibrahim.khalil}@rmit.edu.au
[2] Qatar University, Doha, Qatar
abdelaziz.bouras@qu.edu.qa

Abstract. We present a formal model for smart contract workflow using Colored Petri-Net in the context of a blockchain-based healthcare supply chain in this paper. Ensuring traceability of products is a crucial issue in a smart healthcare supply chain. Blockchain and smart contracts are two enabling technologies that ensure the traceability of products and prevent data tampering in the smart healthcare supply chain. In a blockchain-based supply chain, a workflow of smart contracts needs to created and executed based on the input data. The selection of smart contracts in the workflow is data-driven and dynamic. Hence, it is necessary to verify the correctness of the dynamic execution of smart contracts. In this paper, we develop a Colored Petri-Net based formalism to verify the correctness of dynamic behaviors of the smart contract workflow. We conduct experiments to evaluate the performance of our proposed model.

Keywords: Blockchain · Formal model · Smart contract ·
12 healthcare supply chain · Colored petri-net

1 Introduction

With the help of Internet-of-Things (IoT) and smart devices, the smart supply chain can play an essential role during the pandemic situation, such as COVID-19. For example, keeping records of pharmaceutical products in the whole supply chain process in a contactless manner can be a perfect example of the smart supply chain in healthcare. However, supply chain participants can tamper data if they fail to comply with the product handling policy. Therefore, it is necessary to ensure the traceability of the supply chain data and prevention of data tampering throughout the process.

Blockchain provides data traceability and protection from tampering at the same time [12,13]. Hence, the blockchain technology has become a new norm in different applications such as supply chain [15], healthcare [10,17], smart grid [2],

© ICST Institute for Computer Sciences, Social Informatics and Telecommunications Engineering 2020
Published by Springer Nature Switzerland AG 2020. All Rights Reserved
N. Park et al. (Eds.): SecureComm 2020, LNICST 336, pp. 391–402, 2020.
https://doi.org/10.1007/978-3-030-63095-9_25

and smart transport [1, 6, 7, 9]. Data are stored in the blockchain as a transaction [16]. At present, *smart contract* [3] is an essential part of blockchain-based systems. Smart contracts are a great advancement in blockchain technology [11]. A smart contract is a computer program that is executed automatically when a certain condition is satisfied. In a blockchain-enabled smart supply chain, business rules are abstracted as smart contracts and deployed in the blockchain networks. Smart contracts validate blockchain transactions before they make any changes to the distributed ledger.

In this paper, we address the issue of verifying the correctness of smart contract execution that is dynamic in nature and data-driven. The blockchain-based smart healthcare supply chain (SHSC) involves many stakeholders such as producers, distributors, logistics service providers, retailers, and consumers. All stakeholders are connected to a blockchain network to ensure traceability, transparency, integrity, and trust by preventing data modification. Business contracts among stakeholders are stored in multiple smart contracts. These smart contracts are executed whenever a particular condition is met. For example, a payment smart contract, between a supplier and customer, processes the payment to the supplier if x units of a pharmaceutical item are delivered to the customer. However, the execution of smart contracts may be dependent on data. For instance, a supplier may not deliver the required x units of the product. Assume that y units are delivered at first, and z units are delivered later, such that $x = y + z$. Hence, two different blockchain transactions are generated with the respective number of delivered items. Hence, the payment smart contract should process the payment only if the sum of units delivered is equal to x. Here, the execution of the payment smart contract is data-driven and behaves dynamically. As a supply chain task is a complex task by nature, we need a series of smart contracts, called *smart contract workflow*, from different participants to fulfill a particular supply chain task. Hence, it is necessary to verify if a generated smart contract workflow is complying with different dynamic conditions in SHSC.

The primary objective of this paper to develop a model that would verify the correctness of the execution of smart contracts with the dynamic behavior in the blockchain-based SHSC. In this paper, we model the dynamic behaviors of smart contracts in a workflow based on the business rules using Colored Petri-Net (CP-Net). Colored Petri-Net [5, 18] is a version of Petri-Net. CP-Net is a popular formalization method that is used for modeling the dynamic behavior of entity [14]. This formalization is being used to check the soundness of smart contracts [4, 8, 19] in blockchain-based systems. CP-Net allows us to describe the smart contract behavior and logic through different tokens as colors [4]. Dynamic conditions of smart contracts can be expressed, and vulnerabilities in smart contracts can be detected easily in CP-Net. Overall, unnecessary loss is avoided in blockchain-based SHSC.

The rest of the paper is organized as follows. Section 2 discusses some of the related works. Section 3 describes the proposed Colored Petri-Net based formalism for smart contract workflow. Experimental results and performance of the proposed framework are analyzed in Sect. 4. We conclude the paper in Sect. 5.

2   Related Work

In this section, we discuss some of the Colored Petri-Net based formal modeling approaches for smart contracts in blockchain systems.

The research work in [8] proposes a Colored Petri-Net based formal verification method that identifies smart contracts' logical vulnerabilities in the blockchain system. Initially, the smart contract models with possible attackers based on hierarchical CP-Net. Next, the smart contract models are executed for validating the functional correctness. Authors in [8] demonstrate that the CP-Net-based formalism can detect the smart contract's logical vulnerabilities as well as the non-logical vulnerabilities in the contracts, such as the limitations of the smart contract development platform.

Authors in [4] present a multilevel modeling solution for smart contracts for analyzing the security of smart contracts. The model improves bytecode's program logic rules in the first place. Next, the Hoare logics are used for creating a CP-Net model. The wrong execution paths are shown by the model to analyze the security of a smart contract.

However, none of the aforementioned works model the data-driven dynamic behaviors of smart contract workflow, which is necessary for the safe execution of smart contracts in blockchain-based SHSC.

3   Proposed Model

In this section, we discussed our proposed Colored Petri-Net based modelling of smart contract workflow for the blockchain enabled SHSC.

3.1   Overview of Data-Driven Smart Contract Composition

In SHSC, smart contracts take data in terms of transactions and pass data to functions that implement business rules. Each function has at least one pre-condition and post-condition known as *guard conditions*. The blockchain network should verify an input value of the guard condition before smart contracts are deployed to the blockchain.

As a task in the supply chain is complex in general, a smart contract may not be enough to execute all of the business rules when a blockchain transaction is generated. Hence, multiple smart contracts need to be selected and composed to execute all business rules. Smart contract composition may be performed based on the data that is provided in the transaction. Therefore, data-driven compositions of smart contracts are required to fulfill a supply chain task in the SHSC.

In SHSC, we introduce four types of smart contract composition logics:(1) *sequential*, (2) *aggregation*, (3) *split*, and (4) *loop*. An overview of each of the composition logic is illustrated in Fig. 1. Assume that the composability between two smart contracts are represented using the operator "→". In the *sequential composition logic*, a smart contract SC sends a data x to another smart contract

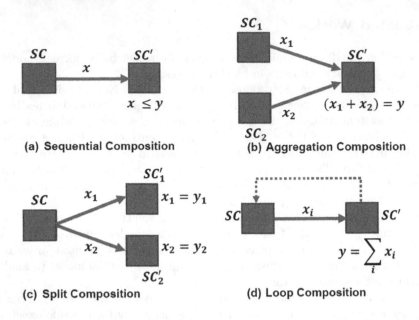

Fig. 1. overview of data-driven smart contract composition logic

SC'. Smart contracts SC and SC is sequentially composable (i.e., $SC \rightarrow SC'$) if $x = y$, where y is the expected value by SC' (see Fig. 1(a)). Assume that a smart contract SC' requires a data x_1 from the smart contract SC_1 and x_2 from another smart contract SC_2 such that $y = x_1 + x_2$, where y is the expected data in SC'. Here, $(SC_1 \uplus SC_2) \rightarrow SC'$ is called *aggregation composition* of smart contract (see Fig. 1(b)), and "$\uplus$" is the aggregation operator. A *split composition* is a composition logic where a smart contract SC sends data to multiple smart contracts. Assume that a smart contract SC sends a data x_1 to a smart contract SC'_1 and x_2 to another smart contract SC'_2. Now, $(SC'_1 \parallel SC'_2) \rightarrow SC$ is a split composition (see Fig. 1(c)), and "$\parallel$" is the split operator. A *loop composition logic* can be defined as a series of sequential composition between two smart contracts SC and SC' which can be represented as $SC \xrightarrow{i} SC'$. Here, "$\xrightarrow{i}$" indicates that the sequential composition $SC \rightarrow SC'$ should be repeated i times (see Fig. 1(d)). The smart contract SC sends data x to the smart contract SC' unless $y = \sum_i x$, where y is the expected data at SC'.

3.2 Colored Petri-Net Formalism of Composite Smart Contracts

In this section, we present Colored Petri-net formalism of different types of data-driven smart contract compositions.

Coloured Petri Net (CP-net) has several places. Every place in the net has a corresponding value type. The set of value types is called a color set. Each of the tokens in a place has a value that belongs to that type. Every single arc has a variable and transition has a *precondition* and a *postcondition*. These preconditions and postconditions are called the guard. A precondition of an input arc of a transition is an expression with multiple variables. These variables are independent. A postcondition is an expression with variables of both input arcs and output arcs. A transition in a CP-net is enabled if and only if for each input place a token can are a well-established process modeling technique that has formal semantics. These semantics are used to model and analyze several processes, including protocols, manufacturing systems, and business processes.

We assume that a Colored Petri net (CP-Net) represents the behavior of a smart contract that works based on input data. The CP-Net for smart contracts consists of one input place and one output place. The input place is used for absorbing information, and the output place is used for emitting information. Combinedly, the CP-Net with input and output places facilitates the definition of the composition operators and the analysis as well as the verification of specific properties (e.g., reachability, deadlock, and liveness). Each event is activated when a particular token is obtained. In addition, the output place will have a certain number of tokens once the required events are fired. Tokens in CP-Net may have different colors representing the preconditions of smart contracts being executed. At any given time, a smart contract can be in one of the following states: initial, ready, processing, postponed, failed, or finished. When a smart contract is in the ready state, a token is in its corresponding input place, whereas the finished state means there is a token in the corresponding output.

Definition 3.1 (Smart Contract Net). A Smart Contract Net (SC-Net) is a CP-Net, i.e., a tuple $SCN = (P, T, F, \Sigma, C)$ where:

- P is a finite set of places such that $P = P_I \cup P_D$, where:
  - P_I is the set of internal places, and
  - P_D is the set of data places. Assume that $\triangleleft p$ and $p \triangleright$ are source and sink places, respectively. For $\forall \triangleleft p, p \triangleright \in P_D$.
- T is a finite set of transitions representing the operations of the service,
- $F \subseteq (P \times T) \cup (T \times P)$ is a set of directed arcs representing flow relation and (P_I, T, F) is a work flow net. (P_I, T, F) has two special places: i and o. Place i is a source place: $\triangleleft i = \emptyset$ and Place o is a sink place: $o^\triangleright = \emptyset$. If we add a transition t to (P_I, T, F) which connects place o with i (i.e., $\triangleleft t = i$ and $t^\triangleright = o$), then the resulting Petri net is strongly connected.
- Σ is the set of color sets.
- C is the color function. Assume that $E = \{e\} \in \Sigma$ is the color set that has only one possible value which stands for the control token in (P_I, T, F). C is defined from P to Σ such that $\forall p \in P_I, C(p) = e$.

Here, the smart contract net is a Colored Petri net. Internal places P_I represent the internal control logic. Data places P_D represent the data exchanged between services. The internal places are tagged with color e that stands for the control token in (P_I, T, F). The data places are tagged with the color sets that represent data types. The function F works as a guard function. The condition of the function F must be satisfied by a color value in E to trigger an event.

Based on the definition of the smart contract net stated above, a smart contract can be defined as follows:

Definition 3.2 (Smart Contract). A Smart Contract is a tuple $SC = <addr, owner, A_{pre}, G, tran, type, dom, desc, C, SCN >$ where:

- $addr$ - is the unique address of the smart contract,
- $owner$ - is the ID of owner of the smart contract,
- A_{pre} - the set of attributes and their values representing the initial state before the execution,
- $G = \{G_1, G_2, \ldots, G_f\}$, where G is the set of f number of functions G_i in the smart contract,
- $tran$ - is the transaction containing meta data that needs to be verified by the blockchain,
- $type$ - is a constant value representing the type of the smart contract,
- dom - is the domain of operation the smart contract. For example, if the smart contract contains the functions related to the manufacturing then the domain of the smart contract is manufacturer. Other possible domains can be distributor, retailer, and consumer in SHSC.
- $desc$ - is the textual description of the smart contract.
- CM - is a set of its component smart contracts such that $CM = \{CM_1, CM_2, \ldots, CM_m\}$, where CM_i is the i-th smart contract in CM and m is the number of component smart contracts involved in the smart contract. If $CM = \{\}$, then SC is a component smart contract. Otherwise, SC is a composite smart contract, and
- $SCN = (P, T, F, \Sigma, CM)$ is the smart contract net modelling the dynamic behavior of the smart contract using a CP-Net.

We assume that any two smart contracts (SC and SC') that are eligible for any of the aforementioned data-driven compositions have the same type and domain description as mentioned in the Colored Petri-net formalism of smart contract (see Definition 3.2).

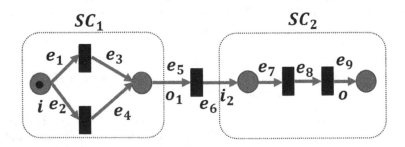

Fig. 2. Colored petri-net modelling of sequential composition of SC_1 and SC_2

Definition 3.3 (Sequential Composition). A sequential composition (S_{SC}) of smart contracts SC_1 and SC_2 is a tuple $S_{SC} =< A_{pre}, G, tran, type, CM, SCN >$ where:

- $CM = CM_1 \cup CM_2$
- $SCN = (P, T, F, \Sigma, C)$ such that
  - $P = P_1 \cup P_2$,
  - $T = T_1 \cup T_2 \cup \{t\}$,
  - $F = F_1 \cup F_2 \cup \{(o_1, t), (t, i_2)\}$,
  - $i = i_1$ and $o = o_2$,
  - $P_I = P_{I_1} \cup P_{I_2} \cup (o_1, t)$,
  - $P_D = P_{D_1} \cup P_{D_2} \cup (i_2, t)$,
  - $\Sigma = \Sigma_1 \cup \Sigma_2$,
  - $C = C_1 \cup C_2$.

Given two smart contracts SC_1 and SC_2, the invocation of SC_2 depends on the output data of SC_1. Therefore, the color function $C(o_1), C(i_2) \in C$ must satisfy $C(i_2) \subseteq C(o_1)$. Otherwise, the second smart contract SC_2 cannot be invoked by the first smart contract SC_1. Hence, the sequence composition of smart contracts would fail. Figure 2 presents the CP-Net of sequence composition of smart contracts.

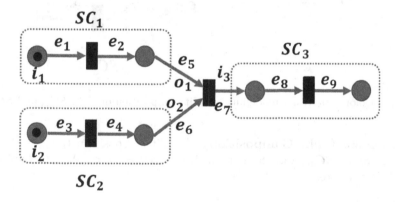

Fig. 3. Colored petri-net modelling of aggregation composition of SC_1, SC_2, and SC_3

Definition 3.4 (Aggregation Composition). An aggregation composition (A_{SC}) of smart contracts SC_1, SC_2, and SC_3 that is denoted as:

$$A_{SC} =< A_{pre}, G, tran, type, CM, SCN >, \text{ where:}$$

- $CM = CM_1 \cup CM_2 \cup CM_3$
- $SCN = (P, T, F, \Sigma, C)$ such that
  - $P = P_1 \cup P_2 \cup P_3 \cup i, o$,
  - $T = T_1 \cup T_2 \cup T_3 \cup \{(t, i_1), (t, i_1), (t, o)\} \cup \{t\}$,

- $F = F_1 \cup F_2 \cup F_3 \cup \{(t, i_1), (t, i_2), (o_1, t), (o_2, t), (t, i_3), (o_3, t)\}$,
- $i = \{i_1, i_2, o_1, o_2\}$ and $o = \{o_1, o_2, o_3\}$,
- $P_I = P_{I_1} \cup P_{I_2} \cup P_{I_3} \cup \{(o_1, t), (o_2, t)\}$,
- $P_D = P_{D_1} \cup P_{D_2} \cup P_{D_3} \cup (i_3, t)$,
- $\Sigma = \Sigma_1 \cup \Sigma_2 \cup \Sigma_3$,
- $C = C_1 \cup C_2 \cup C_3$.

Assume that three smart contracts (SC_1, SC_2, and SC_3) are given. The invocation of SC_3 depends on the output data of SC_1 and SC_2. Therefore, the color function $C(o_1), C(o_2), C(i_3) \in C$ must satisfy $C(i_3) \subseteq \{C(o_1) \cup C(o_2)\}$ to activate the execution of SC_3. Otherwise, the aggregation composition of smart contracts would fail. Figure 3 presents the CP-Net of aggregation composition of smart contracts.

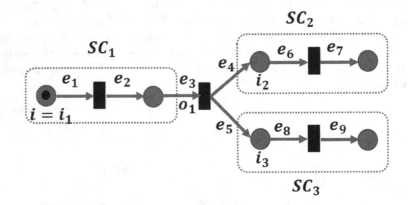

Fig. 4. Colored petri-net modelling of split composition of SC_1, SC_2, and SC_3

Definition 3.5 (Split Composition). A split composition (SP_{SC}) of smart contracts SC_1, SC_2, and SC_3 is a tuple $SP_{SC} =< A_{pre}, G, tran, type, CM, SCN >$ where:

- $CM = CM_1 \cup CM_2 \cup CM_3$
- $SCN = (P, T, F, \Sigma, C)$ such that
    - $P = P_1 \cup P_2 \cup P_3 \cup i, o_1, o_2$,
    - $T = T_1 \cup T_2 \cup T_3 \cup \{(t, i_1), (t, o_1), (t, o_2)\} \cup \{t\}$,
    - $F = F_1 \cup F_2 \cup F_3 \cup \{(t, i_1), (o_1, t), (t, i_2), (o_2, t), (t, i_3), (o_3, t)\}$,
    - $i = \{i_1, o_1\}$ and $o = \{o_1, o_2, o_3\}$,
    - $P_I = P_{I_1} \cup P_{I_2} \cup P_{I_3} \cup \{(o_1, t)\}$,
    - $P_D = P_{D_1} \cup P_{D_2} \cup P_{D_3} \cup \{(t, i_1), (o_1, t), (o_2, t), (o_3, t)\}$,
    - $\Sigma = \Sigma_1 \cup \Sigma_2 \cup \Sigma_3$,
    - $C = C_1 \cup C_2 \cup C_3$.

For any three given smart contracts (SC_1, SC_2, and SC_3), the invocation of SC_2 and SC_3 depends on the output data of SC_1. Therefore, color functions $C(o_1), C(i_2), C(i_3) \in C$ must satisfy $\{C(i_2) \cup C(i_3)\} \subseteq C(o_1)$ to activate the execution of SC_2 and SC_3. Otherwise, the split composition of smart contracts would fail. Figure 4 presents the CP-Net of split composition of smart contracts.

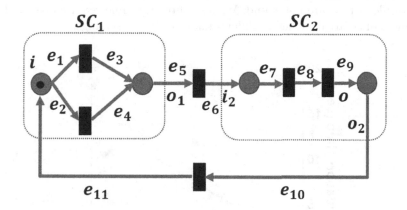

Fig. 5. Colored petri-net modelling of loop composition of SC_1 and SC_2.

Definition 3.6 (Loop Composition). A loop composition (L_{SC}) of smart contracts SC_1 and SC_2 is a tuple $L_{SC} =< A_{pre}, G, tran, type, CM, SCN >$ where:

- $CM = CM_1 \cup CM_2$
- $SCN = (P, T, F, \Sigma, C)$ such that
  - $P = P_1 \cup P_2$,
  - $T = T_1 \cup T_2 \cup \{(t, i_1), (o_2, t), t\}$,
  - $F = F_1 \cup F_2 \cup \{(t, i), (o_1, t), (t, i_2), (o_2, t), (t, i_1), (o, t)\}$,
  - $i = \{i_1, o_2,\}$ and $o = \{o_1, o_2\}$,
  - $P_I = P_{I_1} \cup P_{I_2} \cup \{(o_1, t), (o_2, t)\}$,
  - $P_D = P_{D_1} \cup P_{D_2} \cup (i_1, t), (i_2, t)$,
  - $\Sigma = \Sigma_1 \cup \Sigma_2$,
  - $C = C_1 \cup C_2$.

Given two smart contracts SC_1 and SC_2, the invocation of SC_2 depends on the output data of SC_1 and vice versa. Therefore, the color function $C(i_1), C(o_1), C(i_2), C(o_2) \in C$ must satisfy $C(i_2) \subseteq C(o_1)$ and $C(i_1) \subseteq \{C(i) \cup C(o_2)\}$. Figure 5 presents the CP-Net of loop composition of smart contracts.

4   Experimental Results and Performance Analysis

In this section, we discuss the performance of our proposed framework for modeling the blockchain-based supply chain management system. We conduct several experiments to generate different smart contract workflows and investigate the performance. We use synthetic supply chain data to generate several supply chain workflows. The performance is investigated in terms of the ability to identify workflows that are not sound. We also show the time required to check the soundness of smart contract workflows under different settings.

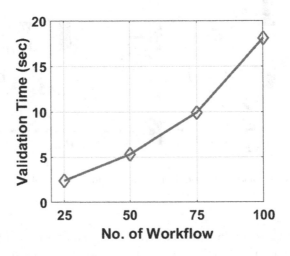

Fig. 6. Validation time (sec) for different number of smart contract workflows requested at a time.

All experiments were executed using a desktop PC with an Intel i5-6600 quad-core CPU without hyperthreading in Windows 10 operating system. We created a JAVA based server program using Apache Tomcat 8.0 to handle simultaneous requests and Petri-net based workflow validation tasks. We consider a collection of 500 smart contracts of different types from different stakeholders.

Table 1 shows the correctness of the validation process of different number of smart contract workflows. The smart contract workflows, conforming the Colored

Table 1. Correctness of soundness checking.

No. of workflow	Sound	Not sound	Correctness
25	24	1	100%
50	43	7	100%
75	69	6	100%
100	88	12	100%

Petri-Net based formalism, are referred as *sound*. Non-conforming workflows are referred as *not-sound*. Results show that our proposed framework identifies the conforming and non-conforming workflows with 100% accuracy.

Figure 6 shows the validation time for different number of simultaneous smart contract workflow validation requests. The validation time is measured in seconds. According to the result shown in Fig. 6, the validation time increases almost exponentially with the increment of validating workflows.

5 Conclusion

In this paper, we present a smart contract workflow validation model for blockchain-based supply chains for smart healthcare. At first, data-driven smart contract composition for the workflow is discussed. Next, a formal model is proposed to analyze the correctness of smart contract workflow before executing the actual blockchain network for different input data. The key benefit of the framework is that it minimizes the cost of smart contract execution. Experimental results demonstrate that the validation task can be performed efficiently for multiple simultaneous validation requests. Our formalism technique can be used to capture dynamic behaviors in any blockchain-based supply chain and other systems. However, we plan to model more complex dynamic behaviors in future work.

Acknowledgement. This work is part of the NPRP11S-1227-170135 project. The authors would like to express their gratitude to the QNRF (Qatar Foundation) for its support and funding for the project activities.

References

1. Ahmed, S., Rahman, M.S., Rahaman, M.S., et al.: A blockchain-based architecture for integrated smart parking systems. In: 2019 IEEE International Conference on Pervasive Computing and Communications Workshops (PerCom Workshops), pp. 177–182. IEEE (2019)
2. Bhattacharjee, A., Badsha, S., Shahid, A., Livani, H., Sengupta, S.: Block-phasor: a decentralized blockchain framework to enhance security of synchrophasor. In: IEEE Kansas Power and Energy Conference, Manhattan, Kansas, USA (2020)
3. Bistarellia, S., Mazzanteb, G., Michelettib, M., Mostardab, L., Sestilib, D., Tiezzib, F.: Ethereum smart contracts: analysis and statistics of their source code and opcodes. Internet Things **11**, 100198 (2020)
4. Duo, W., Xin, H., Xiaofeng, M.: Formal analysis of smart contract based on colored petri nets. IEEE Intell. Syst. **35**, 19–30 (2020)
5. Entezari-Maleki, R., Etesami, S.E., Ghorbani, N., Niaki, A.A., Sousa, L., Movaghar, A.: Modeling and evaluation of service composition in commercial multiclouds using timed colored petri nets. IEEE Trans. Syst. Man Cyber. Syst. **50**(3), 947–961 (2020)
6. Kudva, S., Badsha, S., Sengupta, S., Khalil, I., Zomaya, A.: Towards secure and practical consensus for blockchain based vanet. Inf. Sci. (2020). https://doi.org/10.1016/j.ins.2020.07.060

7. Kudva, S., Norderhaug, R., Badsha, S., Sengupta, S., Kayes, A.: Pebers: practical Ethereum blockchain based efficient ride hailing service. In: IEEE International Conference on Informatics, IoT and Enabling Technologies (2020)

8. Liu, Z., Liu, J.: Formal verification of blockchain smart contract based on colored petri net models. In: 2019 IEEE 43rd Annual Computer Software and Applications Conference (COMPSAC), vol. 2, pp. 555–560. IEEE (2019)

9. Maskey, S.R., Badsha, S., Sengupta, S., Khalil, I.: Bits: blockchain based intelligent transportation system with outlier detection for smart city (2020)

10. Rahman, M.S., Khalil, I., Arachchige, P.C.M., Bouras, A., Yi, X.: A novel architecture for tamper proof electronic health record management system using blockchain wrapper. In: Proceedings of the 2019 ACM International Symposium on Blockchain and Secure Critical Infrastructure, pp. 97–105 (2019)

11. Ream, J., Chu, Y., Schatsky, D.: Upgrading blockchains: smart contract use cases in industry. Retrieved December **12**, 2017 (2016)

12. Scholl, H.J., Pomeshchikov, R., Rodríguez Bolívar, M.P.: Early regulations of distributed ledger technology/blockchain providers: a comparative case study. In: Proceedings of the 53rd Hawaii International Conference on System Sciences (2020)

13. Swan, M.: Blockchain: Blueprint for a New Economy. O'Reilly Media Inc, Sebastopol (2015)

14. Tan, W., Fan, Y., Zhou, M., Tian, Z.: Data-driven service composition in enterprise SOA solutions: a petri net approach. IEEE Trans. Autom. Sci. Eng. **7**(3), 686–694 (2009)

15. Tian, F.: An agri-food supply chain traceability system for china based on RFID & blockchain technology. In: 2016 13th International Conference on Service Systems and Service Management (ICSSSM), pp. 1–6. IEEE (2016)

16. Vakilinia, I., Badsha, S., Arslan, E., Sengupta, S.: Pooling approach for task allocation in the blockchain based decentralized storage network. In: 15th International Conference on Network and Service Management, IEEE (2019)

17. Yue, X., Wang, H., Jin, D., Li, M., Jiang, W.: Healthcare data gateways: found healthcare intelligence on blockchain with novel privacy risk control. J. Med. Syst. **40**(10), 218 (2016). https://doi.org/10.1007/s10916-016-0574-6

18. Zhang, L., Yao, S.: Using the c-net for formalizing workflow patterns. In: 2010 Second International Conference on Information Technology and Computer Science, pp. 102–105 (2010)

19. Zupan, N., Kasinathan, P., Cuellar, J., Sauer, M.: Secure smart contract generation based on petri nets. In: Rosa Righi, R., Alberti, A.M., Singh, M. (eds.) Blockchain Technology for Industry 4.0. BT, pp. 73–98. Springer, Singapore (2020). https://doi.org/10.1007/978-981-15-1137-0_4

Malware Classification Using Attention-Based Transductive Learning Network

Liting Deng[1,2], Hui Wen[1,2(✉)], Mingfeng Xin[1,2], Yue Sun[1,2], Limin Sun[1,2], and Hongsong Zhu[1,2]

[1] Beijing Key Laboratory of IOT Information Security Technology, Institute of Information Engineering, CAS, Beijing, China
{dengliting,wenhui,xinmingfeng,sunyue0205,sunlimin,zhuhongsong}@iie.ac.cn
[2] School of Cyber Security, University of Chinese Academy of Sciences, Beijing, China

Abstract. Malware has now grown up to be one of the most important threats in the internet security. As the number of malware families has increased rapidly, a malware classification model needs to classify the samples from emerging malware families. In real-world environment, the number of malware samples varies greatly with each family and some malware families only have a few samples. Therefore, it is a challenge task to obtain a malware classification model with strong generalization ability by using only a few labeled malware samples in each family. In this paper, we propose an attention-based transductive learning approach to tackle this problem. To extract features from raw malware binaries, our approach first converts them into gray-scale images. After visualization, an embedding function is used to encode the images into feature maps. Then we build an attention-based Gaussian similarity graph to help transduct the label information from well-labeled instances to unknown instances. With end-to-end training, we validate our attention-based transductive learning network on a malware database of 11,236 samples with 30 different malware families. Comparing with state-of-the-art approaches, the experimental results show that our approach achieves a better performance.

Keywords: Malware classification · Tranductive learning · Attention mechanism · Deep learning

1 Introduction

Malware has now become one of the most important threats in the internet security. The cyber threat report from SonicWall shows that there were 10.52 billion malware attacks in 2018, an increasing of 22% from 2017 [1]. This emphasizes the importance of developing robust and efficient approaches to detect as

N. Park et al. (Eds.): SecureComm 2020, LNICST 336, pp. 403–418, 2020.
https://doi.org/10.1007/978-3-030-63095-9_26

well as classify malicious samples. Traditionally, malware analysis methods can be divided into two main categories including static approaches and dynamic approaches. In static approaches, malware is analyzed by signatures without executing. However, the attackers can easily tweak the available malware and create their own versions to bypass the detection. As even a small change of code can cause the change of signature, static approaches would fail to detect these malware variants. In dynamic approaches, malware is analyzed in a controlled environment such as a virtual environment, simulator, and sandbox. Although dynamic approaches can solve the code obfuscation problem by executing, they are time consuming and need significant efforts from security experts with proper experiences.

As the above hand-crafted malware analysis approaches need a lot of effort to extract features, new methods are adopted to improve the efficiency. Since Krizhevsky et al. [2] achieved the first place in ImageNet competition using deep Convolutional Neural Network (CNN), researchers have introduced deep learning methods into almost every field including malware classification. Benefited from deep learning technology, features can be learned automatically and malware classification model can be built without security experts. Raff et al. (2018) [3] embedded the malware raw bytes into fixed length and performed malware classification with both CNN and Recurrent Neural Networks (RNNs). Quan et al. (2018) [4] proposed a Convolutional Neural Network-Bi Long Short-Term Memory (CNN-BiLSTM) architecture. Taking the raw binaries as input, their approach achieved a high accuracy of 98.2% in classifying nine malware families.

Although deep learning-based approaches can efficiently obtain ideal classification results, they need large amounts of samples for training. However, when setting up the malware database, we found the number of samples in different malware families varies greatly. With the rapidly emerging of malware families, it is almost impossible to collect malware samples from all the existed families. Therefore, we introduce a few-shot learning method to learn the classification model with strong generalization ability from few malware samples. In few-shot learning, the training instances are randomly divided into support set and query set. If each of N unique classes contains K labeled instances as the support set, the target few-shot problem is called N-way K-shot [5]. In each episode, the few-shot learning network learns from the labeled instances which are in the support set and predicts the malware families for the unlabeled instances which are in the query set. The concept of few-shot learning (FSL) was proposed by Fei-Fei et al. (2006) [6]. And FSL is also called one-shot learning if there is only one labeled instance in each unique class of the support set. By using three known categories to derive a priority, they developed a Bayesian learning framework and achieved a detection performance of around 70–95% on images from 101 categories. Vinyals et al. (2016) [7] proposed matching networks, which used a cosine similarity matrix following the embedding function to predict classes for the unlabeled points. Snell et al. (2017) [8] proposed prototypical networks, which computed the mean of the support instances of each unique class in the embedding space as class prototype. Then they predicted the labels of query set by finding the nearest prototype for embedded query instances. Sung et al. (2018)

[5] proposed Relation Network (RN) which can label the instances of query set by computing relation scores between the query images and each instance in the support set. Liu et al. (2018) [9] produced Transductive Propagation Network (TPN) to propagate labels from labeled instances to unlabeled instances. Their experiments showed the state-of-the-art results on *miniImageNet* [10] and *tieredImageNet* [11].

Considering similar malware samples have similar image textures, Nataraj et al. (2011) [12] transferred the raw malware binaries into gray-scale images and used GIST [13,14] to do a wavelet decomposition. By choosing k-Nearest Neighbors (kNN) with Euclidean distance for classification, their method achieved an accuracy of 98% with 25 malware families, a total of 9,458 samples. Kalash et al. (2018) [15] obtained 98.52% and 99.97% accuracy on Malimg and Microsoft malware datasets by using a CNN based on VGG-16 [16]. Ding et al. (2018) [17] converted the bytecodes exacted from each Android APK file into an image. Of the total 3,962 malware samples in fourteen families, they obtained an accuracy of 94% with four convolutional layers. Inspired by these results, we also visualize the malware binaries into gray-scale images as data preprocessing.

To the best of our knowledge, few researchers have attempted to use few-shot learning methods on malware classification task. Trung et al. (2018) [18] converted the API calls into vectors via word2vec. They proposed a Memory Augmented Neural Network (MANN) [19] with Least Recently Used Access (LRUA) to classify the unlabeled malware. However, their test dataset had only 430 malicious samples in 5 ransom families. Besides, they compared the experimental results with traditional machine learning methods but not with the few-shot learning methods. In this paper, we propose an attention-based transductive learning network, which can learn the label information from the few samples in each malware family. We evaluate the effectiveness of our method with traditional machine learning methods, deep learning methods and some state-of-the-art few-shot learning methods. Our main contributions are:

- We develop an attention-based transductive learning network for malware classification which can propagate information from labeled instances to unlabeled instances through an attention-based Gaussian similarity graph.
- We set up a malware database with 11,236 samples in total 30 malware families.
- We conduct our approach with traditional machine learning, deep learning and few-shot learning experiments on our collected malware database. As our proposed method has a strong generalization ability, the classification accuracies are increased by more than 60% compared with the traditional machine learning methods and 50% compared with the deep learning methods. In addition, comparing with several state-of-the-art few-shot learning methods, we can also achieve the best performance in 5-shot and 10-shot learning experiments.

The rest of this paper is organized as follows. In Sect. 2, we describe our malware classification approach called attention-based transductive learning network in detail. The experiments are presented in Sect. 3. We conclude the whole paper in Sect. 4.

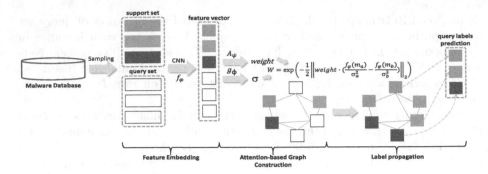

Fig. 1. The overview of the proposed attention-based transductive learning network.

2   Proposed Method

In this section, we will introduce the proposed attention-based transductive learning network, which can be divided into two parts: malware visualization and model learning. With this approach, we can efficiently achieve the malware classification task by just learning a few malicious instances in each family. The overview of the proposed method is shown in Fig. 1.

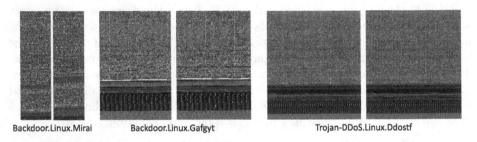

Backdoor.Linux.Mirai   Backdoor.Linux.Gafgyt   Trojan-DDoS.Linux.Ddostf

Fig. 2. We can see that different malware samples appear visually similar from a given family and distinct from those belonging to different families. The images are rescaled for better visualization.

2.1   Malware Visualization

We consider this part as the data preprocessing module. Inspired by Nataraj et al. (2011) [12], gray-scale images of different malware samples appear visually similar from a given family and distinct from those belonging to different families. We provide some examples extracted from various families that support this observation in Fig. 2. Therefore, as shown in Fig. 3, we transfer the collected raw malicious binaries into gray-scale images. We first read the binary file in each 8-bits as unsigned integers which can exactly represent the gray value from 0 to 255. As the input of the CNN need to be a fixed size, we then resize every gray-scale images into 64×64. After this data preprocessing module, our raw malware database can be converted into the database with gray-scale images.

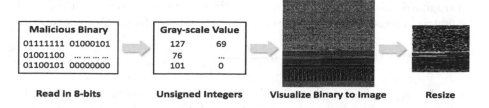

Fig. 3. The process of malware visualization module.

2.2 Model Learning

We illustrate our attention-based transductive learning model in Fig. 1, which consists of three components: feature embedding function with CNNs; Gaussian similarity graph based on attention mechanism; and label propagation algorithm which flows the label information from support set to the query set.

In each episode, we randomly select N malware families with K labeled instances from each of N as the support set $S = \{(m_i, y_i)\}_{i=1}^{l} (l = N \cdot K)$. Similarly, we select T labeled instances in each of these N families for the query set $Q = \{(m_j, y_j)\}_{j=1}^{p} (p = N \cdot T)$. The aim of our model is to learn information from the support set S and minimize the loss between prediction and the query set Q.

Feature Embedding. After malware visualization, we put the 64×64 grayscale images into feature embedding function f_φ to extract features from the input, where φ represents the parameters of the function. The f_φ includes four convolutional blocks where each block starts with a 2D-convolutional layer with the filter size of 64 and a 3×3 kernel. The convolutional layer is followed by a batch-normalization layer, a ReLU function and a 2×2 2D-Max-Pooling layer (see Fig. 4). Remarkably, we use f_φ to the instances in both support set and query set. So we get $f_\varphi(m_s)$ and $f_\varphi(m_q)$ as the output of the feature embedding function where m_s and m_q represent the images from support set and query set.

Fig. 4. Detailed architecture of each convolutional block in feature embedding function.

Attention-Based Graph Construction. The output $f_\varphi(\cdot)$ of the feature embedding function is a 64-channel 4×4 image. We then flatten $f_\varphi(\cdot)$ and concatenate the feature vectors of support set and query set. In this way, if we set $N = 5$ for selected malware family number, $K = 5$ and $T = 15$ as the number of support and query instances in each of the unique families, we can get the feature matrix of 100×1024. To represent the similarity between each vector of the matrix, we choose a Gaussian similarity formulation for graph construction:

$$W_{ij} = exp\left(-\frac{E(f_\varphi(m_a), f_\varphi(m_b))}{2\sigma^2}\right) \tag{1}$$

where $f_\varphi(m_a)$, $f_\varphi(m_b)$ $(a, b \in [1, (N \cdot K + N \cdot T)])$ represent each vector in the feature matrix, σ is a scale parameter and $E(\cdot, \cdot)$ is defined as a distance computation function. As W_{ij} deeply depends on σ, we need for optimal this parameter to achieve the best performance. Therefore, we use a scale select function g_ϕ to get σ for each feature vector, where ϕ represents the parameters of the function.

With learning an independent σ for each feature vector, the Gaussian similarity formulation can be converted as follows:

$$W_{ij} = exp\left(-\frac{1}{2}E\left(\frac{f_\varphi(m_a)}{\sigma_a^2}, \frac{f_\varphi(m_b)}{\sigma_b^2}\right)\right) \tag{2}$$

For function $E(\cdot, \cdot)$, we simply choose the Euclidean distance formula. Inspired by Woo et al. (2018) [20], different pixels contribute differently to the final classification accuracy. So we need to show the importance of each feature value after extracting them from each malicious instance by $f_\varphi(\cdot)$. Therefore, we introduce an attention mechanism A_ψ to our Gaussian similarity graph, where ψ contains the parameters of the function. The output of A_ψ is a *weight* vector which shapes the same as the feature vector. By using the Euclidean distance and adding the attention mechanism, similarity formulation can finally be defined as follows:

$$W_{ij} = exp\left(-\frac{1}{2}\left\|\boldsymbol{weight} \times \left(\frac{f_\varphi(m_a)}{\sigma_a^2} - \frac{f_\varphi(m_b)}{\sigma_b^2}\right)\right\|_2\right) \tag{3}$$

The detailed structure of the attention mechanism based graph construction module is shown in Fig. 5. In general, the module consists of two main functions which are the scale select function g_ϕ and the attention mechanism function A_ψ. For g_ϕ, it contains a convolutional block, a fully-connected layer, a ReLU non-linear function and a fully-connected layer. And the convolutional block is composed of a 3×3 convolutional layer with 1 padding, a batch-normalization

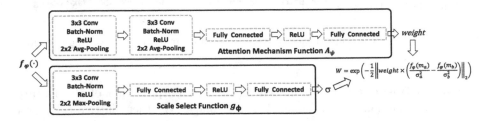

Fig. 5. Detailed architecture of the attention-based Gaussian similarity graph construction module.

layer and a ReLU activation function followed by a 2×2 max-pooling layer. For A_ψ, it contains two convolutional blocks, a fully-connected layer, a ReLU non-linear function and a fully-connected layer. And each of the convolutional blocks is composed of a 3×3 convolutional layer with 1 padding, a batch-normalization layer and a ReLU activation function followed by a 2×2 max-pooling layer. Specially, inspired by kNN that each instance can be represented by its nearest k neighbors, we choose the top k of similarity scores for each instance in W_{ij}.

To accelerate the convergence of our network, we normalize the similarity matrix W_{ij} symmetrically. The formulation of symmetric normalized Laplacian is $L = D^{-1/2}WD^{-1/2}$, where D is defined as the diagonal matrix $D = diag(d_1, d_2, \cdots, d_i, \cdots, d_n)$. Indicating the sum of the i-th row of W, d_i is called the degree of vertex i. Finally, we obtain our attention-based Gaussian similarity graph L, which is a $(N \cdot K + N \cdot T) \times (N \cdot K + N \cdot T)$ symmetric matrix.

Label Propagation Algorithm. In this part, we describe how to get labels of the query set from the support set. The detailed process is shown in Fig. 6.

First, we build a label matrix $Y^L \in \mathbb{R}^{(N \cdot K) \times N}$ for the support set, where N is the number of selected malware families and K represents the instances in each family of the support set. We define $i \in (N \cdot K)$ as the instance number and $j \in N$ as the family number. By using one-hot encoding, $Y_{ij}^L = 1$ if the label of m_i is j and $Y_{ij} = 0$ otherwise, where m_i represents the instance of the support set. Accordingly, we build a label matrix $Y^U \in \mathbb{R}^{(N \cdot T) \times N}$ for the query set, where T represents the instances in each malware family of the query set. As all the instances of the query set are initially unlabeled, we define Y^U as a zero matrix. For convenience, we concatenate the matrix Y^L and Y^U into a new matrix $Y^P \in \mathbb{R}^{(N \cdot K + N \cdot T) \times N}$.

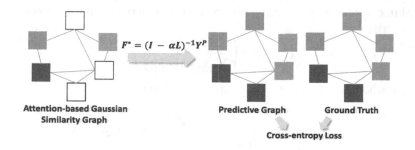

Fig. 6. The detailed process of label propagation algorithm.

According to Zhou et al. (2004) [21], each unlabeled instance in the query set can be labeled in a convergent sequence $\{F(t)\}$ iteratively. $F(0)$ is supposed to be Y^P. We use the formulation as follow to iterate the matrix Y^P:

$$F(t+1) = \alpha LF(t) + (1 - \alpha)Y^P \tag{4}$$

where α is a parameter in the range of 0 to 1, L is the symmetric normalized Laplacian matrix as mentioned above. And $F(t)$ indicates the predictive label matrix in the t-th iteration. Through the Eq. (4), we can get the general formula:

$$F(t) = (\alpha L)^{t-1}Y^P + (1-\alpha)\sum_{n=0}^{t-1}(\alpha L)^i Y^P \tag{5}$$

Considering the ranges of the variables in the formulation, we can get the limit values when t tends to be the positive infinite:

$$\begin{cases} \lim_{t\to+\infty}(\alpha L)^{t-1} = 0, \\ \lim_{t\to+\infty}\sum_{n=0}^{t-1}(\alpha L)^i = (I - \alpha L)^{-1} \end{cases} \tag{6}$$

Therefore, the Eq. (5) can be simplified as follows:

$$F^* = \lim_{t\to+\infty}F(t) = (1-\alpha)(I-\alpha L)^{-1}Y^P \tag{7}$$

where I is the identity matrix. Because $(1-\alpha)$ denotes to a constant value, we use $F^* = (I - \alpha L)^{-1}Y^P$ as the approximate equation. For this reason, we can now directly obtain the predictive label matrix F^* without iterations. And this equation is used to do the label prediction in the actual experimental studies.

After obtaining the predictive label matrix F^*, we choose the position of the max value in each vector as the label of each query instance. Then we use these predictive labels to calculate the accuracy of our network comparing with the ground truth. In addition, the classification loss is computed between the ground truth labels (in both support set and query set) and F^*. The cross-entropy method is chosen as the loss function. By using softmax followed by a logarithmic operator, we transfer the predictive matrix F^* into a probabilistic score matrix.

$$P_{ij} = log\left(\frac{exp(F^*_{ij})}{\sum_{j=1}^{N} exp(F^*_{ij})}\right) \tag{8}$$

Then the whole loss function is computed as follows:

$$J(\varphi, \phi, \psi) = -\frac{1}{N \cdot (K+T)}\sum_{i=1}^{N\cdot(K+T)}\sum_{j=1}^{N} D(gt, j)P_{ij} \tag{9}$$

where gt is the label value of ground truth and $D(\cdot,\cdot)$ is a position function defined in Eq. (10):

$$D(gt, j) = \begin{cases} 1 & gt = j \\ 0 & gt \neq j \end{cases} \tag{10}$$

Remarkably, the loss of our learning network is dependent on the parameters φ, ϕ and ψ.

3   Experiments

In this section, we first describe the collected malware database in detail. Then we represent the hyper parameters used in the experiments of our attention-based transductive learning network. Finally, we evaluate our approach with traditional machine learning methods, deep learning methods and state-of-the-art few-shot learning methods on our malware database.

3.1   Malware Dataset

We crawl 11,236 well-labeled malicious samples with 30 categories from several malware information sharing platforms such as MalShare [22], Hybrid-Analysis [23] and VirusSign [24]. After visualizing all the malware binaries, we can obtain

Table 1. Detail information of the malware database.

Malware family	Train samples	Test samples
AdWare.Win32.iBryte	607	261
Downloader.Win32.LMN	240	103
AdWare.Win32.MultiPlug	144	63
Trojan-DDoS.Linux.Ddostf	65	28
Backdoor.Linux.Gafgyt	905	388
Linux.Lightaidra	137	52
Backdoor.Linux.Mirai	108	41
Trojan.Kryptik	158	68
Trojan.MSIL.Crypt	237	102
Trojan.MSIL.Inject	91	40
Trojan.Win32.Generic	147	63
Backdoor.Win32.Androm	55	25
Trojan.JS.Agent	196	84
Trojan.Script.Generic	47	28
Trojan.SuspectCRC	218	94
Trojan.VB.Crypt	79	34
Trojan.VBS.Agent	84	37
AdWare.Win32.Generic	1740	747
Trojan.Win32.Agentb	125	54
Trojan.Win32.Crypt	393	169
Trojan.Win32.Lethic	64	28
Trojan.Win32.Emotet	45	26
Trojan.Win32.Filecoder	60	26
Trojan.Win32.Agent	68	30
Trojan.Win32.MicroFake	58	25
RiskTool.Win32.Generic	60	26
Backdoor.Win32.Hlux	72	31
Trojan.Win32.Ransom	1295	556
Backdoor.Linux.Tsunami	300	129
Trojan-DDoS.Linux	53	27

a database of 11,236 well-sorted gray-scale images. The detail of the database is listed in Table 1. We load our malware database and split it into two sets: 7,851 samples for training and 3,385 samples for testing.

3.2   Experiment Configuration

To make a better comparison with other few-shot learning approaches, we use the same feature embedding function f_φ with the same parameters as other few-shot learning methods [5,8]. In addition, we randomly select N ($N = 5, 10, 20, 30$) families in the total 30 malware families. Refer to the conclusion mentioned by Zhou et al. (2004) [21], the parameter k of top k values for each instance in W_{ij} is set to 20. And α is set to 0.99 [21], which denotes the hyper-parameter of label propagation information. All the instances are randomly generated from the malware database. With end-to-end training, we initialize the learning rate to 10^{-3} and cut in half every 20 epochs while each epoch has 100 batches. Adam optimization is applied for training.

The experiments are based on a 64-bit Ubuntu 16.04 system. We use PyTorch (version 1.2.0) framework to implement our model and NVIDIA Tesla V100 to accelerate the computation. The training model for 5-shot and 10-shot cost 1010.13 s and 1201.37 s while 1-shot costs 847.46 s. Due to the less training time, we can update our model efficiently with new malware families and samples.

3.3   Experimental Results

In this part, we evaluate and verify the effectiveness of our attention-based transductive network with three groups of comparison experiments. We compare the proposed approach with traditional machine learning methods, deep learning methods and some state-of-the-art few-shot learning methods. We treat the gray-scale images as input in all groups of experiments. The best performance in each experimental setting is depicted in bold.

Compare with Traditional Machine Learning Methods. In the first group of experiments, we compare our approach with several traditional machine learning methods. In our approach, we treat the support set as training data and query set as the test data in each episode. We predict the accuracies of query set after training 100 epochs while each epoch has 100 episodes. In each traditional machine learning method, we choose the same number of malware samples as our approach for training and testing. Therefore, we randomly select 5 instances in each unique family for training and 15 instances for testing. To stabilize the accuracies for each of the traditional machine learning methods, we train for 10000 episodes. By choosing N ($N = 5, 10, 20, 30$) in the all 30 malware families, Table 2 describes the results comparing the proposed approach with SVM, kNN, Random Forest (RF) and Decision Tree (DT).

As shown Table 2, our approach reaches the classification accuracies of more than 90% in all the experiments. In addition, even compared with the second best score in 5-way experiment, the accuracy of our approach is 60% better. This group of experiment shows that our approach has a strong feature extraction ability in multi-class malware classification problem. Comparing with the traditional learning methods, our proposed network can achieve the best performance by learning only a few malware samples.

Table 2. The classification accuracies compared with traditional machine learning methods.

Model	5-way	10-way	20-way	30-way
SVM	59.50%	47.71%	38.64%	34.34%
kNN	50.49%	37.05%	27.47%	23.70%
RF	49.61%	37.81%	29.83%	26.66%
DT	44.92%	34.26%	27.20%	24.55%
Our approach	**95.33%**	**94.63%**	**93.33%**	**92.56%**

Compare with Deep Learning Methods. In the second group of experiments, we compare our approach with two malware classification methods in recent researches using the deep Convolutional Neural Network. Espoir et al. (2017) [25] designed a network with three-layers CNN and two fully connected layers while Gurumayum et al. (2020) [26] built a network with two CNN layers and a fully connected layer. They both got over 97% classification accuracies on their own malware datasets. Therefore, we compare the performance of malware classification between our approach and theirs when training only a few samples. In our approach, we use the same experimental settings as the first group of experiments. For each deep learning method, we also choose the same number of malware samples as our approach for training and testing. In each epoch, we randomly select 5 instances in each unique family for training and 15 instances for testing. And we train the model for 100 episodes in each training step. To stabilize the accuracy, we test 1000 epochs and average the results. By choosing N (N=5,10,20,30) in the all 30 malware families, Table 3 shows the results comparing our approach with two deep learning malware classification methods.

Compared with results in the first group of experiments (Table 2), we can see that the deep learning methods get better accuracies than the traditional machine learning methods. It indicates that the deep learning methods have stronger ability of feature selection. With the increasement of selected malware families N (N=5,10,20,30), our approach shows more robust in multi-class malware classification while the accuracies of deep learning methods decrease obviously. In addition, even compared with the second best score in 5-way experiment, the accuracy of our approach is 50% better. Therefore, our approach can learn the family features more efficiently from a few numbers of malware samples.

Table 3. The classification accuracies compared with deep learning methods.

Model	5-way	10-way	20-way	30-way
Espoir et al. [25]	63.42%	52.28%	41.55%	37.20%
Gurumayum et al. [26]	60.81%	49.71%	38.74%	34.49%
Our approach	**95.33%**	**94.63%**	**93.33%**	**92.56%**

Compare with State-of-the-art Few-Shot Learning Methods. In the third group of experiments, we compare our approach with some state-of-the-art few-shot learning methods in malware classification task. By choosing $N(N = 5, 10, 20, 30)$ categories in the all 30 malware families, Table 4, Table 5 and Table 6 describe the classification accuracies comparing our approach with Matching Networks [7], Relation Networks [5] and Prototypical Networks [8]. We use the common training and testing settings in few-shot classification task. In testing phase, we randomly generated $K + T$ samples in random N families from the testing set. The model parameters are finetuned by K instances and evaluated by the rest T instances in each unique family for in each testing episode.

To make a better comparison with other few-shot learning approaches, we use the same parameters as the other few-shot learning methods [5,8] in Table 4. So the number of support set in each unique malware family is $K = 5$ while the number of query set in each unique family is $T = 15$. From Table 4, We can notice that the proposed method achieves the best results in all the N-way 5-shot experiments. This experiment shows that the proposed attention-based transductive learning network achieves the highest classification accuracies and is more suitable for malware classification task.

Table 4. The classification accuracies compared with state-of-the-art few-shot learning methods ($K = 5$).

Model	5-way	10-way	20-way	30-way
Matching networks [7]	66.98%	59.54%	47.46%	45.07%
Relation networks [5]	67.83%	56.46%	48.41%	44.28%
Prototypical networks [8]	73.46%	61.69%	50.44%	45.76%
Our approach	**75.41%**	**63.15%**	**52.48%**	**50.41%**

Moreover, we also try to set $K = 10$ as the number of support set in each unique malware family while the number of query set in each unique family is still 15. By using more 5 instances for training in each malware family, our approach can still achieve the best performance in all experiments (Table 5). Compared with the results in the N-way 5-shot experiments above (Table 4), we can find that the accuracies of our approach are 2–3% higher. This experiment indicates that our network can achieve a stronger generalization ability by learning from a few more instances in each malware family.

Finally, we also try to extend our approach to N-way 1-shot experiments. By just learning one labeled instance from each selected malware family, we still use $T = 15$ as the number of query set in each unique malware family. As seen from Table 6, our approach can still achieve the best performance in 5-way and 10-way experiments. However, Matching Network [7] performs better than our approach in 20-way and 30-way experiments. These results are explicable because Matching Network [7] is specifically designed for one-shot learning.

Table 5. The classification accuracies compared with state-of-the-art few-shot learning methods ($K = 10$).

Model	5-way	10-way	20-way	30-way
Matching networks [7]	68.94%	60.52%	48.80%	45.41%
Relation networks [5]	73.84%	59.92%	50.68%	44.49%
Prototypical networks [8]	76.57%	64.06%	53.74%	48.14%
Our approach	**77.95%**	**66.73%**	**55.53%**	**51.39%**

Table 6. The classification accuracies compared with state-of-the-art few-shot learning methods ($K = 1$).

Model	5-way	10-way	20-way	30-way
Matching networks [7]	60.22%	52.64%	**50.61%**	**49.28%**
Relation networks [5]	64.43%	51.84%	42.38%	36.55%
Prototypical networks [8]	63.97%	55.26%	43.83%	38.63%
Our approach	**66.89%**	**55.67%**	45.14%	39.83%

With the increasing of epochs, we show the curve of classification accuracy (Fig. 7) and loss value (Fig. 8) for each approach in 5-way 5-shot. As shown in Fig. 7, our approach can finally achieve the best performance after 100 epochs while each epoch contains 100 batches. For Fig. 8, we choose cross-entropy loss function for the proposed approach and Prototypical Network [8] while MSE (Mean-Square Error) and NLL (Negative Log Likelihood) loss for Relation Network [5] and Matching Network [7].

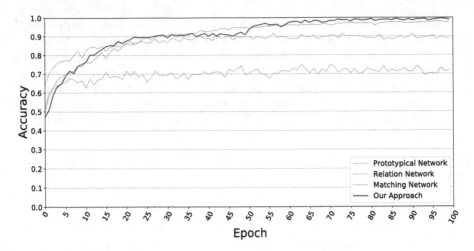

Fig. 7. Training accuracy curve with the increasing of epochs in 5-way 5-shot.

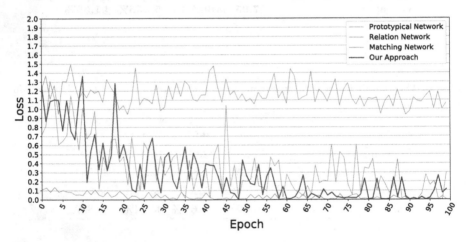

Fig. 8. Training loss curve with the increasing of epochs in 5-way 5-shot.

4   Conclusion

In this paper, we collect 11,236 malware samples from the real-world environment and build a malware database. To solve the problem of few labeled samples of malware classification and improve the generalization ability, we propose a novel malware classification approach called attention-based transductive learning network. By training with few malware samples, our approach performs the classification accuracies of 60% more than traditional machine learning methods and 50% more than the recent deep learning malware classification methods. Comparing with some few-shot learning approaches, we also achieve the highest classification accuracies in few-shot experiments and a considerable performance in the one-shot experiment.

Acknowledgement. This work was supported by the National Key R&D Program of China(Grant No. 2018YFC1201102, Grant No. 2017YFB0802804) and Key Program of National Natural Science Foundation of China (Grant No. U1766215).

References

1. Sonicwall cyber threat report. https://www.sonicwall.com/resources/white-papers/2019-sonicwall-cyber-threat-report/
2. Krizhevsky, A., Sutskever, I., Hinton, G.E.: Imagenet classification with deep convolutional neural networks. In: Advances in Neural Information Processing Systems, pp. 1097–1105 (2012)
3. Raff, E., Barker, J., Sylvester, J., Brandon, R., Catanzaro, B., Nicholas, C.K.: Malware detection by eating a whole exe. In: Workshops at the Thirty-Second AAAI Conference on Artificial Intelligence (2018)
4. Le, Q., Boydell, O., Mac Namee, B., Scanlon, M.: Deep learning at the shallow end: malware classification for non-domain experts. Digital Invest. **26**, S118–S126 (2018)
5. Sung, F., Yang, Y., Zhang, L., Xiang, T., Torr, P.H., Hospedales, T.M.: Learning to compare: relation network for few-shot learning. In: Proceedings of the IEEE Conference on Computer Vision and Pattern Recognition, pp. 1199–1208 (2018)
6. Fei-Fei, L., Fergus, R., Perona, P.: One-shot learning of object categories. IEEE Trans. Pattern Anal. Mach. Intell. **28**(4), 594–611 (2006)
7. Vinyals, O., Blundell, C., Lillicrap, T., Wierstra, D. et al.: Matching networks for one shot learning. In: Advances in Neural Information processing systems, pp. 3630–3638 (2016)
8. Snell, J., Swersky, K., Zemel, R.: Prototypical networks for few-shot learning. In: Advances in Neural Information Processing Systems, pp. 4077–4087 (2017)
9. Liu, Y., et al.: Learning to propagate labels: Transductive propagation network for few-shot learning (2018). arXiv preprint arXiv:1805.10002
10. Ravi, S., Larochelle, H.: Optimization as a model for few-shot learning (2016)
11. Ren, M., et al.: Meta-learning for semi-supervised few-shot classification (2018). arXiv preprint arXiv:1803.00676
12. Nataraj, L., Karthikeyan, S., Jacob, G., Manjunath, B.: Malware images: visualization and automatic classification. In: Proceedings of the 8th International Symposium on Visualization for Cyber Security, ACM, p. 4 (2011)
13. Torralba, A., Murphy, K.P., Freeman, W.T., Rubin, M.A.: Context-based vision system for place and object recognition (2003)
14. Oliva, A., Torralba, A.: Modeling the shape of the scene: a holistic representation of the spatial envelope. Int. J. Comput. Vision **42**(3), 145–175 (2001)
15. Kalash, M., Rochan, M., Mohammed, N., Bruce, N.D., Wang, Y., Iqbal, F.: Malware classification with deep convolutional neural networks. In: 2018 9th IFIP International Conference on New Technologies, Mobility and Security (NTMS), IEEE pp. 1–5 (2018)
16. Simonyan, K., Zisserman, A.: Very deep convolutional networks for large-scale image recognition (2014). arXiv preprint arXiv:1409.1556

17. Ding, Y., Wu, R., Xue, F.: Detecting android malware using bytecode image. In: Xiao, J., Mao, Z.-H., Suzumura, T., Zhang, L.-J. (eds.) ICCC 2018. LNCS, vol. 10971, pp. 164–169. Springer, Cham (2018). https://doi.org/10.1007/978-3-319-94307-7_13

18. Tran, T.K., Sato, H., Kubo, M.: One-shot learning approach for unknown malware classification. In: 2018 5th Asian Conference on Defense Technology (ACDT), IEEE pp. 8–13 (2018)

19. Santoro, A., Bartunov, S., Botvinick, M., Wierstra, D., Lillicrap, T.: Meta-learning with memory-augmented neural networks. In: International Conference on Machine Learning, pp. 1842–1850 (2016)

20. Woo, S., Park, J., Lee, J.-Y., Kweon, I.S:.Cbam: Convolutional block attention module. In: Proceedings of the European Conference on Computer Vision (ECCV), pp. 3–19 (2018)

21. Zhou, D., Bousquet, O., Lal, T.N., Weston, J., Schölkopf, B.: Learning with local and global consistency. In: Advances in Neural Information Processing Systems, pp. 321–328 (2004)

22. MalShare. https://www.malshare.com

23. Hybrid-Analysis. https://www.hybrid-analysis.com

24. VirusSign. https://www.virussign.com

25. Kabanga, E.K., Kim, C.H.: Malware images classification using convolutional neural network. J. Comput. Commun. $6(1)$, 153–158 (2017)

26. Sharma, G.A., Singh, K.J., Singh, M.D.: A deep learning approach to image-based malware analysis. In: Das, H., Pattnaik, P.K., Rautaray, S.S., Li, K.-C. (eds.) Progress in Computing, Analytics and Networking. AISC, vol. 1119, pp. 327–339. Springer, Singapore (2020). https://doi.org/10.1007/978-981-15-2414-1_33

COOB: Hybrid Secure Device Pairing Scheme in a Hostile Environment

Sameh Khalfaoui[1,2]($\boxtimes$), Jean Leneutre[2], Arthur Villard[1], Jingxuan Ma[1], and Pascal Urien[2]

[1] EDF R&D, 7 Boulevard Gaspard Monge, 91120 Palaiseau, France
{sameh.khalfaoui,arthur.villard,jingxuan.ma}@edf.fr
[2] LTCI, Télécom Paris, Institut Polytechnique de Paris, Paris, France
{jean.leneutre,pascal.urien}@telecom-paris.fr

Abstract. Due to the scalability limitations, the secure device pairing of Internet of Things objects cannot be efficiently conducted based on traditional cryptographic techniques using a pre-shared security knowledge. The use of Out-of-Band (OoB) channels has been proposed as a way to authenticate the key establishment process but they require a relatively long time and an extensive user involvement to transfer the authentication bits. However, the context-based schemes exploit the randomness of the ambient environment to extract a common secret without an extensive user intervention under the requirement of having a secure perimeter during the extraction phase, which is considered as a strong security assumption.

In this paper, we introduce a novel hybrid scheme, called COOB, that efficiently combines a state-of-the-art fast context-based encoder with our Out-of-Band based scheme. This protocol exploits a nonce exponentiation to achieve the temporary secrecy goal needed for the authentication. Our method provides security against an attacker that can violate the secure perimeter requirement, which is not supported by the existing contextual schemes. This security improvement has been formally validated in the symbolic model using the TAMARIN prover. Based on our implementation of the Out-of-Band channel, COOB enhances the usability by reducing the pairing time up to 39% for an 80-bit OoB exchange while keeping an optimal protocol cost.

Keywords: Internet of Things · Security · Secure device pairing · Out-of-band channel · Context-based pairing · Formal methods

1 Introduction

With the growing demand for personal gadgets and sensors, the use of a decentralized device-to-device (D2D) communication system has become a necessity for numerous applications in the context of Internet of Things (IoT) like Smart-Homes, Intelligent Transportation Systems (ITS) and Smart Metering and Mon-

© ICST Institute for Computer Sciences, Social Informatics and Telecommunications Engineering 2020
Published by Springer Nature Switzerland AG 2020. All Rights Reserved
N. Park et al. (Eds.): SecureComm 2020, LNICST 336, pp. 419–438, 2020.
https://doi.org/10.1007/978-3-030-63095-9_27

itoring (SMM). This decision is based on the inefficiency of a centralized communication solution to meet the scalability and the interoperability goals. Therefore, the protection of this communication channel requires the use of a secure key establishment protocol between the devices, known as *Secure Device Pairing* (SDP). This process ensures that the communicating nodes agree on the same symmetric encryption key, which represents an initial trust establishment between devices that have no pre-shared knowledge (a certificate, a shared password or a symmetric key). The no prior secret condition is motivated by two reasons. The first one is the unfeasibility of exploiting a Public Key Infrastructure (PKI) due to the growing numbers of heterogeneous IoT devices. The second reason is the *Zero-Trust* policy that disapproves of trusting the manufacturer with delivering the initial pre-shared pairing keys to avoid any vulnerabilities or breaches related to a third party.

Two main techniques are used to achieve these goals. The first one uses a pre-authenticated auxiliary channel that is also known as a location limited or a human assisted channel [3]. However, in this work we will refer to it as an *Out-of-Band* (OoB) channel. These channels suffer from low data-rates, which results in a long pairing time. This drawback can severely affect the user-experience. Therefore, the optimization of this usability criteria is considered a necessity for such protocols. The second technique ensures authentication through a proof of co-presence based on the randomness of the ambient environment. This method is better known as *Context-based Pairing* or *Zero-Interaction Protocols* (ZIP) [11]. Even though this type of pairing schemes is optimal in terms of usability and user-friendliness, it demands a safe zone where no attacker is assumed present to avoid any risks related to facing a well-equipped adversary. This can be quite hard to guarantee by a regular user and quite easy to take advantage of by an adversary that can hide a sensor in that, allegedly, safe environment.

In this work, we propose a novel device pairing scheme that is able to efficiently combine an existing fast contextual key agreement protocol with an authenticated Out-of-Band channel. Our hybrid protocol, called COOB, has two distinct components. The first one is a contextual module where we take advantage of any fast and reliable contextual key agreement technique. The second component is a protected OoB channel that guarantees at least the authenticity and the integrity of the exchanged information. This design provides a security improvement in comparison with the existing context-based schemes since it is robust against a powerful contextual attacker. This adversary can sense and even control the ambient environment surrounding the two legitimate devices. Furthermore, it provides a usability improvement by reducing the protocol completion time in comparison with the existing pairing schemes that rely solely on a low data-rate OoB channel. In addition, COOB maintains a reduced cryptographic cost of only two hash computations for each device. In order to reach this level of optimality, a nonce exponentiation is exploited while constructing the Diffie-Hellman public keys to temporarily hide their real values, as described in Sect. 3.3.

The main contributions of this paper are summarized as follows:

(I) We design a novel hybrid pairing protocol that efficiently combines a contextual based and an Out-of-Band based pairing techniques to enhance the security and the usability aspects.

(II) We evaluate the security of our scheme by providing a proof estimating the attack success probabilities under two adversary models. Also, we formally validate the security of our design in the symbolic model using the TAMARIN prover.

(III) We implement the Out-of-Band protocol on two Raspberry Pi 4B. Then, we conduct a time efficiency analysis to estimate the usability improvement provided by the contextual module.

The rest of this paper is organized as follows. Section 2 discusses relevant work to OoB and context-based pairing schemes and highlights the limitations of each category. Section 3 describes our protocol along with the assumptions and the threat model taken into account. Section 4 evaluates the security of our scheme and formally validates its robustness in the symbolic model using the TAMARIN prover. Section 5 describes the protocol implementation on the Raspberry Pi 4B and outlines the results of the time efficiency estimation and, lastly, Sect. 6 concludes our work.

2   Related Work

Numerous secure device pairing solutions rely on an Out-of-Band channel with specific security properties to send information that validates what has been exchanged on the In-Band channel, referred to as the In-Band channel. This is due to the unfeasibility of performing the authentication based on a single channel that is controlled by a Dolev-Yao intruder [9], as demonstrated in [7] using BAN Logic analysis [6]. This powerful adversary is assumed to have a perfect knowledge of the protocol and he is able to overhear, block, delay, replay and forge any transmission over that channel. However, he is not able to perform any computational attacks against the cryptographic functions. As a consequence of adopting this intruder model, the usage of the In-Band channel without having pre-shared secrets is not sufficient to provide the desired security guarantees for the key exchange process. Therefore, there is a need for an auxiliary communication link on which the authentication of the exchanged keys can happen. These channels can be constructed based on audio, visual or haptic transmissions. Due to their special nature and their communication properties, they provide an initial level of security that is sufficient to primarily guarantee the integrity of the data and the demonstrative identification [3], which is ensuring that the communicating devices on these channels are the intended ones for pairing. Other security objectives might be provided in some cases such as the confidentiality and the data origin authenticity. These assumptions on the OoB channel reduce the attacker capabilities in comparison with his abilities on the In-Band channel. In this context, we adopt the Out-of-Band security classification in the work of

Mirzadeh et al. [25] that defines the three following categories: the *confidential* channel which eliminates all attacker capabilities, the *protected* channel that limits the adversary powers to intercepting, blocking and delaying the messages which breaks the confidentiality assumption and affects the guarantee of the message reception. Finally, the *authentic* channel grants the attacker the additional capabilities to replay messages that were exchanged in previous sessions which violates the data freshness guarantee [30].

Some proposals such as Secure Simple Pairing (SSP) [4] and Push Button Configuration (PBC) [2] exploit the short-range radio communications, such as the Near Field Communication (NFC), as an Out-of-Band channel. Unfortunately, this technology is not secured against an attacker that is sufficiently close to the pairing objects as demonstrated in the work of Akter et al. [1]. Thus, we will not consider it as a secure option of an OoB channel. In the work of Fomichev et al. [10], a selection of pairing proposals that rely on Out-of-band channels have been thoroughly described based on their nature (radio [2,4], visual [26,36], acoustic [13,32] or haptic [21,27]), the degree of the user involvement and the application context of the pairing. The latter criteria classes the pairing use-cases into categories that have related security threats and objectives. The significant limitations of these channels are their low data-rates and their need for a extensive user intervention. The former drawback is due to the quality of the interfaces on the commercial IoT products, which makes the transfer of long hashes or keys not possible. Some of the proposed schemes rely on the human user to *setup* the devices for the exchange, to *relay* an information from one device to another, to *compare* a short authentication string on both objects or to simply *generate* a secret PIN and to enter it in both devices [10]. As an example, the security of the pairing scheme MANA III [12] is based on the confidentiality of the PIN entered by the user. Even though the confidential OoB channels are not considered as a reliable option due to the feasibility of eavesdropping attacks on the acoustic, the visual and the haptic transmissions using side-channel analysis techniques [14]. Another prominent threat in the protocol design is the predictable human input. This vulnerability is considered as a *Human-factor error* that, if not well designed, might compromise the effective security of the protocol [17].

Due to the usability challenges related to the use of Out-of-Band channels such as the long pairing completion time and the extensive human involvement as shown in [17,20], the research focus has shifted toward a more autonomous authentication technique based on a proof of co-presence. These protocols use the randomness of the ambient environment to extract a contextual information on both devices within a specific area called the *authentication zone*. This parameter represents the area where the legitimate devices are required to be placed in order to enhance the usability of the protocol by minimizing the errors when sensing the environment. The contextual information can be either used to extract a key for encryption later on [23], a fingerprint of the device location [15] or as a way to encode a secret between the pairing parties [34]. Based on the close proximity assumption, the two objects are expected to have similar measurements of the chosen environmental metrics, which will result in a similar contextual security parameters. The choice of the metrics should be based on aspects such as: the **location dependency** that explains the changes in the contextual measurements when we change the position of the sensor, the **static randomness** that guarantees the extraction of contextual information with a sufficient entropy when the devices are static and finally, the **unpredictability** aspect that guarantees the unfeasibility of a prediction attack on the contextual measurements. There are multiple context-based schemes that use the audio as a source of randomness such as [18,29]. In the work of Schürmann et al. [29], the authors used an audio fingerprint of the energy fluctuation between the frequency bands coupled with a fuzzy commitment [16] in order to exchange a key between two co-located devices. Also, the work of Karapanos et al. [18] exploits the acoustic environment by computing a similarity score using the average of the maximum cross-correlation of audio samples applied on a set of one-third octave bands. This result is then compared to a fixed threshold to decide the co-presence of the devices. This metric is based on the unpredictability of the acoustic signals received in the dynamic scenarios where these schemes were tested. Unfortunately, this choice does not satisfy most of the previously mentioned criteria such as the location dependency and the static randomness in quite environments. In the work of Fomichev et al. [11], it has been proven that the microphones heterogeneity increases drastically the error rates of the contextual pairing, which makes the scheme less robust against contextual attacks. Also, we can never discard the risk of *audio amplification*, as discussed in [29], where the adversary uses a directional microphone to amplify the audio signals, which makes him able to reconstruct the fingerprint and get hold of the shared secret.

Another variant of contextual protocols relies on a number of metrics from the ambient radio environment as a proof of physical proximity such as the *Receiver Signal Strength Indicator* (RSSI) [23,28] and the *Channel State Information* (CSI) [33,34]. These protocols are based on the assumption that devices within a close range and using a high frequency radio technology perceive the same unpredictable changes in the signal strength in short periods of time. Therefore, they are able to extract high entropy contextual information that can be ultimately used in exchanging a secret or deriving an encryption key. This hypothesis satisfies our three main criteria mentioned above but it has been recently proven in [31] that the RSSI can be manipulated by the adversary. This attack has been demonstrated using a fake Wi-Fi access point on which the transmission power is adapted to the location of the target device so that it computes the wanted signal strength indicator. On the other hand, the CSI measurements represent the propagation of the signal in terms of scattering, fading and power decay with respect to their physical location. This metric becomes rapidly de-correlated between two devices as the distance between them increases. It is also highly unpredictable due to its dependency on the ambient environment as shown in [34]. Such properties of the CSI are used to provide a high random bit generation rate that can reach hundreds of bits per second. The authenticity and the confidentiality of the secret are guaranteed against a passive attacker outside the *safe zone* but its resilience in the face of an active adversary is still considered under investigation since it has been theoretically proven feasible by the work of Zafer et al. [35]. In this paper, we combine the two types of secure device pairing protocols in order to benefit from the fast contextual secret agreement in the context-based schemes to reduce the pairing completion time in comparison with the protocols relying solely on the low data-rate Out-of-Band channels. Also, we exploit the advantages of the Out-of-Band channels in terms of security under a threat model which deals with an ambient environment controlled by the attacker. Such strong intruder represents the Achilles' heel of any existing contextual scheme, especially without the requirement of human interactions such as performing some pattern of movement or taping, as suggested in [15].

3   COOB

3.1   System Model

Our protocol is based on two main building blocks: a *contextual module* and an *Out-of-Band module*. These two components are used in an optimal manner to benefit from the advantages of both types of pairing. Our scheme does not rely on a specific sensing technology or a precise choice of an Out-of-Band channel. It takes as an input a *reliable* and *fast* contextual key agreement protocol and a *protected* OoB channel that guarantees the integrity and the authenticity of the information transmitted. The human interaction needed is only limited to placing the devices in close proximity and pushing a button, which is used as a way to provide user feedback about the correctness of the pairing process. This modular design gives the protocol two main advantages: an *adaptive nature* to the recent enhancements in both research directions and a *flexibility* toward the existing interfaces on the constrained objects. In the upcoming protocol description, we will apply a contextual extractor proposed in [34] due to its fast generation rate and a visual communication channel for the Out-of-Band module.

3.2   Assumptions and Threat Models

We take into account the scenario where two devices, Alice and Bob, try to pair by authenticating their public Diffie-Hellman keys exchanged over the In-Band channel. We assume that the *discovery* phase, where the two devices gain knowledge of each other, has been correctly established by the user. The details of this phase are considered out of the scope of this work. The target devices of our protocol need, based on the choice of the contextual part, a Bluetooth module to communicate on the In-Band channel and a Wi-Fi chipset able to extract the CSI measurements. Also, we need, based on the choice of the Out-of-Band channel, a LED and a button as interfaces on the initiator device, named Alice, a LED and a light-sensor as interfaces on the enrollee, named Bob. Additionally, we need enough computational power to handle the Diffie-Hellman key computations [8].

We take into account the existence of a powerful Dolev-Yao [9] adversary that is able to control both the In-Band channel and the ambient environment surrounding the pairing participants such as the audio, the radio (Wi-Fi, Bluetooth and GPS) and even the physical environment (temperature, humidity, altitude and their combinations). This capability is not limited to a single target device since we assume that the attacker can be in the same context as all of the legitimate objects for an unlimited period of time. Furthermore, in our analysis we consider the feasibility of computational attacks that are targeting the cryptographic functions that rely solely on a short secret as the source of randomness. This assumption makes the security evaluation of our scheme more realistic with respect to the use of short secrets to perform the ad-hoc pairing. Therefore, we assume the existence of two kind of attackers in our evaluation: the first one is an **ordinary contextual intruder** that is not able to suppress any existing contextual information and is not allowed inside a pre-defined *safe zone* fixed by the pairing scheme assumptions. The second one is a **sophisticated contextual intruder** that is able to sense and ultimately control the ambient environment, which makes him aware of the secret extraction outcome in both devices. The latter threat model might seem unrealistic but it has been proven in [31] that such attacks, against co-presence authentication systems, are possible using a form of a "ghost-and-leech" technique [19]. Due to the close proximity of the pairing parties, the adversary might use a leech and a ghost at the same place. The leech plays the role of an eavesdropping device that senses the environment and send it back to the attacker using a fast digital communication, i.e a microphone or a photo-sensor. On the other hand, the ghost plays the role of a device that controls the environment, i.e a speaker or a laser.

3.3 Our Proposal

In this section, we present a novel approach that combines an Out-of-Band based scheme with a context-based protocol to provide a usability improvement in term of reducing the pairing time in comparison with the previously proposed OoB-based protocols relying on a low-bandwidth Out-of-Band channel. Furthermore, our approach presents a security enhancement against a sophisticated contextual attacker without an extensive user involvement, which is not supported by the previously proposed contextual schemes. Our protocol takes advantage of a DH exponentiation that temporarily hides the real values of the public keys in order to reach the optimal security provided by our two hash verifications. Furthermore, this technique avoids the additional use of cryptographic commitment schemes to minimize the communication and computation costs required, as detailed in Sect. 3.3.

Our proposal is split into two main steps. First, we will briefly introduce, in the background Sect. 3.3, the contextual module where we will highlight the key aspects of the TDS protocol [34] used in our scheme. Then, we will explain our choice of the Visible Light Communication (VLC) as our Out-of-Band channel. Secondly, we will present the exchanges of our protocol, COOB, that combines the two previously mentioned blocks in an optimal manner in terms of time, communication and computational efficiency by exploiting the advantages of a nonce exponentiation technique.

Background

Contextual Module

As mentioned above in Sect. 3.1, we will apply the fuzzy extractor used in the work of Xi et al. [34] that exploits the channel state readings from a Wi-Fi access point that is publicly agreed upon. Due to the close proximity of the two legitimate devices (within an authentication zone $0.4\lambda \approx 5$ cm), they receive highly correlated CSI amplitude measurements as highlighted in Fig. 1. The sensing of the ambient environment will be initiated by each device respectively at the beginning of the discovery phase.

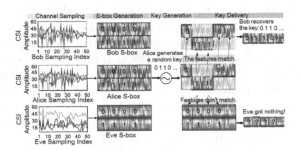

Fig. 1. The main steps of TDS [34]

After gathering a sufficient number of samples, Alice will try to synchronize the sampled data with the other device by sending a sequence of values to Bob marking the beginning of the valid samples that will be used in the encoding process. The S-box in our case will represent a $(2 \times l)$-matrix where l is the bit-length of the secret. Each element of the matrix will include a number $m \times n$ of CSI samples that uniquely represent a bit value 0 or 1, where m is the number of sub-carriers used and n is the number of measurements per sub-carrier. Thus, two consecutive $m \times n$ samples need to be distinct in order to reflect a 0 or a 1 bit. After uniquely identifying each block of the matrix, an l-bit secret is independently generated by Bob and then, for each bit, he sends its corresponding block in the S-box. As an example, if the secret starts with the sequence 0110 then Bob will send the first 0-block, the second 1-block, the third 1-block and the fourth 0-block as illustrated in Fig. 1. Since Alice has computed a similar S-box due to the reception of similar CSI samples, she will decide whether the received i^{th} block represents a 0 or a 1 bit value based on a comparison with her i^{th} column in her matrix. However, the adversary will not be able to reconstruct the original message due to his different measurements, which result in a different matching box. In this design, we will use Reed-Solomon (RS) codes to ensure that Alice can correct a number of bits fewer than a fixed limit. This will guarantee the reconstruction of the secret by only a legitimate device inside the *authentication zone*. Readers willing to learn more about the TDS scheme can consult the original paper [34].

To simplify the protocol description in the upcoming sections, we will model this technique as a fuzzy-commitment scheme [16] that uses two similar contextual bit-values r_{c_a} and r_{c_b} generated respectively by Alice and Bob. These two variables will represent the S-box process of encoding and decoding based on the CSI features. The transfer of the blocks V_b by Bob will be modeled as $V_b = r_{c_b} \oplus Encode(r_b)$ where $Encode(.)$ is the Reed-Solomon encoding function. This message will be decoded on the other side using r_{c_a} as follows: $r_b = Decode(r_{c_a} \oplus V_b)$ where $Decode(.)$ is the Reed-Solomon decoding function. The feasibility of this modeling is due to the similarity between the concept of representing a bit by multiple random information and the idea of hiding its value using a random contextual bit and an XOR operation.

Out-of-Band Module
In our proposal, we need two Out-of-Band channels that limit the attacker capabilities to blocking, delaying and eavesdropping on the transmissions. These channels will be differentiated based on their nature and their degree of human interaction as described in Sect. 2. The first Out-of-Band channel will have the purpose of exchanging an authentication parameter and the second one will serve as a final validation step of the pairing. Due to the constrained nature of our target devices, we decided to choose a simple unidirectional visible light OoB channel based on a LED on the initiator (Alice) and a light sensor on the enrollee (Bob). This choice is based on the nature of the channel since it is hard for an attacker to replay or forge a message without being detected by the user. Also, it is less susceptible to the ambient noise than the acoustic or the haptic channels and easier to setup due to the close proximity assumption. For the second one, we decide to include a very limited user action represented by pushing a button on Alice after receiving a signal from Bob. This signal can vary between a vibration, a sound or a simple LED blink. This choice of human-aided channel will provide the user with an explicit feedback about the state of the pairing process.

Protocol Description
After the discovery phase, the devices become aware of each other and agree on the Diffie-Hellman public parameters (the cyclic group $\mathbb{G}$, the generator g and a big prime p). At the same time, they start sensing the environment in order to collect a sufficient number of samples to perform the contextual encoding and decoding operations. They generate their ephemeral DH private keys (a and b), two secret l-bit nonces (r_a and r_b) and they dpublic keys ($g^{a-r_a} \bmod p$ and $g^{b-r_b} \bmod p$). In addition, Alice generates a hashing key K_h to avoid any exhaustive search attempts on the nonce r_a using a simple hash output $h(ID_A, ID_B, g^a, r_a)$. To simplify the expressions, we will refer to the DH keys as g^{a-r_a} and g^{b-r_b}, without the modulus operation. In Fig. 2, we represent the In-Band exchanges by the black circles ●, while the blue ● and the red circles ● refer, respectively, to the Out-of-Band exchanges that are intended to perform the verification and the validation of the pairing.

Alice initiates the pairing process, as depicted in Fig. 2, by sending g^{a-r_a} to Bob along with its identifier ID_A and the keyed hash $h_{K_h}(ID_A, ID_B, g^a, r_a)$ in the message ❶ on the In-Band channel. Afterwards, she begins the construction of her S-box using the CSI values that come after the sequence S_A, which has been shared with Bob for synchronization purposes. At this point, the enrollee starts constructing his S-box using the CSI values that come after S_A. This operation is modeled by the construction of a contextual nonce r_{c_b}. Then, he transmits the parameters ID_B, g^{b-r_b} along with the fuzzy commitment scheme $V_b = r_{c_b} \oplus Encode(r_b || [g^{a-r_a}]_i^{i+l-1})$ to Alice in the message ❷ on the In-Band channel. The parameter i is computed as follows $i = r_b \ modulus \ (|g^{a-r_a}| - l)$ where the values $|g^{a-r_a}|$ and $[g^{a-r_a}]_i^{i+l-1}$ represent, respectively, the number of bits and an l-bit truncation of the modified public key g^{a-r_a} starting at the bit number i. At the reception of the previous message, Alice extracts the secret parameter $\hat{r}_b$ using her contextual parameter r_{c_a} as follows $\hat{r}_b || \widehat{[g^{a-r_a}]}_i^{i+l-1} = Decode(r_{c_a} \oplus \widehat{V}_b)$. Then, she verifies the correctness of the reconciliation of $\hat{r}_b$ based on the verification of $\widehat{[g^{a-r_a}]}_i^{i+l-1}$. The l-bit verification of g^{a-r_a} is used to improve the contextual mismatch detection time, which provides a way to enhance the usability in the case of an inattentive user placing the devices far apart. At this point, Alice sends the XOR of the three values $\hat{r}_b, r_a$ and $\widehat{[g^b]}_{\hat{j}}^{\hat{j}+l-1}$ in the message ❸ over the protected OoB channel. The parameter $\hat{j}$ is computed as follows $\hat{j} = \hat{r}_b \ modulus \ (|g^b| - l)$ and the symbol $\hat{x}$, in our description, represents an expected value x that is suspected to be modified by the adversary. Subsequently, Bob recomputes $\hat{r}_a = r_a \oplus \hat{r}_b \oplus \widehat{[g^b]}_{\hat{j}}^{\hat{j}+l-1} \oplus r_b \oplus [g^b]_j^{j+l-1}$ and sends to Alice a keyed hash $h_K(ID_A, ID_B, \hat{g}^a, g^b)$, using the shared key $K = (g^{a-r_a} . g^{\hat{r}_a})^b$, in the message ❹ on the In-Band channel. Then, Alice verifies the keyed hash received in the previous message and she confirms the verification by sending the hashing key K_h to Bob in the message ❺ on the In-Band channel. Finally, Bob verifies the keyed hash received in message ❶. Then, he provides a signal to the user, in the message ❻, to notify Alice of his validation by asking him to push a button on the other device.

The reason behind the use of the nonce exponentiation is to temporarily hide the real values of the legitimate devices DH public keys from the attacker. This secrecy is needed to guarantee the correctness of the hash verification of Alice. To better explain this requirement, we will describe an attack scenario. First, we start by assuming that we use the real DH keys instead of the hidden ones. The adversary injects his own DH public key g^x in the message ❷. At this point, the adversary has a perfect knowledge of the secret DH key computed by Alice, $K_A = g^{xa}$. Therefore, he has all the parameters needed to recompute the keyed hash sent in message ❹ which will lead to bypassing the verification on Alice's side even when the value of Bob's nonce in the contextual commitment, sent in message ❷, has not been revealed by the attacker. As a consequence, the use of the real values of the DH public keys bounds the protocol security to a single hash verification instead of two. Thus, we will have only l bits of

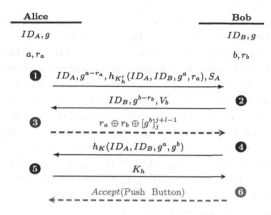

Fig. 2. COOB: Hybrid key agreement scheme (Color figure online)

security when we used $2l$ bits of authenticated exchanges against an ordinary contextual intruder which is not optimal. One possible solution to this issue is to use a commitment scheme, which needs two separate messages to provide the temporary secrecy property for a single public key. This requirement adds in a computation and communication cost of 4 exchanges for the two keys. This complexity can be easily avoided using the DH exponentiation to hide the public values while relying on a fuzzy commitment scheme that is based on a random ambient information source. Also, this contextual technique makes the ordinary contextual attacker unable to reveal the values of the nonces for the entire protocol run with the exception of a successful random guess. Accordingly, this provides a permanent confidentiality of these security parameters instead of a temporary property. This approach makes the protocol optimal in term of security with less computational cost than the first proposal and, most of all, without adding a communication cost.

This novel approach combines two pairing techniques using two short nonces as a way of hiding the legitimate DH public keys from the attacker in order to prove their authenticity later on based on two hash verifications. The values r_a and r_b are protected by the discrete logarithm problem, which makes it hard for an adversary to retrieve them from the keys g^{a-r_a} and g^{b-r_b}, especially without the knowledge of the private keys a and b. To the best of the authors' knowledge, COOB is the first scheme that combines the contextual and the OoB based pairing. This has been made possible using the exponential challenge-response technique that hides Alice's DH public key g^a. This security measure makes the adversary unable to recompute the keyed hash and fail to bypass the verification. Our hybrid protocol relies on a very constrained set of human interactions that consists of placing the devices in close proximity and pushing a button on the initiator (Alice) to confirm the pairing.

There are two main advantages with respect to each category of pairing mechanisms. **In comparison with the previously proposed context-based schemes**, we provide an attack success probability of 2^{-l} against a sophisticated contextual attacker that is able to violate the safe zone without detection and to completely control the environment. **In comparison with the same OoB-based protocol structure that only uses the Out-of-Band channel to transfer** $2 \times l$ **bits**, we provide less pairing completion time due to the fast generation of the contextual information relying on TDS [34], which takes at maximum 2 s to agree on a 256-bit key. However, an average time of 8.6 s is required for a 6-digit numerical comparison, performed by the user, with a 10% mismatch rate related to human factor errors, as stated in the work of Kumar et al. [20]. The usage of automated pairing schemes that are highly preferred by the study participants, such as HAPADEP [32] and Blinking Lights [26], scores between 10.6 and 28.8 s only for exchanging a 15-bit authentication string. Therefore, for sending $2l$ bits on the out-of-Band channel, we would need twice the time, which is not convenient for the user.

4   Security Analysis

4.1   Security Evaluation

We begin our analysis by assuming, at this moment, that the attacker is **outside the safe zone**, which makes him unable to predict or to collect the same contextual information measured by the two legitimate devices. Therefore, he is unable to send his own contextual commitment.

A MitM attack scenario starts by blocking the message of Alice ❶ and by replacing it with the following construction: $ID_A, g^{a'-r'_a}, h_{K'_h}(ID_A, ID_B, g^{a'}, r'_a)$, where x' represents an attacker induced value. Then, the adversary blocks the message ❷ and sends to Alice his own version: $ID_B, g^{b'-r'_b}, V_e$. The parameter V_e can be a legitimate contextual commitment computed by Bob or an old one replayed by the attacker. Afterwards, Alice retrieves the nonce $\hat{r}_b = Decode(r_{c_a} \oplus V_e)$ and sends the message ❸, that contains the value $r_a \oplus \hat{r}_b \oplus [g^{\widehat{b'-r'_b+\hat{r}_b}}]_{\hat{j}}^{\hat{j}+l-1}$, over the protected Out-of-Band channel which guarantees the integrity and the authenticity. Subsequently, Bob retrieves $\hat{r}_a$ using the following equation:

$$\hat{r}_a = r_a \oplus \hat{r}_b \oplus [g^{\widehat{b'-r'_b+\hat{r}_b}}]_{\hat{j}}^{\hat{j}+l-1} \oplus r_b \oplus [g^b]_{\hat{j}}^{j+l-1} \tag{1}$$

Using $\hat{r}_a$, Bob recomputes the public key of Alice $\widehat{g^a} = g^{a'-r'_a+\hat{r}_a}$ and the DH secret key $\widehat{K_B} = g^{ba'}$. Then, he uses it to compute the second verification hash $h_{\widehat{K_B}}(ID_A, ID_B, g^{a'-r'_a+\hat{r}_a}, g^b)$ and sends it to Alice in the message ❹. The initiator verifies the hash using her key $K_A = g^{a(b'-r'_b+\hat{r}_b)}$ and sends the hashing key K_h to Bob in the message ❺, which will be blocked and replaced by K'_h. At this moment, Bob is able to verify the keyed hash received in the message ❶ using the parameter K'_h induced by the adversary, the nonce $\hat{r}_a$ and the public key $\widehat{g^a} = g^{a'-r'_a+\hat{r}_a}$.

The easiest way for the attacker to bypass the hash verification of Alice, **hash verification I**, is to block the message ❹ and recompute the initiator key $K_A = g^{a(b'-r'_b+\hat{r}_b)}$ but he can only compute $K_E = g^{b'(a-r_a+r'_a)}$. This means that the optimal solution for the attacker is to use the legitimate contextual information $V_e = V_b$ in order to have the equality $\hat{r}_b = r_b$ and to satisfy the equation

$$r'_b = r_b \tag{2}$$

As for the hash verification of Bob, **hash verification II**, the attacker needs to satisfy the following equation when constructing the message ❶:

$$r'_a = \hat{r}_a \tag{3}$$

To summarize the results of the previous security analysis, the attacker needs to satisfy two main conditions

$$\begin{cases} r'_a = \hat{r}_a \\ r'_b = r_b \end{cases}$$

The parameters r'_a and $\hat{r}_a$ are completely independent as shown in Eq. 1, which means that we have an attack success probability $P_{s_B} = 2^{-l}$. The same property applies on the values r'_b and r_b, which provides an attack success probability of $P_{s_A} = 2^{-l}$.

The two verifications are sequential, which means that the execution of the second phase depends on the success of the first one. Therefore, the total success probability of the whole MitM attack is $P_s = P_{s_A} \times P_{s_B} = 2^{-2l}$. This analysis is better highlighted in Table 1 where the assumptions on Eq. 3 and Eq. 2 are made and the corresponding success probabilities are computed. In this context, $m_A = |h_K(ID_A, ID_B, \widehat{g^a}, g^b)|$ and $m_B = |h_{K_h}(ID_A, ID_B, g^a, r_a)|$ were used to express the probability of a collision on the hash functions. Based on this analysis, the MitM attack success probability is bounded by 2^{-2l}.

In the case of an **ordinary contextual attacker**, we will have the same results as the ones indicated in Table 1. This fact is explained by the confidentiality assumption on the contextual information, which protects the parameters r_a and r_b from being revealed by the adversary.

In the case of a **sophisticated contextual attacker**, he has the capacity to gain knowledge of Bob's secret r_b based on computing an S-box similar to the

Table 1. MitM attack success probability

Verification phases	$r'_a = \hat{r}_a$ & $r'_b \neq r_b$	$r'_a \neq \hat{r}_a$ & $r'_b \neq r_b$	$r'_a \neq \hat{r}_a$ & $r'_b = r_b$	$r'_a = \hat{r}_a$ & $r'_b = r_b$
Hash verification I	✗	✗	✓	✓
Hash verification II	✗	✗	✗	✓
Upper bound of the successful attack probability	2^{-m_A}	$2^{-(m_A+m_B)}$	2^{-m_B}	2^{-2l}

ones constructed by the legitimate devices. Even though he knows Bob's true DH public key g^b and Alice's secret based on the message ❸, he still has to satisfy Eq. 3, which still guarantees the mutual authentication with an attack success probability $P_s = 2^{-l}$. To the best of the authors' knowledge, this property is not maintained by any context-based protocol relying on the unpredictability aspect of the ambient environment.

4.2   Formal Validation

To validate the correctness of the protocol in the symbolic model, we perform a formal verification using the TAMARIN prover [24], a powerful validation tool for security protocols. In our analysis, we begin with the evaluation of the confidentiality of the secret keys and nonces of Alice and Bob. Then, we evaluate an authentication property referred to as *injective agreement* [22]. This lemma verifies that the protocol guarantees to Alice that if she completes a protocol run with Bob to agree on a key K, then Bob has been apparently running the protocol with Alice and the two devices agreed on the same value. This property will be tested in both ways to guarantee a mutual authentication as mentioned in our code[1]. The multiple-session attack was not considered in our evaluation since we have no persistent secret during multiple protocol executions. These assumptions reflect the consequences of a Man-in-the-Middle attack where the adversary performs the actions described in Sect. 4.1.

This tool adopts the Dolev-Yao intruder model on its public channel, which grants the attacker with a complete control over it. Thus, it satisfies our attacker model requirements on the In-Band channel. However, the protected Out-of-Band channel is modeled in the tool such that it prevents the attacker from forging or replaying any messages. As for the *blocking* and the *delaying* actions, the adversary is already able to temporarily or permanently stop the process of sending an information, even on the protected channel. Our sophisticated contextual attacker is represented as a Dolev-Yao intruder that has perfect knowledge of contextual information of the two devices, r_{c_a} and r_{c_b}, which grants him a perfect reconstruction of the nonce r_b. Even though there is a lack of a modular exponentiation in the tool, we can model, to a certain degree, these operations to reach the full capabilities of the intruder. Nonetheless, the XOR properties were recently modeled in TAMARIN v1.4.1 but the tool does not support multiple executions of this operation, as required in message ❸ on the Out-of-Band channel. This computational burden is caused by the multiple algebraic properties of the XOR. To ease the computation, we modeled our own approximation of the XOR operation using a simpler constructor functions $xorc(.,.)$ to apply the operation on two variable inputs.

To guarantee the correctness of the protocol execution, a set of restrictions must be indicated in the TAMARIN model. We enforced the use of an initialization rule that provides all the devices with the same contextual information. We

---

[1] The TAMARIN model of COOB can be found in https://github.com/ samehkhalfaoui/COOB-TAMARIN-model/blob/master/COOB_model.spthy.

imposed also the uniqueness of the private DH keys and of the authentication nonces to avoid any multi-session attack. Finally, we apply the hash equality restriction that stops the protocol run when the hash verification does not hold, which represents the case of an attack detection.

Table 2. COOB evaluated properties in the symbolic model

Property	Result	
	Ordinary contextual attacker	Sophisticated contextual attacker
Secrecy of r_c	✓	✗
Secrecy of r_a	✓	✗
Secrecy of r_b	✓	✗
Secrecy of Alice's key	✓	✓
Secrecy of Bob's key	✓	✓
Alice-to-Bob injective agreement	✓	✓
Bob-to-Alice injective agreement	✓	✓

The results of the lemmas highlighted in Table 2 validate the robustness of our protocol in the symbolic model even in the presence of a sophisticated contextual attacker that can break the secrecy of the authentication nonces during the protocol run. The outcomes are either ✓ when the property is validated or ✗ when the property does not hold and an attack trace is provided by the tool. We use the automated proofs with the default heuristic and the default proof tree exploration. The validation lasts 84 mins and is conducted on a computer with an Intel(R) Core™ i5 − 9400H CPU @ 2.5 GHz × 8 processor, 32 GB of RAM, running Ubuntu 18.04.4 LTS.

Moreover, this analysis shows that an attacker will not be able to mount an MitM attack resulting in the agreement on different keys on each device and guarantees the secrecy of the computed key has been validated for both Alice and Bob. Therefore, this analysis validates the mutual authentication property between the legitimate pairing parties chosen by the user and the secrecy of the communication link established for the post pairing phase. The case of multi-session attacks has not been addressed in this validation for two reasons. First of all, it adds significant computation cost due to the unbounded number of sessions that needs to be considered. Secondly, our scheme regenerates fresh parameters at the beginning of each session, which makes the assumption of having persistent security knowledge between two distinct protocol runs invalid. Therefore, relying on the security parameters from an earlier execution of the scheme is considered as a MitM attack where the adversary is trying to guess the appropriate nonce values, as explained in Sect. 4.1.

5   Implementation

5.1   Experimental Setting

We implement COOB using Python 2 on two Raspberry Pi 4B. This choice of cards is mainly motivated by the simplicity of the extraction and the manipulation of the CSI measurements for a future implementation of the contextual module. The first Raspberry Pi is connected to a source of light, for example an LED, and the second one is connected to a photo-resistor in order to construct a protected visual OoB channel. We use the Elliptic Curve Diffie-Hellman (ECDH) key exchange protocol based on a Koblitz curve secp256k1, SHA-256 for hashing and Bluetooth as our In-Band channel. As for the choice of the elliptic curve domain parameters, we use by default in our implementation the recommended specifications provided in [5].

The Out-of-Band module apply an On-Off Keying (OOK) modulation and it takes 0.2 s to send one bit value. This transmission rate is explained by the choice of the photo-resistor and the capacitor at the receiving side as shown in Fig. 3. This RC light detection circuit is used because of the digital nature of the Raspberry Pi pins and their inability to read analogue inputs. Therefore, the charging time of the RC circuit is used as a reference when applying an internal counter to detect the existence of a light pulse when compared with a threshold computed with regard to the ambient luminosity level at the time of pairing.

Fig. 3. Visual Out-of-Band channel design

The contextual module is assumed to apply a reconstruction threshold that represents the maximum number of bits that can be corrected by the Reed-Solomon codes during the secret reconciliation phase. We fixed the value of the threshold to 20% of the total hidden value bit-length $|r_b| + |[g^{b-r_b}]_j^{j+l-1}| = 2 \times l$ to tolerate any encoding errors by the legitimate devices. This fault tolerance is expected to increase the contextual secret message bit-length $|V_b| = \lceil 2.4 \times l \rceil$ while providing a more reliable encoding scheme.

5.2   Preliminary Performance Evaluation

For the moment, we compute an estimation of the time needed by the chosen contextual module, based on the published results of the TDS protocol performance in the work of Xi et al. [34], in order to approximate the pairing time required by our hybrid protocol COOB. First, we refer to a metric denoted *bit generation rate* that represents the number of secret bits that are agreed upon by both devices over the whole protocol execution time. This measure includes the time required for the CSI information extraction, the S-Box computation and the transfer of the encoded bits. For a distance separating the two devices ranging between 3 and 4 cm, the TDS secret bit generation rate ranges between 100 to 180 bits per second for multiple scenarios, both static and mobile. In our analysis, we take the average value of 140 bits per second to approximate the required time for pairing to estimate the performance COOB in comparison with an OoB-based pairing protocol that transfers $2l$ bits. These two scheme provide the same level of security. In order to clearly evaluate the performance of our scheme, we compare it to the same protocol design in terms of exchanges, key manipulation and cryptographic primitives but without the contextual module. The pairing time of the $2l$-bit Out-of-Band scheme was averaged over 10 protocol runs that were conducted for a number of bits l varying between 16 and 80 bits. The results were analyzed to provide a time percentage gain that reflects the added value of our modular hybrid design.

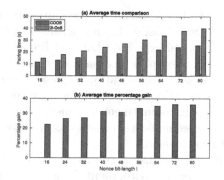

Fig. 4. Pairing time performance comparison: COOB vs 2l-OoB scheme

As highlighted in Fig. 4-(a), the pairing time imposed by a solely OoB-based scheme that sends $2l$ bits on the Out-of-Band channel grows rapidly to reach 40 s for a bit-length $l = 80$ bits. Our implemented OoB-based protocol achieves a better performance compared to the published usability results in the work of Kumar et al. [20] that take on average 28.8 s for $l = 15$ bits on a visual channel. Therefore, we will be using our OoB pairing protocol performance results to conduct a more realistic comparative study. Our hybrid scheme takes advantage of the fast contextual agreement module to keep the required association time within a reasonable limit equal to 25 s. This comparison is better described using a time percentage gain that reflects COOB pairing time reduction while maintaining the same level of security. This time optimization ranges between 22 and 39%, as shown in Fig. 4-(b), for a nonce bit-length l between 16 and 80. In a high security level scenario, a higher secret bit-length is required for both the DH keys and the nonces, which makes the use of a typical OoB-based scheme extremely unsuitable. Furthermore, the risk of dealing with a sophisticated contextual attacker prevents the use of a context-based pairing scheme. These inconveniences can be mitigated using COOB since the time gain can exceed 50% of the whole pairing time required by the other OoB-based schemes and a level of security can be assured by the use of an Out-of-Band channel that only transfers half of the authentication bits.

Our hybrid design guarantees a optimal pairing time in comparison with the other schemes that rely on low-bandwidth Out-of-Band channels. This time reduction enhances the usability aspect of the device pairing process without demanding an extensive user involvement. Also, this can also be handy in the case of a group device pairing where the time of use of an Out-of-Band channel grows linearly with the number of paired devices. Thus, applying our pairwise pairing scheme to this scenario will provide a further time optimization in comparison with the use of multiple OoB communications.

6   Conclusion

In this paper, we designed a hybrid secure device pairing protocol that efficiently combines the use of an Out-of-Band channel with an existing fast contextual encoding scheme. Our protocol exploits a Diffie-Hellman nonce exponentiation approach, applied in the context of device pairing, that achieves the temporary secrecy goal desired in the key authentication process. The use of this technique results in an optimal computation and communication cost in comparison with the traditional cryptographic commitment schemes. This technique imposes an optimal computation and communication cost in comparison with the traditional cryptographic commitment schemes.

COOB provides security against a sophisticated contextual attacker that completely controls the ambient environment. This adversary model is not supported by the existing context-based device pairing protocols. In addition, we formally validated our design in the symbolic model using the TAMARIN prover. Furthermore, our scheme reduces the pairing time up to 39% compared to the OoB-based schemes by relying on a state-of-the-art fast contextual pairing protocol. This optimization enhances the usability and the reliability aspects in comparison with the existing OoB-based schemes.

Acknowledgement. This work was supported by the SEIDO lab (The joint research laboratory for Security and Internet of Things between EDF R&D and Télécom Paris.). The authors would like to thank Dr. Ivan GAZEAU for his support in the formal verification of the protocol.

References

1. Akter, S., Chakraborty, T., Khan, T.A., Chellappan, S., Al Islam, A.A.: Can you get into the middle of near field communication? In: 2017 IEEE 42nd Conference on Local Computer Networks (LCN), pp. 365–373. IEEE (2017)

2. Alliance, W.F.: Wi-fi simple configuration technical specification, version 2.0. 5 (2014)
3. Balfanz, D., Smetters, D.K., Stewart, P., Wong, H.C.: Talking to strangers: Authentication in ad-hoc wireless networks. In: NDSS. Citeseer (2002)
4. Bluetooth, S.: Bluetooth core specification v5. 0. Bluetooth Special Interest Group: Kirkland, WA, USA (2016)
5. Brown, D.R.: Recommended elliptic curve domain parameters. Standards Efficient Cryptogr. Group Ver 1 (2010)
6. Burrows, M., Abadi, M., Needham, R.M.: A logic of authentication. Proc. Royal Soc. London. A. Math. Phys. Sci. **426**(1871), 233–271 (1989)
7. Claycomb, W.R., Shin, D.: Extending formal analysis of mobile device authentication. J. Internet Serv. Inf. Secur. **1**(1), 86–102 (2011)
8. Diffie, W., Hellman, M.: New directions in cryptography. IEEE Trans. Inf. Theor. **22**(6), 644–654 (2006). https://doi.org/10.1109/TIT.1976.1055638
9. Dolev, D., Yao, A.: On the security of public key protocols. IEEE Trans. Inf. Theory **29**(2), 198–208 (1983)
10. Fomichev, M., Álvarez, F., Steinmetzer, D., Gardner-Stephen, P., Hollick, M.: Survey and systematization of secure device pairing. IEEE Commun. Surv. Tutorials **20**(1), 517–550 (2017)
11. Fomichev, M., Maass, M., Almon, L., Molina, A., Hollick, M.: Perils of zero-interaction security in the internet of things. Proc. ACM Interactive, Mobile, Wearable and Ubiquitous Technol. **3**(1), 10 (2019)
12. Gehrmann, C., Mitchell, C.J., Nyberg, K.: Manual authentication for wireless devices. RSA Cryptobytes **7**(1), 29–37 (2004)
13. Goodrich, M.T., Sirivianos, M., Solis, J., Tsudik, G., Uzun, E.: Loud and clear: human-verifiable authentication based on audio. In: 26th IEEE International Conference on Distributed Computing Systems (ICDCS 2006), p. 10. IEEE (2006)
14. Halevi, T., Saxena, N.: Acoustic eavesdropping attacks on constrained wireless device pairing. IEEE Trans. Inf. Foren. Secur. **8**(3), 563–577 (2013)
15. Jin, R., Shi, L., Zeng, K., Pande, A., Mohapatra, P.: Magpairing: Pairing smartphones in close proximity using magnetometers. IEEE Trans. Inf. Foren. Security **11**(6), 1306–1320 (2015)
16. Juels, A., Sudan, M.: A fuzzy vault scheme. Designs, Codes and Cryptography **38**(2), 237–257 (2006)
17. Kainda, R., Flechais, I., Roscoe, A.: Usability and security of out-of-band channels in secure device pairing protocols. In: Proceedings of the 5th Symposium on Usable Privacy and Security, p. 11. ACM (2009)
18. Karapanos, N., Marforio, C., Soriente, C., Capkun, S.: Sound-proof: usable two-factor authentication based on ambient sound. In: 24th {USENIX} Security Symposium ({USENIX} Security 15), pp. 483–498 (2015)
19. Kfir, Z., Wool, A.: Picking virtual pockets using relay attacks on contactless smartcard. In: First International Conference on Security and Privacy for Emerging Areas in Communications Networks (SECURECOMM 2005), pp. 47–58. IEEE (2005)
20. Kumar, A., Saxena, N., Tsudik, G., Uzun, E.: A comparative study of secure device pairing methods. Pervasive Mob. Comput. **5**(6), 734–749 (2009)
21. Lee, K., Raghunathan, V., Raghunathan, A., Kim, Y.: Syncvibe: fast and secure device pairing through physical vibration on commodity smartphones. In: 2018 IEEE 36th International Conference on Computer Design (ICCD), pp. 234–241. IEEE (2018)

22. Lowe, G.: A hierarchy of authentication specifications. In: Proceedings 10th Computer Security Foundations Workshop, pp. 31–43. IEEE (1997)
23. Mathur, S., Miller, R., Varshavsky, A., Trappe, W., Mandayam, N.: Proximate: proximity-based secure pairing using ambient wireless signals. In: Proceedings of the 9th International Conference on Mobile Systems, Applications, and Services, pp. 211–224 (2011)
24. Meier, S., Schmidt, B., Cremers, C., Basin, D.: The TAMARIN prover for the symbolic analysis of security protocols. In: Sharygina, N., Veith, H. (eds.) CAV 2013. LNCS, vol. 8044, pp. 696–701. Springer, Heidelberg (2013). https://doi.org/10.1007/978-3-642-39799-8_48
25. Mirzadeh, S., Cruickshank, H., Tafazolli, R.: Secure device pairing: a survey. IEEE Commun. Surv. Tutorials 16(1), 17–40 (2013)
26. Saxena, N., Ekberg, J.E., Kostiainen, K., Asokan, N.: Secure device pairing based on a visual channel. In: 2006 IEEE Symposium on Security and Privacy (S&P'06), pp. 6-pp. IEEE (2006)
27. Saxena, N., Uddin, M.B., Voris, J., Asokan, N.: Vibrate-to-unlock: Mobile phone assisted user authentication to multiple personal RFID tags. In: 2011 IEEE International Conference on Pervasive Computing and Communications (PerCom), pp. 181–188. IEEE (2011)
28. Scannell, A., Varshavsky, A., LaMarca, A., De Lara, E.: Proximity-based authentication of mobile devices. Int. J. Secur. Networks 4(1–2), 4–16 (2009)
29. Schürmann, D., Sigg, S.: Secure communication based on ambient audio. IEEE Trans. Mob. Comput. 12(2), 358–370 (2011)
30. Sen, J.: Security in wireless sensor networks. Wireless Sensor Netw. Current Status and Future Trends 407, 408 (2012)
31. Shrestha, B., Saxena, N., Truong, H.T.T., Asokan, N.: Sensor-based proximity detection in the face of active adversaries. IEEE Trans. Mob. Comput. 18(2), 444–457 (2018)
32. Soriente, C., Tsudik, G., Uzun, E.: HAPADEP: human-assisted pure audio device pairing. In: Wu, T.-C., Lei, C.-L., Rijmen, V., Lee, D.-T. (eds.) ISC 2008. LNCS, vol. 5222, pp. 385–400. Springer, Heidelberg (2008). https://doi.org/10.1007/978-3-540-85886-7_27
33. Xi, W., Li, X.Y., Qian, C., Han, J., Tang, S., Zhao, J., Zhao, K.: Keep: fast secret key extraction protocol for d2d communication. In: 2014 IEEE 22nd International Symposium of Quality of Service (IWQoS), pp. 350–359. IEEE (2014)
34. Xi, W., et al.: Instant and robust authentication and key agreement among mobile devices. In: Proceedings of the 2016 ACM SIGSAC Conference on Computer and Communications Security, pp. 616–627. ACM (2016)
35. Zafer, M., Agrawal, D., Srivatsa, M.: Limitations of generating a secret key using wireless fading under active adversary. IEEE/ACM Trans. Networking 20(5), 1440–1451 (2012)
36. Zhang, B., Ren, K., Xing, G., Fu, X., Wang, C.: Sbvlc: Secure barcode-based visible light communication for smartphones. IEEE Trans. Mob. Comput. 15(2), 432–446 (2015)

A Robust Watermarking Scheme with High Security and Low Computational Complexity

Liangjia Li[1], Yuling Luo[1,2]($\boxtimes$), Junxiu Liu[1], Senhui Qiu[1,3], and Lanhang Li[1]

[1] School of Electronic Engineering, Guangxi Normal University, Guilin 541004, China
yuling0616@gxnu.edu.cn
[2] Guangxi Key Lab of Multi-source Information Mining and Security,
Guangxi Normal University, Guilin 541004, China
[3] Guangxi Key Laboratory of Wireless Wideband Communication and Signal
Processing, Guilin 541004, China

Abstract. Implementing a watermarking algorithm with high security and low computational complexity is a challenge, especially at a limited distortion level. A novel watermarking scheme is proposed in this paper, which is based on Tent-Logistic-Cosine Map (TLCM) and Direct Current (DC) coefficient modification. Firstly, the watermark is encrypted by a matrix obtained from TLCM. Then, the cover image is divided into non-overlapping 4×4 sub-blocks and some blocks are selected randomly. Thereafter, the DC coefficients of selected blocks are calculated directly in the spatial domain without performing two-dimensional discrete cosine transform. Finally, using the proposed watermark embedding procedure, DC coefficients of selected blocks are updated according to the encrypted watermark bits. Results show that the proposed watermarking algorithm has high security and low computational complexity at a limited distortion.

Keywords: Watermark · TLCM · DC coefficient · Spatial domain

1 Introduction

Digital data is continuously transmitted and shared owing to the recent advancements in Internet technologies, which makes the copyright infringement issue serious. To resolve this problem, digital watermarking schemes [1–6] and image encryption schemes [7–10] are presented. In this paper, the watermarking scheme is investigated as it is considered to be an effective copyright protection method [11]. Watermarking technology is used to embed digital information into digital content. Then, the copyright can be proved via the extracted digital information from the digital content by related computing operations [4]. There are two methods to insert the watermark: spatial domain insertion and transform domain insertion [12]. Specifically, the former is that the pixel values of cover

© ICST Institute for Computer Sciences, Social Informatics and Telecommunications Engineering 2020
Published by Springer Nature Switzerland AG 2020. All Rights Reserved
N. Park et al. (Eds.): SecureComm 2020, LNICST 336, pp. 439–454, 2020.
https://doi.org/10.1007/978-3-030-63095-9_28

image are changed directly to embed a watermark, which has lower computation but the ability of resisting to geometric and image processing attacks is relatively weaker [13]. The latter is that the transform coefficients of the cover image are used to embed the watermark. The latter has better robustness but its computation complexity is higher than the former [14]. Therefore, many watermarking schemes are based on the transform domain. For example, Discrete Cosine Transform (DCT) is commonly used in watermarking schemes [15–17]. However, it is a recent research hotspot to design a watermarking algorithm that can simultaneously satisfy the advantages of two watermark embedding methods [18]. For example, in [1], a new watermarking method based on Direct Current (DC) coefficients is designed. Firstly, the luminance Y of 512×512 colour image is partitioned into non-overlapping 8×8 blocks. Then, the DC coefficients of all blocks calculated in spatial domain are used to embed 64×64 binary watermark. In [2], the watermarking technology is also based on pixel domain. The binary watermark with size of 64×64 is encrypted by a chaotic sequence which is generated via iterating generalized Logistic map. Then the grey cover image is partitioned into non-overlapping 8×8 blocks and the encrypted watermark is embedded into the DC coefficients of all blocks.

Security is also the main consideration for designing watermarking schemes [19,20]. Therefore, one-dimensional (1D) chaotic maps are widely used in digital watermarking schemes to improve security due to their complex dynamical behaviour [21,22]. However, some watermarking schemes have been proved that the embedded watermark can be extracted by an attacker due to the limited key space of the chaotic system [23]. Specifically, in [21], the watermark is scrambled by the chaotic sequence of Logistic map. Then, the 2-level wavelet transform is performed on the cover image and the scrambled watermark is embedded into the approximation coefficients. However, the security of this algorithm is not high because the embedded watermark can be extracted by an attacker. In [22], the embedding positions are determined by combining Logistic map and Arnold cat map, and the initial conditions of chaotic systems are used as secret keys. But the embedded watermark can also be removed. Based on aforementioned discussion, by combining Tent-Logistic-Cosine Map (TLCM) and DC coefficient modification, a novel watermarking algorithm with high security and low computational complexity at a limited distortion level is designed in this paper. The designed scheme is based on previous works [1,2]. The main contributions of this work are as follows: (1) The 512×512 grey cover image is divided into non-overlapping 4×4 sub-blocks, and some blocks are used for embedding watermark, which can improve the imperceptibility. (2) The proposed watermark embedding procedure can further improve the robustness. (3) The binary watermark is encrypted via the proposed watermark encryption scheme, which can achieve higher security. (4) The DC coefficients of selected blocks are computed in pixel domain, which can shorten the execution time. (5) Three state-of-the-art watermark schemes are chosen for a comparative study, and the proposed technology outperforms other algorithms in both imperceptibility and robustness.

The rest of this paper is organized as follows. The basic knowledge of TLCM and mathematical theoretical analysis about 2D-DCT are provided in Sect. 2. The proposed watermark scheme is given in Sect. 3. Experimental results and performance analysis are reported in Sect. 4. Finally, Sect. 5 presents the conclusion.

2 Preliminaries

2.1 Chaotic Systems

TLCM is a 1D chaotic map by combing Tent map, Logistic map and Cosine map [24]. Moreover, it has been demonstrated that TLCM has more complex dynamical behaviour than its seed maps. The control parameter $u \in [0, 1]$. TLCM is defined by

$$x_{n+1} = \begin{cases} \cos\left(\pi\left(2u x_n + 4(1-u)x_n(1-x_n) - 0.5\right)\right), & \text{if } x_n < 0.5, \\ \cos\left(\pi\left(2u(1-x_n) + 4(1-u)x_n(1-x_n) - 0.5\right)\right), & \text{if } x_n \geq 0.5. \end{cases} \quad (1)$$

2.2 Mathematical Theoretical Analysis

(a) DC coefficient is obtained in pixel domain. DCT is used to transform real numbers into frequency domain. A transformed matrix can be obtained by performing DCT. In transform matrix, the coefficient in the upper left corner is named as DC coefficient, whereas remainders are the Alternating Current (AC) coefficients. Suppose the size of matrix $f(\varphi, \omega)$ is $s \times t$, ($\varphi = 0, 1, 2, \ldots, $ s-1, $\omega = 0, 1, 2, \ldots, $ t−1), the 2D-DCT of $f(\varphi, \omega)$ is introduced by

$$\mathcal{F}(u, v) = c_u c_v \sum_{\varphi=0}^{s-1} \sum_{\omega=0}^{t-1} f(\varphi, \omega) \cos \frac{\pi(2\varphi + 1)u}{2s} \cos \frac{\pi(2\omega + 1)v}{2t}, \quad (2)$$

where $\mathcal{F}(u, v)$ is DCT coefficient of $f(\varphi, \omega)$, u ($u = 0, 1, 2, \ldots, s-1$) is horizontal frequency, v ($v = 0, 1, 2, \ldots, t-1$) is vertical frequency, c_u and c_v are two compensation factors and they are given by

$$c_u = \begin{cases} \sqrt{1/s}, u = 0, \\ \sqrt{2/s}, 1 \leq u < s-1, \end{cases} \quad (3)$$

and

$$c_v = \begin{cases} \sqrt{1/t}, v = 0, \\ \sqrt{2/t}, 1 \leq v < t-1. \end{cases} \quad (4)$$

The inverse 2D-DCT is given by

$$f(\varphi, \omega) = c_u c_v \sum_{\varphi=0}^{s-1} \sum_{\omega=0}^{t-1} \mathcal{F}(u, v) \cos \frac{\pi(2\varphi + 1)u}{2s} \cos \frac{\pi(2\omega + 1)v}{2t}. \quad (5)$$

According to Eq. (2), when u = 0 and v = 0, the DC coefficient of 2D-DCT can be obtained directly by

$$\mathcal{F}(0,0) = \frac{1}{\sqrt{st}} \sum_{\varphi=0}^{s-1} \sum_{\omega=0}^{t-1} f(\varphi, \omega). \tag{6}$$

Thus, the DC coefficient $\mathcal{F}(0,0)$ can be obtained directly by calculating the average of all values of the matrix in spatial domain, and the specific result is detailed in [1].

(b) Modifying DC coefficient in spatial domain. Each value in the matrix will be updated after executing inverse 2D-DCT if the DC coefficient is changed. The relation between the changed amount of DC coefficient and each value update in spatial domain is discussed below. According to Eq. (5), the inverse 2D-DCT can be written by

$$f(\varphi, \omega) = \frac{1}{\sqrt{st}} \mathcal{F}(0,0) + f(\varphi, \omega)^{AC}, \tag{7}$$

where $f(\varphi, \omega)^{AC}$ denotes the reconstructed matrix from AC coefficients. If the DC coefficient is altered and the altered amount is recorded as Δ_m, the modified DC coefficient $\mathcal{F}(0,0)^{\sim}$ can be obtained by

$$\mathcal{F}(0,0)^{\sim} = \mathcal{F}(0,0) + \Delta_m. \tag{8}$$

Therefore, the recovered matrix $f(\varphi, \omega)^{\sim}$ is written by

$$f(\varphi, \omega)^{\sim} = \frac{1}{\sqrt{st}} \mathcal{F}(0,0)^{\sim} + f(\varphi, \omega)^{AC}. \tag{9}$$

According to the Eq. (7) and Eq. (8), Eq. (9) is written as

$$\begin{aligned} f(\varphi, \omega)^{\sim} &= \frac{1}{\sqrt{st}} \mathcal{F}(0,0)^{\sim} + f(\varphi, \omega)^{AC} \\ &= \frac{1}{\sqrt{st}} [\mathcal{F}(0,0) + \Delta_m] + f(\varphi, \omega)^{AC} \\ &= \frac{\Delta_m}{\sqrt{st}} + \frac{1}{\sqrt{st}} \mathcal{F}(0,0) + f(\varphi, \omega)^{AC} \\ &= \frac{\Delta_m}{\sqrt{st}} + f(\varphi, \omega) \end{aligned} \tag{10}$$

Therefore, if the changed amount of DC coefficient is Δ_m, the recovered matrix can be obtained directly by adding $\frac{\Delta_m}{\sqrt{st}}$ to each value in the original matrix without performing inverse 2D-DCT.

3   The Proposed Watermarking System

3.1   Watermark Encryption Scheme

A binary matrix generated by TLCM is used to encrypt the watermark, which can enhance the watermarking scheme security. The watermark and the encrypted watermark are shown in Fig. 1. Suppose the size of binary watermark W is m × n, watermark encryption process is as follows. Firstly, the TLCM is iterated for m × n/8 times, and a chaotic sequence $x = (x_1, x_2, \ldots, x_{m \times n/8})$ is obtained. Then, x is quantified by $x' = \text{floor} \left(\text{mod} \left(x \times 10^{14}\right), 256\right)$, where floor($\cdot$) denotes rounding down function. Furthermore, the decimal sequence x' is converted into corresponding binary sequence and the length is 1 × m × n, labelled as $x'' = (x_1'', x_2'', \ldots, x_{m \times n}'')$. Besides, the x'' is reshaped into m × n two-dimensional matrix, and the result is labelled as x_R'' which is used for watermark encryption. Finally, the encrypted watermark W_E is obtained by performing $W_E = W \oplus x_R''$, where $\oplus$ is XOR operation.

Fig. 1. Watermarks: (a) Original watermark; (b) Encrypted watermark.

3.2 Watermark Embedding

In this section, the watermark embedding process is given. Specifically, the M × N gray cover image C is divided into non-overlapping 4 × 4 blocks. Each sub-block is embedded with one-bit watermark information, so the number of sub-blocks and the number of watermark bits should meet $M/4 \times N/4 \geq m \times n$. The flow chart of the watermarking embedding is shown in Fig. 2 and its detailed embedding process is as follows.

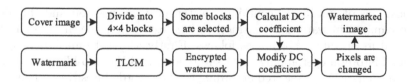

Fig. 2. The flow chart of watermark embedding.

Step 1. The m × n binary watermark W is encrypted by performing the steps of Sect. 3.1. The encrypted watermark is recorded as $W_E(s, t)$, where s = 1,2,...,m, t = 1,2,...,n and (s, t) denotes the coordinates of encrypted watermark bits.

Step 2. The M × N gray cover image C is divided into non-overlapping 4 × 4 sub-blocks $B_{i,j}$, where i = 1, 2, \ldots, M/4, j = 1, 2, \ldots, N/4, (i, j) represents the coordinates of sub-blocks.

Step 3. m × n blocks are randomly selected according to a given key and their positions are recorded.

Step 4. DC coefficient of each selected block is calculated directly in pixel domain, which is expressed by $DC = \left[\sum_{p=1}^{4} \sum_{q=1}^{4} B_{i,j}(p,q) \right] /4$, where (p,q) denotes the coordinates of pixel values in the block.

Step 5. According the encrypted watermark W_E, if $W_E(s,t) = 1$, DC coefficient of selected block is modified by

$$\begin{cases} DC_1 = \text{floor} \left(\frac{DC}{\alpha} \right) \alpha + \gamma\alpha, \\ DC_2 = \left[\text{floor} \left(\frac{DC}{\alpha} \right) + 1 \right] \alpha + \gamma\alpha, \end{cases} \tag{11}$$

where DC_1 and DC_2 are two different modified DC coefficients, respectively, α is scaling factor, γ is fine-tuning coefficient and $\gamma \in [0,1]$. If $W_E(s,t) = 0$, DC coefficient of selected block is modified by

$$\begin{cases} DC_1 = \left[\text{floor} \left(\frac{DC}{\alpha} \right) - 1 \right] \alpha + (1-\gamma)\alpha, \\ DC_2 = \text{floor} \left(\frac{DC}{\alpha} \right) \alpha + (1-\gamma)\alpha. \end{cases} \tag{12}$$

Step 6. Select the optimal modified DC coefficient DC_{opt} according to the rules: if $|DC_1 - DC| \le |DC_2 - DC|$, $DC_{opt} = DC_1$, or else, $DC_{opt} = DC_2$.

Step 7. The changed amount of selected block is calculated by $DC_{ch} = DC_{opt} - DC$, where DC_{ch} denotes changed amount of DC coefficient.

Step 8. The DC_{ch} is distributed averagely to all pixels of the block. Then, the block with one-bit watermark information is obtained by $B_{i,j}^{w} = B_{i,j} + DC_{ch}/4$, where $B_{i,j}^{w}$ is the watermarked sub-block.

Step 9. Repeating the steps 4–8 until all the selected blocks are embedded with encrypted watermark bits. Finally, the watermarked image C^w is obtained.

3.3   Watermark Extraction

The positions of sub-blocks containing watermark information and the matrix x_R'' are required in watermark extraction. The extraction flowchart is shown in Fig. 3 and its specific steps are as follows. Firstly, the watermarked image C^w is divided into non-overlapping 4 × 4 sub-blocks, and the sub-blocks containing watermark bits $B_{i,j}^{w}$ are selected according to the recorded positions. Thereafter, calculate DC coefficient of $B_{i,j}^{w}$ by $DC^w = \left[\sum_{p=1}^{4} \sum_{q=1}^{4} B_{i,j}^{W}(p,q) \right] /4$, where DC^w denotes the DC coefficient which contains one-bit watermark information. Furthermore, according to the extracted rule, if $\text{mod} \left(\text{round} \left(DC^W \right), \alpha \right) < \alpha/2$, the extracted watermark bit is 1, otherwise the extracted watermark bit is 0, where round($\cdot$) rounds the element to the nearest integer. Repeating the step 2 and step 3 until all the watermark bits W_E^* are extracted from C^w. Finally, the embedded watermark W^* is recovered by performing $W^* = W_E^* \oplus x_R''$.

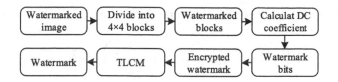

Fig. 3. The flow chart of watermark extraction.

4 Experiment Simulation and Analysis

In this section, the main required performances for a watermarking algorithm, including imperceptibility, robustness, security and computational complexity are analysed. The 64×64 watermark in Fig. 1(a) and eight 512×512 grey cover images in Fig. 4 are used to test. The performance's metrics definitions, simulation results are given in the following subsections.

Fig. 4. Cover images: (a) Lena; (b) Boat; (c) Man; (d) Peppers; (e) F16; (f) Lake; (g) Elaine; (h) House.

4.1 Metrics

Imperceptibility is measured by Peak Signal-to-Noise Ratio (PSNR) and Structural Similarity Index Measure (SSIM). SSIM ranges in [0,1]. A higher PSNR and SSIM indicate that the algorithm has a high imperceptibility. According to [14], the imperceptibility is acceptable when PSNR $\geq$ 37dB and SSIM $\geq$ 0.93. The PSNR is defined by

$$\text{PSNR}(C, C^w) = 10 \lg \frac{C_{\max}^2}{\text{MES}}, \tag{13}$$

where $C_{\max}$ is the maximum pixel value in C, MES refers to the mean square error between C and C^w, which is defined by

$$\text{MES} = \frac{1}{M \times N} \sum_{i=1}^{M} \sum_{j=1}^{N} \left[C(i, j) - C^w(i, j) \right]^2, \tag{14}$$

where M × N represents the size of C and C^w. Moreover, SSIM is calculated by

$$\text{SSIM}(C, C^w) = \frac{(\mu_C \mu_{C^w} + d_1)(\sigma_{CC^w} + d_2)}{(\mu_C^2 + \mu_{C^w}^2 + d_1)(\sigma_C^2 + \sigma_{C^w}^2 + d_2)}, \tag{15}$$

where μ_C and μ_{C^w} are the averages of C and C^W, σ_C^2 and $\sigma_{C^w}^2$ are the variances of C and C^W, σ_{CC^w} is the covariance between C and C^w, d_1 and d_2 are two variables.

In addition, Normalized Correlation (NC) and Bit Error Rate (BER) are utilized to measure the robustness of the extracted watermark. The ranges of NC and BER are both in [0,1]. When the NC value equals 1 or the BER value equals 0, the extracted watermark is consistent with the original one. NC is defined by

$$\text{NC}(W, W^*) = \frac{\sum_{i=1}^{m} \sum_{j=1}^{n} W(i,j) \cdot W^*(i,j)}{\sqrt{\sum_{i=1}^{m} \sum_{j=1}^{n} [W(i,j)]^2} \cdot \sqrt{\sum_{i=1}^{m} \sum_{j=1}^{n} [W^*(i,j)]^2}}, \tag{16}$$

where m, n represent the length of W and W^*, respectively. In addition, BER is defined by

$$\text{BER}(W, W^*) = \frac{\sum_{i=1}^{m} \sum_{i=1}^{n} W(i,j) \oplus W^*(i,j)}{m \times n}. \tag{17}$$

4.2 Imperceptibility and Robustness Analysis

The imperceptibility is a vital performance for watermarking scheme. When the imperceptibility is acceptable, other performances can be discussed further. The watermark is embedded into eight cover images by using the proposed scheme, and Fig. 5 gives the experimental results. Results show that the PSNRs of eight watermarked images are greater than 42 dB and their SSIMs are larger than 0.98. Moreover, both PSNR and SSIM are significantly larger than acceptable values 37 dB and 0.93, respectively, which indicates that the proposed method has excellent imperceptibility.

Figure 6 presents the PSNR comparison for three watermarked images obtained by the proposed algorithm and three state-of-the-art schemes [2–4]. From the Fig. 6, the PSNRs of three watermarked images obtained by this work are higher than other algorithms. Especially compared with [3], the 512 × 512 grey cover image can only contain a 32 × 32 binary watermark in their work, while the 512 × 512 grey cover image can embed with a 64 × 64 binary watermark in this work. The watermark capacity of this work is four times than that of [3], and the PSNR of this work is still higher than [3]. Therefore, it is proved again that the proposed method has excellent imperceptibility.

The robustness is another important feature of watermarking scheme. Therefore, the robustness is further investigated when the invisibility is acceptable. In this work, the robustness is evaluated by using different attacks, including

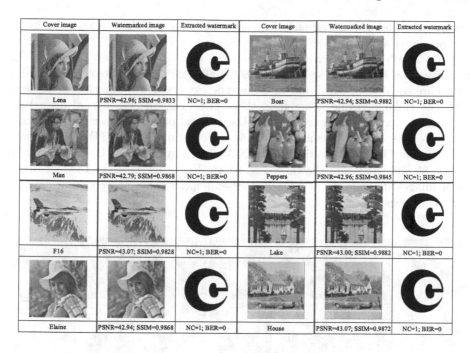

Cover image	Watermarked image	Extracted watermark	Cover image	Watermarked image	Extracted watermark
Lena	PSNR=42.96; SSIM=0.9833	NC=1; BER=0	Boat	PSNR=42.94; SSIM=0.9882	NC=1; BER=0
Man	PSNR=42.79; SSIM=0.9868	NC=1; BER=0	Peppers	PSNR=42.96; SSIM=0.9845	NC=1; BER=0
F16	PSNR=43.07; SSIM=0.9828	NC=1; BER=0	Lake	PSNR=43.00; SSIM=0.9882	NC=1; BER=0
Elaine	PSNR=42.94; SSIM=0.9868	NC=1; BER=0	House	PSNR=43.07; SSIM=0.9872	NC=1; BER=0

Fig. 5. Experimental results.

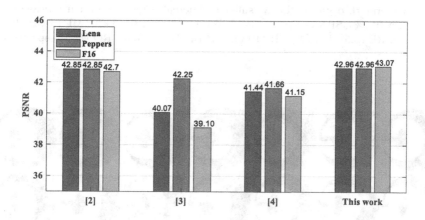

Fig. 6. PSNR comparison.

Gaussian Noise (GN), Speckle Noise (SN), Salt & Peppers Noise (SPN), Average Filter (AF), Wiener Filter (WF), Gaussian Low-pass Filter (GLPF), Median Filter (MF), JPEG compression (JPEG), Rescaling (RE), Cropping (CR), Motion Blur (MB), Sharpening (SH) and Rotation (RO). Figure 7 shows the watermarked image "Lena" under aforementioned attacks. Fig. 8 shows the extracted watermarks from the watermarked images "Lena" under those attacks by using the proposed algorithm, and their corresponding NC and BER are listed in Table 1. The NC values are greater than 0.9 and BERs are less than 11.89%. Especially for JPEG (QF = 70) and RE (2) attacks, the NCs are equal to 1 and BERs are equal to 0, which indicate that the extracted watermark is consistent with the embedded one. Therefore, there is no obvious perceptual distortion between the extracted watermark and the original one. For other cover images, similar results are also obtained, and their corresponding NC and BER are shown in Fig. 9 and Fig. 10, respectively. The NCs shown in Fig. 9 are basically greater than 0.85 and the BERs shown in Fig. 10 are basically less than 15% for other cover images. Therefore, the proposed scheme has a superior behaviour against various attacks.

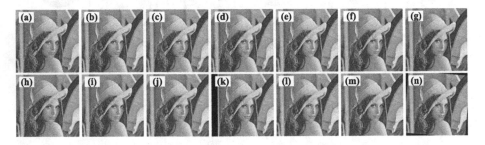

Fig. 7. Watermarked image "Lena" suffered different attacks, and a–n represent GN (0.02%), SN (0.1%), SPN (1%), AF (3×3), WF (3×3), GLPF (3×3), MF (3×3), JPEG (QF = 70), RE (0.5), RE (2), CR (10%), MB (4, 7), SH (0.8), RO (5°), respectively.

Fig. 8. Extracted watermark from watermarked image "Lena" under different attacks, and a–n represent GN (0.02%), SN (0.1%), SPN (1%), AF (3 × 3), WF (3 × 3), GLPF (3 × 3), MF (3 × 3), JPEG (QF = 70), RE (0.5), RE (2), CR (10%), MB (4, 7), SH (0.8), RO (5°), respectively.

Table 1. NC and BER (%) of watermark extracted from cover image "Lena" under various attacks.

Attack index	Description	NC	BER
a	GN (0.02%)	0.9971	0.29
b	SN (0.1%)	0.9840	1.61
c	SPN (1%)	0.9079	9.23
d	AF (3 × 3)	0.9040	5.59
e	WF (3 × 3)	0.9762	2.39
f	MF (3 × 3)	0.9799	2.03
g	GLPF (3 × 3)	0.9554	4.49
h	JPEG (QF = 70)	1	0
i	RE (0.5)	0.9823	1.78
j	RE (2)	1	0
k	CR (10%)	0.9437	5.67
l	MB (4, 7)	0.8813	11.89
m	SH (0.8)	0.9998	0.02
n	RO (5°)	0.9474	5.27

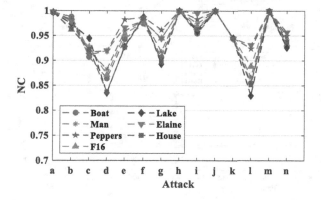

Fig. 9. NCs of extracted watermarks for different watermarked images.

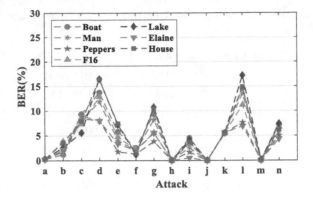

Fig. 10. BERs of extracted watermarks for different watermarked images.

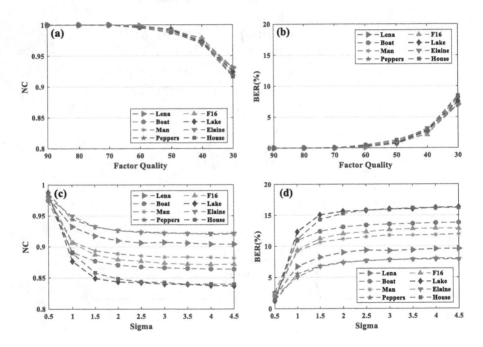

Fig. 11. The NCs and BERs of extracted watermark under JPEG and GLPF attacks with different parameters. (a) NCs under JPEG; (b) BERs under JPEG; (c) NCs under GLPF; (d) BERs under GLPF.

Besides, the robustness is further evaluated by using JPEG and GLPF attacks with dynamic parameters, and Fig. 11 shows the NCs and BERs of extracted watermarks. Figure 11 (a) and (b) represent the JPEG attacks, and the JPEG's quality factor is set from 90 to 30 with a step of −10. As the quality factor decrease, the NCs slowly decrease and the BERs slowly increase. Even the quality factor reaches 30, the NCs are larger than 0.9 and BERs are less than 10%. Moreover, when the quality factor is larger than 70, the NC of extracted watermark is 1 and BER is 0. Figure 11 (c) and (d) represent the results under the GLPF attack, and the parameter sigma is set from 0.5 to 4.5 with a step of 0.5 under 3×3 filter window size. Results show that the NCs of extracted watermark are greater than 0.84 and BERs are lower than 16% for eight cover images. Thus, the proposed algorithm has great ability to defend against JPEG and GLPF attacks.

What's more, the robustness of this work is compared with two related works to prove the great robustness of this scheme. Table 2 and Table 3 present the BER comparison of this work and two state-of-the-art methods for cover image "Lena" [2,3]. As shown in Table 2, the BERs of extracted watermark are lower than [2] under various attacks. Especially for GN (0.02%) and SH, BER is 14.16% under GN (0.02%) and BER is 32.3% under SH in [2], while BER is 0.29% under GN (0.02%) and BER is 0.02% under SH in this work. The BER comparison with [3] is presented in Table 2. The results show that the BERs in this work are also lower than [3]. Especially for JPEG (QF = 70) and SH, BER is 2.05% under JPEG (QF = 70) and BER is 0.1% under SH in their work, while BER is 0 under JPEG (QF = 70) and BER is 0.02% under SH in this work. Therefore, the proposed algorithm has good performance in both imperceptibility and robustness.

4.3 Security Performance Analysis

Since the embedded watermark is encrypted by the matrix x_R'', it is necessary to perform XOR operation between extracted watermark and x_R'' to get the final correct watermark. In this paper, the binary matrix x_R'' is generated by iterating the TLCM. Specifically, the initial value x_1 and control parameter u of the TLCM are related to x_R''. If the x_1 and u are wrong, a wrong matrix x_R'' is obtained. Then, the extracted watermark cannot be recovered correctly by

Table 2. BER (%) of [2] and this work for cover image "Lena".

Attack	[2]	This work
GN (0.02%)	14.16	0.29
SPN (1%)	27.19	9.23
MF (3×3)	5.53	4.49
GLPF (3×3)	8.52	2.03
SH	32.30	0.02
JPEG (QF = 70)	0	0
JPEG (QF = 80)	0	0
RO (10°)	7.18	7.18
RO (45°)	19.49	12.65
CR (Centre)	9.91	1.61
CR (Top left corner)	21.09	12.40
CR (Top right corner)	22.31	12.92

Table 3. BER (%) of [3] and this work for cover image "Lena".

Attack	[3]	This work
JPEG (QF = 20)	20.70	9.70
JPEG (QF = 30)	15.82	6.98
JPEG (QF = 50)	7.91	0.98
JPEG (QF = 70)	2.05	0
SPN (1%)	16.50	9.28
SPN (2%)	22.17	15.84
SH	0.10	0.02
RE (2)	0	0

using wrong x_R''. In other words, the correct watermark cannot be obtained even the attacker knows the watermark embedding algorithm. Besides, the accuracy of computer is limited, assuming it is 10^{-15}. Thus, the entire key space is 2^{104} in this work, which has reached the required key space 2^{100} [25]. The x_1 and u used in this paper cannot be simultaneously found by force attack. Therefore, the proposed algorithm has high security.

4.4 Computational Complexity Analysis

This section analysis the computational complexity. Table 4 gives the running time comparison of two different methods during embedding and extraction processes. The results indicate that the proposed scheme is faster than the performing true 2D-DCT in terms of both watermark embedding and extraction processes. Specifically, the average total time of watermark embedding and extraction of this work is ~5 times faster than that of conventional DCT.

Table 4. Times comparison of conventional DCT and this work [unit: second].

Image	Conventional DCT			This work		
	Embedding	Extraction	Total	Embedding	Extraction	Total
Lena	0.2538	0.1590	0.4128	0.0325	0.0441	0.0766
Boat	0.2231	0.1803	0.4034	0.0376	0.0402	0.0778
Man	0.2053	0.1514	0.3567	0.0390	0.0448	0.0838
Peppers	0.2246	0.1582	0.3828	0.0331	0.0403	0.0734
F16	0.2096	0.1492	0.3588	0.0316	0.0443	0.0759
Lake	0.2261	0.1483	0.3744	0.0332	0.0394	0.0726
Elaine	0.2252	0.1502	0.3754	0.0359	0.0440	0.0799
House	0.2156	0.1817	0.3973	0.0362	0.0407	0.0769
Average	0.2230	0.1598	0.3827	0.0349	0.0422	0.0771

5 Conclusion

In this work, a novel robust watermarking scheme with high security and low computational complexity watermarking scheme is proposed. To achieve high security, the watermark is encrypted by a binary matrix obtained via TLCM before it is embedded into the cover image. In the meantime, the cover image is divided into non-overlapping 4×4 sub-blocks and some blocks are selected to embed with watermark, which can improve the imperceptibility. In watermark embedding process, the DC coefficient is calculated directly in spatial domain to shorten the execution time. Experimental results demonstrate that the proposed watermarking algorithm has high security, low computational complexity, good imperceptibility and great robustness. Future work will investigate the colour watermarking scheme.

Acknowledgments. This research is supported by the National Natural Science Foundation of China under Grants 61801131 and 61661008, the Guangxi Natural Science Foundation under Grants 2017GXNSFAA198180, the funding of Overseas 100 Talents Program of Guangxi Higher Education, 2018 Guangxi One Thousand Young and Middle-Aged College and University Backbone Teachers Cultivation Program, Research Fund of Guangxi Key Lab of Multi-source Information Mining & Security (19-A-03-02), Research Fund of Guangxi Key Laboratory of Wireless Wideband Communication and Signal Processing, and the Young and Middle-aged Teachers' Research Ability Improvement Project in Guangxi Universities under Grant 2020KY02030.

References

1. Su, Q., Niu, Y., Wang, Q., Sheng, G.: A blind color image watermarking based on DC component in thespatial domain. Optik **124**(23), 6255–6260 (2013)
2. Parah, S.A., Loan, N.A., Shah, A.A., Sheikh, J.A., Bhat, G.M.: A new secure and robust watermarking technique based on logistic map and modification of DC coefficient. Nonlinear Dyn. **93**(4), 1933–1951 (2018). https://doi.org/10.1007/s11071-018-4299-6
3. Kang, X., Zhao, F., Lin, G., Chen, Y.: A novel hybrid of DCT and SVD in DWT domain for robust and invisible blind image watermarking with optimal embedding strength. Multimedia Tools Appl. **77**(11), 13197–13224 (2017). https://doi.org/10.1007/s11042-017-4941-1
4. Ko, H.J., Huang, C.T., Horng, G., WANG, S.J.: Robust and blind image watermarking in DCT domain using inter-block coefficient correlation. Inf. Sci. **517**(1), 128–147 (2020)
5. Ali, M., Ahn, C.W.: An optimized watermarking technique based on self-adaptive DE in DWT-SVD transform domain. Signal Process. **94**(1), 545–556 (2014)
6. Rajani, D., Kumar, P.R.: An optimized blind watermarking scheme based on principal component analysis in redundant discrete wavelet domain. Signal Process. **172**(1), 1–15 (2020)
7. Luo, Y., Lin, J., Liu, J., Wei, D., Cao, L., Zhou, R.: A robust image encryption algorithm based on chua's circuit and compressive sensing. Signal Process. **161**(1), 227–247 (2019)

8. Luo, Y., Cao, L., Qiu, S., Lin, H., Harkin, J., Liu, J.: A chaotic map-control-based and the plain image-related cryptosystem. Nonlinear Dyn. **83**(4), 2293–2310 (2015). https://doi.org/10.1007/s11071-015-2481-7

9. Luo, Y., Tang, S., Liu, J., Cao, L., Qiu, S.: Image encryption scheme by combining the hyper-chaotic system with quantum coding. Optics Lasers Eng. **124**(1), 1–13 (2020)

10. Luo, Y., Ouyang, X., Liu, J., Cao, L.: An image encryption method based on elliptic curve elgamal encryption and chaotic systems. IEEE Access **7**(1), 38507–38522 (2019)

11. Makbol, N.M., Khoo, B.E., Rassem, T.H., Loukhaoukha, K.: A new reliable optimized image watermarking scheme based on the integer wavelet transform and singular value decomposition for copyright protection. Inf. Sci. **417**(1), 381–400 (2017)

12. Zhang, L., Wei, D.: Image watermarking based on matrix decomposition and gyrator transform in invariant integer wavelet domain. Signal Process. **169**(1), 1–18 (2020)

13. Chan, C.K., Cheng, L.: Hiding data in images by simple LSB substitution. Pattern Recogn. **37**(3), 469–474 (2004)

14. Liu, J., Huang, J., Luo, Y., Cao, L., Yang, S.: An optimized image watermarking method based on HD and SVD in DWT domain. IEEE Access **7**(1), 80849–80860 (2019)

15. Hsu, L.Y., Hu, H.T.: Robust blind image watermarking using crisscross inter-block prediction in the DCT domain. J. Visual Commun. Image Representation **46**(1), 33–47 (2017)

16. Parah, S.A., Sheikh, J.A., Loan, N.A., Bhat, G.M.: Robust and blind watermarking technique in DCT domain using inter-block coefficient differencing. Digital Signal Process. A Rev. J. **53**(1), 11–24 (2016)

17. Das, C., Panigrahi, S., Sharma, V.K., Mahapatra, K.K.: A novel blind robust image watermarking in DCT domain using inter-block coefficient correlation. AEU - Int. J. Electron. Commun. **68**(3), 244–253 (2014)

18. Byun, S.W., Son, H.S., Lee, S.P.: Fast and robust watermarking method based on DCT specific location. IEEE Access **7**(1), 100,706–100,718 (2019)

19. Cayre, F., Fontaine, C., Furon, T.: Watermarking security: theory and practice. IEEE Trans. Signal Process. **53**(10), 3976–3987 (2005)

20. Wang, Y.G., Zhu, G., Kwong, S., Shi, Y.Q.: A study on the security levels of spread-spectrum embedding schemes in the WOA framework. IEEE Trans. Cybern. **48**(8), 2307–2320 (2018)

21. Liu, N., Li, H., Dai, H., Guo, D., Chen, D.: Robust blind image watermarking based on chaotic mixtures. Nonlinear Dyn. **80**(3), 1329–1355 (2015). https://doi.org/10.1007/s11071-015-1946-z

22. Habib, S.M., Ries, S., Max, M.: A blind chaos-based watermarking technique. Secur. Commun. Netw. **7**(4), 800–811 (2014)

23. Chen, L., Chen, J., Zhao, G., Wang, S.: Cryptanalysis and improvement of a chaos-based watermarking scheme. IEEE Access **7**(1), 97549–97565 (2019)

24. Hua, Z., Zhou, Y., Huang, H.: Cosine-transform-based chaotic system for image encryption. Inf. Sci. **480**(1), 403–419 (2019)

25. Murillo-Escobar, M.A., Cruz-Hernández, C., Cardoza-Avendaño, L., Méndez-Ramírez, R.: A novel pseudorandom number generator based on pseudorandomly enhanced logistic map. Nonlinear Dyn. **87**(1), 407–425 (2016). https://doi.org/10.1007/s11071-016-3051-3

Selecting Privacy Enhancing Technologies for IoT-Based Services

Immanuel Kunz$^{(\boxtimes)}$, Christian Banse, and Philipp Stephanow

Fraunhofer AISEC, Garching, Germany
{immanuel.kunz,christian.banse,philipp.stephanow}@aisec.fraunhofer.de

Abstract. The rising number of IoT devices enables the provisioning of novel services in various domains, such as the automotive domain. This data, however, is often personal or otherwise sensitive. Providers of IoT-based services are confronted with the problem of collecting the necessary amount and quality of data, while at the same time protecting persons' privacy using privacy enhancing technologies (PETs). Selecting appropriate PETs is neither trivial, nor is it uncritical since applying an unsuitable PET can result in a violation of privacy rights, e.g. according to the GDPR. In this paper, we propose a process to select data-dependent PETs—i.e. technologies which manipulate data, e.g. by distorting values—for IoT-based services. The process takes into account two perspectives on the selection of PETs which both narrow down the number of potentially applicable PETs: First, a data-driven perspective which is based on the data's properties, e.g. its longevity and sequentiality; and second, a service-driven perspective which takes into account service requirements, e.g. the precision required to provide a particular service. We then show how the process can be applied for automotive services proposing a taxonomy for automotive data and present an exemplary application.

In this way, we aim at providing a reproducible method of selecting PETs that is more specific than existing approaches, and which can be applied both as a standalone process and complementary to existing ones.

Keywords: Privacy enhancing technologies · Automotive data · Privacy-Preserving IoT

1 Introduction

The increasing amount of IoT devices is enabling the provisioning of many novel services, like predictive maintenance and usage-based insurance. These services collect data from a multitude of IoT devices with the purpose of processing the data in a remote backend. Commercial solutions for implementing such services

---

© ICST Institute for Computer Sciences, Social Informatics and Telecommunications Engineering 2020
Published by Springer Nature Switzerland AG 2020. All Rights Reserved
N. Park et al. (Eds.): SecureComm 2020, LNICST 336, pp. 455–474, 2020.
https://doi.org/10.1007/978-3-030-63095-9_29

are already available provided, e.g., by Amazon Web Services[1] for general IoT services, and by BMW for the automotive domain[2].

Yet, IoT data often contains personal or otherwise sensitive information and it is in the interest of the user as well as the service provider to preserve users' privacy when collecting this data. The need for privacy protection results from legal requirements regarding the collection of personal data, e.g. the General Data Protection Regulation (GDPR). Two of its central principles are *data minimization* and *purpose limitation*, and it makes violations against these principles punishable by considerable fines. Also, the GDPR demands that personal data is secured appropriately and that certain rights are provided to the data subjects, e.g. to access and rectify their personal data. Therefore, minimizing processing and storage of personal data seems only reasonable when acting as an IoT service provider who wants to minimize this liability.

A multitude of general and specialized techniques to protect personal data, usually referred to as *Privacy Enhancing Technologies* (PETs), has been researched and developed in the past. Selecting suitable PETs for a given set of data, however, is not trivial. First, not all PETs are applicable to any type of data, e.g. to numeric or categorical data. Second, service providers usually require collected data to satisfy certain properties to conduct meaningful analysis, for instance, regarding its precision.

Research in the area of privacy requirements engineering focuses on risk-driven approaches [5,18] where data flows throughout a system are analyzed and privacy risks are identified which are then mitigated using appropriate PETs. Yet, there is not a clear mapping of privacy risks to mitigative PETs, so they can often only suggest large amounts of PETs that are potentially applicable, leaving the actual selection to the user. For some types of PETs it is still possible to make a more granular selection taking into account whether they can be applied in a *meaningful* manner, i.e. if a PET can practically be applied to the data type, and if the results are *usable* considering the service's purposes.

In this paper, we propose a process to select PETs for IoT-based services which aims at providing a more granular selection process. It focuses on data-dependent PETs, i.e. such technologies whose applicability depends on the characteristics of the data that is processed, and takes also into account service-specific requirements. As such, it complements existing risk-driven approaches. Its contribution is twofold:

– A general process for the selection of data-dependent PETs including data-driven and service-driven elicitation criteria, and
– a proposal for its application in the automotive domain including a taxonomy of automotive data that is mapped to applicable PETs.

The remainder of this paper is structured as follows: The following section describes the classes of PETs that we cover with our approach. Next, Sect. 3 describes the selection process including the relevant criteria we identified for a

---

[1] https://aws.amazon.com/iot/.
[2] https://aos.bmwgroup.com/.

data-driven and service-driven elicitation of PETs. Section 4 presents our application of the process to the automotive domain proposing a taxonomy for automotive data and presents an example. Section 5 discusses the process based on several requirements, such as reproducibility. Finally, Sect. 6 describes related work and Sect. 7 concludes the paper.

2   Background: Data-Dependent PETs

Many IoT-based services face considerable privacy challenges due to several reasons. First, IoT devices often generate large amounts of data that can be personal or otherwise sensitive, e.g. location data and usage statistics. Second, devices like the ones used in connected cars and smart homes, are often used throughout several years. And third, they are usually owned by the same person or group of persons over that time period which allows the creation of long-term tracking profiles. These conditions make it difficult to satisfy privacy goals like anonymity of users and unlinkability of individual data items.

A multitude of PETs has been proposed in the past to solve these problems. While different types of PETs exist, in this paper we focus on those whose applicability directly depends on their input data. This dependency results from the fact that these PETs manipulate data somehow, for instance by modifying, replacing or deleting values. Other types of PETs, e.g. based on encryption techniques or based on usage control, usually can be applied independently from the kind of data that is processed, and are not considered in this paper.

The following enumeration is extracted from an existing collection of PETs by Hundepool et al. [15]. They also map these PETs to two kinds of data they can process: continuous and categorical data. Continuous data is numeric data on which arithmetic operations can meaningfully be applied, while categorical data assumes values from a finite set on which arithmetic operations do not make sense. Note that categorical data can additionally be ordinal meaning that it can be sorted in a meaningful order. This enumeration and their mapping to continuous and categorical data forms the basis for our approach.

This way, we do not analyze specific PET-algorithms, but treat a PET as a function taking either continuous- or categorical-valued inputs and generating a privacy-enhancing output. Our analysis therefore does not consider any specific PET algorithm but only classes of PETs. Still, it aims at preserving their semantics without loss of generality.

We further categorize the PETs into *deterministic distortion* PETs, i.e. PETs which manipulate data using deterministic values, and *randomized distortion* PETs, i.e. PETs which manipulate data using randomized values.

Deterministic Distortion—Recoding. Recoding techniques aim at reducing the precision of data. As such, they implement a form of discretization, for example by summarizing two categorical values or by rounding numeric values. Hence, they can be applied to both categorical and continuous data [15]. Special types of recoding techniques are top and bottom recoding where the top and/or bottom values in a set are summarized into one category. These techniques require that the values can be ranked, i.e. they are either continuous, or they are categorical and ordinal.

Deterministic Distortion—Suppression. This technique means the removal of a value or a group of values and can be applied to both value types as well. One way to apply suppression is to use *local suppression* meaning that one particular value is suppressed, e.g. with the aim to eliminate an identifying combination of values (see Fischetti and Gonzáles [9]). Another possibility is to suppress certain attributes, e.g. when they contain identifying information, or certain records, e.g. when they represent easily identifiable outliers.

Deterministic Distortion—(Micro-)Aggregation. Aggregation techniques take a set of values and replace them by a statistic. Various micro-aggregation techniques are presented in [15]. When applying micro-aggregation to continuous data, records are clustered, i.e. a number of groups with a certain minimum size are built, and the values are replaced by their respective group average. Concerning categorical data, micro-aggregation can only be applied for ordinal values since only in this case can the data be assigned to groups of similar values (see Torra [27]).

Randomized Distortion—Swapping. With this technique, values of a continuous or categorical attribute are swapped between records. Hence, they are preserved within the data set and allow certain statistical analyses but cannot be traced back to a certain data subject. This is useful when sensitive attributes exist in the data set whose distribution is interesting but their connection to other entries of its original record is not necessary (see Moore [19]).

Randomized Distortion—Noise Masking. Noise masking aims at distorting data by adding a randomized value to, or multiplying it with, the original value. Different techniques exist that preserve certain statistical properties within a data set when applying noise masking, see for example Domingo-Ferrer et al. [7]. Practically, it can only be applied to continuous data since it requires the possibility to perform arithmetic operations.

Randomized Distortion—Post-randomization Method (PRAM). This method, proposed by Gouweleeuw et al. [4], can only be applied to categorical values. It changes each value independently with a certain probability. This way, its application results in a diminished certainty of the linkability between two attributes. Still, meaningful statistics can be computed afterwards—depending on the probability that has been applied in the method and the size of the data set.

Randomized Distortion—Synthetic Data. Three approaches can be distinguished to introduce synthetic data into a data set which are generally applicable to both continuous and categorical data. In the first approach, the data set is fully replaced by synthetic data, yet preserving certain properties, like the distribution of an attribute (see e.g. Rubin [24]). The second approach partially replaces original data with synthetic data, for example by only replacing sensitive values (see Little [17]). The third approach, combines original and synthetic data into a *hybrid* data set containing either more original data or more synthetic data (first proposed by Dandekar et al. [3]).

In the next section, a process for the selection of these PETs is proposed, considering how data types and service requirements influence their applicability.

3   A Process for the Selection of PETs in IoT-Based Services

The goal of the process proposed in this Section is to present a systematic way of eliciting a usable set of PETs for a given set of data. More concretely, we aim at fulfilling three requirements. First, the set of PETs it suggests for a given set of data and service requirements should be reproducible. Second, it should be applicable as a standalone process as well as be applicable to the results of other approaches, such as LINDDUN (see Sect. 6). Third, it should facilitate data minimization: it should guide users of the process towards selecting a set of PETs such that their application results in the minimal quantity and quality of data that is still sufficient to fulfill the service's purposes. We discuss the fulfillment of these requirements in Sect. 5.

The typical environment we assume for this process to be applied in is an IoT-based service, i.e. a service which continuously collects a pre-defined set of data from several data-generating devices. Such a service may, e.g., offer a predictive maintenance service using data generated by industrial IoT devices. Note that some of the criteria we propose here deterministically suggest or oppose a certain PET, while others only strengthen or weaken the applicability of certain PETs to some extent.

Figure 1 shows our selection process consisting of the following four steps:

1. *Service description:* The service is described including its actors and data required to provide the service.
2. *Data-driven PET-elicitation:* The applicability of the PETs presented in the last Section is assessed based on several data-dependent criteria. This way, *practically applicable* PETs are elicited. In Sect. 4.1, we will show how this can be done proposing a taxonomy for automotive data.
3. *Service-driven PET-elicitation:* The set of PET candidates is further refined based on the requirements of the automotive service towards the data. This step considers the required data precision as well as other requirements resulting in a *usable* set of PETs.
4. *PET-selection:* From the resulting set of usable PETs, a combination is selected.

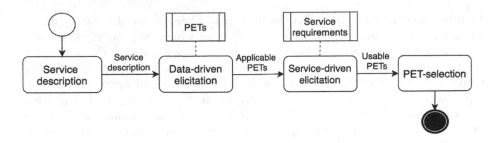

Fig. 1. The PET-selection process. It takes two inputs—a list of PET candidates and a list of service requirements—and provides a set of usable PETs.

3.1   Step 1: Service Description

In this first step, the service is described, including its participants, the required data and its processing purposes. The participants include the service provider, the users and possibly subcontractors. This step captures whose personal data is processed and by whom. The data that is required to run the service represents an input to the data-driven elicitation (Step 2). The description of its purposes is needed as an input to the service-driven elicitation (Step 3) since they reveal the requirements that the service has towards the data. Finally, out of the required data, it is identified which data needs to be protected, e.g. anonymized or pseudonymized.

To decide this, it is helpful to distinguish between the categories *identifying* and *quasi-identifying* information as well as *confidential* and *non-confidential* information, as proposed by Hundepool et al. Note that these categories are not necessarily disjoint.

- **Identifiers:** This category includes directly identifying information like full name, exact address etc.
- **Quasi-identifiers:** quasi-identifiers are sets of variables that can identify a person if combined, possibly with external information (see Dalenius [2] and Samarati [25]). The problem that quasi-identifiers pose is that every variable is potentially part of a quasi-identifier and consequently they cannot be excluded from any dataset.
- **Confidential variables:** This is sensitive, but usually not identifying, information for instance someone's religion or health conditions.
- **Non-confidential variables:** This kind of information contains non-sensitive information, for example the country of residence.

It is always use case-dependent whether certain data needs to be protected to preserve users' privacy. Still, the categorization above suggests that identifiers should be removed and confidential, i.e. sensitive, information should be unlinkable to a person. A more complex and use case-dependent task is to specify the quasi-identifiers and to decide which of their variables should also be removed or distorted.

3.2   Step 2: Data-Driven Elicitation

Step 2 of the process elicits PETs based on the data characteristics and proposes several criteria to that end. Every criterion either specifies that a certain class of PETs is applicable, has limited applicability to some extent, or is not applicable. Their relevance is evaluated for all data that was defined in step 1. This way, the list of possibly applicably PETs is narrowed down in a bottom-up elicitation. We also give some examples from the automotive domain to illustrate the criteria.

Continuous and Categorical Data. One simple criterion in the elicitation of data-dependent PETs is the given data's value type. In Sect. 2, we have described that PRAM only accepts categorical, and noise masking only accepts continuous data. Other PETs, in contrast, can be applied to both (i.e. recoding, suppression, aggregation, swapping, synthetic data).

Set Size. Set size refers to the number of values the data can assume. With a decreasing set size, the applicability of PETs in general decreases as well. The reason is that a small set size does not leave much possibility for distorting a value. For example, noise masking can only be applied using a small randomized value in the case of a small set size. So, either only a small distortion is applied—leaving a greater possibility to infer sensitive information—or a greater distortion is applied—resulting in a strongly decreased information content. For instance, appropriately distorting data that expresses a vehicle's engaged gear is more difficult than distorting data expressing the vehicle's horsepower. A further example is data that only expresses a binary value, e.g. a crash sensor which only measures if a crash has occurred or not.

Ordinal and Nominal Data. As seen in Sect. 2, among categorical data, ordinal and nominal data can be distinguished. *Nominal* categorical values cannot be compared to each other apart from equality. *Ordinal* categorical values can be ranked such that a minimum and maximum can be found and different values can be compared. Consider, for instance, a car which generates data about its driving mode, e.g. *eco* and *sport*, and about the seat positions. While the driving modes can only be compared for equality, different seat positions can be ranked and their differences can be quantified.

If the data is categorical, but not ordinal, aggregation PETs cannot be applied [15].

Data Longevity. This criterion expresses how often a specific data value changes. The longer a value lives, the more limited is the applicability of randomized distortion PETs since the resulting data may allow to infer properties of the raw data in the long-term. Applying, for instance, noise masking to a sensitive attribute with a constant distribution, may allow to infer the raw value in the long term. Also the appropriate parametrization of randomized distortion PETs becomes more difficult for long-lived data.

Value Sequences. Some kinds of data can only assume values in a specific sequence, like the state of a car's assistance system. In this case, the applicability of randomized distortion PETs, such as swapping, is limited since the resulting values can exhibit a non-valid sequence. This limitation also concerns suppression since suppressed values may be reconstructed using the expected value sequence.

Metadata and Identifiers. Data may transport identifiers and other metadata that is required for a correct transmission and linkability of data items. This data therefore does not transmit information that is directly required for the service's purposes.

When anonymizing identifiers, randomized distortion PETs are technically applicable, but not in a meaningful way. A MAC address, for example, contains an identifier for the device's manufacturer. Applying a randomized distortion PET like noise masking to this address would result in an anonymization of the manufacturer but would also result in falsely identifying a different manufacturer. The identity information, however, is the only information contained in this data and would effectively be erased by a randomized distortion. Other techniques, like recoding, can still be applied in a meaningful way, e.g. by masking a number of digits of an identifier.

In Sect. 4.1 we show how a taxonomy of the data can be built based on these criteria. This way, a direct mapping of data categories to applicable PETs can be established.

3.3 Step 3: Service-Driven Elicitation

The data-driven elicitation in step 2 results in a set of meaningfully applicable PETs. Yet, this set does not allow any statement about the usefulness of the candidate PETs considering the purposes of the service. For instance, an applicable PET may be suppression which, however, may not only suppress sensitive data, but also important information for the service's processing purposes. Therefore, also a service-driven elicitation—based on the service's requirements towards the data utility—can be conducted to further specify which PETs are useful. This step can be seen as a top-down mapping since it is based on the service's requirements.

Three criteria for the service-driven elicitation are examined in the following.

Value Precision. One service-dependent criterion is the required precision of collected values since it determines the scope in which PETs may be used. Value precision can be changed, for example, by rounding values to a certain decimal place or by masking the last digits of an identifier. The precision of categorical data can only be changed by generalizing the values, i.e. by finding new, more general categories that comprise two or more original ones. Also, PETs that distort values using random values, like noise masking and PRAM, reduce the values' precision. In contrast, applying synthetic data, suppression or aggregation does not preserve the original values at all.

In case a service requires high precision of collected data, this criterion therefore limits the applicability of all PETs seen in Sect. 2 except swapping since swapping preserves all exact values and only swaps them between records. In contrast, a scenario in which a service does not require exact values but rather requires statistics about the data, endorses the application of randomized distortion PETs. Synthetic data, for instance, can be designed to manipulate data while preserving certain statistical properties.

Data Freshness. Data freshness expresses how long ago data has been generated. High requirements towards data freshness, e.g. requiring near real-time data, can limit the applicability of aggregation PETs since their application relies on collecting data from one or multiple data sources introducing a certain latency into the processing.

Attribute Dependency. A further criterion that influences the usefulness of PETs concerns the dependency between attributes. If a service provider needs to collect a certain combination of attributes, it may not be possible to obtain meaningful results when processing them independently from each other using different PETs. Consider, for example, a connected car generating distance and speed data. If the service's purpose is to infer a correlation between the two kinds of data, the data's usefulness may be reduced if the distance data would be perturbed using noise masking but the speed data would be recoded using generalization.

Such a set of data can also originate from multiple vehicles. Consider, for example, a fleet of vehicles whose average fuel consumption shall be determined. In this case, too, the statistic cannot be reliably computed anymore if the vehicles' consumption values have been processed using different PETs. In some case-specific, this problem can be avoided altogether if data is collected on a higher level of abstraction, i.e. the inference computations are done locally, inside the vehicle.

A special case of attribute dependency concerns the identifiability of users, i.e. the requirement to associate certain data items with a particular person or a group. If only the data values are needed, e.g. for statistical analysis, identification of a user is not necessary which suggests the suppression or pseudonymization of the identifier. Hence, if data needs to be traceable to a certain individual, the applicability of suppression and pseudonymization is limited. It may, however, be the case that identifying attributes need to be collected by a service together with other attributes. If there is no dependency between the two, swapping can be a useful PET since it can be used to break the link between identifying values and other, otherwise sensitive, values and still preserve them within the data set.

3.4   Step 4: PET-Selection

After the two elicitation steps, a set of usable classes of PETs results from which appropriate ones can be selected. This last selection step poses the question of how to select PETs from a set of usable ones. In the following, we briefly describe criteria that may be relevant for this question. As it is highly application- and use case-specific, however, we consider a further investigation out of scope for this paper.

To select a final set of PETs, a service provider may consider the implementation cost and complexity of the PETs. If, for instance, suppression results as an option, it may be considered first, since it is relatively easy to implement and reliably protects the respective data. Also, the service provider may want the collected data to satisfy certain privacy metrics, like k-anonymity, that result from legal requirements or internal compliance requirements. These metrics may only be satisfiable by certain PETs.

Furthermore, it is possible that step 3 results in an empty set of useful PETs, i.e. there is no possibility to anonymize the given set of data such that it still meets the service's requirements. In this case, the consequence may be that the service provider needs to obtain the users' consent to the collection and processing of the raw personal data. Otherwise the service may simply not be implementable.

4   Selecting PETs for Automotive Services

In this section, we show how the process proposed above can be applied in the context of IoT-based automotive services. As seen in Sect. 3.2, the meaningful applicability of PETs depends on the data's characteristics, such as *set size*, *longevity*, and *value sequences*. In what follows, we propose a taxonomy for automotive data that is created based on the criteria we proposed, and we map the resulting categories to applicable PETs. This way, we aim at providing a domain-specific data-driven elicitation that can generally be applied to IoT-based services in the automotive domain. Finally, we show an exemplary application of the process which uses this taxonomy for the data-driven elicitation step.

4.1   A Taxonomy for Automotive Data

In the following, we present our taxonomy for automotive data and discuss to what extent the PETs described above are applicable for their processing. It comprises the categories of *Communication Metadata*, *Vehicle Attributes*, *Stream Data*, *State Variables*, *Event Data* and *Complex Data*. The mapping is summarized in Table 1 (at the end of this Subsection).

Communication Metadata. Communication metadata includes data that is needed for the transmission of messages, for instance: SIM card ID, IP address, MAC address, Bluetooth address and Vehicle Identification Number (VIN). While this data is numeric, it is actually categorical data since these identifiers assume values from a finite set and follow a fixed format that usually does not allow to perform arithmetic operations on them. This consideration influences the applicability of PETs as explained in Sect. 3.3.

Vehicle Attributes. Vehicle attributes include rather long-lived data that describes the vehicle, for example: Transmission information (e.g. number of gears), fuel type (e.g. gasoline, diesel, electric, hybrid), engine information (e.g. number of cylinders, battery type, construction type), vehicle dimensions (e.g. width, length, height), tire and wheel dimensions (e.g. diameter and width) and number of doors and seats.

Vehicle attributes are similar to communication metadata since they also assume values from a finite set and meaningful arithmetic operations cannot be performed on them, i.e. they pertain to the categorical value type. Yet, they also differ from communication data. First, they are often not numeric, and second, the application of randomized distortion PETs can yield meaningful results. In comparison to a MAC address, for example, the number of seats in a vehicle can be perturbed using a PET like PRAM. Still, the applicability of these PETs is limited due to the data's longevity and limited set size.

Vehicle attributes can, for instance, be used to fingerprint a vehicle for tracking purposes since they expose long-lived information.

Stream Data. This category contains data that is generated continuously by sensors, for example: Location, temperature (e.g. cabin, outside, motor), pressure (e.g. tire pressure), speed, distance (e.g. LiDAR, RADAR, ultrasound), battery status (e.g. charging cycles), steering angle and yaw rate.

This data is continuous, therefore all PETs except PRAM can be used to process it. A special kind of stream data is location data. It has a high privacy-relevance since it often reveals identifying and sensitive information about users. A number of specialized PETs exist for anonymizing location data, which can also be classified according to the PET classes included in our approach. For example, existing works have proposed recoding techniques [8,12,13], synthetic data [16] and aggregation PETs [6] for location data.

As an example, consider a predictive maintenance service which analyzes stream data to recognize anomalies in the generated data. It can use this data to predict when certain sensors or parts need to be replaced or maintained, for instance suggesting an oil or tire change.

State Variables. State variables express the state of a system, for example of an assistance system or the state of cabin settings. Examples are: Assistance systems (e.g. system state of cruise control, adaptive cruise control, lane-keeping assistance), cabin settings (e.g. positions of seats, mirrors, steering wheel), infotainment usage data (e.g. used media types and infotainment services), driving mode (e.g. eco, sport) and light settings (e.g. daytime running light, long distance light).

State variable data is categorical. Similar to communication metadata and vehicle attributes, it can be processed using recoding while the application of other techniques is either limited or not given at all. It still differs from other data categories since it is rather short-lived. Consider, for example, the light setting: It is often changed by a rotary switch where the setting can only be changed to one of its neighboring settings. This way, a sequence for the light setting is implicitly established.

For example, this data may be used in a car-sharing service which automatically prepares the cabin settings, for instance seat and mirror positions, for the driver's preferences when she rents a vehicle.

Event Data. This data is sensor data that is generated irregularly indicating that a certain event has taken place, for example: Automatic safety belt tightening, diagnostic trouble codes, ESP intervention, lane departure warning, fatigue warning and emergency assist.

Event data can be treated as categorical data. Yet, it can only assume one value rendering most PETs non-applicable. Event data can neither be recoded— e.g. no generalized categories can be found—nor can the data be perturbed by noise masking, swapping or PRAM since the one possible value cannot be changed or replaced. Neither can aggregation be applied since no statistics of the data's values can be built. The only class of PETs which can be applicable without limits is synthetic data. Using synthetic data, events can be generated which preserve the original events' statistical properties, e.g. average time elapsed between occurrences, while at the same time masking their real occurrences.

For instance, crash detection data can be used by an application that triggers an automatic emergency call. The automatic safety belt tightenings can further be used to infer information about the driving behavior of the driver.

Complex Data. This category summarizes data which cannot be assigned to any of the above categories and is thus not included in Table 1. Consider, for example, combined data structures collected from various sources, e.g. represented as n-tuples, potentially requiring the application of a different PET to each n-th element. Further examples of complex data are image and sound data used for voice assistants and for inward-facing and outward-facing cameras. Their privacy-enhancement cannot be ensured by reducing precision since this does not necessarily ensure that persons recorded by a camera or a microphone are properly de-identified. Hence, specialized PETs are required for their anonymization, such as proposed in [1] and [23]. Other examples for complex data are: Installed applications, account information (e.g. user names, passwords, payment information), voice and video recordings, contact list, call history and data induced by the driver (e.g. query data for location-based services).

Table 1 summarizes the results of the mapping showing which classes of PETs (recoding, suppression, aggregation, swapping, noise masking, PRAM and synthetic data) are applicable to which automotive data categories (communication metadata, vehicle attributes, stream data, state variables, event data, location data). X represents *applicable*, *(X)* represents *limited applicability* and a gray box represents *not applicable*. Note that the general mapping between PET classes and value types is taken from [15] (as described in Sect. 2), and the granular mapping of automotive data categories to PET classes is our contribution (as described in Sect. 4.1).

Table 1. Applicability of PET classes to automotive data categories. The mapping of the general applicability of value types (categorical, continuous) to PET classes is taken from Hundepool et al. [15]; our contribution extends this mapping to the automotive data categories and proposes a granular discussion of their grade of applicability.

Automotive data	Value type	PET classes						
		Det. Dist.			Rand. Dist.			
		Recod.	Suppr.	Aggr.	Swapping	Noise M.	PRAM	Synthet.
Metadata	Cat	X						
Vehicle Attr.	Cat	X	(X)	(X)	(X)	(X)	(X)	(X)
Stream data	Cont	X	X	X	X	X		X
State vars	Cat	X			(X)		(X)	(X)
Event data	Cat							X
Location	Cont	X	(X)	X	(X)	(X)		(X)

4.2 Example Process Application

In the following, we describe a fictitious example service to show how the process proposed above can be applied in a real-world scenario.

In our example, we consider an insurance company as the service provider who wants to collect data about the driving behavior of customers to offer a risk-based payment model. To calculate the risk-based price for the user, the service provider wants to collect a set of data from the customers' vehicles.

1) Service Description. In this first step, the required data as well as the actors in the service are described. The actors in this example include the insurance company as the service provider as well as the service users who are assumed to be the owners of the vehicles from which data is collected. To determine the driving behavior of the driver, the service provider wants to collect data about the vehicle's speed, the operating times (e.g. driving times in the morning or the evening) as well as data about the interventions of the Electronic Stability Control (ESC) assistance system. Also, the insurance company wants to know the vehicle's horsepower (HP) as vehicles with a higher number of HP are associated with a higher risk of causing accidents.

While this data is not directly identifying, it can be classified as sensitive as it reveals information about the concerned person's driving behavior.

2) Data-Driven Elicitation. The data-driven elicitation represents the second step of our selection process, identifying applicable PETs for the required data. First, speed data can be categorized as stream data since it is generated continuously by the respective sensors. Hence, all considered classes of PETs except PRAM are applicable. The vehicle's operating times can be seen as a status variable that assumes values from the sequence of possible time values. It can therefore best be processed using recoding techniques. Third, the ESC interventions represent event data since they represent irregularly generated events. They can be processed using the PETs synthetic data or, applied to its timely occurrences, aggregation. Fourth, the vehicle's HP pertains to the category of vehicle attributes. Due to its longevity, only recoding PETs are applicable here.

3) Service-Driven Elicitation. In the third process step, the service requirements towards the data are considered to further specify the set of applicable PETs. The first criterion concerns the value precision the service provider requires to be able to provision the service. Regarding the speed data, the service provider does not need to know exact speed values but rather speed intervals in which the vehicle is operated. We assume that the required precision for the speed data equals to intervals of 20 km/h. Similarly, the HP is only needed in intervals of 20 HP to evaluate the risk that car model induces. The operating times of the vehicle are required only to infer the time of day, i.e. day- or night-time. Lastly, the ESC interventions are required as the exact number of occurrences in the preceding month.

Data freshness is the second criterion of the service-driven elicitation considering how fast the service provider needs the data after it has been generated. In our example, the service provider does not have any freshness requirements since the risk assessment can also be conducted on old data. Also, the third criterion, value dependency, does not further narrow down the set of applicable PETs.

4) PET-Selection. From the set of meaningfully applicable PETs that result from the service-driven elicitation, in step 4 it can be selected as follows.

All speed data can be rounded down to the nearest multiple of 20 km/h to meet the service provider's minimal requirement towards the precision of the data, i.e. a recoding technique can be applied. Applying randomized distortion PETs is possible as well, e.g. by applying additive noise masking with a randomized value between −10 and +10.

The only meaningfully applicable class of PETs for the horsepower value is recoding PETs. Since the required precision equals intervals of 20 km/h, a rounding PETs with this granularity can be applied.

Concerning the status variable of operating times, the service provider is especially interested in the information at which times of the day the vehicle is operated. Therefore, a generalization is suggested to the values *day time* and *night time*. Other PETs are not usable here. For example, applying a randomization with PRAM would result in an easily reversible sequence where the variable can be matched with the actual time of day when the data was received.

The event data showing ESC interventions can be processed using an aggregation of the events, e.g. building a statistic of the average occurrences in a certain time frame. Alternatively, synthetic data could be generated to mimic the real occurrences of the events preserving relevant statistics.

In this Section we have shown a case study of the application of our process building a taxonomy of automotive data and using it in a concrete example. While this case study is specific to the automotive domain, we expect our process to be equally well applicable to other IoT-related domains. Considering the proposed taxonomy, it can be transferred, for instance, to smart home appliances as well as these devices also generate stream data (e.g. a fridge's temperature), event data (e.g. a finished washing machine), state variable data (e.g. the lighting state) and metadata and they may as well possess long-lived attributes.

5 Discussion

In what follows, we discuss to what extent the proposed process can satisfy the three requirements we defined in Sect. 3, namely its *reproducibility*, its *applicability* as a standalone process as well as complementary to other approaches, and its ability to facilitate *data minimization*.

5.1 Reproducibility

Since the reproducibility of the process depends on the reproducibility of the two elicitation steps 2 and 3, we discuss this requirement for these two steps. Meanwhile, step 1 only provides the service description and the selection in step 4 is not examined in detail in this paper.

Step 2 provides data-driven criteria which indicate to what extent certain PETs are applicable. On the one hand, these criteria are not completely unambiguous since in some cases, they only indicate a "limited" applicability which does not allow a deterministic decision. On the other hand, we have described the application-specific criteria which determine the applicability if it is limited, e.g. regarding the PETs' parametrization. For example, if the data values at hand follow a specific sequence, swapping can only be applied if the resulting states still contain sufficient randomness. The results of step 2 are therefore reproducible to the extent where a limited applicability might be evaluated differently by different users.

Step 3 includes service-driven criteria, like precision and freshness of the data. These criteria are more use case-dependent. For instance, a high value precision limits the applicability of most PETs. It is, however, use case-dependent how the required value precision influences the usability of a PET. The service-driven criteria therefore rather provide guidelines for service providers that have to be evaluated using the specific purpose and data at hand. As such, their reproducibility depends on how a user of the process evaluates the degree of precision and freshness the service requires.

In summary, the process steps are reproducible to the point where application-specific criteria need to be considered. Given the same set of input data, step 2 results in a reproducible set of applicable and non-applicable PETs, while a result of limited applicability may be interpreted differently by different users. Step 3 includes two criteria that also may be evaluated differently by different users since their evaluation depends on the specifics of the service.

To further enhance the reproducibility of the process, it may be beneficial to make the results of the single process steps more comparable. To that end, appropriate metrics could be defined for the PETs to make the selection and parametrization of a certain PET comparable to other use cases. For instance, identifying a metric that measures the randomness in a state variable sequence would make the evaluation of the applicability of noise-masking PETs more comparable and its application more reproducible given a certain set of requirements.

5.2   Standalone and Complementary Applicability

The proposed process is applicable as a standalone process given a service description which includes the required data and its purposes. Applying the process standalone can be especially useful if it is integrated into the requirements engineering process during a system design. The process can be applied early on in the system design to assess whether useful PETs can be found for the required data and to assess to what extent the data collection can be minimized. Since its applicability does not require a complete system design or data flow analysis, it may be applied many times for such an assessment during a system design.

The process can, however, also be applied complementary to other existing approaches (see Sect. 6). As such it may be utilized to narrow down a list of potentially applicable PETs that have been elicited from a risk analysis. In the following, we first discuss how our process compares to existing approaches and then explain how a complementary application can be conducted.

One difference between risk-driven approaches and our process is that risk-based approaches suggest a list of PETs based on privacy threats. As such, they do not elicit *practically applicable* PETs—which is ensured in our approach by the data-driven elicitation—but suggest PETs that generally may apply to the identified threats. Furthermore, they leave the service-driven elicitation to the user applying the approach.

The LINDDUN methodology, proposed by Deng et al. [5], defines six steps to systematically approach the elicitation of privacy requirements. LINDDUN is an acronym for the considered privacy threats which are linkability, identifiability, non-repudiation, detectability, disclosure of information, unawareness of users as well as policy and consent non-compliance. Following this methodology, first a Data Flow Diagram (DFD) is created and privacy threats are identified. Then, threats are prioritized, mitigation strategies are established and in the last step PETs are selected. Note that we do not discuss policy and consent compliance here since they do not influence the selection of data-dependent PETs.

Consider again the example application described above, where data about operating times, ESP interventions and the vehicle's HP is collected. When identifying threats for these data flows, none of the threats described above can be excluded. Two trips may, for instance, be linkable if the driver has consistently high numbers of ESP interventions due to her driving style. Apart from this, a vehicle may always be identifiable by the metadata that is included in a message. Consequently, a risk-driven approach generates a considerable number of threats for the data flows and will suggest a large number of potentially applicable PETs. Here, the proposed process can narrow down the list of PETs to the ones which are practical and usable.

A complementary application can be conducted based on the data flows that are identified in the risk-based approach. LINDDUN, for example, includes the creation of a data flow diagram. This diagram can also be used as the service description which corresponds to the result of step 1 of our process. Furthermore the process takes two inputs as illustrated in Fig. 1: PET candidates and the service requirements. As PET candidates, the results from the risk-based analysis are used. Note, however, that only data-dependent PETs can be taken into account here. The service requirements are needed as input to step 3. We assume these to be known since a service description including necessary data flows is already required for the risk-based analysis.

5.3 Data Minimization

The proposed process goes beyond the decision of collecting certain data items or not, but aims at selecting data-dependent PETs that can limit the quantity of data—e.g. suggesting suppression—as well as the quality of data—e.g. suggesting randomized distortion PETs—to what is necessary for the service's purposes. It does so by applying data-driven as well as service-driven criteria to the PET elicitation. The process is, however, limited to the PETs it is scoped to (see Sect. 2). Also, the appropriate minimization of data collection depends on the parametrization of the chosen PETs. Still, we would argue that it provides many important criteria towards data minimization as it is required by various data protection regulations, such as the GDPR which requires the collection of personal data to be "limited to what is necessary in relation to the purposes for which they are processed" (Article 5).

6 Related Work

6.1 Privacy Requirements Engineering

Existing work on privacy requirements engineering focuses on risk-based approaches. In Sect. 5, we have already discussed LINDDUN.

A further approach by Luna et al. [18] is called *Quantitative Threat Modeling Methodologies*. Here, similar to LINDDUN, first a DFD is created and it is mapped to privacy and security threats. Next, possible misuse case scenarios are examined, i.e. use cases from the perspective of an attacker. In a fourth step, the threats are quantified using attack trees and finally, mitigation strategies are chosen. The methodologies of Deng et al. and Luna et al. are both based on the threat modeling approach developed by Microsoft called STRIDE [22].

Oliver [21] proposes a privacy requirements framework. It describes ontological structures for the description of data and system properties, like information types (e.g. location or identifier) and usage types (e.g. advertising or profiling). From these, privacy requirements can be generated.

Spiekermann and Cranor [26] identify three types of system activities from which privacy requirements can be deduced: data transfer, data storage and data processing. Additionally, they include user expectations and behavior, as well as the threat model—which can vary between users—in their requirements analysis. Furthermore, they differentiate between two basic approaches in engineering privacy requirements, namely *privacy by architecture* and *privacy by policy*.

In comparison to these mostly risk-driven approaches, our selection process is data- and service-driven. As such, it can complement risk-driven approaches since it does not target specific privacy threats but aims at providing a more granular selection. Following the classification by Notario et al. [20], our process is a *goal-oriented* approach rather than a *risk-based* one.

6.2   Categorizing Automotive Data

A further contribution of this paper is a taxonomy of automotive data. Existing proposals focus on building taxonomies according to the functional parts of a car rather than for the applicability of PETs.

One similar approach to categorizing automotive data was proposed by Hornung [14] who identifies four categories: local data (e.g. Bluetooth ID, MAC addresses), environment data (e.g. concerning the infrastructure and the weather), third-party data (e.g. about installed applications) and personally-identifiable information (e.g. biometric data and voice recordings). He also suggests other categories based on the complexity of data which are: vehicle attributes (e.g. model), communication data (e.g. Car-2-Car communication), sensor data (e.g. temperature), processed data for the driver (e.g. navigation data) and infotainment data.

The GENIVI Alliance[3] suggests a list of automotive data specifying the value type and unit in a tree structure[4]. Version 2.0 of this specification defines as top-level branches vehicle parts, like drive train and chassis, but also concrete signals like drive time and ambient air temperature which do not directly pertain to any of these vehicle parts. Hence, these categories are especially useful in the design of on-board automotive software systems where it is important to have a well-arranged structure that provides access to the required data.

Concerning concrete sensor data, Fleming [10,11] lists automotive sensors and categorizes them based on their functionality or the respective vehicle part power train, chassis or body.

In comparison to these approaches, our taxonomy proposed in Sect. 4.1 is based on data-driven criteria for the applicability of PETs.

---

[3] https://www.genivi.org.
[4] https://github.com/GENIVI/vehicle_signal_specification.

7   Conclusion and Future Work

In this paper, we have proposed a process for the selection of PETs, focusing on two subproblems of the PET selection problem. First, we have focused on specific classes of PETs, namely PETs which manipulate data. Second, we have focused on IoT-based services establishing data-driven and service-driven criteria for the elicitation of PETs. We have shown that within this scope the applicability of PETs can be elicited more granularly than in previously proposed approaches. We have then shown how the process may be applied specifically for the automotive domain proposing a novel taxonomy for automotive data. We have furthermore discussed to what extent the proposed process satisfies reproducibility, standalone and complementary applicability, as well as data minimization.

Future work includes the development of criteria for the elicitation of other types of PETs, e.g. PETs based on encryption-techniques or based on usage-control, and further criteria for the selection of PETs in step 4 of the process. Also, we will examine the application of our selection process to other domains, such as smart homes and medical devices. We further plan to extend the process integrating the quantification of privacy using metrics like k-anonymity (as discussed in Sect. 5), and improve its usability by transforming it to an iterative approach.

Acknowledgment. This work was partly funded by the Bavarian Ministry of Economic Affairs and Media, Energy and Technology, within the project Bayern-Cloud.

References

1. Birnstill, P., Ren, D., Beyerer, J.: A user study on anonymization techniques for smart video surveillance. In: 12th International Conference on Advanced Video and Signal Based Surveillance (AVSS), pp. 1–6. IEEE (2015)
2. Dalenius, T.: Finding a needle in a haystack or identifying anonymous census records. J. Off. Stat. **2**(3), 329 (1986)
3. Dandekar, R.A., Domingo-Ferrer, J., Sebé, F.: LHS-based hybrid microdata vs rank swapping and microaggregation for numeric microdata protection. In: Domingo-Ferrer, J. (ed.) Inference Control in Statistical Databases. LNCS, vol. 2316, pp. 153–162. Springer, Heidelberg (2002). https://doi.org/10.1007/3-540-47804-3_12
4. De Wolf, P.P., Gouweleeuw, J., Kooiman, P., Willenborg, L., et al.: Reflections on PRAM. In: Statistical Data Protection, pp. 337–349. Citeseer (1998)
5. Deng, M., Wuyts, K., Scandariato, R., Preneel, B., Joosen, W.: A privacy threat analysis framework: supporting the elicitation and fulfillment of privacy requirements. Requir. Eng. **16**(1), 3–32 (2011). https://doi.org/10.1007/s00766-010-0115-7
6. Domingo-Ferrer, J.: Microaggregation for database and location privacy. In: Etzion, O., Kuflik, T., Motro, A. (eds.) NGITS 2006. LNCS, vol. 4032, pp. 106–116. Springer, Heidelberg (2006). https://doi.org/10.1007/11780991_10
7. Domingo-Ferrer, J., Sebé, F., Castellà-Roca, J.: On the security of noise addition for privacy in statistical databases. In: Domingo-Ferrer, J., Torra, V. (eds.) PSD 2004. LNCS, vol. 3050, pp. 149–161. Springer, Heidelberg (2004). https://doi.org/10.1007/978-3-540-25955-8_12

8. Duckham, M., Kulik, L.: A formal model of obfuscation and negotiation for location privacy. In: Gellersen, H.-W., Want, R., Schmidt, A. (eds.) Pervasive 2005. LNCS, vol. 3468, pp. 152–170. Springer, Heidelberg (2005). https://doi.org/10.1007/11428572_10

9. Fischetti, M., González, J.J.S.: Models and algorithms for optimizing cell suppression in tabular data with linear constraints. J. Am. Stat. Assoc. **95**(451), 916–928 (2000)

10. Fleming, W.J.: Overview of automotive sensors. Sens. J. **1**(4), 296–308 (2001)

11. Fleming, W.J.: New automotive sensors—A review. Sens. J. **8**(11), 1900–1921 (2008)

12. Hoh, B., Gruteser, M., Xiong, H., Alrabady, A.: Enhancing security and privacy in traffic-monitoring systems. Pervasive Comput. **5**(4), 38–46 (2006)

13. Hoh, B., Gruteser, M., Xiong, H., Alrabady, A.: Preserving privacy in GPS traces via uncertainty-aware path cloaking. In: Proceedings of the 14th ACM Conference on Computer and Communications Security, pp. 161–171. ACM (2007)

14. Hornung, G.: Verfügungsrechte an fahrzeugbezogenen Daten [Rights of disposition for vehicle-related data]. Datenschutz und Datensicherheit-DuD **39**(6), 359–366 (2015)

15. Hundepool, A., et al.: Statistical Disclosure Control. Wiley, Hoboken (2012)

16. Kido, H., Yanagisawa, Y., Satoh, T.: An anonymous communication technique using dummies for location-based services. In: Proceedings of the 2005 International Conference on Pervasive Services, ICPS 2005, pp. 88–97. IEEE (2005)

17. Little, R.J.: Statistical analysis of masked data. J. Off. Stat. **9**(2), 407 (1993)

18. Luna, J., Suri, N., Krontiris, I.: Privacy-by-design based on quantitative threat modeling. In: 7th International Conference on Risks and Security of Internet and Systems (CRiSIS), pp. 1–8. IEEE (2012)

19. Moore, R.: Controlled data-swapping techniques for masking public use microdata sets. US Census Bureau [Custodian] (1996)

20. Notario, N., et al.: PRIPARE: integrating privacy best practices into a privacy engineering methodology. In: Security and Privacy Workshops, pp. 151–158. IEEE (2015)

21. Oliver, I.: Experiences in the development and usage of a privacy requirements framework. In: 24th International Requirements Engineering Conference (RE), pp. 293–302. IEEE (2016)

22. Potter, B.: Microsoft SDL threat modelling tool. Netw. Secur. **1**, 15–18 (2009)

23. Qian, J., et al.: VoiceMask: anonymize and sanitize voice input on mobile devices. arXiv preprint arXiv:1711.11460 (2017)

24. Rubin, D.B.: Statistical disclosure limitation. J. Off. Stat. **9**(2), 461–468 (1993)

25. Samarati, P.: Protecting respondents identities in microdata release. Trans. Knowl. Data Eng. **13**(6), 1010–1027 (2001)

26. Spiekermann, S., Cranor, L.F.: Engineering privacy. Trans. Softw. Eng. **35**(1), 67–82 (2009)

27. Torra, V.: Microaggregation for categorical variables: a median based approach. In: Domingo-Ferrer, J., Torra, V. (eds.) PSD 2004. LNCS, vol. 3050, pp. 162–174. Springer, Heidelberg (2004). https://doi.org/10.1007/978-3-540-25955-8_13

Khopesh - Contact Tracing Without Sacrificing Privacy

Friedrich Doku[1]($\boxtimes$)(iD) and Ethan Doku[2](iD)

[1] University of Pittsburgh, Pittsburgh, PA, USA
frd20@pitt.edu
[2] Irondale High School, New Brighton, MN, USA
2021dokue58@moundsviewschools.org

Abstract. Secure contact tracing has proven challenging to implement, because even if a user's contact data is encrypted, it is still difficult to hide the user's metadata, which could be used to determine a user's identity, furthermore, many existing contact tracing software implementations may require a user to send sensitive information such as location data to be processed by a central authority. Current systems such as DP-3T [9] and COVIDSafe [10] do not provide anonymity or much privacy protection. It is also not guaranteed that the data collected will not be used for marketing, commercial gain, or law enforcement.

Khopesh is a new secure contact tracing system that offers strong privacy guarantees, hiding both a user's contacts and location data. This is made possible through the use of identity-based encryption, mix networks, and a novel technique called secure-contact contract signing, which enables groups of users to view each other's reports.

Keywords: Anonymity · Privacy · Communication

1 Introduction

In the wake of the Covid-19 virus, we find that the world is underprepared to track the spread of pandemics. Existing methods to track the spread of the virus heavily rely on the government to deploy large-scale surveillance operations to track people. These existing methods provide users with almost no privacy and anonymity whatsoever. However, many of these contact tracing services allow users to opt-in or opt-out, but if governments expect the number of users using contract tracing apps to increase, the designers need to design protocols with stronger privacy guarantees. Users should not have to sacrifice their privacy to help stop the spread of the Covid-19 virus, and companies should not be able to take advantage of the current situation to increase their profits.

Many users would like secure contact tracing, but current contact tracing software does not guarantee privacy. Even if the data is encrypted, adversaries can still learn a lot about a user based on metadata, which can be observed

© ICST Institute for Computer Sciences, Social Informatics and Telecommunications Engineering 2020
Published by Springer Nature Switzerland AG 2020. All Rights Reserved
N. Park et al. (Eds.): SecureComm 2020, LNICST 336, pp. 475–486, 2020.
https://doi.org/10.1007/978-3-030-63095-9_30

through traffic analysis. Contact tracing software needs to be designed for security, adding encryption on top of an insecure protocol does not make it more secure.

Covid-19 is indeed a pandemic, and current tracing technology, such as COVIDSafe [10], VirusRadar [1], etc, help monitor the spread of Covid-19 and provide users with some security. However, these systems still do not provide users with anonymity.

This paper presents Khopesh, a secure contact tracing system that protects the identity and contact data of its users. Khopesh efficiently tracks the spread of infectious diseases like Covid-19 while providing users with anonymity and privacy. Khopesh can keep its users completely anonymous as long as two users are active. Furthermore, it is still possible for a user to know whether a friend or family member has been infected with the virus despite their anonymity. Khopesh does not collect location data for contact tracing.

Khopesh keeps passive adversaries that monitor network traffic from learning the identity of its users by exploiting a mixnet. Users will generate a random permutation of mixer public keys. Next, they will onion-encrypt their report data with the public keys in the order determined by the permutation and send it to the mixnet, which will shuffle reports and decrypt layers of encryption before sending it to a mailbox server where users will download their reports. Khopesh operates in rounds, and each round users will follow this process.

Khopesh's drawback is that to protect its users from a passive attacking adversary that monitors network traffic, it must make some performance sacrifices. For example, Khopesh's users must download and decrypt many reports before viewing their reports because many users will share a mailbox, and inside each mailbox are encrypted reports for specific users. This downloading and decrypting of reports exploits significant amounts of bandwidth and CPU resources.

Nevertheless, Khopesh is still more secure than traditional contact tracing systems. Khopesh may use more computing resources than other contract tracing systems, but the extra computing resources are all used to protect a user's personal information, providing Khopesh with stronger privacy guarantees.

All in all, we make the following contributions:

- Analyze the design of Khopesh, a secure contact tracing system that keeps its users anonymous and their contacts protected.
- Introduce a novel technique called secure-contact contract signing, which allows users to form groups and share their reports securely.

2   Threat Model and Goals

Khopesh aims to keep its users anonymous and their contacts private, while effectively tracing the spread of infectious diseases. In this section, we describe Khopesh's threat model and goals.

2.1   Threat Model

Khopesh's design assumes that a passive attacking adversary is monitoring all of Khopesh's traffic, controls all but one of Khopesh's mixer servers (users do not need to know which one), and controls an arbitrary number of users. We also assume that the adversary can block, delay, or inject traffic. A user, Alice, sending reports through Khopesh should have their communication protected as long as one mixer is uncompromised. Since users will send their reports over multiple rounds, we assume that the adversary may interfere with the users more than one round. The adversary's goals include finding out who is in the network and who is sending reports to whom.

All cryptographic assumptions are standard (the adversary will be unable to break cryptographic primitives). We assume secure public key encryption, hash functions, and key-exchange mechanisms. We assume that Khopesh's mixer public keys are known to all users.

Finally, we assume that honest Khopesh servers and users correctly implement the Khopesh protocol, and no data leakage exists through side channels. In the case of a server or client being controlled by an adversary, it is assumed that they are not following the protocol, but honest servers and users are assumed to be running bug-free implementations of Khopesh.

Khopesh is not a fault-tolerant system. Khopesh can recover from minor server failures, but it does not protect against server component failures or denial-of-service attacks. Since we do not cover availability attacks on Khopesh, we will leave this out of scope.

Cryptographic Primitives. Khopesh relies on the following cryptographic primitives.

Identity Based Encryption. Khopesh exploits the Boneh-Franklin Identity-Based encryption scheme [5] to create public and private key pairs for secure-contact contracts and for users, which consists of the following algorithms:

- $(mk, params) \leftarrow \mathsf{Setup}(k)$. Generates the system parameter $params$ and the master-key mk, from a security parameter k.
- $(d) \leftarrow \mathsf{Extract}(params, mk, ID)$. Generates the user's private key d given the $params$, mk, and the user's id ID.
- $(C) \leftarrow \mathsf{Encrypt}(params, ID, M)$. Encrypts a message M from $params$ and ID to create a ciphertext C
- $(M) \leftarrow \mathsf{Decrypt}(params, C, d)$. Decrypts C from d, $params$, and mk to generate M.

XSalsa20 Authenticated Encryption. Khopesh exploits XSalsa20, which provides immunity to timing attacks. Each mixnet server and user in Khopesh uses XSalsa20 for encrypting and decrypting reports.

- $(C) \leftarrow \mathsf{AEncrypt}(n, M, pk)$. Encrypts a message M from a public key pk and a cryptographic nonce n to create a ciphertext C
- $(M) \leftarrow \mathsf{ADecrypt}(n, pk, C, sk)$. Decrypts C from the recipients pk, private key sk, and n.

2.2   Goals

Khopesh has three primary goals.

Correctness. Informally, Khopesh is correct if every honest user can successfully send her report to the central authority, and the central authority can process that data and inform users about infected users.

Anonymity. Khopesh achieves the goal of keeping the identity of its users anonymous if the passive attacking adversary described in Sect. 2.1 is unable to uncover the identity of Khopesh's users by no more than random guessing.

Privacy. Khopesh achieves the goal of protecting privacy if users can have their contacts hidden from the passive attacking adversary described in Sect. 2.1 and can inform other trusted users of their current status.

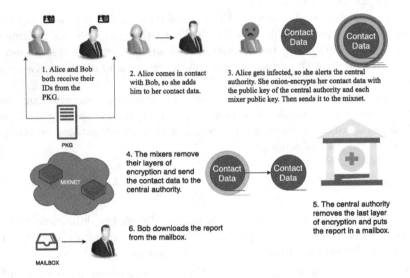

Fig. 1. An overview of Zephyr's protocol.

3   Design

We will now explain the details of Khopesh and how it protects itself from the passive attacking adversary that is described in Sect. 2.1.

3.1   Private Key Generators

Traditional key distribution servers leak data about who a user is communicating with based on the public-key the user receives from the server. To avoid key distribution, Khopesh exploits a private key generator (PKG), which is a trusted third-party server that is responsible for generating the IDs of users and private keys for secure-contact contracts using IBE.

When users start the Khopesh protocol, they will first authenticate themselves by sending their phone numbers to the PKG. Once the PKG has received the user's phone number, it will send a text message containing a unique code to the user's phone. Once the user returns the code to the PKG, the PKG will send the user her ID, which is a hash of their encrypted phone number using a cryptographically secure string as the public key.

To create a secure-contact contract, the users will authenticate themselves again but instead receive a shared ID and private key. The shared ID is computed by hashing an encrypted concatenation of each group member's phone number with a cryptographically secure string as the key. The PKG will store each user's ID and shared ID.

3.2   Mixnet

Khopesh exploits a mixnet to prevent reports from being traced back to their senders.

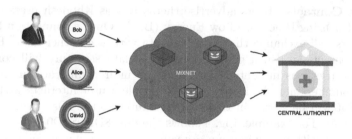

Fig. 2. Users send their data through a mixnet.

Once a mixer in the mixnet has received reports, it will shuffle them, remove layers of encryption, and send them to the next mixer. Figure 2 shows a group of users Bob, Alice, and David each has onion-encrypted their reports with mixer public keys in different orders after first encrypting their reports with the central authority's public key. Each report passes through the mixnet, and the last mixer to decrypt the final layer of encryption of a report sends the report to the central authority. As long as one mixer is honest, an adversary will be unable to figure out the destination of a user's report because each mixer shuffles their reports before sending them to the next mixer.

It is necessary to make sure that mixers are shuffling the reports. If the reports are not shuffled, it will be easier for adversaries to figure out the identities of Khopesh's users. To ensure that mixers are not misbehaving, Khopesh exploits zero-knowledge shuffle proofs for verifying the shuffling process of each mixer. These proofs prove that each shuffle output is a permutation of each shuffle input without revealing any knowledge of the permutation.

3.3   Mailboxes

Mailboxes are publicly known memory locations that reside in the central authority. Mailboxes provide Khopesh's users with greater identity protection because each mailbox is determined by the user's phone number modulus the number of mailboxes, which means that several users will share the same mailbox. Adversaries will be unable to figure out the identity of a user because every other user will download their reports from the same server, creating no distinction between other users.

The central authority will send all infection reports to a single mailbox and shared reports (reports created with secure-contact contracts) will be placed into the mailboxes of their recipients.

3.4   Users

We will now describe how users operate in Khopesh.

Receiving Contacts. Users advertise themselves as Khopesh users and scan for each other using Bluetooth Low Energy (BLE). Once a connection has been formed, users will exchange their contact data with each other using BLE and store the contact data in a general tree. This data structure will contain all the people a user was in contact with and any indirect interactions. However, the phone numbers nor the identity of the people a user interacts with will be stored. What will be stored in the data structure are the IDs of each person a user encounters. For example, Fig. 4 shows the user 8DK9S0D0 (Alice) who has been in contact with multiple users. As you can see, the names/phone numbers of all of the connected users are not shown. Alice's indirect connections are the two leaf nodes that are under the user with the ID D7G9ZZQ2 (Fig. 3).

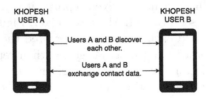

Fig. 3. Khopesh BLE handshake.

This general tree data structure makes it easy for users to receive reports about possible infections. If the central authority releases a report that a user has been infected, other users can check if they have been possibly infected by searching their trees for the infected user's ID.

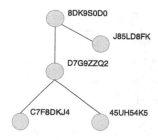

Fig. 4. Structure of user contacts.

Receiving Infection Reports. When a user gets infected, she will send her report through the mixnet to the central authority with a flag that shows that she has the virus. The central authority will send this report to a report mailbox, which is the mailbox Bob used to download Alice's infection report in Fig. 1. Users will download this report mailbox, which will contain the IDs of users that have the virus. If a user finds one or more of these IDs in their contact data, there is a chance they could have the virus.

Sending Reports. To protect their contact reports from being traced back to their identity, infected users are required to send their reports to be processed through the mixnet before reaching the central authority. At the end of each round, users will encrypt their report with the central authority's public key. Next, they will generate a random permutation of mixer public keys and encrypt their reports with each public key in the order determined by the generated random permutation, forming encapsulated layers of encryption. Upon adding a layer of encryption, a user will add the destination IP address of the mixer that is to decrypt the encrypted layer.

When reports are sent, any known information about a user's contacts such as names and phone numbers will be removed. The central authority will only be able to view the user's ID.

Secure-Contact Lists. Secure-contact lists enable groups of users to share their contact reports with each other securely. By sharing contact reports users in the group will be able to check the likelihood that group members have been infected. The creator of the contract will send a request to the PKG. The PKG will then show the contract to each user after authenticating them by sending a code to their phone as described in Sect. 3.1. If every user agrees to the contract then the contract is valid, and users in the group will be able to view each other's reports. Now users can use the shared public key to encrypt their reports. Users will add the mailbox address to their reports and send the to the central authority just as they would for an infection report. The central authority will place the reports in the mailboxes. If all users on the contract do not agree to the contract, it is invalid, and the group will not form (Fig. 5).

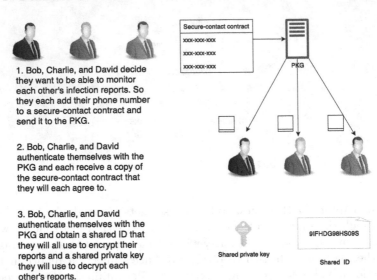

1. Bob, Charlie, and David decide they want to be able to monitor each other's infection reports. So they each add their phone number to a secure-contact contract and send it to the PKG.

2. Bob, Charlie, and David authenticate themselves with the PKG and each receive a copy of the secure-contact contract that they will each agree to.

3. Bob, Charlie, and David authenticate themselves with the PKG and obtain a shared ID that they will all use to encrypt their reports and a shared private key they will use to decrypt each other's reports.

Fig. 5. An overview of secure-contact contracts.

4   Analysis

4.1   Correctness

If the protocol is carried out faithfully, then Khopesh's mixers will shuffle the reports, and the last mixer will send the reports to the central authority for processing. Infection reports will be placed in the user's mailboxes. Thus, Khopesh satisfies the correctness property.

4.2   Sender Anonymity

Sender anonymity relies on the verifiability and zero-knowledge property of the verifiable shuffle. In the mixnet, every upstream mixer is the prover, and every downstream mixer is the verifier of the verifiable shuffle. Verifiability ensures that the protocol is carried out correctly. If it is not, the verifier will halt and throw an error. Apart from this, every honest mixer's permutation is unknown to the adversary. Therefore, the final permutation of the reports will also be unknown to the adversary, so the adversary will be unable to link the report to a user.

To protect itself from N-1 attacks, Khopesh's mixnet implements Mixminion's [6] "timed-dynamic-pool" batching strategy; mixers process reports every t seconds but wait until they have a threshold of reports before beginning processing.

4.3   Receiver Anonymity

The anonymity of mailbox downloads depends on whether or not the adversary knows which mailbox a user uses. If the adversary does know the mailbox of a user, receiver anonymity is still achieved to an extent because the user could be any user that uses that mailbox. However, if the adversary does not know the mailbox a user uses, then full receiver anonymity is achieved because the user could be any user in the network.

4.4   Privacy

Secure-Contact Contracts. Khopesh's secure-contact contracts enable users to create groups where each member can view the reports of each other group member. Communication to and from the PKG is encrypted, so an adversary will be unable to tamper with the secure-contact contract. All users are shown the list and choose to agree to the contract. If one or more users disagree, the contract will be invalid, and the group will not form. The privacy of secure-contact contracts depends on the integrity of each user in the group. If one user in the group leaks another group member's report, privacy is lost.

Regular Reporting. Traditional reporting (no secure-contact contracts) does not leak any information to the adversary. Users send their reports to the mixnet, and the mixnet sends their reports to the central authority for processing.

Bluetooth Sending. Reports contain no information about any user since phone numbers are removed from reports before being sent to other users. Only IDs of users remain and these cannot be linked to any user's phone number. Even if the adversary obtains these contact reports they will only be able to find relationships between anonymous users.

5   Limitations and Vulnerabilities

5.1   Bluetooth

Using Bluetooth to detect other users can lead to an increased number of false positives because the distance between users is not very accurate. To solve this problem, Khopesh could use Bluetooth localization techniques to improve location accuracy [2,11].

5.2   Verifiable Shuffling

Khopesh implements Bayer and Groth's [4] verifiable shuffle algorithm, which takes 2 min to prove and verify 100,000 reports. This is a fast algorithm, but it has not been optimized for Khopesh; its current implementation does not exploit parallelism, which is a performance loss for Khopesh. This implementation could be made faster by including support for multiple cores.

5.3   Forward Secrecy

Khopesh's current design does not include forward secrecy. This allows an adversary to collect reports of users from the mailboxes and decrypt them later once she has obtained a user's private key. To mitigate this, Khopesh could regenerate keys every round. However, this means users would have to reauthenticate themselves to receive their new private keys from the PKG.

5.4   PKG Attacks

Khopesh's PKG creates the private keys for secure-contact contracts and users and also authenticates users, which makes it a potential target. If the PKG is compromised, an adversary will be able to view all the phone numbers of users that will authenticate themselves with their phone numbers in the future. However, the phone numbers of current users will be protected as long as they do not create a secure-contact contract, which requires reauthentication.

6   Implementation

A prototype of Khopesh is available at https://github.com/MutexUnlocked/khopesh. The prototype implements every component of Khopesh's protocol, including a user prototype for Android smartphones.

7   Evaluation

Our evaluation quantitatively answers the following question:

- Can Khopesh support a large amount of users and reports?

7.1   Experimental Setup

To answer the above question, we ran an experiment on DigitalOcean Droplet servers (Linux-based virtual machines). All servers used had an Intel Xeon Skylake 2.7 GHz CPU with 4 cores, 8 GB of RAM, and 1 Gbps of network bandwidth. The servers run Linux version 5.7.7.

We use the following parameters in our experiment. Our mixnet consisted of 3 mixers, 1 PKG, and a central authority each corresponding to one VM. All reports are premade with a fixed size of 1192 bytes (including 144 bytes of encryption overhead). To ensure that clients do not bottleneck, clients are simulated using 4 additional VMs. Each user sends their reports regularly (no secure-contact contracts).

7.2   Server Performance

Figure 6 shows that Khopesh scales linearly with the number of users and reports. The end-to-end latency for Khopesh includes authentication with the PKG, processing reports with the mixnet, and sending reports to the central authority.

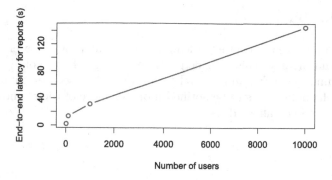

Fig. 6. Performance of Khopesh's protocol when varying the number of online users. Every user sends a report every round.

8   Related Work

8.1   Covid-19 Tracing Protocols

BlueTrace [3] is a privacy-preserving contact tracing protocol that is also the foundation for Covid-19 tracing apps such as COVIDSafe [10]. BlueTrace protects the contacts of users. However, it gives health authorities the power to obtain and use personally-identifiable information of infected users. In contrast, Khopesh's central authority is unable to view any information associated with users, which includes phone numbers. The central authority only processes the hashes of encrypted phone numbers.

DP-3T [9] is a decentralized Covid-19 tracing protocol that protects the contacts of users, thus, providing users with more privacy and security than traditional centralized Covid-19 tracing systems. However, DP-3T is subject to the targeted identification attack [8]. In contrast, Khopesh is not vulnerable to any such attack and keeps its infected users and non-infected users equally anonymous.

8.2   Protocols that Provide Anonymity

Khopesh implements a free-route mixnet similar to Mixminion's [6] mixnet, for example, both mixnet designs rely on TLS over TCP for communication between mixers. However, Khopesh's mixnet does not provide the same flexibility as Mixminion. For example, replies and message forwarding are not supported. In Khopesh every report that travels through the mixnet is treated the same.

Alpenhorn [7] is a protocol used for initiating connections between two users without leaking metadata. Khopesh uses Alpenhorn's idea of using IBE to create private keys for its users without revealing much metadata. However, Alpenhorn's PKG implements forward secrecy, making it safer from attackers that later compromise a user's private key.

9   Conclusion

Khopesh is a new secure contact tracing system that provides users with both anonymity and privacy. This is made possible through the use of identity-based encryption, mix networks, and a novel technique called secure-contact contract signing, which enable users to be notified if one or more of their contacts, whom they trust, have been affected.

References

1. Virusradar (2020). https://virusradar.hu/
2. Almaula, V., Cheng, D.: Bluetooth triangulator. Final Project, Department of Computer Science and Engineering, University of California, San Diego, pp. 1–5 (2006)
3. Bay, J., et al.: Bluetrace: a privacy-preserving protocol for community-driven contact tracing across borders. Technical Report, Government Technology Agency-Singapore (2020)
4. Bayer, S., Groth, J.: Efficient zero-knowledge argument for correctness of a shuffle. In: Pointcheval, D., Johansson, T. (eds.) EUROCRYPT 2012. LNCS, vol. 7237, pp. 263–280. Springer, Heidelberg (2012). https://doi.org/10.1007/978-3-642-29011-4_17
5. Boneh, D., Franklin, M.: Identity-based encryption from the weil pairing. In: Kilian, J. (ed.) CRYPTO 2001. LNCS, vol. 2139, pp. 213–229. Springer, Heidelberg (2001). https://doi.org/10.1007/3-540-44647-8_13
6. Danezis, G., Dingledine, R., Mathewson, N.: Mixminion: design of a type III anonymous remailer protocol. In: 2003 Symposium on Security and Privacy, 2003, pp. 2–15. IEEE (2003)
7. Lazar, D., Zeldovich, N.: Alpenhorn: Bootstrapping secure communication without leaking metadata. In: 12th USENIX Symposium on Operating Systems Design and Implementation (OSDI 16), pp. 571–586. USENIX Association, Savannah, GA, November 2016. https://www.usenix.org/conference/osdi16/technical-sessions/presentation/lazar
8. Tang, Q.: Privacy-preserving contact tracing: current solutions and open questions. arXiv preprint arXiv:2004.06818 (2020)
9. Troncoso, C., et al.: Decentralized privacy-preserving proximity tracing, April 12 2020. https://www.github.com/dp-3t/documents/raw/master.DP3T%20White%20Paper.pdf
10. Watts, D.: Covidsafe, Australia's digital contact tracing app: the legal issues. Australia's Digital Contact Tracing App: The Legal Issues (May 2, 2020) (2020)
11. Zafari, F., Gkelias, A., Leung, K.K.: A survey of indoor localization systems and technologies. IEEE Commun. Surv. Tutorials **21**(3), 2568–2599 (2019)

Author Index

Printed in the United States
By Bookmasters